Teaching
Elementary
Language Arts

second edition

Teaching Elementary Language Arts

Trenton State College **Dorothy Rubin**

HOLT, RINEHART AND WINSTON

New York   Chicago   San Francisco   Dallas   Montreal   Toronto   London   Sydney

With love to my understanding, helpful, and supportive husband, Artie, my delightful daughters, Carol and Sharon, and my precious granddaughter, Jennifer.

Library of Congress Cataloging in Publication Data

Rubin, Dorothy.
  Teaching elementary language arts.

  Includes bibliographical references and index.
  1. Language arts (Elementary) I. Title.
LB1575.R82 1980   372.6′044   79-20044
ISBN 0-03-053236-1

ACKNOWLEDGMENTS

Cover photographs by Russell Dian and James Silliman

The author wishes to thank the Ewing Township and Lawrence Township schools, who allowed the photographs in the book to be taken there.

Fig. 1.3, p. 7 used by permission of the National Newspaper Syndicate. Fig. 4.3, p. 23 is reprinted with permission; Copyright, Los Angeles Times.   P. 25 "Carnival" cartoon reprinted by permission of NEA.   Pp. 33–34, quotations from J. W. Getzels and P. W. Jackson, *Creativity and Intelligence.* Copyright © 1962, John Wiley & Sons, Inc. Reprinted by permission of John Wiley & Sons, Inc.   P. 399–400, the "Teacher Evaluation," reprinted by permission of the publisher, Phi Delta Kappa, Inc., January 1962. Fig. 5.1, p. 52 reprinted by permission of the National Education Association. Pp. 59–60 reprinted from the November 1967, issue of *Education.* Copyright 1967, by the Bobbs-Merrill Company, Inc., Indianapolis, Indiana.   P. 61 from the English Language Arts Program prepared by the Language Arts Curriculum Committee, Dr. Howard VanderBeek, Chairman, Malcolm Price Laboratory School, University of Northern Iowa, Cedar Falls, Iowa.   P. 79 "A Teacher . . . Grades," *Journal of Education,* vol. CXXXVI, March 1954, pp. 171–172. Copyright by the Trustees of Boston University, Boston, Mass. P. 80, from John Crawford and Richard French, "An Evaluation . . . Secondary Schools," *Journal of Education,* vol. CXXXVI, March 1954, pp. 169–171. Copyright by the Trustees of Boston University, Boston, Mass.   P. 82, "African Dance," Copyright 1926 by Alfred A. Knopf, Inc., and renewed 1954 by Langston Hughes. Reprinted from *Selected Poems* by Langston Hughes, by permission of the publisher.   P. 83, Walter de la Mare, "The Huntsman," by permission of The Literary Trustees of Walter de la Mare and The Society of Authors and their representatives.   Pp. 90–92 from *How to Be A Puppeteer* by Eleanor Boylan. Copyright © 1970 by Eleanor Boylan. Reprinted by permission of the publishers, Saturday Review Press/E. P. Dutton & Co., Inc.   Table 6.1, p. 97 Mildred C. Templin, *Certain Language Skills in Children; Their Development and Interrelationships.* Child Welfare Monograph Series #26 University of Minnesota Press Mpls. © 1957 by the University of

Preface

A book for the 1980s must be one that reflects the times. It must help teachers to be more current, more effective, more creative, more understanding of the variety of children in the classroom, more knowledgeable, more accountable, and better teachers. *Teaching Elementary Language Arts* is intended to be such a book. The second edition retains all of the features of the first edition that have made it such a popular book among professors, students, and in-service teachers, while broadening its scope and coverage. New chapters have been added to help teachers to implement the language arts ideas, materials, and methods presented in the book and to help them plan and accommodate the special children they will probably encounter in their regular classrooms. Although the breadth and scope of *Teaching Elementary Language Arts* have increased, its substantiveness and readability have not been compromised. The text *also* still emphasizes the blend of theory and practice and the interrelatedness of the language arts including reading.

In order to understand the "whys" of teaching methods and practices in the area of language arts, one should comprehend those psychological foundations and researches on which this book is based. However, this is not a "theory" text, since a practical approach is emphasized throughout to help teachers effectively implement the language arts program. The material is presented so that it will be enjoyable as well as informative.

The text develops or presents psychological principles and/or historical perspectives in the language arts, followed by exercises that illustrate practical applications of these principles in classroom teaching situations.

Part One deals with the foundation on which a good language arts program should be built. Unless teachers are aware of individual differences, of how language is acquired by the child, and of the importance of creativity in the life of a child, they will not be able to implement the proposed language arts program well. In Part Three, material is presented which will allow teachers to gain insight into themselves as teachers, to be perceptive of the physical environment in their classrooms, and to be aware of the complex of variables operating in the world of their students. These factors—combined with knowledge of the evaluative process, teaching methods, materials, knowledge of the characteristics of special children and their unique cognitive learning styles, organizational patterns, and principles of good classroom management—will help make better teachers.

Evaluation of teachers, students, and the language arts program, as it is analyzed in Part Three, is treated as an important on-going process which should be in evidence at the beginning, middle, and end of the total program.

Part Two contains the subject matter of the language arts and discusses both the development and implementation of skills that a good language arts teacher needs. All the chapters in Part Two have examples of performance objectives for the teacher. Model lesson plans are given as further illustrations.

In this text the child is the focal point around which the teacher orchestrates language arts activities, providing a learning environment which allows a child the freedom to participate, interact, and experience.

"Sensitivity" has become a key word in education—and that is all to the good. But unless teachers know basic skills and have the ability to implement these skills, there will be no real teaching.

It should be emphasized that this book does not dictate one approach to the language arts. Controversies are explained from several viewpoints, in order to help teachers see through an "either/or" dichotomy and utilize elements from each that best suit the needs of students. By explaining and analyzing the various outlooks and methods prevalent in the language arts field, a practical approach to teaching is developed throughout the text.

Organization of the Book

Recognizing the importance of language and building the elements of listening, speaking, reading, and writing are basic tenets for a language arts program. This mere recognition does not ensure that such areas will become integral parts of the language arts program or of the desired learnings of the student. To make the language arts program an integral part of the student's experiences, this book attempts to put teachers in the "driver's seat." The schema given in Parts One and Three will allow teachers to see themselves as dynamic persons in the classroom. Without such key people there would be no language arts program. Teachers must become effective classroom managers, for it is they who will guide students in acquiring vital language arts skills.

The four chapters in Part One are short enough to be covered in one or two class sessions. Part Three "Preparing for Instruction," also contains short chapters. It emphasizes the importance of the evaluative process and hopefully insures for ongoing evaluation throughout the program. It presents the teacher as the manager of the language arts program, who is able to plan and make decisions based on the needs and readiness levels of his or her students. How to organize for instruction and various classroom organizational patterns are discussed, and scenarios to illustrate the concepts are presented. An emphasis on individual differences and teaching the special child is made so that teachers will be better prepared for their role.

The subject matter chapters of the language arts, in Part Two, have certain common elements: a list of teacher competencies, an introduction, thought questions the reader will be able to answer after having read the chapter, diagnostic checklists, a summary, lesson plans, and questions for discussion. It should be clearly understood that the competencies presented at the beginning of the chapters are not inclusive sets. Part Three provides techniques that will help readers generate their own selected competencies and student behavioral objectives appropriate to specific situations.

The author wishes to acknowledge her gratitude to John Mahaney and Lauren Procton for their valuable suggestions, creative editing, and support. She also wishes to thank Herman Makler for being such a kind, patient, considerate, and helpful production editor. Special thanks must go to her daughter Sharon for her very helpful and perceptive comments and suggestions.

Princeton, N.J.   D.R.
January 1980

Contents

5   Aural Responsiveness—Listening,   **43**

6   Oral Communication and Speech Improvement,   **73**

7   Word Recognition and Approaches to Reading: Selected Areas,   **115**

part two

The
Subject Matter
of the
Language Arts

41

part three

Preparing
for
Instruction

389

appendices

The Foundation of the Language Arts

one

Introducing the Language Arts

EXAMPLES OF TEACHER COMPETENCIES*

1. The teacher will be able to state the components of language arts.
2. The teacher will be able to describe and give examples of how the language arts are interrelated.
3. The teacher will be able to define *decoding* and *encoding* and give examples of each.
4. The teacher will be able to define *communication* and *language* and explain the relationship between language and communication.
5. The teacher will be able to explain the relationship between communication and nonverbal behavior.
6. The teacher will be able to explain the importance of correct interpretation of culturally different children's nonverbal behavior.

What Are the Language Arts and How Are They Interrelated?

Language arts are listening, speaking, reading, and writing.

Did you know that elementary-school children spend about 57 percent of their time supposedly listening; that is, 57 percent of the time in elementary school someone is speaking and the students may or may not be engaged in the act of listening?

After you have finished reading Chapter 5 of this book, you will be able to make the children's listening time in class more effective and you will also comprehend how listening affects the other language arts areas. Perhaps, you will become a better listener yourself.

*The examples of teacher competencies presented at the beginning of each chapter in this book usually will not include the standard that will be used to measure the success of the performance or the conditions under which the behavior is to be performed. (*See* Chapters 15 and 18.)

How shy children can be encouraged to engage in oral expression more freely is an important part of the language arts also. The solution to this problem as well as other speech-related questions will be found in Chapter 6.

Do you think you would be able to encourage your students to read on their own? You will know how to do so after finishing Chapter 9.

And how many activities can you think of to make written expression more enjoyable for your students? Examples of such stimulating activities will be found in Chapters 10 and 11.

Now you know that the major components of language arts are listening, speaking, reading, and writing, but you still are not aware of the wide range of topics included in each area. To help you to visualize the composition and organization of the subject matter of the language arts, as presented in this textbook, see Table 1.1.

Although the language arts areas in this book are divided into separate chapters in order to make them more comprehensible, it is important to recognize and stress the interrelatedness of the language arts. This fundamental relatedness can be deduced from observations of children's development of oral and written expression, which follows the sequence listening, speaking, reading, and writing. To reinforce the importance of this sequence in the reader's mind, this book follows the same sequential order. And because of this developmental sequence a problem encountered in one segment of the language arts will usually carry over to another, while proficiency in one segment usually facilitates the acquisition of another area. For example, in order for children to be able to speak correctly, they must be able to hear sounds correctly, and the sounds must convey meaning for them.

A young child kept asking his mother for carrots every Sunday after he came home from Sunday School. Finally, his mother decided to ask the child's Sunday School teacher about this phenomenon. The teacher had no explanation to give the mother. When they asked the child he said that the teacher had said, "Eat carrots for me." The teacher realized the child was misinterpreting "He careth for me," to mean eat carrots for me.

Many teachers know of similar examples. One of the most common substitution errors made is "My country 'tis a bee, sweet land of liver tree," for "My country 'tis of thee, Sweet land of liberty."

The Pledge of Allegiance to the Flag is also often misheard and therefore misrecited. For example, children have been heard to say, "I pledge allegiance to the . . . for Richard Stanz" and "one nation invisible. . . ."

Decoding and Encoding in the Language Arts

The language arts, which employ common word symbols, involve the intake (listening and reading) and the outgo (speaking and writing) of language. *Encoding* and *decoding* are technical terms that explain what takes place in the acts of listening, speaking, reading, and writing. For example, when you speak, you encode the sounds so that they are meaningful; when you listen, you decode the meanings. Writing is the encoding of sounds in graphic (written) symbols;

table 1.1   Subject Matter of Language Arts

while reading is the decoding of the graphic form.

Figure 1.1 portrays the encoding and decoding process as it is used in communicating messages. In this model Speaker A first conveys a message to Listener B, who, after decoding and interpreting the message, becomes Speaker B. Speaker B then conveys a message to Listener A, who decodes and interprets the message and becomes Speaker A again. The communication cycle is now complete.

The same sequence would be followed for writing and reading, substituting writer for speaker and reader for listener, as is shown in the model.

Communication and Language

When Confucius was asked what he would do if he had the responsibility for administering a country, he said that he would improve language. If language is not correct, he stated, then what is said is not what is meant; if what is said is not what is meant, then what ought to be done remains undone; if this remains undone, morals and arts would deteriorate; if morals and arts deteriorate, justice will go astray; if justice goes astray, the people will stand about in helpless confusion.

CONFUCIUS (*c.* 551–479 B.C.)

You can well imagine what would happen if there was no language. Would there be any communication? In answering this question one would have to say it depends on the definition of "language," which is used by different people to mean many different things. One can talk of kinesics, which involves gestures that may or may not accompany speech as language; or one can speak of the language of flowers, bees, and so on. However, in *linguistics*, which concerns itself with the science of language, the term "language" refers to human speech. Whenever the term is used in this book, it will refer to human speech. Since kinesics and the others mentioned are nonvocal and nonlingual, they would not be considered language by most linguists. (See the following section and Chapter 6 for more on kinesics.)

figure 1.1   *Model of Encoding and Decoding in Communication*

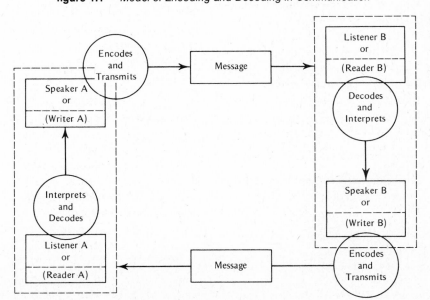

Language is a learned, shared, and patterned, arbitrary system of vocal sound symbols with which people in a given culture can communicate with one another. From this definition it can be stated that language is vocal, requiring commonality of agreement on the vocal sounds chosen to stand for ideas or objects. The term "patterned" in the definition of language refers to the recognition that word meanings depend on the placement of the words in a sentence. For example, in the following sentences the words "train" and "left" have different meanings based on the way they are placed in the sentences:

1. *Train* your dog to lift his *left* paw.
2. Since I *left* so late, I may miss my *train*.

Let us look at another example involving commonality of meaning. If two persons are conversing with one another and Individual A says to Individual B: "They put my dog on the litter," B might have difficulty in understanding A because "litter" has many different meanings. Does "litter" refer to a "stretcher" or does it mean "disorder"? It is difficult to discern the meaning of "litter" from the context (the words surrounding a word that can shed light on its meaning) of this sentence. However, if Individual A says: "They carried my dog on the litter to place him in the ambulance," there would be less chance for confusion because both people would be able, from the context of this sentence, to recognize a commonality of meaning for the noise "litter."

Communication could not take place unless a consensus of word meanings existed between Individuals A and B.

Would the following dialogue between Alice and Humpty Dumpty be considered communication?

"And only *one* for birthday presents, you know. There's glory for you!"

"I don't know what you mean by 'glory,' " Alice said.

Humpty Dumpty smiled contemptuously. "Of course you don't—till I tell you. I meant 'there's a nice knockdown argument for you.' "

"But 'glory' doesn't mean 'a nice knockdown argument,' " Alice objected.

"When *I* use a word," Humpty Dumpty said in rather a scornful tone, "it means just what I choose it to mean—neither more nor less."

"The question is," said Alice, "whether you *can* make words mean so many different things."

"The question is," said Humpty Dumpty, "which is to be master—that's all."[1]

Would communication always take place if individuals have a consensus of word meanings? The answer would have to be, "It depends," for the term "communication" also seems to evoke a number of different meanings. To some persons, watching television, reading a book, or listening to a lecture all involve communication. This may be due to the fact that a dictionary defines communication as "the act of imparting, conferring or delivering from one to another; as, the communication of knowledge, opinions, or facts."[2] This definition is not very precise because it implies that communication can be a one-way process; that is, merely giving. However, in order for communication to take place, there must be an *exchange* of ideas; there must be a sharing of common understanding between or among individuals. For effective communication students must learn that:

1. Language is man-made.
2. Language changes.
3. Language is a system of sounds.
4. Sounds are arranged into words.
5. The method of sound production helps to convey meaning.
6. Words are made up of vocal sounds plus meaning.
7. Words are organized into patterns which convey unique meanings.

[1]Lewis Carroll, *Through the Looking Glass* (New York: Grosset & Dunlap), pp. 216–217.

[2]*Webster's New Twentieth-century Dictionary, Unabridged,* 2d ed. (Cleveland, Ohio: World, 1970), p. 367.

8. There are no right or wrong words for things, but common usage is employed in word meanings.

9. New words are derived as a society advances.

From the preceding we can state that:

1. Words are merely noises, unless meaning commonly agreed on by humans is attached to them.

2. Lack of common word meanings between speaker and listener or between writer and reader will result in faulty communication.

This textbook is concerned with helping readers to be more perceptive to the world around them via the language arts. The more proficient students are in listening, speaking, reading, and writing, the more able they will be to contribute to the culture in which they live and the more they can benefit from that culture.

Humans advance through language. Helen Keller, who became blind and deaf in early infancy, exemplified the importance of language, its interrelationships, and what a phenomenal feat is involved in the child's acquisition of language. In her own words she describes her awakening to language:

As the cool stream gushed over one hand she [Helen Keller's teacher] spelled into the other the word water, first slowly, then rapidly. I stood still, my whole attention fixed upon the motions of her fingers. Suddenly I felt a misty consciousness as of something forgotten—a thrill of returning thought; and somehow the mystery of language was revealed to me. I knew then that "w-a-t-e-r" meant the wonderful cool something that was flowing over my hand. That living word awakened my soul, gave it light, hope, joy, set it free! . . .

I left the well house eager to learn. Everything had a name, and each name gave birth to a new thought. As we returned to the house every object which I touched seemed to quiver with life. That was because I saw everything with the strange, new sight that had come to me.[3]

Communication and Nonverbal Behavior

Human communication is actually a combination of words and gestures. Walburga .von Raffler-Engel, a world-renowned linguist who has done extensive research in the area of nonverbal behavior, feels that the nonverbal component is as vital to communication as words. Engel differentiates between and among *body language, kinesics*, and *social movements*. *Body language* is used to express the mood of an individual. For example, people walking back and forth or fidgeting with their hands are expressing signs of nervousness or anxiety. *Kinesics* is associated with message-related body movements. Kinesics either accompanies speech or

[3]Helen Keller, *The Story of My Life* (New York: Doubleday, 1954), p. 36.

SMIDGENS

is used in place of speech. For example, American speakers may communicate that they feel someone is crazy by *saying* that, while at the same time making circular movements around their temples, or just by making circular movements around their temples without speaking. *Social movements* are those body movements that children may be taught, whereas kinesic motions usually are those acquired with verbal language. Greetings are in the category of social movements, and so methods of greeting one another would vary with cultural groups. Black Americans may use the highly stylized "soul handshake," other Americans may merely shake hands, the Japanese may greet each other with a bow, and so on.[4]

Unless teachers who are working with children from various cultures recognize that differences exist in the nonverbal behavior between and among cultures, communication may not take place. For example, for Germans, the kinesic motion or gesture for showing that someone is "nutty" is to touch their foreheads with their index fingers; for Americans, however, it is to make circular movements around the temple. Another example in the social movements area shows how misunderstanding can take place because of lack of communication due to nonverbal behavior: Many Chicano and black children are taught that it is a sign of respect to look down while speaking to an elder; it is considered a sign of respect *not* to look the person in the face. Other Americans are generally taught that well-bred persons look directly at the person to whom they are speaking. American teachers who see a child looking down while they are speaking to him or her usually infer that the child is either discourteous or not paying attention. Misreading of a child's nonverbal behavior will cause confusion for a child and put up barriers between a child and a teacher that need not exist.

[4]Walburga von Raffler-Engel, "We Do Not Talk Only With Our Mouths," *The Language Quarterly* 4 (December 1977): 1–3.

Summary

The various areas of language arts—listening, speaking, reading, and writing—are interrelated, and children develop command over language in the sequential order listed. The language arts involve intake (or decoding) and outgo (or encoding) of language, and a communication model for these processes was presented earlier in the chapter.

After defining language as the learned, shared, and patterned, arbitrary system of vocal sound symbols used in communication, the components for effective interchange were listed with emphasis on common word meanings. Also, the importance of nonverbal behavior to human communication was emphasized, and the terms *body language*, *kinesics*, and *social movements* were explained.

SELECTED BIBLIOGRAPHY

Destefano, Johanna S., *Language, the Learner and the School*. New York: Wiley, 1978.

Fraenkel, Gerd. *What Is Language?* Boston: Ginn, 1965.

Funk, Hal D., and DeWayne Triplett, eds. *Language Arts in the Elementary School: Readings*. Philadelphia: Lippincott, 1972.

How We Communicate (filmstrip). Jamaica, N.Y.: Eye Gate Media, 1976.

Knapp, Mark. *Nonverbal Communication in Human Interaction*, 2d ed. New York: Holt, Rinehart and Winston, 1978.

Miller, G. A. *Language and Communication*. New York: McGraw-Hill, 1951.

von Raffler-Engel, Walburga. "Developmental Kinesics: Cultural Differences in the Acquisition of Nonverbal Behavior," in *Child Language*. New York: International Linguistic Association, 1975, pp. 195–204.

———. "We Do Not Talk Only With Our Mouths." *The Language Quarterly* 4 (December 1977): 1–3.

———. "On the Structure of Nonverbal Behavior." *Man-Environment Systems* 8 (1978): 60–66.

Whorf, B. L. *Language, Thought, and Reality*. Cambridge, Mass.: Technology Press, 1956.

two

Understanding the Individual Differences of Children

EXAMPLES OF TEACHER COMPETENCIES

1. The teacher will be able to state some individual differences that affect language development and school achievement.
2. The teacher will be able to define *intelligence.*
3. The teacher will be able to describe the role of intelligence tests in a school program based on individual differences.
4. The teacher will be able to state some sex differences that may affect language learning.
5. The teacher will be able to explain how cultural factors may affect sex differences.
6. The teacher will be able to explain why children who speak a dialect of English or a foreign language may have communication difficulties in school.
7. The teacher will be able to explain how socioeconomic factors may influence language development.
8. The teacher will be able to explain how family composition may affect language development.

The classic fable of "The Animal School" illustrates the importance of recognizing that individual differences exist among students.

THE ANIMAL SCHOOL

Dr. G. H. Reavis

Once upon a time the animals decided they must do something heroic to meet the problems of a "New World." So they organized a school. They adopted an activity

9

curriculum consisting of running, swimming, and flying. To make it easier to administer the curriculum it was decided that all of the animals should take all of the subjects.

The duck was excellent in swimming. In fact, he was far better than his instructor, but he could not do more than make passing grades in flying and was very poor in running. Since he was so slow in running, he had to remain after school and drop swimming in order to practice running. This was kept up until his web feet were badly worn and he was only average in swimming. But average was acceptable in the school—so nobody worried about that except the duck.

The rabbit started at the top of the class in running, but had a nervous breakdown because of so much make-up work in swimming. The squirrel was excellent in climbing until he developed frustration in the flying class where his teacher insisted that he start from the ground up instead of from the treetop down. He also developed "Charlie Horses" from over-exertion and then got a "C" in climbing and a "D" in running.

The eagle was indeed a problem child and was disciplined severely. In the climbing class, he beat all others to the top of the tree, but insisted on using his own way to get there. At the end of the year an abnormal eel that could swim exceedingly well, run, climb, and fly a little, had the highest average and was made valedictorian.

The prairie dogs stayed out of school and fought the tax levy because the administration refused to add digging and burrowing to the curriculum. They apprenticed their child to a badger and joined with the groundhogs and gophers to start a very successful private school.

Does this little Fable have a moral?

Introduction

A good language arts program cannot exist unless teachers take the individual differences of their students into account. Perceptive teachers sensitive to the uniqueness of each of their students will be better able to plan a program based on their students' needs. Because the principle of providing for the individual differences of students is the backbone of the language arts program, this chapter is being presented in Part One. Throughout this book the necessity for providing for the individual differences of students is emphasized.

Some important individual differences that influence language development and, consequently, school achievement are shown in Figure 2.1. (No weighting of the relative importance of the factors is given.) This chapter will explain how these factors may affect individual school performance.

Why humans behave as they do is a fascinating question. For example, why is it that two children with similar Intelligence Quotient (IQ) scores have different achievement behaviors? We cannot discuss the cause of children's behavior in any substantive way in this text, but many excellent books are devoted specifically to this topic. (See bibliography.) Yet it is important for the language arts teacher to have some understanding of the various factors that make up individual difference and we will consider some of these now.

Intelligence

It is difficult to pick up a newspaper, journal, or magazine without finding some reference to achievement or intelligence. Usually when intelligence—specifically an intelligence test—is brought up, the atmosphere becomes highly

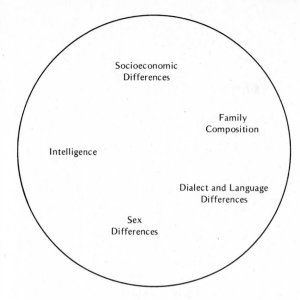

figure 2.1   *Individual Differences*

charged. Hardly anyone seems to regard IQ objectively.

Intelligence refers to the ability to reason abstractly or to solve problems. Since intelligence is a construct—that is, it is something which cannot be directly observed or directly measured—testing and research have necessitated an operational definition. Such a definition coined in the early part of the century is still much quoted: "Intelligence is what the intelligence test measures."[1] There are a variety of tests designed to measure intelligence, yet no test exists which actually measures intelligence. In other words, intelligence tests cannot adequately determine an individual's absolute limits or the potential of the intelligence. Yet many persons, both lay and professional, actually behave as if the intelligence test will tell all.

This state of affairs may be due to the nature-nurture controversy. Advocates of the nature side believe that heredity is the sole determiner of intelligence, and that no amount of education or the quality of the environment can alter intelligence. Those who believe in the nurture side claim that intelligence is determined in great part by the environment. For them, intelligence can be affected if the child is exposed to different environments and education. Most professionals take an in-between position, saying that intelligence may be determined by an interaction between heredity and environment. "Heredity deals the cards and environment plays them."[2] Yet the heredity theory dies hard.

The majority position which believes that intelligence is determined by some combination of heredity and environment brings up the question as to *which* factor is more important. Conflicting studies reported in this area attribute different percentages to each factor. The controversy continues to rage, as does the confusion surrounding what intelligence tests are measuring.

Most intelligence tests are highly verbal and studies have shown that persons who do well on vocabulary tests also seem to do well on intelligence tests.[3] If a child has language problems—or if a dialect of English or a language other than English is spoken at home—the child could easily have difficulty in performing well in school. IQ tests are valid mainly for a middle-class standard English curriculum, and they predict the ability of an individual to do well in such environments. The positive correlation or agreement between individuals' IQs and their ability to do work in school is neither very high nor low. There are factors other than IQ which determine an individual's success in school. One very important factor for school success is *motivation*—the desire, drive, and sustained interest to do the work.

The IQ test is an imperfect tool which helps teachers and parents to understand the abilities

[1]E. G. Boring, "Intelligence as the Tests Test It," *New Republic* 35 (1925): 35–37.

[2]Lee J. Cronbach, *Educational Psychology* (New York: Harcourt, Brace, 1954), p. 204.

[3]Leona Tyler, *The Psychology of Human Differences* (New York: Appleton-Century-Crofts, 1965), p. 80.

of children better. If students are doing very well in school, and if, according to their IQ scores, they are only supposed to be doing average work, one would be misusing the IQ test by thinking, "Stop, you're not supposed to be doing that well."

The IQ test also helps show teachers the wide range of levels of ability in their classes. If teachers are aware of the wide span of mental age of their students, they can design a program based especially on individual needs. (See Chapter 17.)

However, teachers are cautioned not to see the IQ test as a perfect predictor of a child's ability to do work in school, for there are other factors, discussed in the remainder of this chapter, which influence school achievement.

Sex Differences

Are females really the weaker sex? Why are there more male underachievers in elementary school grades? Why are there more remedial readers among boys than girls? Why do males usually receive poorer grades in school than females? Since there are more adult males in important positions in society, does this mean that males are smarter than females?

There are vast differences between males and females besides the obvious physical ones. Females seem to have a biological precocity evident from birth onward.[4] The skeletal development of girls is superior to boys at birth, and this physical superiority continues until maturity.[5] Males, however, give off more carbon dioxide than females,[6] which means that boys need to take in more food and consequently

produce more energy. Even though the male matures later than the female, his oxygen intake is greater and continues so throughout life.[7] It has been hypothesized that sex differences in behavior may be due to these differences in metabolism.

These factors may affect the readiness levels of children in listening, speaking, reading, and writing—the language arts. Teachers must realize that some primary-grade boys may not be as mature as some girls of the same chronological age. They should not be expected to do equally well on tasks that necessitate the use of specific hand muscles—such as handwriting. Similarly, teachers should not expect these more immature male students to be able to "sit still" as long as some more mature female students, or to have a comparable attention span. Teachers should know that, although studies reveal no significant differences between males and females in general intelligence,[8,9] there are differences in specific aptitudes. For example, it has been consistently shown that girls usually surpass boys in verbal ability. From infancy to adulthood, females usually express themselves in words more readily and skillfully than males. Researches show that in general girls seem to learn to talk a little earlier; are usually somewhat superior during the preschool years in articulation, intelligibility, and correctness of speech sounds; and that they learn grammar and spelling more readily and are less likely to be stutterers.[10]

Interestingly, comparisons of males and females on a variety of tests have made it clear that girls and women do not have larger vocabularies than boys and men. Males in general,

---

[4]Amram Scheinfeld, *Women and Men* (New York: Harcourt, Brace, 1944), pp. 58–71.

[5]J. M. Tanner, "Physical Growth," in *Carmichael's Manual of Child Psychology*, 3d ed., Paul H. Mussen, ed. (New York: Wiley, 1970), p. 109.

[6]Stanley M. Garn and Leland C. Clark, Jr., "The Sex Difference in the Basal Metabolic Rate," *Child Development* 24 (September–December 1953): 215–224.

[7]Ibid., p. 222.

[8]Scottish Council for Research in Education, *The Intelligence of a Representative Group of Scottish Children* (London: University of London Press, 1939).

[9]Scottish Council for Research in Education, *The Trend of Scottish Intelligence* (London: University of London Press, 1949).

[10]Tyler, pp. 243–244.

according to the studies, are superior in mathematical ability and in the area of science, but in the area of rote memory females are usually superior.[11] Males' superiority in quantitative reasoning and science may be due to a culture bias.

It has been hypothesized, and the evidence is mounting, that the language differences observed between the sexes in the early years may also be due to cultural factors. For example, mothers might spend more time with young females during the day than with young males, since it would be "sissy stuff" for boys to help Mommy clean the house. As a result, there would be more verbal interaction between the mother and daughter.

Although the female "gains" in the area of language facility, she may also be adding a liability. Her parents may reward behavior that does not correlate very well with achievement; that is, she may be learning to be more docile, to have less initiative, to be less independent, and also to be less aggressive.

Boys may have their problems too. Usually reared by females, and seeing males only for a short time in the evening, they may have more difficulty in role identification. They are often pressured into being "rougher" or "tougher" than they would like, in order to satisfy a parent's stereotype of what a male should be.

It is to be hoped that by recognizing that sex differences exist, teachers will be more aware of the halo effect[12] and can be on the alert for it. For example, girls typically receive higher grades in school than boys in the area of overall "work" achievement because teachers tend to rate girls higher on such specific traits as deportment and handwriting.

Furthermore, girls are known to be more perceptive of the external environment than boys,[13] so that they can "size up" teachers more readily and therefore are more able to give teachers what they think is wanted.

Many changes are taking place in today's cultural attitudes toward male and female roles in society. There is a strong movement to counter sexism in textbooks, and legislation is being enacted which will give females more options. For example, girls can now compete in the formerly all-male bastion of the Little Leagues. More mothers are continuing to pursue their careers while the children are very young, utilizing day care centers or nursery schools. Although the parent surrogates in these centers are still usually female, the one-to-one relationship that the child formerly enjoyed is not present.

It will be interesting to note whether or not sex differences shown in test results will remain in spite of the impact of the movement to counter sexism in texts and in certain aspects of society. Perhaps these and other influences will change the results of earlier research on sex differences, not only in the interest and learning spheres, but also in the biological realm. Now that many women are working and competing with males, insurance companies may have to revise their actuarial tables for females in which women had longer life expectancy than males after the childbearing years.

By recognizing the existence of sex differences, teachers will be able to plan more effectively for students. They will be more able to dispel sex-stereotyping myths, which not only hinder effective planning but also interfere with the learning process. Their own thinking concerning sex differences may perhaps be changed to avoid a number of sex-stereotyping pitfalls. They will recognize that all girls are not alike and that all boys are not similar. Children are

---

[11]Ibid., pp. 244–245.

[12]The halo effect is a response bias which contaminates an individual's perception in the area of rating; that is, a person may rate another individual high on general characteristics because of one or two good impressions or rate the person low overall because of one or two bad impressions.

[13]Witkin, H. A., et al., *Personality through Perception* (New York: Harper & Row, 1954).

not plastic prototypes of one another but unique entities. Not all boys are aggressive and competitive; nor are all girls docile, dependent, and verbal.

Dialect and Language Differences

Children who speak a variation or dialect of English or another language are not inferior to children speaking standard English, nor is their language inferior. Research by linguists (persons who study language) has shown that many variations of English are highly structured systems and not accumulations of errors in standard English. Children speaking in a dialect of English have no difficulty communicating with one another. However, any dialect which differs from standard English structure and usage will usually cause communication problems for children in school and in society at large. Many expressions used by children who speak a variation of English may be foreign to teachers, and many expressions used by teachers may have different connotations for the students. The similarities between the dialects of English and standard English can also cause misunderstandings between the students and teachers because both groups may feel they "understand" what the others are saying when, in actuality, they do not.

Children who come from homes where a language other than English is the dominant one may also have language difficulties when they enter school unless they are truly bilingual. The dictionary definition of bilingual states that one must be "capable of using two languages."[14] However, many schoolchildren who speak a language other than standard English at home are not bilingual. These children may hear only "noises" when they first enter school, because the English sounds have little or no meaning for

them. They will often confuse the language spoken at home with their newly acquired English and vice-versa. It is not a question of one language being better than or preferred over another, but rather one of helping children to get along in the dominant social, economic, and political culture and to become a part of it. Unless students learn to communicate in standard English as well as in a dialect or another language, they will have difficulty in finding their "places in the sun" in the economy.

More will be said about this topic in several upcoming chapters, in particular in the section on teaching English as a second language in Chapter 6.

Home Environment

Socioeconomic class, parents' education, and the neighborhood in which children live are some of the factors which shape children's home environments. Studies have shown that the higher the socioeconomic status, the better the verbal ability of the child.[15] Children who have good adult language models and are spoken to and encouraged to speak will have an advantage in the development of language and intelligence. Parents who behave in a warm, democratic manner and provide their children with stimulating educationally oriented activities, challenge their children to think, encourage independence, and reinforce their children, are preparing them very well for school.

Children who come from homes where parents have only an elementary-school education, where many people live in a few rooms, and where unemployment among the adults in the home is common will usually be at a disadvantage in language learning. (See Chapter 3.)

Teachers should also be aware of the adult

---

[14]*Webster's New Twentieth-century Dictionary*, Unabridged, 2d ed. (Cleveland, Ohio: World, 1970), p. 182.

[15]Walter D. Loban, *Language Development: Kindergarten through Grade Twelve*, Research Report No. 18 (Urbana Ill.: National Council of Teachers of English, 1976).

composition of the child's home environment. Whether a child is reared by both parents, a single parent, a servant, by grandparents, or by foster parents will affect the child's attitudes and behavior. A child who is reared by a female single parent may behave differently from one reared by a male single parent, for instance. The death of one parent or of another family member will usually cause emotional stress in the child. A divorce can be a traumatic experience for children. Teachers who are aware of the home environment and are sensitive to sudden changes in this important area are in a better position to understand and help such students.

How many children are born into a family and the order in which these children are born affect the achievement levels of individuals, at least to some degree. Research is still being done on these factors, but it has been hypothesized that firstborn children do better both in school and in life than other children in the family. Children without siblings have been shown to be more articulate for the most part than a child who is a product of a multiple birth (like twins or triplets) or a singleton (one child born at a time) who has other brothers and sisters.[16]

Studies have shown that the only child, who is more often in the company of adults, has more chances of being spoken to by the grown-ups around him than is the case when there are many children in the family. Then, too, twins seem to have less need to communicate with others because they have a close relationship.

Singletons with siblings also have "interpreters" near at hand; that is, older siblings who can often understand a younger child's messages so well that the younger child need not attempt to express himself more effectively.

All of these factors form part of the learning climate in the home and influence the degree and amount of learning in the school.

[16]Mildred A. Dawson and Miriam Zollinger, *Guiding Language Learning* (New York: Harcourt Brace Jovanovich, 1957), pp. 36–37.

Summary

Intelligence can be defined as the ability to reason abstractly and to solve problems, but there seems to be no hard and fast way of measuring either intelligence or how well a child will do in school. There are, however, a number of factors that a teacher must recognize when the teacher is concerned about the individual differences in children. One such factor is sex difference, particularly the differences in growth and learning abilities between young boys and girls. Another difference is in the home life of the child. In some homes more than one language is spoken, in others a dialect prevails. Also, the differences in the education of a student's parents, the socioeconomic class of the family, the neighborhood in which a student lives, and the composition of the family must be recognized as making for differences and should be taken into account if the teacher is to give each pupil the best possible education.

Since research generalizations are often based on averages, we tend many times to talk of "average" children, but they don't really exist. It must be emphasized—and often—that each child is an individual who reacts differently because of many variables which make the student separate and unique, with his or her special assets, liabilities, and needs.

SELECTED BIBLIOGRAPHY

Anastasi, Anne. *Individual Differences*. New York: Wiley, 1965.

Anderson, Gary J. "Effects of Social Climate on Individual Learning," *American Educational Research Journal* 7 (1970): 135–152.

Bloom, Benjamin S. *Stability and Change in Human Characteristics*. New York: Wiley, 1964.

Cronbach, Lee J. "How Can Instruction Be Adapted to Individual Differences?" in *Learning and Individual Differences*, Robert M. Gagné, ed. Columbus, Ohio: Merrill, 1967.

Cuban, Larry. *To Make a Difference: Teaching in the Inner City*. New York: Free Press, 1970.

Deutsch, M., I. Katz, and A. R. Jensen, eds. *Social Class, Race, and Psychological Development*. New York: Holt, Rinehart and Winston, 1968.

Howe, Florence. "Sexual Stereotypes Start Early." *Saturday Review*, October 16, 1971, p. 76.

Hurlock, Elizabeth B. *Child Growth and Development*, 5th ed. New York: McGraw-Hill, 1978.

Jensen, Arthur R. *Environment, Heredity, and Intelligence;* compiled from the *Harvard Educational Review*. Cambridge, Mass.: President and Fellows of Harvard College, 1969.

Lugi, James O., and Gerald L. Hershey. *A Multidisciplinary Approach to Psychology of Individual Growth*. New York: Macmillan, 1974.

Maccoby, Eleanor E., ed. *The Development of Sex Differences*. Stanford, Calif.: Stanford University Press, 1966.

Maccoby, Eleanor E., and Carol M. Jacklin. *The Psychology of Sex Differences*. Stanford, Calif.: Stanford University Press, 1974.

Rosenthal, R., and L. Jacobson. *Pygmalion in the Classroom*. New York: Holt, Rinehart and Winston, 1968.

Smart, Mollie S., and Russell C. Smart. *Children: Development and Relationships*, 3d ed. New York: Macmillan, 1977.

Smith, Louis M., and William Geoffrey. *The Complexities of an Urban Classroom*. New York: Holt, Rinehart and Winston, 1968.

Sprinthall, Richard C., and Norman A. Sprinthall, *Educational Psychology: A Developmental Approach*. Reading, Mass.: Addison-Wesley, 1977.

Tyler, Leona E. *Individual Differences: Abilities and Motivational Direction*. Englewood Cliffs, N.J.: Prentice-Hall, 1974.

three

Understanding Language and Concept Development in the Child

Relationship of Language to School Achievement and Other Factors

When young children first come to school, we can wonder what their chances are for success. Will they achieve or will they become roll-call statistics in the nonachievement ledger?

The answers to these questions depend on the children's past experiences, as well as the difference factors discussed in Chapter 2. Figure 3.1 illustrates how the quality of language development depends on the interrelationships of the basic ingredients—which are the factors of intelligence, home environment, sex differences, cultural differences, and family make-up.

Children who are advanced in language development tend to achieve better in school than those who are not.[1] Studies show that high-achieving readers come from homes with enriched verbal environments, whereas low-achieving readers come from homes in which little conversation takes place with the parents.[2] This report on the language ability of "disadvantaged children" comes from an English writer:

> Twenty-four children of one-and-a-half to two years old, living in an orphanage, were divided into two groups, matched for "measured intelligence"—as far as it could be measured at that age: what is clear is that both groups showed *low* ability. Each of the twelve in one group was sent to be looked after by an adolescent girl living in a mental home: the other group was left at the orphanage. After two years the group that had been living with the girls showed extraordinary increases in measured intelligence (well over twenty points), while those in the orphanage showed a *decrease* of similar proportions. What is more astounding still is that after *twenty-one years*, the experimenter was able to trace the children and discovered that the average of the final school achievement of the group looked after in infancy by the girls was twelfth grade (work normal for seventeen-to-eighteen-year-olds) whereas the average for the other group was fourth grade (work normal for nine-to-ten-year-olds).[3]

The importance of having someone to talk to, especially in the crucial years from two to five, has been substantiated by many studies. From these, as well as from the discussion in Chapter 2, it can be seen how closely interrelated are the areas of language, intelligence, early home environment, and school achievement. Furthermore, one can begin to realize how language plays a vital role in the development of intelligence and the reality of success in school.

Let us now turn to the development of language.

Language Development Theories

There is no general agreement among linguists, who are individuals engaged in the systematic study of language, on how a child acquires language. One group claims that language is not innate or inborn. According to this group, the child possesses general abilities for learning, but no specific ability for the learning of language. For them, all language is learned by experience. Another group claims that the human brain is biologically suited for language development. Based on this view, the human brain is unique in its ability to acquire language, which is, thus, an innate human characteristic. All that is necessary for the development of language is to be exposed to it. (For books on language theories see Bibliography.)

Regardless of which theory one advocates, most would agree that the acquisition of language is a most important aspect of the child's intellectual development during the preschool years. Young children must determine, solely from the speech around them, the rules that govern language usage, so that they are able to understand and to produce well-constructed sentences. Amazingly, this difficult and complex task is accomplished by almost all children!

Stages in Language Development

A theoretical model describing the process of language learning consistent with recent research, but not dependent on the innateness

[1]Walter D. Loban, *Language Development: Kindergarten through Grade Twelve*, Research Report No. 18 (Urbana, Ill.: National Council of Teachers of English, 1976).

[2]Esther Milner, "A Study of the Relationship between Reading Readiness in Grade One School Children and Patterns of Parent-Child Interaction," *Child Development* (June 22, 1951): 95–112.

[3]James Britton, *Language and Learning* (Middlesex, England: Penguin, 1970), pp. 94–95.

[4]E. Brooks Smith, Kenneth S. Goodman, Robert Meredith, *Language and Thinking in School*, 2d ed. (New York: Holt, Rinehart and Winston, 1976), pp. 17–26.

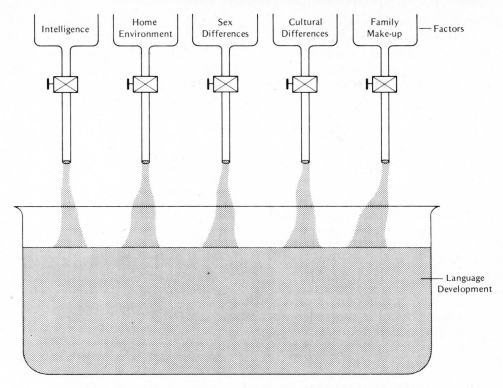

figure 3.1 *Factors Affecting the Language Development of the Child*

assumption, follows.[4] In this model children's language development is divided into a number of stages that overlap; that is, children enter into higher stages well before they have completed earlier (lower) stages. The age at which children enter the various stages is dependent on individual differences. The ages given are approximations and are supplied by the author of this text.

Stage One—Random

In the random stage, children are involved in a variety of vocalizing, cooing, gurgling, babbling, and make most of the sounds that they will need in articulation later on. Children vary the way they use their lips, mouths, and tongues. The sounds children produce are a chance assortment, but adults hear them as the *phonemes* (smallest units of speech sounds) of language. Often children's babbling is composed of con-

sonant-vowel links, such as Ma-ma-ma or Da-da-da. These first sounds are usually greeted with joy and delight by children's parents. No matter how unintelligible the sounds, the parents will perceive them to be words meaning "Mama" and "Daddy." Parents are excited because they feel that their children have spoken. They will many times repeat the sounds of "Ma ma" and "Da da," and reward the children with extra attention and smiles every time they produce these sounds. Such reinforcement usually causes children to repeat the response.

Stage Two—Unitary

In the unitary stage children develop deliberate units of language which are often limited to one syllable. The length of each utterance is a function of the child's level of physical development and control over his or her sound-producing mechanism, since the processes of language development and physical maturation are simultaneous. For example, one-year-old children usually have only a one-digit word span (the children can only retain and repeat one digit). The word that the children use is an abbreviation for their association with the total situation. Single words are used to convey whole sentences. Sometimes a single utterance is used to signify a variety of adult sentences. For example, "See" may mean "I see you" or "Let me see it."

Children's early forms of speech include those words which convey a major meaning from the speech heard; children's speech has been described as "telegraphic."[5] Children are able to get and convey the message even though it is beyond their digit span. In telegraphic speech, when the children use more than one word, the word order of adult speech is preserved.

How are children able to extract the most meaningful words from fairly complex utterances? One explanation is that content words are those that parents may have practiced with the children one at a time. For example, the parents may use association; that is, they pair a real apple with the word sound "apple." When the children repeat the word the parents may reinforce them by smiling and saying "Good." Content words also receive the most stress in a sentence, and may therefore be the easiest to discern.

Stage Three—Expansion and Delimiting

In expanding speech children go from one or two syllable utterances to adult language structure. At approximately eighteen or twenty months children's first two-word utterances usually appear. These consist of words from two

[5]Roger Brown and Ursula Bellugi, "Three Processes in the Child's Acquisition of Syntax," *Harvard Educational Review* 34 (1964): 133–151.

classes. The first, called the pivot class, is small, contains words of high frequency, and may be in either the first or second position, but is usually fixed in one or the other. First or second position merely refers to the place of the word in a given sentence. The second, called the open class, contains all other words. In speaking, the children combine a single pivot word with other words. For example, "See Mommy," "See Daddy," "See kitty," "See baby." Some two-word utterances may serve a number of speech purposes. For example, "Mommy play," might mean "Mommy is playing" or "I want Mommy to play with me."

Researchers in language development, considering the problem of how children's telegraphic speech becomes elaborated, supposed that a constant exposure to adult speech may be a sufficient basis for children to enlarge their own speech. However, parents also tend to imitate children's speech. If a child says "Kitty drink," the parent is apt to say, "Yes, the kitty is drinking his milk." The parents help children to see that their utterances are correct for the situation and add other appropriate language elements which are grammatical.

If parents "overload" the information that is presented to children at this stage by using too many words, the children will probably not get the message. For example, Gertrude L. Wyatt, an authority on language problems, writes of twins who were having difficulty in speaking because their mother flooded them with too much information. The boys were looking at a picture book with their mother when this dialogue took place:

Steve: How do aya-pa go?
Mother: (who has understood Steve's question): It takes an elephant fifteen years to reach mature size. Elephants are mammals with an enormous appetite.

The language pattern that the mother presented did not fit the boys' stage of development. As a result, communication between mother and sons broke down. The mother's rapid speech and sophisticated vocabulary had overloaded the boys' receiving systems to the point where they were unable to distinguish and remember single sounds and sequences of sounds.[6]

By thirty-six months of age some children are using varieties of complete English sentences. Through the gradual expansion of speech, the child, by about four years of age, has mastered the features of adult speech.

Stage Four—Structural-Awareness

So that children can express their increasingly abstract ideas and feelings they must come to the stage of structural awareness, where they are able to generalize and find pattern and order in speech. As children begin to use plurals and to vary their verb forms, the most common type of mistake they make indicates that the rules they follow are overgeneralized and do not include exceptions. For example, irregular verbs are regularized, making the past tense of "I go," "I goed."

Stage Five—Automatic

In the automatic stage children have internalized grammar, so that they can generate a large number of sentences that are grammatical although they cannot explain why by conscious reasoning. Children are usually at this stage when they are ready to enter kindergarten.

Stage Six—Creative

At the creative stage children are involved in inventing their own language. Although many of the phrases they use may be trite, expressing

the attitudes of their peer group or community, they fulfill the children's needs.

Figure 3.2 illustrates the language development stages just discussed.

Summary

It appears that children learn language by *association* (pairing the real object with the sound of the word), *reinforcement* (any positive stimulus, such as praise, which usually causes the individual to repeat a given response), *imitation* (children's attempting to voice the sounds initially voiced by the parent figures), and *elaboration* (expanding a word into a complete sentence).

Children may have difficulty in acquiring language if they are not exposed to elaborated speech patterns: if, for example, a language other than English is spoken at home or if they are not listened to. (See Chapter 6 for a discussion of the child's development of articulation.)

Concept Development

Concept development is closely related to language development. Unless children attain the necessary concepts, they will be limited in all aspects of the language arts.

A group of stimuli with common characteristics is a concept. These stimuli may be objects, events, or persons. Concepts are usually designated by their names, such as books, war, men, women, animals, teachers, and so forth. All these concepts refer to classes (or categories) of stimuli. Some stimuli do not refer to concepts; Miss Dawn, the hairdresser, Hemingway's "The Killers," World War II, and the Super Bowl are examples. These are particular (not classes of) stimuli, persons, or events.[7]

---

[6]Gertrude L. Wyatt, "In the Beginning Is the Word," *New York Times*, October 19, 1969.

[7]John P. DeCecco, *The Psychology of Learning and Instruction: Educational Psychology* (Englewood Cliffs, N.J.: Prentice-Hall, 1968), p. 388.

Creative stage

(72 months)

Child able to invent his own language as ability to conceptualize and think abstractly increases. Words used to express uniqueness of life as seen by specific group or individuals. Trite clichés are used.

Automatic stage, kindergarten level

Child able to communicate in his society, has internalized grammar of the language. He has a large vocabulary, can generate many utterances, can tell whether utterance is correct or not but not able to explain why.

(60 months)

Words and phrases take on meaning. Child experiments with language; as a result it becomes more ungrammatical than in prior stage. Makes errors by overgeneralizing. *Example*: "I goed" for "I went." Develops ability to generalize, to find patterns and order in language. *Example*: "I see you." "I see ball." "I see Mommy."

Structural-awareness stage

(48 months)

Child has acquired a large vocabulary. Language of child has features of adult speech.

Expansion and delimiting stage

Utterances are becoming more precise. Collection of utterances are expanded from one or two syllables to fuller ones. *Example*: "Wanna play" to "I want to play." Word order of adult speech is maintained. Two-word utterances may serve purpose for many sentences.

(24 months)

Pivot words are used with all other words. *Example*: "See Mommy." "See baby." "See ball."

Unitary stage

Child imitates parents. Speech is abbreviated. Single words used for whole sentences. *Example*: "Play, play," for "Play with me." Develops units of language. Word *play* may serve the purpose of many sentences. Uses sound purposefully to express a need.

(12 months)

Acquires ability to use sound as attention getter. Babbling still prevalent.

Random stage

Vocalizations resemble phonemes of adult speech. Random assortment of sound produced by child is not language. Babbling. *Example*: Ma-Ma-Ma. Cooing.

figure 3.2 *Model of language development stages showing the close overlap of any one stage with the immediately neighboring stages (ages are approximated and supplied by the author).* *Source:* Adapted from Smith, Goodman, and Meredith (1976).

FIGMENTS   **By Dale Hale**

figure 3.3   *Language development and concept development are closely related. Not understanding one meaning of the word* toast, *the boy incorrectly interprets adult speech.*

Concepts are needed to reduce the complexity of the world. When children learn that their shaggy pets are called dogs, they tend to label all other similar four-footed animals as "dogs." This is because young children overgeneralize, tending to group all animals together, and have not yet perceived the differences between and among various animals. Unless children learn to discern differences, the class of words that they deal with will become exceptionally unwieldy and unmanageable. However, if children group each object in a class by itself, this too will bring about difficulties in coping with environmental stimuli, because it will also be such an unwieldy method.

Piaget and Concept Development

Concept development is closely related to cognitive (thinking) development. Jean Piaget, a renowned Swiss psychologist, has written on children's cognitive development in terms of their ability to organize (which requires conceptualization), classify, and adapt to their environments.

According to Piaget,[8] the mind is capable of intellectual exercise because of its ability to cat-

egorize incoming stimuli adequately. Schemata (structured designs) are the cognitive arrangements by which this takes place. As children develop, and take in more and more information, it is necessary to have some way to categorize all the new information. This is done by means of schemata, and, as children develop, their ability to categorize grows too. That is, children should be able to differentiate, to become less dependent on sensory stimuli, and to gain more and more complex schemata. Children should be able to categorize a cat as distinct from a mouse or a rabbit. They should be able to group cat, dog, and cow together as animals. Piaget calls the processes which bring about these changes in children's thinking *assimilation* and *accommodation*.

Assimilation does not change an individual's concept but allows it to grow. It is a continuous process which helps the individual to integrate new, incoming stimuli into existing schemata or concepts. For example, when children tend to label all similar four-footed animals as dogs, the children are assimilating. They have assimilated all four-footed animals into their existing schemata.

If the child meets stimuli which cannot fit into the existing schema, then the alternative is either to construct a new category or to change the existing category. When a new schema or

[8]Jean Piaget, *The Origins of Intelligence in Children* (New York: International Universities Press, 1952).

concept is developed, or when an existing schema is changed, this is called accommodation.

Although both assimilation and accommodation are important processes that the child must attain in order to develop adequate cognition, a balance between the two processes is necessary. If children overassimilate, they will have categories that are too large to handle and, similarly, if they overaccommodate, they will have too many categories, as we have already seen. Piaget calls the balance between the two *equilibrium.* A person having equilibrium would be able to see similarities between stimuli and thus properly assimilate them, and would also be able to determine when new schemata are needed for adequate accommodation of a surplus of categories.

As children develop cognitively they proceed from more global (generalized) schemata to more particular ones. For the child there are usually no right or wrong placements, but only better or more effective ones. That is what good education is all about.

Concepts are necessary to help students acquire increasing amounts of knowledge. For example, in school, as one proceeds through the grades, learning becomes more abstract and is expressed in words, using verbal stimuli as labels for concepts. Many teachers take for granted that those spoken concept labels are understood by their students, but this is not always so. Many times these concepts are learned either incompletely or incorrectly. This example illustrates incomplete concepts for the tourist and immigrant.[9]

All tourists may be obviously American whereas all the immigrants may be obviously Mexican. The tourists may be well dressed, the immigrants poorly dressed, and so on. If the natural environment is like a grand concept-formation experiment, it may take the child a long time to attain the concepts *tourist* and *immigrant;* indeed, the environment may not be as informative as the usual experimenter since the child may not always be informed, or reliably informed, as to the correctness of his guesses. No wonder a child might form the concept that a tourist is a well-dressed person who drives a station wagon with out-of-state license plates!

When children come to school the teacher must assess their concept-development level, then help them to add the attributes necessary and relevant for the development of particular concepts, while aiding them to delete all those concepts that are faulty or irrelevant.

Concept Development in Primary Grades K–3

Preschool children learn concepts, for the most part, from direct experience. Unless young children have had direct sensory experiences, they will have difficulty in concept development.

When children enter kindergarten they may know the following concepts: above and below, on top of, underneath, next to, the middle one, start, stop, go, come, sit, stand, and so on. They may not know this type of concept: the one before, the next one, double, like, and unlike, nor are they likely to recognize grapheme-phoneme (letter-sound) correspondences or number names for quantities.[10]

Kindergarten children are learning to group many objects. Different kinds of apples—such as Delicious, McIntosh, Cortland, and Greening apples—would all go under the class Apples. Also, pears, apples, bananas, plums, and so forth would go under the class Fruit.

In the primary grades children are learning simple concepts such as over and under, big and little. The pupils learn to classify things such as dog and animals, days and weeks, pennies and money, and so on, proceeding from a concrete to a more abstract level. For example, a child can name his or her dog "Champ," who is a pet, and as a pet it is also in the class of animals.

[9]John Carroll, "Words, Meanings and Concepts," *Harvard Educational Review* 34 (1964): 194.

[10]Robert M. Gagné, *Conditions of Learning* (New York: Holt, Rinehart and Winston, 1965).

© 1974 by NEA, Inc.

"YOU GOTTA SPEAK PLAIN ENGLISH TO MY MOM! YOU ASK FOR BREAD AND YOU GET BREAD ... ASK FOR MONEY!"

As children grow in their use of listening, speaking, and reading skills, their concept development continues. They learn that some words designate different levels of things and feelings. They put on their *coats*. They put *coats* of paint on the toy. These two uses illustrate a homograph. The children learn about different kinds of elevators, forms, cities. They develop the relational concepts of afraid, brave, proud, faraway, and so on. They learn the meaning of figures of speech, such as: "The trees trembled in the night" or "The wind roared its disapproval." The students should also learn the concepts of *synonyms* (words that mean the same or nearly the same) and *antonyms* (words that mean the opposite) in isolation and in context.

Concept Development and the Educationally Disadvantaged Child[11]

In the case of educationally disadvantaged children teachers cannot assume that certain concepts have already been attained. For example, most teachers would take for granted that the term "pet" is a concrete, clearcut name that all children could easily learn. However, this may not be so. Many children from a low socioeconomic area in Washington, D.C., did not know the word "pet." To the children living in this area "pet" was an abstraction, because a child living in an overcrowded apartment does not usually have a pet. In order to have a dog one must obtain a license, feed the pet, give it medical attention, have a place for it to stay, and so on. Although children who live in low socio-economic environments may have rich, expressive vocabularies of their own, they will not be the same vocabulary that is predominantly used in middle-class schools and curriculums.[12]

In helping educationally disadvantaged children to develop concepts, the teacher must help them to attain concepts which are of greatest concern, interest, and use to them. It is claimed by some authorities that these children use adjectives better than verbs, that they are able to express themselves better in spontaneous or

[11]The term "disadvantaged" is applied to those students who come from low socioeconomic status homes. These children are disadvantaged in school because they may lack the concept-development experiences and the vocabulary that is needed in order to achieve well in school.

[12]Edgar Dale, "Vocabulary Development of the Underprivileged Child," *Elementary English* 42 (November 1965): 778–786.

unstructured situations than in formal ones, that they understand more language than they use, and that they have the verbal ability to fantasize.[13] Using these descriptive factors as a guide, the teacher could create a program to help such children attain the concepts necessary for developing cognitive processes and the language arts.

An informal inventory test of concepts in the primary grades, such as the one on pages 26–29, could be developed and easily administered to the whole class as a paper-and-pencil test, or it can be given orally to individual students, whichever is more convenient in the classroom situation.

Another method to determine whether chil-

dren have the concept of opposites would be for the teacher to ask each child to give some opposites for the following words:

no	good	fat
boy	mommy	go
happy		

In order to determine whether the children understand the concepts of left and right, the teacher could play the game "Simon Says" with the children and employ directions using the words "left" and "right." The teacher could also observe whether children understand the concept of "first" and "last" by asking children to name who is first in line or who is last in line. The teacher can learn much about the concept development of students by using such informal techniques.

[13]Frank Riessman, *The Culturally Deprived Child* (New York: Harper & Row, 1962).

EXAMPLE OF AN INFORMAL INVENTORY TEST OF CONCEPTS FOR PRIMARY-GRADE STUDENTS

For each concept the teacher will orally state the tested term in the context of a sentence. The children will show they understand the concept by correctly checking or putting a circle around the picture that best describes the concept. Before beginning, the teacher should make sure that all children understand the symbol for a check (✔) and that they can draw a circle around an object.

1. Concept *over*. Concept in sentence: The check (✔) is over the ball.

Directions:

Put a circle around the picture that shows a (✔) is over a ball. (Again, the teacher should put a (✔) on the board to make sure children understand this term. The teacher should make a circle on the board to make sure children understand this concept as well.)

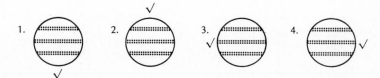

2. Concept of *under*. Concept in sentence: The check (✔) is under the ball.

Directions:

Put a circle around the picture that shows a (✔) is under a ball.

1.   2.   3.   4.

3. Concept of *squares*. Sentence: Which picture shows a square?

Directions:

Put a check in the square.

4. Concept of *triangle*. Sentence: Which picture shows a triangle?

Directions:

Put a check in the triangle.

5. Concept of *most*. Sentence: Which box has the most balls?

Directions:

Draw a circle around the box that has the most balls.

1. 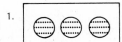   2.    3.

6. Concept of *least.* Sentence: Which box has the least balls?

Directions:

Draw a circle around the box that has the least balls.

7. Concept of *smallest.* Sentence: Which ball is the smallest?

Directions:

Draw a circle around the smallest ball.

8. Concept of *largest.* Sentence: Which ball is the largest?

Directions:

Draw a circle around the largest ball.

9. Concept of *opposites.*

Directions:

Draw a circle around the picture that is the opposite of the word that I am going to say. (For example, the teacher says, "What is the opposite of girl?")

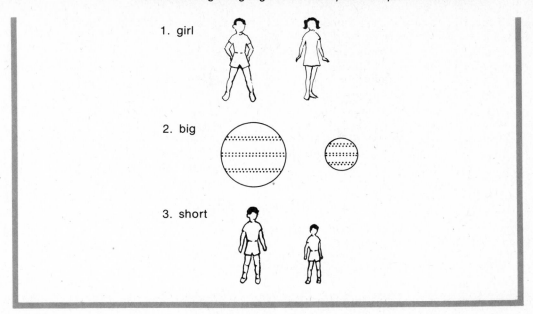

1. girl

2. big

3. short

Summary

Success in school depends in great part on children's language development. Whether language is an innate ability, as some authorities believe, or is a result of a human brain uniquely able to acquire language, young children learn to speak the language of those around them and furthermore learn the grammar involved in producing well-constructed sentences. This is generally accomplished in six interlocking stages for which a model is given in the text. In order to grow in their use of language, children must also begin to develop concepts by which they group words and organize them. Piaget has evolved the terms assimilation and accommodation to describe the changes in thinking. As their ability to develop new concepts grows, children are learning and gaining knowledge.

It is important for teachers to identify the level of concept development among the children in their class, and a simple series of tests is given for this purpose. Particularly with children from low socioeconomic areas, teachers must not make assumptions about concept development, but must determine actual levels.

SELECTED BIBLIOGRAPHY

Brown, Roger, and Ursula Bellugi. "Three Processes in the Child's Acquisition of Syntax." *Harvard Educational Review* 34 (1964): 133–151.

Caramazza, Alfonso, and Edgar Zurif. *Language Acquisition and Language Breakdown*. Baltimore, Md.: Johns Hopkins University Press, 1978.

Carroll, John B. *Language and Thought*. Englewood Cliffs, N.J.: Prentice-Hall, 1964.

Chomsky, Noam. *Language and Mind*, enl. ed. New York: Harcourt Brace Jovanovich, 1972.

Dale, Philip S. *Language Development*. Hinsdale, Ill.: Dryden, 1972.

De Villiers, Jill G., and Peter A. De Villiers. *Language Acquisition*. Cambridge, Mass.: Harvard University Press, 1978.

Fagan, Edward R. *English and the Disadvantaged*. Scranton, Pa.: International Textbook, 1969.

Hardy, William G. *Communication and the Disadvantaged Child*. Baltimore, Md.: Williams & Wilkins, 1970.

Labov, William. *Sociolinguistic Patterns*. Philadelphia, Pa.: University of Pennsylvania Press, 1973.

Loban, Walter D. *Language Development: Kindergarten through Grade Twelve*. Research Report No. 18. National Council of Teachers of English, 1976.

McNeill, D. *The Acquisition of Language: The Study of Developmental Psycholinguistics*. New York: Harper & Row, 1970.

Piaget, Jean. *The Language and Thought of the Child*. New York: Harcourt, Brace, 1926.

Rosen, Connie. *The Language of Primary School Children*. New York: Penguin, 1973.

Smith, E. Brooks, Kenneth S. Goodman, and Robert Meredith. *Language and Thinking in School*, 2d ed. New York: Holt, Rinehart and Winston, 1976.

Stross, Brian. "Language Acquisition and Teaching." *Language Arts* 55 (September 1978): 749–755.

Vygotsky, L. S. *Thought and Language*, trans. E. Hanfmann and G. Vakar. Cambridge, Mass.: M.I.T. Press, 1962.

Wadsworth, Barry J. *Piaget for the Classroom Teacher*. New York: Longmans, 1978.

Williams, Frederich, ed. *Language and Poverty*. Chicago: Markham, 1970.

four

Developing Creativity in the
Language Arts Program

EXAMPLES OF TEACHER COMPETENCIES

1. The teacher will be able to explain why the language arts teacher should be well acquainted with creativity.
2. The teacher will be able to state several definitions of creativity.
3. The teacher will be able to state some ways that are used to measure creativity.
4. The teacher will be able to explain the relationship between creativity and intelligence.
5. The teacher will be able to describe the creative process.
6. The teacher will be able to describe how creativity can be nurtured in the classroom.
7. The teacher will be able to describe brainstorming and explain how to use it in the classroom.

I see the mind of a five year old, . . . as a volcano with two vents, destructiveness and creativeness. And I see that to the extent that we widen the creative channel we atrophy the destructive one. . . .[1]

SYLVIA ASHTON-WARNER

[1]Sylvia Ashton-Warner, *Spinster* (New York: Simon & Schuster, 1959), p. 221.

The Young Child and Creativity

It is said that children come to school curious, uninhibited, filled with enthusiasm and the desire to know, but as they proceed through school, these talents are squelched. Carl Rogers, a well-known clinical psychologist, claims: "In education we tend to turn out conformists, stereotypes, individuals whose education is

31

'completed,' rather than freely creative and original thinkers."[2] Another psychologist, H. A. Anderson, says: "Creativity was in each of us as a small child. In children creativity is a universal. Among adults it is almost nonexistent."[3] Others decry the stifling of the child's natural gifts by surrounding adults and blame them for destroying the child's ability to create.[4]

These statements imply that our schools are not assuming the responsibility which John Dewey, an eminent philosopher and educator, felt was an especially crucial one—that of giving free rein to the child's imagination and allowing it to flourish.[5]

Language arts teachers must be well acquainted with creativity. A good physical environment is a necessary first step in helping to establish an atmosphere where creativity can reign. (See "Classroom Physical Environment" in Chapter 15.) But more is needed to encourage and stimulate creativity. Teachers must have some understanding and insight into the creative process itself. They must also have a knowledge of techniques which will spark the creativity in students.

How Is Creativity Defined and Measured?

Confusion exists about the meaning of the term "creativity" because it can mean so many different things to so many different people. Some define creativity as "something new." Yet what may be new to one may not be new to another. If we use a definition such as this, anyone, regardless of intellectual capacity, can be considered creative. Other definitions of crea-

tivity are based on that of divergent thinking— for example, the many different ways of doing things, which has been derived from J. P. Guilford's three-dimensional model of intelligence and which represents intellect in terms of operations, content, and products.

However, since the dimension of creativity is not measured on IQ tests, E. P. Torrance, an educational psychologist at the University of Georgia, developed tests of creative thinking, which he based on his investigations of classroom situations where he felt creativity was fostered. Torrance defines creativity "as the process of becoming sensitive to problems, deficiencies, gaps in knowledge, missing elements, disharmonies, and so on; identifying the difficulty; searching for solutions, making guesses, or formulating hypotheses about the deficiencies; testing and retesting these hypotheses and possibly modifying and retesting them; and finally communicating the results."[6] The tests are supposed to measure fluency or the number of relevant ideas; flexibility or the number of shifts in thought or changes in categories of response; originality or the number of statistically infrequent responses; and elaboration or the number of different ideas employed in working out the specifics of an overall idea.

S. J. Parnes, President of Creative Education Foundation at Buffalo University, gave his definition at a symposium on creativity in the early sixties: a combination of imagination plus knowledge plus evaluation. Although there is no universally agreed on definition of creativity, Parnes' seems to incorporate all the necessary elements. It also delimits and qualifies a broad definition, whereby anything new to the individual connotes creativity. It seems reasonable that the more knowledge individuals have, no matter in what area, the more able they will be to generate many different ideas—if they have the requisite

[2]Carl Rogers, "Toward a Theory of Creativity," in *Creativity and Its Cultivation*, Harold H. Anderson, ed. (New York: Harper & Row, 1959), p. 69.

[3]Ibid., p. xii.

[4]Hughes Mearns, *Creative Youth* (New York: Doubleday, Page, 1926), p. viii.

[5]John Dewey, *The Child and the Curriculum and the School and Society* (Chicago: University of Chicago Press, 1902), p. 61.

[6]E. P. Torrance, "Scientific Views of Creativity and Factors Affecting Its Growth," in *Creativity and Learning*, Jerome Kagan, ed. (Boston: Houghton Mifflin, 1967), pp. 73–74.

imagination. Similarly, the more intelligent the individuals, the more able they will be to evaluate their product. Therefore, an individual who is more intelligent is bound to be more capable of greater creativity than someone who is less intelligent—all other things being equal. In actuality, since "other" variables are rarely equal it does not necessarily follow that people of great intelligence will be more creative than people of less intelligence.

J. W. Getzels and P. W. Jackson's study of two groups of students, one of which was composed of supposedly high creatives who were not gifted and the other of which was composed of gifted students who were not highly creative, was of great significance because it brought the concept and importance of creativity to the attention of educators. The researchers found that the high IQ group was not necessarily the high creative group and, although both groups of students achieved equally well, different characteristics distinguished the two groups. After studying the data more closely, it was found that all the students had relatively high IQs and were able; for example, the mean IQ of the high creative group was 127; whereas the mean IQ of the high intelligence group was 150.[7]

Some persons have used this study in their claim that one does not need to be intelligent in order to be creative. This is not so when we define creativity in an absolute sense. For example, the discovery of a new vaccine or a new technique in surgery would necessitate special knowledge and intelligence, but other factors are needed to make one truly creative. The characteristics which distinguish one group of able students from another include those salient features which may determine creative behavior. High creatives are more concerned with their "self-ideal" and are not as influenced by impositions from the teacher or society. A sense of

humor was another factor, according to the Getzels and Jackson study, which set high creatives apart from high gifted students. For example, children were asked to write an autobiography, parts of which are given here.[8]

High Creative Subjects

In 1943 I was born. I have been living without interruption ever since. My parents are my mother and father—an arrangement I have found increasingly convenient over the years. My father is Dr. _____ physician and surgeon—at least that's what the sign on his office door says. Of course, he's not anymore for Dad's past the age where men ought to enjoy the rest of his life. He retired from Mercy Hospital Christmas before last. Got a fountain-pen for 27 years of service. . . .

I was transferred from another world, or "hatched" as you might call it, at a very young age (0 for a fact). I called my mammy and she came runnin'! Den dat dok came an' he done took me and ah' squealed with fright. O' course I couldn' see anythin' anyhoo. (I was done borned in dat place dey call "Bellview," now what would ah' be doon' dere?) Den I grown up fur' three (3) yer' before my brudder was bornded. He is de' durndist critter ah' eveh' saw podnah'. At this time in my life you can see I played a cowboy, with my mudder as a injun. She never was the same cause ah used to hit her with a frin' pan. . . .

High IQ Subjects

I was born in Hartford, Connecticut on April 7, 1943. My sister Mary was born 6 years later and my brother Paul a year and a half after that. Because of their close age they have never had to worry about what to do. Today my sister is in 2nd grade, my

---

[7]J. W. Getzels and P. W. Jackson, *Creativity and Intelligence: Explorations with Gifted Students* (New York: Wiley, 1962), p. 24.

[8]Ibid., pp. 100–101.

brother in 1st. The only change in our family was the addition of a dog Terry who is very important to us. . . .

My autobiography is neither interesting nor exciting and I see very little reason for writing it. However I shall attempt to write a certain amount of material which would be constructive. I was born May 8, 1943, in Atlanta, Georgia, U.S.A. I am descended from a long line of ancestry which is mostly Scotch and English, with a few exceptions here and there. Most of my recent ancestors have lived in the southern U.S. for a good while, though some are from New York. After being born, I remained in Georgia six weeks, after which I moved to Fairfax, Virginia. During my four-year stay there, I had few adventures of any kind, other than accidently setting fire to my brother's bed. . . .

Another test using a projective technique (a method in which the individual tends to put himself into the situation depicted) presented a picture stimulus to the students perceived as a man sitting in an airplane reclining seat on a return trip. Here are samples of the comments given by a high IQ subject and a high creative subject.[9]

High Creative Subject

This man is flying back from Reno where he has just won a divorce from his wife. He couldn't stand to live with her anymore, he told the judge, because she wore so much cold cream on her face at night that her head would skid across the pillow and hit him in the head. He is now contemplating a new skidproof face cream.

High IQ Subject

Mr. Smith is on his way home from a successful business trip. He is very happy

[9]Ibid., p. 39.

and he is thinking about his wonderful family and how glad he will be to see them again. He can picture it, about an hour from now, his plane landing at the airport and Mrs. Smith and their three children all there welcoming him home again.

A possible explanation for the difference in response between the two groups may be that very able students, who are achievement oriented and grade conscious, will attempt to "size up" the teacher at the beginning of the term, try to "figure out" what is wanted and then attempt to give the teacher exactly that. It's not that these students are not able to be creative but that they have learned while going to school that "creativity" is not rewarded; and they act accordingly. They have been conditioned not to be divergent.

When students are asked to write their autobiographies, most students probably just state their vital statistics. This may show that high IQ children answer in what they feel is the expected direction. The question is: Would they answer in this way if they were encouraged to be creative?

The Creative Process

Creativity cannot be commanded. It needs time. If teachers want to help students to be creative, they must have an understanding of this process.

According to psychologists there seem to be four stages to the creative act for most people: (1) preparation, (2) incubation, (3) illumination, and (4) verification.[10]

Preparation involves all the necessary background experience and skills an individual must have in order to be creative in a given area. As was previously mentioned, in Parnes' definition

[10]G. Wallas, *The Art of Thought* (New York: Harcourt Brace, 1926).

The more knowledge and imagination individuals have, the more creative they can be.

of creativity "knowledge" is an important ingredient; the more knowledge people have, the more able they are to be creative. Creativity and knowledge of basic skills are not mutually exclusive. They work hand in hand. The teacher can help students by making sure all are receiving the necessary tools. Those who say, "Let them just create; knowledge gets in the way," and so forth, are not helping to set the proper stage to prepare for creativity. An engineer-lawyer discussing engineering education says:[11]

Engineering education should encourage students to strive for the mastery of fundamentals, the discovery of the relatedness of things, and the cultivation of excellence. But it should also be a

[11]Daniel V. DeSimone, "Education for Innovation," *Spectrum* IEEE 5 (January 1968): 83.

creative experience, stimulating the imagination of students and helping them to prepare themselves for the contests and the challenges of an imperfect world. It should encourage them to believe they can do the "impossible" from time to time, even if it means doing violence to precedent.

The importance of recognizing the tools necessary for creativity has been sidetracked because of the overuse and misuse of the term "creativity." Persons who have achieved in the creative area usually devote a great portion of their lives to the field in which they work. Competency and creativity demand good preparation.

Incubation is the second step in the creative process. This stage is not visible. It is the time when individuals appear to be thinking about anything but the problem, yet they may actually be mulling it over in their minds.

In the following line drawing, how many squares do you see?

Most people say sixteen. Ask them to look again. They are usually puzzled.

Hint:

What is the definition of a square? Now look again. How many do you see now? At this point some call out seventeen, eighteen, or nineteen. They are getting the idea. They are looking beyond the obvious.

Solution:

There are thirty different squares: sixteen each of 1 x 1; nine each of 2 x 2; four each of 3 x 3; and one of 4 x 4.

How clever are you?
How many know their Roman numerals well? Think of Roman numeral nine, then subtract three. By adding one symbol to Roman numeral nine, you should be able to come up with the answer.
After some time the teacher often has to provide the answer. IX is put on the board, and an "S" is added before the number to produce six.

Illumination is that moment of insight when a spark is lit and a solution seems at hand. A Nobel Prize winning scientist describes illumination this way:[12]

. . . I just wander about, without especially clear ideas or preconceived notions so far as I know, and now and then something pops up—boom!— something that is entirely new, that leads to new lines of research.

Verification is the final stage, where the "hunch" (the hypothesis) is subjected to testing and refinement. The same Nobel Prize winner describes his manner of work:[13]

But while I am working I usually do not know where I am going. I just follow hunches. I dream up all sorts of theories at night and then disprove them in the laboratory the next day. Checking a hunch, sometimes I see some discrepancy, something unexpected—then I follow it up. Success depends on whether the hunch was good or bad.

Nuturing Creativity

Creativity is not something which "just happens." If we want divergent thinkers (persons who can see many different ways to solve problems) and individuals who are and continue to be intelligent risk-takers, we must create an environment that values these traits and we must involve students in creative experiences. If teachers are not creative—if they are fright-

[12]Albert Szent-Gyorgyi, "The Strategy of Life," *Science and Technology* (New York: International Communications, June 1966), p. 49.
[13]Ibid., p. 49.

ened and bothered by divergency—they will be unable to create the proper physical, emotional, and intellectual climate essential for the development of creativity.

A creative atmosphere is one which pervades everything that is done in the classroom. On the first school day the manner in which the students are greeted will determine, to a certain extent, how free students will feel to be different.

Teachers must provide stimulating activities for students when they first begin school. Torrance has developed a tentative hierarchy of creative skills which he feels might be taught to children. His six levels range from the young child's learning to produce new combinations through the manipulation of sounds, colors, and shapes to the child's being able to carry through the sequence of creative problem-solving.[14]

On page 36 are some exercises that have been used with intermediate-grade students, as well as with college language arts students, on the first few days of class. They help to establish rapport, to awaken many students as to how "set" they are, and also to show how the verbal behavior of the teacher influences students.

To illustrate how rigid many students are, and how a teacher's verbal behavior influences students, it can be shown that beginning with the question of how clever someone is can cause anxiety, especially on the first day of class when a student wants to make a good impression. This challenge may bring about less effective functioning. The second question about how well the students know Roman numerals, and a repetition of the words, can cause students to think about an answer in the area only of Roman numerals, where their minds have been "set."

Another exercise in creative thinking designed to avoid rigidity is to put this dot matrix on the board:

. . .

. . .

. . .

Tell the students to connect the dots with four straight lines going through each dot only once and without lifting the pencil from the paper. To solve this new problem students must use a very important clue, that of *going beyond*. Most people confine themselves to the set of the original square, but the problem can only be solved if one goes beyond.

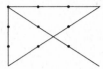

These activities help students recognize how "set" they are and encourage creativity in the class.

Brainstorming

Brainstorming (generating many different ideas without inhibition) is a technique that has been popularized in business and industry. It can be used very effectively in the classroom situation to help stretch students' imaginations. The process is an excellent way to break the ice among students on any level. It helps them to work together while creating an atmosphere conducive to creativity.

Certain principles must be followed so that brainstorming will be truly effective:

1. Anything goes.
2. No criticisms.
3. Build on another's ideas.

It has been found that those who generate the most ideas in a brainstorming session most often also have the ideas of highest quality.[15]

Before getting students involved in group-brainstorming, they should try self-brainstorming. Students can be given a stimulus to which they must react, "stretching their imaginations"

[14]E. Paul Torrance, *Encouraging Creativity in the Classroom* (Dubuque, Iowa: W. C. Brown, 1970), pp. 40–53.

[15]Alex F. Osborn, *Applied Imagination*, 3d ed. (New York: Scribner's, 1963), p. 156.

while observing the three principles listed here. They can write down all of their ideas and, after a few minutes, time is called. The student with the greatest quantity of ideas reads his or her list to the whole class. If someone in the class has an idea not on this original list, that idea is added. (This also makes for a very good listening activity for students.) Only after all the ideas have been stated does evaluation take place.

In group-brainstorming students choose one person who is a very fast writer to record oral ideas called out as soon as they are thought up. The same principles prevail for group-brainstorming as for self-brainstorming. But in the group the temptation to criticize must be overcome. These topics could be used for both group- and self-brainstorming sessions:

1. Many different uses of a brick.
2. Many different uses of a pin.
3. Many different uses of a paper clip.
4. Many different uses of a coat hanger.
5. Many different uses of a paper bag.
6. Many different uses of a button.
7. Many different uses of a rubber band.
8. Many different uses of a pencil.
9. Many different uses of a block.
10. Many different uses of a paper carton.
11. State all elements that an "ideal school" would have.
12. State what you would build on the moon, if you were going there on a trip.
13. State all the kinds of automation devices you can think of.

Students should be helped to understand that "different uses" does not include, for example: "A brick can be used to build a house. A brick can be used to build a wall. A brick can be used to build a chimney." It would include such things as: "A brick can be used as a bed warmer, to write with, to carve out and use as an ashtray, to use as a missile," and so on.

Brainstorming activities can lead to a number of very exciting language arts projects. In one fifth-grade class, students were group-brainstorming the many different uses of a half-pint

milk carton. After they had evaluated some of their ideas, many of the children wanted to carry them out. As a result, a number of new groups were formed. One group made puppets and a stage out of the cartons. Then they started to write scripts for their puppets. The Fifth Grade Thespian Group was born. They not only gave original shows to their own class but also presented shows for many of the other classes. The kindergarten children enjoyed them, and upper-grade children looked forward to these informal productions as well. Announcements to advertise coming attractions were written by the Thespian Group, which was usually joined by other children who helped with artwork and new productions.

Some students made robots and other imaginary creatures out of the milk containers and wrote stories about them.

Brainstorming, while helping to establish a nonthreatening environment, can also be a springboard to creative writing! (See Chapter 11.)

In summary, a good language arts program cannot exist without the necessary ingredient of creativity. When creativity is a living process that permeates the teaching–learning activities, the classroom atmosphere is charged with electricity and becomes a very special place.

This poem describes how creativity in a child can be almost thwarted. If you were this child's teacher, how would you have reacted?

GREEN SKY, BLUE GRASS

Oh happy day,
Oh day so bright,
Let me catch you,
Just for a moment,
And let me feel you!

Yes, I'll draw you,
My happy day, with
Bright, happy colors.
Pretty day, I'll draw you
With a green sky and blue grass—
All in a smiling sea of yellow.

Happy and oh so free,
Let me draw you!

Then I heard a laugh,
A snicker, a sneer.
"Green sky, blue grass?
Everyone knows that
Grass is green and
Skys are blue and
Seas aren't yellow and . . ."

But I didn't hear any more,
Because I had lost my happy day—
It disappeared so fast
I didn't see it go.
And I was sad and tired
And didn't know what to do.

Then I heard another voice,
A bright, happy voice,
Like my day.
And it said, "What a pretty picture!
What beautiful colors!"

And then I found
My happy, carefree day again.
My pretty day with
Green skies and
Blue grass in a
Sea of yellow.
And I had caught my day.
And for a moment I was free
Like my day.

S.A.R.

Summary

Whatever the ingredients of creativity are, they are difficult to measure. Most studies have shown that creativity and intelligence seem to go together, but a high IQ does not guarantee imagination, humor, or creative ability. Time and understanding seem to be involved in the four-stage model of the creative act given in this text. These stages include preparation, incubation, illumination, and verification. When creativity is recognized, it can be nurtured by the teacher. Getting students to go beyond rigid mind sets, to brainstorm either by themselves or in groups, and to develop activities and new ways of looking at things are some suggestions for making the classroom a special place.

SELECTED BIBLIOGRAPHY

Barron, F. X. *Creative Persons and Creative Process*. New York: Holt, Rinehart and Winston, 1969.

De Mille, Richard. *Put Your Mother on the Ceiling*. New York: Penguin, 1976.

Getzels, J. W., and P. W. Jackson. *Creativity and Intelligence: Explorations with Gifted Students*. New York: Wiley, 1962.

Getzels, J. W., and G. F. Madaus. "Creativity," in R. L. Ebel, ed., *Encyclopedia of Educational Research*. New York: Macmillan, 1969, pp. 267–275.

Guilford, J. P. "Traits of Creativity," in *Creativity and Its Cultivation: Interdisciplinary Symposia on Creativity*, H. H. Anderson, ed. New York: Harper and Brothers, 1959, pp. 142–161.

Lowenfeld, Viktor, and W. Lambert Brittan. *Creative and Mental Growth*, 6th ed. New York: Macmillan, 1975.

Newell, A., J. C. Shaw, and H. A. Simon. "The Processes of Creative Thinking," in *Contemporary Approaches to Creative Thinking*, H. E. Gruber, G. Gerrell, and M. Wertheimer, eds. New York: Atherton, 1962, pp. 63–119.

Osborn, Alex F. *Applied Imagination: Principles and Procedures of Creative Problem-solving*, 3d ed. New York: Scribner's, 1963.

Parnes, S. J. "The Literature of Creativity, Part II." *Journal of Creative Behavior* 1 (1967): 191–240.

Stanley, Julian C., ed. *Gifted and the Creative: A Fifty-Year Perspective*. Baltimore, Md.: Johns Hopkins University Press, 1978.

Taylor, C. W., ed. *Creativity: Progress and Potential*. New York: McGraw-Hill, 1964.

Torrance, E. P. "Priming Creative Thinking in the Primary Grades." *Elementary School Journal* 62 (1961): 34–41.

Torrance, E. P. *Rewarding Creative Behavior: Experiments in Classroom Creativity*. Englewood Cliffs, N.J.: Prentice-Hall, 1965.

Torrance, E. P., and Myers, R. E. *Creative Learning and Teaching*. New York: Harper & Row, 1970.

Upton, Albert, et al. *Creative Analysis*, rev. ed. New York: Dutton, 1978.

Summary of Part One

A schema by which to develop a firm foundation for a language arts program has been presented. So that teachers can effectively implement this program they must have knowledge of diversity among their students. Since language, intelligence, and students' early home lives are closely related, teachers must have an understanding of this relationship and the factors which might hinder or facilitate achievement in school. Chapter 3 on language and concept development provides teachers with the background knowledge needed in this area. And Chapter 4 helps teachers understand that knowledge and nurturing of the creative process further enhance the intellectual environment for learning.

Part One: Suggestions for Thought Questions and Activities

1. What would the world be like if all written matter were completely destroyed? What kind of communication would we have? What would happen to the educational establishment?

2. Imagine that you were moving to another planet. Determine the kind of community you would set up and the kind of education you would establish. Analyze and evaluate your plan.

3. Try to communicate with another person without speaking. Get a number of people to team up with a partner and attempt to establish some form of communication without speaking. Then set up a communications system. Analyze what procedures you had to follow to set up the system.

4. At the first class meeting, have students who do not know one another form groups of four to six. Have the students talk among themselves to learn about each other's likes, interests, backgrounds, names, and so forth. After a while have the students put each of their names on a slip of paper. The group as a whole, using a part of each person's name, creates a new word with a meaning that somewhat reflects each person in the group. Each newly created word must conform to a part of speech so that when it is combined with the other newly created words to form a sentence it will be structurally correct and make sense. After the sentence with the newly created words is put on the board for the class, each member is introduced using the newly created word and what it stands for. Example:

Persons in Group	Word Created	Part of Speech	Meaning of Word
John	Jonic	Adjective	Cheerful
Michael	Pechael	Verb	Likes
Deidre	Eido	Noun	Individual
Cynthia	Thial	Adjective	Social
Jennifer	Enniferings	Noun	Events

A jonic eido pechaels thial enniferings.
A cheerful individual likes social events.[16]

Ask students to explain what they have learned about language from this activity.

5. Given two hypothetical children, X and Y, construct a comparison chart showing how one child's chances for success in school are better than the other child's chances because of certain noneducative factors. State five factors and describe each factor.

6. Choose a preschool child from among your acquaintances. Observe and record the verbal behavior of this child during a one-hour play period. Discuss your observations with the class.

7. Use brainstorming techniques to make a list of the many different topics that could be used for brainstorming activities in the language arts.

---

[16]Adapted from Kenneth Cadenhead, "Using Language in a Special Way to Get Acquainted," *Language Arts* 53 (October 1976): 772–773.

part two

The
Subject Matter
of the
Language Arts

five

Aural Responsiveness—Listening

EXAMPLES OF TEACHER COMPETENCIES

1. The teacher will be able to state the various levels of listening and the factors which affect each level.

2. The teacher will be able to state exercises which will enhance students' listening skills.

3. The teacher will be able to prepare lesson plans based on the listening needs and readiness levels of students.

4. The teacher will listen to students, and act positively by planning adequate time for children to express themselves.

5. The teacher will listen to students, and act positively by incorporating their ideas into the planning of lessons.

6. The teacher will be able to prepare lessons in the area of critical listening, so that students will gain the skill to detect propaganda and bias in oral presentations.

7. The teacher will be able to determine whether students value, appreciate, or have an interest in gaining skills in listening by observing whether pupils voluntarily become involved in listening activities, such as the taping of sounds in the classroom. Further evidence would be if they show that they pay attention when others speak by being able to answer questions or state irrelevancies or deceptions about what was presented orally.

8. The teacher will be able to state effective practices which would aid children who speak nonstandard English to listen more effectively.

9. The teacher will be able to state conditions which would provide an atmosphere conducive to effective listening.

10. The teacher will be able to organize the classroom environment so that students can listen with a minimum of distraction. This will be evidenced by observing students' attention span while others are speaking and by students' responses to oral questions.

Introduction

Gilbert and Sullivan, in their comic opera *Pirates of Penzance*, illustrate the dire consequences that can occur from faulty listening. In the opera we learn how Frederic, the well-born hero, has been wrongly doomed to a life of piracy by Ruth, his nursemaid:

I was a stupid nursery-maid,
  on breakers always steering,
And I did not catch the word aright,
  through being hard of hearing.
Mistaking my instructions, which
  within my brain did gyrate,
I took and bound this promising
  boy apprentice to a pirate.
A sad mistake it was to make,
  and doom him to a vile lot:
I bound him to a pirate—you—
  instead of to a pilot!

The importance of listening is evident in many ways in our everyday lives: for example, the telephone; the sound motion picture (which replaced silents); the prominent place in home entertainment of radio and television; and the dubbing of foreign films with oral text replacing written subtitles to make them more acceptable to worldwide audiences. Can one imagine the world without oral communication?

The child's initial learning of language comes through listening; it is the foundation for the sequential development of language arts. If children do not listen effectively, they almost assuredly will have difficulty in all other areas of the language arts. If children hear "dat" for "that" or "dis" for "this," they will say "dat" and "dis." Later, when they have to read "that" or "this," they may have difficulty because these words are not in their listening experience. The written symbol would not remind them of a sound with which they are familiar. Similarly, if children cannot read the word "that" and it is not in their listening capacity, they will not be able to write it. If children are going to communicate effectively, they must learn to hear even subtle differences and similarities among sounds.

An individual's adequate development of listening skills is important for advanced learning and thinking. By listening to the ideas of others, we can compare them with our own, which helps us to become more critical thinkers. By learning to listen to others, students are better able to discern the purpose of the speakers, the way they organize their ideas, and their use of developmental materials. Such students are better prepared to resist double-talk and meaningless generalizations and to acquire new information.

A study comparing personalities with the way in which they listened concludes that:

The ideal listener primarily keeps an open, curious mind. He listens for new ideas everywhere, integrating what he hears with what he already knows. He is also self-perceptive and thus listens to others with his total being or self. Thus he becomes personally involved with what he hears. Being this aware he is not willing to blindly follow the listening crowd. He maintains conscious perspectives on what is going on instead. He looks for ideas, organization and arguments but always listens to the essence of things. Knowing that no two people listen the same, he stays mentally alert by outlining, objecting, approving, adding illustrations of his own. He is introspective but he has the capacity and desire to critically examine, understand and attempt to transform some of his values, attitudes, and relationships within himself and with others. He focuses his mind on the listening and listens to the speaker's ideas, but he also listens with feeling and intuition.[1]

Listening is to language arts as the sense of seeing is to the art of painting. Before artists are able to express themselves in some esthetic form, they must first have perceived the world around them visually. Only then can they begin

[1]Elizabeth Mae Pflaumer, "A Definition of Listening," in *Listening: Readings*, ed. Duker (Metuchen N.J.: Scarecrow Press, 1971), pp. 46–47.

Listening is an important skill that needs to be developed in young children.

to build and integrate these images into a more meaningful perception of their experiences. In a like manner, listening is basic to the language arts. The embryonic language artists must first accumulate listening experiences so that they can build, integrate, and assimilate these experiences and be able to express themselves more meaningfully.

After you have finished reading this chapter you should be able to answer the following questions:

1. How important is listening? Why?
2. How are listening skills developed?
3. Can listening skills be taught? How?
4. What are some teaching tactics?
5. What should a teacher know about the various levels of listening? Why?
6. What are some listening activities which would enhance listening at the various levels?
7. What is an effective listener?
8. What should a teacher know about the relationship of nonstandard English and the development of effective listening skills?

The Relationship of Listening to Other Language Arts Areas

Listening as Decoding

Listening is the intake of language. The listener is involved in decoding a message from the speaker. The listener hears sound symbols which are called *phonemes*. These are analogous to the Morse code, for the listener must be able to decode the various sounds which stand for symbols. In order to decode, listeners must be able to hear differences between and among the various sounds of their language. If you were to ask a salesperson about the price of an item and were told fifty cents a pound, how can you be sure that the salesperson didn't say ninety cents a pound or five dollars a pound? You might say, "Because with my ears I heard that person say fifty cents rather than ninety cents. Fifty cents sounds *different* from ninety cents."

The buyer-listener might think he or she heard fifteen rather than fifty cents because of the similarity of the sounds. The emotional bias toward wanting to hear the lower price could also influence the listener.

Phonemes have no meaning in themselves except as they are combined into a specific pattern to form a *morpheme*, which is the smallest word unit. Morphemes are combined into an arrangement which gives the sentence its unique meaning. The listener must be able to assimilate the flow of sound symbols into meaningful concepts or no communication can occur. If a listener heard the sentence: "I blibed the blob," the sounds cannot be assimilated into meaningful concepts because "blibed" and "blob" are nonsense words. Similarly, if listeners heard the delightful poem "Jabberwocky" recited by Alice in *Through the Looking-Glass*, they would be as perplexed as Alice was concerning its meaning. Read one stanza and see if you agree.

> 'Twas brillig, and the slithy toves
> Did gyre and gimble in the wabe.
> All mimsy were the borogoves,
> And the mome raths outgrabe.

(See Chapter 1 for further amplification of decoding.)

Auditory Discrimination and Memory Span

Auditory discrimination, which is the ability to distinguish between sounds, is essential for the acquisition of language and for learning to read. The essence of what speech clinicians have learned concerning auditory discrimination is summarized as:

1. There is evidence that the more nearly alike two phonemes are in phonetic (relating to speech sounds) structure, the more likely they are to be misinterpreted.
2. Individuals differ in their ability to discriminate among sounds.
3. The ability to discriminate frequently matures as late as the end of the child's eighth year. A few individuals never develop this capacity to any great degree.
4. There is a strong positive relation between slow development of auditory discrimination and inaccurate pronunciation.
5. There is a positive relationship between poor discrimination and poor reading.
6. While poor discrimination may be at the root of both speech and reading difficulties, it often affects only reading or speaking.
7. There is little if any relationship between the development of auditory discrimination and intelligence, as measured by most intelligence tests.[2]

For children who speak a nonstandard dialect of English or for whom English is a second language, it is well to bear in mind that the acquisition of speech sounds for any given dialect is learned very early in life and is usually established by the time the child starts school. These children especially need help in auditory discrimination.

Auditory memory span is essential for individuals who must judge whether two or more sounds are similar or different. In order to make such comparisons, the sounds must be kept in memory and retrieved for comparison. Auditory memory span is defined as "the number of discrete elements grasped in a given moment of attention and organized into a unity for purposes of immediate reproduction or immediate use."[3]

[2]Joseph W. Wepman, "Auditory Discrimination, Speech and Reading," *Elementary School Journal* 60 (1960): 326.

[3]Virgil A. Anderson, "Auditory Memory Span as Tested by Speech Sounds," *American Journal of Psychology* 52 (1939): 95.

A deficiency in memory span will hinder effective listening.

Listening and Reading

In the elementary grades, when children are primarily involved in learning to read so that they can read to learn, students of low and average achievement usually prefer to listen rather than to read independently. These children gain more comprehension and retention from listening, because of the important added cues they receive from the speaker, such as stress given to words or phrases, facial expressions, and so on.[4] Children who are very able and who have had success in reading achievement prefer to read, because these children can set their own rate of reading for maximum comprehension and retention. They don't wish to be constrained by the fixed oral rate of word production of the teacher.

The case where students can understand a passage when it is orally read to them, but can not understand it when they read it themselves indicates that the words are in the students' listening capacity, but that they have not gained the skills necessary for decoding words from their written forms.

It may be that some words are in the children's listening capacity (for example, they know the meaning of the individual words when they are said aloud), but they still might not be able to assimilate the words into a meaningful concept. The instructor will have to help these children in concept development and in gaining the necessary reading comprehension and listening skills. A person who does not do well in listening comprehension skills will usually not do well in reading comprehension skills. Help in one area usually enhances the other, because both listening and reading contain some important similar skills.

Research done on the relationship between reading and listening has shown that practice in listening for detail will produce a significant gain in reading for the same purpose.[5] Another investigation found that children who did poorly in comprehension through listening were also poor in reading comprehension.[6]

Although there are many common factors involved in the decoding of reading and listening—which would account for the relationship between the two language arts areas—listening and reading are, nonetheless, separated by unique factors. The most obvious being that listening calls for *hearing*, whereas reading calls for *seeing*. As has already been stated, in the area of listening, the speakers are doing much of the interpretation for the listeners by their expressions, inflections, stresses, and pauses. Similarly, the listeners do not have to make the proper grapheme (letter) -phoneme (sound) correspondences because these have already been done for them by the speakers. It is possible for students to achieve excellent listening comprehension, but not achieve as well in the area of reading.

Readers must first make the proper grapheme-phoneme correspondences and must then organize these into the proper units to gain meaning from the words. Readers must also be able to determine the shades of meaning implied by the words, to recognize any special figures of speech, and finally to synthesize the unique ideas expressed by the passage.

The relationship between listening and reading ability is succinctly summarized by these four rules:

---

[4]Robert Ruddell, "Oral Language and the Development of Other Language Skills," *Elementary English* 43 (May 1966): 489–498.

[5]Annette P. Kelty, "An Experimental Study to Determine the Effect of Listening for Certain Purposes upon Achievement in Reading for those Purposes," *Abstracts of Field Studies for the Degree of Doctor of Education* 15 (Greeley: Colorado State College of Education, 1955): 82–95.

[6]William E. Young, "The Relation of Reading Comprehension and Retention to Hearing Comprehension and Retention," *Journal of Experimental Education* 5 (September 1936): 30–39.

1. When auding[7] ability is low, reading ability tends more often to be low.

2. When auding ability is high, reading ability is not predictable.

3. When reading ability is low, auding ability is not predictable.

4. When reading ability is high, auding ability is, to a very small extent, predictable—and likely to be high.[8]

Listening and Speaking

Studies with deaf and hard-of-hearing children reveal that their speech has been severely retarded. Many children with hearing problems have often been improperly diagnosed as being mentally retarded because of their language difficulty. It would not be far off the mark to say, "We speak what we hear."

From descriptive studies of children's acquisition of language, it has been found that they learn language from the speech around them. Children learn the rules that govern usage of words so that they can comprehend and produce properly constructed speech. Since skill in listening is so very closely related to speech development and, subsequently, effective oral development, knowledge of the various aspects of listening becomes essential for the proper understanding of the development of speech.

The Development of Listening

"Listen! Listen to me!" Children want to be heard. Whether their parents spend time listening to them, whether they encourage them to express themselves will affect the kind of listening the children are able to do, as well as influence their oral expression.

By the time children come to school they have emerged from an egocentric view of the world, where everything they do and say concerns *me*, *my*, or *I*. In this egocentric world, children speak in parallel, in a collective monologue. They are not in the role of listeners, and so there is no communication. According to Jean Piaget, the eminent Swiss psychologist, not until children need to be social do they need to become logical in their speaking.

Read the following noncommunicative egocentric speech of a preschooler:

Mlle. L. tells a group of children that owls cannot see by day.
Lev: "Well, I know quite well that it can't."

Lev (at a table where a group is at work): "I've already done 'moon' so I'll have to change it."
Lev picks up some barley-sugar crumbs: "I say, I've got a lovely pile of eyeglasses."
Lev: "I say, I've got a gun to kill him with. I say, I am the captain on horseback. I say, I've got a horse and a gun as well."[9]

If children are to learn effectively in school, they must first learn to listen. Since they have spent their early childhood years in egocentric thought, they have not developed this skill adequately. When children come to school they participate in dialogue, which is a giving and receiving of ideas between two persons. Though they must listen, children still need someone to listen to them.

When Lev emerged from egocentric speech, he was able to engage in a communicative conversation with other children of his age:

Pie: (6.5) "Now you shan't have it [the pencil] because you asked for it."
Hei: (6.0) "Yes I will, because it's mine . . ."
Pie: "Course it isn't yours. It belongs to everybody, to all the children."
Lev (6.0): "Yes, it belongs to Mlle. L. and all the children, to Ai and to My too."

---

[7]*Auding* refers to the highest level of listening. It is defined as listening plus comprehension. The term "listening" is many times used to mean auding.

[8]John Caffrey, "The Establishment of Auding-age Norms," *School and Society* 70 (November 12, 1949): 310.

[9]Jean Piaget, *The Language and Thought of the Child* (London: Routledge & Kegan Paul, 1959), pp. 18–19.

Pie: "It belongs to Mlle. L. because she bought it and it belongs to all the children as well."[10]

Dialogue between children and their classmates and between teachers and children is very important in children's development of listening skills and in making their thinking more objective. Teachers should listen to children; observe them at play and work; introduce new materials and ideas to them; add information; raise questions; allow opportunities for children to raise questions as well; and *talk* with children about what they see, think, and feel. It is essential that teachers show they respect their pupils' ideas and act as models of "good listeners" for them. Children must have sufficient practice or "play" in the intake and outgo of language. Unless children are given ample opportunities to engage in listening and "being listened to," they may not develop their listening ability adequately.

Different Levels of Listening[11]

In order to have a better understanding of the hierarchical and cumulative nature of listening, a discussion of the various levels of listening is necessary. *Hearing* is the lowest level in the hierarchy of listening.[12] Hearing refers to sound waves being received and modified by the ear. Someone in the process of hearing physically perceives the presence of sounds, but would not be able to make out what the sounds are; they would merely be noise. Hearing, being a purely physical phenomenon, cannot be taught.

Listening is in the middle of the hierarchy of listening, in which individuals become aware of sound sequences. They are able to identify and recognize the sound sequences as known words, if the words are in their listening capacity.

Auding is at the highest level of the hierarchy and involves not only giving meaning to the sounds but assimilating and integrating the oral message. An individual at the auding level would be able to gather the main idea of a spoken passage, discern analogies and inferences, and perform all the other high-level comprehension skills that are usually associated with reading. Creative problem-solving as well as critical listening are also skills included in this level. Although we are looking at each level as a separate entity, the act of listening is not divided into parts, but functions as a whole.

Factors Influencing Hearing—The Lowest Level

Auditory Acuity Auditory acuity has to do with the physical response of the ear to sound vibrations. If individuals have organic ear damage, they will not be able to hear properly, if at all, depending on the extent of the damage. Auditory acuity is the ability to respond to various frequencies (tones) at various intensities (level of loudness).

Human speech comprises frequencies ranging from 125 to 8000 Hertz (Hz).[13] The intensity or loudness level found in everyday speech will range typically from 55 decibels (faint speech) to 85 decibels (loud conversation). When hearing is tested, a person's ability to hear is checked across the entire speech-frequency range. If persons require more than the normal amount of volume (d.b. level) to hear sounds at certain frequencies, they are most probably exhibiting a hearing loss. The most critical frequencies for listening to speech lie in the frequency range between 1000 and 2500 Hertz, because the majority of word cues are within this range.

[10]Ibid., p. 71.
[11]Stanford E. Taylor, *Listening: What Research Says to the Teacher* (Washington, D.C.: National Education Association, 1969).
[12]Unless otherwise qualified, such as in the discussion on the hierarchy of listening, whenever the term "listening" is used in this text it will refer to auding, the highest level of listening.

[13]*Hertz* is the accepted international scientific word for "cycles per second," named after the great nineteenth-century German physicist, who proved the existence of electromagnetic waves.

Frequencies above 2500 Hertz contribute to the fineness with which we hear such sounds as:/b, d, f, g, s, t, v, sh, th, zh /(Webster's symbols).

An audiometer is used for precise measurement of hearing loss by audiologists. But teachers can make a lot of informal measurements on their own. Teachers can observe their students to notice if any of the following behavior is present:

Does the child appear to be straining to push himself or herself closer to the speaker?

Does the child speak either very softly or very loudly?

Does the child have difficulty in following simple directions?

Does the child turn up the sound of the record player or tape recorder?

Does the child have difficulty pronouncing words?

Does the child seem confused?

Although these questions could be posed for a number of other problems, a teacher should have the student checked for possible hearing loss if one or more of these symptoms are manifested.

Auditory Fatigue   This is a temporary hearing loss due to continuous or repeated exposure to sounds of certain frequencies. A monotonous tone or droning voice will have the effect of causing auditory fatigue. It has been shown that exposure to continuous loud noises over an extended period of time could be permanently harmful to an individual's hearing ability. Listening to music at a very high volume or being constantly exposed to cars and trucks rumbling through highway tunnels can have deleterious effects on hearing.

Binaural Considerations   When individuals are in the presence of two or more conversations, they must be able to direct their attention to only one of the speakers in order to be able to get the essence of what is being said. The more readily listeners are able to separate the sound sources, the more they will be able to get

messages correctly. *Binaurality* thus refers to the ability of listeners to increase their reception sensitivity by directing both ears to the same sound.

Masking   *Masking* occurs when other sounds interfere with the message being spoken. Background noises drowning out a speaker or noisy classrooms or simultaneous group discussions will retard hearing ability.

Factors Influencing Listening—The Middle Level

Listening involves the way in which one identifies and recognizes sounds. Unless people are attentive to sounds, they will not understand their meaning, and meaning of sounds is an important part of listening. Sustained attention is concentration. If individuals are physically or mentally unwell, their chances for attending, and thus listening, are slim. Speakers play an important role in maintaining sustained attention. If they are boring, disliked, or unenthusiastic, they will not be as readily listened to as speakers who are interesting, liked, enthusiastic, and who use motivating techniques. Similarly, the physical environment of the classroom plays an important role in maintaining sustained attention. If the room is too hot or cold, if the chairs are uncomfortable, if there are provisions for writing, if the lighting is adequate and free of glare, if the acoustics are good, and if there are visual distractions—all these play a part in whether listening occurs.

Factors Influencing Auding—The Highest Level

Auding is the highest level of listening, as we have seen. It is not only the ability to discriminate between one word and another, or one syllable and another, but it involves the individual's ability to assimilate the spoken message using an individual's total experience. The thinking skills used during auding are quite similar to those employed during speaking, reading, and writing. Since the average speaking rate is 150 words per minute, the individual has time to formulate thoughts about what is being said, if what is being said is in the experience of the auditor. If the words are not in the listener's listening capacity, or if the topic is beyond the scope of his or her experiences, the listener will not understand what is being said. An individual who knows nothing about linguistics will have difficulty in comprehending an advanced lecture on this topic. A person with a background in linguistics may also have difficulty with the lecture if the words being used by the speaker are not familiar.

Figure 5.1[14] on page 52 depicts the three stages of hearing, listening, and auding.

Critical Listening—An Important Auding Skill

We are living at a time when individuals, from early childhood onward, are daily exposed to a plethora of news, advertisements, and information from the mass media. From past experiences we have learned that what is presented as fact may actually be suspect. One way that teachers can help to lessen the impact of propaganda or half-truths is to emphasize critical listening skills in the classroom. Critical listening refers to that high level of listening skill whereby the individual is able to detect bias, propaganda, and so on in oral presentations. *Critical listening* is "the process of examining spoken materials in the light of related, objective evidence, comparing the ideas with some standard or consensus, and then concluding or acting upon the judgment made."[15]

Critical listening incurs special difficulties that arise from face-to-face relationships. The speaker's voice, gestures, and the general reaction of the audience can influence the listeners' thinking and interpretation. The listeners must also adjust their intake of information based on a pace set by the speaker.

These statements may seem contradictory to what was previously discussed concerning differences between reading and listening. It was earlier stated that the speaker's voice, expressions, mannerisms, and so on enhance comprehension for the listeners by helping them with certain cues that are not present while reading. However, for *critical* listening, the speaker's voice, gestures, expressions, and so on may actually impede the exercise of the critical faculty of listening because of the particular persuasiveness of the speaker. Such a speaker may be able to sway even antagonistic audiences to a one-sided view. An example would be the almost hypnotic effect that Adolf Hitler had on his German audiences at mass meetings during the 1930s.

Critical listening requires that students be able to engage in many levels of thinking, while still being effective listeners. The thinking skills include those in the cognitive domain, such as knowledge, comprehension, application, analysis, synthesis, and evaluation.

In the primary grades the teacher should be establishing the foundation for effective critical listening. Children must have many experiences all through school in working at various cognitive levels, as well as training in listening concentration skills and in listening comprehension skills.

Students should be helped to know what to note about a speaker, so that they can detect the presence of propaganda or bias. They also should be taught methods of logical reasoning so that they can detect fallacies in the speaker's arguments.

The Institute for Propaganda Analysis has identified several devices or basic techniques of propaganda (see Table 5.1 on page 59). The teacher could tape-record speeches using each

[14]Taylor, op. cit., p. 5.
[15]Sara Lundsteen, "Teaching and Testing Critical Listening," in *Elementary School Language Arts: Selected Readings*, Paul C. Burns and Leo M. Schell, eds. (Chicago: Rand McNally, 1969), p. 158.

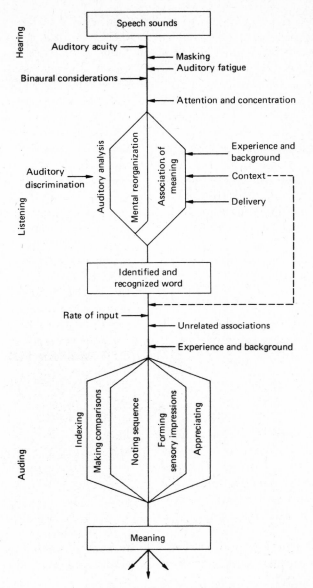

Speech sounds

Hearing

Auditory acuity ———→ ←—— Masking
←—— Auditory fatigue

Binaural considerations ———→ ←—— Attention and concentration

Listening

Auditory discrimination ———→

Auditory analysis

Mental reorganization

Association of meaning ←—— Experience and background

←-- Context ----

←—— Delivery

Identified and recognized word

Rate of input ———→ ←------

←—— Unrelated associations

←—— Experience and background

Auding

Indexing

Making comparisons

Noting sequence

Forming sensory impressions

Appreciating

Meaning

figure 5.1   *The Total Act of Receiving Auditory Communication*

of these propaganda strategies and have students decide what tactic is being used and give examples.[16]

[16]Adapted from Thomas R. Lewis and Ralph G. Nichols, *Speaking and Listening* (Dubuque, Iowa: W. C. Brown, 1965), pp. 56–58.

The questions that listeners should ask themselves about a speaker include information concerning the "newness" of the material being presented, its relevance, the competence of the speaker, the sources of information, and the stance of the speaker. (See Chapter 8 for a discussion on critical reading.)

Purposes for Listening

People read for different purposes; they listen for different purposes, too. "It might be extremely unprofitable to listen creatively or casually to an emotionally charged appeal requiring action of some sort by the listener. It would be extremely unpleasant to always listen to social conversations critically. Therefore, the individual must not only learn to listen carefully, but learn to listen appropriately in order to get the most [or the least] from what is heard."[17]

In a conversation with a friend we are attentive listeners. In listening to a story being read, we may listen for the main idea, a sequence of events, specific details, supporting evidence, and so on. However, in listening to a dramatic presentation we may merely listen with appreciation. When listening to a politician or a commercial, we should listen critically.

Listening for Appreciation

Teachers should set aside some time every day for appreciative listening. During this time the emphasis should be completely on enjoyment. Appreciative listening is listening for deriving pleasure and enjoyment from poems, stories, music, or any other art form that fits some mood, feeling, or interest. The skill of appreciative listening should be developed in early childhood. Children who are accustomed to listening for appreciation will be better able to enhance their learning–listening ability by sharpening their concentration and memory skills.

Young children enjoy listening to stories, poems, music, and to the delightful sounds of language itself. (See Chapters 8 and 11.) Teachers can help children appreciate the works of others by creating a good affective environment and by helping children to identify with the

---

[17]John Gilbert Way, "Teaching Listening Skills," *The Reading Teacher* (February 1973): 474.

mood of the poem or music. For example, the teacher can play a polka record. After the record is played, the teacher should elicit from the children how the music made them feel. Did it make them feel good? Did it make them feel happy? Did it make them feel like dancing? Poetry is another excellent vehicle for developing appreciative listening. Young children learn very early that many Mother Goose poems are as good as music because they help you run, skip, jump, trot, gallop, swing, and hop.

Children delight in poems that stress alliteration. Alliteration is the repetition of (usually) the initial consonant sound or sounds in two or more neighboring words or syllables. Young children are fascinated by alliteration because it seems to tickle their sound sense. Because of this, tongue twisters are especially relished by children. Who hasn't enjoyed listening to and saying, "She sells seashells at the seashore"?

Onomatopoeia is another poetic technique that appeals to children's ears. Onomatopoeia is the use of words whose sound suggests the sense of the word. For example, in Langston Hughes' poem "African Dance," you can hear and feel the beating of the drums from the following:

And the tom-toms beat,
And the tom-toms beat.

Of course, rhythm and rhyme are also loved by children. What child hasn't delighted in Dr. Seuss' *The Cat in the Hat?* What child or adult hasn't enjoyed listening to Edward Lear's amusing limericks?

There was an Old Man with a beard,
Who said, "It is just as I feared!—
  Two Owls and a Hen,
  Four Larks and a Wren,
Have all built their nests in my beard!"

Listening to stories that are well read or well told is also an excellent means to help develop appreciative listening skills. Being transported to another land, century, or world can challenge our imaginations and uplift our souls. (See section on "Nonstandard English and Its Implications for Instruction" in this chapter for further discussion on the importance of reading stories aloud to children.)

Nonstandard English and Listening

The teaching of standard English to children who speak other languages or dialects is a complex process involving all the language arts areas, but it begins with listening. Since listening is basic to any constructive learning, this section is included here. Further amplification will be presented in Chapter 6.

When children who speak nonstandard English come to school they may face special difficulties since they may have trouble both in understanding what other people say to them and in being understood by these people. Since listening and the whole range of aural and oral communications are so important to success in school—and so important to the development of good skills in reading, thinking, and problem-solving—it is imperative that attention be given immediately to improving the listening skills of such pupils. These children must be helped with the basic listening skills, and with setting the purpose of the listening they do. The sooner these children get help, the greater their chances for later success will be.

As has been stated many times in this text, language is acquired from the utterances of the adults who surround the child. Therefore the listening process determines the child's output, namely, speech. As a result, children who hear standard English would learn to speak standard English; whereas culturally different children, who hear another dialect or language, would learn to speak what they hear. Although we must recognize that differences exist in language and help children to learn standard English, at the same time we must maintain their dignity and self-respect and be careful not to extend value judgments preferring one language or dialect over another.

It is probably true that facility in standard English is necessary for academic success and for admission into the higher economic community of the culture, but that does not mean that nonstandard English is "bad," nor that the persons who speak it are not worthy. There must be no implication that one language or dialect is inferior to another; learning standard English should be looked on as a useful added skill.

Since it is very important for the teacher to help all children to be able to listen to and discriminate among speech sounds which may be strange or foreign to them, it would help teachers to have a better understanding of the difficulties involved if they recognized some language differences. Teachers who know the phonological and syntactic features of nonstandard English will be better able to appreciate the differences between the listening environment of the standard speaker and that of the child who speaks a nonstandard dialect. The teacher with an understanding of dialects will be able to comprehend the child's message and will be more accepting of the child; such a teacher will also be better prepared to plan listening training lessons for this child.

Since there are many dialects of English, and since a student could have grown up with an entirely different language, no attempt will be made to summarize the differences in language here. The important thing to be stressed is attitude. Teachers must demonstrate by their attitudes that one language is as good as another, that it is just as useful for people to learn someone else's language as it is for children who speak nonstandard English to learn standard English. Everyone in the classroom can learn from everyone else. Unless the complete classroom environment—physical, emotional, social, and intellectual—reinforces this attitude, very valuable learning opportunities will be lost and actual damage to some students might be done.

The teacher must lead the way. Find out what

kinds of language differences exist in the community; check with other professionals who know such communities for information about the varieties of nonstandard English likely to be encountered. Find people who can tutor these languages or dialects, read books and articles on them, listen to recordings, or develop other learning tools. You will find a bibliography of some available materials at the end of this chapter, but that is only a starting point. New materials are being produced almost daily. The process of teaching and learning is continuous and serious. If it is not, that attitude cannot help but be communicated to the entire classroom.

Nonstandard English and Its Implications for Instruction

So that children can learn standard speech, they must first feel a need to do so. To be successful they must be able to hear differences between sounds. If they only hear nonstandard speech at home, from their peers, and in the school environment, they will not have a need to learn, nor will they hear the differences necessary for learning. Children should be encouraged to express themselves as often as possible early in their school careers, in kindergarten or in preschool organized activities. Children should not be criticized. They should not be told, "No, that's wrong. Say it this way." The teacher should repeat the children's sentences in standard English so that they can hear the sentence in a standard structural pattern. When a child says, "Her a good girl," the teacher might say, "Yes, she is a good girl." Unless children learn to hear differences in both the patterns of speech and in the phonemes, they will not be able to reproduce them in standard English. Similarly, unless they learn to hear the sounds and patterns of standard English, they will usually have difficulty in reading and writing.

Schools seem to have had very little effect on teaching the patterns of standard English speech to speakers of nonstandard English, as evidenced by the fact that many students leave school knowing only the same speech patterns with which they entered. If a new pattern is to be learned, the process must begin as soon as the children enter school. Such children must have instructors who speak standard English exceptionally well.

In order to help children who speak nonstandard English to develop sound differentiations, auditory discrimination exercises among initial consonants, final consonants, and phonograms or graphemic bases (successions of graphemes that occur with the same phonetic value in a number of words such as *ight*, *ake*, *at*, *et*, and so on) should be emphasized. Here are some examples of exercises:

Auditory Discrimination Activities   "Listen carefully! I am going to say some words that begin like *b*aby and *b*all. Listen and try to pick out all those words that start just like *b*aby and *b*all." Say such lists of three words as:

*b*ook	cake	*b*ox
*b*ang	*B*obby	hat
*b*anana	candy	*b*icycle
*b*aseball	apple	dog

"Now listen carefully; I may be tricky. Does everyone know what tricky means? Yes, it means to fool someone. Well, I may try to fool you. I am going to state a group of words and you will have to pick out all those words which begin like book. Now here's the tricky part. There may be some groups of words that have no words starting like book—cookie, dog, chicken. Are there any words that start like book in that list? No. That's correct. Good! Let's begin."

farm	cow	bear
box	land	school
girl	drum	letter
boy	Tom	bait
cracker	train	drum

"Now, listen carefully as I say some words. Which ones sound alike?"

man   can   tan   book

"Yes, man, can, and tan sound alike. Good. Now listen again."

look   book   cook   man

"Yes, look, book, cook sound alike. Good! Now listen again."

cake   bake   lake   boy

"Listen carefully. I have a riddle for you."

The word I am thinking of rhymes with lake.
It also rhymes with bake.
When mother makes it, I love to eat it.
Who knows what it is?

"Very good! It's cake. Listen again."

The word I am thinking of rhymes with man.
It also rhymes with can and tan.
When I am very hot I use it.
Who knows what it is?

"Yes. Very good! It's a fan. Listen again."

The word I am thinking of rhymes with mat.
It also rhymes with hat and fat.
It likes to drink milk and says, "Meow."
Who knows what it is?

Other activities could involve the taping of standard and nonstandard English sentences which children are asked to group to determine whether they can discriminate between standard and nonstandard English:

Nonstandard pattern: "She didn't have no money."
Standard pattern: "She didn't have any money."

It is essential that the objective of the lesson is made clear to the children at the start, and that only one pattern is introduced at a time.

In order to give them practice, for overlearning purposes, a good motivating technique is to make this activity into a game. The pupils can be divided into two, three, or four groups. The tape recorder plays four or five sentences in a nonstandard pattern and then four or five similar sentences in standard English. The children on the first team have to differentiate between them and then state all the sentences in the standard pattern. The same procedure is followed for teams two, three, and four. Different sentences are used for each team.

The teacher can also tape children's conversations. Before playback, the teacher can ask the children to listen for their voices. Next, he or she can have them all say a number of simple sentences in standard English, which would also be taped. The teacher then can play these back so that the children can listen to themselves speaking standard English.

A number of studies[18,19] have found that children who speak nonstandard English make significant gains toward standard English when they are involved in a rich oral program, one that stresses the reading aloud of stories and the active involvement of the children in related oral activities. Teachers, beginning with kindergartners, should plan a program for linguistically different children which should include the regular and continuous listening to storybooks based on their students' interest and concept development levels. Speech stimulating activities such as choral speaking, creative dramatics, discussion, storytelling, and so on should follow the listening to a story so that the children can have an opportunity to express themselves. (See Chapter 6 for more on speech stimulating activities.)

A rich oral program is a necessary first step to prevent reading failure because it helps prepare the children for reading. The closer the children's language is to the written symbols encountered in reading, the greater their chance

[18]Dorothy Strickland, "A Program for Linguistically Different Black Children," Eric # ED 049 355, April 22, 1971.

[19]Bernice E. Cullinan, Angela M. Jaggar, and Dorothy Strickland, "Language Expansion for Black Children in the Primary Grades: A Research Report," *Young Children* 29 (January 1974): 98–112.

of success. Hearing standard English in the context of something meaningful with which they can identify helps the children to gain "facility in listening, attention span, narrative sense, recall of stretches of verbalization, and the recognition of new words as they appear in other contexts."[20]

Classroom Management for Listening Training

Time Spent in Oral Communication

There must be a balance between oral (speaking) and aural (listening) activities in school. The teacher must understand that first-grade children are not used to sitting still for long periods of time. They need a rhythm of rest and activity. Although there are individual differences in the attention spans of children, expecting children to spend forty-five minutes to one hour at their desks while listening is most unrealistic. Young children become restless after ten to fifteen minutes of listening.

Most teachers do not seem to realize how much time children spend "listening" in school. When teachers are asked to list those areas in which schoolchildren spend the most time, they usually state reading and give a low listing to listening. But research has shown that children in elementary school listen at least 57.5 percent of class time.[21] This percentage rises to about 90 percent in high school. As early as 1926, before the advent of television, a researcher stated: "Listening ability is the most frequently used of the forms of communication. Of the total time spent in communication with verbal symbols, it occupies almost three times as much

time as reading, and four times as much as writing."[22] Of the time spent in communication through verbal symbols by adults, 42.1 percent is spent in listening, 31.9 percent in talking, 15.0 percent in reading, and 11.0 percent in writing. Of the total waking time spent in such communication, 29.5 percent is spent in listening, 21.5 percent in talking, 10.0 percent in reading, 6.9 percent in writing, 2.7 percent in miscellaneous activities, and 29.4 percent in no form of communication.[23]

Although research has substantiated the importance of listening and has shown that students spend the most time in this area, many schools still lack programs for the sequential development of this important skill. It is often either taken for granted that students can "listen" without any aid, or it is assumed that students are somehow gaining the necessary skills. With the present emphasis on reading, due to the increasing number of reading failures in school, it is felt by some that more time should be given to reading than to listening. Ironically, the lack of training in listening skills may well be impeding the development not only of reading but also of speaking and writing.

Providing the Listening Environment

The relationship and importance of listening to language arts and other subject-matter courses have been established. In order to succeed in many different activities, both in and out of school, one must be able to listen! Teachers cannot make the assumption that just because their students have the ability to hear, they will be good listeners. Good listening takes training. Teachers should incorporate listening training sessions into each school day to insure that listening skills will be systematically developed. Listening lessons are an essential part of the

[20]Dorothy H. Cohen, "The Effect of Literature on Vocabulary and Reading Achievement," *Elementary English* 45 (February 1968): 217.

[21]Miriam E. Wilt, "A Study of Teacher Awareness of Listening as a Factor in Elementary Education," *Journal of Educational Research* 43 (April 1950): 626–636.

[22]Paul T. Rankin, "The Measurement of the Ability to Understand Spoken Language" (Ph.D. diss., University of Michigan, 1926); *Dissertation Abstracts* 12 (1952): 848.

[23]Ibid., pp. 847–848.

child's curriculum and should not be neglected or taken for granted. However, no listening skills can be developed unless the child's hearing organs are functioning properly. Even if there are no organic hearing difficulties, there may be other factors which will affect adequate listening.

An environment must be provided where students feel free to share their ideas with one another and are able to listen to others without distraction. Some of the factors which affect both the quality of living in the classroom and the listening climate include the physical, emotional, social, and intellectual environments.

The physical environment refers to any observable factors in the setting which could affect the behavior of an individual. A desirable physical environment would include an arrangement of classroom furniture which is best suited for ongoing listening activities. The furniture should be functional, comfortable, and easily movable. The sound and noise level from the outside or neighboring classrooms should be minimal. The room should be properly ventilated, with a comfortable temperature and humidity range. There should be a proper glareless lighting level. Materials—such as tape recorders, earphones, and record players—should be easily accessible. A specific area should be set aside for individuals or a group of children who can use these materials without disturbing other children. A good physical environment contributes to the good overall quality of classroom living and helps set the stage for a satisfactory emotional, social, and intellectual environment.

The emotional environment should be one in which children do not feel threatened, and where they are not fearful or overly anxious. A warm, friendly, nonthreatening atmosphere is set by the teacher's acceptance, respect, and understanding of each child. A teacher who is consistent and fair, as well as stable and emotionally mature, will help provide an effective place to study. Discipline techniques—any technique used to control a misbehavior—must be fair, firm, clear, and administered without anger. Outbursts of anger, threats, or arbitrary and willful punishments must be avoided.

The social environment is somewhat dependent on the presence of a positive emotional environment, so that students will be more accepting of others. Children who gain recognition and approval in the classroom are more ready to give recognition and approval to others. Teachers can learn about the social relations of the children in their classes by means of a sociogram, a map or chart showing the interrelationships of the children in the classroom, identifying those who are "stars" or "isolates."[24] By means of the sociogram, the teacher can group children more effectively. Teachers who encourage students to express themselves, to explore many ways of solving problems, to make intelligent guesses, who are open-minded, and who allow for mistakes are helping to establish a good intellectual environment.

Students who feel comfortable with one another, who are not threatened, who are secure and physically comfortable will be more ready to learn and better able to listen.

Setting Purposes for Listening in the Classroom

The teacher should help children to set purposes for the various kinds of listening that they will be doing. "Show and tell" listening is different from critical listening. In the former, where a child shares some event or idea with the class, the listeners are involved in appreciative listening; in the latter the listeners are involved in making comparisons, judging whether the speaker is qualified, evaluating what is being said, and looking for biases.

Organizing and Planning for Listening

Teachers should plan to spend at least fifteen minutes of each school day in listening training

[24]See Appendix C for information on the use and construction of the sociogram.

table 5.1   Basic Propaganda Techniques

Type of Propaganda	Examples
1. Name-calling: Denouncing a person by tagging him or her with a widely condemned label.	Facist, chisler, Red, and so on.
2. Glittering generalities: Seeking acceptance of ideas by associating them with words widely accepted and approved.	Freedom, businesslike, American, Christian, democratic, and so on.
3. Transfer: Citing respected sources of authority, prestige, or reverence in such a way as to make it appear they approve the proposal.	The home, the Constitution, will of the people, public education, the church, the flag, and so on.
4. Testimonial: Using testimonials from famous people to build confidence in a product.	For TV commercials—actors, athletes, personalities, and so on.
5. Card-stacking: Building on half-truths.	Through careful selection of favorable evidence and an equally careful omission of unfavorable or contrary evidence.
6. Plain folks: Seeking favor through establishing someone as "just one of the boys."	Presidential candidates photographed in Indian war bonnets or politicians shown milking cows, and so on.
7. Bandwagon: Going along; since everybody is doing some certain thing, we ought to do it too.	A commercial saying: "The majority of people eat Crunchies. Are you one of these?"

activities. The listening lesson should be based on the needs, interests, and readiness levels of the pupils. Some of the activities would involve the whole class; whereas others might involve a group of children or only one child. The students can participate not only in the planning of some of the lessons but also in providing ideas for them.

Teaching Tactics in Listening

Some effective "teaching tactics" which teachers can use to develop good listening habits in their students are given below.

1. *In the first place, children need to recognize that the teacher places a high value on good listening habits.* Teachers should make it clear that attentive listening is sincerely appreciated. A comment to the class such as, "It certainly is helpful to have a class that listens so thoughtfully to the opinions of the other children," is a positive approach which gives status to good listening.

2. *Capitalize on that last "five-minute period" of the day.* This is the time to briefly review the highlights of the day so that the children will have some-

thing constructive to tell their parents when asked, "What did you do in school today?" These last five minutes not only promote thoughtful listening, they also provide an excellent opportunity to develop good relations with the parents.

3. *Develop a good speaking voice and help the children to do likewise.* The voices of both teacher and children reflect honest interest in what is being said. A pleasant voice coupled with evident enthusiasm invites others to listen. Thus it is evident that the speaker, too, plays an important part in developing the art of listening. For this reason, oral reports especially should always be most carefully prepared.

4. *Sometimes give tests orally.* Instead of having children always given tests which involve reading, have them write answers to test items which you dictate.

5. *Avoid being a "parrot."* Oftentimes some of the children will pay little attention to what is being said by their classmates or the teacher. In such instances some teachers will repeat these statements or questions "so that everyone can hear." This practice may encourage some of the children not to listen in the first place. However, there may be times when pupils' comments or questions may truly not be understood and in these instances the pupils themselves should be called upon for clarification.

6. *If a pupil has been absent, have another pupil summarize for him or her what was done while the pupil was gone.* This practice will encourage pupils to listen thoughtfully in order to recall the main points of a report or a discussion. In turn, the absent pupil will be inclined to listen carefully to the summary, and thus the practice is a good experience for both pupils.

7. *Afford children opportunities to listen to a variety of sources.* Children should not only listen thoughtfully to the teacher and to the other children's "talk" but to other sources such as playbacks on the tape recorder, television, sociodramas, assembly programs, radio, dramatizations, dialogues, and oral reports. Listening to oral reading by the pupils might especially be stressed, as it seems to have been largely overlooked in recent language arts programs.

8. *Guide the children in making a chart listing the characteristics of a good listener.* Such standards as (1) asks intelligent questions and (2) respects speakers' rights to their opinions might illustrate points in *The Good Listener's Code.*

9. *Have the children discuss* why *they should be good listeners.* This experience in calling forth their own reasons may help the children convince themselves as to the importance of listening well. It would be especially helpful if they list and debate the *whys of good listening.*

10. *Encourage pairs of children to interview each other about their hobbies.* Following these interviews, the children could report the findings of their interviews to the entire class.

11. *Ask children to give oral summaries of what has been discussed or reported.* This activity fosters interest and gives purpose to the listening situation.

12. *Provide the children with ample practice in writing from dictation.* Start with short sentences and gradually increase the length and difficulty. Normally, say the sentences only once. If the children wish, they may utilize their personal form of shorthand. After a paragraph has been dictated, ask the children to point out the main idea and perhaps a key word.

13. *By using the sociodrama, have a group of children dramatize both good and poor listening situations.* In terms of the negative, one sociodrama could show an inattentive, restless audience; listeners being disturbed by an inattentive pupil; speakers who do not understand their subjects or who use distracting mannerisms or poor voice projection. *Of course,*

dramatizations or sociodramas in which the "positive" approach is used are very important and should follow the negative presentation. Following these presentations, class discussion should bring out a number of important points connected with effective listening.

14. *Use the tape recorder.* Many occasions lend themselves to the use of this instrument. For example, a tape recording could be made of a class discussion followed by the pupils noting and evaluating the main points made during the discussion. Then, when the tape is played back, they could compare the main points which they had listed with what they now hear for a second time.

15. *Help children recognize the importance of listening carefully for names when they are being introduced to others.* Good listening habits pay dividends in this listening situation—and encourage the practice of listening carefully in order to remember.

16. *Be a good listener yourself.* By the process of osmosis children often do as they see others do. When the teacher listens with sincere interest to what the children themselves say, the latter will catch the habit of both attentiveness and courtesy in listening. Perhaps this is the most important method of all in helping children to become courteous, thoughtful listeners.[25]

Informal Teacher Assessment of Listening Skills

The informal assessment is not concerned with determining organic ear malfunctions. If a teacher feels that a student is having difficulty, which might be physiological, he or she should go through the proper referral procedures and inform the principal, school nurse, and parents so that the child can be properly diagnosed by professionally trained personnel. Many times a child is diagnosed as having a "hearing impairment" problem and labeled as having perceptual learning problems when the difficulty is not due to physiological factors but to experiential ones.

In order to determine the student's level of

[25]Guy Wagner, "What Schools Are Doing: Teaching Listening," *Education* (November 1967. Copyright 1967 by Bobbs-Merrill, Indianapolis, Ind.): 184–186.

listening at the auding level, the teacher could easily develop a diagnostic instrument by choosing paragraphs based on the student's concentration and vocabulary ability according to grade levels. The paragraphs can vary in length from grades one to six. A grade one selection would be approximately 25 words, whereas a grade six paragraph would be approximately 125 words. The number of comprehension questions asked would depend on the specific grade level or ability levels of students. For the first grade the teacher could ask three or four questions, whereas in sixth grade, six or seven questions could be asked. From these tests the teacher can determine whether there is a listening problem common to all students or to just a few.

Listening Activities for All Children*

Although many opportunities may present themselves each day for excellent listening activities, the teacher should also plan these activities. The boxed material here lists listening skills that students at various grade levels should attain. Teachers can use this as a checklist to determine whether enough opportunities have been provided to students for developing listening skills. Examples of activities are also presented so that teachers can develop exercises on their own.

*Although activities are being presented at specific levels they can be adapted for any grade level.

PRIMARY-GRADE LEVEL LISTENING SKILLS

During or by the end of the *kindergarten–primary* years the child . . .

Responds to simple verbal questions, directions, and statements.
Listens with comprehension to short discussions.
Listens critically, recognizing gross discrepancies and distinguishing fact from fancy.
Recognizes words that rhyme.
Listens and matches tones.
Listens and responds to rhythm in music.
Locates the source of a sound.
Identifies voices of peers and others.
Listens in order to reproduce sounds, such as animal noises.
Becomes sensitive to rhyme and rhythm in poetry.
Appreciates beauty in the language or in poetry.
Begins to see word pictures in poetry and prose.
Can hear most likenesses and differences in beginning, final, and medial sounds.
Follows sequential development of a story.
Remembers order of events in correct sequence up to five steps.

Derives meaning from intonation.
Identifies with the characters in literature.
Shows increased attention span.
Grows in awareness of the value and the use of words.
Shows enrichment of ideas.
Listens for a specific purpose: details—funny part—exciting part—word pictures—sequence—main ideas—comparisons.
Learns to be a good member of an audience.
Increases ability to make inferences.
Listens in order to relate, to compare, and to apply information.
Senses effective speech on the part of others.
Recognizes oral clues.
Begins to determine the purpose of the speaker.
Recognizes onomatopoeic terms.
Raises pertinent questions in discussion.
Perceives cause and effect relationships.
Responds emotionally, sensing the feeling of the speaker or story character.[26]

Some examples of activities for developing or improving these skills follow.

[26]*Curriculum Bulletin of the Malcolm Price Laboratory School,* University of Northern Iowa, Iowa City, Iowa.

Auditory Discrimination Activities

Present three words to children with similar initial consonant sounds and one word with a different initial consonant sound. Have children state the words with similar consonant sounds. Present three words to children with similar final consonant sounds and one word with a different consonant sound. Have children state word with different final consonant sound. State four words to children of which three are rhyming words and one is not. Have children state the three rhyming words.
Have children listen to tape of city sounds.
Have children pick out all the sounds they hear.
Have children listen to tape of country sounds.
Have children pick out all the sounds they hear.
Have children listen to tape of school sounds.
Have children pick out all the sounds they hear.

Concentration Exercises— Auditory Memory

These concentration exercises can be adapted for any grade level. In kindergarten and grade one the teacher can use these activities:

Following Directions Orally

"Listen carefully. I am going to tell you a few things to do. Let's see who can do them all correctly. Is everyone listening? Fine. When I point to you, that pupil should do all the things that I have told him or her to do. Ready, here we go.

"Stand up, raise your right hand, and put number six on the front chalkboard.
"Stand up, go to the back of the room, and hop on your right foot."

The teacher can either increase or decrease the number of directions according to the ability levels of the students.
Some other concentration activities that could be used at the primary-grade levels include following directions and specific subject-matter skills. Since the purpose of the activity is to determine concen-

tration skill, the instructor should make sure that the children know the meanings of all the words in the activities and that they understand and can apply the concepts.
The following exercise involves squares, circles, triangles, and numbers. The children have received this sheet:

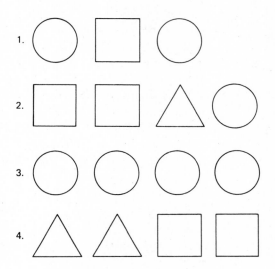

Instruction

"Listen carefully. We are going to see how well we can listen and follow directions. Before beginning, we will do one together. On the board I have put a square, a circle, and a triangle. I will state some directions to you. I will then call on someone to follow them. Is everyone listening? Good! Put a three in the circle, a one in the square, and a four in the triangle."
After the teacher has called on someone to do the example, these instructions are given:

1. Put a cross in the first circle, a dot in the last circle, and a one in the square.
2. Put a check in the second square, a one in the first square, and a three in the triangle.
3. Put a two in the second circle, a three in the first circle, and a one in the last circle.
4. Put a four in the first triangle, a six in the second square, and a two in the second triangle.

Sample Listening Comprehension Activities

1. Children listen to a short story and suggest titles for it.
2. Teacher reads a sequence of words in random order which can be categorized. Children then select the categories.
3. Students are presented with the following questions or statements, and they must determine who is talking.

Who Is Talking?

Inference Activities

1. Number, please?
2. Calling all cars.
3. It is time to go to bed.
4. Always read silently first.
5. All aboard!

INTERMEDIATE-GRADE LEVEL LISTENING SKILLS

During or by the end of the *intermediate* years the child . . .

Shows increasing desire to learn through listening, as an individual and as a member of a group.
Shows increasing responsibility for listening efficiently and effectively.
Responds to more complicated verbal questions, directions, and statements.
Listens to peers, as well as to instructors and other speakers, to get information and knowledge and to develop understanding.
Recognizes and respects the needs of others for group listening.
Accepts responsibility of raising questions when the ideas of the speaker have not been understood.
Shows increased skill in offering constructive criticism when reacting to reports, comments, and other activities of classmates and teachers.
Follows an argument, a discussion, a problem-solving situation, and so on in order to contribute effectively to the development of group understandings.

Responds emotionally to good poetry and prose.
Is gaining sympathetic understanding of people of other times and other places through listening to good literature.
Is gaining understanding of life through vicarious experiences in listening.
Begins to recognize the use of words in influencing the listener.
Shows increased awareness of shades of meaning of words.
Identifies, enjoys, and uses figures of speech.[27]

Examples of some activities to develop listening concentration and comprehension skills at the intermediate-grade level follow.

Concentration Exercises—Auditory Memory

DIGIT SPAN FORWARD

In order to develop concentration, which is sustained attention, digit-span exercises are given based on a graduated level of difficulty. The instructor should caution students that concentration demands an individual's complete attention. It would be a paradox for someone to be relaxed and concentrating at the same time. Students must focus all their efforts on the stimuli being presented. The teacher should instruct students in the following way: "Listen carefully. I am going to say some numbers and when I am through I want you to write them exactly the way I have said them. I will state the numbers only once and at a rate of one per second. All right, let's begin. Remember, listen carefully and do not write them until I am finished giving you the whole sequence."

Following is a sample list of numerals at a span from 2 to 9. This exercise can be used with younger children after they have learned to write the digits 0 to 9. A teacher can also use these exercises in the early grades in another way. The teacher would instruct young children to: "Listen carefully. I am going to say a group of numbers and right after I stop, I will point at someone and that child will repeat them. Let's all listen and see whether the numbers are *exactly* the way I said them."

[27]Ibid.

Numbers for Digits Forward

Span

(2) 85

(3) 374

(4) 7295

(5) 52874

(6) 362915

(7) 8514739

(8) 16952738

(9) 739584162

DIGIT SPAN BACKWARD

Exercises involving the repetition of digits backward are more difficult and demand more concentration than repeating digits forward. Since many students have difficulty with this exercise a few examples should be given by the teacher before starting. The level at the beginning of the exercise should assure success for all students. The teacher says: "Listen carefully. I am going to say some numbers, and I want you to be able to repeat them backward. For example, if I should say 7-3-1, you should say 1-3-7. Since we are going to work with the whole class (or a group of students), rather than saying the numbers backward, you will write them backward. Do not first write them forward and then turn them backward. You must write them backward immediately. Ready now; listen carefully." The rate is one per second.

Numbers for Digits Backward

Span

(2) 61

(3) 195

(4) 9583

(5) 94158

(6) 483692

(7) 5836192

(8) 18362749

The instructor can use the norms in Table 5.2 to determine the level of students. The norms should also serve as a guide for preparing concentration exercises for various age levels.

A sample activity to improve direction following and concentration skills is given below. The instructor can adapt the exercise according to the readiness levels of students. Before proceeding with the activity, the teacher must be sure that all the vocabulary words are in the listening capacity of the children so that the children can state the meanings of all the words in the directions. This exercise can also serve as a review to determine whether children are able to use the words when they are presented orally in a sentence. Students receive the two boxed diagrams on a sheet of paper.

The teacher instructs the students to "Listen carefully while I give you some directions. Do not start to follow the directions until after I have finished reading the whole sentence to you."

table 5.2 Terman 1937 Revision Norms for Digits Forward and Digits Backward[28]

Year Level	Digits Forward	Digits Backward
2½	2	—
3	3	—
4½	4	—
7	5	3
9	5	4
10	6	4
12	6	5
14	7	5
*SA I	7	6
SA II	8	7
SA III	9	7

*Superior Adult

[28]Table compiled from data contained in Lewis M. Terman and Maud A. Merrill, *Measuring Intelligence* (Boston: Houghton Mifflin, 1937), and prior work by Terman.

Directions

1. In Box 1 circle the second letter of the second word, and in Box 2 put a dot in the center figure.
2. In Box 2 put a check in the second triangle, and a cross on the first letter of the third word in Box 1.
3. Put a dot in the first circle in Box 2, a cross in the last figure in Box 2, and a circle around the second letter of the last word in Box 1.[29]

Verbal Memory Exercise

"Listen carefully. I will state pairs of words one after the other. I will then state only one word from each pair and you will have to tell me the mate of the word. For example, I will say:

man/woman
apple/cake

[29]From Dorothy Rubin, *Reading and Learning Power* (New York: Macmillan, 1980.)

When I say 'man' alone; you will have to say 'woman.'
When I say 'apple' alone; you will have to say 'cake.'

The teacher can increase the pairs of words from two to three to four and so on. This activity can be made into a game, or the whole class or a group of children, depending on the grade level, can write the words.

Sample Listening Comprehension Activities

1. Read a story to the students. Have them give the main idea of the story.
2. Read a short story in which events are in an illogical order; have children order them logically.
3. Listen to a political speech. Have children point out any use of appeals to emotion.
4. Read short paragraphs and have children write what would happen next.

Student's Name:
Grade:
Teacher:

Diagnostic Checklist for Aural Responsiveness (Listening)

PART 1

| Listening (organic) | Observation Dates |

Symptoms
1. The child is absent due to ear infection.
2. The child speaks very softly.
3. The child speaks very loudly.
4. The child speaks in a monotone.
5. The child complains of noises in head.

6. The child turns head to one side to hear.
7. The child reads lips while listening.
8. The child asks to have things repeated.
9. The child cups hand behind ear to listen.

PART 2

Auditory Discrimination (samples)	Yes	No

1. The child can state whether the following sets
   of words are similar or different:

Tim	Tom
bit	bet
none	none
fan	van
saw	saw
down	pawn

2. The child can state another word that begins
   like

   four.
   Tom.
   pan.
   some.
   down.

3. The child can state another word that ends
   like

   look.
   jump.
   can.
   pot.

4. The child can state another word that rhymes
   with

   look.
   fat.
   tan.
   bake.

5. The child can give the letter that stands for
   the first sound heard in

   bury.
   mother.
   zone.
   curb.
   label.
   jewel.
   yell.

6. The child can give the two letters that stand for the first two sounds heard in

       plan.
       twin.
       stone.
       swan.
       float.
       snag.
       cry.
       glove.

7. The child can give the two letters that stand for the first sound heard in

       chair.
       shame.
       thumb.
       phone.

8. The child can give the letter that stands for the last sound heard in

       plan.
       mom.
       rug.
       hare.
       buzz.
       lake.

PART 3

Listening Concentration (samples)	Yes	No

1. The child has difficulty in repeating sets of digits in proper order:

       a. forward
       b. backward

2. The child has difficulty in following given sets of directions.

PART 4

Listening Comprehension (samples)*	Yes	No

1. Literal listening: The child, after listening to a passage, can answer questions that relate to information explicitly stated in the passage.

2. Interpretive listening: The child, after listening to a passage, can answer questions dealing with
   a. finding the main idea.
   b. generalization.
   c. "reading between the lines."
   d. reasoning cause and effect.
   e. conclusions.
   f. semantic variation of meaning.

3. Critical listening: The child, after listening to a passage, can answer questions dealing with
   a. propaganda.
   b. fact or opinion.
   c. fantasy or reality.
   d. objectivity or subjectivity.

4. Creative listening: The child, after listening to a passage, can answer questions dealing with divergent thinking.

PART 5

Listening for Appreciation	Yes	No
5. The child voluntarily chooses to listen to records, tapes, and so on.		

*The length and difficulty of the selection used is determined by the grade level. Also, this is not an inclusive list of listening comprehension skills.

Summary

It has been established that listening is the foundation of the language arts program, and its relationship to the other language arts areas has been discussed. The development of listening skills in the child, as well as the hierarchical nature of listening—which includes hearing, listening, and auding—were presented. The development of critical listening, which is necessary to detect bias and propaganda, was explored and shown to be an important listening skill. Emphasis on this skill in the schools was advocated because of the constant exposure of the public to special pleading in the mass media. It was also suggested that teachers set aside some time every day for appreciative listening, which is listening for enjoyment. In addition, some of the differences between nonstandard English and standard English were presented, so that the teacher could better prepare and plan listening training lessons for students who speak nonstandard English. Specific suggestions for listening training for such students were also given.

The second half of the chapter was concerned with the instruction and development of students as effective listeners. Classroom management and environments conducive to the teaching of listening skills were discussed. Numerous teaching tactics and listening training exercises were presented, variations of which can be used with children at all grade levels. A Diagnostic Checklist for Aural Responsiveness (Listening) was also presented.

Now that you have read this chapter you should be able to attain the teacher competencies presented at the beginning of this chapter.

As a further aid, two examples of listening lesson plans follow. Using these as a guide, see if you can construct a plan of your own.

LESSON PLANS*

Lesson Plan I—Listening

Lower-Primary-Grade Level

I. Objectives
   A. The children will be able to recognize five everyday sounds through using their auditory discrimination.
   B. The children will be able to match five similar sounds through using their auditory discrimination.
II. Preliminary Preparation
   A. Make up bulletin board entitled "Sounds Around Us." Have pictures of things that make familiar sounds—which the children will hear on tape—on the bulletin board, covered. Later, as children identify sounds that they heard on the tape, the appropriate pictures can be uncovered.
   B. Other materials to be kept on hand are sound boxes and tapes of familiar sounds.
III. Procedure
   A. Introduction
      1. "Can someone tell me what we use our eyes for? How about our noses? Our mouths?"
      2. "What do we use our ears for? What are some sounds that we hear in school every day?"
      3. "Today we're going to use only our ears, so let's put our heads down, close our eyes, and listen very carefully to the sounds we are going to hear. Afterward, we'll talk about the sounds we have heard."
      4. Play the tape which has various sounds that the children can readily recognize (for example, car horn, door closing, telephone ringing, water running, and so on).
      5. "All right, let's lift our heads up and open our eyes. Who can tell me one sound that he or she heard?"
      6. Call on various children to name the sounds. Uncover the pictures on the bulletin board as the object is named.
      7. "Can anyone tell me what we can call all of these things we heard?" (sounds)
      8. "Can anyone tell me what the word *explorer* means? Well, today we're also going to be explorers, explorers of sound."
   B. Development

*Lesson plan formats will vary to show flexibility in style.

---

1. Show class ten boxes previously prepared (five are striped and five are plain).

2. Have five children come to the front of the room. Give each child one of the plain boxes.

3. "Although these boxes look the same, they each have something different in them, so that when they are shaken they make different sounds. Let's listen!" Have children shake boxes one at a time.

4. Have five different children come up and hold the striped boxes. Repeat the same procedure as above.

5. "Did anyone notice anything as he or she listened to the sounds of the plain boxes and the sounds of the striped boxes? Did any of the boxes have the same sounds?"

6. "This is our job. Each of the plain boxes has a sound that matches a sound of one of the striped boxes. I'm going to shake one plain box at a time. Listen very carefully to the sound it makes, then we'll have the striped boxes shaken one at a time to see who can discover which box matches the one that I just shook."

7. "This is how we are explorers; we have to discover which box matches which."

8. As the class makes its decisions, write their guesses on the board. At the end of the lesson check to see if the results are correct. If not, go back over the material.

C. Summary

1. "Today we heard many different sounds. Why were the sounds different?" (different objects)

2. "Earlier in the lesson I said that we were going to be explorers. What did we explore today?"

3. "On the way home from school today keep your ears open and see how many new sounds you hear, and if you can tell what is making the sound."

4. "Tomorrow morning we can talk about the sounds we heard."

Lesson Plan II—Listening

Intermediate-Grade Level

Behavioral Objectives

1. The students will be able to identify the various sounds presented on the tape recorder.

2. The students will be able to state the mood that certain recorded sounds suggest.

3. The students will be able to state how certain sounds give us information.

Preparation

Have blinds or curtains closed. Have tape recorder ready and children seated in a circle around the recorder.

Introduction

"We have been involved with many different kinds of listening exercises. We have talked about how important it is to listen and how some people are better listeners than others because they have had to depend more on this sense than on the sense of sight. Today we're going to be involved with a special listening activity. Will everyone please close his or her eyes." [While their eyes are closed, turn off the lights.] Play eerie music on the tape recorder playback. After a minute turn off the tape and ask the children to open their eyes. [Keep lights out.] Ask whether anyone can tell you what they thought of when they heard the music played. If they were seeing a movie what would they expect to happen if they heard such music? Tell the students that this special listening activity involves their ability to identify many different familiar sounds when presented on the tape recorder. They will also hear many different kinds of sounds and music presented in films, and they will have to determine what they think will happen or is happening when these sounds are played.

Development

Tell the children to listen carefully and see if they can pick out and remember all the sounds that are played. When the tape recorder is stopped, one student will identify and remember one of the sounds and then that person will call on someone else to identify another sound. The children will continue to call on one another until they have identified all of the sounds. Say: "Is everyone ready? Good! Now, listen carefully!"

The sounds presented are: car honking, children talking, dishes being washed, leaves rustling in the wind, people walking, people running, running water, keys moving on a key chain, the jingling of coins in a pocket, and a bowling ball hitting pins. After all the sounds have been identified, the students are asked if they can think of any sounds they would like to record. They can then record some familiar school sounds and have other children guess what the sounds are.

Now tell the students that the sounds they are going to hear are usually heard in movies and on the radio to help to set the mood of a story. "Listen carefully and tell me what else the music says to us." Play the tape with sad music, happy music, eerie music, gay music. The following recordings can be used:

Sad music—Chopin's "Dirge"
Happy music—Music from the movie *Snow White and the Seven Dwarfs:* "Whistle While You Work"
Eerie music—"Night on Bald Mountain"—Moussorgsky, arranged by Rimski-Korsakov
Gay music—Any waltz by Strauss or "The Beer Barrel Polka."

After each mood piece is played, children are encouraged to tell how it makes them feel and also to state what they would expect to happen if they heard this music in a film, on the radio, on television.

Summary

Pull main points of lesson together by restating the objectives and having the students determine whether these have been achieved.

Suggestions for Thought Questions and Activities

1. Develop a listening activity for fun, perhaps one involving directions to be followed by primary-grade students. By intermediate-grade students.

2. There are children in your classroom who never seem to pay attention and who hardly ever follow directions. How would you go about determining what their problems are? How would you try to help them overcome these problems?

3. Develop a *creative* lesson plan on some aspect of listening.

4. List some creative listening activities.

5. Prepare some critical listening questions for intermediate-grade students which could be used with a particular short oral selection of your own choosing.

6. Prepare some creative listening questions for the same selection as in Question 5.

7. Discuss those factors which should be taken into account in determining whether a good listening environment exists for learning.

8. State some skills you would like your students to achieve that were not presented in this chapter.

9. Prepare a lesson plan in listening to use with children who speak nonstandard English.

10. Explain how you would develop an appreciative listening program in the primary grades. In the intermediate grades.

11. Create a learning center for the development of critical listening skills.

SELECTED BIBLIOGRAPHY

Carlson, Bernice Wells. *Listen! And Help Tell the Story*. Nashville, Tenn.: Abingdon Press, 1965.

Cayer, Robert. *Listening and Speaking in the English Classroom: A Collection of Readings*. New York: Macmillan, 1971.

Duff, T.S., and M.L. Clark. *Listening in the Primary School: Views and Practices of Australian Teachers*. Australia Council for Educational Research Ser.: No. 99, 1976.

Duker, Sam. *Listening: Readings*. Metuchen, N.J.: Scarecrow Press, 1966.

————. *Teaching Listening in the Elementary School: Readings*. Metuchen, N.J.: Scarecrow Press, 1971.

Faber, Carl A. *On Listening*. Pacific Palisades, Calif.: Perseus Press, 1976.

Hall, Edward T. "Listening Behavior: Some Cultural Differences," *Phi Delta Kappan* 50 (1969): 379–380.

Lundsteen, Sara. *Listening: Its Impact on Reading and the Other Language Arts*. Champaign, Ill.: National Council of Teachers of English, 1972.

Oakland, Thomas. *Auditory Perception: Diagnosis and Development for Language and Reading Abilities*. Seattle, Wash.: Special Child Publishers, 1971.

Pronovost, Wilbert. *The Teaching of Speaking and Listening in the Elementary School*. New York: Longmans, Green, 1959.

Rubin, Dorothy. "Developing Listening Skills," in *The Primary Grade Teacher's Language Arts Handbook*. New York: Holt, Rinehart and Winston, 1980.

————. "Developing Listening Skills," in *The Intermediate Grade Teacher's Language Arts Handbook*. New York: Holt, Rinehart and Winston, 1980.

Schwartz, Alvin. *A Twister of Twists, A Tangler of Tongues*. New York: Lippincott, 1972.

Sheldon, Harry J. "Wanted: More Effective Teaching of Oral Communication," *Language Arts* (September 1977): 665–667.

Stammer, John D. "Target: The Basis of Listening," *Language Arts* (September 1977): 661–664.

Sund, Robert B., and Arthur A. Carin. *Creative Questioning and Sensitivity: Listening Techniques, 2d ed*. Columbus, Ohio: Charles E. Merrill, 1978.

Taylor, Stanford. *Listening: What Research Says to the Teacher*. Washington, D.C.: National Education Association, 1973.

Wagner, Guy. *Listening Games: Building Listening Skills with Instructional Games*. Darien, Conn.: Teachers Publishing Corp., 1962.

six

Oral Communication and Speech Improvement

EXAMPLES OF TEACHER COMPETENCIES

1. The teacher will listen to students and incorporate their ideas into oral expression lessons.

2. The teacher will listen to students and act positively by providing time for oral expression activities.

3. The teacher will be able to state methods for enhancing development of oral communication.

4. The teacher will be able to prepare lessons for oral communication based on the needs and readiness levels of students.

5. The teacher will be able to state the differences between conversation and discussion.

6. The teacher will be able to state conditions which would provide an atmosphere for creative dramatics.

7. The teacher will be able to prepare lessons in the area of creative dramatics.

8. The teacher, working with students, will identify a set of criteria to aid in evaluating a good discussion and an effective oral report.

9. The teacher will help children to gain skill in making and using puppets for oral expression activities.

10. The teacher will be able to state differences between speech correction and speech improvement.

11. The teacher will be able to state the most often found articulatory–speech problems in children.

12. The teacher will be able to plan and execute a lesson on sound-production education.

13. The teacher will be able to determine whether students value, appreciate, or have an interest in speech improvement by observing whether students

speak clearly, with expression, and whether they voluntarily become involved in speech stimulation activities.

14. The teacher will be able to prepare oral activities for children who speak another language or nonstandard English.

There is all the difference in the world between having something to say and having to say something.

JOHN DEWEY

Introduction

Talking wasn't allowed in the school I went to. You only spoke if you were called on to recite or answer a question. Anyone caught talking at other times was looked on with disdain by the teacher. A chronic violator of the silence rule was usually severely disciplined.

Fortunately, times have changed. We recognize the importance of oral expression, and we recognize that school is a place for talking—for giving free play to children's communicative instincts. A classroom in which children can spontaneously interact with one another and teachers is necessary for oral communication. A good classroom should not be silent. It should be one in which children's ideas are heard, respected, encouraged, and shared.

Children need many opportunities to express themselves, to try out ideas, and to get feedback. When children interact with adults, they are testing their own language. Children's language grows when it receives reinforcement from adults, and children's self-concepts are enhanced when they feel that what they have to say is valuable. Listening to children and respecting what they have to say encourages them to engage in more conversations. The more conversations that children engage in, the better listeners they become because to engage in a meaningful conversation, they must listen to the speaker. (See Chapter 5.)

Chapter 6 is concerned with the classroom teachers' ability to provide an effective oral communication and speech improvement program which is also *fun* for the students. This chapter is divided into three parts. Part One presents the oral expression (speech stimulation) activities such as finger play, choral speaking, puppetry, and so on, which are vital to all oral communication and speech improvement programs. Part Two is concerned with speech improvement. The topics and materials of this part are designed to help teachers who may feel inadequate in the speech improvement area to gain confidence in their ability to present a good speech improvement program in the classroom. The development of speech sounds and proper sound production (articulation) in the child is coupled with a game approach so that learning is fun. Teachers are also shown how to determine standards of speech normality in their students. In order to make the teacher aware of the kinds of speech defects that separate the average child from the speech-handicapped child, a listing and description of these defects are presented.

In Part Three a special section on Teaching English as a Second Language (TESL) is included to help teachers when they are confronted with this need.

After you have finished reading this chapter you should be able to answer these questions:

1. How can a teacher organize the classroom for the development of effective oral communication?

2. What types of activities are included in an oral communication program?

3. What oral expression activities can primary-grade level children participate in?

4. What oral expression activities can intermediate-grade level children participate in?

5. What kinds of activities should the teacher include in a speech improvement program for primary or intermediate students?

6. How can television be made part of the communicative process?

7. What are the differences between speech improvement and speech correction?

8. What is the classroom teacher's role in the area of speech disorders?

9. Do all children develop speech sounds at the same age? Elaborate on the answer.

10. What are the most common speech defects in children?

11. How can teachers help children correct speech defects?

12. What is TESL?

13. Do you feel it is necessary to have TESL programs in the schools? Give reasons to support your response.

Classroom Environment Conducive to Effective Oral Expression

The necessity for providing a good physical, emotional, social, and intellectual environment was discussed in Chapter 5 and is applicable here. An environment in which listening occurs without distractions will also be one which is more conducive to oral expression. If students know that others are listening to them, they will be motivated to speak effectively in order to convey their messages.

Physical Environment

Classroom desks and chairs should be arranged so that all students can see and hear the speaker. Obstacles obstructing students' view should be removed, for they act as deterrents to both speakers and listeners who are trying to communicate. If the speakers' expressions and manner—their total nonverbal behavior—are effective in relaying the message, then the whole class should be able to see as well as hear them. Speakers faced with an audience that is constantly twisting and turning in their seats will be distracted. Speakers who feel they have lost their audience may lose confidence and this will affect their delivery.

A classroom that is too warm or too cold or is drafty or one that is peppered with posters or displays may distract the audience and prevent speakers from performing at their highest level of competence.

Emotional Environment

So that children will volunteer to give oral reports or talks or become involved in discussions, creative dramatics, puppetry, and so on, they must be in a nonthreatening environment. They must feel that what they have to say is important and that others want to listen to them. They must be secure about not being ridiculed or criticized. The classroom situation must be friendly, sympathetic, and understanding.

Social Environment

Children who feel accepted by their peers and teacher will more often volunteer to engage in oral expression activities. The teacher who is aware of the individual personalities of students and who uses a sociogram (see Appendix) to discover more about the students' social relationships can more intelligently assemble groups for discussions, group reports, and so on.

Teachers should also recognize that their own behavior toward students influences the children's behavior toward those same students.

In the primary grades boys and girls usually work and play together indiscriminately, but by the intermediate grades this pattern alters to a more deliberately homogeneous sex pattern. During the past two decades, this primary-grade pattern seems to be changing. In many first-, second-, and third-grade classes boys will only choose boys for play and social interaction, while girls will only choose girls. Teachers should be aware of this phenomenon in their classrooms and act accordingly when they group children for oral expression activities.

Intellectual Environment

Students who are in an intellectually stimulating environment and are engaged in a variety of activities will have many things to talk about, discuss, and report on.

Oral Expression Activities (Speech Stimulation Activities)

When children come to school they have usually acquired adult language patterns and are engaging in meaningful oral expression. The teacher needs to encourage children's language development with activities that stimulate speech.

Speech stimulation activities involve the speech arts. They not only help to develop better speech, voice, and body movements necessary for effective speech, but are also enjoyable activities in which children usually love to participate. A variety of activities should be incorporated in the oral communication program in order to provide for all students' needs and interests.

The oral expression (speech stimulation) activities included here are:

Conversation.
Telephoning.
Discussion.
Giving talks.
Choral speaking.
Finger play.
Creative dramatics.
Puppetry.
Storytelling.

Some special activities on role playing, pantomime, nonverbal behavior, haptics, and voice usage are also included.

Conversation

Socialization is a process that prepares an individual to live in society. Human beings are social animals. The better we know one another, the better we are able to get along with one another. It is through social discourse such as conversation that we learn more about our friends and neighbors and, many times, about ourselves as well. The need to converse with one another is seen daily in any classroom, whether it is a university graduate class or a kindergarten. When an instructor is interrupted during a class period and must stop to talk to a visitor or leave the class for a short while, what happens? Practically anyone can predict the students' behavior in this situation. They start talking to one another. No prompting is necessary, sometimes to the dismay of the teacher. Children naturally like to talk, to exchange pleasantries, ideas, comments, and so on. The teacher must understand this need in students and provide not only an environment where students will feel free to engage in spontaneous, informal, and nonstructured talks with one another but also provide time for this to take place.

Since children as well as adults spend most of their time in conversational oral discourse, teachers should help students to be more adept at this skill. Being a good conversationalist helps individuals to be freer to communicate with others and thus plays a large role in enhancing self-concept.

Telephoning

Can you imagine life without the telephone? Would you agree that hardly a day goes by when you do not make use of the phone? Many children speak on the phone for a variety of purposes at very early ages; however, this does not mean that they use the phone well or effectively. Teachers ought to help children communicate better through use of the telephone.

Primary-grade children should learn how to answer the telephone in a courteous and pleasant manner. They should learn how to dial the operator's number and, in case of an emergency, how to dial the police department's number, the fire department's number, or the hospital's number. The children should learn how to state their message in a direct and calm manner. Simulated conversations using the teletrainer,* which is available through many local telephone business offices, can help children be better telephone users. Examples of scenarios for simulated telephone conversations follow. Each scenario requires two children—the caller and the receiver of the call—and the teacher, who will operate the teletrainer switchboard. (If teletrainer equipment is not available, the teacher can have the children engage in simulated telephone conversations using toy phones.) In each scenario, the child must dial the number correctly, speak clearly, use good telephone manners, and role play the part for the suggested scenario.

Scenarios

Child calls the fire department to report a fire.

Child calls the police to report that his or her dog is missing.

*The teletrainer is an amplifier and control unit that produces a dial tone, ringing, and a busy signal, and completes the circuit between the two phone units by means of a long cord.

Child calls information for help in finding an out-of-town telephone number.

Child calls the operator to report reaching a wrong number.

Child calls a friend to find out about a homework assignment.

Child calls a friend to invite the friend for dinner.

Child calls a sick friend to find out how the friend is feeling.

Child phones his or her parents to tell them that he or she will be late.

Child calls the doctor because someone has just become very ill, and no one else is home.

Intermediate-grade level children should continue to acquire telephoning skill. Following are examples of scenarios for simulated conversations and role playing. If teletrainer equipment is used, the teletrainer switchboard can be operated by one of the students.

Scenarios

Child dials long-distance information to get a telephone number.

Child dials the operator to report reaching a wrong number on an in-state long-distance call.

Child calls the police to report a serious accident.

Child calls a business firm to leave a message for one of his or her parents.

Child calls the operator to report receiving a wrong number on an out-of-state call.

Child uses the yellow pages of the telephone directory to find a business firm that sells a special item that he or she needs—the child phones a few business firms to find out whether they have the special item, the cost of the item, and other pertinent information about the item.

Child calls the newspaper editor to report something exciting that happened at school.

Discussion

Although the terms "conversation" and "discussion" are used interchangeably, and children engage in informal discussions during work and play, differences exist between the two. As already stated, conversation is informal, spontaneous, and nonstructured, whereas classroom discussions are usually formal, more structured, directed, involved with specific purposes, and demand the cooperation of many persons.

Group Discussions in the Primary Grades   Group discussions can be initiated by a number of stimuli. Every day innumerable opportunities present themselves for group discussions. The children may have had a story read to them which has caused some excitement or controversy. They may have seen a television show or movie that has stimulated them, or some event in the news may have sparked a need for clarification or discussion. In order to make discussions meaningful and beneficial, certain standards should be set by the students and the teacher.

1. Everyone must respect the rights of each person to voice or state his or her opinion.
2. When someone is speaking, all persons should be courteous and attentive.
3. Speakers have the responsibility to make themselves heard, to stick to the point, and to speak clearly so that they can be understood.
4. All persons should try to contribute to the discussion.
5. Individual children should try not to dominate the discussion.

Group Discussions in the Intermediate Grades   In the intermediate grades all of these standards would also apply. However, there are some more advanced skills that such children should develop.

1. Everyone should develop the ability to participate in meetings conducted according to a basic parliamentary procedure.
2. Each child should learn to act as a leader in a discussion by:
    a. keeping all speakers on the topic.
    b. helping all to contribute, sometimes by asking questions.
    c. not allowing a few people to dominate.
    d. not letting arguments begin.
    e. not allowing emotions to rule.
    f. pulling main points of discussion together.

3. Children should learn to disagree politely.
4. All persons should be able to listen for supporting evidence related to the main topic of discussion.

A listing of the various forms of discussion is given below for teachers:

1. Informal Discussion: This can evolve at any time in the classroom with or without apparent leadership. It usually includes a grouping of some children who have a common interest or problem.
2. Round Table: This takes place without an audience. A number of members informally discuss something under the direction of a leader.
3. Panel Discussion: Approximately four to eight equally informed participants, under the direction of a leader, engage in a discussion before an audience. The topic or problem is informally presented from many views. A question-and-answer period from the audience usually follows.
4. Dialogue: An expert is questioned by another individual who is also well informed in the area. Television programs use this format when interviewing public figures. Teachers can employ this technique when a guest, who is an authority on a specific topic, is invited to visit the classroom. Some students can take a special assignment to become more informed in this area, and then act as the expert in questioning the guest.
5. Debate: Two different sides of an issue are presented in a formal manner. Provisions for full class participation can be achieved by allowing questions from the floor. For an effective debate the students involved must be well informed.

Time for Talks

Time should be set aside each week for special talks given by individuals on topics of interest. Talks not only help students to present ideas in a logical and sequential fashion but also give them practice in using appropriate voice quality, rhythm, rate, and volume, and in speaking in front of an audience. They can also practice good body posture, facial expressions, gestures, and body movements during talks.

Informal Oral Reporting   In the primary grades informal oral reporting is the most frequent talk activity. "Show and tell" is a first-grade activity in which pupils share some event with their classmates or tell about some new acquisition. Although some teachers use sharing time at the beginning of the school day to "calm children down," it can be an excellent technique to draw out the shy child and to give more aggressive children an opportunity to stand in the limelight. In order to gain the attention of the group, children soon learn that they must have something interesting to say; they also must be able to say it so that others will continue to listen.

From "show and tell" sharing, primary-grade children can be encouraged to share some information about a television show that they especially like, a movie that they have just seen, or a story that they have either read or had read to them.

Teachers should not only encourage this type of oral reporting, they should really assist children who are presenting the talks to make them enjoyable for listeners. Teachers, by asking specific questions, will help the reporter not only to recall some pertinent facts but will also keep rambling to a minimum.

Reinforcement should be given, praising the student for an interesting point or some descriptive phrases that help listeners to get a better picture of what is being said.

Formal Oral Reporting   In the intermediate and upper grades students present formal reports. These differ from informal oral reports in that they require study and preparation of background material.

When primary-grade children give formal oral reports, the length of time for the talk should be just a few minutes and preparation should also be limited in scope. It should be stressed that those second- and third-grade pupils who are reading at a fifth- or sixth-grade level are able to do research with help from the teacher, and give oral reports that will provide an opportunity for enrichment for them.

Certain standards should be set for talks in

order to make them worthwhile and meaningful. These guidelines might be beneficial for both the teacher and students in the primary grades:

TEACHER'S EVALUATION CHART FOR TALKS IN THE PRIMARY GRADES

I. Is the subject appropriate for the child and the audience?

   1. Does the child appear interested in the subject?
   2. Does the child appear to know the subject?
   3. Does the class appear interested in the subject?

II. Is the talk organized so the group can understand it easily?

   1. Does the child express a complete thought?
   2. Does the child tell things in the right order?
   3. Does each statement contribute to the main thought?
   4. Does the child use words which express his or her ideas clearly and accurately?

III. Is the child at ease (free from distracting mannerisms)?

   1. Does the child keep twisting and turning?
   2. Does the child keep repeating himself or herself?
   3. Does the child keep turning away from the audience?

IV. Does the child use acceptable voice tones and articulation?

   1. Can the child be heard easily?
   2. Is the child's voice pleasing to hear?
   3. Does the child speak at a suitable rate?
   4. Does the child's voice express the meaning of the words?
   5. Does the child use accurate articulation?
   6. Does the child use distinct enunciation?
   7. Does the child use acceptable pronunciation?[1]

[1] Adapted from Elizabeth Chase Read, "A Teacher-administered Rating Chart for Talks in the Primary Grades," *Journal of Education* 136 (March 1954): 171–172.

TEACHER'S EVALUATION CHART FOR TALKS IN THE INTERMEDIATE AND UPPER GRADES

I. Is the subject appropriate for the child and the audience?

    1. Does the child appear interested in the subject?

    2. Does the child appear to know the subject?

    3. Does the class appear interested in the subject?

II. Is the speaker's main point and organization clear?

    1. Does the speaker state the main point clearly?

    2. Does the speaker select a main point that can be explained in the time limit?

    3. Does the speaker use examples or reasons or facts to make the point clear?

    4. Does the speaker develop the main point in a clear order?

    5. Does the speaker summarize the main point clearly at the end of the talk?

    6. Does the speaker select words which express the ideas clearly?

III. Does the speaker make the talk interesting?

    1. Does the speaker arouse the interest of the audience at the beginning of the talk?

    2. Does the speaker keep the attention of the audience during the talk?

    3. Does the speaker use appropriate pictures, objects, or chalkboard diagrams?

IV. Does the speaker present a poised appearance?

    1. Does the speaker appear to be at ease?

    2. Does the speaker use appropriate posture and body actions?[2]

[2]Adapted from John Crawford and Richard French, "An Evaluation Chart for Talks or Oral Reports in the Secondary Schools," *Journal of Education* 136 (March 1954): 169–171.

Oral Communication through Choral Speaking

Choral speaking helps children to improve their speech while having fun. It is a way of saying aloud, in unison, a poem or a prose selection by a group trying to catch the spirit and rhythm of the piece. The selection must be one which lends itself to unison speaking.

Participation in this activity helps students not only to appreciate good literature but to gain a better understanding of poetry. In order to give a good rendition of a poem, students must be able to interpret the mood and thought of the selection.

Choral speaking also helps shy youngsters to "forget themselves" and become less self-conscious. Once children have gained confidence in their ability to speak, they will be less reticent to speak before an audience.

The teacher can employ choral speaking effectively in kindergarten, with appropriate material that will help children enjoy the sounds and rhythm of poetry.

Types of Choral Speaking   There are various types of choral speaking in which children can take part. In *Line-a-Child*, individual children speak different lines. For example, in the following Mother Goose Nursery Rhyme, "Solomon Grundy," the entire class could speak the first and eighth lines, while six individual children speak the second, third, fourth, fifth, sixth, and seventh lines. For further interest a contrast of voices can be used so that children with light, bright voices speak the first three lines, and children with rich, heavy voices speak the last three lines.

SOLOMON GRUNDY

All children	Solomon Grundy born on Monday,
1st Child	Christened on Tuesday,
2d Child	Married on Wednesday
3d Child	Very ill on Thursday,
4th Child	Worse on Friday,

5th Child	Died on Saturday,
6th Child	Buried on Sunday,
All children	This is the end of Solomon Grundy.

MOTHER GOOSE

Other selections from Mother Goose that can be used with *Line-a-Child* choral speaking include "Here Sits the Lord Mayor"; "One, Two, Buckle My Shoe"; "This Little Cow"; and "For Want of a Nail." Other good choices would be:

ONE AND ONE

1st Voice	Two little girls are better than one,
2d Voice	Two little boys can double the fun,
3d Voice	Two little birds can build a fine nest,
4th Voice	Two little arms can love mother best,
5th Voice	Two little ponies must go to a span,
6th Voice	Two little pockets has my little man,
7th Voice	Two little eyes to open and close,
8th Voice	Two little ears and one little nose,
9th Voice	Two little elbows dimpled and sweet,
10th Voice	Two little shoes on two little feet,
11th Voice	Two little lips and one little chin,
12th Voice	Two little cheeks with a rose shut in,
13th Voice	Two little shoulders, chubby and strong,
14th Voice	Two little legs running all day long.

MARY M. DODGE

THE OWL

1st Voice	When cats run home and light is come,
2d Voice	And dew is cold upon the ground,
3d Voice	And the far off stream is dumb,
4th Voice	And the whirling sail goes round;
All	Alone and warming his fair wits, The White Owl in the belfry sits.
5th Voice	When merry milkmaids click the latch,
6th Voice	And rarely smells the new-mown hay,
7th Voice	And the cock hath sung beneath the thatch
All	Twice or thrice his roundelay; Alone and warming his fair wits, The White Owl in the belfry sits.

ALFRED, LORD TENNYSON

In antiphonal poems the heavy and light voices speak to each other. The Mother Goose rhymes "Willy Boy, Willy Boy"; "Baa Baa Black Sheep"; "Little Girl, Little Girl"; "Pussy Cat, Pussy Cat"; "Jennie Come Tie"; and "Little Dog, Little Dog" are examples of this type of verse. Other examples are:

"LADY MOON"

1st Half Class	Lady Moon, Lady Moon, where are you roving?
2d Half Class	"Over the sea."
1st Half Class	Lady Moon, Lady Moon, whom are you loving?
2d Half Class	"All that love me."
1st Half Class	Are you not tired with rolling, and never Resting to sleep? Why look so pale and so sad, as forever Wishing to weep?
2d Half Class	"Ask me not this, little child, if you love me; You are too bold: I must obey my dear Father above me, And do as I'm told."
1st Half Class	Lady Moon, Lady Moon, where are you roving?
2d Half Class	"Over the sea."
1st Half Class	Lady Moon, Lady Moon, whom are you loving?
2d Half Class	"All that love me."

LORD HOUGHTON

ONCE I CAUGHT A FISH

1st Half Class	1, 2, 3, 4, 5
2d Half Class	Once I caught a fish alive,
1st Half Class	6, 7, 8, 9, 10,
2d Half Class	I let him go again.
1st Half Class	Why did you let him go?
2d Half Class	Because he bit my fingers so.
1st Half Class	Which finger did he bite?
2d Half Class	The little finger on the right.

ANON.

HOW MANY SECONDS IN A MINUTE?

1st Half Class	How many seconds in a minute?
2d Half Class	Sixty, and no more in it.
1st Half Class	How many minutes in an hour?
2d Half Class	Sixty for sun and shower.
1st Half Class	How many hours in a day?
2d Half Class	Twenty-four for work and play.
1st Half Class	How many days in a week?
2d Half Class	Seven both to hear and speak.
1st Half Class	How many weeks in a month?
2d Half Class	Four as the swift moon runn'th.
1st Half Class	How many months in a year?
2d Half Class	Twelve, the almanac makes clear.
1st Half Class	How many years in an age?
2d Half Class	One hundred, says the sage.
1st Half Class	How many ages in time?
2d Half Class	No one knows the rhyme.

CHRISTINA G. ROSSETTI

WHAT DOES THE HAIL SAY?

1st Half Class	What does the hail say?
2d Half Class	Knock! Knock!
1st Half Class	What does the rain say?
2d Half Class	Pit! Pit!
1st Half Class	What does the sleet say?
2d Half Class	Sh! Sh!
1st Half Class	What does the wind say?
2d Half Class	Whoo! Whoo!

ELEANOR SMITH

In *cumulative choral reading* a small group reads one section and is joined by a second group which reads the second section; they are joined by a third group which reads the third section. Usually no more than five groups should be used to build the cumulative effect. The emphasis in this kind of reading becomes more forceful and the poem usually sounds louder and faster with each group and line. Here is an example of a poem that can be used with cumulative choral reading:

AFRICAN DANCE

Small group 1	The low beating of the tom-toms,
Groups 1 and 2	The slow beating of tom-toms,
Groups 1–3	Low . . . slow.
Groups 1–4	Slow . . . low—
Groups 1–5	Stirs your blood.
All	Dance!
Group 1, softly	A night-veiled girl
Groups 1 and 2, softly	Whirls softly into a
Groups 1–3, softly	Circle of light
Groups 1–4, softly	Whirls softly . . . slowly,
Groups 1–5, softly	Like a wisp of smoke around the fire—
Groups 1–5	And the tom-toms beat,
Groups 1 and 2	And the tom-toms beat,
Groups 1–4	And the low beating of the tom-toms
Groups 1–5	Stirs your blood.

LANGSTON HUGHES

The reading emphasis of "African Dance" should grow more forceful, and the poem should become louder and faster with each line, indicating the increasing intensity of the drum beat. In the second verse, there should also be an increasing intensity of feeling, but the reading should be more melodious and softer than in the first verse. In the last stanza the voices should reach an explosive crescendo.

When class members speak the refrain while one or several students tell the story they are *refrain speaking*. Verses that lend themselves to this type of choral speaking are:

A FARMER WENT TROTTING

1st Group	A farmer went trotting upon his grey mare,
All	Bumpety, Bumpety, bump!
1st Group	With his daughter behind him so rosy and fair,
All	Lumpety, lumpety, lump!
2d Group	A raven cried "croak!" and they all tumbled down,
All	Bumpety, bumpety, bump!
2d Group	The mare broke her knees, and the farmer his crown,
All	Lumpety, lumpety, lump!
3d Group	The mischievous raven flew laughing away,
All	Bumpety, bumpety, bump!
3d Group	And vowed he would serve them the same the next day,
All	Lumpety, lumpety, lump!

MOTHER GOOSE

THE WIND

1st Group	I saw you toss the kites on high And blow the birds about the sky; And all around I heard you pass, Like ladies' skirts across the grass.
All	O wind, a-blowing all day long, O wind, that sings so loud a song!
2d Group	I saw the different things you did, But always you yourself you hid. I felt you push, I heard you call, I could not see yourself at all—

All	O wind, a-blowing all day long, O wind, that sings so loud a song!
3d Group	O you that are so strong and cold, O blower, are you young or old? Are you a beast of field and tree, Or just a stronger child than me?
All	O wind, a-blowing all day long, O wind, that sings so loud a song!

ROBERT LOUIS STEVENSON

Part speaking presents a selection by groups of students in such a way that the sequence and continuity of ideas expressed in the poem are maintained. Each group speaks a part of the selection, the groups being divided according to the kinds of voices indicated by the poem; for example, low voices would read a part appropriate for heavy voices, whereas higher voices would read a part that calls for light voices.

This poem by Walter De La Mare lends itself to part speaking:

THE HUNTSMEN

1st Group	Three jolly gentlemen, In coats of red, Rode their horses Up to bed.
2d Group	Three jolly gentlemen Snored till morn, Their horses champing The golden corn.
3d Group	Three jolly huntsmen, At break of day, Came clitter-clatter down the stairs And galloped away.

In *unison speaking* the group reads the entire poem where it maintains one mood or one theme throughout. The students then decide what divisions they wish to make, which help portray the meaning of the poem more clearly to the audience. Unison or group choral reading is not a separate technique or form but merely uses any or all types of choral reading for the most effective casting of a poem.

A Choral-speaking Technique   To proceed with a choral-speaking program teachers should first attempt to release the class from tension, for *relaxation* is necessary for effective choral speaking. Breathing exercises can be used to relax students, and help them to learn to breathe properly. Breathing activities—such as puffing, blowing, sighing, and yawning—while emphasizing swelling at the waist or belt line on the intake of air should help to discourage shoulder and upper-chest breathing. Another relaxing activity has children responding to the teacher's oral reading of a poem with rhythmical body movements. The teacher's reading should bring out the rhythms and music of the poem.

After these "warm up" activities students are ready for choral reading. During this phase the teacher presents meaningful segments of a selection to students, who silently follow the reading by making the proper lip and mouth movements. The segments are presented again, and this time the pupils whisper the lines. Finally, pupils recite the lines as the teacher silently mouths or whispers them.

Finger Plays

Finger plays are speech stimulation activities especially suitable for kindergarten and first-grade children. If they are properly presented, they can be most effective in helping children to learn sequential order in speaking and to develop good body movements and gestures. Finger play is an excellent medium for the shy or withdrawn child who is reticent to speak. Since finger-play activities can be presented with the participation of the whole group, children who have speech difficulties usually participate.

Finger plays involve simple rhyming stories which are readily dramatized. Here are some suggestions for presenting finger-play activities.

Steps in Learning Finger Plays

1. Teacher presents finger-play activity to be learned by children.
2. Children thoroughly learn the rhyme that accompanies the finger-play activity.
3. Next, children learn the finger actions.
4. The rhyme and the finger actions are joined. The teacher softly and slowly accompanies the students' recitation.
5. The children, without the teacher, are asked to perform the first line of the finger play, then the second line, and so on until all the lines have been individually completed.
6. The children perform the whole finger-play activity by themselves.

Teachers should act as encouragers, reinforcers, and helpers. So that finger play can be both fun and educationally worthwhile, children must feel free to participate. Children should be invited to participate, but they should not be pressured if they are reluctant. If teachers are enthusiastic and generous in their praise, they will soon have everyone in the class involved.

Here are some examples of simple finger-play activities.[3,4]

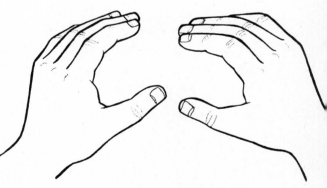

Here is a pumpkin, big and round;
(*Fingers form circle*)

[3]The length of the finger-play activity will depend on the individual differences of the students.
[4]James Neal Blake, *Speech Education Activities for Children* (Springfield, Ill.: Charles C. Thomas, 1970), p. 35.

Here is a kitty, soft and brown;
(Fists on top of each other with two fingers up)

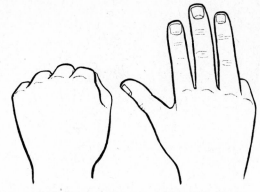

Four little bunnies were as frisky as could be
One ran down a hill, and then there were three.

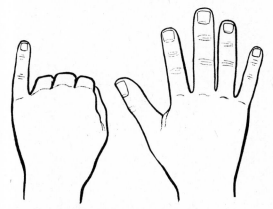

Six little bunnies found a little hive;
One chased a bee, and then there were five.

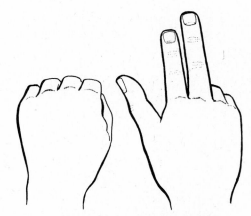

Three little bunnies had nothing to do;
One chased a bug, and then there were two.

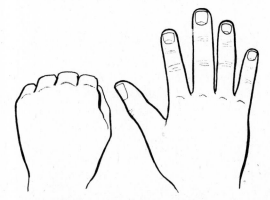

Five little bunnies hurried to the store;
One got lost, and then there were four.

Two little bunnies sat warming in the sun;
One found a carrot, and then there was one.

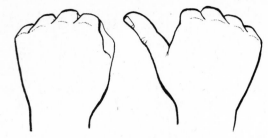

One little bunny knew when to run;
He heard a dog bark, and then there was none.

FIREMEN

Ten brave firemen
(*Ten fingers are held straight up*)
Sleeping in a row.
(*Fingers are held out flat*)
Ding goes the bell
(*Clap hands*)
Down the pole they go.
(*Hands go down an imaginary pole*)
Jumping on the engine.
(*Make driving motions*)
Oh! Oh! Oh!
Putting out the fire
(*Pretend to hold hose*)
Sh! Sh! Sh!
Home so slow.
(*Driving motion slowly*)
Back to bed again
(*Hands form pillow*)
All in a row.
(*Fingers are held out flat*)

I'M A HAPPY CHILD

Eyes to see with.
(*Point to eyes*)
Ears to hear with.
(*Point to ears*)
Nose to smell with.
(*Point to nose*)
Teeth to chew.
(*Point to teeth*)
Feet to run with.
(*Point to feet*)
Hands to work with.
(*Hold up hands*)
I'm a happy child, aren't you?
(*Point to neighbor*)

HICKORY, DICKORY, DOCK

Hickory, Dickory, Dock!
The mouse ran up the clock;
The clock struck one
The mouse ran down
Hickory, dickory, dock!

Let the left arm and hand raised over the head be the tall grandfather clock. The right hand is the mouse. The mouse runs up the clock as the rhyme is spoken. Both hands are clapped together once over the head with the third line. Then the mouse runs down the clock.

Creative Dramatics and Speaking

Creative dramatics offers many opportunities for the development of the "creative spirit," and lends itself as well to the improvement of voice, vocabulary, and diction. This is a natural for children, because their play is so full of pretending, imagination, and imitation.

It is important at the outset to distinguish creative dramatics from play productions. Creative dramatics is for the child, not for an audience; it is informal. In this form it is usual for children to make up their own story and dialogue. The teacher can help stimulate creative dramatics by setting a certain scene and having students act out the parts.

Here are suggestions for children five through seven years of age.

Procedure The teacher might ask: "How many have heard Mother or Father call the dentist? What did they say? Who can pretend that they are a mother or father calling the dentist?"

The conversation would probably go something like this:

Imitates dialing a telephone.
"Is this Dr. Jones?"
"I would like to make an appointment to have my teeth checked.
"May I have one this week? One tooth is bothering me.
"Thank you."

A dramatization of a boy or girl feeding a dog can be motivated by the teacher in the same way: "How many children have a dog or cat? How many have fed them? Show us how you did it."

Dramatizations

"Here, Shawn; here, Shawn; here, Shawn. Look what I have for you. It's a nice bone. We had rib roast today and Mother gave me this bone. No, don't jump all over me. I'll give it to you. Here you are. Look at him run with it. He's afraid somebody will take it away from him."

Other possibilities would include:

Someone cutting the grass.
Someone watering the lawn.
Someone cleaning the house.
Child putting sick doll to bed.
Child running a lemonade stand.
Child calling friends to come to play.
Child going to bed.
Child getting up and dressing.
Children visiting the zoo.

Someone shopping at the supermarket.
Child eating supper.
Child building an airplane.

Self-consciousness at the beginning can be reduced by allowing several children to dramatize the same thing at the same time, encouraging each child to act as he or she thinks best and not imitating what the others are doing. As they develop in dramatic ability and gain confidence, one child may perform alone. Gradually more difficult situations can be acted such as:

Two children talking about a game.
Several children playing going to the library.
One child being a storekeeper while others come to buy.
Several children giving a simple circus performance.
Children dramatizing animals, while other children visit the zoo and talk about the habits and actions of the animals.

The teacher can tell a story and then have the children act it out supplying their own dialogue. Poems can be acted out by the children as well. Many Mother Goose rhymes are excellent acting sources for kindergarten and first-grade children. Such characters as Humpty Dumpty, Jack and Jill, Little Miss Muffet, Mary and her lamb, and Georgie Porgie are fun to portray. The opportunities for creative dramatics are bounded only by the creative limitations of the teacher.

By second grade many children can be more independent in creative dramatics. They can take the initiative in choosing a story that they would like to "act out" for the class. A group of second graders might decide to present "The Three Billy Goats Gruff"—a favorite with most children. The performers should be encouraged to make all decisions concerning casting, props, and number of rehearsals. The teacher's role is that of questioner, suggester, encourager, and reinforcer. The teacher can ask questions to stimulate children's thinking about a problem or can make some positive suggestions for solving the problem. The children should be encouraged to try their ideas, but they should know that the teacher is available for assistance if needed. The children's efforts should be praised and their endeavor should be shown as worthwhile.

Role Playing—An Extension of Creative Play

Role playing is a form of creative dramatics that is natural to children. They either choose or are appointed to specific roles; the scenario is set; but the dialogue is spontaneously developed. In a fifth- or sixth-grade class the scenario might be a discipline problem serious enough to warrant calling both parents to school. A meeting is set up in the principal's office. The child, the mother, the father, the teacher, and the principal are present. The players have been told the scenario. It is up to them to act out the drama.

Role playing often helps teachers gain insights into the feelings of students, and to discover what is important to them. This technique can also help students develop keener perception of how it feels to be in certain situations.

The teacher is cautioned, when choosing children to play particular roles, against obvious assignments; for example, having an "isolate" play a popular student or the "star" in the classroom play an "isolate." Discretion must be used in role playing so that students are not embarrassed or ridiculed. Children should not be forced to play a role in which they might feel uncomfortable.

Pantomime

Pantomime is creative dramatics without speech. Students use only their faces and bodies to convey a thought or action. Pantomime usually helps students become more sensitive to

what they see. It also helps them to learn about the importance of facial expressions and body movements in conveying and receiving messages.

Primary-grade pupils seem to use pantomime naturally in their everyday activities. They especially enjoy playing "make-believe" or "pretend" type of games in which they imitate some person, animal, or object. These children can pantomime many everyday situations such as:

Waking up in the morning.
Getting dressed.
Eating lunch.
Reading a book.
Sweeping the floor.

Intermediate-grade students might try more difficult themes such as:

Playing baseball.
Showing enthusiasm.

Exhibiting fear.
Being too hot.
Being too cold.
Crying.
Acting bored.
Feeling tired.
Moving through a crowded bus.
Having a difficult time conversing on the telephone.

When pantomiming, students must carefully think about and analyze the moods, situations, or ideas they wish to act out in order to determine how best to convey them. Imitation of facial expressions and body movements requires keen observation.

"Reflections" is a good game to use with pantomime for both primary- and intermediate-grade students. This game uses sets of two players in which one student is the "mirror" and the other is the "image." The "image" students make different faces or body movements which the "mirror" students reflect.

Nonverbal Behavior: Its Role in Oral Communication and Creative Dramatics

Man communicates both verbally and nonverbally, and the total message lies in the combination of the two modalities.[5] (See Chapter 1.) Kinesics, the gestures which may or may not accompany speech, help to convey and clarify meaning. For example, an arched eyebrow tells us that a person is skeptical about what is being said, and could be verbally saying, "Do you really want me to believe that?" Upturned palms combined with a shrug of the shoulders tells us that a person is confused. That person might be verbally saying, "I don't know." Body movements portray a person's moods and feelings as

readily as words. For example, a person's body stance can tell us whether he or she is anxious or relaxed. Following are some suggestions for activities that can help students be more perceptive to the messages conveyed by nonverbal behavior:

1. Students can videotape some persons while role playing. Students then can view the tape to identify the kinesic motions that individual role players use while speaking, the *vocal* nonverbal behaviors (ohs, ahs, screams, and so forth, that are vocal but express no words by themselves), and other body movements.
2. Students can view a foreign film and record some of the representative nonverbal behavior of the actors and actresses.
3. Children from different cultural backgrounds can try to communicate some message using some form of nonverbal behavior.
4. Students, with eyes closed, listen to a videotaping of two persons talking. The students then open their eyes and view the videotape. The students are asked to compare the listening and viewing of the tapes to determine whether they were able to get the complete message from only listening. If videotapes are not available, two students can role play the two sequences for the class.
5. Students can view television shows to observe the various kinds of facial gestures and body movements that individuals use when they speak.

Haptics: Nonverbal Communication through Touch   The study of *haptics*, nonverbal communication through touch, is relatively new; most of the research in this area has been done mainly with visually impaired or handicapped children. Haptics offers many possibilities for helping all kinds of students to become more sensitive to the effect that "touch" has on communication. When one is speaking, "a touch" at the right time helps convey meaning, for different ways of touching may convey different feelings or meanings. A pat on the back by a parent to a child and a pat on the behind by a football player to another player after a good

[5]Walburga von Raffler-Engel, "Total Communicative Redundancy: The Neglected Factor in Foreign Language Research," paper presented at the Los Angeles Second Language Research Forum, 1978.

scrimmage both mean "well done." A handshake or the touching of hands are forms of greeting.

Videotaping spontaneous class conversations during recess can allow students to observe how touch aids communication. Students can then role play different kinds of touch techniques and have their classmates interpret what they are trying to convey.

Puppetry

Some children—who are reluctant to participate in storytelling, creative dramatics, or role playing—find puppetry a fine outlet for creative expression. Through the manipulation of puppets, these children overcome much of their shyness and fear of speaking in front of an audience. By projecting their feelings and thoughts into the puppets, they make them come alive.

Puppetry is a means of acting by using one's hands. The hands become the characters. The suggestions listed here could aid puppeteers in giving a successful performance.

Suggestions to Students on How to Be a Good Puppeteer

1. Know your script or story by heart if you are performing in front of an audience without a stage. Even when performing behind a stage, know the script or story very well. (Puppets may, of course, be used in a more informal manner; that is, children can use puppets in different situations in which the dialogue is completely spontaneous.)
2. Keep your eyes on the puppet.
3. Move the puppet that is talking, and have other puppets looking at the one that is speaking.
4. Help puppets make expressions by moving their heads and bodies. For example, a sad puppet would be turned slowly away from the audience, whereas a happy puppet might be bouncing up and down looking at the audience. Your voice will also help to convey the desired effect.
5. Avoid jerky movements with your puppets. Let

them make graceful entrances and exits. Do not just snatch them out or pop them in.

In the primary grades many Mother Goose poems and fairy tales lend themselves well to dramatizations with puppets. Intermediate-grade pupils might also use fairy tales, as well as their favorite stories from children's literature. They might want to write their own plays or stories and make puppets needed for the characters in the play.

Once puppet shows have been created, they can be taken to a wider audience—other classes, parents, a home for the aged—where the show's impact can be evaluated by the audience and where the students involved can achieve a sense of pride in what they have accomplished.

Making Puppets Primary-grade children can make stick puppets and hand puppets, which are both easy to construct and manipulate. Only biodegradable and recyclable material should be considered for building puppet-show sets or creating the puppets themselves. This helps children to develop an ecological con-

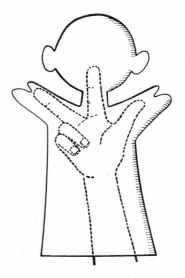

science and become more sensitive to their environment.

Stick puppets can be constructed from cardboard by stapling the front and back of the figures together over a long thin stick. Hand puppets from vegetables—such as potatoes, carrots, yams, and turnips—or from bags, socks, Styrofoam, and Spongex can also be easily made.

One type of hand puppet consists of a head and loose garments and usually has no legs. The index finger fits into the neck (see illustration),[6] and the thumb and forefinger fit into the sleeves; the garment conceals the hand.

A hand puppet can also be made of a sock, handkerchief, or paper bag, which covers the hand. Here are some suggestions for making hand puppets.[7]

[6]Eleanor Boylan, *How to Be a Puppeteer* (New York: McCall, 1970), p. 13.

[7]Ibid., pp. 20–21.

A sock can be fashioned into a puppet in two ways: Simply put your hand into it, as you would into the mitten, and work your fingers for a mouth; or, stuff the toe of the sock with soft material (such as nylon stockings) and tie it loosely where you want the neck, leaving room to insert your index finger. Sew on features and a piece of cloth around the "chin" to cover your hand. Like this:

Line the palm of a mitten with red cloth and sew on two button eyes where your knuckles are. If you like, add yarn whiskers or yarn hair sewn to the wristband. This puppet makes an interesting "creature" of any kind. Floppy ears can make it a dog; a cardboard horn on the tip of the nose will make it a unicorn. Should you want to make this puppet on a larger scale, instead of a mitten use a piece of material which fits over your arm like a loose sleeve and terminates at your fingers in two sections, the bottom for your thumb and the top for your fingers. Add the red mouth lining, eyes, hair, ears, etc., and you will have a more elaborate, long-necked creature, such as a giraffe or dragon. Like this:

For a paper-bag puppet, draw a face at the bottom of the bag where it folds flat, making sure that the mouth is in the center of the crease. Then put your hand into the bag and open and shut the crease so that the mouth "speaks." Like this:

A Styrofoam ball and a popsicle stick make a delightful puppet. Take a piece of cloth about eight or nine inches square and, holding the stick erect, drape the cloth over it; thrust the covered end of the stick into the ball. Like this:

Storytelling

The traditional definition of storytelling is "the oral interpretation of literature and folklore." In the traditional definition, no props or theatrical tricks are used. The storyteller, the story, a place to tell the story, and a receptive audience are all that is needed. Today, a number of persons combine storytelling with creative dramatics or use puppets or other props to help them to convey their story. Whatever technique of storytelling the storyteller uses, the key is in finding a story that is just right for that person— a story that the storyteller enjoys. Storytellers must also use the language of the story well, and their voice, gestures, and body movements must all work together to convey that certain magic that good storytellers have.

Storytelling is an art that can be learned. Teachers should not only encourage their children to be storytellers, but they too should set an example for their students.

Every week the teacher and students can plan for sharing and storytelling. Children may either relate their experiences or tell a story to the class. In the primary grades students should be encouraged to relate their experiences without much emphasis on form. However, by the intermediate grades the teacher and students can set some guidelines for storytelling. Here are some suggestions:

1. Only tell stories with which you are very familiar.
2. Prepare a list of characters.
3. Outline the action and plot.
4. Keep the story moving.
5. Use your voice and body to help to tell the story.
6. Look at your audience.

Voice Usage Activities

To help pupils improve their voice quality and to learn about the varieties of pitch, a tape recorder should be used so that students can listen to themselves. The teacher should plan systematic periods for voice-speech improvement and help students establish a relaxed and easy attitude. They should also be helped to listen with awareness and attention.

"The Three Bears" is a good story to use in the primary grades for teaching volume, pitch, or voice quality. Children act out the story, interchanging the roles of father, mother, and baby bear.

Activity for Developing a Pleasing Voice Quality An example of an activity for developing a pleasing voice quality in early-primary-grade students follows:

Teacher reads story.

"Lenny the Tiger liked to eat a lot. The problem was that every time he ate a lot, he became very very sleepy. He would become so sleepy after he ate that he would fall asleep wherever he was. If anyone tried to awaken Tiger, he would be very angry, because then he would yawn all day long."

TEACHER: "Can you describe Tiger?"
CHILD: "He liked to eat a lot and he always fell asleep."
TEACHER: "Can you tell us what he did all day after he was awakened?"
CHILD: "He would yawn."
TEACHER: "Let's all yawn like Tiger."
(All the children yawn.)
TEACHER: "How do you think Tiger sounded when he was angry? Who would like to sound like Tiger and say, 'Leave me alone!'"
CHILD: "Leave me alone."
TEACHER: "Good, let's all say, 'Leave me alone.'"
CHILDREN: "Leave me alone!"
TEACHER: "Let's say 'Leave me alone' in an angrier voice."
CHILDREN: "Leave me alone."
TEACHER: "How did your throats feel when you said that? Did they hurt? Did you feel your muscles tighten? Let's yawn again."
(The children yawn.)

TEACHER: "How did that feel? Did your throats feel easy and relaxed?"
CHILDREN: "It felt easy."
TEACHER: "When we talk, should we allow our throats to become tight?"
CHILDREN: "No."
TEACHER: "Good, when we talk, our voices should not be hurting but should feel easy. Our throats should not be tight; they should be relaxed."

Television: Making It Part of the Communicative Process

It is a fact that children spend a great amount of time watching television. Preschool children may average about four hours a day, and nine- and ten-year-olds may average about four to six hours a day.[8] Rather than bemoaning this state of affairs, let us channel children's enjoyment of television into constructive instructional paths. (See "Television Reporting" in Chapter 10.)

Television requires listening and viewing; communication requires interaction—an exchange of ideas. The challenge is to make television part of the communicative process rather than a one-way process. How to do this is, of course, the key. Some suggestions follow which may be helpful. These suggested activities can be used with both primary- and intermediate-grade level children unless otherwise specified. Obviously the materials used would vary according to the ability levels of the children involved.

1. Use television in the classroom.
   a. Have children discuss the shows that they watch and why they watch the shows that they do.

[8]Aletha H. Stein, "Mass Media and Young Children's Development," *71st Yearbook for the National Society for the Study of Education*. Part II. Ira J. Gorden, ed. (Chicago: University of Chicago Press, 1972), pp. 181–202.

b. If videotapes and video cassettes are available, you might tape a favorite situation comedy and watch it together. A discussion should follow of the characters, plot, dialogue, and message that the writer is trying to convey.

c. Watch some special educational program together. Prepare students for the program. Set purposes for the viewing. Follow up with a discussion.

d. Listen to a tape recording of two different commercials which promote two different products. Then view a videotape of the same two commercials. Discuss which medium is more effective in getting its message across.

2. Correlate out-of-school television viewing with your language arts program.

a. Discuss the various commercials that appear on television and what makes them so memorable.

b. Analyze the most popular commercials to try to determine why they became so popular.

c. Discuss the propaganda tactics used in different commercials seen on television. (intermediate-grade level)

d. Have students watch a number of television news shows at home, and have them read a number of newspapers. Then have them make a comparison/contrast between the two mediums concerning the coverage of news, sports, entertainment, weather, and so on. (intermediate-grade level)

e. Encourage students to write a script for their favorite television character.

f. Encourage children to role play their favorite television characters in a given scenario.

g. Encourage students to present a puppet show based on their favorite television program or their favorite characters.

h. Have students watch a play or special television movie based on a book. Then have students read the book on which the television show is based. The students can compare the television production with the book.

i. Students can present character sketches to the class portraying the main character of a television show, and the rest of the class is challenged to figure out who the character is.

j. Some students could present a scene from a television show and then challenge the rest of the class to name the show.

Speech Improvement

Most of us are aware of George Bernard Shaw's play *Pygmalion (My Fair Lady)*, and of how a great transformation takes place in the heroine due mainly to improvement in her speech. Professor Higgins' technique as the story's speech therapist was so effective in bringing about the desired verbal changes in Eliza, the ragged cockney flower girl, that she was able to enter the English upper class at least for a time. This beguiling story demonstrates that good speech can be learned, provided that one is motivated enough to want to learn. The play dramatically underlines the maxim that we are judged by what we say *and how we say it*.

Shaw's play has a happy ending, but in reality it would be difficult to improve and correct someone's speech at Eliza's age, unless, like Eliza, one spent night and day doing nothing else.

Fortunately, speech improvement programs are part of, and integrated with, many ongoing elementary-school programs. More knowledge of the development of language in the child and the important interrelatedness of speech to all other language arts learning have stimulated teachers to use speech improvement programs. These not only include speech sound education (articulation) but also help students to express themselves more clearly and audibly and to use their voices and bodies as assets in conveying a message.

While all children need and can benefit from speech improvement programs, only a small percentage may need speech correction or speech therapy. Special speech correction is needed for those who exhibit speech defects that distract listeners and distort or entirely lose the speaker's message. Although speech correction is in the domain of the school speech clinician, the classroom teacher can also provide some correction when it is developmental in nature. The separation of "speech improvement" from "speech correction" can be misleading, because some speech improvement does involve correction. The confusion can be overcome if one thinks in terms of degree. While classroom teachers can help some children who show inadequately developed speech, they cannot help those with more severe developmental problems, as well as those with other kinds of disorders.

To summarize, the term "speech improvement" is used when the ongoing classroom program is discussed; "speech correction" is applied to children who are helped by a clinician.

Classroom teachers are not expected to be, nor should they be, speech diagnosticians. They should recognize children's speech problems and whether these can be helped in the regular classroom or should be referred to the school clinician for special help.

Although the school clinician serves as a consultant to the speech improvement program, the clinician's primary responsibility is in clinical speech services: to identify the children who require special services; provide those services through identification and selection of children for therapy and a clinical program of diagnosis, direct and indirect remedial methods, and consultative services.[9]

The Teacher's Role in Speech Improvement

In Chapter 15 the teacher is discussed as the key person in the classroom. Effective or not, the teacher will make a difference in the kind of education the children get. In the speech area the teacher has a double-barreled effect: first, by guiding the speech improvement program through the school year; and second, by serving as a model of (one would hope) desirable speech for many children. One of the skills that mark an excellent teacher is good speech, together with the ability to communicate orally. In all activities in which teachers engage—including directions given in class—whether intentionally or not, they set examples for students on how to speak. Teachers must, therefore, be conscious of their speech patterns, their mannerisms, their speech delivery, their diction, and the overall effect their speech has on students.

Teachers should attempt to evaluate their speech behavior critically. Videotape is an excellent tool to use for self-assessment purposes. (See Chapter 15.) Teachers can tape themselves while engaged in different activities at various times of the day to determine how they measure up as speech models. Here are some questions to ask yourself in self-evaluation:

When I speak, do my actions, facial expressions, and gestures enhance or distract from my delivery?

Do I appear bored or am I "alive" and enthusiastic?

Do I speak loudly enough for everyone to hear, or is my voice too loud?

Would I enjoy listening to myself? For example, does my voice have variety?

Do I pronounce my words clearly and carefully?

Am I confusing my audience because I am not sure enough about my topic?

Is the information that I am giving reliable and accurate?

How new is it?

Have I chosen the words at the level of my audience?

Am I logical?

Do I keep repeating myself?

Is my vocabulary varied?

Do I talk too much?

Do I try to understand other people's points of view?

Do I listen to others?

[9]Clayton L. Bennett, "Communications Disorders in the Public Schools," in *Handbook of Speech Pathology and Audiology*, Lee Edward Travis, ed. (New York: Appleton-Century-Crofts, Meredith Corp., 1971), p. 978.

Do I try to bring humor into my talks?
Do I present information in interesting ways?

A good teacher does not have to be a speech expert to be aware of the relationship of speech to other language arts areas. A child who has difficulty in speaking will have difficulty with reading, writing, spelling, phonics, and so on.

> If a wide gap exists between the language used by the child every day and the language of the books which he is trying to read, he cannot possibly succeed until that gap is closed. The beginner who says, "Me dot one"; the older child who persists in saying, "I seen," "This one is gooder," "I've gaven it to him," makes slow progress in reading until spoken language improves.[10]

Nor does the teacher have to be a speech pathologist to recognize the most common speech problems children bring to school. As has been said, the teacher should know which problems can be handled in class and which should be referred to professionals. The good teacher designs a school speech program so as to include both correction of faulty speech habits and helping children communicate more effectively through oral expression. Children must learn to recognize that people with overt speech problems sometimes cannot assume leadership roles because of their inability to express themselves adequately or to address an audience.

Development of Speech Sounds in Children

Before teachers can wisely plan the speech improvement program best suited to the needs of their students, they should know something about the chronological development of speech sounds. Studies have shown that children at suc-

cessive ages should be able to "produce correctly" each of the English sounds. The words "produce correctly" mean that the child can make the specific articulatory or phonetic movements so that they are acceptable to a linguistic community. (While children are acquiring speech sounds, they are also involved in the more complex activity of learning a language with all its rules or subsystems of rules. (See Chapter 3.)

Studies have shown that infants at various ages utter a certain number of phonemes (smallest units of speech sounds). The average child utters approximately seven phonemes at about months one and two, and twenty-seven phonemes at about twenty-nine and thirty months. Researchers have also reported that vowel sounds are more frequent than consonant sounds in infants before their first year. After one year of age the infant makes more consonant than vowel types of utterances, and by age two and one-half the child's vowel repertoire equals that of an adult.

The consonant sound development of the child includes only four in the first two months of life; by approximately five or six months about six more consonant sounds appear. By twenty-nine or thirty months the child's consonant profile approximates that of an adult.[11]

In order to learn a system of phonemes one must be able to produce phonetic features such as voicing, nasality, and so on. According to linguists, the phonetic features are already in children's repertoires when they start to learn the phoneme system of English.

Table 6.1 compares the ages at which children acquire consonant speech sounds.

These results tend to show that there is a relationship between phoneme development and age, in that some sounds are produced earlier than others. They also indicate that by age eight most sounds are produced correctly.

---

[10]Gertrude Hildreth, "Interrelationships among the Language Arts," *The Elementary School Journal* 48 (June 1948), p. 539.

[11]Harris Winitz, *Articulatory Acquisition and Behavior* (New York: Appleton-Century-Crofts, 1969), pp. 9–14.

table 6.1 Comparison of the Ages at which Subjects Correctly Produced Specific Consonant Sounds in the Templin, the Wellman, and the Poole Studies*

	Age Correctly Produced		
Sound	Templin (1957)	Wellman and others (1931)	Poole (1934)
m	3	3	3.5
n	3	3	4.5
ŋ	3	—[a]	4.5
p	3	4	3.5
f	3	3	5.5
h	3	3	3.5
w	3	3	3.5
j	3.5	4	4.5
k	4	4	4.5
b	4	3	3.5
d	4	5	4.5
g	4	4	4.5
r	4	5	7.5
s	4.5	5	7.5[b]
ʃ	4.5	—[c]	6.5
tʃ	4.5	5	—[c]
t	6	5	4.5
θ	6	—[a]	7.5[b]
v	6	5	6.5[b]
l	6	4	6.5
ð	7	—[c]	6.5
z	7	5	7.5[b]
ʒ	7	—[c]	6.5
dʒ	7	6	—[c]
hw	—[a]	—[a]	7.5

*In the Wellman and others and Templin studies a sound was considered mastered if it was articulated correctly by 75 percent of the subjects. The criterion of correct production was 100 percent in the Poole study.
[a]Sound was tested but was not produced correctly by 75 percent of the subjects at the oldest age tested. In the Wellman data the "hw" reached the percentage criterion at 5 but not at 6 years, the medial "ŋ" reached it at 3, and the initial and medial "θ" and "ð" at 5 years.
[b]Poole (Davis, 1938), in a study of 20,000 preschool and school-age children, reports the following shifts: "s" and "z" appear at 5.5 years, then disappear and return later at 7.5 years or above; "θ" appears at 6.5 years and "v" at 5.5 years.
[c]Sound not tested or not reported.
Source: M. C. Templin, *Certain Language Skills in Children, Their Development and Interrelationships, Institute of Child Welfare, Monograph Series,* no. 26, vol. 54. (Minneapolis: University of Minnesota Press, 1957), p. 53.

Other speech sound studies have not produced evidence that an orderly sequence of sound development takes place, that is, that any one sound must precede or follow a given other sound.

Variables Affecting Articulatory Development

It should be noted that individual differences may exist in children's ability to articulate specific sounds. Certain variables may influence when a child produces a sound. For example, a number of studies have shown a low positive correlation between intelligence and articulatory errors. This correlation is an inverse one and is more pronounced for those with IQs below 70, that is, the lower the IQ, especially below 70, the greater the chance for articulatory errors.

Studies of the relationship between socioeconomic status and articulatory development have revealed more articulatory errors among children from lower socioeconomic classes. However, this relationship is similar to that between intelligence and articulation; it, too, is a low positive one.

Ordinal position studies (order of birth) have found that first-born children articulate better. Studies of intersibling age difference found that articulation improved with increased age difference. The greater the difference between the ages of siblings, the better the articulation. An only child's articulation is better than that of a child from a home with many siblings. The explanation for these findings might be that first-born children, only children, and siblings with a larger intersibling age difference have a greater opportunity to spend time with their parents while learning phoneme production.[12]

Teachers should be aware that IQs below 70, birth order, and socioeconomic status are factors

[12]Ibid., pp. 141–147.

which may impede the articulatory development of the children in their classrooms and should make allowance for such differences.

Children's Speech Problems

Children who have difficulty in speaking or who have a speech problem will avoid speaking. To some they may appear shy or introverted, but they may really be frustrated. Rather than causing themselves embarrassment or embarrassing those around them, they may prefer to remain silent. This will affect their work in school, their relations with their peers and other figures, and their feelings about themselves. They will be limited in their activities because social intercourse is the most common form of human communication. And they will be at a disadvantage in making themselves understood. They will refuse to speak on the telephone, and discussions and talks will be avoided.

A speech problem may on occasion actually be detrimental to one's own or someone else's health. The mother of a ten-year-old girl who is a stutterer said that one day, while the girl was with her grandfather, he had severe pains in his chest, indicating a possible heart attack. The girl was terrified. Although he asked her to please phone his doctor, whose number was on the table, the child could not speak into the receiver. Most ten-year-olds would be terrified under these circumstances, but they would be able to use the phone and call the doctor, mother, or ambulance. This is an example of a child who needs special help in speech correction and who should be referred to a speech clinician.

Children who use "dat" for "that" and "dis" for "this" in their daily speech do not need speech therapy, unless they cannot make the "th" sound. They have learned to speak this way from adult figures around them. Similarly, children who come from another part of the country where a different dialect is spoken may sound "different" to their classmates, but they should not be categorized as having a speech defect. (See Chapter 5 for a discussion of nonstandard English. Also, give special attention to the section "Teaching English as a Second Language" in this chapter.) Some children—whose voices are noticeably thin or weak, or who speak without inflection—may be doing so as the result of a poor self-concept and not necessarily as a result of a speech defect.

Many children come to school with infantile speech habits. Since they have been speaking that way for a long while they will need motivation and help in overcoming such habits. These children must recognize that they have a problem and then learn how to correct the habit. They will need the teacher's patience, understanding, and protection from ridicule.

The classroom teacher can also help with some simple lisping problems. If a child is still lisping at the end of first grade, he or she should be referred for special help. Stuttering is a more difficult problem and usually requires special work, since it is most often caused by a complex of variables which may involve both emotional and physiological factors.

The teacher should be careful not to confuse some barriers to effective communication with speech defects. Examples of such barriers, which could apply to any speaker, are:

1. Nonstandard pronunciation and use of language.
2. Poor oral reading.
3. A type of speech prevalent in a different section of the country.
4. Incorrect articulation due to immaturity.
5. A psychological disturbance which shows itself in speech.

Usually, these speech difficulties can be handled by the regular classroom teacher with the aid of a speech therapist or specialist.[13]

[13]Jon Eisenson and Mardel Ogilvie, *Speech Correction in the Schools* (New York: Macmillan, 1963), pp. 2–3.

Types of Speech Defect[14]

Speech defects usually cannot be handled in an ordinary classroom. They include:

1. Articulatory defects.
2. Stuttering.
3. Voice defects.
4. Cleft palate speech.
5. Cerebral palsy speech.
6. Retarded speech development.
7. Language impairment associated with brain damage.
8. Speech defects due to impaired hearing.

This questionnaire is provided for teachers as an aid in determining whether students have any speech defects. A preponderance of "yes" answers would indicate that the teacher should consult with a speech therapist.

[14]Ibid., p. 4.

ANALYSIS OF SPEECH DEFECTS[15]

Articulatory Defects

Does the child substitute one sound for another?
Does the child omit sounds?
Does the child distort sounds?
Is the child very hard to understand?

Stuttering

Is the child disturbed by his or her dysfluency?
Does the child repeat sounds or syllables or words more than classmates?
Is the child's speech decidedly arhythmical?
Does the child block frequently?
Does the child have difficulty in getting his or her words out?

Vocal Difficulties

Is the child's voice noticeably unpleasant in quality?
Is the child's pitch higher or lower than most of the child's classmates'?
Is the child's voice monotonous?
Is the child's voice husky?
Is the child's voice too loud?
Is the child's voice too weak?
Is the child difficult to hear in class?

[15]Ibid., pp. 10–12.

Cleft Palate Speech

Is there an obvious cleft of the teeth ridge or palate?
Is the child's voice excessively nasal?
Are the child's /p/,/b/,/t/,/d/,/k/, and/g/ inaccurate?
Are some of the child's other consonants distorted?

Cerebral Palsy Speech

Does the child have obvious tremors of the musculature in phonation and breathing?
Is the child's speech slow, jerky, and labored?
Is the child's rhythm of speech abnormal?

Delayed Speech

Is the child's speech markedly retarded in relation to that of the child's classmates?
Does the child omit and substitute sounds substantially more than classmates?
Does the child use shorter and simpler sentences than those of classmates?
Does the child use fewer phrases and prepositions than classmates?

Language Impairment

Is the child's comprehension of language markedly retarded?

Does the child seem to be inconsistent in the ability to understand as well as to use language? Is the profile of the child's linguistic abilities uneven? (For example, can the child read much better than spell? Is the child surprisingly good in arithmetic and yet quite poor in either reading or writing?)

Speech Defect Due to Impaired Hearing

Does the child have frequent earaches and colds?

Does the child have running ears?

Does the child omit sounds or substitute one sound for another?

Does the child distort sounds?

Does the child speak too loudly?

Does the child speak too softly?

Does the child frequently ask you to repeat what you have said?

Does the child turn his or her head to one side as you speak?

Does the child watch you closely as you speak?

Does the child make unusual mistakes in the spelling words you dictate?

Does the child misinterpret your questions or instructions frequently?

Does the child do better when given written instructions than when given oral instructions?

Does the child seem more intelligent than his or her work indicates?

The teacher must accept a child whatever the problem or handicap, and help other children to encourage the child to become an effective, contributing member of the class. The child with a speech problem must be made to feel respected and wanted. Although such a child is usually aware of the speech defect, the child should not feel that he or she is being singled out negatively because of it.

Articulatory Problems

Articulatory problems are the most frequently found speech defects in children. Teachers can provide sound production education training in their regular classrooms. Articulatory problems are most often caused by faulty learning rather than an oral or dental malformation. Speech therapists have discovered that the most frequently occurring articulatory errors are likely to center around eight consonant sounds: /r, s, l, sh, h, th, ch, f/. Of these, the /r/, /s/, /l/, and /th/ usually are most difficult for primary-grade children.

It is interesting to note that the consonant sounds are most difficult for children. It appears that vowels are, on the whole, mastered early.

Some of the articulatory difficulties arise due to the substitution, distortion, ommission, or slighting of phonemes in children's speech sound production. When teachers become aware of some of these errors they should refer the children to speech clinicians. However, some errors can be taken care of with a program in speech sound education in the regular classroom. (See suggested activities for this area in the section "Developing the Speech Improvement Program.")

Voice Usage in Oral Expression

A good speaking voice should be easily heard, pleasing, and should express meaning and mood. Five vocal skills which a child's voice must have in order to be pleasing and expressive are:[16]

1. A pleasing voice quality.
2. Adequate volume.
3. Variety in duration of words.
4. Appropriate phrasing and smoothness.
5. Variety of pitch.

[16]Wilbert Pronovast and Louise Kingman, *The Teaching of Speaking and Listening in the Elementary School* (New York: Longmans, Green, 1959), p. 111.

Not only does a child imitate the language of the people in the surrounding environment, but his or her voice is also an imitation of someone's voice at home. When the child comes to school he or she may decide to choose the teacher as a model. Therefore, it must be stressed again that the teacher has the responsibility to serve as a good example.

A number of factors affect a child's voice usage. A child who is aggressive may speak loudly and harshly; whereas a shy, timid child may speak quietly. Physical illness or emotional tension will also be reflected in the child's voice.

Developing the Speech Improvement Program

Planning for Speech Improvement

In order to be able to plan a program appropriate to the needs of particular students, the teacher must first evaluate their speech performance. The chart on page 102 serves as a guide for cataloging a pupil's speech faults in both the primary and intermediate grades.

To use this instrument the teacher can either listen to the speech sounds and patterns of students during ordinary classroom activities, and mark the chart appropriately; or tape some special oral activity in which students' production of speech sounds and patterns is noted.

Pupil-Teacher Planning for Speech Improvement   After the teacher has determined that there will be time devoted each day for speech improvement activities and has chosen a number of possible activities based on children's needs, the teacher should invite the students to participate in the planning and final selection of activities and topics. If the students participate in determining when the special talks, creative dramatics, or work with puppets will occur, and if they have a say in the kinds of activities they will be doing, the chances for a successful speech program will be enhanced.

Including the children in the planning process does not mean that teachers abdicate their role in the classroom. Both teachers and students should have a voice in the allocation of time as well as the choice of topics. If differences arise and choices need to be made, the teachers and students should give reasons for their choices.

Time Spent in Speech Improvement Activities

Since almost all children need help in speech improvement, the program should be one which is related to many ongoing classroom activities. Speech activities can be integrated with the language arts, as well as with many other subject areas. Almost all school activities afford time for oral expression, when pupils should be encouraged to talk about matters which interest them. Time should be set aside each day for talks which would involve individual children, or a group, or the whole class. The amount of time spent in this area will depend on the specific grade level and activity. In the first grade the teacher might set aside fifteen minutes a day for special talks, while in the second grade twenty minutes might be set aside. In third and fourth grades twenty-five to thirty minutes might be allotted for talks, and in fifth and sixth grades the allotment could be thirty to thirty-five minutes.

There is no set rule for time allotment. Teachers must take the needs, interests, and readiness levels of their students into account when planning such activities. In some first-grade classes, where the children are very immature and their attention span is quite short, fifteen minutes could be too long. In another first-grade class, composed of more mature children with a longer attention span, fifteen minutes might not be long enough.

The time spent in any area should be just enough so that pupils do not become restless. Spending a shorter amount of time in an activity and stopping while students are still interested

Child's Name _____
Grade _____ Date _____

INVENTORY OF SPEECH PROBLEMS

1. Is voice:
   a. loud?   _____
   b. too low?   _____
   c. nasal?   _____
   d. hoarse?   _____
   e. monotonous?   _____
   f. pitched abnormally high?   _____
   g. pitched abnormally low?   _____

2. Is rate of speech:
   a. too slow?   _____
   b. too rapid?   _____

3. Is phrasing poor?   _____

4. Is speech hesitant?   _____

5. Is there evidence of articulatory difficulties such as:
   a. distorting sounds?   _____
   b. substituting one sound for another?   _____
   c. omitting sounds?   _____

6. Is there evidence of vocabulary problems such as:
   a. repetition of phrases?   _____
   b. limited vocabulary?   _____

7. Is there evidence of the child's negative attitudes
toward oral communication such as:
   a. does not engage in discussions or conversations?   _____
   b. does not volunteer to give a talk or oral report?   _____

helps to insure that they will look forward to the next speech improvement activity.

Avoiding Sex Stereotyping in Choice of Speech Topics and Activities

The specific interests of boys and girls are in large part determined by what society categorizes as masculine or feminine. Boys are expected to like mechanical devices, cars, science, and so on; girls are supposed to like dolls, playing house, and being a "mommy." Both activity categories are fine; but many boys and girls have interests that diverge from the expected.

Teachers must avoid classifying oral expression activities or topics for discussion as either masculine or feminine. When planning lists of topics for class discussions with students, they should avoid making such remarks as: "Oh, this is a topic that will be fun for boys," or "Girls would really enjoy working in this area." Teachers should display equal enthusiasm for all topics and show that they will allow pupils to choose any one which interests them. Students will perform much better if they have chosen a topic because of genuine interest rather than because it is expected.

Speech Sound Education Activities

The teacher can use Table 6.2, which lists forty sounds of the English language, as a guide for working with speech sound education. Two sets of symbols for these sounds are shown—the International Phonetic Alphabet symbols (IPA) and *Webster's Dictionary* symbols. A word is given with each sound in the initial, medial, and final positions (if possible), as well as a sentence illustrating the specific sound.

A sound can be presented in isolation and the children can imitate the sound first in a group response and then with responses from individual children. Another technique useful in determining which sounds need emphasis for the students would be to have them tape-record a number of words and sentences which have each of the sounds.

Whichever technique the teacher chooses, the important factor is to determine those sounds with which students need help. After teachers have determined sounds that need special attention, they should spend only a few minutes each day on the sounds in isolation. Spending a few minutes daily on isolating the sound allows for intensive concentration on one particular sound. The effect can be just as good as spending a longer period of time on speech activities which are not as concentrated or focused.[17] A procedure for utilizing this technique follows.

Correctly present the sound and have the chil-

dren imitate it. Then give words which have the sound in different positions, and have the children imitate these. Next present a sentence which has a number of words illustrating the sound, and again have the children imitate them.

Teachers should not introduce new sounds until children have adequately learned the one being practiced. The type of presentation and the number of sounds will be determined by the needs and abilities of the children. Before introducing a new sound, the previous ones should be reviewed. At this time the teacher should also present some auditory discrimination activities to ascertain whether children can hear differences among the various sounds that they have practiced. Teachers might also encourage students to generate words in which the various practiced sounds are represented.

Each sound may also be presented to the class with a distinct personality and character of its own. With its own face, gesture, name, and personality it becomes separate and distinct from all others. Here is one method for exploring the "geography" of the mouth:

During the process of identifying speech sounds, the geography of the mouth is explored, bit by bit. Having the children make the sound *silently* is an excellent way of introducing them to the placement of mouth, tongue, teeth, or lips for that particular sound. The geography of the mouth can further be explored by tongue gymnastics. Children are invariably delighted with "tongue tales" of various kinds. These stories, told by the teacher, require the children to follow along and supply all actions and sound effects through tongue movements. Many teachers are familiar with the story of Mrs. Tongue, who spends most of her time cleaning her house (the mouth). The energetic and industrious woman even sweeps the ceiling (the palate), the walls (sides of the mouth), the stairways (teeth), and shakes her broom (the tongue) with vigor outside her home. She then looks on the roof for her lost kitten (tongue pointed toward nose). After taking one last "peek" (grooving the tongue) for her lost cat, she returns into the home and shuts the door (lips).

[17]Blake, op. cit. pp., 20–21.

table 6.2   Sounds of the English Language

IPA Symbol	Webster's Symbol*	Position in Words Initial	Position in Words Medial	Position in Words Final	Sentences
1. [i]	/ē/	eat	feel	we	We eat peas and green beans.
2. [I]	/ĭ/	it	hit		It is Billy's kitten. Sit in the kitchen.
3. [eɪ]	/ā/	ache	cake	say	Jane ate cake today.
4. [ɛ]	/ĕ/	egg	head		Let me get the hen's egg.
5. [æ]	/ă/	at	ran	spa	The cat ran after the fat rat.
6. [ʌ]	/ū/	up	fun		To run and play in the sun is fun.
7. [ɑ]	/ä/	are	car	bah	The car is at the farm.
8. [ɔ]	/ò/	all	wall	awe (gnaw), saw	The ball went over the wall.
9. [ou]	/ō/	oh	cold	so	Oh! Oh! Oh! My nose is cold.
10. [U]	/ù/	ooze	book		Put the good book up. Cookies are good.
11. [u]	/ü/		moon	you (too)	Soon you can see the moon, too.
12. [aU]	/aù/	out	loud	now	The brown cow is out now.
13. [aɪ]	/ī/	I	side	buy	White mice might be fun.
14. [ɔi]	/oi/	oyster	toil	boy	Roy took his toy from the boy.
15. [ʃ]	/ər/	err	dirt	sir	Curt first heard the bird.
16. [ə]	/ə/	about	colonist	banana	We ate about three bananas.
17. [r]	/r/	ran	around	ear	Round and round and round the rabbit ran.
18. [l]	/l/	look	dollar	all (ball)	The girls are in the library. The boys play ball.
19. [m]	/m/	me	mama	arm	Mama, may I give the hammer to Sam?
20. [n]	/n/	no	penny	in	The man with the funny nose is a clown.
21. [ŋ]	/ng/		singer	sing (ring)	The ring was found when the school bell rang.
22. [j]	/y/	you	onion		William, you may not go into the barnyard yet.
23. [w]	/w/	we (was)	away		We walk this way on the sidewalk.
24. [h]	/h/	he	anyhow		He hid his hat at home.
25. [p]	/p/	pie	happy	cup	Please play in this place until supper.
26. [b]	/b/	be	number	Bob	Bobby has a rubber ball.
27. [t]	/t/	to	letter	it	Tad is Tom's pet turtle.
28. [d]	/d/	do	daddy	hand	Daddy weeded the garden yesterday.
29. [k]	/k/	car	cookie	ask	Carl drinks cocoa for breakfast.
30. [g]	/g/	go	buggy	egg	The little girl dug in her garden.
31. [f]	/f/	foot	coffee	if	Fred forgot to feed the calf after he came home.
32. [v]	/v/	voice	river	give	Eva and Virginia live in the lovely valley.
33. [θ]	/th/	thank	birthday	teeth	Ruth, Beth, and Arthur are going on Thursday.
34. [ð]	/th/	that	other	breathe	Mother and Father like cold weather.
35. [s]	/s/	see	pencil	bus	Sally sings songs on the sofa.
36. [z]	/z/	zoo	music	is	A zebra lives in the zoo. Rose likes music.
37. [ʃ]	/sh/	she	dishes	wish	Shirley's shoes are shiny when she polishes them.
38. [ʒ]	/zh/		measure		The treasure was hidden from vision.
39. [tʃ]	/ch/	child	teacher	speech	Charles reached for the teacher's chalk.
40. [dʒ]	/j/	John	pages	age	John and Jim jumped over the hedge.

Not all dictionaries use the same symbols to represent sounds.

The tongue, versatile as it is, can be a merry-go-round, a telephone pole, a slide, a pinwheel. It can hump and point and click and curl. By its use, the children can discover all the hills, valleys, and ridges inside their mouths, both in silence and in the production of sounds. The tongue movement which belongs with each speech sound can be stressed, along with the other parts of the speech apparatus which might be used.

Thus, children learn to identify a sound not

only by its visual and auditory clues but by its placement as well. Identification and recognition of each sound should be sought through all these channels. Children will soon learn to recall a sound through any one of its various clues. They will be able to remember a sound by the name of the sound alone, by the gesture associated with that sound, or by the position of the lips and tongue as the sound is seen but not heard. They will be able to interrelate all these factors with the auditory impression of the sound.

In order to obtain such identification of the various sounds, the children as a group must be interested in learning these sound characteristics. Drill on sounds alone will not produce any such sustained interest. What will?

First of all, each sound is presented separately. It is given a name. This name not only distinguishes the particular sound from all others in the alphabet of sounds but also hints at some other characteristic of the sound. It may be an auditory characteristic, such as calling the ssss sound Timmy Teakettle or Sammy Snake. It may be a visual characteristic, such as a finger raised to the lips for the "be quiet" sound, shhh. It may be a tactile sensation, such as holding the hand to the larynx to feel the vibration when a zzzzz is produced. All of these methods may be used to aid in the identification of a single sound.[18]

Teaching English as a Second Language (TESL)

There is a story currently circulating which relates the tale of a mother mouse attempting to teach her baby mice how to get along in the great outside world. The mother mouse teaches the children how to avoid traps, how to retrieve the bait from traps without getting caught, and other similar activities, and on the final day of instruction, she says: "You know, children, a cat lives in this house—and the cat is your enemy. Today I am going to show you how to handle the cat." The mother mouse then lines up the baby mice at the entrance to their home in the baseboard of a large

room, and she proceeds to run out in plain view of the baby mice and attract the attention of the cat. The unwary cat, very much surprised by the bold behavior of the mouse, is about to pounce on her when the mother mouse rears back on her hind legs and in a shrill high voice says: "Arf, arf." At this juncture every hair on the cat stands on end, he turns tail, and runs wildly in the opposite direction; whereupon the mother mouse turns and smiling broadly at her children says, "You see, children, it pays to speak a second language."[19]

When children enter school they bring with them the language of their environment, of their family, home, and neighborhood. This first language learning they have acquired is the most deeply rooted, regardless of what other language learning they achieve later in their lives.

Defining "Culturally Different" and "Culturally Disadvantaged"

The rejection of the child's language "may more deeply upset him than the rejection of his skin. The latter is only an insult, the former strikes at his ability to communicate and express his needs, feelings—his self."[20] The language of children who do not speak standard English has been an effective means of communication for them until they come to school. If such children are made to feel inferior because of their language, by a teacher who constantly attacks their speech for being incorrect, they may not attempt to learn standard English.

To understand the complexity of the language problem better, it would help to differentiate between such terms as "culturally deprived" and "culturally different," which are often used to label groups of children in one culture. Although culturally deprived children may also be culturally different children, the definition of

[18]Charles Van Riper and Katherine G. Butler, *Speech in the Elementary Classroom* (New York: Harper & Brothers, 1955), pp. 64–65.

[19]Virginia W. Jones, "Training Teachers of English for Alaska's Native Children," *Elementary English* 48 (February 1971): 198.

[20]E. Brooks Smith, Kenneth S. Goodman, and Robert Meredith. *Language and Thinking in the Elementary School* (New York: Holt, Rinehart and Winston, 1970), p. 48.

culturally deprived includes the background of a poverty-level home, in which the parents are illiterate and where they may seem to be indifferent to them. The children lack the rich experiences of storytelling, trips, cultural endeavors, and so on. "Culturally-deprived" children may live in either the city or the suburbs. They may or may not be users of nonstandard English. The "culturally different" child is one whose parents were usually born in a country other than the United States and who speak a language other than English. Although the child may be United States born, English is not the dominant language spoken in the child's home.

All children, regardless of whether they are "culturally disadvantaged" or "culturally different," must be able to communicate at the aural–oral level in standard English before they are able to read effectively. A factor to recall, emphasized in Chapter 5 ("Listening"), is that persons who speak nonstandard English are not "bad," nor is their language inferior. But if one is to be successful in school and in society, standard English is an important requisite.

Defining TESL

Teaching English as a Second Language (TESL) concentrates on helping children who speak another (foreign) language or nonstandard English to learn standard English as another language. It does not do away with their own languages but adds another.

Although the teaching of ESL is recommended for children who speak nonstandard English, the crucial question is whether the techniques for teaching ESL to these students should be similar to those for students who speak another (foreign) language. There is no unanimous agreement on this question. There *is* agreement that much inappropriate education provided for linguistically different populations stems from a widespread lack of good instruction in *oral language*. Although different techniques may be found feasible while working with different groups of children who do not speak standard English, the aural–oral approach is one that can be used with all groups.

TESL *Programs* In most in-service programs teachers are expected to use audiolingual techniques and are given assistance in their use. The concept of appropriate and inappropriate speech is stressed, rather than that of correct or incorrect speech. Elementary-grade students do not read materials they have not first learned orally.

In some schools TESL programs consist of heterogeneous grouping and special classes where the children receive language instruction individually or on a group basis. If there are only a few children on a given grade level who are non-English speaking, they are assigned to a classroom where the teacher provides for the special needs of these students. If "there are fifteen to twenty or so pupils who speak a minimum of English within a grade range of two or three years, the formation of a temporary (approximately three months) 'orientation class' can be considered." These students will be transferred to an appropriate regular classroom after they have reached a functional level of ability in speaking English.

A number of resource people may be used with TESL students ranging from special language teachers to corrective reading teachers. The approach is again the aural–oral one; in these programs it is suggested that all instruction be given in English.[21]

Some schools are also using a bilingual–bicultural approach in which instruction is given in both English and another language. Content areas, such as math, are presented in the home-learned tongue. However, English as a second

---

[21]Peter D'Arrigo, "Variables and Instructional Arrangements for the Non-English Speaking Child in the School Program," *Elementary English* 49 (March 1972): 405–409.

language is taught to non-English speaking children and the other language is taught to English-speaking children.

These points must be noted by TESL teachers:[22]

1. The structure of the dominant language and English—differences in their phonology, morphology, and syntax.
2. The interference points between the child's mother tongue, the dominant language, and English.
3. A variety of approaches and techniques for teaching English as a second language.

TESL *Lessons*   Although the TESL lessons vary according to the grouping of the children, there are a number of elements common to lessons. They usually consist of a basic dialogue presented orally by the teacher. The sentences in the dialogue, which are based on the readiness levels of the class, are usually repeated two or three times without student response.

Here is a method that the teacher can use to encourage class participation:[23]

1. The teacher models (provides the pattern) for the first sentence and gestures to the whole group;
2. The whole group repeats the sentence;
3. The teacher repeats the first sentence and gestures to each preformed small group in turn who repeat the same sentence;
4. The teacher next encourages individual responses by his or her own repetition.

The pattern is repeated for each sentence of the dialogue. An example of simple dialogue might be the following. (It should be remembered that each sentence must be introduced and repeated in a manner already described.)

Good day.
Good day.
How are you?
I am fine.

The children are also given opportunities to use their new basic dialogue in role-playing situations.

Drill exercises follow the same method of instruction as the basic dialogue, except that pupils must provide the sentence pattern from one previously learned. For example: A sentence has been introduced—"This is a book." The children follow the same method as for developing basic dialogue. Then the teacher holds up a ball. A child, group of students, or the whole class then repeats the learned pattern including the new element, and states, "This is a ball." This method would be used to learn question-answer type of responses, to shorten or to expand responses, and to generate student sentences.

Teachers who use such techniques as role playing, audiovisual aids, concrete materials, and other multimedia approaches to teach English as a second language will enlarge their chances for success. Students enjoy games or gamelike activities, which provide practice for students in ways that are fun.

An activity that might be used to develop speaking and listening skills involves directions. In the game, "My turn, your turn," the teacher states some directions. The teacher points at a child and says, "Your turn." The child must then repeat and carry out the instructions.

Another activity includes "mystery" boxes. Numerous commonplace objects are put in the "mystery" box. Children must select an item from the box, state what it is, and compose a sentence in standard English naming the item.

The activities that are chosen should emphasize the aural–oral approach, stimulate interest, and encourage student participation. (See Chapter 5 on "Nonstandard English and Its Implications for Instruction.")

Parental Involvement in TESL   An important factor in helping students learn standard English, when they have been speaking nonstandard English or another language, would involve in-

---

[22]Adapted from Paul Wasserman and Susan Wasserman, *"No Hablo Inglés," Elementary English* 49 (October 1972): 833.
[23]Ibid., pp. 834–835.

Student's Name:
        Grade:
        Teacher:

**Diagnostic Checklist for Oral Communication and Speech Improvement
(See specific inventory checklists that are given within the chapter.)**

	Yes	No
Speech (general): The child's speech is		
1. distinct.		
2. inaudible.		
3. monotonous.		
4. expressive.		
Nonverbal Communication: The child		
1. uses facial expressions effectively.		
2. uses hands effectively.		
3. uses body movements effectively.		
Vocabulary (general): The child's vocabulary is		
1. meager.		
2. rich.		
3. accurate.		
4. incorrect.		
Sentences		
1. The child uses incomplete sentences.		
2. The child uses simplistic sentences.		
3. The child uses involved sentences.		
4. The child uses standard English.		
5. The child uses a variation of English.		
6. English is not the dominant language for the child.		
The child engages in conversation freely.		
The child respects other persons when he or she is speaking.		
The child enters into class discussions.		
The child can describe in his or her own words an event that has occurred.		
The child freely engages in these activities:		
1. creative dramatics		
2. role playing		
3. choral speaking		
4. finger play (primary grades)		

5. puppetry
6. pantomime
7. "show and tell" (primary grades)
8. informal reports
9. formal reports (intermediate grades)
10. debates (intermediate grades)
11. storytelling

cluding parents in the school programs for teaching ESL. Perhaps a program could be developed where the parents are also given ESL instruction. The more people in the family who are active in the language program, the more successful the child will be in mastering standard English.

Summary

This chapter has provided the teacher with the necessary background information and activities for carrying out an oral communication and speech improvement program in the regular classroom. The teacher's role and the importance of the teacher as a good speech model were emphasized, and the ingredients necessary to provide a nonthreatening environment conducive to oral expression were given. Articulatory development, as well as the factors that may affect it—such as socioeconomic status, intelligence, number of siblings, order of birth—were also discussed. The more practical aspects of an oral communication and speech improvement program were presented, including the setting aside of time each day for speech training, organizing for oral expression, and the types of oral expression activities used in the speech program. Speech sound production (articulation) activities, which are both fun and purposeful, were detailed. Oral expression activities or speech stimulation activities—talks, discussions, conversation, choral speaking, finger play, creative dramatics, role playing, and pup-

petry—were explained in a way that would enable teachers to employ them in class. TESL, for children who do not speak English or who speak nonstandard English, was described in order to acquaint teachers with methods and techniques used to aid such children in speaking standard English. Helpful suggestions which teachers could use in their classrooms, even if a special TESL program does not exist in the schools, were also given. A Diagnostic Checklist for "Oral Communication and Speech Improvement" was also presented.

Now that you have read this chapter, you should have mastered the teacher competencies presented at the beginning of this chapter.

Two examples of speech lesson plans follow on pages 110–112. Using these as a guide, see if you can construct a plan of your own.

Suggestions for Thought Questions and Activities

1. You have children in class who are very quiet. They follow directions and are able to do the required work. Would you call on them often? Explain your answer. What would you do to engage these children in more interaction sessions? Because children are quiet, does this necessarily mean they have problems? Explain your answer.

2. Develop a creative lesson plan in the area of speech improvement. What elements would go into the plan? How would it develop? What goals do you have in mind?

3. The school in which you are teaching has a

LESSON PLAN I

Grade Level: Early Primary Grades

Objectives

1. The students will be able to correctly recite the words and sounds in proper sequence of Edward Lear's alphabet rhymes.
2. The students will be able to differentiate among different sounds orally presented.

Introduction

"Yesterday we were talking about a book that I read to you. Who remembers the name of it? Yes! Good! It was called *May I Bring a Friend?*[24] Now, who remembers what it was about? Yes, it was about animals visiting the king and queen. Do you remember how carefully we had to listen so we could remember the exact order in which they visited, and then make our picture story? Who still remembers the order? Very good! Listen carefully to the music that is played on the tape recorder while Jane shows the picture story to us. The music should make all of the sounds that the animals make.

"Today we are going to learn some rhymes which are 'ear ticklers.' Listen carefully and tell me why I said that they will tickle your ears."

Development

Lear's rhymes are presented to the class. After the children have heard the verses, the children are asked why the teacher called them ear ticklers. (Because of the sounds.) They may also be called tongue twisters.

A familiar example of a tongue twister can be given—"She sells seashells by the seashore." The teacher explains that to be able to recite this verse, the class must make their mouths and tongues do exactly what they want. They will have to speak clearly and not too fast, or their tongues will run away from them. The Lear poem is recited again, and the class is asked to listen. The children are then asked to give another reason why they had to listen carefully. (Because it's like the first verse. In order to know in what order the words appear it is necessary to listen carefully.) The first line of the poem is said aloud by the teacher: "A was once an apple-pie." The whole class repeats the line. The teacher then says:

Pidy
Widy
Tidy
Pidy
Nice insidy,
Apple pie!

The whole class repeats the verse. Both parts are then put together and the class repeats both parts. The same procedure is followed for verses B, C, and D.

[24]Beatrice Schenk De Regniers, *May I Bring a Friend?* (New York: Atheneum, 1964).

The children are next divided into four groups. Each group recites its part in proper sequence. The teacher practices verse A with the first group, verse B with the second group, verse C with the third group, and verse D with the fourth group. Now the groups say the verses one after another, each group reciting only its part. The children's recitation can be taped and played back so that they can hear themselves. They then discuss the taping of their production.

Summary

The teacher asks the children what they did. A new poem was learned and recited on tape. Careful listening let them learn their parts and know what came next.

LESSON PLAN II

Grade Level: Intermediate Grades

Objective

The students, after listening to a tape recording of various sounds, will be able to create characters and dialogue to match the sounds.

Introduction

"Who remembers some of the things we've been doing in creative dramatics? Yes, good. We have listened to stories and then acted them out. We've also created our own characters and had our classmates try to guess who we were. Listen to this tape recording for a moment."

Play some eerie music.

"What does this remind you of? Yes, I agree, it sounds scary. Today, we're going to listen to various sounds on the tape and from these create characters and dialogue that would seem to match the sounds."

Development

"Let me play this eerie sound again. If we were to create a character to match this sound, what kind of character could we make up? How do you think he or she would sound or speak? What do you think he or she would say? Let's think about this for a moment and develop a character together. Any suggestions? Good! We could have a 'mad scientist,' who has just created a 'non-being.' How would he sound? What would he say? How would he act? Who would like to play this role for us? Look at all these hands. I see we have lots of potential 'mad scientists.'

"Judy, would you like to try? Good.

"Harry, would you like to try? Good.

"Now that we seem to have the idea, I'm going to have you go into groups of four. I will play various sounds on the tape and then each group will decide on the character that they think best matches the tape, the way he or she would sound, and what he or she would say. We'll present our characters after each sound taping. Are there any questions? Fine. Let's go into the same groups we were in for the puppet activity."

(Students in groups listen to sounds, create characters, and present them to the class.)

Summary

"What have we done today? Who can briefly summarize it for us? Good. We've listened to tape-recorded sounds and we've created characters and dialogue to match the sounds. Were we successful? Yes, we were able to do this. Who has some ideas on how to follow up on this activity?

"Very good! Do all of you want to take John's suggestion?

"Fine, then each group, using its own tape recorders, will try to tape a sound and have the rest of us create characters for the sound."

large percentage of children who speak nonstandard English and come from low-income families. You have been appointed to a special school committee which is to determine the kind of program that should be developed so that these children gain proficiency in standard English. What kind of program would you advocate, and what is your rationale for setting up this program?

4. Develop some stimulating situations to encourage creative dramatics in the primary and intermediate grades.

5. Develop some activities which will initiate oral-interaction sessions among primary-grade and intermediate-grade students.

6. Discuss techniques that will help to develop "good speakers."

SELECTED BIBLIOGRAPHY

General

Cayer, Roger. *Listening and Speaking in the English Classroom.* New York: Macmillan, 1971.

Egland, George. *Speech and Language Problems: A Guide for the Classroom Teacher.* Englewood Cliffs, N.J.: Prentice-Hall, 1970.

Hopper, Robert, and Rita J. Naremore. *Children's Speech: A Practical Introduction to Communication Development,* 2d ed. New York: Harper & Row, 1978.

Keppie, Elizabeth. *Speech Improvement through Choral Speaking.* Magnolia, Mass.: Expression Co., 1973.

Pronovost, Wilbert. *The Teaching of Speaking and Listening in the Elementary School.* New York: Longmans, Green, 1959.

Rasmussen, Carrie. *Speech Methods in the Elementary School.* New York: Ronald Press, 1962.

Riper, Charles van. *Speech in the Elementary Classroom.* New York: Harper & Brothers, 1955.

Rubin, Dorothy. "Developing Speaking Skills," in *The Primary Grade Teacher's Language Arts Handbook.* New York: Holt, Rinehart and Winston, 1980.

———. "Developing Speaking Skills," in *The Intermediate Grade Teacher's Language Arts Handbook.* New York: Holt, Rinehart and Winston, 1980.

Travis, Lee E., ed. *Handbook of Speech Pathology and Audiology.* New York: Appleton-Century-Crofts, 1971.

Winitz, Harris. *Articulatory Acquisition and Behavior.* New York: Appleton-Century-Crofts, 1969.

Creative Dramatics

Bordon, Sylvia. *Plays as Teaching Tools in the Elementary School.* West Nyack, N.Y.: Parker, 1970.

Chambers, Dewey. *Literature for Children: The Oral Tradition; Storytelling and Creative Drama,* 2d ed. Dubuque, Iowa: W. C. Brown, 1977.

Cheifetz, Dan. *Theater in My Head*. Boston: Little, Brown, 1971.

Heinig, Ruth. *Creative Dramatics for the Classroom Teacher*. Englewood Cliffs, N.J.: Prentice-Hall, 1974.

Kamerman, Sylvia. *Dramatized Folk Tales of the World*. Boston: Plays, Inc., 1971.

Kolczynski, Richard C., and Sister Angeline Cepelka, C.S.A. "Creative Dramatics: Process or Product?" *Language Arts* 54 (March 1977): 283–286.

McIntyre, Barbara. *Informal Dramatics: A Language Arts Activity for the Special Pupil*. Pittsburgh: Stanwix House, 1963.

Schattner, Regina. *Creative Dramatics for Handicapped Children*. New York: John Day, 1966.

Wright, Lin. "Creative Dramatics and the Development of Role-taking in the Elementary Classroom." *Elementary English* 51 (January 1974): 89–93.

Nonverbal Behavior

Gay, K. *Body Talk*. New York: Scribner's, 1974.

Gilbert, A. G. *Teaching the Three Rs Through Movement Experiences: A Handbook for Teachers*. Minneapolis, Minn.: Burgess, 1977.

Thompson, James. *Beyond Words: A Nonverbal Communication in the Classroom*. New York: Scholastic Book Services, 1973.

von Raffler-Engel, W. *Children's Acquisition of Kinesics* (a color film). Scarsdale, N.Y.: Campus Film Distributors, 1974.

Wood, Barbara. *Children and Communication: Verbal & Non-Verbal Language Development*. Englewood Cliffs, N.J.: Prentice-Hall, 1976.

Pantomime and Mime

Albert, David. *Pantomime: Elements and Exercises*. Topeka, Kans. University Press of Kansas, 1971.

Walker, Katherine. *Eyes on Mime: Language Without Speech*. New York: John Day, 1969.

Finger Plays

Colville, M. Josephine. *The Zoo Comes to School: Finger Plays and Action Rhymes*. New York: Macmillan, 1973.

Hogstrom, Daphne. *Little Boy Blue: Finger Plays Old and New* (gr. k–2). Racine, Wisc.: Western Publishing, 1976).

Poulssen, Emilie. *Finger Plays* (gr. k–1). New York: Hart, Inc., 1977.

Shely, Patricia. *All-Occasion Finger Plays for Young Children*. Cincinnati, Ohio: Standard Publishing, 1978.

Puppets

Alkema, Chester. *Puppet-making*. New York: Sterling, 1971.

Boylan, Eleanor. *How to Be a Puppeteer*. New York: McCall Publishing, 1970.

Gates, Frieda. *Easy to Make Puppets* (gr. k–3). Chippewa Falls, Wisc.: Harvey House, 1976.

Luckin, Joyce. *Easy to Make Puppets* (gr. 3–10). Boston: Plays, Inc., 1975.

Weiger, Myra. "Puppetry." *Elementary English* 51 (January 1974): 55–65.

Storytelling

Bauer, Caroline Feller. *Handbook for Storytellers*. Chicago: American Library Association, 1977.

Bergold, Sharon. "Children's Growth of Competence in Storytelling." *Language Arts* 53 (September 1976): 658–662.

Chambers, Dewey. *Literature for Children: The Oral Tradition; Storytelling and Creative Drama*, 2d ed. Dubuque, Iowa: W.C. Brown, 1977.

Groff, Patrick. "Let's Update Storytelling." *Language Arts* 54 (March 1977): 272–277; 286.

Pellowski, Anne. *The World of Storytelling*. Ann Arbor, Mich.: Bowker, 1977.

Wagner, Joseph. *Children's Literature through Storytelling*. Dubuque, Iowa: W.C. Brown, 1970.

Teaching English as a Second Language

Allen, Virginia G. "The Non-English Speaking Child in Your Classroom." *The Reading Teacher* 30 (February 1977): 504–508.

Axelrod, Jerome. "Some Pronunciation and Linguistic Problems of Spanish Speaking Children in American Classrooms." *Elementary English* 51, (February 1974): 203–206.

Dillard, Joey L. *Black English*. New York: Random House, 1972.

Fishman, Joshua A. *Bilingual Education: An International Sociological Perspective*. Rowley, Mass.: Newbury House, 1976.

Hess, Karen, et al. *Dialects and Dialect Learning*. Urbana, Ill.: National Council of Teachers of English, 1973.

Johnson, Laura S. "Bilingual Bicultural Education: A Two-Way Street." *The Reading Teacher* 29 (December 1975): 231–239.

Labov, W. *The Study of Non-standard English*. Urbana, Ill.: National Council of Teachers of English, 1970.

McLaughlin, Barry. *Second Language Acquisition in Childhood*. New York: Halsted Press, 1978.

Stewart, W. A., ed. *Non-standard Speech and the Teaching of English*. Washington, D.C.: Center for Applied Linguistics, 1964.

Yawkey, Thomas D. "Teaching Oral Language to Young Mexican-Americans." *Elementary English* 51 (February 1974): 203–206.

seven

Word Recognition and Approaches to Reading: Selected Areas

EXAMPLES OF TEACHER COMPETENCIES

1. The teacher will be able to state ways in which reading is related to the other language arts areas.
2. The teacher will be able to define reading.
3. The teacher will be able to state and explain the necessity for defining the act of reading.
4. The teacher will be able to state the components of reading as presented in this chapter.
5. The teacher will be able to state the steps involved in planning a language-experience reading story.
6. The teacher will be able to describe the guided instructional approach used in most basal reading series.
7. The teacher will be able to describe the individualized reading approach.
8. Teachers will observe their students and determine what phonic skills they need in order to be better decoders.
9. Teachers will observe their students and determine what syllabic word attack skills their students need.
10. The teacher will be able to determine whether students value, appreciate, or have an interest in gaining phonic skills by observing whether pupils use the decoding skill while reading independently.

Introduction

David is a quiet boy with an endearing smile. He is small in stature and not well-dressed; he is determined to learn to read. Although he is in the fourth grade, David cannot read. "I want to read," he told his teacher. "My father bring one big book when he came home at night. He say it for me to read. I read. You see." David has hope, so he comes to school each day. But how much longer will he do so? Will he succeed in entering and mastering the land of books filled with those magic symbols called words? Will he unlock these symbols and discover the wonders of far-off places? David is waiting. Will we, as teachers, be able to help him?

It would be both foolhardy and presumptuous to assume that one or two chapters in a language arts text could perform the Herculean task of preparing teachers to help the Davids of this country learn to read. Special reading courses are needed for that. Most schools of education have at least one required course in reading for their education majors, to give special emphasis and importance to reading. But this does not mean that reading must or should be separated from the rest of the language arts area. As a matter of fact, reading is so closely related to the other language arts that a problem in one area will overflow into others. (*See* Chapters 5 and 6.)

Chapters 7 and 8 present a few selected topics in reading that are of particular interest to the language arts teacher. After you have read this chapter you should be able to answer these questions:

1. How is reading related to the other language arts areas?
2. Why is it important to learn to read?
3. What are some approaches to teaching reading?
4. How does the language-experience approach incorporate all the language arts areas?
5. What skills are taught in phonic instruction?
6. What are consonant and vowel digraphs?
7. What are diphthongs and consonant blends (clusters)?

The Relationship of Reading to Other Language Arts Areas

The interrelatedness of the various language arts areas to reading cannot be emphasized enough. Students meeting difficulties in one facet will generally carry the problem over to another aspect of the language arts. If we ask why David, in the fourth grade, is not reading, his teacher claims that he was tested the year before and was found to have impaired hearing. Digging into the problem further, we find that David has been "tested" by another teacher in the school, who knew little about the study of hearing. When David's teacher is asked if referrals had been made for more professional opinions and testing, we are told that it doesn't really pay to bother, because all special personnel from the psychologist to the remedial reading teachers are overloaded and the teacher would only be wasting his time.

By pinning the label "hearing impairment problem" on David the teacher is psychologically relieved of his responsibility. But David has not yet lost his determination to learn to read. He does not have a hearing problem. He has a language problem, which might be mistaken for a hearing impairment difficulty in the third or fourth grade. David comes from a bilingual home where Spanish is the dominant language. He has difficulty discriminating between sounds in English; therefore he needs help in auditory discrimination. If David does not hear English words correctly, how can he be expected to say them correctly, or, for that matter, read or write them? To David, many of the words in English are mere noises, because the words are not in his listening vocabulary. David needs help in learning the English language.

To help David and others like him to become

more competent in English, a teacher must know the methods of teaching English as a second language using aural–oral approaches before involving a child in the act of reading. Such children must learn to "listen," so they will be able to make auditory discriminations. (See Chapters 5 and 6.) The teacher must also determine whether children have adequate visual perception. The concept of left and right, which is so important for learning to read, should also be established.

Bilingual children must be helped to build concepts which they have not previously developed. They should be given concrete objects and their labels, and helped to develop the concepts of opposites, rhyming, size, relativity, similarity, and so on. Nothing can be taken for granted. (See Chapter 3.)

Let us now take up the particulars of how listening, speaking, and writing are closely related to reading.

Listening

In order to be able to recognize expressions in print, students must have heard these phrases correctly in the past. Reading comprehension depends on comprehension of the spoken language. Students who are sensitive to the arrangement of words in oral language are more sensitive to the same idea in written language. Listening helps to enlarge a student's vocabulary. It is through listening that pupils learn many expressions they will eventually see in print. Listening takes place all the time. Teachers orally explain word meanings and what the text says. Students listen to other children read orally, talk about books, and explain their contents.

Speaking

Students read with greater ease things that they have talked about. Oral statements in class discussion can be recorded and become reading material for pupils. Through oral language, teachers can learn about the interests of students and build on these in choosing books. Students share favorite stories and passages with others by reading aloud. Many times, pupils will dramatize a story they have found in their reading. Voice sound production activities are based on words in the reading selections. Discussion topics also may emanate from stories.

Reading

Reading helps students acquire knowledge and often furnishes the stimulus for creative writing. From reading, students gain knowledge of the vocabulary and sentence structure used in both speaking and writing, and they are helped to develop a language sense.

Writing

Many similar phonic skills are used in speaking, reading, and writing. Writing reinforces word recognition and sentence sense and increases familiarity with words. Many reading experiences require writing skills. Knowledge of sentence structure, punctuation, and spelling are necessary for effective writing. Students generally do not write words that are not in their reading vocabulary.

Through writing, students are able to gain a better understanding of the author's task in getting his or her ideas across. Writing makes students keener analyzers of reading.

The Importance of Learning to Read

The significance of children's early years in reading achievement has been amply documented; however, this should not be used as an excuse for not helping children when they come to school. Rather than putting blame on social, political, and economic factors, over which teachers and children have little control, more should be done in the schools.

The importance of learning to read in the early grades cannot be overstated. The longer children remain nonreaders, the less likely are their chances to get up to their grade levels or their ability levels, even with the best remedial help. Underachievers in reading tend to have many emotional and social problems, and these are compounded as the child goes through school.

Teachers want to help children to learn—that is their intent. Those teachers who cannot help students soon lose confidence in themselves, and their own self-concept is impaired. This feeling eventually gets picked up by their students. As was stated earlier, it would be an impossible task to prepare teachers to help all children to learn to read in one or two reading chapters. However, by making teachers more aware of the interrelationship of reading to other language arts areas, they will be better able to integrate reading with the rest of the teaching program and to recognize that aid in one area reinforces another. Aware teachers will provide more reading opportunities for their students,

figure 7.1 *A teacher working with a group of students.*

as well as strengthen their foundation for reading. Reading in the elementary grades should not be relegated to that one period during the day specifically devoted to the reading group.

Defining Reading

John is able to decode correctly all the words in a passage; however, he cannot answer any questions on the passage. Is John reading? Susie makes a number of errors in decoding words, but the errors she makes do not seem to prevent her from answering any of the questions on the passage. Is Susie reading? Maria reads a passage on something about which she has very strong feelings; she has difficulty answering the questions based on the passage because of her attitudes. Is she reading? José can decode the words in the passage, and he thinks that he knows the meaning of all the words; however, José cannot answer the questions on the passage. Is José reading?

To answer the questions just posed, we would have to state: They depend on our definition of reading. A definition of reading is necessary because it will influence what goals will be set in the development of the reading program. A teacher who sees reading as a one-way process, consisting simply of the decoding of symbols or the relating of sounds to symbols, will develop a different type of program than one who looks upon reading as getting meaning from the printed page.

There is no single, set definition of reading. As a result, it is difficult to define it simply. A broad definition, that has been greatly used, is that reading is the bringing to and getting of meaning from the printed page. This implies that readers bring their backgrounds, their experiences, as well as their emotions, into play. Students who are upset or physically ill will bring these feelings into the act of reading, and this will influence their interpretative processes. A person well versed in reading matter will gain more from the material than someone less knowledgeable. A student who is a good critical thinker will gain more from a critical passage than one who is not. A student who has strong dislikes will come away with different feelings and understandings from a pupil with strong likings.

By defining reading as the bringing to and getting of meaning from the printed page, Susie is actually the only child who is reading because she is the only one who understands what she is reading. Although John can verbalize the words, he has no comprehension of them. Maria can also decode the words, but her strong feelings about the topic presented in the selection have prevented her from getting the message that the writer is conveying. José can decode the words and knows the meanings of the individual words, but either he is not able to get the sense of the whole passage, or he does not know the meaning of the words in another context.

Reading as a Total Integrative Process

By using a broad or global definition of reading, we are looking upon reading as a total integrative process that includes the following domains: (1) the *affective*, (2) the *perceptual*, and (3) the *cognitive*.

The affective domain includes our feelings and emotions. The way we feel influences greatly the way we look upon stimuli on a field. It may distort our perception. For example, if we are hungry and we see the word *fool*, we would very likely read it as *food*. If we have adverse feelings about certain things, these feelings will probably influence how we interpret what we read. Our feelings will also influence what we decide to read. Obviously, attitudes exert a directive and dynamic influence on our readiness to respond.

In the perceptual domain, perception can be defined as giving meaning to sensations or the ability to organize stimuli on a field. How we organize stimuli depends largely on our background of experiences and on our sensory receptors. If, for example, our eyes are organically defective, those perceptions involving sight would be distorted. In the act of reading, visual perception is a most important factor. Children need to control their eyes so they move from left to right across the page. Eye movements influence what the reader perceives.

Although what we observe is never in exact accord with the physical situation,[1] readers must be able to accurately decode the graphemic (written) representation. If, however, readers have learned incorrect associations, this will affect their ability to read. For example, if a child reads the word "gip" for "pig" and is not corrected, this may become part of his or her perceptions. If children perceive the word as a whole, in parts, or as individual letters, this will also determine whether they will be good or poor readers. The more mature readers are able to perceive more complex and extensive graphemic patterns as units. They are also able to give meaning to mutilated words such as

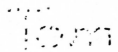

Perception is a cumulative process which is based on an individual's background of experiences. The perceptual process is influenced by physiological factors as well as affective ones. As already stated, a person who is hungry may read the word *fool* as *food*. Similarly, a person with a biased view toward a topic being read may delete, add, or distort what is being read.

Betts presents a number of factors upon which the perceptual process of decoding writing into speech is dependent:[2]

---

[1]Julian E. Hochberg, *Perception* (Englewood Cliffs, N.J.: Prentice-Hall, 1964), p. 3.

[2]Emmett A. Betts, "Linguistics and Reading," *Education* 86 (April 1966): 457–458.

1. Motivation, e.g., the attitudinal factor *need* to identify the unknown part or parts of a particular word.

2. Attention as a powerful selector of stimulus information to be processed and as a constant feature of perceptual activity.

3. Set, a determiner of perception, which, among other things, causes the pupil to regard reading as a poverty-stricken word-calling process or as a thinking process.

4. Grouping of stimuli into recognizable syllables, phonograms, and other patterns for making optimum use of a limited span of attention.

5. Meaning, both structural and referential, needed for the closure of perception.

6. Contrast, such as the contrastive letter patterns which represent contrastive sound patterns.

7. Feedback, a circular process, from the examination of letter groupings of the written word to the sounds of the spoken word; for example, the *application* of word perception skills to the written word during silent reading.

8. Closure, as in the identification of the word *noise* after the usual sound represented by *oi* is recalled.

9. Kinesthesis, as it operates in inner speech and in word learning.

The cognitive domain includes the areas involving thinking. Under this umbrella we would place all the comprehension skills. Persons who have difficulty in thinking (the manipulation of symbolic representations) would obviously have difficulty in reading. Although the cognitive domain goes beyond the perceptional domain, it builds and depends on a firm perceptual base. That is, if readers have faulty perceptions, they will also have faulty concepts.

Reading Approaches

Although there are many approaches to the teaching of reading, only the language-experience approach, which utilizes all of the language arts areas, the basal reader approach, which is probably the most used in the country, and the individualized reading approach, which is probably the most difficult to implement, are being presented. These three are being presented together because many teachers usually use a combination of the three approaches in the teaching of reading.

The Language-Experience Approach

The language-experience approach utilizes the experiences of children. It is a nonstructured emerging reading program, based on the inventiveness of both teacher and students. In sharp contrast to approaches predetermined by exact guidelines and materials, the language-experience approach to reading brings together all the language arts skills. Persons advocating this approach do not attempt to distinguish between the reading program and other language activities.

In the language-experience approach children's speech determines the language patterns of what they will read, and the children's experiences determine the content. The emphasis is not on decoding from the printed page but rather on speaking to express a thought, followed by the encoding of that thought into written form. Since the written material is made up of the children's experiences, they will have more of an incentive to learn to read it. A word of caution is in order. The teacher must be careful to determine whether the children can actually decode the written symbols or whether they have just memorized what they have said. The children may act as though they are reading, but they may not be making any grapheme–phoneme associations.

The teacher using the language-experience approach must also help students gain facility in word recognition skills. One difficulty is that word attack skills are often neglected, because the needs of the children are not as clearly recognized as when other approaches are used. Nor does the experience approach have a sequential, predetermined guide. As a result, the teacher must know the sequence of skills and teach them as part of the program. The word attack skills needed for independence in the language-experience approach are similar to those necessary for any other approach—configuration, phonics, structural analysis, context clues, and so on. And all the skills which make an effective reader should be emphasized.

Teachers do not have to use an exclusive language-experience approach for their whole reading program. Even for the very experienced teacher, it is not recommended that this be the only approach. A varied reading program is the most likely to be successful for the greatest number of students.

The Experience Story   One tool used as a basic teaching technique is the experience story, which provides for the development and expression of concepts on a very personal and meaningful level. It has the added virtue of permitting growth in most of the language skills.

The experience story is written cooperatively after the class has had a real or vicarious learning experience. The technique is useful with all students at various ability levels. When used with able students, it provides a model against which individuals can evaluate their own writing efforts. The time spent on the experience story may vary from one class period to several days, depending on the complexity of the concept and the ability of the class.

Types of Experiences Used for Experience Stories

The opportunities are unlimited, but the best are those which provide for the development of meaning in a stimulating discussion. Examples include picture description and interpretation; map explanation and interpretation; report on a field trip; summaries of answers to problems; summaries of stories, television shows, and movies; original stories; explanation of the facilities in a new school; descriptions of holidays or special events.

Steps in the Development of an Experience Story

Readiness. The teacher structures the actual experience for the group or individual. Following the experience, the teacher guides a discussion during which the class or the child:

Reviews the experience.
Uses the vocabulary to be utilized in writing the story.
Lists the important points to be included in the story.
Sets up standards for the construction of the story.

Writing the Story. The pupils suggest sentences which are discussed and probably improved before being written on the board by the teacher. Then the organization follows. A listing is made of the important points described, based on the natural sequence of the experience. The entire story is read, evaluated, and improved by the class working together.

The Individualized Reading Approach

The individualized reading approach has been undertaken in the instruction of reading to better satisfy the individual differences of students. The characteristics usually associated with individualized reading include the individual pupil-teacher conference, self-selection of books, self-pacing in reading, record-keeping, and the availability of a wide variety of books and other reading materials. Individualized reading programs may vary from a completely individualized approach to ones using some group instruction as part of the program. When the individualized approach was first initiated, the teacher was supposed to only work in a tutorial manner with the child, that is, in a one-to-one relationship. Children were supposed to choose their own books, were supposed to work at their own pace, and were taught the skills of reading in relation to what they were reading rather than in a sequential order. Although some teachers may still follow a completely individualized reading program, many have modified the program to include some group instruction to allow for more teacher-pupil contact. Also, many teachers help children choose their books, and skill development is also generally presented in a more sequential manner. Whether individualized reading is practiced alone, in conjunction with another approach, or in some other modified form, the one constant that remains for all is the easy accessibility of a wide range of books based on the interests and reading levels of the students.

The Basal Reader Approach

The basal reader approach is probably the most common approach used by elementary-grade teachers to teach reading. Although the basal reader approach may not be the whole reading program, it is usually a prominent part of it. Teachers seem to feel more secure with a reading series than with an approach that is less structured, more open-ended, and not based on a sequential development of skills.

Comparison of Programs for the 1980s with Earlier Programs   The basal reader series published in the late 1970s for the 1980s seem to be more sensitive to needs and interests of students than earlier series. In the newer series there appear to be more provisions for individual differences, and reading is looked upon as part of the total language arts program rather than a separate component of it. Teachers are also cautioned to accommodate for dialect and language differences. Helping students to become independent readers is recognized as more important than before, and an effort is made to guide children beyond the textbook. The stories that are chosen tend to be based on the developmental needs and interests of students, and an attempt is made to avoid sexist, ethnic, and racial biases in the stories. There also seems to be more of an emphasis on the development of higher level comprehension skills than in earlier series. (See Chapter 8.)

Materials   Although some of the basal series may incorporate one or two unique features, such as the inclusion of an early childhood component or the incorporation of a language-experience approach in the teaching of beginning reading, the materials used are generally more alike than different. The readers for the basal reader series start with book material from the pre-readiness level to about the seventh or eighth grade. In the latest series, the children's books are marked according to reading levels rather than grade levels, and in the Teacher's Edition, a chart relates the levels to their traditional grade equivalents. The number of levels in the individual series may vary because some programs have an early childhood component, some have more than one book at one level, and some may not go beyond the sixth grade. Although the latest basal series may vary in how they indicate their specific reading levels, they are alike in that they no longer use grade levels. Although the system that is now used is less obvious than the previous one in which books were designated by their exact grade levels, children should be able to easily figure out the system. (Obviously 2 is higher than 1 and B is higher than A.) The books are all based on graduated levels of difficulty, and they have a controlled vocabulary—a basal vocabulary in which the number of different words that appear in the reader is modest, but the rate of their recurrence is high.

Each series usually includes the pupil's books, the pupil's workbook or skillbook that parallels each level of the pupil's book, and a Teacher's Edition. The Teacher's Edition is looked upon as a resource book, and usually it contains all the information necessary for a complete reading program. Every detail from the objectives of the lesson to the presentation of vocabulary to supplementary and optional materials is presented. All questions and answers presented in the lesson are also included. Nothing is left to chance. The Teacher's Edition usually includes a full-color reproduction of the reader's page and a reproduction of the workbook page. Many times the Teacher's Edition also includes full-size, reproducible supplementary worksheets. Provision for informal evaluations is provided as well.

Although the authors of the basal reader programs claim that success of their program does not depend on the optional materials, each program seems to have a wealth of these materials available. The wide range of materials includes Language Activity Kits, soft-cover trade books, games, cards, and all kinds of tests.

Instructional Technique: Guided Reading

The teaching technique used with the basal reader programs is a guided or directed one. Although each program may vary in the number of steps it uses to present the lesson, in the use of terminology to describe each step, or in the sequence of presenting steps, most lessons have the following common factors:

1. Preparing for Reading
Learn a new phonic, word structure, or study skill (depending on level of book)
Review known vocabulary
Learn new words needed to read selection
Set purposes for reading selection
Use motivating technique to stimulate interest in story
Relate to past experiences of children

2. Guided Silent Reading (Comprehension Skill Development)
Questions and statements are used as motivating techniques to direct children to read silently

3. Guided Oral Reading (Comprehension Skill Development)
Questions and statements are used as motivating techniques to read orally

4. Discussion of Material Read (Comprehension Skill Development)

5. Follow-up Activities (Comprehension and/or

Vocabulary, Phonic, Structural Analysis, or Study Skill Development)
(Teachers can use the same guided approach in teaching a reading lesson not using a basal reader series.)

Commentary The basal reader series is fine to use as one approach in the reading program. It should, however, not be the whole program. Unfortunately, many teachers use the Teacher's Edition as an end in itself, never deviating from it and never attempting any of their own creative ideas. Even the editors of some of the latest series would frown on this. Workbooks or skillbooks also should not be used as ends in themselves or as busywork. The teachers should use the workbooks or skillbooks as diagnostic instruments to identify those children who are having difficulty with certain skills and those children who are ready to advance to more difficult skills. If teachers have properly instructed the children in the use of the workbook and if they act as guides, the workbook can help the children in developing independence.

One of the greatest disadvantages of the basal reader program, which paradoxically is also hailed as one of its greatest advantages, is that of the controlled vocabulary. The concept of controlled vocabulary is used in basal readers so that children can overlearn a number of basic words. This is fine for some children, but highly able children are ready to expand their reading vocabulary more quickly. The words that are presented in beginning readers are usually limited and not challenging enough for gifted children.

Even though the latest basal reader series are attempting to provide for more individual differences, and they have in the past decade significantly increased their vocabulary loads, teachers still need to use some individualized approaches to better accommodate the individual differences of their students. It appears that the best reading program is one that incorporates an eclectic–pragmatic approach. In such a program, teachers use skill and ingenuity to mold many approaches into a workable whole. They are not afraid to discard any approach that does not seem to work for the students, and they incorporate reading with the rest of the language arts program.

The Importance of Decoding in Reading

As we have seen, students who have difficulty in listening will have problems in oral language, as well as in reading. Since reading is a process of interpreting printed symbols that are based on arbitrary speech sounds, it depends on a foundation of previously learned speech symbols. Usually, beginning readers have a substantial oral vocabulary before they begin to read, when they learn that each word they speak or listen to has a printed symbol. Students who become effective readers must be able to automatically decode written symbols which represent speech sounds. Inability to do this will prevent readers from bringing to or getting any message from the printed page.

Defining Phonics

Phonics, which is the study of relationships between the letter symbols (graphemes) of a written language and the sounds (phonemes) they represent, is a method used in teaching word recognition in reading. It is a pedagogical term. Phonics is used in the classroom as an aid to decoding words. It helps students gain independence and reliance in reading, but it is only one aspect of the reading process.

Learning Phonic Skills

Learning phonics is necessary so that children are able to gain independence in reading. If children do not learn phonic analysis and synthesis, they will be at a disadvantage in learning to read. The teacher, however, must not assume that all children can learn to make the proper grapheme–phoneme relationships. Some children can benefit from another method of word recognition. It should be recognized that phonics is but one part of word recognition, which itself is but one part of the whole reading program.

The best way for teachers to understand how children learn phonic word attack skills is to experience the phenomenon themselves. To simulate this experience, teachers must know the steps involved. First the child learns a few sight words. Then, when the child learns that some words look alike and/or sound alike, the mastering of phonic word attack skills has begun. This task is not a simple one. Here is a technique which helps put the teacher into the "skin" of the child learning word attack skills.

In the illustration which follows you will learn a new set of phonic signals. English speech will be represented by symbols other than those of the usual Roman alphabet. Play along with the game. When you finish, you will better understand the task which children face and which you help them master.[3]

[3]Carl J. Wallen, *Word Attack Skills in Reading* (Columbus, Ohio: Merrill, 1969), pp. 13–18.

Step One

Objective: Learn sight words.

Learn to pronounce the six words below at sight. Test yourself by covering the pictures.

Step Two

Objective: Test yourself on knowledge of sight words.

Match words and pictures. Check yourself by referring back to Step One.

Step Three

Objective: Test auditory discrimination readiness.

Answer the following questions with *yes* or *no*.

1. Do the two words represented by the pictures have the same ending sound?

2. Do the two words represented by the pictures have the same ending sound?

3. Do the two words represented by the pictures have the same beginning sound?

Step Four

Objective: Test visual discrimination readiness.

Circle the *words* in each column which have the same letters in the same places as those underlined in the word at the top of the column. Column I has been completed.

Step Five

Objective: Use phonic word attack to pronounce a new word.

Follow the directions given below.

1. Pronounce these three words.
2. How do the three words look alike?
3. How do the three words sound alike?

4. Pronounce these three words.
5. How do the three words look alike?
6. How do the three words sound alike?

7. Here is a new word.
8. How does it look like the other two groups of words?
9. Can you pronounce the new word?

(If you cannot pronounce the new word, do Steps One, Two, Three, and Four again. Then follow the directions given in Step Five.)

Notice that you pronounced the new word by comparing the look of the new word with the look of familiar words. You assumed that if words have a similar spelling they will have a similar pronunciation.

Thus: 1. *oride*   probably begins like or and rhymes with hide.
2. *smeek*   probably begins like smile and rhymes with seek.
3. *virgule*   probably begins like virtue and rhymes with mule.

In phonic word attack the child compares new words with familiar ones. When he finds words having a similar spelling he assumes that the words will also have a similar pronunciation. Phonic signals are the letters and groups of letters which the reader compares. The reader learned two nonsense phonic signals in the previous exercise and used them in applying phonic word attack to the new word.

Phonic Signals Learned

New Word Attacked

A Developmental Sequence of Phonic Instruction

Although the teaching of phonics will vary according to the needs and readiness levels of the students, in a developmental sequence certain skills must be achieved before others. So that teachers can properly diagnose the needs and readiness levels of their students in phonics, teachers must be proficient in this area.

Following is an outline of the developmental sequence of phonic instruction. Each area listed will be defined, and examples for each skill will be presented.

1. Auditory discrimination.
2. Visual discrimination.
3. Sounds of initial consonants and written representations of initial consonants.[4]
4. Substitution of initial consonants in sight vocabulary words.
5. Final consonants and their substitution in sight vocabulary words.
6. Consonant clusters (blends) *(bl, st, str)*.
7. Initial consonant blends (clusters); final consonant blends (clusters).
8. Initial consonant digraphs *(th, ch, sh)*.
9. Final consonant digraphs *(ng, gh)*.
10. Silent consonants *(kn, pn, wr)*.
11. Vowel sounds.

[4]Consonants are usually taught before vowel sounds.

    a. Long vowel sounds.
    b. Short vowel sounds.
12. Effect of final *e* on vowel.
13. Double vowels.
    a. Digraphs.
    b. Diphthongs.
14. Vowel controlled by *r*.
15. Special letters and sounds.
16. Syllabication.
    a. Meaning of syllable.
    b. Syllable phonics.
        i. Open syllable.
        ii. Closed syllable.
        iii. Final *e* in last syllable.
    c. Rules.
        i. Double consonant vc/cv.
        ii. Vowel-consonant-vowel v/cv.
        iii. Consonant with special *le* c/cle or v/cle.
    d. Accent.

Auditory and Visual Discrimination

As has already been stated, unless children are able to hear sounds correctly, they will not be able to say them correctly, read them, or write them. Not only must children be able to differentiate between auditory sounds and visual symbols in order to be ready for reading, they must also learn that the sounds they hear have written symbols.

Since they must have good auditory and vi-

AUDITORY DISCRIMINATION

Directions:

Listen carefully and see if you can tell which pair of words are the same.

can　　can
hurt　　hut

Directions:

Listen carefully and give me another word that begins like:

T—Top　　＿＿＿＿＿＿＿＿＿　＿＿＿＿＿＿＿＿＿

C—Car　　＿＿＿＿＿＿＿＿＿　＿＿＿＿＿＿＿＿＿

Directions:

Listen carefully and give me another word that ends like:

AY—Day　＿＿＿＿＿＿＿＿＿　＿＿＿＿＿＿＿＿＿

OW—Cow　＿＿＿＿＿＿＿＿＿　＿＿＿＿＿＿＿＿＿

VISUAL DISCRIMINATION

Directions:

Draw a circle around the word that is like the first word:

far　　fun　　fix　　car　　far

Directions:

Draw a circle around all groups of letters and groups of numbers that are alike. This exercise is excellent for picking up reversals.

tio　　toi　　iot　　ito　　tio　　ot

3523　　2533　　2452　　3523　　5234　　3352

sual discrimination, these samples of exercises should help in determining such discrimination.

Initial Consonants

Initial consonants are single consonants (one speech sound represented by one letter). For example: b(bird), g(go), k(kite), p(pet), t(Tom), y(yellow), z(zoo).

Presentation Teachers should not present initial consonants in isolation from words. Since letters do not have sounds, but are merely representations of them, it is not correct to refer to the sound of *b* or *g*. Teachers may state a number of words beginning with the initial consonant. They may ask the children to listen to the words "ball," "book," and "bee." They should write the words on the board. Then they should ask how "ball," "book," and "bee" are similar. They all have the same beginning letter *b*. They all start with the same sound. Teachers can then give a list of words that begin with *b* and ask students to state some others that start like "big," "book," and "balloon."

For variety, the children can be given a series of words which begin with the same initial consonant and be told to match these words with those in a second column that start with the same letter by drawing a line from one to the other. For example:

Substitution of Initial Consonants After children have learned to recognize and are able to state single consonants, they are ready to substitute those in already learned words to generate new words. The new words must be in their listening capacity; that is, they must have heard the word and know the meaning of it in order to be able to *read* it. For example, chil-

dren have learned the consonant letter *c* and they also know the word "man." They should then be able to substitute *c* for *m* and come up with the word "can."

Final Consonants and Substitution of Final Consonants

Final consonants are similar to the list given for initial consonants, except that they appear at the end of the word. Examples of the most frequent single consonants are: b(rob), d(road), g(pig), k(brook), l(tool), m(mom), n(hen), p(top), r(car), s-z(has), t(hot).

Some teachers teach final consonants at the same time that they teach initial consonants. This approach is preferable, since teachers are working with a particular sound that they want the children to "overlearn"; that is, they want students to be able to recognize and state the sound-letter combination over an extended period of time. By emphasizing the initial and final consonants in words, the children are gaining extra practice in both the particular sound and the letter which represents the sound being studied. Since the children have learned that the letter *Gg* stands for a certain sound, and can recognize this sound in "girl, "go," "game," "get," and so on, they should also be given words such as "pig," "log," "leg," "tag," and so on, to see whether they can recognize the same sound at the end of the word.

In order to gain skill in the substitution of final consonants, the children are given a list of words that they can already decode and recognize—such as "bat," "pet," "let," "tan." Then they are asked to substitute the final letter *g* in all the words to make new words. For example, "bat" would become "bag," "pet" would become "peg," "let" would become "leg," and "tan" would become "tag." Pupils can also be asked to substitute other consonants to make new words. For example, *d* for *g* in "bag" to make "bad," and *d* in let to make "led."

Consonant Clusters (Blends)

Consonant clusters are simply a way of combining the consonant sounds of a language. Clusters are a blend of sounds. (In some basal reader series, the term *consonant cluster* has replaced the term *consonant blend*.)

Initial Consonant Blends (Clusters)

Consonant blends (clusters) are a combination of sounds, not letters. They are two or more consonant sounds blended together so that the identity of each sound is retained. For example: bl(blame), pl(play), cr(crack), tr(try), sk(skate), sl(sled), sm(smile), sn(snow), sp(spot), sw(swim), scr(scream), str(stream), spr(spread), spl(splash).

Many times words with blends are presented in the first grade at the primer and reader levels in basal readers, but are not formally taught until second grade. The teaching of the initial consonant blends depends on the readiness levels of the children, who may be at the stage where they can benefit from added instruction in order to help them more readily decode words. The children must be able to recognize, sound, and substitute initial consonants in words before proceeding to blends. They should be given a list of sight words that have blends, such as spin, snow, play, stop, asked to say these words and then tell what sounds they hear at the beginning of the words. They should also be asked to say a list of words such as go, get, me, and mother, and then be asked what the difference between the two groups of words is. The children should be able to discern that in the group consisting of play, stop, and spin, they were able to hear two consonant sounds rather than one. Thus the concept of a blend is introduced. The teacher should then give the children exercises similar to those presented in the section on initial consonants. For example, the pupils could be given a list of words which they may not necessarily know as sight words:

1	2	3	4
black	big	mother	happy
ball	play	great	broom
blue	draw	farm	track
chain	down	spin	grow
train	go	run	help

Teachers would tell the children to underline only those words they pronounce—such as black, play, spin and broom.

This exercise can also be used to see how well children listen, follow directions, and recognize blends. For example, the teacher can instruct the children to *listen carefully* and not to do anything until she has completed the sentence. Then, she can say: Put a circle around black and a cross on blue. Put a circle around draw and a line under play. Put a line under great and a circle around spin. Put a cross on track and a circle around broom.

Final consonant blends are usually taught after initial consonant blends, using similar techniques.

Initial Consonant Digraphs

Consonant digraphs usually consist of two consonants which represent one speech sound. For example, ch(chair), sh(show), th(thank), ph(phone).

Final Consonant Digraphs

Examples of final consonant digraphs are: th(booth), ng(sing), sh(mash), ch(cinch), gh(rough). Note: It is possible to have a diagraph represent one of the sounds in a cluster. In the word "cinch," *nch* represents a cluster (blend) because *nch* represents a blend of *two* sounds. The letter *n* represents a sound, and the digraph *ch* represents another sound.

Silent Consonants

Silent consonants refer to two consonants in which one is silent. Examples are: kn(know), gh(right), wr(wreck). These are analogous to consonant digraphs, since the two consonants represent one speech sound.

Vowel Sounds

Working with vowel sounds is more difficult than working with consonants because of the inconsistency of vowel sounds. There are exceptions for almost every vowel rule. Most children have met many of the vowel rules in sight words, and have learned to pronounce the words properly before they are able to state the rule. Vowel rules are generally not taught until the end of the first or until the second grade. Again, the discussion as to when to teach vowel rules would depend on the readiness level of the pupils in the class. The purpose of teaching vowel rules is to help students become more proficient in analyzing words, so that they can be more effective independent readers.

Should long or short vowels be taught first?[5] Since the long vowel sound is the name of the vowel, children might have less difficulty in hearing this sound. Therefore, it would be better to start with long vowel sounds, even though there are more words with short vowel sounds.

Whichever kind of vowel is taught first, it is important that the teacher use the children's background of experiences to help them acquire new skills.

Teachers should familiarize children with the schwa sound, represented by (ə) of the phonetic alphabet. The schwa is important in phonic instruction because it frequently appears in the unstressed (unaccented) syllables of words with more than one syllable. (See section on "Special Letters and Sounds.")

---

[5]Although some linguists frown at the use of the terms "long" and "short" vowels, because they claim there are only gradations of vowel sounds, it is helpful to use these terms in the teaching of phonics.

Long Vowel Sounds—a e i o u (and sometimes) y

In teaching this concept, attention should be drawn to the sound element. A number of sight words illustrating the long vowel sound can be placed on the board:

āpe	bē	gō
āge	hē	nō
Āpril	ēven	ōpen
āte	mē	

The children are told to listen to the words as they are sounded. Can they hear the name of any of the vowels in the words? If they can, they can tell which ones they hear. After they correctly state the vowel they heard, "saying its name," it is explained that these vowels are called long vowels and they are marked, for example, ā.

A list of words containing long vowels should be read to the children and the students should then say which vowel is long in each word. They can be given a list of words and asked to mark all the vowels which are long, after everyone has said the words aloud. For example:

āble	gāme	hāte	mōst
boy	get	hid	nāme
cāke	girl	hīde	nō
come	gō	man	nōte
father	hat	mē	pet

After children have had practice in recognizing long vowel sounds in spoken words the teacher presents written exercises in which the children must work independently at marking the long vowel sound. The words in these exercises should all be sight vocabulary words—those the children have already met and are able to recognize.

Y represents a long vowel sound when it occurs at the end of a word or syllable, and when all the other letters in the word or syllable are consonants. For example: by, cry, baby, deny. Note that *y* in these words represents different vowel sounds. It stands for a long *i* sound in one-syllable words containing no other vowels. (See section on "Special Letters and Sounds.")

Short Vowel Sounds

Since the children have already had practice in long vowel sounds, a list of words with short vowel sounds can next be placed on the board and each one pronounced:

not	get	man
got	let	can
pin	put	mad
tin	cut	cap
met	hat	had

The list containing long vowels can be presented so that children can hear the differences between long and short vowel sounds. The children's attention should also be brought to the *position* of the short vowel in such words as:

fat	man	net	got
mat	mad	get	not
cat	can	let	
hat		pet	

Children should be helped to notice the vowel rule—*a single vowel in the middle of a word or syllable is usually short*. Since this concept is taught at the end of the first or the beginning of second grade, the introduction of the term "syllable" would usually be deferred. The concept of closed syllable is reviewed in the intermediate grades in conjunction with syllabication.

Words like gō, nō, mē, and hē should also be noticed. The vowels are all long; there is only one vowel in the word; and *a vowel at the end of a one-vowel word (or syllable) usually has the long sound*.

The Effect of the Final *e*

Words that the children know as sight words should be listed on the board and sounded:

note	cake	cute
made	take	mile

The children are asked to listen to the vowel sound, and it is stressed that in each of the sounded words the first vowel stands for a long sound. The children are then asked to notice what all the words have in common: all of the words have two vowels; one of the vowels is an *e*, which is always at the end of the word, and this *e* always has a consonant preceding it; the first vowel is always long, and the final *e* is always silent. The teacher then lists the following words on the board:

hat	cap	tub
kit	Tim	rob
can	not	hug
tap	cut	hop

The students read the words, tell what the vowel is, and what kind of vowel sound the word has. The teacher then asks the children to put an *e* at the end of each of the words, so that the word list becomes:

hate	cape	tube
kite	time	robe
cane	note	huge
tape	cute	hope

The pupils are asked to read the words aloud. If they need help, the teacher reads the word. Again they are asked to notice what all of the words have in common and what happened to the words when the final *e* was added to each of them.

The teacher, through observation and discussion, helps children develop the final *e* rule which states that *in words or syllables contain-*

ing two vowels, separated by a consonant, one of which is a final e, the first vowel is usually long and the final e is silent.[6]

Some practice exercises include a list of words to which children are instructed to add a final *e* to make a new word. The children then use both words in a sentence to show that they understand the difference in meaning between them. Another exercise shows their ability to recognize differences between words:

Directions:

Put in the correct word.

1. He _____ himself. (cut, cute)
2. She is _____. (cut, cute)
3. I _____ you like my pet. (hop, hope)
4. I like to _____ on my foot. (hop, hope)
5. My friend's name is _____. (Tim, time)
6. What _____ is it? (Tim, time)

Double Vowels

Digraphs Two vowels adjacent to one another in a word (or syllable) stand for a single vowel sound and are called vowel digraphs. For example: *ea, oa, ai, ei, oe, ie* in words like beat, boat, hail, receive, believe. In first grade the children usually learn the rule that when two vowels appear together, the first is usually long and the second is silent. This usually does hold true for a number of vowel combinations such as *ai, oa, ea,* and *ee;* however, there are exceptions to this rule, such as *ae, uy, eo, ew.* These digraphs are sounded as a single sound, but not with the long sound of the first. Some examples are sew, buy, yeoman, Caesar. Note that in the word "believe," it is the *second* vowel which is

---

[6]When we say that a letter is silent, we mean that it does not add a sound to the syllable; however, it is just as important as any other letter in the syllable. It signals information about other letters, and it helps us to determine the sound represented by other letters.

long. Some vowel digraphs combine to form one sound that is not the long sound of either vowel. For example, in the words "neighbor," "weigh," and "freight," the digraph *ei* is sounded as a long *a,* and in the word "sew" the digraph *ew* is sounded as a long *o,* with the *w* acting as a vowel. Note that in the word "rough" the digraph *ou* is not sounded as a long vowel.

Diphthongs Diphthongs are blends of vowel sounds beginning with the first and gliding to the second. The vowel blends are represented by two adjacent vowels. Examples include *ou, oi, oy, ow.* Some of these diphthongs can be confusing to children because the *ou* in "house" is a diphthong but the *ou* in "rough" is not a diphthong but a digraph. Note that in the word "how" the *w* acts as a vowel in the diphthong *ow.* (Even though a diphthong is a *blend* of two vowel sounds, for syllabication purposes you should consider it as one vowel sound.)

Vowel Controlled by *r*

A vowel followed by *r* in the same syllable is controlled by the *r.* As a result, the preceding vowel does not have the usual long or short vowel sound. Examples: car, fir, or, hurt, perch. If a vowel is followed by *r,* but the *r* begins another syllable, the vowel is not influenced by the *r.* Examples, ī • rāt$\not{e}$, tī • rād$\not{e}$.

Review of Vowel Rules

1. A long vowel is one which sounds like the name of the vowel.
2. A single vowel followed by a consonant in a word or syllable usually has a short vowel sound.
3. A single vowel at the end of a word or syllable usually has a long vowel sound.
4. A vowel digraph consists of two adjacent vowels with one vowel sound. Many times the first vowel is long and the second is silent. There are exceptions, such as believe, in which the two vowels form a single sound where the first vowel is not long, and weigh, in which the two vowels form a single sound but neither vowel is long.
5. In words or syllables containing two vowels separated by a consonant, and one vowel is a final *e,*

the first vowel is usually long and the final *e* is silent, as in bāke̸.

6. A vowel followed by *r* is controlled by the consonant *r*.

7. When *y* is at the end of a word containing no other vowels, the *y* represents the long sound of *i*, as in my, sky.

8. Diphthongs are blends of vowel sounds beginning with the first and gliding to the second, as in boy, boil, house.

Review Exercise

Clues to Vowel Sounds   Here are five clues that will help in determining which vowel sound you would expect to hear in a one-syllable word:

1. A single vowel letter at the beginning or in the middle is a clue to a short vowel sound—as in hat, let, it, hot, and cup.

2. A single vowel letter at the end of a word is a clue to a long vowel sound—as in we, by, and go.

3. Two vowel letters together are a clue to a long vowel sound—as in rain, day, dream, feel, and boat.

4. Two vowel letters, one of which is a final *e*, are a clue to a long vowel sound—as in age, ice, bone, and cube.

5. A vowel letter followed by *r* is a clue to a vowel sound that is neither long nor short—as in far, bird, her, horn, care, and hair.

In the blank before each word write the number of the statement in the list that would help you determine the vowel sound in the word.

—— she	—— grave	—— curb
—— pill	—— plot	—— up
—— oak	—— drain	—— pair
—— lung	—— harsh	—— coax
—— mane	—— whine	—— charm
—— hurl	—— freak	—— plead
—— bean	—— ask	—— flag

Special Letters and Sounds

Y   As already mentioned, *y* is used both as a consonant and a vowel. When *y* is at the beginning of a word or syllable it is a consonant.

Examples: yes, yet, young, your, canyon, graveyard. In the words canyon and graveyard, *y* begins the second syllable; therefore it is a consonant.

When *y* acts as a vowel, it represents the short *i* sound, the long *i* sound, or the long *e* sound. *Y* usually represents the short *i* sound when *y* is in the middle of a word or syllable that has no vowel letter. Examples: hymn, gym, synonym, cymbal. *Y* usually represents the long *i* sound when it is at the end of a single-syllable word that has no vowel letter. Examples: by, try, why, dry, fly. *Y* usually represents the long *e* sound when it is at the end of a multisyllabic word. Examples: baby, candy, daddy, family.

C and G   Some words beginning with *c* or *g* can cause problems because the letters *c* and *g* each stand for both a hard and a soft sound. The letter *g* in gym, George, gentle, and generation stands for a soft *g* sound. A soft *g* sounds like *j* in Jack, jail, and justice. The initial letter *c* in cease, center, cent, and cite stands for a soft *c* sound. A soft *c* sounds like *s* in so, same, and sew. The initial letter *g* in go, get, game, gone, and garden stands for a hard *g* sound. The initial letter *c* in cat, came, cook, call, and carry, stands for a hard *c* sound. A hard *c* sounds like *k* in key, king, kite, kettle. Note that the letter *c* represents a sound that is either like the *s* in see or like the *k* in kitten.

Q   The letter *q* is always followed by the letter *u* in the English language. The *qu* combination represents either one speech sound or a blend of two sounds. At the beginning of a word, *qu* almost always represents a blend of two sounds, *kw*. Examples: queen, quilt, quiet, queer, quack. When *qu* appears at the end of a word in the *que* combination, it represents one sound, *k*. Examples: unique, antique, clique.

The Schwa (ə)   The *schwa* sound is symbolized by an upside down *e* (ə) in the phonetic (speech) alphabet. The schwa sound frequently appears in the unstressed (unaccented) syllables of words with more than one syllable. The schwa, which usually sounds like the short *u* in but, is represented by a number of different vowels. Examples: believe (bə • ḻēvⱴ), police (pə • lēs), divide (də • vīdⱴ), robust (rō • bəst), Roman (rō • mən). In the examples the italicized vowels represent the schwa sound. Although the spelling of the unstressed syllable in each word is different, the sound remains the same for the different vowels. (Note: The pronunciations presented here come from *Webster's New Collegiate Dictionary*, but it should not be inferred that these are the only pronunciations for these words. Pronunciations may vary from dictionary to dictionary and from region to region.)

Syllabication—Intermediate Grades

A syllable is a vowel or a group of letters containing one vowel sound. Syllabication of words is the process of breaking known an unknown multisyllabic words into single syllables. This is important in word recognition because in order to be able to pronounce the word, a child must first be able to syllabicate it. Knowledge of syllabication is also helpful in spelling and writing. In attacking multisyllabic words, the pupil must first analyze the word, determine the syllabic units, apply phonic analysis to the syllables, and then blend them into a whole word.

Syllabication Rules

Since a multisyllabic word must be syllabicated before applying phonic analysis, syllabication rules will be given first. The vowel rules that the students have learned since first grade should be reviewed, because these same rules will be used in the application of phonic analysis.

Rule 1: Vowel followed by two consonants and a vowel (vc/cv). If the first vowel in a word is followed by two consonants and a vowel, the word is divided between the two consonants.

Examples: but/ter can/dy com/ment

Rule 2: Vowel followed by a single consonant and a vowel (v/cv). If the first vowel is followed by one consonant and a vowel, the consonant usually goes with the second syllable.

Examples: be/gin ti/ger fe/ver pu/pil

An exception to the v/cv syllabication rule exists. If the letter *x* is between two vowels, the *x* goes with the first vowel rather than with the second one.

Examples: ex/it ex/act ox/en

Rule 3: Vowel or consonant followed by a consonant plus *le* (v/cle) or (vc/cle). If a consonant comes just before *le* in a word of more than one syllable, the consonant goes with *le* to form the last syllable.

Examples: sam/ple can/dle an/kle bun/dle pur/ple daz/zle bea/gle ca/ble

Rule 4: Compound words. Compound words are divided between the two words.

Examples: girl/friend base/ball

Rule 5: Prefixes and suffixes. Prefixes and suffixes usually stand as whole units.

Examples: re/turn kind/ly

Phonics Applied to Syllabicated Syllables

After the word has been divided into syllables, the student must determine how to pronounce the individual syllables. The pronunciation is determined by whether the syllable is open or closed, and whether it contains a vowel digraph or diphthong:

Open syllable—one which contains one vowel and ends in a vowel. The vowel is usually sounded as long, as in gō.

Closed syllable—one which contains one

vowel and ends in a consonant. The vowel is usually sounded as short, as in mat.

Application of Vowel Rule to Syllabication Rule 1—Double Consonant Rule (vc/cv)

The closed-syllable vowel rule would apply to a syllable that contains one vowel and ends in a consonant. The vowel sound is usually short.

Examples: mit/ten cot/ton af/ter fas/ten

Application of Vowel Rule to Syllabication Rule 2—Vowel Consonant Vowel Rule (v/cv)

The open-syllable rule would apply to a syllable that contains one vowel and ends in a vowel. The vowel sound is usually long.

Examples: bē/gin tī/ger ō/ver fā/tal dē/cide pū/pil

Application of Vowel Rule to Syllabication Rule 3—Special Consonant *le* Rule (v/cle) or (vc/cle)

If the syllable is closed as in "sad/dle" and in "can/dle" then the vowel sound is usually short in the first syllable since it ends in a consonant. If the syllable is open as in "fā/ble" and "bū/gle" then the vowel sound is usually long in the first syllable, since it ends in a vowel. The letter combinations containing *le*—such as *cle*, *ble*, *gle*, *dle*, *kle*, *ple*, *tle*, and so on—usually stand as the final syllable. The final syllable is not accented; it is always an unstressed syllable containing the schwa sound.

Examples: sĭm/ple fā/ble săd/dle
ăp/ple bū/gle căn/dle

Accenting Words

In order to pronounce words of more than one syllable the students must syllabicate the word, apply phonic analysis, and then blend the syllables into one word. In order to be able to blend the syllables into one word correctly, stu-

dents must know something about accenting and how accents affect vowel sounds. Pupils should know that unaccented syllables are usually softened, and that there may be differences between pronunciation of homographs (words that are spelled the same but have different meanings) due to a difference in accent.

Example: con'duct (noun) con duct' (verb)

Accenting and accent marks are taught in conjunction with syllabication in the intermediate grades. Since children at this level do not meet too many words which require a secondary accent, the teaching emphasis should be on the primary accent.

Procedures for Teaching Accenting

A number of two-syllable words are placed on the board and syllabicated:

pi/lot	a/ble	ap/ple	va/cant
den/tist	rea/son	help/ful	bot/tle
sub/due	wi/zard	wis/dom	tai/lor
lo/cal	co/lumn	jour/nal	

The teacher explains that even though students are able to syllabicate the individual words, and are able to apply the proper phonic analysis, in order to be able to pronounce the words correctly, they still must know something about accenting the words.

Students are asked to listen while the teacher pronounces each word, to determine which syllable is stressed. The teacher then asks individual students to volunteer to pronounce the words, and explains that the syllable which is sounded with more stress in a two-syllable word is called the accented syllable. The teacher explains that the accent mark (') is used to show which syllable is stressed, that is, spoken with greater intensity or loudness. This mark usually comes right after and slightly above the accented syllable. The teacher further explains that the dictionary has a key to pronunciation of words, and that the marks that show how to pronounce words are called *diacritical marks*. The most frequent diacritical marks are the breve (˘) and the macron (¯), which pupils have already met as the short and long vowel sounds. The accent (′) is also in the class of diacritical marks.

A list of words correctly syllabicated are put on the board:

pi′ lot	a′ ble	ap′ ple	pro′ gram
rea′ son	help′ ful	bot′ tle	jour′ nal
wis′ dom	tai′ lor	lo′ cal	den′ tist

Syllabication and vowel rules are then reviewed. The two-syllable words in the list above are all accented on the first syllable. Another group of words in which the second syllable is stressed are then listed:

ap point′	pro ceed′	as tound′
sub due′	pa rade′	po lite′
re ceive′	com plain′	pro vide′

Students are again asked to listen while each word is pronounced to determine which syllable is being stressed and to see if they notice any similarity among all the second syllables. They should notice that all stressed second syllables have two vowels. From their observations they should be able to state the following generalization: *In two-syllable words the first syllable is usually stressed, except when the second syllable contains two vowels.*

In three-syllable words it is usually the first or second syllable which is accented, as in an′ ces tor, cap′ i tal, ho ri′ zon. (See the discussion on stress in Chapter 14.)

These skills for decoding of words are useful for all children, including those who speak nonstandard English. However, for those speaking nonstandard English (or a foreign language) the teacher must be especially certain to utilize the aural–oral approach before attempting to teach reading. (*See*, for example, sections in Chapter 5 and 6.) Obviously, the child must have the words that are to be decoded in both his hearing and speaking vocabularies in order to make the proper grapheme–phoneme associations.

Children who speak nonstandard English or a foreign language will need more practice in auditory discrimination and sound production education, as was outlined in the previous chapters, before being able to read. This approach will facilitate the acquisition of phonic and word attack skills which will help these children to become proficient and independent readers. As was stated earlier, individual differences will determine when an approach is "preferable" with a given child or group. Teachers must be cautioned against attempting to teach such skills to all children, for they are not all able to learn phonic or syllabication rules. Students at low-ability levels usually have difficulty with syllabication and accenting.

Linguistics and Phonics

Linguistics, which is the scientific study of language, is not a new science. However, its influence on reading instruction and in particular on beginning reading was not pronounced until the 1960s. Although there are many branches of linguistics, only those subdivisions which directly relate to the area of phonics will be discussed. (See Chapter 14 for more on linguistics.) Phonology, which is a branch of descriptive linguistics, is the study of the sound system of language and consists of the related studies of phonetics and phonemics. Phonology is the division that is the most closely related to the area of phonics.

Since the terms "phonics," "phonetics," and "phonemics" are often confused, definitions of the three follow.

Phonics involves the study of relationships between the letter symbols (graphemes) of a written language and the sounds (phonemes) they represent. It is a method used in teaching word recognition in reading, that is, it belongs in the area of pedagogy.

Phonetics, a branch of linguistics, is the study of the nature of speech sounds. According to Betts, phonetics includes:

1. How speech sounds are produced by tongue, teeth, vocal bands, and other parts of the speech mechanism.

2. The perception of speech sounds by the hearing mechanism.

3. The variant pronunciation and varying usage of speech sounds in different regions of a country or of the world.

4. The system of speech symbols—their symbolic nature—for communication of messages.

"Applied" phonetics includes:

1. Correction of defective speech.
2. Teaching a "standard" speech in a given region.
3. Devising symbols to represent speech sounds;

for example, one pronunciation of "call" is transcribed via the phonetic symbols [kol]; "hat" as [hat].[7]

Phonemics "deals with the problems of discovering which phonemes are part of the conscious repertoire of sounds made by speakers of a language or dialect."[8] "The phonemic system is that group of phonemes used by speakers of a language to put their utterances together."[9] A *phoneme* is the smallest unit of sound that a

[7]Emmett Albert Betts, "Confusion of Terms," *The Reading Teacher* (February 1973): 454–455.
[8]Burt Liebert, *Linguistics and the New English Teacher* (New York: Macmillan, 1971), p. 82.
[9]Ibid., p. 84.

Student's Name:
Grade:
Teacher:

Diagnostic Checklist for Word Recognition Skills

	Yes	No
1. The student uses: a. context clues. b. picture clues (graphs, maps, charts).		
2. The student uses configuration clues (the shape of the word).		
3. The student uses known phonograms or graphemic bases (a succession of graphemes that occurs with the same phonetic value in a number of words *[ight, id, at, ad, ack]*) to try to unlock unknown words.		
4. The student uses phonic analysis by recognizing a. consonants. i. single consonants: initial, final ii. consonant blends (clusters) (*br, sl, cl, st,* and so on) iii. consonant digraphs (*th, sh, ph, ch,* and so on) iv. silent consonants (kn, gn, pn)		

    b. vowels.
      i. short vowels (cot, can, get, and so on)
      ii. long vowels (go, we, no, and so on)
      iii. final silent *e* (bake, tale, role)
      iv. vowel digraphs (*ea, oa, ie, ei, ai,* and so on)
      v. diphthongs *(oi, oy)*
    c. the effect of *r* on the preceding vowel.

5. The student is able to apply the following syllabication rules to words:
    a. vowel consonant/consonant vowel rule *(vc/cv)* (but/ter, can/dy)
    b. vowel consonant/vowel rule (v/cv) (na/tive, ca/bin)
    c. special consonant *le* rule (vc/cle) or (v/cle) (ca/ble, can/dle).

6. The student is able to apply phonic analysis to syllabicated words with
    a. an open syllable (no/ble).
    b. a closed syllable (pi/lot).
    c. a vowel digraph (re/main).
    d. a diphthong (foi/ble).
    e. a silent *e* (re/bate).

7. The student is able to apply the following accent rule to two-syllable words:
    Accent falls on the first syllable except when the second syllable has two vowels (tailor, career).

8. The student is able to use structural analysis to recognize (See Chapter 8 for an elaboration of the terms above.)
    a. compound words (grandmother, caretaker).
    b. the root or base of a word (turn, state).
    c. suffixes *(tion, al, ic, y).*
    d. prefixes *(re, un, non).*
    e. combining forms *(bio, cardio, auto).*
    f. derivatives.
      i. root plus prefix (return)
      ii. root plus suffix (turned)
      iii. root plus prefix and suffix (returned)

Student's Name:
Grade:
Teacher:

Diagnostic Checklist Test for Word Recognition Skills

Auditory Discrimination	Yes	No

1. The student is able to listen to a set of words and state which pair are the same:

Ted Ted		
cap cap		
bud but		
out out		
shell shall		
bit bet		
send sand		

2. The student is able to listen to a word and state another word that begins like

b: boy.		
r: ran.		
m: mine.		
p: pencil.		

3. The student is able to listen to a word and give another that ends like

k: clock.		
t: hat.		
d: card.		
t: plant.		

Visual Discrimination

The student is able to do the following visual discrimination activities:

1. Following are a number of letters. Choose the letter that is different from the first one in the line:

Example: E   E   *D*   E   E

a.	U	R	U	U	U	U	
b.	P	P	P	P	P	D	
c.	d	d	d	b	d	d	
d.	p	p	p	p	d	p	

2. Following are a number of letters. Choose the letter that is the same as the first one in the line:

Example: R   S   S   T   *R*

a.	D	B	D	B	O	S	
b.	B	R	D	D	B	P	
c.	M	N	M	N	O	R	
d.	O	C	O	P	R	B	

3. Following are a number of words. Draw a circle around the word that is the same as the first word:

Example: fun   far   fix   fat   (fun)   fall

a.	was	saw	sat	won	wet	was
b.	bark	dark	bark	hard	barn	bar
c.	other	order	ought	other	about	ether
d.	saw	set	sun	sat	saw	was

4. Following are groups of numbers. Draw a circle around the number group that is the same as the first in the line:

Example: 716   617   (716)   176   617

a.	319	913	139	319	193
b.	481	184	841	481	148
c.	1325	5312	2153	1532	1325
d.	9164	9164	1649	9461	4619

5. Following are groups of letters. Draw a circle around the letter group that is the same as the first in the line.

Example: iot   tio   (iot)   oit   oti

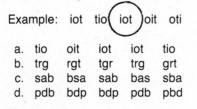

a.	tio	oit	iot	iot	tio
b.	trg	rgt	tgr	trg	grt
c.	sab	bsa	sab	bas	sba
d.	pdb	bdp	bdp	pdb	pbd

Word Analysis Test—Auditory	Yes	No

1. The student is able to state the number of syllables in each word.

   ("Listen carefully. Each of the words I am going to pronounce has one or more than one syllable. Tell me the number of syllables you hear in each word.")

   a. vocabulary (5)
   b. bicycle (3)
   c. baby (2)
   d. reached (1)
   e. mother (2)

2. The student is able to state the vowel sound heard in each word.

   ("Listen carefully. Tell me the vowel sound you hear in each word.")

a. bake (ā)	f. use (ū)
b. coat (ō)	g. leap (ē)
c. pit (ĭ)	h. neck (ĕ)
d. hen (ĕ)	i. pine (ī)
e. bat (ă)	j. lip (ĭ)

   a.
   b.
   c.
   d.
   e.
   f.
   g.
   h.
   i.
   j.

Word Analysis Test—Visual		

The student is able to pronounce the following nonsense words.
("Can you pronounce the following nonsense words?")

   a. l o a p (l ō ᶿ p)
   b. h a k e (h ā k ¢)
   c. c h i n e (c h ī n ¢)
   d. p h a t (f ă t)
   e. l i p o (l ī p ō)

speaker uses to distinguish one utterance from another.

Both phonemics and phonetics are more concerned with the analysis of the sound system of language than with pedagogy.

Linguists' Definition of Vowels and Consonants

Phonemes are classified into consonants and vowels and then are further divided into *voiced* or *voiceless* sounds. All vowels are voiced.

Whether a sound is voiced or voiceless can be determined by placing your hand over your larynx (Adam's apple) and making the sound. For example, for the sound [b] vibrations can be felt, whereas for the sound [p], no vibrations can be felt.[10]

Phonemes are also categorized "according to the point of articulation, the place in the oral cavity where the speech stream is modified."[11] Vowel sounds can be produced when "the air stream passes comparatively freely through the oral cavity, being modified mainly by the position of the tongue." Consonants "result when, in speaking, the outgoing breath stream is either partially or completely obstructed by the organs of speech."[12]

A phoneme is a class of sounds, not a distinct and separate sound. There are a number of variations within any phoneme and each variation is called an *allophone*. However, persons speaking the native language are not aware of the differences.

Recording of Phonemic Symbols and Phonetic Symbols

Since many of the phonemes of the language are written with letters of the alphabet, in order to distinguish between letters and representa-

tion of sounds, specific brackets are used.

Phonemes are written between slashes (//), whereas phonetic symbols are written within square brackets ([ ]).

For example, the letter *b* stands for the second letter of our alphabet and is part of the graphemic (written) system of English, but the symbol [b] stands for a sound, part of the phonetic (spoken) system of language, and the phonemic symbol / b / stands for the sound which belongs to a particular language.

Summary

Chapter 7 has presented selected topics in reading of particular relevance to the total language arts picture. The relationship of reading to the total language arts program was explored and a discussion of how the definition of reading can influence the reading program was undertaken. The presented definition looks upon reading as a total integrative process. Reading as a total integrative process includes the affective, perceptual, and cognitive domains.

Then reading approaches were presented. Since the language-experience approach emphasizes the interrelatedness concept, this approach was discussed, with suggestions given for the development of an experience story. Also discussed were the basal reader and the individualized reading approaches.

Phonics, which is an aspect of word-recognition skills and is used in other language arts areas, was discussed. A sequential development of phonic instruction and syllabic word attack skills was presented. A diagnostic checklist and a diagnostic checklist test for word recognition skills were also presented.

Now that you have read Chapter 7, you should have mastered the teacher competencies for reading presented at the beginning of the chapter.

Two examples of reading lesson plans follow. Using them as a guide, see if you can construct a third one.

---

[10]Ibid., p. 76.
[11]Ibid., p. 78.
[12]Anna D. Cordts, *Phonics for the Reading Teacher* (New York: Holt, Rinehart and Winston, 1965), p. 138.

LESSON PLAN I—PRIMARY GRADES

Behavioral Objectives

1. The students will be able to recognize words containing "at."
2. The students will be able to state eight words that end in "at," which have different initial consonants.
3. The students will be able to read eight words that contain "at."

Preliminary Preparation

Drawing paper, crayons.
Chairs arranged in a semicircle near the chalkboard.

Introduction

"Yesterday we talked about and played a game with some family words. What family did these words belong to? Yes, the 'ake' family. Who can give me some words belonging to that family? Yes, 'make,' 'lake,' 'take,' 'cake,' and 'rake.' Very good. Today we're going to meet words which belong to another family, and I am going to tell you a funny story about this family. Listen carefully to this story because you are going to help me tell the story, create an ending for it, and then draw some special pictures about it."

Development

Once, a long time ago, there lived a cheerful and friendly animal called Kippa Kappa. He lived in outer space in a village called Kippa Kump, near the earth's moon. Although Kippa Kappa was cheerful and friendly, he was very lonely because he had no friends. One day Kippa Kappa told his mother and father that he was leaving Kippa Kump in order to travel to other villages in search of friends.

Kippa Kappa started on his journey. He walked and walked. Soon he became tired and hungry. He stopped and, lo and behold, he saw his favorite moon food growing. What do you think Kippa Kappa's favorite moon food is? In case you don't know, moon food is very different from earth food. On the moon, words are eaten as food. Kippa Kappa's favorite moon food is a word with "at" in it. How many children can help Kippa Kappa pick some of his favorite food? Let's see. Kippa Kappa picked a "bat" and ate it. Does that have an "at" in it? Yes, but Kippa Kappa is still very hungry, so he picked a "fat" and a "mat" and ate them. "Um mm, these are good," said Kippa Kappa. In order to satisfy his hunger, Kippa Kappa must eat eight delicious foods with "at" in them. How many has he already picked? Yes, he's picked three. How many more does he need? Yes, he now needs five more. Let's list the three on the board, and then let's help Kippa Kappa find five more moon goodies to eat.

Have the children think of other initial consonants that they can use with "at." As they state the words, list them on the board; for example, cat, hat, pat, rat, sat, and so on. Give the children word clues if they have difficulty thinking of some of the words.

Now ask the children how they think the story will end. Tell the group that the end depends on them, and let them supply the ending.

Lastly, tell the children to draw a picture of one of Kippa Kappa's favorite foods and label it. The children can also draw a picture of Kippa Kappa and write a sentence about eating a word containing "at."

Summary

"What have we done today?" Have each child tell the name of the "at" word he drew a picture of, and hang the "at" chart made by the children in the reading area as a reference. Discuss the next family words the children will learn.

Note: This lesson should be taught to a group of no more than nine children at a time.

LESSON PLAN II—INTERMEDIATE GRADES

Behavioral Objectives

1. Students will be able to define "syllable" correctly.
2. Students will be able to analyze the act of syllabication to determine which is done first—syllabication or phonic analysis.
3. Students will be able to state the syllabication rules.
4. Students will be able to state the following vowel rules: final "e" rule, vowel digraph, diphthong, open syllable, closed syllable.

Preparation

On the board are listed the following nonsense syllables:

crono	lattle	tremmle	noin
prene	peomeat	cranmeto	sloy
platebe	creit	troper	
ploat	slatter	labebe	
cobe	nolbeit	brune	

Introduction

There are a number of nonsense words on the board. How many of them can you pronounce? In order to be able to pronounce words properly what do you have to know? Do you syllabicate first, or do you put in vowel rules first? We've been working with individual syllabication rules and vowel rules. Let's see if we can apply what we've learned.

Development

Ask students: "Who can tell me what they think we should do? Why don't you experiment first on your own." After a while ask for volunteers to pronounce the words put up on the board. After each word is pronounced, ask the student to tell how he or she syllabicated the word. Ask other students if they agree with the syllabication. After each word the teacher should give immediate knowledge of results, and make sure that the nonsense words have been pronounced and syllabicated correctly. At this point the teacher should ask the students to again review the definition of a syllable, which is a vowel or a group of letters with a vowel sound. The teacher should ask the students why they think nonsense syllables were used in the lesson. It is hoped that some will state that nonsense syllables are used so that students are not influenced by known words and most importantly because all rules would apply without exception.

The next question is concerned with syllabication rules. Ask the students to see if they can come up with the syllabication rules they have already learned by looking at the nonsense syllables that have been syllabicated. It is hoped that the students will come up with the three syllabication rules which would then be listed on the board next to the nonsense syllables.

cro/no	slat/ter	noin
prene	lat/tle	
ploat	sloy	

Syllabication Rules　　　　　　　　　　　　　　　　　　*Vowel Rules*

Vowel consonant vowel (v/cv)—consonant goes with second vowel　　　　silent "e" rule

Vowel consonant consonant vowel rule (vc/cv)—divided between two consonants　　　　open syllable　closed syllable

Special consonant "le" rule—consonant goes with "le" to form a syllable　　　　vowel digraph　diphthong

After the children have derived the syllabication and the vowel rules, ask them what they did in order to be able to pronounce the multisyllabic nonsense words. Did they apply the vowel rule first or the syllabication rule?

Put two more examples on the board: "rommo" and "romo." Ask the children to syllabicate these two nonsense syllables, rom/mo and ro/mo. Since "rom" ends in a consonant, it is a closed syllable and therefore the "o" is short. Since "ro" ends in a vowel, it is an open syllable and therefore the "o" is long.

Go back to the original question, "To pronounce a multisyllabic word, what must you do first?" The children should say, "Syllabicate, because you do not know whether it will be an open or closed syllable until after you have syllabicated." Give a few more examples to make sure that the children understand this concept. Now ask the children for examples when they *would not* syllabicate first.

Put the following nonsense words on the board: depe, tope, doap, croap, rute, noin, sloy, teip. Ask the students to tell why they would not syllabicate these words first. Ask what depe, tope, and rute have in common. It is hoped that the students will note that these are all one-syllable words with the silent "e" rule. The silent "e" rule states that in words or syllables containing two vowels, one of which is the final "e," the first vowel is usually long and the final "e" is silent. In "depe," "tope," and "rute" there are two vowels, one of which is a final "e," as we have noted. Therefore, the first vowel is long and the "e" is silent.

In "croap," "doap," and "teip" the combinations "oa" and "ei" are vowel digraphs. A vowel digraph is a vowel combination making one vowel sound. The nonsense words "doap," "croap," and "teip" are one-syllable words containing vowel digraphs, whereby the first vowel is usually long and the second is silent. It should be stated that there are some exceptions, and sometimes the second vowel in a vowel digraph is long and the first is silent. It should also be emphasized that the vowel digraph and silent "e" rule are present in other than one-syllable words, as the class has already seen.

In "noin" and "sloy" the combinations are diphthongs. They are one-syllable words, so they too are not syllabicated.

Summary

Pull together the main points of the lesson. Have children state the syllabication and vowel rules. Have them state why they would syllabicate first. Have a number of children come to the board and make up nonsense syllables, which other children have to syllabicate and pronounce. As a further review, hand out the sheet of words below and have the students syllabicate them. After the list has been checked, the students should be told that tomorrow they will be working with accenting. In order to properly pronounce words of two or more syllables, they should also know something about accents.

DO YOU KNOW HOW TO DIVIDE WORDS INTO SYLLABLES?

Here are three clues that will help you:

1. can dy, mit ten: first vowel element followed by two consonants and a vowel.
2. o pen, bea con, la dy: first vowel element followed by a single consonant.
3. bu gle, rum ble, strug gle: final le preceded by a consonant.

Look at each word below and decide where the first syllable ends. Draw a line between the first and second syllable of the word. Put the number of the clue listed above on the line to show how you know where the first syllable ends. The first three words are done for you.

garbage __1__	able _____	master _____
handle __3__	collar _____	pronounce _____
pupil __2__	nimble _____	giggle _____
hobby _____	mirror _____	maple _____
bacon _____	eager _____	pepper _____
elbow _____	pilot _____	shuffle _____
wrinkle _____	snuggle _____	lazy _____
tiger _____	person _____	bundle _____

baby _____	reason _____	corner _____
table _____	acorn _____	after _____
borrow _____	cargo _____	nature _____
tailor _____	rifle _____	captain _____
purpose _____	simple _____	amble _____
tangle _____	notice _____	iron _____

*This lesson would be used with a group of very able students.

Suggestions for Thought Questions and Activities

1. You have just been appointed to a special primary-grade reading committee. Your task is to acquaint the teachers with the language-experience approach to reading. How would you do this so that teachers would want to incorporate this type of approach into their reading programs?

2. Can you defend the use of phonic instruction in your school? What would your arguments and rationale be?

3. There is talk in your school of separating reading from the rest of the language arts program and perhaps having a special teacher for reading instruction. How do you feel about this? Present arguments pro or con.

4. Explain the place of phonics in the language arts program.

5. Develop a creative lesson plan in the area of phonics.

6. Think up some activities that would be fun and would help primary graders to recognize and name initial consonants.

7. Present a lesson that would help primary-grade children understand the concept of open and closed syllables. How would you be able to determine whether your lesson was successful?

8. Make a comparison/contrast of three different basal reader programs developed for the 1980s. Choose a similar level for all three programs.

9. Choose a basal reader program developed for the 1980s. Compare this basal reader program with the ones prepared ten and twenty years before. Use the *same* basal series and use the *same* level for the comparison.

SELECTED BIBLIOGRAPHY

Reading Method Books

Aukerman, Robert. *Approaches to Beginning Reading*. New York: Wiley, 1971.

Dallmann, Martha, et al. *The Teaching of Reading*, 5th ed. New York: Holt, Rinehart and Winston, 1978.

Durkin, Dolores. *Teaching Them to Read*, 3d ed. Boston: Allyn and Bacon, 1978.

Hall, Mary Anne. *Teaching Reading as a Language Experience*, 2d ed. Columbus, Ohio: Merrill, 1976.

Harris, Albert and Edward R. Sipay. *How to Teach Reading: A Competency-Based Program*. New York: Longmans, 1978.

Heilman, Arthur. *Principles and Practices of Teaching Reading*, 4th ed. Columbus, Ohio: Merrill, 1977.

Smith, Frank. *Understanding Reading*, 2d ed. New York: Holt, Rinehart and Winston, 1978.

Smith, Nila Banton. *Reading Instruction for Today's Children*. Englewood Cliffs, N.J.: Prentice-Hall, 1963.

Stauffer, Russell. *The Language-experience Approach to the Teaching of Reading*. New York: Harper & Row, 1970.

Veatch, Jeannette. *How to Teach Reading with Children's Books*. New York: Scholastic Citation, 1978.

Wallen, Carl J. *Competency in Teaching Reading*. Chicago: Science Research Associates, 1972.

Zintz, Miles. *The Reading Process: The Teacher and the Learner*. Dubuque, Iowa: W.C. Brown, 1975.

Phonics

Bagford, Jack. *Phonics: Its Role in Teaching Reading*. Iowa City, Iowa: Sernoll, 1967.

Dechant, Emerald. *Linguistics, Phonics and the Teaching of Reading*. Springfield, Ill.: C C Thomas, 1969.

Durkin, Dolores. *Strategies for Identifying Words: A Workbook for Teachers & Those Preparing to Teach*. Boston: Allyn and Bacon, 1976.

————. *Phonics, Linguistics and Reading*. New York: Teachers College Press, 1972.

Gans, Roma. *Guiding Children's Reading Through Experiences*. New York: Teachers College, Columbia University, 1941.

————. *Fact and Fiction about Phonics*. Indianapolis: Bobbs-Merrill, 1964.

Heilman, Arthur. *Phonics in Proper Perspective*, 3d ed. Columbus, Ohio: Merrill, 1976.

Linguistics and Reading

Bloomfield, Leonard, and Clarence L. Barnhart. *Let's Read: A Linguistic Approach*. Detroit, Mich.: Wayne State University Press, 1961.

Dechant, Emerald. *Linguistics, Phonics and the Teaching of Reading*. Springfield, Ill.: C C Thomas, 1969.

Durkin, Dolores. *Phonics, Linguistics, and Reading*. New York: Teachers College Press, 1972.

Fries, Charles. *Linguistics and Reading*. New York: Irvington Press, 1963.

Goodman, Kenneth. *The Psycholinguistic Nature of the Reading Process*. Detroit, Mich.: Wayne State University Press, 1973.

Smith, Frank. *Psycholinguistics and Reading*. New York: Holt, Rinehart and Winston, 1973.

Wardhaugh, Ronald. *Reading: A Linguistic Approach*. New York: Harcourt, Brace & World, 1969.

Relationship of Reading to Other Language Arts Areas

Rupley, William H. "Language Development and Beginning Reading Instruction." *Elementary English* 52 (March 1975): 403–407.

Shepherd, Richard. "Oral Language Performance and Reading Instruction." *Elementary English* 51 (April 1974): 544–546; 560.

Smith, Nila Banton. "Early Language Development: Foundation of Reading." *Elementary English* 52 (March 1975): 399–402; 418.

Walden, James, ed. *Oral Language and Reading*. Urbana, Ill.: National Council of Teachers of Reading, 1969.

eight

Reading Comprehension, Vocabulary Expansion, and Diagnosis: Selected Areas

Introduction

TEACHER X: John, in what year does this story take place?

JOHN: In 1945.

TEACHER X: Good.

TEACHER W: Maria, what conclusion can you draw from the story you have just read?

MARIA: Humans are at times inhumane.

TEACHER W: Good.

TEACHER S: Susan, how do you feel about the author's portrayal of the main character?

SUSAN: The character is portrayed in an unrealistic manner because . . .

TEACHER S: Good.

TEACHER Y: Tom, can you supply an ending to the story we have just read that is different from the author's?

TOM: I'll try. Everyone had left. He was now alone. However, he . . .

TEACHER Y: Good.

Although the questions posed by Teachers X, W, S, and Y are all comprehension questions, there is a wide range of difference in the difficulty of their questions. Teachers who persist in asking only questions similar to the one asked by Teacher X are hindering their students and not helping them reach higher levels of thinking. Background knowledge of reading comprehension is important for teachers to be able to develop a reading program that includes higher levels of cognition.

After you have finished reading this chapter you should be able to answer the following questions:

1. What are the categories of reading comprehension as presented in this chapter?
2. What are some of the reading comprehension skills?
3. What is the "main idea of a paragraph"?
4. How do you find the main idea of a paragraph?
5. What is "inference"?
6. How do context clues help in getting word meanings?
7. What are "analogies"?
8. What do you need to know to complete analogy proportions?
9. Why do you have to set purposes for reading?
10. What is "skimming"?
11. Why is skill in vocabulary expansion important?
12. What is the place of the dictionary in vocabulary expansion?
13. Why would you help students to learn combining forms?
14. How does the definition of reading influence the reading diagnostic program?
15. What is an informal reading inventory?
16. How do you determine who is a disabled reader?

Reading Comprehension

Reading comprehension is a complex intellectual process involving a number of abilities. The two major abilities involve word meanings and reasoning with verbal concepts.

Various writers have suggested different lists of skills that they feel are basic to understanding. The skills usually listed are as follows:

1. The ability to associate meaning with the graphic symbol.
2. The ability to understand words in context and be able to select the meaning that fits the context.
3. The ability to read in thought units.
4. The ability to understand units of increasing size (the phrase, clause, sentence, paragraph, and whole selection).
5. The ability to acquire word meanings.
6. The ability to select and understand the main idea.
7. The ability to draw inferences.
8. The ability to evaluate what is read, that is, to recognize literary devices and to identify the tone, mood, and intent of the writer, and so on.[1]

Obviously, the presented skills are not all at the same level; for instance, it is certainly easier to state the meaning of a word than to evaluate a passage.

[1]Henry P. Smith and Emerald V. Dechant, *Psychology in Teaching Reading* (Englewood Cliffs, N.J.: Prentice-Hall, 1961), pp. 213–214.

Categorizing Reading Comprehension

Comprehension involves thinking. As there are various levels in the hierarchy of thinking, so are there various levels of comprehension. Higher levels of comprehension would obviously include higher levels of thinking. The following model adapted from Nila Banton Smith divides the comprehension skills into four categories.[2] Each category is cumulative in that each builds on the others. The four comprehension categories are: (1) literal comprehension, (2) interpretation, (3) critical reading, (4) creative reading.

Literal Comprehension Literal comprehension represents the ability to obtain a low-level type of understanding by using only information explicitly stated. This category requires a lower level of thinking skills than the other three levels. Answers to literal questions simply demand that the pupil recall from memory what the book says.

Interpretation Interpretation is the next step in the hierarchy. This category demands a higher level of thinking ability because the questions in the category of interpretation are concerned with answers that are not directly stated in the text but are suggested or implied. To answer questions at the interpretive level, readers must have problem-solving ability and be able to work at various levels of abstraction. Obviously, children who are slow learners will have difficulty working at this level as well as in the next two categories. (See Chapter 17.)

The interpretive level is the one at which the most confusion exists when it comes to categorizing skills. The confusion concerns the term *inference*. The definition of inference is: Something derived by reasoning; something that is not directly stated but suggested in the state-

ment; a logical conclusion that is drawn from statements; a deduction; an induction. From the definition we can see that inference is a broad reasoning skill and that there are many different kinds of inferences. All of the reading skills in interpretation rely on the reader's ability to "infer" the answer in one way or another. However, by grouping all the interpretive reading skills under inference, "some of the most distinctive and desirable skills would become smothered and obscured."[3]

Some of the reading skills that are usually found in interpretation are as follows:

> determining word meanings from context
> finding main ideas
> "reading between the lines" or drawing inferences[4]
> drawing conclusions
> making generalizations
> recognizing cause and effect reasoning
> recognizing analogies

Critical Reading Critical reading is at a higher level than the other two categories because it involves evaluation, the making of a personal judgment on the accuracy, value, and truthfulness of what is read. To be able to make judgments, a reader must be able to collect, interpret, apply, analyze, and synthesize the information. Critical reading includes such skills as the ability to differentiate between fact and opinion, the ability to differentiate between fantasy and reality, and the ability to discern propaganda techniques. Critical reading is related to critical listening because they both require critical thinking. (See "Critical Listening—An Important Auding Skill" in Chapter 5.)

Creative Reading Creative reading uses divergent thinking skills to go beyond the literal comprehension, interpretation, and critical-

---

[2]Nila Banton Smith, "The Many Faces of Reading Comprehension," *The Reading Teacher* 23 (December 1969): 249–259; 291.

[3]Ibid., pp. 255–256.

[4]Although, as already stated, all the interpretive skills depend on the ability of the reader to infer meanings, the specific skill of "reading between the lines" is the one that teachers usually refer to when they say they are teaching *inference*.

reading levels. In creative reading, the reader tries to come up with new or alternate solutions to those presented by the writer.

Helping Children Acquire Comprehension Skills

All children need help in developing higher level reading comprehension skills. If teachers persist in asking only literal-type comprehension questions that demand a simple convergent answer, higher level skills will not be developed.

Unfortunately, much of what goes on in school is at the literal comprehension level. Teachers usually ask questions that require a literal response and children that answer this type of question are generally looked upon as being excellent students. It is to be hoped that this will change now that many reading task forces across the country are emphasizing the teaching of higher level comprehension skills.

Rather than asking a question that would call for a literal response, the teacher must learn to construct questions that call for higher levels of thinking. This should begin as early as kindergarten and first grade. For example, the children are looking at a picture in which a few children are dressed in hats, snow pants, jackets, scarves, and so on. After asking the children what kind of clothes the children in the picture are wearing, the teacher should try to elicit from his or her students the answers to the following questions: "What kind of day do you think it is?" "What do you think the children are going to do?"

This type of inference question is at a very simple level because it is geared to the readiness and cognitive development level of the children. As the children progress to higher levels of thinking they should be confronted with more complex interpretation or inference problems. It is important that the teacher work with the children according to their individual readiness levels. The teacher should expect all of the chil-

dren to be able to perform, but should avoid putting them in situations which frustrate rather than stimulate them.

Critical reading skills are essential for good readers. Teachers can use primary graders' love of fairy tales to begin to develop some critical reading skills. For example, after the children have read "Little Red Riding Hood," the teacher can ask such questions:

1. Should Little Red Riding Hood have listened to her mother and not spoken to a stranger? Explain.
2. Would you help a stranger if your mother told you not to speak to a stranger? Explain.
3. Do you think a wolf can talk? Explain.
4. Do you think that this story is true? Explain.
5. Do you think Little Red Riding Hood is a good girl? Explain.

Creative reading questions are probably the most ignored by teachers. To help children in this area, teachers need to learn how to ask questions that require divergent rather than convergent answers. A teacher who focuses only on the author's meaning or intent and does not go beyond the text will not be encouraging creative reading. Some questions which should stimulate divergent thinking on the part of the reader would be the following:

1. After reading "Little Red Riding Hood," can you come up with another ending for the story?
2. After reading about John, can you come up with a plan for the kind of vacation he would like?
3. After reading the story about the cat that escaped from the well, can you come up with some ideas as to how he was able to escape?
4. Based on your reading about John and his family, what kind of trip would you plan to make them happy?

Divergent answers, of course, require more time than convergent answers. Also, there is no one correct answer.

Following is a short reading selection and examples of the four different types of meaning questions. These are being presented so that the teacher can have practice in recognizing the different types of questions at the four levels.

One day in the summer, some of my friends and I decided to go on an overnight hiking trip. We all started out fresh and full of energy. About halfway to our destination, when the sun was directly overhead, one-third of my friends decided to return home. The remaining four of us, however, continued on our hike. Our plan was to reach our destination by sunset. About six hours later as the four of us, exhausted and famished, were slowly edging ourselves in the direction of the setting sun, we saw a sight that astonished us. There, at the camping site, were our friends who had claimed that they were returning home. It seems that they did indeed go home, but only to pick up a car and drive out to the campsite.

The following are the four different types of meaning questions:

Literal comprehension: What season of the year was it in the story? What kind of trip were the persons going on?

Interpretation: What time of day was it when some of the people decided to return home? How many persons were there when they first started out on the trip? In what direction were the hikers heading when they saw a sight that astonished them? At what time did the sun set?

Critical reading: How do you think the hikers felt when they reached their destination? Do you feel that the persons who went home did the right thing by driving back to the site rather than hiking? Explain.

Creative reading: What do you think the exhausted hikers did and said when they saw the four who had supposedly gone home?

An Emphasis on Some Important Comprehension Skills

This section presents some comprehension skills that need special emphasis. Because of the ambiguity of language, the first portion of this section will deal with *homographs*. Unless teachers can help students discern that words have multiple meanings and help them to determine the correct meaning from the sentence context, students will not be able to read. Because *context clues* are a vital aid to comprehension, a brief discussion of some often used context clues is also being presented. *Finding the main idea of a paragraph* is the comprehension skill on which teachers probably spend the most time. It is also a skill that is many times taken for granted—it is assumed that pre-service teachers can find the main idea of a paragraph and that teachers can help their students do the same. This assumption is often not borne out. The last two portions of this section deal with *inference and analogies*, which are often neglected by teachers because of their own insecurities in these areas.

Determining Meanings of Homographs[5]

Because many words have more than one meaning, the meaning of the word is determined by how the word is used in a sentence. You must help students to be careful to use correctly those words with many meanings. In the following pairs of sentences, notice how the same italicized word conveys different meanings:

That is a large *stack* of books.
Stack the books here.

The *train* had a lot of passengers.
Do you *train* your own dog?

The dogs *bark* at night in my neighborhood.
The *bark* of the tree is peeling.

From these, you can see that the way the word is used in the sentence will determine its meaning. Words that are spelled the same but have different meanings are called *homographs*. Some homographs are spelled the same but do not sound the same. For example, *refuse* means "trash," but it also means "to decline to accept." In the first sentence, *refuse* (ref ′ • use)

[5]Dorothy Rubin, *The Vital Arts—Reading and Writing* (New York: Macmillan, 1979).

meaning "trash" is pronounced differently from *refuse* (re • fuse') meaning "to decline to accept" in the second sentence. In reading you can determine the meaning of *refuse* from the way it is used in the sentence (context clues). For example:

1. During the garbage strike there were tons of uncollected *refuse* on the streets of the city.
2. I *refuse* to go along with you.

(See Chapter 12 for a further discussion of homographs. See also Chapter 1.)

As already shown, readers should be able to grasp the meaning of homographs from the sentence context (the words surrounding a word that can shed light on its meaning). For example, note the many uses of *capital* in the following sentences.

That is a *capital* idea.
Remember to begin each sentence with a *capital* letter.
The killing of a policeman is a *capital* offense in some states.
Albany is the *capital* of New York State.
In order to start a business, you need *capital*.

Each of the preceding sentences illustrates one meaning for *capital*.

In sentence 1 *capital* means "excellent."
In sentence 2 *capital* means "referring to a letter in writing that is an uppercase letter."
In sentence 3 *capital* means "punishable by death."
In sentence 4 *capital* means "the seat of government."
In sentence 5 *capital* means "money or wealth."

The sample activity below challenges students to recognize that some words are spelled the same but have different meanings determined by their placement in a sentence.

Context Clues

Sentence context also helps readers figure out words that are not homographs. For example, in the following sentence see if you can figure out the meaning of *hippodrome:*[6]

[6]Dorothy Rubin, *Gaining Word Power* (New York: Macmillan, 1978).

EXAMPLES OF HOMOGRAPHS (USING SAME WORD WITH DIFFERENT MEANINGS)

Fill in the blanks in each of the following sentences with *one word* that will make sense in each place.

1. _____ your ticket to the man so that you can get into the _____.
2. Although he was usually a(n) _____ runner, he did not run _____ after his long _____, and he had difficulty keeping a(n) _____ grip on the rope.
3. The _____ wearing a(n) _____ said that he would _____ the valuables with his life.
4. The newspaper _____ mentioned how a(n) _____ supporting a building had broken and fallen on a(n) _____ of soldiers.

Answers: (1) show, (2) fast, (3) guard, (4) column.

SMIDGENS   by Bob Cordray

©1975 National News Syndicate

In ancient times the Greek people would assemble in their seats to observe the chariot races being held in the *hippodrome*.

From the context of the sentence, you should have realized that *hippodrome* refers to some arena (place) where races were held in ancient Greece.

Sometimes readers can actually gain the definition of the word from the sentence or following sentences. For example:

> The house had a cheerful atmosphere. At any moment I expected *blithe* spirits to make their entrance and dance with joy throughout the house.

From the sentences, readers can determine that *blithe* refers to something joyful, gay, or merry.

Alert readers can also use contrasts or comparisons to gain clues to meanings of words. For example, try to determine the meaning of *ethereal* in the following sentence:

> He was impressed by the *ethereal* grace of Jane's walk rather than Ellen's heavy-footed one.

If you guessed *"light and airy"* for the meaning of *ethereal*, you were correct. You know that *ethereal* is somehow the opposite of *heavy*. This is an example of contrasts.

In the next example, see how comparisons can help you:

> Maria was as *fickle* as a politician's promises before election.

In this sentence *fickle* means "not firm in opinion" or "wavering." Because politicians try to court all their constituents (voters) before an election, they often are not firm in their opinions, make many promises, and are wavering. By understanding the comparison, readers can get an idea of the meaning of *fickle*.

Good readers use all these clues to help them to determine word meanings.

Finding the Main Idea of a Paragraph[7]

In reading and writing, finding the main idea is very useful. In reading, the main idea helps you to remember and understand what you have read. In writing, the main idea gives unity and order to your paragraph.

The main idea of a paragraph is the central thought of the paragraph. It is what the paragraph is about. Without a main idea, the paragraph would just be a confusion of sentences. All the sentences in the paragraph should develop the main idea.

To find the main idea of a paragraph, you must find what common element the sentences share. Some textbook writers place the main idea at the beginning of a paragraph and may actually put the topic of the paragraph in bold print in order to emphasize it. However, in literature this is not a common practice. In some paragraphs the main idea is not directly stated but implied. That is, the main idea is indirectly stated, and you have to find it from the clues given by the author.

[7]Rubin, *The Vital Arts—Reading and Writing*.

Although there is no foolproof method for finding the main idea, there is a widely used procedure that has proved to be helpful. In order to use this procedure you should know that a paragraph is always written about something or someone. The something or someone is the topic of the paragraph. The writer is interested in telling his or her readers something about the topic of the paragraph. To find the main idea of a paragraph, you must determine what the topic of the paragraph is and what the author is trying to say about the topic that is special or unique. Once you have found these two things, you should have the main idea. This procedure is useful in finding the main idea of various types of paragraphs.

Reread the preceding paragraph and state its main idea. *Answer:* A procedure helpful in finding the main idea of a paragraph is described.

Now read the following passage from "Fight Fat with Behavior Control" by Michael J. Mahoney and Kathryn Mahoney, in *Psychology Today* (May 1976). After you have read the passage, choose the statement that *best* states the main idea.

In our society, food is often connected with recreation. We go out for coffee, invite friends over for drinks, celebrate special occasions with cakes or big meals. We can't think of baseball without thinking of hot dogs and beer, and eating is so often an accompaniment to watching TV that we talk of TV snacks and TV dinners. Just as Pavlov's dogs learned to salivate at the sound of a bell, the activities we associate with food can become signals to eat. Watching TV becomes a signal for potato chips; talking with friends becomes a signal for coffee and doughnuts; nodding over a book tells us it's time for pie and milk.

1. Watching TV signals a need for food.
2. All persons connect food with recreation.
3. Eating is a social activity.
4. Recreation, in our society, often serves as a signal for food.
5. In all societies food is often connected with recreation.

The answer is statement 4. Statement 1 is a fact in the paragraph but it is too specific to be the main idea. Statement 2 is too general. The paragraph is not discussing all persons. Statement 3 can be inferred from the paragraph, but it is not the main idea of the paragraph. Statement 5 is too general. Statement 4 is what the paragraph is about. The sentences in the paragraph elaborate this idea by giving examples of various recreations that are connected or associated with food.

SPECIAL NOTE: The main idea is a general statement of the content of the paragraph. You must be careful, however, that your main idea statement is not so general that it goes beyond the information that is directly or indirectly given in the paragraph.

Drawing Inferences[8]

Many times writers do not directly state what they mean but present ideas in a more indirect, roundabout way. That is why inference is called the ability to "read between the lines." *Inference* is defined as *understanding that is not derived from a direct statement but from an indirect suggestion in what is stated*. Readers draw inferences from writings; authors make implications or imply meanings.

The ability to draw inferences is especially important in reading fiction, but it is necessary for nonfiction, also. Authors rely on inferences to make their stories more interesting and enjoyable. Mystery writers find inference essential to the maintenance of suspense in their stories. For example, Sherlock Holmes and Perry Mason mysteries are based on the ability of the characters to uncover evidence in the form of clues that are not obvious to others around them.

Inference is an important process that authors rely on. Good readers must be alert to the ways that authors encourage inference.

[8]Ibid.

©1956 United Features Syndicate, Inc.

Implied Statements   As has been said already, writers count on inference to make their writing more interesting and enjoyable. Rather than directly stating something, they present it indirectly. To understand the writing, the reader must be alert and be able to detect the clues that the author gives. For example, in the sentence *Things are always popping and alive when the twins, Herb and Jack, are around,* you are given some clues to Herb's and Jack's personalities, even though the author has not directly said anything about their personalities. From the statement you could make the inference that the twins are lively and lots of fun to be around.

You must be *careful,* however, that you *do not read more* into some statements than is intended. For example, read the following statements and put a circle around the correct answer. *Example:* Mary got out of bed and looked out of the window. She saw that the ground had some white on it. What season of the year was it? (a) winter, (b) summer, (c) spring, (d) fall, (e) can't tell.

The answer is "(e) can't tell." Many persons choose "(a) winter" for the answer. However, the answer is (e) because the "something white" could be anything; there isn't enough evidence to choose (a). Even if the something white was snow, in some parts of the world, including the United States, it can snow in the spring or fall.

Good readers, while reading, try to gather clues to draw inferences about what they read. Although effective readers do this, they are not usually aware of it. As Sherlock Holmes says in *A Study in Scarlet,* "From long habit the train of thought ran so swiftly through my mind that

I arrived at the conclusions without being conscious of intermediate steps."

Recognizing Analogies[9]

Analogies are relationships between words or ideas. In order to make the best use of analogies, or to supply the missing term in an analogy proportion, you must know not only the *meanings* of the words but also the relationship of the words or ideas to one another. For example, "*doctor* is to *hospital* as *minister* is to _____." The answer is, of course, *church.* The relationship has to do with specialized persons and the places with which they are associated. Another example one could try would be: "*beautiful* is to *pretty* as _____ is to *decimate.*" Although you know the meanings of *beautiful* and *pretty* and you can figure out that beautiful is more than pretty, you will not be able to arrive at the correct word to complete the analogy if you do not know the meaning of *decimate. Decimate* means "to reduce by one-tenth" or "to destroy a considerable part of." Because the word that completes the analogy must express the relationship of more or greater than, the answer could be *eradicate* or *annihilate,* because these words mean "to destroy completely."

Some of the relationships that words may have to one another are similar meanings, opposite meanings, classification, going from particular to general, going from general to particular, degree of intensity, specialized labels, characteristics, cause-effect, effect-cause, func-

[9]Rubin, *Gaining Word Power.*

tion, whole-part, ratio, and many more. The preceding relationships do not have to be memorized. You will gain clues to these from the pairs making up the analogies; that is, the words express the relationship. For example: *"pretty* is to *beautiful"*—the relationship is degree of intensity; *"hot* is to *cold"*—the relationship is one of opposites; *"car* is to *vehicle"*—the relationship is classification. The following is an analogy activity.

Find the relationship between a pair of words and then complete each analogy with the *best* word. There are more words given in the word list than you need.

Word List: sun, moon, light, cold, kilometer, pour, year, rate, ship, day, compass, rain, cards, blizzard, doe, time, era, kind, drove, dame, ram, century, place, ewe, love, cub, binary, meter, ecstasy, chirp, moo, friend, hate, millimeter.

1. *Happy* is to *sad* as *night* is to _____.
2. *Rain* is to *downpour* as *snow* is to _____.
3. *Horse* is to *mare* as *deer* is to _____.
4. *Chicken* is to *rooster* as *sheep* is to _____.
5. *Sad* is to *miserable* as *joy* is to _____.
6. *One* is to *thousand* as *meter* is to _____.
7. *Hint* is to *disclose* as *drip* is to _____.
8. *Distance* is to *odometer* as *direction* is to

_____.

Answers: (1) day, (2) blizzard, (3) doe, (4) ram, (5) ecstasy, (6) kilometer, (7) pour, (8) compass.

Reading for Different Purposes: An Emphasis on Skimming[10]

Setting purposes for reading is a crucial factor in reading. Students need to learn that they read for different purposes. If they are reading for pleasure, they may either read quickly or slowly based on the way they feel. If they are studying or reading information that is new to them, they

[10]Dorothy Rubin, *Reading and Learning Power* (New York: Macmillan, 1980).

will probably read very slowly. If, however, they are looking up a telephone number, a name, a date, or looking over a paragraph for its topic, they will read much more rapidly. Reading rapidly to find or locate information is called *skimming*. All skimming involves fast reading; however, there are different kinds of skimming. Skimming for a number, a date, or name can usually be done much more quickly than skimming for the topic of a paragraph or to answer specific questions. (Some persons call the most rapid reading *scanning* and the less rapid reading skimming.) Teachers should help students recognize that they read rapidly to locate some specific information, but that once they have located what they want, they may read the surrounding information more slowly.

Skimming is an important skill because it is used so often throughout one's life, and it is many times the only way to get a job done in a reasonable amount of time. Some skimming activities for upper-intermediate-grade level students follow:

1. Skim newspaper headlines for a particular news item.
2. Skim movie ads for a particular movie.
3. Skim tape or record catalogs for a specific title.
4. Skim the yellow pages of the phone book for some help.
5. Skim the television guide to find a particular show.

Vocabulary Expansion

Good vocabulary and good reading go hand in hand. Unless readers know the meanings of words, they will have difficulty in understanding what they are reading. It should be stressed that just knowing the meanings of the words will not ensure that individuals will be able to state the meanings of sentences, nor does knowing the meanings of sentences assure that readers can give the meanings of whole paragraphs, and so forth. However, by not knowing the meanings

figure 8.1 *An illustration of interrelationships among language, concepts, and cognitive development. Since Punkin Head did not know what a hare or tortoise is, he could not understand the story told to him by Tiger. Punkin Head must be able to differentiate these animals from others which may have some similar characteristics. At a higher cognitive level, he must also be able to conceptualize why the tortoise beat the hare in the race, and thereby comprehend the meaning of the adage: "Slow and steady wins the race."*

of the words, the individual's chances of being able to read well are considerably lessened. Without an understanding of words, comprehension is impossible.

As children advance in concept development, their vocabulary development must also advance because the two are interrelated. (See Chapter 3.) Children deficient in vocabulary will usually be deficient in concept development. Studies have shown that "vocabulary is a key variable in reading comprehension and is a major feature of most tests of academic aptitude. . . ."[11]

Most teachers are aware of the importance of building sight vocabulary, and word attack skills are a large part of the beginning reading

[11]Walter M. MacGinitie, "Language Development," in *Encyclopedia of Educational Research*, 4th ed. (London: Collier-Macmillan Ltd., 1969), p. 693.

program. (See Chapter 7.) However, the vocabulary development which concerns the building of a larger meaning vocabulary is often neglected. (See also Chapter 3 and "Determining Meanings of Homographs" in this chapter.)

Primary-Grade Children

The development of vocabulary is too important to the success of a child in school to be left to chance. Teachers should, therefore, provide a planned vocabulary expansion program for children when they first enter school.

For a vocabulary program to be successful, the teacher must recognize that individual differences exist between the amount and kind of words that kindergarten and first-grade children have in their listening capacity (ability to understand a word when it is spoken). Some children come to school with a rich and varied vocabulary, whereas others have a more limited and narrow vocabulary. Some children may come to school with a rich and varied vocabulary that can be used with their peers and at home, but it may not be one that is very useful to them in school. For example, some children may possess a large lexicon of street vocabulary and expressions, and some others may speak an English dialect that contains its own special expressions and vocabulary.

Teachers should recognize also that young children's listening vocabulary is larger than their speaking vocabulary and obviously larger than their reading and writing vocabulary. All four areas of vocabulary need to be developed. However, since children first learn language through the aural–oral approach, the teacher should begin with these areas first.

Reading literature aloud to children is a viable means of increasing vocabulary and reading achievement.[12] (See the section on "Nonstandard English and Its Implications for Instruction" in Chapter 5.) The teacher should choose books that appeal to children. The authors of these books must be aware of what is important to a child and what is likely to be confusing so that they can build meaning out of words through the kind of imagery that makes sense to a child. For example, in *Mike Mulligan and His Steam Shovel*, the meaning of *steam shovel* is clarified by giving numerous examples in which a steam-shovel is used. In Margaret Wise Brown's book *The Dead Bird*, the meaning of *dead* is given by a description of the bird's state.[13]

Vocabulary of the Senses All children enjoy words that appeal to the senses. Young children especially enjoy the words that they can

almost taste and feel when they say them because of their sounds. As preschoolers they savored many words by repeating them very slowly over and over again; the sounds of the words were fun to say. Now, as primary-grade students, teachers can take advantage of children's delight in words that appeal to the senses by helping them develop a vocabulary of senses. (See Chapter 11 for "Poetry of the Senses" and Chapter 5 for "Listening for Appreciation.")

A technique a teacher can use is to ask children to give a word for various animal sounds. For example, a cow "moos," a cat "meows," a dog "barks" or "bays," a sheep "baas," a chick "peeps," and a bull "bellows." Then a word can be given for the sounds of nature. For example, the wind "howls," the brook "babbles," the trees "rustle," and so on. This technique can be continued for the sense of sight, of touch, and so on.

Vocabulary Consciousness In the primary grades children are beginning to meet words that are spelled the same but which have different meanings, based on their context in the sentence. Pupils learn that the word *saw* in "I saw Jane" does not carry the same meaning as in "Dick will help Father saw the tree." When primary graders recognize that "saw," "train," "coat," and many other words have different meanings based on surrounding words, they are beginning to build a vocabulary consciousness. This consciousness grows when children begin asking about and looking up the meanings of new words they come across in their everyday activities.

Teachers ought to challenge primary-grade level children's budding vocabulary consciousness in enjoyable ways. One way to do this is to use word riddles or fun-with-word activities. Examples:

1. From a six-letter word for what you put on bread, remove two letters to get what a goat does with his horns.

---

[12]Dorothy H. Cohen, "The Effect of Literature on Vocabulary and Reading Achievement," *Elementary English* 45 (February 1968): 209–213; 217.

[13]*See* Dorothy H. Cohen, "Word Meaning and the Literary Experience in Early Childhood," *Elementary English* 46 (November 1969): 914–925, for a listing of books and examples.

2. To a four-letter word for something liquid that falls from the sky, add two letters to make a kind of damage you can do by twisting a part of the body.

3. From a five-letter word for an animal with a shell, take one letter away to make a word for something that holds things together.

4. The plural of an insect, when you add a letter to it, becomes something you wear.

Answers for *Fun With Words:* (1) butter, butt (2) rain, sprain (3) snail, nail (4) ants, pants

Intermediate-Grade Children

As students become more advanced in reading, more words which previously only had one meaning are being met in new and strange situations. In the intermediate grades, students should be guided to a mastery of vocabulary. If they are fascinated with words, they generally want to know the longest word in the dictionary, and many enjoy pronouncing funny or nonsense-sounding words such as "supercalifragilisticexpialidocious." These students should be helped to:

1. Become aware of words they do not know.

2. Try to guess the meaning from the context and their knowledge of word parts.

3. Learn the most used combining forms.

4. Jot down words that they do not know, and look them up in the dictionary later.

5. Keep a notebook and write down the words they have missed in their vocabulary exercises, giving them additional study. Learn to break words down into word parts in order to learn their meaning.

6. Maintain interest in wanting to expand vocabulary.

Defining Word Part Terms

In order to help students to use word parts as an aid to increasing vocabulary, some terms should be defined. There are a great number of words in our language which combine with other words to form new words, for example,

"grandfather" and "policeman" (compound words). You may also combine a root (base) word with a letter or a group of letters either at the beginning (prefix) or end (suffix) of the root word, to form a new, related word; for example, "replay" and "played." "Affix" is a term used to refer either to a prefix or a suffix.

In the words replay and played, "play" is a root or base, *re* is a prefix, and *ed* is a suffix. A *root* is the smallest unit of a word that can exist and retain its basic meaning. It cannot be subdivided any further. Replay is not a root word because it can be subdivided to play. Play is a root word because it cannot be divided further and still retain a meaning related to the root word.

Derivatives are combinations of root words with either prefixes or suffixes or both. *Combining forms* are usually defined as roots borrowed from another language that join together or that join with a prefix, a suffix, or both a prefix and a suffix to form a word. Many times the English combining form elements are derived from Greek and Latin roots. In some vocabulary books, in which the major emphasis is on vocabulary expansion rather than on the naming of word parts, *combining forms* are defined in a more general sense to include any word part that can join with another word or word part to form a word or a new word.

Vocabulary Expansion Instruction

Vocabulary expansion instruction depends on the ability levels of students, their past experiences, and their interests. If they are curious about sea life and have an aquarium in the classroom, this could stimulate interest in such combining forms as "aqua," meaning water, and "mare" meaning sea. The combining form "aqua" could generate such terms as aquaplane, aqueduct, and aquanaut. Since "mare" means "sea," students could be given the term "aquamarine" to define. Knowing the combining forms "aqua" and "mare," many will probably respond with "sea water." The English term actually means bluish-green. The students can be challenged as to why the English definition of aquamarine is bluish-green.

A terrarium can stimulate discussion of words made up of the combining form "terra."

When discussing the prefix *bi*, children should be encouraged to generate other words that also contain *bi*, such as bicycle, binary, bilateral, and so on. Other suggestions follow.[14]

Write the words "biped" and "quadruped" in a column on the board, along with their meanings. These words should elicit guesses for groups of animals. The teacher could ask such questions as: "What do you think an animal that has eight arms or legs would be called?" "What about an animal with six feet?" And so on. When the animals are listed on the board, the children can be asked to look them up in the dictionary so that they can classify them.

The students can also try to discover the combining forms of the Roman calendar.

Martinus	Sextiles
Aprilis	September
Mais	October
Junios	November
Quintilis	December

Students should discover that the last six months were named for the positions they occupy.

Another set of words made from combining forms describing many-sided geometric figures (polygons) are:

3 sides	trigon
4 sides	tetrahedron
5 sides	pentagon
6 sides	hexagon
7 sides	septagon
8 sides	octagon

When presenting the combining forms *cardio*, *tele*, *graph*, and *gram*, place the following vocabulary words on the board:

cardiograph	telegraph
cardiogram	telegram

After students know that *cardio* means heart and *tele* means from a distance, ask them to try to determine the meaning of *graph*, as used in cardiograph and telegraph. Have them try to figure out the meaning of *gram*, as used in telegram and cardiogram. Once students are able to define *graph* as an instrument or machine, and *gram* as message, they will hardly ever confuse a cardiograph with a cardiogram.

When students are exposed to such activities, they become more sensitive to their language. They come to realize that words are man-made, that language is living and changing, and that as people develop new concepts they need new words to identify them. The words "astronaut" and "aquanaut" are good examples of words which came into being because of space and undersea exploration.

Children come to see the power of combining forms when they realize that by knowing a few combining forms they can unlock the meanings of many words. For example, by knowing a few combining forms, students can define correctly many terms used in the metric system, as well as other words. (See "The Place of Morphology in the Classroom" in Chapter 14.)

deca:	ten
deci:	tenth
cent, centi:	hundred, hundredth
milli:	thousand, thousandth
decameter:	ten meters
decimeter:	1/10 meter
centimeter:	1/100 meter
millimeter:	1/1000 meter
decade:	period of ten years

[14]*See* Loraine Dun, "Increase Vocabulary with the Word Elements, Mono through Deca," *Elementary English* 47 (January 1970): 49–55.

century: period of one hundred years
centennial one hundredth year anniversary
millennium: period of 1000 years.
(*Centi, milli, deci* are usually used to designate "part of.")

Vocabulary Expansion Instruction for Special Students

Working with upper-elementary-grade students who are especially weak in vocabulary requires a relatively structured approach, one that emphasizes the systematic presentation of material at graduated levels of difficulty in ways somewhat similar to those used in the teaching of English as a second language. Each day roots, combining forms, prefixes, and suffixes should be presented with a list of words made up from these word parts. Emphasis is placed on the meanings of the word parts and their combinations into words rather than on the naming of the word parts. For example, *bi* and *ped* are pronounced and put on the chalkboard. Their meanings are given. When "biped" is put on the board, the students are asked by the teacher if they can state its meaning.

The terms presented for study should be those which students will hear in school, on television, or on radio, as well as those they will meet in their reading. The word parts should be presented in an interesting manner, and those that combine to form a number of words should be given. When students see that they are meeting these words in their reading, they will be greatly reinforced in their learning.

To provide continuous reinforcement, daily "nonthreatening" quizzes on the previous days' words may be given. Students should receive the results of such quizzes immediately, so that any faulty concepts may be quickly corrected. The number of words that are presented would depend on individual students.

The possibilities for vocabulary experiences in the classroom are unlimited. Teachers must have the prefixes, suffixes, and combining forms at their fingertips in order to take advantage of the opportunities that present themselves daily. See segment on morphology in the classroom in (Chapter 14 on grammar.)

Sample exercises which teachers should find helpful for stimulating interest in learning new words through combining forms are on page 166.

The Dictionary as a Tool in Vocabulary Expansion

Although children use picture dictionaries in the primary grades more as an aid to writing than in vocabulary expansion, if young readers discover the wonders of the dictionary they can enrich their vocabulary. Primary-grade picture dictionaries consist of words that are generally in the children's listening, speaking, and reading vocabularies. They consist of alphabetized lists of words with pictures and can serve as the children's first reference tool, helping them to unlock words on their own and making them more independent and self-reliant. The children can also learn multiple meanings from a picture dictionary, when they see the word "saw" presented with two pictures which represent a tool and the act of seeing.

In the intermediate grades dictionaries serve more varied purposes and there is emphasis on vocabulary expansion. Children delight in learning new words. If properly encouraged by the teacher, vocabulary expansion can become an exciting hunting expedition, where the unexplored terrain is the vast territory of words.

At any grade level teachers can show by their actions that they value the dictionary as an important tool. If a word seems to need clarification, students should be asked to look it up in the dictionary. Although at times it may seem more expedient to simply supply the meaning, students should be encouraged to look it up for themselves. If pupils discover the meaning of

---

Exercise I

Master some useful combining forms. From the words on each line, figure out the meaning of the combining form(s). Write the meaning. Think of other words with the same combining form:

1. *geo:* geography, geometry, geocentric
2. *anni, annu, enni:* annual, biannual, biennial, anniversary
3. *bio:* biology, biography
4. *auto:* autograph, autobiography
5. *cent, centi:* century, bicentennial, centennial

Answers: (1) earth, (2) year, (3) life, (4) self, (5) hundred, hundredth part of.

Exercise II

Match the meaning in Column One to the combining form in Column Two:

Column One	Column Two
1. earth	a. *auto*
2. year	b. *cent*
3. life	c. *geo*
4. self	d. *bio*
5. hundred	e. *anni*

Answers: (1) c, (2) e, (3) d, (4) a, (5) b.

---

the word on their own, they will be more apt to remember it.

In order to build a larger meaning vocabulary the teacher could use a number of motivating techniques to stimulate vocabulary expansion. Pupils can be encouraged to keep a paper bag attached to their desks in which they put index cards with words on one side and the meanings of the words they have looked up on the other. Sometime during the day students can be encouraged to challenge one another, with one student calling out the meanings of a word and another student supplying the word. This technique should make the dictionary one of the students' most treasured possessions.

A most ingenious technique used by two teachers to stimulate interest in the dictionary involved the "Land of Dictionopolis."[15] Students as citizens of Dictionopolis have a responsibility for learning a number of new words from a variety of areas. The classroom is set up with five booths, which are operated on a rotating basis by students in the classroom. They may choose any three words from any of the five booths. Once words are chosen, they are the pupils' on loan, and they each must take a contract on their word. It is now no longer available to any other

[15]Joan Joy and Marilyn Potter, "Dictionopolis," *Elementary English* 41 (April 1964): 351–361.

pupil. At the end of the week the children must fulfill their contract. If they are successful, the word becomes theirs. If not, the word must be returned to the booth. A more extensive discussion of the dictionary is presented in Chapter 12.

Diagnosis and the Definition of Reading

The definition that is chosen for reading also influences the diagnostic program. If we are looking upon reading as a total integrative process, then diagnosis should also be looked upon as a total integrative process. If a global definition is chosen, then the diagnostic program will be a broad one. (See Chapter 7.) Under a global definition, when one does diagnosis, it is recognized that a reading problem is due to many different causes. Therefore, a diagnosis of a reading problem would include considerations of ecological (environmental), personal, and intellectual factors. Educative factors, as well as noneducative factors, are scrutinized. It is recognized that learning takes place in some kind of relationship, that is, not all children respond in the same way, and not all children respond to the same person. An atmosphere conducive to growth is recognized as important, as well as the maxim that success breeds success. Diagnosis is looked upon as continuous, as underlying prevention as well as remediation, and as interwoven with instruction. The emphasis in diagnosis is on determining the child's reading problems, the conditions causing them, and the methods used to overcome the difficulties. (See the section on "Diagnosis" in Chapter 19.)

The Role of the Teacher in Diagnosis

The role of teachers in a total integrative diagnostic reading program is broad. The teacher must observe individual children, understand individual differences, build readiness for reading, and combine diagnosis with teaching.

Teachers must have knowledge of the various word recognition and comprehension skills at their fingertips and be able to teach these effectively. They must know the techniques of observation and be aware of the factors that influence children's reading behavior. Teachers must be able to administer and interpret such diagnostic techniques as the informal reading inventory and word analysis tests. If teachers cannot construct their own informal diagnostic tests, they should be aware of those that are commercially available. (See next section and bibliography.) Obviously, teachers in a total integrative reading program must be well prepared and well informed.

The Informal Reading Inventory

An informal reading inventory (IRI) is probably one of the most valuable aids to classroom teachers in helping them determine a student's reading problem(s). Elementary classroom teachers usually give an informal reading inventory to individual children who score one or two years below their ability level on a standardized reading test or to children who seem to be having a reading problem, even though they have scored well on a standardized reading achievement test. Although it would be desirable to give each child in the class an informal reading inventory, it just is not possible because of time constraints since an IRI is administered individually.

An IRI usually consists of oral and silent reading passages culled from basal readers from the preprimer to the sixth- or eighth-grade levels. Usually each selection has the following kinds of comprehension questions: factual, inferential, evaluative, and word meanings.

Graded word lists, which are also taken from basal readers and usually consist of twenty-five words from each reading level, are used to determine at what grade level the students should begin reading the oral passages. The students usually begin the word list at two levels below their grade level. The highest grade level at which the children have no errors on the graded word list is the grade level at which they begin reading the oral passage. The children read aloud the oral passage and the teacher records any omission, substitution, insertion, pronunciation, repetition, and hesitation errors. If the children read the oral passage at the independent or instructional level, the children are asked the comprehension questions; they then proceed to reading the silent passage at the same grade level and are asked the questions to the silent passage. The students then go to the next reading grade level, continuing until they reach their frustration levels. (The teacher is interested in finding the students' independent and instructional levels, but this usually cannot be done until the students reach their frustration levels.) If the children make so many word recognition errors in oral reading that they are reading at or close to their frustration level, the teacher reads the passage aloud to the students to determine their comprehension ability. This is called a listening capacity test. (Note: The term "informal" implies that the inventory is teacher-made; however, most IRIs are commercially produced. For more information on IRIs and on how to construct one, see the bibliography.)

The chart below shows the Betts Reading Levels and the percentages for determining them. Although other percentages for the reading levels exist, the Betts Reading Levels are the most frequently used.

Who Is a Disabled Reader?

It is not inconceivable to have a sixth-grade class with a span of reading levels ranging from first grade to eighth grade or above (See Chapter 17.) The teacher in such a class must determine who the disabled readers are. Not all students working below grade level are underachievers. A child reading at a third-grade level in a sixth-grade class may be reading at his or her ability level, whereas another child may not be. Similarly, children reading at their grade levels may be reading far below their ability

Betts Reading Levels

Independent Level	Children read on their own without any difficulty.	Word Recognition—99% or above Comprehension—90% or above
Instructional Level	Teaching level.	Word Recognition—95% or above Comprehension—75% or above
Frustration Level	This level is to be avoided. It is the lowest level of readability.	Word Recognition—90% or less Comprehension—50% or less
Listening Capacity Level*	Highest level at which a pupil can comprehend when someone reads to him or her. (Teacher reads to child if he or she has many word recognition errors to determine comprehension level.)	Comprehension—75%

A difficulty with the comprehension component of most informal reading inventories is that all comprehension questions regardless of difficulty are usually equally valued. Also, the types of comprehension questions may vary from one informal reading inventory to another. Another difficulty exists with the subjectivity involved in the scoring of the IRI. For example, it is not clear whether a student with a score of 65 percent in comprehension should be at the instructional or frustration level. The teacher must determine whether or not to continue testing the child.

*Betts uses the term Capacity Level to designate this level.

levels. A teacher may be pleased that a pupil is working on grade level, but gifted children working on grade level are *not* working up to their ability levels. A gifted child working on grade level is "underachieving." However, a child with a 70 IQ in the third grade working at the second-grade level would be achieving at his or her expectancy level. The expectancy scores presented in the following table are "idealized" ones, that is, there are many other variables that affect ability to read than just the mental age of an individual. (See Chapter 2.) Usually a child with a 70 IQ on an individual IQ test would be working more than one year below grade level. Since a child with a 70 IQ would usually not be able to work in the abstract, that child would have difficulty in doing reading skills involving inference, analogies, and so on.

Reading expectancy formulas help teachers to determine who needs special help. A child's reading expectancy yielded by a reading expectancy formula is compared to his or her reading achievement level yielded by a reading achievement test score. If the child's expectancy level is significantly higher than his or her reading achievement score, further diagnosis should be undertaken. (See "Assessment as Diagnostic" in Chapter 19.)

Summary

Chapter 8 has presented selected topics in the area of comprehension, vocabulary expansion, and diagnosis that are important for the language arts teacher. Reading comprehension was categorized into a hierarchy of four levels: literal comprehension, interpretation, critical reading, and creative reading. After a discussion of each category, suggestions were presented on how to help children acquire comprehension skills in each category. Special emphasis was then given to the following comprehension skills: determining meanings of homographs, using context clues, finding the main idea of a paragraph, drawing inferences, and recognizing analogies. Since individuals read at different rates based on different purposes, and since skimming, which is rapid reading for finding some specific information, is one of the most frequently engaged in reading activites, a section on skimming was presented. Techniques and activities for providing a vocabulary expansion program for students were presented.

The definition of reading was shown to influence the reading diagnostic program; a global definition requires a total integrative diagnostic program, and teachers in a total integrative pro-

Bond and Tinker Formula for Estimating Reading Expectancy*

Years in School times $\dfrac{IQ}{100}$ plus 1			Expected Reading Achievement at End of School Year
(1 x .70) + 1	=	1.7	at end of 1st grade
(2 x .70) + 1	=	2.4	at end of 2nd grade
(3 x .70) + 1	=	3.1	at end of 3rd grade
(4 x .70) + 1	=	3.8	at end of 4th grade
(5 x .70) + 1	=	4.5	at end of 5th grade
(6 x .70) + 1	=	5.2	at end of 6th grade
(1 x 1.20) + 1	=	2.2	at end of 1st grade
(2 x 1.20) + 1	=	3.4	at end of 2nd grade
(3 x 1.20) + 1	=	4.6	at end of 3rd grade
(4 x 1.20) + 1	=	5.8	at end of 4th grade
(5 x 1.20) + 1	=	7.0	at end of 5th grade
(6 x 1.20) + 1	=	8.2	at end of 6th grade

*The Bond and Tinker formula beings at grade one; that is, at the end of grade one the child is considered to have been in school one year.

Student's Name:
Grade:
Teacher:

Diagnostic Checklist for Selected Reading Comprehension Skills

	Yes	No
1. The student is able to state the meaning of a word in context.		
2. The student is able to give the meaning of a phrase or a clause in a sentence.		
3. The student is able to give variations of meanings for homographs (words spelled the same but with more than one meaning, for example, train, mean, saw, sole, and so on).		
4. The student is able to give the meaning of a sentence in a paragraph.		
5. The student is able to recall information that is explicitly stated in the passage. (literal-type questions)		
6. The student is able to state the main idea of a paragraph.		
7. The student is able to state details to support the main idea of a paragraph.		
8. The student is able to summarize a paragraph.		
9. The student is able to answer a question that requires "reading between the lines."		
10. The student is able to draw a conclusion from what is read.		
11. The student can complete analogy proportions.		
12. The student can hypothesize the author's purpose for writing the selection.		
13. The student can differentiate between fact and opinion.		
14. The student can differentiate between fantasy and reality.		
15. The student can detect bias in a story.		
16. The student can detect various propaganda tactics that are used in a story.		
17. The student can go beyond the text to come up with alternate solutions or ways to end a story or solve a problem in the selection.		
18. The student shows that he or she enjoys reading by voluntarily choosing to read.		

Diagnostic Checklist for Oral and Silent Reading

Oral Reading	Yes	No	Specific Errors

1. Word recognition errors.
   The teacher listens to the child while he or
   she is reading orally and records whether the
   child makes any of the following errors:

   a. omissions
   b. insertions
   c. substitutions
   d. repetitions
   e. hesitations
   f. mispronunciations.

2. Manner of reading.
   The teacher observes the child while he or
   she is reading aloud and records whether the
   child exhibits any of the following behaviors:

   a. word-by-word phrasing
   b. finger-pointing
   c. head movement
   d. fidgeting
   e. voice characteristics
      high-pitched
      loud
      soft
      monotonous
   f. other

3. Comprehension.
   (*See* Comprehension Diagnostic Checklist.)

Silent Reading	Yes	No

1. Comprehension.
   (*See* Comprehension Diagnostic Checklist.)

2. Manner of reading.
   The teacher observes the child while he or
   she is reading silently and records whether
   the child exhibits any of the following behaviors:

   a. lip movement
   b. reads aloud
   c. head movement
   d. continually looks up
   e. finger-pointing
   f. other.

gram must be highly knowledgeable ones with skills and techniques at their fingertips. A diagnostic checklist for "Selected Reading Comprehension Skills" and a diagnostic checklist for "Oral and Silent Reading" were also presented.

Now that you have read Chapter 8, you should have mastered the teacher competencies for reading presented at the beginning of the chapter.

Two examples of reading lesson plans follow. Using them as a guide, see if you can construct a third one.

LESSON PLAN I—PRIMARY GRADES

Behavioral Objectives

1. The children, having read a number of fairy tales, will be able to determine whether the tales are based on reality or fantasy.
2. The children will be able to create statements based on reality and statements based on fantasy.

Preliminary Preparation

Picture scenes from a number of fairy tales, such as "Cinderella," "Goldilocks and the Three Bears," "Sleeping Beauty," and "Rumpelstiltskin," should be available.

Introduction

"We've been reading a number of fairy tales. Who can name some?" "Good." "Yes, that's another one." "Yes, 'Cinderella,' 'Hansel and Gretel,' 'Sleeping Beauty,' and 'Jack and the Beanstalk' are others." "What's the name of the one we've just finished reading?" "Good, 'Goldilocks and the Three Bears.' " "Let's look at some pictures I have. Who can tell me what they show?" "Yes, the first picture shows Cinderella's coach turning back into a pumpkin." "Good, the second picture shows Rumpelstiltskin spinning straw into gold." "Yes, the third picture shows the prince awakening Sleeping Beauty, who has been asleep for one hundred years."

"Today we're going to discuss something that all these pictures have in common."

Development

"I know many of you watch television. What are some of the shows you've seen lately?" After children name a number of shows, the teacher asks whether they think it is really possible for Wonder Woman to do the things she does. Also, the teacher asks the children whether they think Superman can really fly. "What do many of the shows that portray animals talking, persons flying, or persons changing into different forms or shapes have in common with the fairy tales we've been reading? Let's look again at the pictures I brought in. If I told you that I had a spinning wheel that could change straw into gold, would you believe me?" "No, of course not." "If I told you that I knew someone who had been asleep for one hundred years, and that the kiss of a handsome young man had awakened her, would you believe me? If I told you that I knew a charming little house in which three bears lived and that the three bears slept in beds and lived just like we do, would you believe me?" "No, of course not." "Can someone tell me what all these pictures have that is the same?" "Yes, that is very good. None of them could really happen. What about many of the cartoon shows that we watch on television and such shows as *Superman* and *Wonder Woman?* Do these people really exist?" "No, of course not.

"When something is not real, we say that it is a fantasy. Fairy tales are all fantasies. Most of the cartoons, *Superman, The Incredible Hulk, and Wonder Woman* are fantasies. Fantasy is make-believe. We've played pretend games. Who can give me some examples? Yes, we've made-believe that we were lots of famous people. When you make-believe, it's not real. Let's make up some fantasies."

After the children share their fantasy statements with one another, ask them to create some statements that are not fantasy but based on reality. Then pass out a ditto sheet to each child. On the ditto sheet have statements such as: The moon has a face; A rug can turn into a flying carpet; Bears can talk; Man can fly; Mr. Toad can drive a car; Bears sleep in beds; Bears eat at a table; Man can fly to the moon in a spaceship. The children must state whether the statements are based on fantasy or reality. Go over the answers with the children.

Summary

Pull the main points of the lesson together. Tell students to try to write their own fantasy story when they go back to their seats, and that the next day they can share their stories with the rest of the group.

LESSON PLAN II—UPPER-INTERMEDIATE GRADES*
(Combining Reading and Writing)

Behavioral Objectives

1. After reading a selection, students will make some inferences about the characters presented in the selection.
2. After making inferences about the characters in the selection, students will create a title for the selection.

Preliminary Preparation

A caricature of "The Man with the Midas Touch" and the story "The Pugnacious Pussycat" are made available for each child.
The following sentences are on the chalkboard:

*This lesson should be used with a group of highly able students.

Everyone who disliked getting into fights avoided the *pugnacious* man.

He was like a *tornado*—knocking down everything in his path.

His dog was as grouchy as a *scorpion* with a hotfoot.

He was a rough-looking brute—*a battle-scarred King Kong.*

The cat hissed like a *viper.*

Introduction

"We've been working with the skill of 'reading between the lines.' What have we called this skill?" "Yes. Good, we've called it inference. Can someone tell me what we mean by 'inference'?" "You're right, it refers to information that is not directly stated in the writing but implied—it's something that's suggested. What else did we say about inference?" "Good! We said that to make an inference we must have sufficient information.

"Last night I saw a show entitled 'The Man with the Midas Touch.' From the title, what would you expect the character to be like?" "Yes, you would infer that he is wealthy, that he has successful business ventures, and that he is quite concerned with money.

"We were obviously influenced by the fairy tale character of King Midas. Well, the fairy tale character did have some relationship to the television character, but there was a twist to it. Look at this caricature I made of 'The Man with the Midas Touch.' What do you think the 'Midas Touch' stood for in the television show?" "Yes, you're right—calamity, disaster, or death. Everyone or everything that the character Mr. Midas came in contact with ended in disaster or death. Obviously, from the title we didn't have enough information to make correct inferences about the character or show.

"Today, we are going to read a story, 'The Pugnacious Pussycat.' After we read the story, we're going to try to draw inferences about the story's characters from the selection, and then we're going to create a new title for the selection."

Development

"Before we begin to read the story, let's go over some words and phrases that are underlined on the chalkboard. Using the context clues, can anyone tell me what *pugnacious* means?" "Very good. It means having an aggressive manner. Does anyone remember the word we met yesterday that would be a synonym for *pugnacious* and *aggressive*?" "Yes, good—*belligerent*. Each of the other sentences has a figure of speech in it. We've worked with this figure of speech. What is it called?" "Yes, it's called a 'simile.' Let's go over each to make sure we understand the comparisons that the author is making." The teacher and students go over each one. After they are finished, the teacher asks the students to read the story silently for the purpose of finding out about the main characters in the story. Have the students state the traits of "Harry, the cat." After this is done, have the students state who the main character in the story is. Have students tell about Bryan. Ask the students whether they think Bryan is bright. Although the author does not directly state that Bryan is bright, what clues are given so that we can make this inference? Have students find clues in the story and read these aloud. After the students have presented character traits of both Harry, the cat, and Bryan, and have found evidence in the story to support their inferences, have them generate new titles for the story.

Summary

Pull together the main points of the lesson. Tell students, "For tomorrow I'd like you to write a short character sketch in which information about a character is implied. You will share your character sketches with one another and then challenge each other to generate good titles for your sketches."

Suggestions for Thought Questions and Activities

1. State the four levels of comprehension presented in this chapter. State one skill for each level, and then prepare an activity for each skill at each level. (primary grades)

2. Do the same as above for intermediate grades.

3. You have just been appointed to a special reading curriculum committee at your school. The committee is charged with developing a dynamic reading comprehension program. What suggestions would you make to the committee on how to proceed?

4. Develop a creative lesson plan on the presentation of word parts to intermediate-grade students.

5. Think up some gamelike activities to present combining forms.

6. Jim and John are both in the middle of the fourth grade. Jim has an IQ of 130, and he is reading on grade level. John has an IQ of 70, and he is reading at about a second-grade level. The teacher decides to give only John an informal reading inventory (IRI) because he is reading below grade level. Do you agree with his or her decision? Explain fully.

SELECTED BIBLIOGRAPHY

Reading Comprehension

Goodman, Yetta, and Dorothy J. Watson. "A Reading Program to Live With: Focus on Comprehension." *Language Arts* 54 (November/December 1977): 868–879.

Rubin, Dorothy. *The Vital Arts—Reading and Writing*. New York: Macmillan, 1979.

———. *Reading and Learning Power*. New York: Macmillan, 1980.

———. *The Teacher's Handbook of Reading–Thinking Exercises*. New York: Holt, Rinehart and Winston, 1980.

Singer, Harry. "Active Comprehension: From Answering to Asking Questions." *The Reading Teacher* 31 (May 1978): 901–908.

Smith, Frank. *Understanding Reading*, 2d ed. New York: Holt, Rinehart and Winston, 1978.

Smith, Nila Banton. "The Many Faces of Reading Comprehension." *The Reading Teacher* 23 (December 1969): 249–259; 292.

Sullivan, JoAnna. "Comparing Strategies of Good and Poor Comprehenders." *Journal of Reading* 21 (May 1978): 710–715.

Thorndike, E. L. "Reading as Reasoning: A Study of Mistakes in Paragraph Reading." *Journal of Educational Psychology* 8 (June 1917): 323–332.

Thorndike, Robert L. "Reading as Reasoning." *Reading Research Quarterly* 9 (1973–74): 135–147.

Vocabulary Development

Burke, Eileen M. "Using Trade Books to Intrigue Children with Words." *The Reading Teacher* 32 (November, 1978): 144–148.

Cuyler, Richard C. "Guidelines for Skill Development: Vocabulary." *The Reading Teacher* 32 (December 1978): 316–322.

Hoban, Tana. *Push, Pull, Empty, Full: A Book of Opposites*. New York: Macmillan, 1972.

Karbal, Harold T. "Keying In on Vocabulary." *Elementary English* 52 (March 1975): 367–369.

Rubin, Dorothy. *Gaining Word Power*. New York: Macmillan, 1978.

———. "Developing Vocabulary Skills," in *The Primary Grade Teacher's Language Arts Handbook*. New York: Holt, Rinehart and Winston, 1980.

———. "Developing Vocabulary Skills," in *The Intermediate Grade Teacher's Language Arts Handbook*. New York: Holt, Rinehart and Winston, 1980.

Vaughan, Sally, et al. "A Multiple-Modality Approach to Word Study: Vocabulary Scavenger Hunts." *The Reading Teacher* 32 (January 1979): 434–437.

Diagnosis of Reading Difficulties

Ekwall, Eldon E. *Diagnosis and Remediation of the Disabled Reader*. Boston: Allyn and Bacon, 1977.

Gilliland, Hap. *A Practical Guide to Remedial Reading*, 2d ed. Columbus, Ohio: Merrill, 1978.

Harris, Larry A., and Carl B. Smith. *Reading Instruction: Diagnostic Teaching in the Classroom*. New York: Holt, Rinehart and Winston, 1980.

Miller, Wilma H. *Reading Correction Kit*, 2d ed. New York: The Center for Applied Research in Education, 1978.

Rupley, William H., and Timothy R. Blair. *Reading Diagnosis and Remediation: A Primer for Classroom and Clinic*. Chicago: Rand McNally, 1979.

Zintz, Miles V. *Corrective Reading*, 3d ed. Dubuque, Iowa: W.C. Brown, 1977.

Informal Reading Inventories (Commercial)

Silvaroli, N. *Classroom Reading Inventory*, 3d ed. Dubuque, Iowa: W.C. Brown, 1976.

Spache, George D. *Diagnostic Reading Scales*. Monterey: California Test Bureau, 1972.

nine

Creative Communication through Children's Literature

EXAMPLES OF TEACHER COMPETENCIES

1. The teacher will be able to select books for the class library based on students' interest and reading ability levels.

2. The teacher will be able to determine reading ability levels based on sentence length and word syllabication.

3. The teacher will be able to state reference books that would aid in choosing books for students and for the class library.

4. The teacher will be able to state factors which will help students in becoming enthusiastic about books.

5. The teacher will be able to state criteria that children should try to meet in the enjoyment of books.

6. The teacher will be able to state the meaning and purpose of "bibliotherapy."

7. The teacher will be able to state necessary criteria for interesting children in poetry.

8. The teacher will be able to state factors which will help students to present book reports.

9. The teacher, planning with students, will determine the standards for orally presented book reports.

10. The teacher, together with students and the school librarian, will plan visits to the school library.

11. The teacher will observe the students' reading habits and act positively by setting aside time each day for recreational reading.

12. The teacher will provide a classroom environment conducive to recreational reading. It should include bulletin boards with recommended booklists, book reports on display, students' artwork depicting scenes in various books, information on award-winning books, a book corner with shelves of reading material at various interest and readability levels, comfortable chairs, and a small rug.

13. The teacher will provide books at the readability and interest levels of culturally different students in class.

14. The teacher will provide books for male and female students that portray both men and women as protagonists in a variety of roles and covering various careers.

15. The teacher will provide books for various racial groups which will be at their interest and readability levels.

16. The teacher will be able to determine whether students value, appreciate, or have an interest in recreational reading by observing whether pupils voluntarily choose books to read.

There is no frigate like a book
   To take us lands away,
Nor any coursers like a page
   Of prancing poetry.
This traverse may the poorest take
   Without oppress of toll;
How frugal is the chariot
   That bears a human soul!

              EMILY DICKINSON

Introduction

STUDENT: "Today I am a princess, tomorrow a scientist, and the next day an astronaut. I don't know what I will be next week. It depends on which book I choose to read."

A good literature program should provide for the varying interests of students at all grade and ability levels. It should help to bring joy, delight, and hope to children. A book is "good" only if children enjoy it; if it helps children to broaden their sights, to better understand themselves and their emotions. A good book satisfies intellectual hunger and helps children to awaken to the intelligent love of the beautiful, which is esthetic appreciation. Literature provides students with such a limitless fertile terrain of vicarious experiences; it is so rich a source of both information and meaningful insights, that its role in the language arts must be examined in considerable depth.

The relationship of literature to the language arts areas is a very close and important one. If students have had an adequate foundation in the areas of listening, speaking, and learning to read, it should manifest itself in the children's literature program in that children will voluntarily choose to read books, and teachers will be more successful in generating enthusiasm, ex-

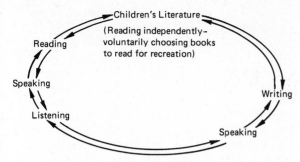

figure 9.1   *Interactive Feedback Loop Model*

citement, and love for books. The more vicarious experiences children have through books, the more they will converse and write, producing reinforcement in various language arts areas. Figure 9.1 is an interactive feedback loop model which shows the reinforcement among some of the language arts areas through children's literature. The figure illustrates how literature acts as a stimulus for writing and reading, and how these, in turn, stimulate oral expression.

The children's literature chapter will include a number of topics which the elementary school teacher will use in order to establish and maintain a good ongoing literature program for all students.

After you have finished reading this chapter you should be able to answer the following questions:

1. Are there many differences between children's and adults' books? Explain.

2. Should children be allowed to read the Hardy Boys and Nancy Drew books? Explain.

3. How would you provide an atmosphere conducive to recreational reading in your classroom?

4. What are some techniques that will interest children in books?

5. How would you help children to select books?

6. What should you know about sex stereotyping in books?

7. What is bibliotherapy? Explain.

8. What kinds of books would you provide for the culturally different child?

9. What should you know about the portrayal of the aged in books?

10. What is the place of book reporting in the children's literature program?

11. Why has poetry been called the stepchild of children's literature? Should this be so? Explain.

12. Are all children able to understand figures of speech? Explain.

13. What should you know about readability formulas?

14. What are some reference books which you could use as an aid in helping your students to choose books?

15. What library skills would you teach to primary- and intermediate-grade level students?

The Background and Development of Children's Literature

In *The Republic* Plato, the fifth century B.C. Greek philosopher, asks: "What kind of education shall we give them all? We shall find it difficult to improve on the time-honored distinction between the training we give to the body and the training we give to the mind and character." Plato is discussing the kind of education that young children should receive in their first stage. He recommends using stories of two kinds, true stories and fiction. He also says:

. . . we start to train the mind before the body. And the first step, as you know, is always what matters most, particularly when we are dealing with those who are young and tender. That is the time when they are taking shape and when any impression we choose to make leaves a permanent mark. Shall we, therefore, allow our children to listen to any stories written by anyone, and to form opinions the opposite of those we think they should have when they grow up? Then it seems that our first business is to supervise the production of stories, and choose only those we think suitable, and reject the rest. We shall persuade mothers and nurses to tell our chosen stories to their children and so mold their minds and characters rather than their bodies. The greater part of the stories current to-day we shall have to reject.[1]

Plato lists explicit kinds of stories which should be rejected, such as those that misrepresent gods and heroes. He would also forbid those in which a father is mistreated by his son, nor would he permit stories of wars and plots and battles among gods. Thus concern about children's reading matter dates back to antiquity.

Plato realized that the early years of children are very important in that what children are exposed to will greatly influence their later life. But Plato's ideas were only a utopian dream.

Not much was actually done concerning children's literature until the second half of the eighteenth century. During this period, children recited "poetry" such as:

> Yes, I was ever born in sin.
> And all my heart is bad within.

Children at this time were treated as miniature adults, and this included the selection of their reading material. Even Shakespeare, whose range of views was so wide, seldom makes use of love of children as a motive. When he does introduce children into one of his plays, he makes them precocious and priggish—children playing at being grown-ups.

In the eighteenth century a number of educational philosophers became interested in the child. As a result, some literature was written specifically for children to both interest and instruct them. But it wasn't until the end of the eighteenth and the beginning of the nineteenth centuries that literary standards for children's literature began to emerge.

Today the pendulum has swung far in the other direction:

Many of my readers seem amazed by the fact that I began to write for children in my late years. The desire to create for them usually manifests itself when the writer is still young himself, not far removed from his own childhood. I was driven to it by deep disenchantment in the literary atmosphere of our epoch. I have convinced myself that while adult literature, especially fiction, is deteriorating, the literature for children is gaining in quality and stature. The child, which until the middle of the 19th century was nothing but a passive and uncritical listener of stories that tired mothers and nannies improvised at his bedside, in our time has become a consumer of great growing literature—a reader who cannot be deluded by literary fads and barren experiments. No writer can bribe his way to the child's attention with false originality, literary puns and puzzles, arbitrary distortions of the order of things, or muddy streams of consciousness which often reveal nothing but a writer's boring and selfish personality. I came to the child because I see in him a last refuge from a literature gone beserk and ready for suicide.[2]

George A. Woods, children's editor of the *New York Times Book Review*, comments on the negative aspects of children's literature in the late 1960s:

The trouble is there's too much produce, too many perishables. Most of the items will get spoiled by the time you get them home; they're half-rotten sitting there on the shelves. They may look good, but inside they're a pulpy mess.

It's that way with children's books: plenty of staples, a lot of lemons, maybe a dozen treats for the palate, only a few for a proper gourmet's fare. . . . An editor in one of the major publishing firms confessed recently that "we could declare a moratorium on putting out picture books for the next ten years and the children of America would not suffer any severe deprivations." [3]

[1]Plato, *The Republic*, trans. H. D. P. Lee (Baltimore: Penguin, 1961).

[2]Isaac Bashevis Singer, "Children's Books," *New York Times Book Review* (November 9, 1969).
[3]George A. Woods, "Children's Books," *New York Times Book Review* (November 3, 1968).

Mr. Woods' feelings in the late 1970s have not changed concerning the fare of books. He feels that most children's books written today are not a celebration of life and joy.

Differences between Children's and Adults' Books

What differentiates children's literature from adult literature? Some persons claim that there is no difference. P. L. Travers has said: "There is no such thing as a children's book. There are simply books of many kinds, and some of them children read."[4] According to Natalie Babbitt, an author of children's books, although everyone can tell a child's book from one for adults, the difficulty lies in discerning the essential nature of the difference. Babbitt does not believe that books for adults are serious while books for children tend to amuse, and she cites *Winnie-the-Pooh, Gone with the Wind,* and *How the Grinch Stole Christmas* as books read by people of all ages who find them both serious in intent and entertaining. Children's books deal with emotions, just as adult books do—love, hate, pride, fear of death, violence, and grief. Among them *Sleeping Beauty, Wind in the Willows,* and *Heidi* all deal with love. *Toad of Toad Hall* is concerned with pride; and *The Yearling* expresses grief. *Charlotte's Web* is unforgettable in its approach to dying and death. *Ali Baba* and *Jack and the Giant Killer* deal with violence. Babbitt claims that the one emotional theme found in children's literature which is not found in adult literature is that of joy, and children's books generally have a "happy ending." She claims that this applies especially to those we remember the longest.[5]

The "happy or satisfying ending" is closely related to "hope"—no matter how unpromising the circumstances, it is not too late. We must all hope, and for children, hope is a part of life.

Setting the Environment for the Enjoyment of Reading in the Classroom

Teachers who are enthusiastic about books will infect their students with that enthusiasm. A teacher who is seen to be deeply immersed in a book during the lunch hour will also have a marked influence on students. But the teacher's responsibility does not end there. The teacher must set the stage, provide the materials, and plan with students for recreational reading.

First, the classroom must be an inviting place to read. It should be airy, light, and physically comfortable. The emphasis on books should be clearly visible. For example, bulletin boards should have recommended booklists at all interest and readability levels. Award-winning books, book jackets from a number of popular children's books, students' recommendations and evaluations of various books, as well as artwork depicting a scene or characters in books, should be on display.

Lots and lots of books should be provided for the children at all interest and readability levels. (See section on choosing books.) Newspapers, magazines, and other printed matter of interest to children should be available. Filmstrips, records, and films of favorite stories should also be kept handy for the children's use.

Next, a special place to read is necessary! A section or corner of the room should be readily accessible to all the students, where a few comfortable chairs, some large comfortable pillows, and a scatter rug are placed. This is the reading corner.

Now, time must be provided so that children can read. This book period is separate from the

[4]Natalie Babbitt, "Children's Books," *New York Times Book Review* (November 8, 1970).
[5]Babbitt, op. cit.

weekly visit to the library and is not dependent on whether children have free time only because they have finished all their "other work." Every day the teacher and children should plan for a book time, when the class just enjoys literature. After the teacher has helped students to choose their books and settle down, the teacher too should read.

Whetting Children's Interest in Books

Studies have shown that reading literature aloud to children helps prepare them for reading. (See "Nonstandard English and Its Implications for Instruction" in Chapter 5 and "Vocabulary Expansion" in Chapter 8.)

During the week there are many opportunities for the teacher to read to students. Books that are chosen to be read in full to the children should be those that will interest all children. For example, one fifth-grade class loved Sherlock Holmes stories; however, the vocabulary was too difficult for a number of the students, even though the stories were at their interest level. Therefore, the teacher either used synonyms for difficult words or defined them. There are a number of books in which the authors seem to be able to use word imagery to clarify the meanings of unfamiliar words. The techniques that the authors use do not take away from the quality of the story as a story but enhance it.[6]

The teachers must read with expression. They should imagine themselves to be actors or actresses and literally "give it their all." If they are reading effectively, the teachers should have gained the complete attention of the students.

Children love to be told stories. For that matter, so do adults. Storytelling is an art, and

must be practiced to be effective. It is different from reading, and many teachers find this difficult and very time-consuming. Some schools have special librarians who are adept at storytelling. (See Chapter 6.)

Another technique that teachers can use to interest children in books is to have several students orally report on books they have read which they feel others would also enjoy. In presenting such reports students must explain why they enjoyed the books, tell about some of the exciting parts, but not give away the endings.

A technique children enjoy using to interest others in books is creative dramatics. A group of students who have read the same book can present skits highlighting exciting parts in the book. (See Chapter 6.)

Children's Interests and Book Selection

The interests and needs of the individual child will determine the kinds of books he or she will read. Because children choose and read books for different purposes, they will need a wide selection.

Most reading interest studies have been based on asking children what they would like to read rather than on what they actually read. A rare study was done on books actually borrowed from the library by children. In grades four through six these books were taken out in order of popularity: *Henry Huggins, Charlotte's Web, Mrs. Piggle Wiggle, Encyclopedia Brown, Homer Price, All-of-a-Kind-Family, The Black Stallion, The Tenggren Tell-It-Again Book, John Henry* (Keats), *The Red Balloon, Stuart Little, The Mouse on the Motorcycle, Dot for Short, Pinocchio,* and *Peter Pan* (abridged by Josette Frank).

It was also reported that jokes and riddles were in first place for nonfiction popularity. A reflection of the times was shown in the chil-

[6]See Dorothy H. Cohen, "Word Meaning and the Literary Experience in Early Childhood," *Elementary English* 46 (November 1969): 914–925, for a listing of books and examples.

dren's choices of sport books. Judo and jujitsu were the favorites.[7]

Since the middle 1970s, an annual bibliography of classroom choices of trade books has been compiled under the direction of the International Reading Association–Children's Book Council Joint Committee. Of all the trade books published in the previous year, approximately 500 are selected by a group of educators. The books are then sent to designated classrooms. A team of specialists keep a record of the children's reactions to the various books. Based on the children's choices, a book is either elected to the bibliography or denied placement on it.[8]

Child Development Characteristics and Book Selection

Teachers who are knowledgeable about the social, emotional, physical, and intellectual development of their students will be better able to help them choose books.

Table 9.1 suggests a listing of books based on children's developmental stages.[9]

Sex Differences in Book Selection

Most of the sex difference studies on children's literature concerned the discovery of boys' and girls' interests in books by either observing the kinds of books they took out or through questionnaires. All such researches were, however, after the fact. That is, boys and girls, by the time they have arrived in school, have already been persuaded by the culture of the kind of interests they should have. The studies confirm and reinforce the enculturation. For example, in a 1950 study of seventh to twelfth graders it was found that boys like fierce adventure stories and mysteries, whereas girls prefer love and sentiment, home and family life stories. A 1967 study corroborated earlier sex difference findings. Fourth-, fifth-, and sixth-grade boys preferred historical fiction, history, social studies, science, and health; whereas girls of similar ages preferred realistic fiction, fanciful tales, biography, recreational interests, and poetry. A 1973 study found that boys' interests had not changed in a decade and that boys have a narrower range of reading interests than girls. Boys prefer books dealing with "excitement," "suspense," and "unusual experiences." "Outdoor life," "explorations and expeditions," "sports and games," and "science fiction" are some of the categories boys listed as their favorites.[10] A 1972 study discovered sex differences expressed in television watching as well as books. Boys chose sports, whereas girls chose social empthay.[11]

This is a time of change in society's attitude toward sex roles. The teacher must be careful not to be caught up in stereotypes. However, what we know about children's attitudes toward choosing books should also be taken into account. For example, it has been found that boys *will not* read "girl books," whereas girls *will* read "boy books." Therefore the ratio of "boy books" should be about two to one in the classroom library collection. Examples of "girl books" are *Little Women* by Louisa May Alcott and many of the Laura Ingalls Wilder books such as *Little House in the Big Woods*.

Since there are more women seeking careers today than ever before, and since many of these careers are in fields once thought to be the sole domain of men, it is necessary for the teacher

[7]Donald J. Bisset, "Literature in the Classroom," *Elementary English* 50 (February 1973): 235.

[8]Children's Book Council Joint Committee, "Classroom Choices for 1979," *The Reading Teacher* 32 (October 1979): 33–52.

[9]Charlotte S. Huck, *Children's Literature in the Elementary School*, 3d ed. updated (New York: Holt, Rinehart and Winston, 1979) pp. 31–36.

[10]J. M. Stanchfield and Susan R. Fraim, "A Follow-up Study on the Reading Interests of Boys," *Journal of Reading* 22 (May 1979): 748–752.

[11]Jane Porter, "Research Report," *Elementary English* 49 (November 1972): 1028–1029.

table 9.1   Books for Ages and Stages

Preschool and Kindergarten—Ages 3, 4, and 5

Characteristics	Implications	Examples
Rapid development of language.	Interest in words, enjoyment of rhymes, nonsense, and repetition and cumulative tales. Enjoy retelling folktales and stories from books without words.	*Mother Goose* Burningham, *Mr. Gumpy's Outing* Gág, *Millions of Cats* Hutchins, *Rosie's Walk* Rockwell, *The Three Bears* Spier, *Crash! Bang! Boom!* Watson, *Father Fox's Pennyrhymes* Wezel, *The Good Bird* *The Gingerbread Boy*
Very active, short attention span.	Require books that can be completed in one sitting. Enjoy participation through naming, touching, and pointing. Should have the opportunity to hear stories several times each day.	Burningham, *A B C* Burningham, *The Cupboard* Carle, *Do You Want to Be My Friend?* Carle, *The Very Hungry Caterpillar* Kunhardt, *Pat the Bunny* Wildsmith, *Puzzles*
Children themselves are the center of their world. Interest, behavior, and thinking are egocentric.	Like characters with whom they can clearly identify. Can only see one point of view.	Buckley, *Grandfather and I* Keats, *The Snowy Day* Preston, *Where Did My Mother Go?* Wells, *Noisy Nora*
Curious about their world.	Stories about everyday experiences, pets, playthings, home, people in their immediate environment are enjoyed.	Cohen, *Will I Have a Friend?* Hoban, *Best Friends for Frances* Keats, *Peter's Chair* Rockwell, *My Doctor*
Building concepts through many first-hand experiences.	Books extend and reinforce children's developing concepts.	Anno, *Anno's Counting Book* Hoban, *Big Ones, Little Ones* Hoban, *Count and See* Jensen, *Sara and the Door* Showers, *The Listening Walk*
Children have little sense of time. Time is "before now," "now," and "not yet."	Books can help children begin to understand the sequence of time.	Burningham, *Seasons* Carle, *The Grouchy Ladybug* Tresselt, *It's Time Now* Zolotow, *Over and Over*
Children learn through imaginative play.	Enjoy stories that involve imaginative play. Like personification of toys and animals.	Burton, *Mike Mulligan and His Steam Shovel* DeRegniers, *May I Bring a Friend?* Ets, *Just Me* Freeman, *Corduroy* McPhail, *The Train*
Seek warmth and security in relationships with adults.	Like to be close to the teacher or parent during storytime. The ritual of the bedtime story begins literature experiences at home.	Brown, *Goodnight Moon* Clifton, *Amifika* Flack, *Ask Mr. Bear* Hutchins, *Good-Night, Owl!* Minarik, *Little Bear* Sharmat, *I Don't Care*

table 9.1   (continued)

Characteristics	Implications	Examples
Beginning to assert their independence. Take delight in their accomplishments.	Books can reflect emotions.	Barrett, *I Hate to Go to Bed* Brown, *The Runaway Bunny* Krauss, *The Carrot Seed* Lexau, *Benjie* Preston, *The Temper Tantrum Book* Watson, *Moving*
Beginning to make value judgments about what is fair and what should be punished.	Require poetic justice and happy endings in the stories.	Bulla, *Keep Running, Allen* Hutchins, *Titch* Piper, *The Little Engine That Could* Potter, *The Tale of Benjamin Bunny* Potter, *The Tale of Peter Rabbit*

Primary—Ages 6 and 7

Characteristics	Implications	Examples
Continued development and expansion of language.	Daily story hour provides opportunity to hear qualitative and creative language of literature.	Preston, *Squawk to the Moon, Little Goose* Steig, *Amos and Boris* Tresselt, *A Thousand Lights and Fireflies* Poetry of Aileen Fisher, Karla Kuskin, David McCord, Stevenson, and others.
Attention span increasing.	Prefer short stories, or may enjoy a continued story provided each chapter is a complete incident.	Flack, *Walter the Lazy Mouse* Lobel, *Frog and Toad Together* Parish, *Amelia Bedelia*
Striving to accomplish skills demanded by adults.	Children are expected to learn the skills of reading and writing. Need to accomplish this at their own rate and feel successful. First reading experiences should be enjoyable.	Cohen, *When Will I Read?* Conford, *Impossible, Possum* Duvoisin, *Petunia* Guilfoile, *Nobody Listens to Andrew* Kraus, *Leo the Late Bloomer*
Learning still based upon immediate perception and direct experiences.	Use informational books to verify experience. Watch guinea pigs, or record changes in a tadpole *prior* to using a book.	Brady, *Wild Mouse* Hoban, *Look Again!* Selsam, *The Amazing Dandelion* Silverstein, *Guinea Pigs, All about Them*
Continued interest in the world around them—eager and curious. Still see world from their egocentric point of view.	Need wide variety of books. TV has expanded their interests beyond their home and neighborhood.	Aliki, *Green Grass and White Milk* Fuchs, *Journey to the Moon* Koren, *Behind the Wheel* Lionni, *Fish Is Fish* Swinton, *Digging for Dinosaurs*

table 9.1 (continued)

Characteristics	Implications	Examples
Vague concepts of time.	Simple biographies and historical fiction may give a feeling for the past, but accurate understanding of chronology is beyond this age group.	Aliki, *A Weed Is a Flower* Dalgliesh, *The Bears on Hemlock Mountain* Hutchins, *Clocks and More Clocks* Turkle, *Obadiah the Bold*
More able to separate fantasy from reality. Developing greater imagination.	Enjoy fantasy. Like to dramatize simple stories.	Ness, *Sam, Bangs, and Moonshine* Sendak, *Where the Wild Things Are* Slobodkina, *Caps for Sale* Tolstoy, *The Great Big Enormous Turnip*
Beginning to develop empathy and understanding for others.	Adults can ask such questions as, "What would you have done?" "How do you think Stevie felt about Robert?"	Hill, *Evan's Corner* Steptoe, *Stevie* Wolf, *Anna's Silent World* Yashima, *Crow Boy*
Have a growing sense of justice. Demand applications of rules, regardless of circumstances.	Expect poetic justice in books.	Freeman, *Dandelion* Hutchins, *The Surprise Party* Udry, *Let's Be Enemies* Zemach, *The Judge*
Humor is developing; enjoy incongruous situations, misfortune of others, and slapstick.	Encourage appreciation of humor in literature. Reading aloud for pure fun has its place in the classroom. Enjoy books that have surprise endings, play on words, and broad comedy.	Allard, *The Stupids Have a Ball* Barrett, *Animals Should Definitely Not Wear Clothing* DuBois, *Lazy Tommy Pumpkinhead* Kuskin, *Just Like Everyone Else* Segal, *Tell Me a Mitzi*
Beginning sexual curiosity.	Teachers need to accept and be ready to answer children's questions about sex.	Gruenberg, *The Wonderful Story of How You Were Born* Mayle, *"Where Did I Come From?"* Sheffield, *Where Do Babies Come From?*
Physical contour of the body is changing. Permanent teeth appear. Learning to whistle and develop other fine motor skills.	Books can help children accept physical changes in themselves and differences in others.	Keats, *Whistle for Willie* McCloskey, *One Morning in Maine* Rockwell, *I Did It*
Continue to seek independence from adults.	Need opportunities to select books of their own choice. Should be encouraged to go to the library on their own.	Ardizzone, *Tim to the Rescue* Steptoe, *Train Ride* Taylor, *Henry the Explorer* Waber, *Ira Sleeps Over*
Continue to need warmth and security in adult relationships.	Books may emphasize universal human characteristics in a variety of lifestyles.	Clark, *In My Mother's House* Gill, *Hush, Jon* Reyher, *My Mother Is the Most Beautiful Woman in the World* Scott, *Sam* Zolotow, *Mr. Rabbit and the Lovely Present*

table 9.1 (continued)

Middle Elementary—Ages 8 and 9

Characteristics	Implications	Examples
Attaining independence in reading skill, may read with complete absorption. Others may still be having difficulty in learning to read. Wide variation in ability and interest. Research indicates boys and girls developing different reading interests during this time.	Discover reading as an enjoyable activity. Prefer an uninterrupted block of time for independent reading. During this period, many children become avid readers.	Blume, *Tales of a Fourth Grade Nothing* Clymer, *My Brother Stevie* Colver, *Bread-and-Butter Indian* Dahl, *Danny: The Champion of the World* Fox, *Maurice's Room* Greene, *Philip Hall Likes Me, I Reckon Maybe* Konigsburg, *From the Mixed-Up Files of Mrs. Basil E. Frankweiler* Robinson, *The Best Christmas Pageant Ever* Schulz, *Hooray for You, Charlie Brown* Selden, *The Cricket in Times Square* Steele, *Winter Danger*
Interest in hobbies and collections is high.	Enjoy how-to-do-it books and series books. Like to collect and trade paperback books. Begin to look for books of one author.	Bond, *A Bear Called Paddington* Cleary, *Ramona and Her Father* Simon, *The Paper Airplane Book* Stein, *The Kids' Kitchen Takeover* Wilder, "Litte House" series
Seek specific information to answer their questions. May go to books that are beyond their reading ability to search out answers.	Require guidance in locating information. Need help in use of library, card catalog, and reference books.	Gallob, *City Leaves, City Trees* Macaulay, *Castle* McWhirter, *The Guinness Book of World Records* Sarnoff, *A Great Bicycle Book*

Later Elementary—Ages 10, 11, and 12

Characteristics	Implications	Examples
Rate of physical development varies widely. Rapid growth precedes beginning of puberty. Girls about two years ahead of boys in development and reaching puberty. Boys and girls increasingly curious about all aspects of sex.	Continued sex differentiation in reading preferences. Guide understanding of growth process and help children meet personal problems.	Blume, *Are You There God? It's Me, Margaret* Blume, *Then Again, Maybe I Won't* Donovan, *I'll Get There, It Better Be Worth the Trip* Ravielli, *Wonders of the Human Body* Winthrop, *A Little Demonstration of Affection*
Understanding and accepting the sex role is a developmental task of this period. Boys and girls develop a sense of each other's identity.	Books may provide impetus for discussion and identification with others meeting this task.	Cleaver, *Trial Valley* George, *Julie of the Wolves* Greene, *A Girl Called Al* Jones, *Edge of Two Worlds* L'Engle, *The Moon by Night*
Increased emphasis on peer group and sense of belonging. Deliberate exclusion of others. Expressions of prejudice.	Emphasize unique contribution of all. In a healthy classroom atmosphere discussion of books can be used for values clarification.	Armstrong, *Sounder* Levoy, *Alan and Naomi* Neville, *Berries Goodman* Westall, *The Machine Gunners*

table 9.1 (continued)

Characteristics	Implications	Examples
Family patterns changing. Highly critical of siblings. By end of period may challenge parents' authority.	Books may provide some insight into these changing relationships.	Byars, *The Pinballs* Hopkins, *Mama* Mann, *My Dad Lives in a Downtown Hotel* Rodgers, *Freaky Friday* Wersba, *The Dream Watcher*
Begin to have models other than parents. May draw them from TV, movies, sports figures, and books. Beginning interest in future vocation.	Biographies may provide appropriate models. Career books may open up new vocations and provide useful information.	Carruth, *She Wanted to Read: The Story of Mary McLeod Bethune* Goldreich, *What Can She Be? A Lawyer* Lee, *Boy's Life of John F. Kennedy* Naylor, *How I Came To Be a Writer* Robinson, *Breakthrough to the Big League*
Sustained, intense interest in specific activities.	Children spend more time in reading at this age than any other. Tend to select books related to one topic; for example, horses, sports, or a special hobby.	Glubok, *The Mummy of Ramose* Graham, *Great No-Hit Games of the Major Leagues* Moeri, *A Horse for X, Y, Z* Ravielli, *What Is Tennis?* Ross, *Racing Cars and Great Races*
Reflecting current adult interest in the mysterious, occult, and supernatural.	Enjoy mysteries, science fiction, and books about witchcraft.	Christopher, *Wild Jack* Duncan, *A Gift of Magic* Hunter, *The 13th Member* L'Engle, *A Swiftly Tilting Planet* Sleator, *Blackbriar*
Highly developed sense of justice and concern for others. Innate sympathy for weak and downtrodden.	Like "sad stories" about handicapped persons, sickness, or death.	Byars, *Summer of the Swans* Greene, *Beat the Turtle Drum* Platt, *Hey, Dummy* Robinson, *David in Silence*
Increased understanding of the chronology of past events. Beginning sense of their place in time. Able to see many dimensions of a problem.	Literature provides the opportunity to examine issues from different viewpoints. Need guidance in being critical of biased presentations.	Frank, *Anne Frank: The Diary of a Young Girl* Hickman, *The Valley of the Shadow* Hunt, *Across Five Aprils* Lester, *To Be a Slave* Tunis, *His Enemy, His Friend* Uchida, *Journey to Topaz*
Search for values. Interested in problems of the world. Can deal with abstract relationships; becoming more analytical.	Valuable discussions may grow out of teacher's reading aloud prose and poetry to this age group. Questions may help students gain insight into both the content and literary structure of a book.	Babbitt, *Tuck Everlasting* Collier, *My Brother Sam Is Dead* Cunningham, *Dorp Dead* Dunning, *Reflections on a Gift of Watermelon Pickle and Other Modern Verse* Engdahl, *Enchantress from the Stars* Kohl, *The View from the Oak* Slote, *Hang Tough, Paul Mather* Wojciechowska, *Shadow of a Bull*

to include books which portray women in such roles, among them: *Maria Mitchell: Stargazer* by Katherine E. Wilkie, the biography of the first astronomy professor at Vassar College; *Challenge to Become a Doctor: The Story of Elizabeth Blackwell* by Leah Lurie Heyn; *What Can She Be? A Veterinarian* and *What Can She Be? A Lawyer* by Gloria and Esther Goldreich; *A Life for Israel: The Story of Golda Meir* by Arnold Dobrin; and *Oh Lizzie! The Life of Elizabeth Cady Stanton* by Doris Faber.

Traditionally, women have been portrayed in literature as mothers and homemakers. Although some persons claim that these are inferior roles, this is not so. It is not easy to be a good parent and homemaker, for they require a great deal of knowledge and skill. It is to be hoped that more books will be written which deal with the parental role in a perceptive way.

Common stereotypes about the sexes have generally been carried over into books. For example, when persons are asked to give masculine and feminine characteristics that are valued, the list to the left is often supplied.[12]

Studies have shown that parents' expectations of their children tend to be similar to the traits in this list. For example, parents tend to see boys as aggressive and more physically vigorous, as adventuresome, as more mechanically inclined, as competitive, and as more noisy than girls, whereas girls are seen as softer and more cuddly, as fragile, as more likely to be frightened, as more well-mannered, and as neater than boys.[13]

Yet many educators, psychologists, and sociologists are realizing that such "traits" are not necessarily biologically determined but may be learned. If females and males are conditioned

Male-valued Traits	Female-valued Traits
Aggressive	Does not use harsh language
Independent	Talkative
Unemotional; hides emotions	Tactful
Objective	Gentle
Easily influenced	Aware of feelings of others
Dominant	Religious
Likes math and science	Interested in own appearance
	Neat in habits
Not excitable in minor crisis	
Active	Quiet
Competitive	Strong need for security
Logical	Appreciates art and literature
Worldly	Expresses tender feelings
Skilled in business	
Direct	
Knows the way of the world	
Feelings not easily hurt	
Adventurous	
Makes decisions easily	
Never cries	
Acts as a leader	
Self-confident	
Not uncomfortable about being aggressive	
Ambitious	
Able to separate feelings from ideas	
Not dependent	
Not conceited about appearance	
Thinks men are superior to women	
Talks freely about sex with men	

to value certain traits, they will conduct themselves accordingly.

Interestingly, the reason that girls will read "boy books" but boys will not read "girl books" is probably that society seems to value "masculinity" more than "femininity." Studies have shown that parents and teachers are usually not

[12]P. S. Rosenkrantz et al., "Sex Role Stereotypes and Self-concepts in College Students," *Journal of Consulting and Clinical Psychology* 32 (1968): 287–295.

[13]E. E. Maccoby and C. N. Jacklin, *The Psychology of Sex Differences* (Stanford, Calif.: Stanford University Press, 1974).

upset when girls engage in boy activities, but parents and teachers generally frown on boys' involvement in girl activities.[14]

Sex-role identity may be more ambiguous for the female who seeks a career. In order to succeed in a career, independence, initiative, agressiveness to a degree, and competitiveness are needed. These are generally characterized as masculine traits, which some females may be loath to assume, and so a conflict arises. How can a female maintain her femininity, but also "make it" in a career? A similar case can be made with males, whose stereotype disallows tenderness, helping at home, and being sensitive to social relations.

Although resistance to departing from sex stereotyping exists, inroads are being made, and teachers are key persons in helping to make these inroads. Teachers who value nonsexist thinking can help their students to change their attitudes toward sexist views.[15]

Change in sex stereotyping of females in books started to become more evident in the early 1970s. For example, the 1973 Caldecott award went to *The Funny Little Woman* by Arlene Mosel, which concerns an inventive Japanese woman who outwits the gods. The Newbery award winner, *Julie of the Wolves*, by Jean George, concerns a thirteen-year-old Eskimo girl, who, married to a simpleton, escapes and with resourcefulness is able to survive by making friends with a pack of wolves.

In these two books initiative and independence are shown as virtues in two females even though they are traits that are usually rewarded in males.

Since the 1960s, science-fiction books, which are usually considered in the male domain, have tended to be oriented toward both sexes, where males and females play central roles. Some books in this category are: Madeleine L'Engle's *A Wrinkle in Time*, Robert O'Brien's *The Silver Crown*, Patricia Wrightson's *Down to Earth*, and H. M. Hoover's *Rains of Eridan* and *The Delikon*.

Although there seems to be a change in the role of females in sports, more needs to be done in this area. Significant sex differences in motor development have been found during children's early years.[16] By the time the children come to school, differences in sport skills appear, and the differences become more marked according to sex type as the children go through school. The marked differences may have been increased by cultural pressure and so teachers should provide books in which girls as well as boys excel in sports.

In the 1970s a number of journals devoted many articles to sexism in children's literature. There were also articles discussing the overuse of the male pronoun in writing, and ways in which to avoid this practice.

When children choose books, the teacher should not differentiate between male and female books. In fact, the teacher should not "push" any book on any child. Books at all interest levels should be made available to all children indiscriminately.

Criteria for Selecting Books

There are a number of factors which should be considered in selecting books for children. Criteria concerned with knowledge of children and what they enjoy in a book include:[17]

1. Theme: What the story is all about.
2. Plot: These grow out of good themes. Children like heroes and heroines who have obstacles to overcome, conflicts to settle, and difficult goals to win.
3. Characterization: As children mature in their

[14]Ibid.

[15]Cristina J. Simpson, "Educational Materials and Children's Sex Role Concepts," *Language Arts* 55 (February 1978): 161–167.

[16]J. E. Garai and A. Scheinfeld, "Sex Differences in Mental and Behavioral Traits," *Genetic Psychology Monograph* 77 (1968): 203, 211.

[17]Huck, op.cit., pp. 6–14.

reading tastes, they go from enjoyment of tales of action with stereotyped characters to characters who are individual, unique, and memorable.

4. Style: A difficult quality to define, but its absence is noticeable in books that are repetitious, boring, labored, and so on.

5. Setting: Concerns time and place of the story. It should enhance the plot, characters, and the theme of the story.

6. Format: Deals with the presentation of material, illustrations, quality of paper used, and binding. The illustrations should be attractive and pleasing to the eye as well as consistent with the story. The quality of the paper should not detract from the reading, and the print of the book should be appropriate for the reader.

Children's Literature and Culturally Different Children

Should literary choice for children be based on the cultural group from which a child comes or on the socioeconomic stratum of their families? Does the reading of good literature help to extend the reader's world?

A study on the reading preferences of inner-city children showed that they like to read about characters in middle-class settings, with positive self-concepts, and in positive group interaction.[18] This is contrary to the idea that they prefer to read stories of inner-city life.

All children, regardless of cultural backgrounds, enjoy "good" literature. For example, numerous research studies of the general as well as the reading interests of children reveal that those from culturally different backgrounds do not vary considerably from others.[19] However, we all like to read books which depict characters from backgrounds similar to our own.

Reading about characters who have similar cultural backgrounds to theirs helps children to develop feelings of self-esteem and worth. It is important to recognize that the treatment of a character in literature may greatly influence individuals' perceptions of themselves. If children constantly see pictures and stories of persons similar to themselves in inferior roles, they may begin to think of themselves as inferior. Similarly, for example, if Caucasians constantly see other racial groups depicted in inferior roles, they may come to think of them in this way. Not only do children from diverse cultural backgrounds need to read about persons in similar cultural groups who have achieved, but it is good for all children to read about other groups of people in a positive way in order to develop better understanding.

If we were to think of all the different racial, religious, and ethnic groups that live in the United States—such as Indian, Mexican, Spanish, French, black, and so on—many children would be considered as culturally different. It was only during the past fifteen years that fiction and nonfiction books began to be published especially for culturally different children.[20] In the *good* literature books, minorities are not portrayed in a stereotyped fashion. They are presented sympathetically and with sensitivity.

Between 1930 and 1968 only forty-nine books with black characters were on the recommended children's literature lists.[21] In the past few years many more books have been published with black protagonists in sympathetic roles. (See bibliography for lists of such books.)

It is understood that the characteristics of "good" literature, which have been discussed previously for all children, are operative for chil-

---

[18]Jerry L. Johns, "What Do Inner-city Children Prefer to Read?" *The Reading Teacher* 26 (February 1973): 462–467.

[19]Patricia Jean Cianciolo, "A Recommended Reading Diet for Children and Youth of Different Cultures," *Elementary English* 48 (November 1971): 781.

[20]List compiled by Emerita Schroer Schulte, "Today's Literature for Today's Children," *Elementary English* 49 (March 1972): 355–363.

[21]Jane Bingham, "The Pictorial Treatment of Afro-Americans in Books for Young Children, 1930–1968," *Elementary English* 48 (November 1971): 880–885.

dren from divergent cultures as well. Regardless of the group to which children belong, the book they read must help them to feel good about themselves. It must help them to view themselves in a positive light, to achieve a better self-concept, and to give them a feeling of worth.

The importance of learning about other groups of people through literature is aptly expressed in the following:

> I never felt the world-wide importance of the children's heritage in literature more than on a day when I stood with Mrs. Ben Zvi, wife of the [then] President of Israel, in the midst of the book boxes she had filled for the centers in Jerusalem where refugee boys and girls were gathered for storytelling and reading of the world's great classics for children. "We want our boys and girls to be at home with the other children of the world," she said, "and I know of no better way than through mutual enjoyment of the world's great stories."[22]

The Black Child and Books: A Special Look

Teachers must be especially perceptive to the needs, interests, and experiences of their black students. Literature is an area which can be effectively used by the knowledgeable teacher. It is important that the black child be given a sense of dignity, worth, and identity, and a feeling that being black is desirable.

> The better books depict black children as individuals whose identity includes name, home life, family, friends, toys, hobbies, etc. In addition, they are black, American, and first-class citizens. These books lead children naturally to the conclusion that differences—in personality, abilities, background—are desirable among people. Books of this sort which have already been published include the "interracial" *Gabrielle and Se-*

lena, by Peter Desbarats, and *Hooray for Jasper,* by Betty Horvath. Charming and individualized black children are the central characters in the Ezra Jack Keats books, *The Snowy Day, Whistle for Willie, Peter's Chair,* and *A Letter to Amy,* as well as in the books *Sam* and *Big Cowboy Western,* by Ann Herbert Scott, and *What Mary Jo Wanted* and *What Mary Jo Shared,* by Janice May Udry. Books like these, on this level, should be so numerous that children will not be able to browse through a library shelf without finding one there.[23]

A book which hinders a child from finding his or her identity, which portrays the child in a stereotyped role, is a book that would be considered poor reading for all children.

When selecting books for a class library, teachers should try to put themselves in the position of the black child and ask: How would I feel if I read this book? Would this book make me come back for another one? Will this book interest me? Are these books on many readability levels? Does the book portray the black child as an individual? Are the adults portrayed in a nonchildlike manner? Are the characters supplied with traits and personalities which are positive? Are the black individuals in various social positions? Would all children, regardless of color, desire to read the book?

If the answers are "Yes," the teacher should choose the book. But even one "no" answer should disqualify the book?

The importance of providing children with books that convey hope and books with which children can identify, because they mirror their lives, cannot be overemphasized. Another factor, which is as important, concerns the image that white children obtain when they read a book about black people. Since children are greatly influenced by what they read, the way

[22]Dora V. Smith, "Children's Literature Today," *Elementary English* 47 (October 1970): 778. '

[23]Judith Thompson and Gloria Woodard, "Black Perspective in Books for Children," in *The Black American in Books for Children: Readings in Racism,* Donnarae MacCann and Gloria Woodard, eds. (Metuchen, N.J.: Scarecrow Press, 1972), p. 23.

that black persons are portrayed in books will have a profound effect on white children's perceptions of black people.

Good books can open doors through which can pass better understanding, mutual respect, trust, and the hope of people living together in harmony and peace.

BIBLIOTHERAPY

If you have ever read a book in which the main character had a problem exactly like yours and if the book helped you to deal better with your problem, you were involved in bibliotherapy.

Reading guidance given by teachers and librarians to help students with their personal problems is regarded as bibliotherapy. Bibliotherapy is the use of books to help individuals to cope better with their problems. The use of books (or bibliotherapy) to help persons is not a new phenomenon. As far back as 300 B.C. Greek libraries bore inscriptions such as "The Nourishment of the Soul" and "Medicine for the Mind." Alice Bryan, a noted librarian, in the late 1930s advocated the use of books as a technique of guidance to help readers "to face their life problems more effectively and to gain greater freedom and happiness in their personal adjustment." [24] However, it probably was not until Russell and Shrodes published their articles on the "Contribution of Research in Bibliotherapy to the Language Arts Program" in 1950 that teachers attempt to bring bibliotherapy into the classroom. Russell and Shrodes discussed their belief that books could be used not simply to practice reading skills, but also to influence total development. They defined bibliotherapy as "a process of dynamic interaction between the personality of the reader and literature—interaction which may be utilized for personality assessment, adjustment, and growth." They also say that this definition:

> . . . is not a strange, esoteric activity but one that lies within the province of every teacher of literature in working with every child in a group. It does not assume that the teacher must be a skilled therapist, nor the child a seriously maladjusted individual needing clinical treatment. Rather, it conveys the idea that all teachers must be aware of the effects of reading upon children and must realize that, through literature, most children can be helped to solve the developmental problems of adjustment which they face. [25]

(For an understanding of the process of bibliotherapy, see references in the bibliography.)

The Uses of Bibliotherapy

Bibliotherapy can be used in both preventive and ameliorative ways. That is, some individuals, through reading specific books, may learn how to handle certain situations before they have taken place. Other persons may be helped through books to overcome some common developmental problem they are experiencing at the time. For whatever purpose bibliotherapy is used, it will only be of value if teachers are knowledgeable of *how* to use bibliotherapy in their classrooms.

In order to use bibliotherapy effectively in the classroom, teachers should know about children's needs, interests, readiness levels, and developmental stages.

Bibliotherapy Themes

The kinds of problems that lend themselves to bibliotherapy are varied. For example, being the smallest child in the class or encountering the first day of school can be devastating to a

---

[24]Alice I. Bryan, "The Psychology of the Reader," *Library Journal* 64 (January 1939): 110.

[25]David Russell and Caroline Shrodes, "Contributions of Research in Bibliotherapy to the Language Arts Program, I," *The School Review* 58 (September 1950): 335.

child. Being an only child may cause difficulty for some children. A new baby may bring adjustment problems for some, and going to the hospital may be a frightening event for others. Moving to a new neighborhood or the simple dislike of a name can cause problems for a number of children. The death of a loved one, the fear of death, or the divorce of parents cause great anxieties on the part of children, and just growing up can be confusing. These are just a few of the problems suitable for bibliotherapy. (See the section on "The Treatment of Death in Children's Literature.")

The Teacher and Bibliotherapy

By reading books that deal with themes such as those stated in the previous section, children can be helped to cope better with their emotions and problems. Perceptive teachers sensitive to their children's needs can help their children by providing the books that deal with the same problems that their children have. However, since teachers are not clinicians, children who are having serious adjustment problems should be referred for help to the guidance counselor or school psychologist. Also, teachers must be careful not to give children who are anxious about a situation a book that would increase their anxiety. A teacher should also not single out a child in front of the class and give him or her a book which very obviously points out that child's defects. It would probably embarrass and upset the child more.

The school librarian and the special reading teacher may be excellent resource persons to help the teacher to choose books for bibliotherapy purposes. For best results, teachers should work very closely with them. Teachers should be familiar, also, with the *Elementary School Library Collection*, which is available in most libraries. This book is an invaluable aid because it has an annotated bibliography of children's books on all themes with both readability

and interest levels indicated, as well as resource books for teachers. (See section on "The Elementary School Library Collection" in this chapter.)

After teachers use the *Elementary School Library Collection* or the aid of librarians to identify some possible books for bibliotherapy, they should peruse the books to determine whether the books meet certain important criteria. Books for bibliotherapy should deal with problems that are significant and relevant to the students. The characters in these books should be "life-like" and presented in a believable and interesting manner. The characters' relationship to others in the book should be equally believable and they should have motives for their actions. The author should present a logical and believable plot using vivid descriptive language, humor, adequate dialogue, and emotional tone. The situations presented by the author should be such that minor problems can be separated from main problems. The episodes in the book should lend themselves to being extracted and discussed so that students can formulate alternate solutions. Also, the author should present enough data so that students can discern generalizations that relate to life situations. The book should also be written in such a manner that the readers' imaginations are so stirred that they can "enter the skin of another."

A good teacher, one who is perceptive to the needs of students and who recognizes the importance of individual differences, will be in a better position to determine when a problem lends itself to being presented to the whole class, or when it should be handled on an individual basis. As was stated earlier, when a teacher wishes to give individual children books for bibliotherapy purposes, the children should not be singled out lest they feel ostracized or humiliated. One chance to help the children choose books could occur during a school library period or a class library period. The teacher and/or school librarian could make a few suggestions to a child. The student could then decide on one by reading the first page of a few of the suggested books.

Another way to interest individual students in books for bibliotherapy purposes would be to choose an episode from a book to read aloud to the class. The chosen episode should present the main character in a problem situation. Also, the protagonist should be one with whom the teacher feels a number of students can identify. After the episode is read, a discussion should take place on how the character resolves his or her problems. The author's solution should not be given. The book may then be offered to those individuals who would like to read it. The teacher using this technique should have a few copies of the book available because many of the students will want to read it.

Many times a teacher may find that a number of children in the class share a similar problem. Therefore, the teacher might want to introduce the problem in some way to the class and use a bibliotherapy technique to help the students to cope with their problem. One technique to use is bibliotherapy and role playing. (See Chapter 6.)

The following is an example of how a teacher can use bibliotherapy and role playing in an upper-primary- or lower-intermediate-grade level class.

Scenario

The teacher overhears a number of children discussing their younger brothers and sisters in rather disparaging terms. Not only do many of the children seem to feel that their younger siblings get more love and attention, but they also seem to feel that they "get away" with much more than they can. The teacher decides to use bibliotherapy and role playing to help the students to adjust and cope better with their problem. After looking through a few books that deal with this theme, the teacher chooses Judy

Blume's *Tales of a Fourth Grade Nothing* to read to the class. This book was chosen because not only does it have most of the criteria discussed earlier, but it lends itself to being read aloud to the class and the story will appeal to less mature as well as more mature students.

Introducing the Problem   The teacher asks the students to draw pictures of their families and of their pets, if they have any, and under each picture write one sentence that describes the member of the family or the pet. After the children have finished, a discussion concerning the pictures takes place. The teacher asks those children who have younger brothers or sisters to tell the class something about them. Those children who have no brothers or sisters should be called upon to tell about their parents or pets. Some other questions the teacher might ask are:

> How did you feel when your mother brought home your new baby brother or sister? If you have no younger brothers or sisters, how do you think you would feel if your mother brought home a younger brother or sister?

Bibliotherapy and Role Playing   The teacher reads aloud Blume's book *Tales of a Fourth Grade Nothing* to the whole class in a week's time. After the book is finished, the students discuss Peter's relationship to his younger brother, Fudge. Students are encouraged to share some of their experiences. After this, the students are told that they are going to do some role playing. Each child who would like to will play the role of Fudge, Peter, the mother, or the father. A scene is set in which Fudge keeps interrupting Peter while Peter is trying to build a model plane. No dialogue is given. The children must spontaneously provide that on their own. After each role-playing scene, discuss what took place with the class, and ask for the role players to give their feelings about the parts. If time permits, have the children reverse roles. It is important that only those children who wish to role play should. No child should ever be forced to role play.

Bibliotherapy and Creative Problem-Solving   Another technique the teacher could have used is bibliotherapy and creative problem-solving. In this method, almost the whole book is read aloud to the class. Before the ending, the students, using clues from the book, try to determine how the main character's problem is resolved. They are encouraged, also, to generate their own solutions. After the ending is read, the students are asked to compare their solutions with the author's. Then they can discuss which they liked better and why.

Bibliotherapy can be effective in helping students to better understand themselves and their feelings. When students realize that other persons have similar problems, they are able to cope better with their own. Bibliotherapy also encourages students to try to seek answers in a positive, intellectual, and logical manner.

Books as an Aid in Bibliotherapy

There are a number of excellent books which deal with some of the problems that children may encounter in today's world. Nan Hayden Agle's *Maple Street* is an enlightening story about a young black girl's desire to improve her street and come to terms with a prejudiced white girl. Mary Calhoun's book, *It's Getting Beautiful Now*, concerns a boy's emotional problems and drugs. Francine Chase's *A Visit to the Hospital* helps both parents and children in preparing for a stay in the hospital. Gladys Yessayan Cretan's *All Except Sammy* portrays a boy's attempts to win the respect of his musical family.

Perceptive teachers, alert to the needs of their students, should be able to aid them in choosing books which help them to cope more effectively with individual problems. As in all matters, the teacher should look for balance in the child's reading habits. A certain degree of escapism is fine, but the child must live in the real world and cannot be in a continuous state of fanciful thinking. (See bibliography for annotated references that will help in selecting literature that portrays life as it is.) Table 9.2 consists of a good sampling of books for bibliotherapy organized by theme.

The Treatment of Death in Children's Literature

Death, like old age, is a subject that in the past has been avoided in most children's books. This may be due to the fact that adults feel children are too young to understand death, so it is best that the topic not be broached. However, young children do think about death, but their perception of it is usually different from that of adults. Perhaps if teachers had a better understanding of children's views of death, they could help their students to cope with their feelings and misconceptions.

Young children do not understand the phenomenon of death:

> The child of less than five years does not recognize death as an irreversible fact. In death he sees life. Between the ages of five and nine, death is most often personified and thought of as a contingency. And in general, only after the age of nine, is it recognized that death is a process happening to us according to certain laws.[26]

Children beyond the age of nine are becoming more logical, better able to deal with the world of reality, and better able to relate to others. They are becoming more aware of what it is to be alive. At the same time, they are also becoming aware of what it might be not to be alive; they are beginning to grasp the concept of death.

Elisabeth Kübler-Ross in the past decade probably has done more to change our views

---

[26]Maria Nagy, "The Child's Theories Concerning Death," *Journal of Genetic Psychology* 73 (1948): 7.

table 9.2

Title	Author	Level	Theme
Here's a Penny	Carolyn Haywood	Upper Primary	Adoption
A Month of Sundays	Rose Blue	Upper Primary/Lower Intermediate	Divorce
My Dad Lives in a Downtown Hotel	Peggy Mann	Upper Primary/Lower Intermediate	Divorce
It's Not the End of the World	Judy Blume	Intermediate	Divorce
Elizabeth Gets Well	Alfons Weber	Primary	Illness (in a Hospital)
A Girl Called Al	Constance Greene	Upper Intermediate	A Child Who Is Different
Dinky Hocker Shoots Smack	M. E. Kerr	Upper Intermediate	A Child Who Is Different
Maple Street	Nan Hayden Agle	Upper Primary/Intermediate	Prejudice
Shawn Goes to School	Petronella Breinberg	Preschool/Early Primary	The First Day of School
Confessions of an Only Child	Norma Klein	Upper Primary/Intermediate	A New Baby
Peter's Chair	Ezra Jack Keats	Preschool	A New Baby
Weezie Goes to School	Sue Felt Kerr	Primary	Youngest Child
Tales of a Fourth Grade Nothing	Judy Blume	Upper Primary/Lower Intermediate	Dealing with a Younger Sibling
Nobody Asked Me if I Wanted a Baby Sister	Martha Alexander	Preschool	Dealing with a Younger Sibling
Sabrina	Martha Alexander	Preschool/Early Primary	Dislike of Name
Then Again, Maybe I Won't	Judy Blume	Upper Intermediate/Young Adult	The Finding of Self
Are You There God? It's Me, Margaret	Judy Blume	Intermediate	The Finding of Self
Nikki 108	Rose Blue	Upper Intermediate	The Finding of Self
The Soul Brothers and Sister Lon	Kristin Hunter	Young Adult	The Finding of Self
Run Softly, Go Fast	Barbara Wersba	Young Adult	Death
The Dead Bird	Margaret Wise Brown	Preschool/Kindergarten	Death
My Grandpa Died Today	Joan Fassler	Primary	Death
Charlotte's Web	E. B. White	Upper Primary/Intermediate	Death
Annie and the Old One	Miska Miles	Intermediate	Death
A Taste of Blackberries	Doris Buchanan Smith	Primary	Death
The Tenth Good Thing about Barney	Judith Viorst	Preschool/Lower Primary	Death

toward death and dying than anyone else. She has also helped us to learn about the stages that dying persons and their loved ones go through. The stages are denial and isolation, anger, bargaining, depression, and acceptance. Although the stages are sequential, a person may go in or out of any stage at any time.

Elisabeth Kübler-Ross feels that children should be raised with an awareness of death. She says that in days of old children were more familiar with death than today because the aged and infirm lived at home. Today, when people become old they rarely are kept at home. She feels that this "deprives the children of an experience of death, which is an important learning experience."[27] She says, further, that "if we help them to face fear and show them that through strength and sharing we can overcome

[27]Elisabeth Kübler-Ross, "Facing Up to Death," in *Readings in Human Development* (Guilford, Conn.: Dushkin Publishing, 1976/77), p. 239.

even the fear of dying, then they will be better prepared to face any kind of crisis that might confront them, including the ultimate reality of death."[28]

If children develop *thanatophobia* (fear of death) or death anxiety, bibliotherapy may be a viable method of helping these children. Perhaps by experiencing death vicariously through their readings, children may be better equipped for the realities of death. *Little Women* gives a very good treatment of death, but many boys would not read it. It is difficult to find as good a treatment of death as *Little Women*, but some good books are being published. These seem to represent a "far healthier and more honest approach than the squeamish skirting of the whole subject that has characterized so much of twentieth-century juvenile literature, for surely this is a vital aspect of life, inseparable from it." [29]

Books on Death

In Lloyd Alexander's *The High King*, death is shown to open doors never thought possible. In Jean George's book, *Who Really Killed Cock Robin*, death is presented as a teaching situation. Madeline Polland's book, *To Tell My People* presents death as a misunderstanding, whereas Barbara Wersba's book, *Run Softly, Go Fast*, portrays death as not the worst part of life because it is only after a father's death that the son gains a better understanding of his parent.

Some other books which teachers might find helpful because of their bibliotherapeutic value are:

Where the Lilies Bloom by Vera and Bill Cleaver, Jr.
Little Women by Louisa May Alcott
The High Pasture by Ruth Harnden
Up a Road Slowly by Irene Hunt

The Big Wave by Pearl S. Buck
The Yearling by Marjorie Kinnan Rawlings

(See bibliography for annotated references that will help in selecting books on the subject of death. See also Table 9.2.)

The Treatment of Old Age in Children's Literature

The treatment of the elderly in children's literature has probably been the most neglected and the most poorly portrayed of all other areas. Interestingly, we are living in an era where a person's life expectancy is the greatest that it has ever been, and as a result the elderly are much more visible and vocal.

Although there is an increased interest in gerontology and in more benefits for the elderly, old age is a topic that the young and middle-aged would prefer to ignore. This is sometimes not too difficult because with the advent of nursing homes and retirement communities, the elderly are probably more segregated from society today then ever before.

> Who can speak for the old? And who speaks to us? . . . No one looks at me—, into my eyes, into the core of me. It is as if I am like all who have lived too long, a being to be tolerated or bypassed or humored.[30]

Stereotypes of the Elderly

Although an analysis of old people in various folk tales shows that the elderly actually are portrayed in various ways, when children were asked how elderly people were shown in fairy stories, the children responded: "They are witches." [31] Obviously, these children have

---

[28]Ibid., p. 241.
[29]Evelyn J. Swenson, "The Treatment of Death in Children's Literature," *Elementary English* (March 1972): 401–404.

[30]"An Old Woman Speaks," in Bert Kruger Smith, *Aging in America* (Boston: Beacon, 1973), p. 2.
[31]Myra Pollack Sadker and David Miller Sadker, *Now Upon a Time: A Contemporary View of Children's Literature* (New York: Harper & Row, 1977), p. 77.

been greatly influenced by the portrayal of the old woman as a mean, cross, wicked hag or witch in such famous fairy tales as "Hansel and Gretel," "Sleeping Beauty," and "Snow White and the Seven Dwarfs."

Barnum, in a study of one hundred randomly selected books, found that the elderly are discriminated against in contemporary young children's literature. She claims that the elderly "appear less frequently than they should, in view of their proportion in the United States population, and are depicted as disadvantaged in many socioeconomic and behavior characteristics."[32] In analyzing books in which the elderly do appear and in which they play a significant part, Barnum claims that the elderly male and female are shown in stereotyped roles. The elderly are rarely shown engaging in notable or exciting activities; they are rarely shown as interesting or active individuals; they are generally shown as passive and incompetent.[33] This is a rather depressing state of affairs.

On the other side, there are books which portray the elderly in another stereotyped way—that of being omniscient. The elderly are shown to be wise and all-knowing in all matters. This idealized version appears in such books as John Houston's *Akavak and the White Archer*.

Some contemporary authors are attempting to portray the elderly in more realistic terms. *A Figure of Speech*, by Norma Fox Mazer, is one such book. It is the sensitive portrayal of an independent old man who lives in a separate apartment but in the same house as his children and grandchildren. Jenny, one of his grandchildren, has a warm relationship with her grandfather. Conflict arises when the grandfather begins to become a little senile about the same time that Jenny's brother returns from college—married and needing a place to live.

Literature can help dispel myths concerning the elderly as well as create them. If books present the elderly in a realistic, compassionate, sensitive, and perceptive manner, it is to be hoped that the negative image that many young people have of the elderly will change to a more positive and realistic one. (See bibliography on "Children and the Aged" for sources that present a bibliography on current books, which offer a positive and acceptable image of the elderly.)

Developing Taste in the Selection of Books

Helping children develop taste in the selection of books is an important goal in the literature program. However, this will not come about by restricting children's reading or insisting that they only read those books selected for them.

The Nancy Drew, Hardy Boys, and Bobbsey Twins books have been the bane of a number of librarians for decades. Some libraries do not have copies, and the mere mention of one of these books may upset some librarians. The books arouse such animosity because they are mass produced in accordance with an exact formula. As a result, the vocabulary, plot, and characters are all stereotyped—all are almost exactly the same. Although these books have no literary value, many children read and seem to enjoy them. The problem confronting teachers is not whether they should demand that children stop reading these books, but how to get them interested in and reading other books.

Good readers eventually become bored with Nancy Drew, the Bobbsey Twins, and the Hardy Boys series because of their sameness, and leave them after reading just a few. However, some children need further stimuli, such as having teachers introduce other books that they think would interest those students. A good method of bringing attention to better books is by reading excerpts aloud from them. The teacher should tell the children something about

[32]Phyllis Winet Barnum, "The Aged in Young Children's Literature," *Language Arts* 54 (January 1977): 29.

[33]Ibid., p. 32.

the book—just enough to whet their appetites. The part chosen to be read should help to arouse the children's curiosity and interest. The manner in which the excerpt is read is very important. The teacher must show genuine enthusiasm, both in reading and in telling about the book. If the teacher has done a good job, most of the students will be trying to get the book to read on their own. The teacher should have several copies of the book immediately available.

Readability and Interest Levels in Choosing Books

There are usually one or two books that are very popular and make the rounds of almost all the children in the class. Although this book may be at the interest level of most of the children, it may not be at all of their reading ability levels. There are always a few children who feel left out because they can't read these books. They may take out the books and either walk around with them or make-believe that they are reading them. By having the book in their possession they may feel they can gain the esteem they crave and need.

The teacher should not embarrass such students, but should carefully choose books similar to the popular one at their reading ability levels, and try to interest them in the substitutes. The teacher should speak individually to such a child and say, "I know how much you like books about heroes. Well, I was looking through this book the other day and I immediately thought of you. I just felt that you would enjoy this book." The teacher should then try to have the student read the first page. Once the child starts by reading the first page, the battle is almost won. The student will usually continue because the book is at both his or her reading ability and interest levels.

The teacher should have an ample supply of books at various readability and interest levels.

To aid teachers in obtaining a proper selection, they can consult the *Elementary School Library Collection*. This reference work gives estimates of children's interest levels and reading difficulties for all the books listed. Having such books available is the essential first part. The other part is helping students choose books based on both their interest and reading ability levels. Unfortunately, as has been shown, a book may be at a child's interest level, but the child may be unable to read it independently. For example, *The Lion* by René DuBois would be of interest to preschool, kindergarten, and first-grade children. However, according to the Spache Readability formula for grades one to three, the book would be near the 3.5 grade level. This means it would have to be read to younger children. At the other end of the scale, there may be students in upper grades with difficulty in reading, who may be at a reading level as low as the pre-primer. These students desperately need books at their interest levels. Fortunately, during the past decade, more books have been published which have the high interest but low readability levels required by such students.

Readability formulas are used to determine the reading difficulty of written material. Most readability formulas are based on both sentence length and syllabication: however, some may also use word lists. Readability formulas do not take other variables—such as experiential background of children, maturation, purpose of reading, and so on—into account. They also do not measure the abstractness of ideas nor the literary style nor quality of the written material. Readability formulas are not absolutely reliable, since different formulas on similar material may not produce the same scores. When a readability formula produces a score of grade four, it does not mean that all fourth graders will be able to read the book. It merely means that a number of fourth graders—approximately five to seven out of ten such readers—will have little trouble with the book.[34] Although readability formulas are imperfect tools, they do have value, for they give some idea of the difficulty of a book for specific groups of readers.

Regardless of which formula teachers use, they should be familiar with the methods for estimating readability. Teachers do not have to work out the exact estimates for each book, but by observing the sentence length and syllables, or sentence length and kinds of words, that is, the difficulty of the words used in a paragraph, they can estimate whether a book is at the proper level for their students to read independently. (See Appendix for examples of readability formulas.)

Although it is difficult to completely ascertain what makes a book easy or hard, the following are "readability pluses" which parents, teachers, and librarians might look for in a book:[35]

Readability is excitement. A punchy beginning. Forceful and colorful language. Variety in style, including both long and short sentences. A subject that appeals to the reader. Interesting pictures and other illustrations.

Readability is familiarity. Plain talk and an informal style, especially for readers with difficulty in standard English. The words and expressions of ordinary speech. The familiar sentence patterns of spoken language. Material that deals with something the reader knows about and has experience with. Unfamiliar ideas explained in terms of familiar ideas.

Readability is clarity. A low percentage of abstract words. Difficult ideas explained and not clumped together. Paragraphs not too long or complicated. Ideas developed in logical order. Introductions and summaries where suitable.

Readability is visibility. Type large enough to read comfortably. Lines not so long that the eye has trouble finding the beginning of the next line. Paper and ink that lets type stand out sharply—

black ink on whitish nonglare paper is best. Plenty of light, without glare. Distance between eyes and print close enough for comfortable reading, but not too close.

Readability is a good book. It's the symmetry and warmth a poem transmits to you. It's a quality that computers find indigestible because it defies precise statistical analysis.

The Elementary-School Library Collection

The *Elementary School Library Collection*, as we have seen, is an invaluable resource with which the teacher should be familiar because it presents children's books with both readability and interest levels, as well as resource books for the teacher.

Following are the symbols used in the *Elementary School Library Collection* to determine interest levels:

N	Preschool in appeal: may be even middle grade in reading difficulty.
N-P	At kindergarten and lower-primary grade in interest and appeal (K–2).
P	At primary-grade level interest (1–3).
P-I	At upper-primary-grade interest level (2–4).
I	At middle-grade interest level (4–6).
I-A	At sixth-grade interest level.
A	Of interest and appeal to mature readers in sixth grade.

The reading difficulty is based on the "Fry Graph for Estimating Readability," except that in the primary grades the revised Spache formula is used. Examples of symbols used in the *Elementary School Library Collection* to represent interest and readability levels are: P–2, I–4, P–6, A–8, P-I–3. The first symbol represents interest level and the second the readability level; (P–2) means primary-grade interest level and second-grade readability level.

[34]Allen M. Blair, "Everything You always Wanted to Know about Readability but Were Afraid to Ask," *Elementary English* 48 (May 1971): 442–443.

[35]Ibid., p. 443.

Below are a number of books of fiction listed in the *Elementary School Library Collection* which are indicated as Phase One books—chosen as indispensable for any library, no matter how small.[36]

Following is an example of the information given in each reference for this section of the *Elementary School Library Collection:*[37]

DALGLIESH, ALICE. Courage of Sarah Noble; illus. by Leonard Weisgard. Scribner © 1954. 52p illus.
> Sarah finds courage to accompany her father into the wilderness, to cook for him while he prepares a home for the family.

---

[36]*The Elementary School Library Collection*, 11th ed., Mary Gaver, ed. (Newark, N.J.: Bro-Dart Foundation, 1977).
[37]Ibid., p. 342.

SUBJ: Indians of North America—Fiction./Frontier and pioneer life—Connecticut—Fiction.
> Ph-1 I-3 $5.95

The listings in the section "Professional Collection" are also indispensable for the language arts teacher. This section includes an annotated bibliography of various kinds of resource books for teachers, ranging from a comprehensive listing of children's books in print, to resource books on specific topics, to a bibliography of resource materials, and to books available to teachers for references.

Following are examples of some of the resource materials:

| *Children's Books in Print* | 1969-v annual | R. R. Bowker |

Title	Author	Interest and Readability Level	Subject
Little Women	Louisa May Alcott	I–A	Girls' fiction
Uncle Mike's Boy	Jerome Brooks	I–6	Loneliness–divorce
A Certain Small Shepherd	Rebecca Caudill	P–1–A	Physically handicapped–joy–sorrow–Christmas
Catch that Pass!	Matt Christopher	I–3	Football fiction
Constance, A Story of Early Plymouth	Patricia Clapp	I–5	Pilgrim Fathers fiction
Poppy Seed Cakes	Margery Clark	P–I–7	New York City fiction
Ellen Tebbits	Beverly Cleary	I–3	School stories
Henry Huggins	Beverly Cleary	P–I–4	Dog stories
Mock Revolt	Vera Cleaver	I–A–6	Family fiction
Away Goes Sally	Elizabeth Coatsworth	I–5	Moving fiction
Bloody Country	James Lincoln Collier	I–5	Wyoming Valley, Pa.–fathers and sons–pioneer life
My Brother Sam is Dead	James Lincoln Collier	I–A–5	United States history–revolution–brothers
Adventures of Pinocchio	Carlo Collodi	I–7	Fairy tales
Come By Here	Olivia Coolidge	I–A–6	Orphan Black fiction
Red Room Riddle, A Ghost Story	Scott Corbett	I–6	Ghost stories
Smoke	William Corbin	1-A–7	Dogs and stepfathers
Courage of Sarah Noble	Alice Dalgliesh	1–3	Frontier life
Door in the Wall	Marguerite DeAngeli	I–7	Physically handicapped
Horse Came Running	Meindert Dejong	I–A–6	Horse story
Wheel on the School	Meindert Dejong	I	Stork story
A Christmas Carol	Charles Dickens	1–A	Christmas story
Four Story Mistake	Elizabeth Enright	1-A–6	Family fiction
Hundred Dresses	Eleanor Estes	P–I–6	Poles in the U.S. Dresses–girls
Wind in the Door	Madelene L'Engle	I–A–7	Science fiction/Fantasies

Black Experience in Children's Books	1974 Rev. ed.	Augusta Baker
Reading Ladders for Human Relations	1972	Virginia M. Reid, ed.
Films Kids Like	1973	Susan Rice
Good Reading for Poor Readers	1974	George D. Spache
Sex Education on Film	1971	Laura J. Singer
Folklore of the North American Indians	1969	Judith C. Ullom
Science Book List for Children	1972	Hilary J. Deason
Complete Book of Children's Play	1970	Ruth E. Hartley
Multimedia Approach to Children's Literature: A Selective List of Films, Filmstrips, and Recordings Based on Children's Books	1972	Ellin Greene, ed.
Arbuthnot Anthology of Children's Literature	1976	May Hill Arbuthnot

Following is a sample of the information given in each reference for this section of the *Elementary School Library Collection:*[38]

CHILDREN'S BOOKS IN PRINT. Bowker, R. R. 1969-v annual.

A comprehensive list of some 40,000 titles in paper and hardcover binding, currently issued and for sale by U.S. publishers as children's books, but "no textbooks, no toybooks, and no workbooks." Three indexes (author, title, illustrator) each give author,

[38]Ibid., p. 497.

title, publisher, date, price and other vital trade information, including price for library bindings and listings of large-type editions.
Includes a list of titles which have gone out of print since the last edition.
—Subject guide. R. R. Bowker 1969-v annual. SUBJ: Children's literature—Bibliography./ Illustrators.

Ph-1 $25.00

Creative Communication with Children through Library Materials

Horn Book Magazine is indispensable to teachers because of its critical reviews of children's books and its articles on authors and illustrators. *School Library Journal* is probably one of the most useful professional journals because of its large number of book evaluations as well as its articles on librarianship. *Language Arts,* formerly called *Elementary English,* usually has a monthly column devoted to reviews of current children's literature and an interview with a well-known children's writer, which language arts teachers should also find most beneficial. At times, articles appear which present annotated bibliographies in specific areas. For example, the November/December 1978 issue of *Language Arts* presented an annotated bibliography of short, easy books for reluctant readers.[39]

The Reading Teacher often has articles on children's literature and often presents annotated bibliographies, which are very helpful for teachers. For example, the April 1978 issue's article entitled "Realistic Literature About the Handicapped" contains an annotated bibliography that teachers might find useful in choosing reading matter for their pupils to prepare them for special children who might be mainstreamed into their classroom.[40] The May 1978 issue has

[39]Alden J. Moe and Carol J. Hopkins, "Jingles, Jokes, Limericks, Poems, Proverbs, Puns, Puzzles and Riddles: Fast Reading for Reluctant Readers," *Language Arts* 55 (November/December 1978): 957–965.
[40]Ruth L. Fein and Adrienne H. Ginsberg, "Realistic Literature About the Handicapped," *The Reading Teacher* 31 (April 1978): 802–805.

an article on "The Interracial Family in Children's Literature," which reviews children's books available on this topic.[41] Each year in the October issue of *The Reading Teacher* a bibliography of children's choices of previous years' books is usually presented. (See section on "Children's Interests and Book Selection.")

The following is a compilation of other references for teachers and parents. An asterisk is placed in front of Nelson's book because it is an especially excellent handbook for teachers. Not only does it feature a variety of stories from other countries but the stories and poems offer a wide diversity of literature topics from the weather to animals, famous people, holidays, and so on.

References for the Adult

American Library Association	*Young Adult Services in the Public Library*
May H. Arbuthnot and others	*Children's Books Too Good to Miss*
Dorothy Broderick	*An Introduction to Children's Work in Public Libraries*
G. Robert Carlsen	*Books and the Teenage Reader*
Phyllis Fenner	*Proof of the Pudding*
Paul Hazard	*Books, Children and Men*
Harriet Long	*Rich the Treasure*
*Mary Ann Nelson	*A Comparative Anthology of Children's Literature*
New York Library Association,	*Films for Children Films for Young*
Childhood and Young Adult Services Division	*Adults Recordings for Children*
Myra Pollack Sadker and David Miller Sadker	*Now Upon a Time: A Contemporary View of Children's Literature*
Ruth Sawyer	*Way of the Storyteller*
Marie Shedlock	*The Art of the Storyteller*
Lillian Smith	*The Unreluctant Years*

Award-winning Books

Who is to judge whether a book has value for children? Are children given a chance to judge the books that they read?

As was stated earlier in this chapter, the criteria to use in determining selection of books for children should include knowledge of children and what they enjoy in a book. Merely saying that a book is an award-winner, as judged by adults, does not mean that the book will be enjoyed by children. It may be that the award-winners chosen by adults have adult values and are reflections of what they think a good book for children should be.

There are awards given to books based on children's nominations: The Georgia Children's Book Award, the Dorothy Canfield Fisher Memorial Children's Book Award, the Junior Book Award, the Young Readers' Choice Award, the William Allen White Children's Book Award, and the Sequoya Children's Book Award. In making these awards, lists of books are first compiled by various individuals concerned with children's literature—such as librarians, teachers, parents, and so on. Students from the fourth through ninth grade then vote on their favorites.

Interestingly, a study using students' judgments found that only four books chosen by stu-

[41]Margo A. Long, "The Interracial Family in Children's Literature," *The Reading Teacher* 31 (May 1978): 909–915.

dents were Newbery Award winners.[42] There were ten similar books chosen by the six award-granting organizations that used children's judgments. It appears that children from different areas have some unanimity of opinion on what they like. Also, all Newbery book winners may not be ones that interest children. This does not mean that major awards, such as the Newbery, should be abolished, but rather that children's choices should also be considered. The main purpose of these awards is to encourage the writing of good children's literature.

The Newbery Medal and the Caldecott Medal

The Newbery Medal is given annually to the book published in the United States which has been voted "the most distinguished literature" for children. The Caldecott Medal is given for the book chosen to be the best picturebook of the year. Following is a listing of the Newbery and Caldecott Medal books chosen since 1965:

Newbery Medal Awards

Title	Author	Year
Shadow of a Bull	Maia Wojciechowska	1965
I, Juan de Pareja	Elizabeth Borten de Trevino	1966
Up a Road Slowly	Irene Hunt	1967
From the Mixed-Up Files of Mrs. Basil E. Frankweiler	E. L. Konigsburg	1968
The High King	Lloyd Alexander	1969
Sounder	William Armstrong	1970
Summer of the Swans	Betsy Byars	1971
Mrs. Frisby and the Rats of NIMH	Robert O'Brien	1972
Julie of the Wolves	Jean George	1973
The Slave Dancer	Paula Fox	
M. C. Higgins the Great	Virginia Hamilton	1975
The Grey King	Susan Cooper	1976
Roll of Thunder, Hear My Cry	Mildred D. Taylor	1977

[42]Manuel Darkatsh, "Who Should Decide on a Book's Merit?" *Elementary English* 51 (March 1974): 353–354.

A Bridge to Terabithia	Katherine Paterson	1978
The Westing Game	Ellen Raskin	1979

Caldecott Medal Awards

Title	Author	Year
May I Bring a Friend?	Beatrice Schenk	1965
Always Room for One More	Sorche Nic Leodhas	1966
Sam, Bangs and Moonshine	Evaline Ness	1967
Drummer Hoff	Barbara Emberley	1968
The Fool of the World and the Flying Ship	Arthur Ransome	1969
Sylvester and the Magic Pebble	William Steig	1970
A Story—A Story	Gail Haley	1971
One Fine Day	Nonny Hogrogian	1972
The Funny Little Woman	Arlene Mosel	1973
Duffy and the Devil	Harvey and Margot Zemach	1974
Arrow to the Sun	Gerald McDermott	1975
Why Mosquitoes Buzz in People's Ears	Leo and Diane Dillon	1976
Ashanti to Zulu: African Traditions	Leo and Diane Dillon	1977
Noah's Ark	Peter Spier	1978
The Girl Who Loved Wild Horses	Paul Goble	1979

Book Reporting

Before discussing the methods of book reporting, the purposes of book reports must be made clear. For many teachers, the main purpose of the book report is to find out whether the child has actually read the book. A teacher who asks students to make a formal, written book report after every book they have read is not being realistic, and is actually discouraging children from reading more. The oral book reports discussed in a previous section were used to stimulate other students' interest in books. The students enjoy giving this kind of report because it is based on books of the students' own choosing, and the reports are voluntarily and enthusiastically given. If the purpose of the book report is to discern whether the students have read a particular book, there are many interesting ways that this can be done that are also fun.

Children can present character sketches portraying the main characters in a book, or they can tell about a character to see if the other children in the class, who have also read this book, know who the character being portrayed or sketched is.

Some students might draw caricatures of some of the book characters or a scene from the book they have read, to see if other students can discover the book they had in mind. The alert teacher will note that this type of activity is a hybrid, and allows for the cross-fertilization of language arts with the visual or graphic arts, thus helping to weld the entire elementary-school program into one cohesive whole. This allows for maximum interplay of the various skills and talents of students, which, in turn, will yield the maximum favorable reinforcing response from the students. The teacher should be constantly on the lookout for such activities.

Whatever activity the children choose in relation to their reading, they should not have to do something for every book they have read.

Written book reports as well as oral book reports have a place in the language arts program, because children have to be able to communicate in writing as well as orally. However, written reports should not deter children from reading. Some teachers choose one book on which everyone must write a report, some give the students a choice of books, and some allow students a completely free choice. The latter two methods, where choice is involved, are better than the forced method. Since many students look on the written book report as an onerous task, it becomes unbearable to some if they cannot at least choose the book. The number of written book reports should be kept to a feasible minimum.

Pillar presents a number of novel approaches to stimulate students to write book reports. The approaches are typed on index cards and available for students. Here are some of them.[43]

1. Pretend you are a puppy and have a chance to be adopted by one of the people in your book. Which one would you choose and why?

2. King Kong has just climbed through your bedroom window. He is trying madly to rip apart the book you have just finished reading. You must act very quickly and defend it. Convince him not to destroy it by citing incidents that you enjoyed. Prove to him that this book is worth keeping.

3. Invite one of the characters in your book to dinner. Tell him or her why you have selected them above the others. Then, leave a note for your mother describing the person and including a few "do's and don'ts" for her to follow so that your guest will feel right at home.

4. You are your book on a shelf in a toy store. What will you say to children to convince them to buy you?

5. Pretend that you are the author of the book you have just finished reading and that it has not yet been published. The editors like your book except for the last chapter. They ask you to write a completely different last chapter. You agree to do so. Remember that it must agree in content and style with the earlier chapters.

6. You are a television commercial writer and have been asked to write a commercial advertising this book to the American public. In not more than two paragraphs, since commercial time is expensive, tell why your book should be read.

7. Since you have the power to transform the major characters in your book into animals and choose to do so, decide upon an animal for each based upon personality traits. Write a letter to each telling why he or she is similar to the animal selected.

8. You are a typewriter that continues to type long after the author has put the final period to a story and retired. Is it that you are changing some of the characters and parts of the plot, or is it that you just can't bear to *see* the story end? What do you have to say?

[43]Arlene M. Pillar, "Individualizing Book Reports," *Elementary English* 52 (April 1975): 467–469.

The main objective for written book reports should be similar to oral ones; that is, to stimulate other children into wanting to read the book. This is the best purpose for having students do book reports. The techniques for writing book reports will be presented in Chapter 10.

Book Wheels

Teachers must be careful about the use of "Book Wheels"—a circle chart divided into a number of segments, each one representing a different kind of book. Many teachers display such charts and insert a student's name in a given section—biography, mystery, poetry— each time a book has been read. The aim is to stimulate students to read as many books as possible, and to have their names inserted in all the sections of the wheel, but the technique can place undue stress and strain on many children. There are children who love to read for enjoyment, reading slowly and savoring each delightful passage. The wheel chart puts pressure on them to speed up. It can become too competitive. There are also some children who may have difficulty in reading and cannot read many books independently. The chart hinders their self-concepts. Often, these children may actually say that they have read books which they have not, because they are embarrassed that their names are not on the chart. A perceptive teacher who wants to use the wheel chart can do so by giving the children their own private charts. Rather than competing with everyone else, the children are thus competing against themselves. Even when the chart is used in this way, the teacher must assure the children that no contest is involved. The chart should only be used to help the students keep a record of their reading.

Poetry, the Stepchild of Children's Literature

> I have a secret from everybody in the
>   world-full-of-people
> But I cannot always remember how it goes.

Research on Poetry in the Schools

If you were to ask children what they like to read least often, the most probable response would be poetry. Why?

From studies it was found that as students advanced through the grades they enjoyed poetry less and less. The reasons given as to why poetry is the stepchild of children's literature are many and varied: the overanalysis of poems,

the overemphasis on memorizing specific poems, using poetry for a discussion of other topics or issues, the difficulty of reading and understanding poems, the improper reading of poems, the sadness or dullness of poems, and so on. As can be seen from some of these reasons, there is no agreement on why poetry is disliked, but there is agreement on the fact that it is disliked.

A number of studies in the early part of the twentieth century tried to determine students' preferences in poetry. Here, too, there was no unanimity of opinion. Some of the reasons given would not be relevant today, such as: Poetry is not in harmony with the main intellectual movements. However, some others would be applicable today:

> (Poetry) used in literature courses is unwisely selected and incorrectly placed for the following reasons: It is selected for literary values that are above pupils' level of appreciation. It is remote from children's life experience and demands an appreciation of the thoughtful, meditative, introspective attitude toward life. It is too difficult for any but the superior pupil. Its difficulty may not only prevent the reading of similar material as a leisure-time activity but may actually set up a negative reaction to all literature.[44]

A more recent study confirms that students enjoyed poetry less as they advanced through the grades. Figurative language and poems depending entirely on imagery were also disliked; however, narrative poems and limericks as well as the use of rhyme, rhythm, and sound increased the children's enjoyment of poetry.[45] Teachers should use this information in planning their poetry program. (See "Listening for Appreciation" in Chapter 5 and "Creating Poetry" in Chapter 11.)

---

[44]Lucy Kangley, "Poetry Preferences in the Junior High School," Contribution to Education No. 75 (New York: Bureau of Publications, Teachers College, Columbia University, 1938).

[45]Carolyn A. Terry, "A National Survey of Children's Poetry Preferences in the Fourth, Fifth, and Sixth Grades" (Ph.D. diss., University of Ohio, 1972).

Poetry's Place in the Curriculum

Poetry does have a place in children's lives and in the curriculum at school. Children's listening experiences should try to cover Mother Goose rhymes, nonsense poems, poems with sensory appeal, and poems that tell a story. Creativity has its origin in children's minds when they begin to respond to the rhythmic beauty of a poem. Enjoyment may be derived from the humor, the fantasy, and the rich store of ideas and emotions which are expressed in poetry. There is a release from tension; there is sheer joy to be had in listening to literature read with feeling and understanding by the teacher.

Teachers should help guide their students to rich experiences through poetry. In order to do this well, teachers must also enjoy poetry. To spread enthusiasm, teachers must be enthused. The choice of poems should be varied, and the study of poetry should not be made prescriptive; for example, children should not be subjected to memorizing poems for the sake of memorizing. If children enjoy a poem and reread it many times for sheer delight, they oftentimes will memorize it simply because they want to. To aid in this process, teachers should be concerned with selecting poems that will appeal to children, that will help them to clarify and extend their appreciation of literature and life.

The children should hear poetry for the sheer delight of it, as they would listen to music. Poetry should be read aloud to hear the sound of the words, the lilt of the rhyme, and the swing of the line. Choral speaking, poetry recordings, and combining poetry and music are examples of exercises which would help to enhance children's enjoyment of poetry.

As the poet William Yeats has said: "I just heard a poem spoken with so delicate a sense of its rhythm, with so perfect a respect for its meaning, that if I were a wise man and could persuade a few people to learn the art, I would never open a book of verse." Teachers should be knowledgeable about children's preferences in poetry so that they can wisely select poems for their students. It has been found that children usually prefer the following:

1. Direct discourse to indirect.
2. Having the place and time clearly indicated so that they can picture the scene in their minds.
3. Humor, but not the satire of adult humor.
4. Sincerity.
5. Lack of moralizing or preaching.

In the presentation of the poem, some principles that would help to instill a continuous liking are:

1. Teachers should read the poem aloud. Like music, the poem should be heard a few times first.
2. Clear up any baffling words that block the children's comprehension.
3. Wait for children's reaction.
4. Plan the uses of poetry in the classroom.
5. Try to choose the right poem at the right time.

Following are some "don'ts" in teaching poetry:

1. Do not overanalyze.
2. Do not overemphasize word practice.
3. Do not confuse singsong rhymes with poetry.
4. Do not approach children below their level.
5. Do not say, "Oh, everybody should love this poem." What appeals to some will not necessarily appeal to others.
6. Do not emphasize memorization.
7. Do not ask children to recite at length.
8. Do not "force" poetry on children.

Examples of Poetry in the Classroom

Many opportunities present themselves for the introduction of poetry in the classroom. The teacher should take advantage of these moments, remembering that not everyone likes the same kinds of poems. During autumn, when the leaves are starting to turn many different colors, and to fall, the teacher could introduce such

poems as James S. Tippett's "Autumn Woods,"
Carl Sandburg's "Theme in Yellow," and Bliss
Carman's "A Vagabond Song," or any of the
following:

THE CITY OF FALLING LEAVES

Leaves fall,
Brown leaves,
Yellow leaves streaked with brown.
They fall,
Flutter,
Fall again.
The brown leaves,
And the streaked yellow leaves,
Loosen on their branches
And drift slowly downwards.
One,
One, two, three,
One, two, five.
All Venice is a falling of Autumn leaves—
Brown,
And yellow streaked with brown.

AMY LOWELL

NOVEMBER NIGHT

Listen . . .
With faint dry sound,
Like steps of passing ghosts,
The leaves, frost-crisp'd, break from the trees
And fall.

ADELAIDE CRAPSEY

THE SEASONS

Autumn marches across the hill
In russet, red, and gold;
Winter steals in soft and still
Crystalline and cold;
Spring is heard in each bird call
Till everything is green;
But summer blazes on every wall
And even heat is seen.

EDNA L. STERLING

Rachel Field's *Roads* is excellent for stirring
the imagination:

A road might lead to anywhere—
To harbor towns and quays,
Or to a witch's pointed house
Hidden by bristly trees.
It might lead past the tailor's door,
Where he sews with needle and thread,
Or by Miss Pim the milliner's
With her hats for every head.
It might be a road to a great, dark cave
With treasure and gold piled high,
Or a road with a mountain tied to its end,
Blue-humped against the sky.
Oh, a road might lead you anywhere—
To Mexico or Maine.
But then it might fool you, and—
Lead you back home again!

A foggy, drizzly day might be a good time to
present Carl Sandburg's *Fog*.

The fog comes
on little cat feet.

It sits looking
over harbor and city
on silent haunches
and then moves on.

Young children especially enjoy poems about
animals.

CAT

The black cat yawns,
Opens her jaws,
Stretches her legs,
And shows her claws.

Then she gets up
And stands on four
Long stiff legs
And yawns some more.

She shows her sharp teeth,
She stretches her lip,
Her slice of a tongue
Turns up at the tip.

Lifting herself
On her delicate toes,
She arches her back
As high as it goes.

She lets herself down
With particular care,
And pads away
With her tail in the air.
MARY BRITTON MILLER

Some poems children enjoy because of the special thought they convey.

A WORD

A word is dead
When it is said,
 Some say.
I say it just
Begins to live
 That day.
EMILY DICKINSON

Children especially enjoy verses such as:

ELETELEPHONY

Once there was an elephant,
Who tried to use the telephant—
No! no! I mean an elephone
Who tried to use the telephone—
(Dear me! I am not certain quite
That even now I've got it right.)

Howe'er it was, he got his trunk
Entangled in the telephunk;
The more he tried to get it free,
The louder buzzed the telephee—
(I fear I'd better drop the song
of elephop and telephong!)
LAURA RICHARDS

A snowy day might be a good time to introduce children to *Stopping By Woods on a Snowy Evening* by Robert Frost, which is usually a favorite of many children.

Robert Frost's "Death of the Hired Man" is a beautiful, sensitive poem which brilliantly portrays the tired and old and ineffectual character of Silas. It is a poem for reading to children in the upper elementary grades, and helps them to realize that poems do not have to rhyme. It is also the kind of poem that, if properly expressed, will produce teary eyes after its reading.

Figures of Speech in Poetry

There is a place for analysis of poems in the language arts program. In poetry, as in prose, if the words are not in the children's hearing capacity, or if they do not understand the ideas, or if the figures of speech are meaningless to the listeners or readers, little enjoyment can take place. Although there are some poems— such as "The Congo" by Vachel Lindsay and "The Raven" by Edgar Allan Poe—which can be enjoyed (the former because of its rhythm and the latter because of its eeriness and ability to create a mood) without knowing the complete meaning, this is not so for the majority.

If the purpose of the lesson is to be analysis of poetry, or the better understanding of figures of speech, this aim should be emphasized and not be confused with poetry appreciation. The children should be helped to understand that in order to appreciate poetry, they must understand the words and figures of speech used in the poems. The reason many children say, "It just doesn't make sense to me," is because many of the words are just noises to them.

The figures of speech most commonly used in poetry are simile, metaphor, and personification. Simile is the comparison of two unlike objects using "like" or "as." Metaphor is also the comparison of two unlike objects, but without using "like" or "as." Personification is the giving of human characteristics and capabilities to nonhuman things such as inanimate objects, abstract ideas, or animals.

In the poem "There Is No Frigate Like a Book" by Emily Dickinson, when a frigate (a ship) is compared to a book, and coursers (swift horses) are compared to a page of prancing poetry, simile is being used. "Prancing poetry" is also an example of personification. The poet says, "This traverse may the poorest take without oppress of toll." "This traverse" is an example of a metaphor in which a journey is being compared to the reading of a book.

Most children in the primary grades would not be able to understand symbolic figures of speech. However, they will be able to get an understanding of imagery in poetry, if the images that are presented in the poem are non-symbolic similes. For example, young children would have no difficulty in understanding this poem by Christina Georgina Rossetti.

WHAT IS PINK?

What is pink? A rose is pink
By the fountain's brink.
What is red? A poppy's red
In its barley bed.
What is blue? The sky is blue
Where the clouds float thro'.
What is white? A swan is white
Sailing in the light.
What is yellow? Pears are yellow,
Rich and ripe and mellow.
What is green? The grass is green,
With small flowers between.
What is violet? Clouds are violet
In the summer twilight.
What is orange? Why, an orange,
Just an orange!

Upper-elementary-grade students enjoy using oxymorons. These are word contradictions, which are used to portray a particular image. For example, "the loud silence was deafening." (See Chapter 11.)

The School Library and Library Skills

The school library should be an integrated part of the students' ongoing activities. A number of schools have designed their physical plants so that the library is actually in the center of the building, easily accessible to all classrooms. The library, properly utilized, becomes the students' storehouse of information and a reservoir of endless delight for them.

The atmosphere in the library should be such that children feel welcome, invited, and wanted. The librarian is the individual who is responsible for setting this tone. A friendly, warm person who loves children and books will usually have a library which has similar characteristics. Children should feel free to visit the library at all times, not just during their regularly scheduled periods.

An enthusiastic and inventive librarian will, by various means, act as an invitation to children to come to the library. Some librarians engage in weekly storytelling activities for all grade levels. Librarians should encourage teachers and children to make suggestions for storytelling, as well as to share the kinds of books they enjoy and would like. The librarian should also act as a resource person in helping the classroom teacher to develop library skills in students. Once students gain the "library habit," it is hard to break, and it will remain with them throughout life.

Following are some of the library skills that children should achieve in the elementary school.

Primary Grades

In the primary grades children are ready to acquire some library skills which will help them to become independent library users. First, the teacher can help primary children to gain an idea of the kinds of books that are available in the library; for example, fiction and nonfiction books. Definitions of the terms should be given, as well as examples of each type of book. For best results, the examples used should be books with which the children are familiar.

Primary-grade children who have learned to read and can alphabetize can also learn to use the card catalogue. They should learn that there are three kinds of cards for each book: an author card, a title card, and the subject card. The teacher should have samples of these for the children to see and handle. By simulating this activity in the classroom, children will be better prepared for actual library activity. Also, their chances for success in using the catalogue properly to find a desired book will be increased. This utilitarian activity can also be programmed to reinforce knowledge of alphabetizing.

Intermediate and Upper-Elementary Grades

By the fourth grade children can learn about other categories of books in the library, such as biographies and reference books.

Reference Books   Children in the elementary grades ask many questions about many topics. Teachers should use some of these questions to help children learn about reference sources. Teachers should help children to understand that it is impossible for one person to know everything today because of the vast amount of knowledge that already exists, compounded each year by its exponential growth. However, a person can learn about any particular area or field if he or she knows what source books to go to for help. For example, the *Readers' Guide to Periodical Literature* will help one to find magazine articles written on almost any subject of interest. There are reference books on language and usage, such as Roget's *Thesaurus of English Words and Phrases*, which would help upper-grade students in finding synonyms and less trite words to use in writing.

The most often used reference book in elementary school, besides the dictionary, is the encyclopedia. Children should be helped to use the encyclopedia as a tool and an aid, rather than as an end in itself. That is, children should be shown how to extract information from the encyclopedia without copying the article verbatim.

In the upper-elementary grades children should learn that there are many reference source books available in the library which can supply information about a famous writer, baseball player, scientist, celebrity, and so forth. The key factor is knowing that these reference sources exist, and knowing which reference book to go to for the needed information.

Teachers can help their upper-grade children to familiarize themselves with these reference books by giving children assignments in which they have to determine what source books to use in fulfilling the assignment.

The Dewey Decimal Classification System

Fifth graders can begin to learn about classifying books in the Dewey Decimal System. Although most colleges and large libraries use the Library of Congress classification system, because it allows for more categories, the Dewey Decimal System is used in most public school libraries. Following are Dewey's ten classifications covering the complete range of areas:

000–099
General Works: encyclopedias, and all other books that summarize knowledge; periodicals; newspapers.

100–199
Philosophy: books on philosophy and psychology (what man has thought about himself and his place in the universe, and how he thinks).

200–299
Religion: books about the different religions and myths of the world.

300–399
Social Science: books on government, law, custom, folklore, family, community, national and international organizations.

400–499
Philology: languages, dictionaries, grammar, prosody.

500–599
Pure Science: mathematics, astronomy, physics, chemistry.

600–699
Applied Science or Useful Arts: medicine, engineering, agriculture, communications (books on inventions, machinery, health, food, industries).

700–799
Fine Arts: music, painting, architecture, sculpture, drawing.

800–899
Literature: (literature of any nation).

900–999
History: history, geography (the story of the people and places of the earth).

Student's Name:
Grade:
Teacher:

Diagnostic Checklist for Creative Communication through Children's Literature

PART ONE

	Yes	No
1. The child voluntarily chooses to read.		
2. The child reads		
a. fairy tales and folk tales.		
b. adventure stories.		
c. sport stories.		
d. biographies.		
e. autobiographies.		
f. nonfiction stories.		
g. mysteries.		
h. science fiction.		
i. poetry.		
j. books depicting various cultures.		
k. books to help him or her cope with an adjustment or emotional problem.		
l. other.		

PART TWO

	Yes	No
1. The child usually finishes the book he or she chooses to read.		
2. The child asks for help in choosing a book.		
3. The child chooses books to read that are at his or her independent reading level.		
4. The child readily shares information about the book he or she reads with others or with the whole class.		
5. The child gives oral reports on books he or she has read.		
6. The child presents written reports to the class on books he or she has read.		
7. The child chooses to dramatize or role play some scenes or characters from books he or she has read.		
8. The child uses ideas that he or she has gained from reading in his or her writings.		
9. The child asks to read to younger children.		
10. The child asks that the teacher read a story to the class.		
11. The child asks to tell a story to a class.		

PART THREE

1. State how many books the child claims he or she reads in a month.		
2. State how many books the child claims he or she attempts to read in a month but doesn't finish.		

Students should know that fiction and biography are two categories which are not classified according to the Dewey Decimal System. Fiction books in most libraries are generally labeled "F" and are arranged in alphabetical order according to author or by title. Biographies about one person are generally labeled "B" or by the number 92. Sometimes the category number 920 is used to indicate collected biographies in which more than one person's life story is given.

Students should also understand the components of the call number, which is used to call the book out of the library stacks. It consists of the class number plus the first initial of the author's surname. For example:

770 (class number)
L (first initial of author's surname).

The teacher can simulate a number of catalogue search activities in the classroom so that students will have greater chances of success when they search the actual card catalogue for specific books. In the fifth and sixth grades, when students are becoming involved in writing reports, library skill will facilitate their independent search for information. (For development of dictionary skills *see* Chapter 12.)

Summary

If teachers have done a good job in other areas of language arts and reading, it will manifest itself in the children's literature program. The teacher who is enthusiastic about books, who provides a good classroom environment, as well as books at all the children's interest and reading ability levels, is setting the stage for a good children's literature program. In choosing books for students, teachers must take into account sex differences and have a knowledge of the interests and needs of culturally different children. The teacher must also be especially perceptive to the black experience in literature. Some knowledge of readability formulas, which are generally based on sentence length and the number of syllables in a word, should aid teachers in choosing books at their students' reading ability levels. There are a number of reference books available which would be of help to the teacher in book selection for students and in selecting any reference materials or aids that they might need. The *Elementary School Library Collection* provides an annotated bibliography, giving both interest and readability levels, as well as reference books, for all teachers' needs in the classroom.

A discussion of the use of books to help students to cope better with their developmental problems was presented, as well as the treatment of old age in children's literature.

A discussion on book reporting, poetry, and library skills was also presented. It was suggested that various types of book reporting be used as stimuli to encourage other students to read, rather than as ends in themselves. Research that has been done on poetry in the schools and an analysis of why it is the stepchild of the literature program were presented. Suggestions on how to incorporate poetry into the classroom, as well as kinds of poems that children might like, were discussed. A section on the librarian and library skills was included because the library, which is the reservoir of knowledge, should be available and easily accessible to all children on their own. A Diagnostic Checklist for "Creative Communication through Children's Literature" was also presented.

Now that you have read this chapter, you should have mastered the teacher competencies presented at the beginning of this chapter. As a further aid, two examples of children's literature lesson plans are presented at the end of this chapter. Using these as a guide, see if you can construct another plan.

LESSON PLAN I

Primary-Grade Level

Behavioral Objective

Students will be able to portray a character in a previously read story so that others in the class can tell who the character is.

Preliminary Preparation

Witch's hat, broom.

Introduction

"We've read many books and stories together this year. Some of you have also told us about your favorite books and stories. If I were to put on this witch's hat and use this broom as my flying aid, would I remind you of someone we read about? Yes, the witch in *The Wizard of Oz*. Now, let's see if you can guess who I am. I'm not going to use any special materials to help me. I'm getting smaller and smaller; oh, I'm so small that I can now step right in. Oh my, who are all those funny looking people? I see so many hands raised. Who am I? Yes, Alice in Wonderland. Now, let's see how many of you can be a character from one of our stories. Although we may speak, we must not name the story or give names of people or places in the story."

Development

Call on a number of children who have raised their hands. Each child acts out a character, while others try to guess who the character is and the name of the story. After a few children have done this, tell the class that we will go into groups and play a little game. "We will see who can get the other groups to guess the character and story. Remember, we can't name anyone in the story."

Children are grouped and each group is told what their story is. The children choose the characters they wish to portray.

After the groups have decided on who their characters are, and how they will portray them, they are presented to the class. The teacher keeps time.

Summary

The teacher elicits from the students what they have done during the lesson. The teacher asks students to think about some new stories that they would like to have read to the class.

LESSON PLAN II

Intermediate-Grade Level

Behavioral Objectives

1. Students will take books out of the library.
2. Students will be able to describe what a character might look like and to give reasons why the character would behave in a certain way.

Preliminary Preparation

Three pictures (differing in body, features, detail) of a possible character. Excerpt from a book (depicting a dilemma).

Introduction

"Today we're going to be looking at some characters from books and seeing if we can guess the kinds of things they would or wouldn't do. Remember the discussion we had on 'The Lady or the Tiger?' * and whether the princess had saved the knight or not? What were some of the reasons we gave for her possible decision? That's right. Now I'm going to read you an excerpt from another book, and I want you to be thinking about the characters and possible clues to their personalities. Also, I have three pictures here (show pictures and stand them up against chalkboard) and I'd like you to be thinking of which picture best describes the main character, if any." (Read excerpt.)

*Synopsis of story provided below.

SYNPOSIS OF "THE LADY OR THE TIGER?" BY FRANK R. STOCKTON

Many years ago a semi-barbaric king punished crime or meted out rewards by decrees of impartial chance. When a subject was accused of a crime of sufficient importance to warrant the notice of the king, notice was given and a day appointed on which the fate of the accused would be determined. All persons would gather on that day and assemble in the galleries, while the accused would be below in the king's amphitheater. In front of the accused were two doors exactly alike and side by side. The person on trial had to choose one. Behind one door was a ferocious, hungry tiger who would spring on its victim and immediately devour him. Behind the other door was a fair and beautiful maiden, who would then become the accused person's bride.

The king's daughter, unknown to the king, was in love with one of his courtiers. When the king discovered this romance he threw the handsome young man into prison, because no subject was allowed to love the princess. The appointed day for the youth's trial came. The princess, known also for her barbaric nature, sat next to her father. She had learned the secret of the doors and knew that her father had chosen one of the fairest and loveliest of all maidens to wed the accused youth if he chose her door. Her lover knew she had learned the secret of the doors and from the arena he looked at her. The princess unnoticed by anyone but the youth raised her right hand. The youth without hesitation opened the right-hand door.

Now the question is this: Did the tiger come out of that door, or did the lady?

Development

What do you think happened? (A few suggestions answered orally.) Yes, those could all have occurred. What about those pictures? Did they match your mental images of the characters? Why or why not? (Answers.) Did any of the things the characters did influence the way you pictured them? Now, I'd like you to write your own ending to the episode, trying to think as the main character would, remembering your mental image of him and explaining why you think he will act as he does. If you like, you can also describe what you would do in the situation.

Summary

We looked at some characters today and tried to discover what they would or would not do in a situation, based on their former actions. Tomorrow we can act out some of our endings, and if some of you would like to read the book to find out how the characters in the book actually acted, you can later report your findings to the class. We can then see how our reasoning and endings compare to the author's. You can keep this in mind while reading any book, and see whether the characters behave in the same way throughout the book.

Suggestions for Thought Questions and Activities

1. Choose and read a book that you feel primary-grade children would enjoy. Give your criteria for choosing the book. Explain how you would present this book to gain the attention and interest of your students. Do the same for the intermediate grades.

2. Choose and memorize the plot of a story that you feel primary-grade children will find entertaining. Present the story in your own words using videotape. Do a critique of your presentation.

3. You teach an intermediate grade in an inner-city school with a large population of children who speak nonstandard English. What criteria would you use in choosing books for these children?

4. You have been appointed to a special school committee whose function it is to determine criteria for choosing books for your school. You have a limited budget. How would you determine the book-buying criteria? What factors would you take into consideration in determining your criteria?

5. You have been appointed to a committee whose responsibility it is to determine the books that children like to read. How would you go about doing this?

6. You have been invited to speak on bibliotherapy. What books would you choose to discuss in your talk?

7. Critically analyze the Newbery Award Books for the past two decades. Look specifically at their portrayal of the following: the elderly, sexism, the culturally different child.

8. Using some of the approaches presented in the chapter as a guide, generate three other creative ways to stimulate students to write book reports.

SELECTED BIBLIOGRAPHY

General Books

Arbuthnot, May. *Arbuthnot Anthology of Children's Literature*. Glenville, Ill.: Scott, Foresman, 1976.

Bettelheim, Bruno. *The Uses of Enchantment: The Meaning and Importance of Fairy Tales*. New York: Knopf, 1976.

Huck, Charlotte, and Doris Young Kuhn. *Children's Literature in the Elementary School*, 3d ed. updated. New York: Holt, Rinehart and Winston, 1979.

Lukens, Rebecca. *A Critical Handbook of Children's Literature*. Glenville, Ill.: Scott, Foresman, 1976.

Root, Shelton L., ed. *Adventuring with Books: Twenty-four Hundred Titles for Preschool—Grade 8*. New York: Citation Press, 1973.

Rudman, Masha. *Children's Literature: An Issues Approach*. Lexington, Mass.: Heath, 1976.

Sadker, Myra P., and David M. Sadker. *Now Upon a Time: A Contemporary View of Children's Literature*. New York: Harper & Row, 1977.

Smith, Dora V. *Fifty Years of Children's Books: 1910–1960, Trends, Backgrounds, and Influences*. Urbana, Ill.: National Council of Teachers of English, 1963.

Sutherland, Zena, ed. *The Best in Children's Books*. Chicago: University of Chicago Press, 1973.

General References, Annotated

Gaver, Mary V., ed. *The Elementary School Library Collection: A Guide to Books and Other Media*, 11th ed. Newark, N.J.: Brodart, 1977. Classified book catalogue listing titles considered to be a minimum collection for a K-6 school library. Also lists professional and audiovisual materials. Contains author, title, and subject indexes.

Haviland, Virginia. *Children's Literature: A Guide to Reference Sources*. Washington, D.C.: U.S. Government Printing Office, 1966. Annotated bibliography of references for children's literature.

Wilson, H. W. *Children's Catalog*, 12th ed. New York: H. W. Wilson, 1971. Part 1—the "classified catalog"—is arranged according to the Dewey Decimal System and gives complete bibliographical data for each title; also recommended grade level and, often, evaluations from reviews. Part 2—the "alphabetical index"—gives author, title, subject, and analytical information.

Special Indexes, Annotated

American Library Association. *Subject Index to Poetry for Children and Young People*. Chicago: American Library Association, 1957. Subject index to poetry for grades K through high school.

American Library Association. *Subject and Title Index to Short Stories for Children*. Chicago: American Library Association, 1955. Index to about 5,000 short stories from 372 books for grades 3–9. Listed under subject with title.

Children's Books in Print. New York: Bowker, 1978. A yearly updating of children's books in print with author, title, and illustrator indexes.

Eastman, Mary. *Index to Fairy Tales, Myths, and Legends, and Supplement 1937–52*. Boston: Faxon, 1926. Indexes to 1,500 folk and fairy tales by subject and title.

Sex Stereotyping in Children's Literature

Adell, Judith, and Hilary D. Klein, eds. *A Guide to Non-Sexist Children's Books*. Chicago, Ill.: Academy Press, 1976.

Mitchell, E. "Learning of Sex Role through Toys and Books." *Young Children* 28 (April 1973): 226–231.

Nadesan, Ardell. "Mother Goose: Sexist." *Elementary English* 51 (March 1974): 375–378.

Sadker, Myra P. "Out of the Pumpkin Shell: The Image of Women in Children's Literature," in *Now Upon a Time: A Contemporary View of Chil-*

dren's *Literature*, ed. by Myra P. Sadker and David M. Sadker. New York: Harper & Row, 1977.

Stavn, Diane, "Reducing the 'Miss Muffet' Syndrome: An Annotated Bibliography." *School Library Journal* 97 (January 15, 1972): 32–35.

Weitzman, Lenore. "Sex Role Socialization in Picture Books for Preschool Children." *American Journal of Sociology* 77 (May 1972): 1125–1150.

Culturally Different Children—Resource Books and Articles

Bresnahan, Mary. "Selecting Sensitive and Sensible Books About Blacks." *The Reading Teacher* 30 (October 1976): 16–20.

Keating, Charlotte Matthews. *Building Bridges of Understanding between Cultures*. Tucson, Ariz.: Palo Verde Publishing, 1971.

Long, Margo A. "The Interracial Family in Children's Literature." *The Reading Teacher* 31 (May 1978): 909–915.

Reid, Virginia M., ed. *Reading Ladders for Human Relations*, 5th ed. Washington, D.C.: American Council on Education, 1972.

Stoodt, Barbara D., and Sandra Ignizio. "The American Indian in Children's Literature." *Language Arts* 53 (January 1976): 17–21.

Sue, Paula Wee. "Promoting Understanding of Chinese-American Children." *Language Arts* 53 (March 1976): 262–266.

Children and the Aged

Constant, Helen. "The Image of Grandparents in Children's Literature." *Language Arts* 54 (January 1977): 33–40.

Larrain, Virginia. *Timeless Voices: A Poetry Anthology Celebrating the Fulfillment of Age*. Millbrae, Calif.: Celestial Arts, 1978.

Sadker, Myra P., and David M. Sadker. "Growing Old in the Literature of the Young," in *Now Upon a Time: A Contemporary View of Children's Literature*, ed. by Myra P. Sadker and David M. Sadker. New York: Harper & Row, 1977. (A bibliography is given.)

Children and the Handicapped

Sadker, Myra P., and David M. Sadker. "Annotated Bibliography of Books Depicting the Handicapped," in *Now Upon a Time: A Contemporary View of Children's Literature,* ed. by Myra P. Sadker and David M. Sadker. New York: Harper & Row, 1977.

Children and Death

Kingston, Carolyn T. *The Tragic Mode in Children's Literature.* New York: Teachers College Press, 1974.

Kübler-Ross, Elisabeth. *On Death and Dying.* New York: Macmillan, 1969.

———.*Questions and Answers on Death and Dying.* New York: Macmillan, 1974.

Reed, Elizabeth. *Helping Children with the Mystery of Death.* Nashville, Tenn.: Abingdon Press, 1970.

"Theme: Learning About Death." (Special Topic) *Language Arts* 53 (September 1976): 673–687; 690–694.

Bibliotherapy

Brown, Eleanor F. *Bibliotherapy and Its Widening Applications.* Metuchen, N.J.: Scarecrow Press, 1975.

Moody, Mildred T., and Hilda K. Limper. *Bibliotherapy: Methods and Materials.* Chicago: American Library Association, 1971.

Rubin, Dorothy. "Bibliotherapy: Reading Toward Mental Health." *Children's House* 9 (September 1976): 6–9.

Rubin, Rhea Joyce. *Bibliotherapy: A Guide to Theory and Practice.* Phoenix, Ariz.: Oryx Press, 1978.

ten

General and Practical Aspects of Writing

EXAMPLES OF TEACHER COMPETENCIES

1. The teacher will be able to explain the relationship of writing to the other language arts areas.

2. The teacher will be able to state the punctuation and capitalization skills that primary-grade level students should be acquiring.

3. The teacher will be able to state the punctuation and capitalization skills that intermediate-grade level students should be acquiring.

4. The teacher will be able to state the kinds of writing skills that primary- and intermediate-grade level students should be acquiring in sentence formation and paragraph development.

5. The teacher will be able to help students acquire skill in outlining.

6. The teacher observes students' written expression and acts positively by preparing lessons based on their needs.

7. The teacher will be able to prepare lessons on letter writing.

8. The teacher and students will cooperatively state criteria for written compositions, which students adhere to while actually writing.

9. The teacher can determine whether students value, appreciate, or have an interest in using the proper mechanics of writing—such as capitalization and punctuation—by observing whether students at the end of the year have improved their mechanical skills.

10. The teacher will be able to determine whether students value, appreciate, or have an interest in revising and proofreading their written work by observing whether they revise and proofread their work.

Introduction

It is taken for granted that the ability to convey thoughts in written form is necessary for social, utilitarian, and business purposes. It is not generally understood, however, that writing may also be a therapeutic aid for emotional release.

Persons who have difficulty in expressing themselves in writing are handicapped in our society. Authorities on social relations have proposed the thesis that socioeconomic status can be determined by the amount and kind of writing that an individual's job requires. It has been hypothesized that the more writing that people must do on their jobs, the higher their socioeconomic status.

In writing, individuals cannot depend on facial expressions, gestures, or tone of voice to help convey the message. As a result, the words, their organization into sentences, and the punctuation signals used must stand on their own. When writing is judged, a judgment is also being made of the writer. The individual's personality, creativity, schooling, and intelligence are literally "put on the line." Although schools cannot inject creativity into students, they can provide stimulating techniques and an atmosphere where individuals are free to be creative. At the very least, the schools at each grade level should help students to improve their writing to a higher level of acceptability each year.

Although students' writings are generally classified into *practical* and *creative* writing, these are not "natural" divisions. Creative as well as practical writing needs to be functional and requires knowledge of writing skills. The separation of the two is usually done for pedagogical purposes. The more knowledge, background, and imagination students have, the better writers they will be.

Practical writing usually means letters, notes, and the necessary mechanics that good writing usually requires. However, even business letters can have some spark which sets them off from others. Wouldn't we all rather receive a creative letter than the more typical cut-and-dried one?

There is no agreement on what constitutes creative writing. When you read something that seems to "get under your skin," that excites, stirs, and makes you "experience," you have probably encountered creative writing.

Regardless of what writing activity children engage in, the teacher must act as a guide, an information center, an encourager, and a stimulator. The teacher must help to adequately prepare students for written expression exercises, provide an atmosphere conducive to writing, base the topics for writing on the interests and needs of students, use motivating techniques which will provide an impetus for writing, and provide ample time for writing in class.

Although, as has already been stated, it is difficult to divide practical and creative writing, it has here been divided into two separate chapters. The first will be concerned with the general aspects of writing applicable to both creative and practical writing. It will also deal with the skills necessary for writing at the elementary-school level. The second chapter on written expression will focus on creative writing in the elementary school and present a special selection of elementary-school children's creative writings.

General Aspects of Writing

Der Techr—
   i no i got som ides but i can't rit em. Hlp.

                                           Don

Knowledge of word usage, coupled with opportunities to write, helps children gain writing proficiency. The discussion on creativity in Chapter 4 is important in helping teachers to understand better how to provide an atmosphere that stimulates creativity. Once children sense that creativity is being rewarded, they will attempt to give freer rein to their imaginations. An emphasis on creativity does not diminish a teacher's responsibility for helping students acquire basic writing skills. Creativity and basic skills reinforce one another. A child who has difficulty in speaking, in spelling, in vocabulary, in writing sentences, in punctuation, and in concept development will have difficulty in communicating through writing.

This chapter is concerned with giving teachers the background they need to help students become more adept in writing for various purposes.

After reading this chapter, you should be able to answer these questions:

1. Are creative writing and basic writing skills mutually exclusive? Explain.
2. How is writing related to other language arts areas?
3. What writing technicalities does a child usually learn in the primary grades? In the intermediate grades?
4. How can writing be correlated to other subject-matter areas?
5. What is the place of the classroom magazine in the writing program?
6. Should teachers correct papers while students are in the process of writing?
7. What is the developmental sequence of writing skills in children?
8. What are the criteria for writing book reports in the primary and intermediate grades?

The Relationship of Writing to Other Language Arts Areas

In order to be able to write effectively, a child must usually go through the developmental sequence of language arts. A child's difficulty in listening will often manifest itself in speaking. This problem may cause other problems in the reading area, and those students who have difficulty in reading will generally have problems in writing. As has been stated innumerable times in this text, the language arts are very closely related to one another, and a problem in one area may well compound itself with problems in other areas.

It is also important to note that any teaching *in* English is the teaching *of* English. Writing permeates all subject-matter areas, as well as all dimensions of the language arts. Students who have difficulty with written expression will be at a disadvantage in most subject-matter areas.

Oral Expression and Written Expression

Oral language is closely related to written language. Some authorities believe that written expression is simply speech "written down." It is known that young children who have difficulty in speaking and expressing themselves will almost assuredly have difficulty with written expression. By age six children are quite set in their pattern of speech, and their writing is a reflection of this speech. Children who do not use expanded sentences or who speak in nonstandard English usually have writing difficulties.

Since oral and written language are closely related, children should have many opportunities to express themselves orally before being expected to write. Through speaking, the teacher can determine the quality of the child's thinking. "The quality of what is expressed in written depends upon the quality of thinking that undergirds it." [1]

Reading and Written Expression

Reading and writing are closely related. Studies show that practice in sentence combining improves reading skills. [2] Practice in reading also helps to improve writing skills. Those students who read widely will have a wider range of experiences to draw on for their own writing than students who read very little or in a narrower

[1] Ruth Strickland, "Evaluating Children's Compositions," *Elementary English* 37 (May 1960): 322–330.
[2] Theone O. Hughes, *Sentence Combining: Means of Increasing Reading Comprehension*, 1975. [ED 112 421]

range. Through reading, the perceptive child develops a more expanded vocabulary, learns figures of speech, and comes in contact with ideas, which are the necessary elements for good writing. (See "Writing" in Chapter 7.)

When, however, children who read a great deal limit their writing only to vicarious experience, they tend to be imitative of the authors they have read. Their writing should reflect their own lives, thinking, and experience.

The experience approach in reading correlates oral and written expression with reading. (See Chapter 7.) This approach is best exemplified in certain British primary schools, where writing is integrated with all the work children do and, therefore, it is not possible to isolate writing as a subject. In these schools writing is a natural outgrowth and expected outcome of whatever children are studying or experiencing at the time. It is "an expression of the very lives children lead." [3]

Vocabulary and Written Expression

Teachers can learn a great deal about students' reading habits by observing the vocabulary they use in writing. There are some students who can pronounce a word correctly, but use the word incorrectly. There are a number of students who are unable to correctly pronounce a word, but can use it correctly in writing. The latter have acquired their vocabulary through reading, and they may greatly surprise their teachers with their written productions.

Although everyone's speaking vocabulary tends to be more limited than their reading or writing vocabularies, there are some students who can express themselves better orally. Teachers should recognize that not all students who are verbal are good writers, and, conversely, not all good writers are good orators.

[3]Howard E. Blake, "Written Composition in English Primary Schools," *Elementary English* 48 (October 1971): 607.

Factors Affecting the Writing Process

Although oral and written language are closely related encoding processes, there are certain factors basic to the writing process which need to be mastered for good writing. To be successful at written expression, an individual must be able to write somewhat legibly, spell, construct sentences and paragraphs, and have knowledge of word usage. Problems in any one of these areas may interfere with the act of creating through writing. Because of the variables involved, the transition from speech to written expression can be a difficult one. For example, in Chapter 13 the problems of learning to manipulate a pencil and attempting to move it fast enough to catch a thought are discussed. Many times the tools which should ease practice of a skill become impediments instead. (See Chapter 13.)

The Sequence of Writing Skills in Children

When children of about two and one-half first put pencil or crayon to paper, they are entering the initial stage of writing. The desire to convey something of one's own on paper is a necessary first step.

Parents should create a stimulating environment for preschoolers, so that children can scribble and express themselves. After preschoolers have committed themselves on paper, they should be encouraged to tell about what they have drawn. Showing enthusiasm about the child's endeavors will reinforce continuance.

Children usually remain in the scribble stage until they master control of specific muscles. Three-year-olds are often able to make circles, showing that they are gaining control of specific hand muscles. By age five, many can construct other geometric figures, such as squares, which require more precision.

Once the child can make figures such as circles, squares, triangles, and variations of these, his or her written expression takes on a "picture form." Kindergarten children may use these figures to "write a story." Some kindergarten children, who have the necessary hand coordination and mental ability, are able to construct letters or words. Some can print their names in some legible form, and write a story about themselves or their families.

In the first half of first grade, when children are occupied with learning to read and to write in manuscript, a great deal of their written expression is imitative; that is, the students copy sentences and short stories that the teacher has written. Even when using the language-experience approach, where the written stories are based on the interest and experiences of the students and are cooperatively developed, unique self-expression is usually lacking.

By the latter half of the first grade, many students have acquired the specific hand motor control necessary for sustained writing, and they often gain enough confidence to write their own stories. Although the story may be only one or two sentences, it is the child's own creation.

As students go through school, they should be accumulating many first-hand as well as vicarious experiences, and the necessary skills they need for written self-expression.

The Writing Environment

The school plant, the curriculum, school materials and books are all inert. They only become activated and part of the dynamic learning situation when the teacher and students use them in an effective manner. An attractive classroom, which is well organized into a number of learning centers, may be a catalyst for students' writing. If the classroom is a place in which exciting things are happening and where children are involved in observing, manipulating, and experimenting, it will also be a place where written self-expression goes on.

The quality of the teacher-pupil and pupil-pupil relationships is important in setting the emotional climate of the classroom. If students and teachers are engaged in cooperative endeavors and students feel secure, they will want to write and share their written ideas with others.

Time for Writing

Students need time to express themselves in written form. Actually writing helps students to be better writers. Five or ten minutes before the lunch hour is not a good time for children to start writing. If teachers spend a great deal of time in preparation and motivating techniques to stimulate the desire to write in children but allow little time for the writing activity itself, the spark, the excitement that has been ignited is hurriedly extinguished. The point to remember is that children should be allowed adequate time to write in class. After getting the proper start in class, many children will work on their own during free time and at home, finishing their compositions because they have become involved with the creative act and want to see the finished product. The option of working on compositions at home should be theirs.

Can Elementary-Grade Students Develop Style in Writing?

Although style in writing is difficult to describe, readers are acutely aware of its absence. The way the writer "turns a phrase," uses words, paints pictures, and incorporates insights are all indications of style.

Before students can achieve originality of style, they must be able to express themselves clearly and logically, have a well-developed vocabulary, and possess good sentence and paragraph sense. These factors may sometimes seem to get in the way of style, and students who prematurely take poetic license with vocabulary and sentence structure for effect may find themselves being "red penciled."

Students at all grade levels should be acquiring vocabulary and writing techniques which will help them eventually to develop their own styles. Some students in elementary school may already have done so; that is, they seem to be able to write with a certain uniqueness despite the lack of many basic skills. Teachers must be ever vigilant for such students. They must encourage them to write, and help them to acquire the skills they will need.

In order to acquire style all students must become sensitive to the many nuances of language. They must know when slang is effective, when a slang term can express some idea or describe something more effectively than another term. Students must be helped to avoid overworking or "beating to death" particular slang words, such as "gross," "cool," or "kicky." When these words are no longer fashionable, they actually convey no meaning because of their vagueness. If writers rely too heavily on slang, they tend to become lazy in word use. In order to develop style, the student must choose words carefully so that exact meaning is conveyed. Effective use of figurative language is important in style development. Children in the intermediate grades are able to work with simile, metaphor, personification, and oxymorons. (See "Figures of Speech" in Chapters 9 and 11.)

While most elementary graders do not as yet have a style of writing, they are in the process of developing such a style of their own. How well they do this depends on a variety of factors, the most important of which is the opportunity to write often.

Should Teachers Correct Papers While Students Are in the Process of Writing?

Teachers may be unsure about whether to correct papers while students are writing. In methods classes they are taught to circulate among their students to "pick up" any errors the students may be making and to help children correct such errors. This practice, though useful

for "functional" writing, should not be enforced during creative writing periods. Ideas are more important than form in creative writing, and a teacher peering over shoulders and picking up spelling, punctuation, and word-usage errors will hinder and inhibit students. The teacher should be available for any help that the children may ask for on their own. In creative writing corrections should be made only after the student has finished and is ready to share the product. When students are involved in "functional" or "practical" writing—such as constructing a business letter, where form is very important—the teacher should walk around the room while the children are working and help with any problems.

If the teacher notices that many students are making similar errors, the most common of these should be presented in a special lesson to

GRIN AND BEAR IT

"Now hand in your composition, Otis, and let's have no more nonsense about the school depriving you of the book and movie rights!"

the entire class or to a particular group. If some children are making unique errors the teacher should go over these with the individuals.

The Classroom Magazine

Alert parents realize that their children are growing in many skills in school. The classroom magazine can be an informative, public-relations vehicle which shows parents what children actually *are* doing in school, and parents delight in seeing children's work in print.

The magazine can also be a motivator stimulating students to want to write and showing how writing is correlated to other subjects. By either displaying children's stories around the room or publishing a monthly magazine, children begin to feel their work is important. They will take pride in what they have written and also be spurred to work harder. Seeing other children's writings, they are better able to judge the quality of their own work.

Evaluation of Compositions

Evaluation is an integral part of the educative process and is most effective when students

1. are involved in the process.
2. understand the purpose of the evaluation.
3. have a need for it.

Evaluation of students' written expression is necessary so that

1. students can determine whether they are improving in writing.
2. students can learn how they are performing relative to other students in the class.
3. teachers can determine how their students compare with other classes.

In the early grades children's compositions are mainly group endeavors in which ideas are dictated to the teacher, who provides capitali-

zation, punctuation, and the arrangement of sentences. This helps to give form to what children are saying. The teacher at this stage should not evaluate with the intent of giving a grade. Spontaneity of expression is more important than form at this level.

The teacher's evaluation of the child's progress is a continuous one. The personality traits that the child shows, the amount of help he needs, his growth in interest, in initiative, in sustained attention to the writing task, in independence, as well as in technical skills of handwriting and spelling are all a part of the evaluation. The teacher's observation of the child's behavior, her anecdotal records, and the writing the child produces form the materials for evaluation. Though the teacher evaluates the child's writing for content and for form, what is happening to the child is more important than what he produces." [4]

By the intermediate grades students' compositions can begin to be evaluated in terms of both content and form, and grades can be given. Merely giving a grade to a paper does not help students; extensive comments about the content and mechanics of the paper are necessary. Encouraging students by praising good ideas, while diagnosing specific writing problems, will do more to help pupils become better writers than awarding a letter or number grade. The teacher, by cooperatively analyzing papers with students, can help them to recognize that, even though their ideas are good, they must be able to express them better in written form or the ideas will not be conveyed to the reader. Although the emphasis for both practical and creative writing should be on ability to express ideas, basic skills are needed. Children must be helped to realize that basic skills and tools— such as command of vocabulary, knowledge of punctuation, sentence sense, and spelling—are needed for effective communication. The teacher will have to be very careful not to inhibit stu-

[4]Ruth Strickland, "Evaluating Children's Compositions," in *Children's Writing: Research in Composition and Related Skills* (Champaign, Ill.: National Council of Teachers of English, 1960–1961), p. 66.

PEANUTS ®
By Charles M. Schulz

dents who simply put down their ideas, even though they lack many of these tools. Pupils should be encouraged to acquire the tools. If the form of the paper is correct but the quality of the ideas is poor, the teacher should help students clarify their thinking through analysis of their ideas.

Teachers and students can recognize that the grading of written compositions is not a science, because of its subjectivity. The same paper graded by different individuals can be awarded any grade in the range of "A" to "F." See Chapter 19 on evaluation.) The teacher must be alert for bias or "set" that may creep into the grading of compositions, and should do everything possible to keep an open mind.

An activity that could be used for the fourth grade and above to exemplify this point can also be fun. A short composition, not one belonging to any student in the class, is read. Mimeographed copies of the composition are then given to each student, and they are asked to grade the composition and make comments they think would help the student who wrote it.

This activity serves three purposes. First, students, by sharing their different grades and comments with the class, will verify the subjectivity involved in grading written papers. Second, by analyzing the paper, students should become more critical of their own writing. Third, some criteria for written composition standards can be set up, which might help students in evaluating their own papers. (See section on "Revision and Proofreading.")

Should a child's composition ever receive a "D" or an "F"? Such a grade means that there is nothing redeemable in the paper—the quality of the writing is poor; the ideas expressed are muddled; the mechanics of writing are non-existent. Rather than give the student a failing grade, the teacher should meet individually with such students to discuss their problems. These particular pupils need all the help and encouragement they can get. There should be no pretense that the papers are good. But teachers should help these students know that they can and are expected to do better. After a complete diagnosis of students' difficulties, a program to eliminate each one of the problems should be developed. These students need many and varied writing activities. Some may have to start with writing sentences or paragraphs. The important factor is that students' difficulties are analyzed and that something is done to alleviate the problems.

Preventive measures are always more effective than remediation. If *all* teachers provide stimulating techniques, give their students many opportunities to express themselves in written form, and provide basic skill development throughout their teaching careers at school, problems can be prevented.

Skills Necessary for Effective Writing

Many people in the United States lack writing mechanics. Studies have shown that "no group of nine-year-olds has mastered the basic conventions of writing, that only the best thirteen-year-olds had and, by age seventeen, better than fifty percent of the teenagers could put together simple sentences, use commas, and express simple ideas in general, imprecise language." However, ". . . young Americans who do well with basic writing mechanics (such as spelling, punctuation, and sentence structure) also tend to write with the most ingenuity."[5]

Punctuation

Children must learn that punctuation marks give the signals needed for clear meaning in writing. In oral expression, stress, pitch, pauses, and even arm waving help clarify meaning. These punctuation signals replace the various intonation patterns that are used orally:

Punctuation Signals

.	period
,	comma
;	semicolon
:	colon
?	question mark
_____	underlining
!	exclamation mark
—	dash
( )	parentheses
[ ]	brackets
" "	quotation marks

The primary- and intermediate-grade designations in the following outline of punctuation skills are merely approximations. Just when students are ready for the next level will be determined by their individual differences.

In the Primary Grades

1. Period at the end of a sentence.
2. Period after abbreviations. (An abbreviation is a shortened form of a word or phrase.)
3. Question mark at the end of interrogative sentence.

4. Comma in dates.
5. Comma after greeting and closing in letters.
6. Periods after numbers in a listing.
7. Periods after Mr., Mrs., and Ms.
8. Period after an initial.
9. Apostrophe in some contractions, such as can't, she's. (A contraction is usually a combination of two words or a shortening of a compound word.)
10. Apostrophe in possessive singular, such as girl's, boy's. (When singular nouns or pronouns show ownership, an apostrophe ['] and *s* are usually added to the nouns.)

In the Intermediate Grades

1. Mastery of all items of previous years.[6]
2. Use of apostrophe in more contractions.
3. Use of apostrophe in singular and plural possessives. (To show ownership for plural nouns ending in -*s* or -*es*, an apostrophe is added after the *s*. Examples: berries' pits; Joneses' home. To show ownership for plural nouns not ending in -*s* or -*es*, an apostrophe and -*s* are added. Examples: the mice's tails, the children's room.)
4. Use of hyphen between syllables in separating a word at the end of the line.
5. Use of exclamation mark to express strong emphasis or emotion.
6. Use of exclamation mark for a command. (Optional. A period is often used.)
7. Use of a comma to separate items in a series.
8. Use of a colon after the salutation in a business letter.
9. Use of a comma to set off a quotation.
10. Quotation marks before and after a quotation.
11. Use of a comma to help make sentences clearer.
12. Use of a comma in figures containing four or more digits. (Optional for four digits.)
13. Use of commas with transitional words—such as however, indeed, that is, for example, in fact, and so on.
14. Use of quotation marks for special words in a sentence.
15. Use of quotation marks to set off the title of a poem, short story, magazine article, chapter, and so on.

---

[5]Jane Porter, "Research Report," *Elementary English* 49 (October 1972): 865.

[6]This will be determined by the individual differences of students and the school situations in which they study.

16. Use of a colon to set off a list of items.
17. Use of a colon in writing time. Example: 9:00 P.M.
18. Underlining the title of a book.

Capitalization

In the Primary Grades   Children in kindergarten and first grade have usually learned that their names start with a "big letter." In learning the letters first graders are presented with both the capital and lowercase letters. During the primary grades children learn many uses for capital letters. In writing sentences they learn that the first word of a sentence begins with a capital letter. They learn that the greeting is always capitalized in letter writing. From letter writing and working with dates they find that the day and month of the year are also capitalized. In writing experience stories with the teacher, they are helped to notice that the title is always capitalized.

Children learn that not only are their own first and last names capitalized but all names are capitalized. Also, titles preceding names are in capital letters; for example, Mr., Mrs., Miss, and Ms. The children discover that the first word of the closing of a letter is capitalized; for example, Yours truly, Your friend, Sincerely yours, and so on. States, cities, and streets are capitalized, and whenever children use "I" in a sentence it should always be capitalized. Primary-grade children also notice that the first word of every line in a poem is usually capitalized (except for the poetry of some modern poets).

In the Intermediate Grades   Before proceeding into intermediate-level capitalization skills, the children should have mastered all the capitalization skills listed for primary-grade students. They will continue to build their capitalization skills by learning that all names of countries, roads, avenues, streets, towns, and so on are capitalized. And, similarly, that any word used as a name would begin with a capital letter; for example, "Mother," "Father," but not "his mother," "her father." Titles of books, poems, stories, movies, and magazines are also capitalized, as well as names of languages, buildings, institutions, and companies. Intermediate-grade level students learn to capitalize the first word of a direct quotation, historical periods, names of nationalities, a direction that names a definite area, and in outlining, the first word of each main topic and subtopic.

Writing Sentences

Learning to write sentences that are clear and make sense is a very important part of the writing program. Before children can write stories or paragraphs, they must be able to write sentences. In order to do this, children must have practice in oral expression. Starting in the primary grades, children are helped to express themselves so that they can "say what they mean"; later they can "write what they mean."

Not only do children need many opportunities to express themselves orally, they also must write sentences for clear written expression. Children in the primary grades learn to write simple questions and statement sentences in the active voice. In the intermediate grades they learn to write exclamatory and imperative compound sentences, which may be in the active or passive voices.

Children in both the primary and intermediate grades must learn that a sentence expresses a complete thought and that it is a significant unit of language.

Intermediate-grade level children learn that a sentence is a word or group of words stating, asking, commanding, supposing, or exclaiming. The sentence contains a subject and a verb that are in agreement in number with one another. It begins with a capital letter and ends with a period (.), a question mark (?), or an exclamation mark (!). For example:

Jennifer is pretty. (statement or declarative sentence)

Who is he? (question or interrogative sentence)
Stop him. (command or imperative sentence)
Help! (expression of great emotion or exclamatory sentence)

Intermediate-grade level children learn that an *interjection* is a word usually used with an exclamation mark to express emotion; it is independent of the rest of the sentence. Examples: Oh! Aha! They also learn that some sentences may be as brief as one word. For example:

Stop.
Go.
Help!

When children are taught to write sentences such as the above, they should be helped to recognize that the subject, *you,* is understood and that the punctuation helps give meaning to the sentences.

In the primary grades children write many different kinds of *simple sentences.* They write simple sentences containing the following:

1. single subject and single verb: "Sharon swims."
2. single subject and compound (two or more) verb: "Sharon runs and swims."
3. compound subject and single verb: "Sharon and Seth swim."
4. compound subject and compound verb: "Sharon and Seth swim and run."

In the intermediate grades, children are learning to write compound sentences. They learn that a compound sentence contains two or more groups of words that can stand alone as sentences. Each group of words must have its own subject and verb. Examples:

My sister is an excellent ball player, and my brother is a good musician.
My sister is a good ball player, but it doesn't interfere with her music.

Each of the compound sentences has two groups of words that can stand alone as a simple sentence because each has a subject and a verb, and each expresses a complete thought. Ex-

amples: My sister is an excellent ball player. My brother is a good musician. My sister is a good ball player. It doesn't interfere with her music.

To combine two sentences into a compound sentence, children learn that they must use a comma with a conjunction such as *and* or *but.*

Primary-grade children, when first learning to write sentences, tend to string many sentences together by adding the conjunction "and." Intermediate-grade children have usually learned to avoid the overuse of conjunctions, but they are more prone to write run-on sentences because of their overuse of the comma. For example, they may not separate the following sentences: "The children all raised their hands." "We started to talk." They may instead put them together with a comma. "The children all raised their hands, we started to talk."

In writing sentences pupils learn to avoid certain unacceptable sentence fragments. For example: *Into the store, When she came, And in a second,* and *Although he is* are not sentences.

In the following list the first sentence is correct, whereas the second example is not.

1. There are a number of birds, such as sparrows, who do not migrate during the winter.
2. There are a number of birds who do not. Such as sparrows.

In order to gain clarity in sentence writing, children must learn that careful placement of words is helpful. For example, how clear are the following sentences?

The girl ran down the street in a green coat.
The baby drank the milk with a smile.

In order to understand the meaning of the sentences better they should be rewritten in the following manner:

The girl in a green coat ran down the street.
The baby, with a smile, drank the milk.

(See discussion on generating sentences in Chapter 14.)

Writing Paragraphs

After children have gained facility in writing sentences, they should be helped to write paragraphs.

A paragraph usually consists of a topic sentence followed by a number of related sentences and usually ends in a concluding statement. The topic sentence is generally the first one in the paragraph. The related sentences tell something about the topic sentence and are arranged in some order to make sense. The beginning of each paragraph is indented.

Paragraphs, like sentences, should have unity and order. If the paragraph is one concerning a sequence of events, then the sentences must be placed in some kind of sequential order. If the paragraph involves an explanation, it must proceed in a logical order such as from cause to effect.

The sentences in the paragraph must also have some kind of coherence so that they flow logically from one to the other. Put another way, sentences must be linked. Some words that help link sentences are *after, then, besides, moreover, however, therefore, as a result,* and *for that reason.* Although linking words are useful connectors, not all sentences in a paragraph need a linking word.[7]

The Topic Sentence[8] The topic sentence is usually the first sentence in a paragraph, and it states what the paragraph will be about by naming the topic. It also usually gives clues to the development of the main idea of the paragraph. (See Chapter 8 for main idea.) From the topic sentence one can anticipate certain events. One can determine that the subsequent sentences will supply supporting details as examples, comparison/contrasts, sequence of events, cause and effect situations, and so on, to support the main idea.

[7]Dorothy Rubin, *The Vital Arts—Reading and Writing* (New York: Macmillan, 1979), p. 129.

[8]Ibid., p. 147.

It is possible for any sentence in the paragraph to be the topic sentence, and some paragraphs may not have a topic sentence. The topic sentence should not be confused with the main idea. The topic sentence usually anticipates both the main idea and the development of the main idea. It may or may not contain the main idea. Even though a topic sentence exists and is stated explicitly (fully and clearly) in the paragraph, the main idea may not be explicitly stated.

The Concluding Sentence A good paragraph does not end with some minor point or detail. It generally ends with some strong point, a conclusive statement, a restatement, or a question relating to what has preceded. In ending a paragraph, try to help students to avoid terms such as *In conclusion, In ending, To sum up,* and so on.

Writing a Composition

Upper-elementary-grade level children are ready to learn how to write good compositions. Teachers should help them to recognize the relationship between reading and writing, and how one enhances the other. For example, as stated earlier in this chapter and in Chapter 7, students who read widely will have a broad range of ideas from which to draw for their own writing. Also, through reading they will come to recognize what skills are necessary to be a good writer.

To write a composition, students must be able to choose a topic that is neither too narrow nor too broad. They must be able to write a topic sentence for an opening paragraph of the composition so that readers will be prepared for what is to follow; they must be able to combine paragraphs so that they are all related to the topic that they have chosen; and they must be able to write a concluding paragraph.

The Opening Paragraph Teachers need to help students learn how important and crucial

the opening paragraph of a composition is because the opening paragraph helps the reader to determine whether he or she wants to continue reading or not. It introduces the reader to the writer and tells something about what the writer wants to say. It also prepares the reader for the rest of the paper. The task is to attract the reader's attention and to get him or her to read on. To do this, the opening paragraph should be brief, to the point, and interesting. The topic sentence, which is usually the first sentence in the opening paragraph, plays an essential role in helping to set the stage for the rest of the paper. (See sections on the topic sentence.)

Teachers could use samples from literature to illustrate their points. For example, the teacher could bring in a short opening paragraph from a magazine or journal article and state: "Read the following paragraph from 'Would You Obey a Hitler?' by Jeanne Reinert, in *Science Digest:*"

Who looks in the mirror and sees a person ready and willing to inflict pain and suffering on another in his mercy? Even if commanded? All of our senses revolt against the idea.

After the students finish reading the paragraph, the teacher says: "Doesn't it capture your attention? Don't you want to continue reading? Let's analyze what the writer has done:

a. The paragraph is short and to the point.

b. The central idea for the composition is contained in the paragraph so that the reader is prepared for what follows.

c. The writer's technique of using questions gains our attention. (Notice that the questions are rhetorical; i.e., they require or expect no response.)

d. The writer tells us something about his or her feelings."

After analyzing the paragraph, the teacher then says: "Following are a couple of beginning paragraphs taken from the autobiographies of famous persons. The opening tactic used by each writer is anecdotal (referring to a short, entertaining account of some happening that is usually biographical). After reading each one, ask yourself these questions:

a. Did it attract my attention?

b. Did it make me want to read more?

c. Was it short and to the point?

d. Did it give me information about what was to follow?

e. Did it tell me something about the author's feelings?

f. Did it set the stage for the rest of the composition?"

From *Molly and Me* by Gertrude Edelstein Berg:

I should probably say that I liked school—it sounds better. But the whole truth is, I didn't. I wasn't interested and there was always something I would rather be doing than sitting in a classroom, like, for instance, sitting at home. Besides, I was scared. It wasn't psychological, it was just the way the school looked.

From *Daybreak* by Joan Baez:

Mother tells me that I came back from the first day of kindergarten and told her I was in love. I remember a Japanese boy who looked after me and wouldn't let anybody knock me around. When they gave us beans to eat in the morning I told him they'd make me sick, and he buried them under the table for me.

After the students have analyzed the paragraphs, the teacher should ask them to write the opening paragraph of their autobiography.

The Topic Sentence of the Opening Paragraph   The topic sentence in the first paragraph of a composition usually sets the stage for the rest of the paper. It is broader than the topic sentences in subsequent paragraphs because it prepares the reader for what is to follow in the whole composition. The topic sentence of the opening paragraph may give the reader the writer's feelings about the subject or some information as to what the composition is about. Whichever method the writer chooses to use, the topic sentence should catch the reader's attention and make him or her want to read on.

The teacher should expose students to topic sentences from opening paragraphs that attract the readers' attention. The students should be asked to find topic sentences from their readings that they think are good ones. Students should also be asked to generate a number of topic sentences on various themes for the opening paragraph of a composition.

The Concluding Paragraph   The concluding paragraph is very special in a composition because it pulls everything in the composition together. It ought to leave the reader with the main thought of the composition and with a feeling of completeness. The writer may use a number of techniques to accomplish this. One method is a simple statement, another is a question, and another is a quotation. (See section on writing paragraphs.) Teachers should help students notice the similarity between the concluding paragraph of a composition and the ending of a paragraph. Also, teachers should help their students try to avoid using such artificial terms as *In conclusion, In sum, Finally*, and so on to begin their concluding paragraph. The terms take away from the creativity of the paragraph and do not add anything significant to it.

To help students gain facility in writing concluding paragraphs, teachers can use the same techniques that were given for gaining skill in writing opening paragraphs and topic sentences for opening paragraphs.

Revision and Proofreading

Both revision and proofreading are important and needed for a "polished" final copy of a paper, but they involve different processes. Revision refers to the creative improvement of an existing script; proofreading is the process of correcting technical writing errors such as punctuation errors, spelling errors, capitalization errors, and the like. Revision and proofreading can be the bane of writers. "Do I have to?" and "Ugh!" usually result when children are asked to rewrite or proofread their papers. If children are shown the purposes of revision and proofreading, these tasks will not be such onerous ones. If an elementary-school class prepares a monthly magazine, which includes most of the activities of the class, it can become the possession of each child, so that everyone wants to contribute. In order to prepare the magazine material, children must have relatively "polished copy"; revision and proofreading are necessary to get final copy from the original draft.

The following Proofreading and Revision Checklist Chart can be kept on display:

1. Have you checked your spelling and looked up any words you are not sure of in the dictionary?

2. Do you have a period at the end of your sentences that should have periods?

3. Do you have a question mark at the end of your sentences which ask a question?

4. Do you have a capital letter at the beginning of all of your sentences?

5. Do you have a capital letter at the beginning of all names of persons and things?

6. Have you capitalized "I" whenever you used it?

7. Have you put in commas when you are listing lots of things?

8. Have you put the apostrophe in the proper place in making contractions—such as can't, don't, isn't, hasn't, I'm?

9. Have you used the apostrophe in the correct place in writing possessives—such as John's, children's, babies', books'?

10. Do all your sentences make sense?

11. Is this the best way to present your ideas?

12. Does each of your paragraphs tell about one main idea?

13. Have you remembered to indent each paragraph?

Book Reporting

Chapter 9 discussed book reporting. It was mentioned that many children look on written book reports as burdensome tasks, which may detract from reading. It was also emphasized that teachers should not require children to do book reports on all books that they read.

Written book reports have a place in the language arts program. In the primary grades the teacher and children can write book reports together when they have all read a book together. The teacher can stimulate this activity by having children tell about some of the things they liked or did not like about the book. The teacher can also ask children if they think other children of about their age would like to read the book. If so, the teacher asks how can they let these children know about the book. Should everything about the book be told? Why not?

At the primary level the book report should include the following:

1. The name of the book.

2. The author of the book.

3. A good beginning sentence that tells something interesting about the book.

4. A number of other sentences that further explain why the book should be read. An example of something funny in the book might be given.

5. A special character in the book can be described.

6. A concluding sentence that further encourages children to want to read the book ends the review.

The report should stimulate interest, but not summarize the whole book so that it need not be read.

In the intermediate grades, even though most of the children's reports are written to stimulate others to want to read the book, children are also learning that they do not like all the books they have read. They must learn to be more impartial in their reports. Although they did not necessarily like the book, this does not mean that someone else will also dislike it. They also have to share enough information to get the audience interested but not tell the whole story and thereby spoil the enjoyment of the book for others.

At the intermediate level (as at all other levels) students who are asked why they liked a book usually reply, "It was interesting" or "It was good." These comments do not help classmates in deciding whether or not to read a book. Here are some suggestions for helping intermediate-grade students write book reports:

1. State name and author of book.

2. What kind of book is it? For example, is it a biography, autobiography, science fiction, war story, mystery, animal story, nature story?

3. Who are the main characters in the story? For

example, who is the hero, the villain? What about the characters—are they lifelike or just stereotypes? Which characters did you like or dislike? Why?

4. Is the setting of the story important? Where does it take place? When does the story take place?

5. Very briefly discuss the plot without giving the whole story away. Tell whether it was fast-moving, humorous, whether there was good suspense, and so on.

6. Did the author paint clear pictures? Did he or she describe characters well?

7. What did you like about the book?

8. Are there any particular people for whom you would especially recommend the book?

The teacher can read sample book reports to the class, and students can volunteer which ones they like best and why. It would be worthwhile for teachers in the intermediate grades to write a book report based on a book that all of their students have read, with the participation of the whole class, or with groups of children. (See Chapter 9 for some novel approaches to stimulate children to write book reports.)

Television Reporting

Television, as all educators know, plays an important part in the lives of children. Teachers can use television viewing as an impetus for writing. Children at both the primary and intermediate grades should be encouraged to discuss the programs they watch and review them by writing critically of particular programs.

At the primary-grade level, first graders can dictate reviews about the shows they have watched either as a group endeavor, using an experience-approach technique, or individually.

At the intermediate level children are able to write their own reports. However, as in book reporting, children should cooperatively develop standards for writing television reviews. (See "Television: Making It Part of the Communicative Process" in Chapter 6.)

Letter Writing

Most adults, and especially children, love to receive letters. Of all writing exercises, letter writing will be one of the most frequently engaged in activities for most individuals. Many different kinds of letters have to be written—friendly letters, business letters, invitations, orders, complaints, requests, regrets, apologies, and so forth.

In the primary grades, letter writing can be correlated with a number of other ongoing activities. When first-grade children are learning the days and months, describing the kind of day it is, learning the phonemes and their graphemic representations, the teacher can use letter writing as an ongoing activity each day to review some of the instruction for the handwriting lesson or as part of an experience story, telling about some event or happening in which the children were involved.

Letters should be brief, and they should be written to someone to whom they might actually be sent. For example, in the beginning of the first grade, letters should consist of only one sentence; for example, telling the name of day. Here are some sample letters for first-grade children:

> Dear Mommy and Daddy,
>   Today is Monday.
>   Love,
>   Sharon

> Dear Daddy,
>   It is raining today.
>   Love,
>   Carol

> Dear Mommy,
>   I can make the letter b.
>   Love,
>   Seth

As children progress through the year, their letters will become progressively longer. Many children learn to read and spell the words that are continuously used in letters. Children should be allowed to bring their letters home. It is a good idea to ask first-grade children to save some of their letters so that they are able to see how well they have progressed during the year. And it is delightful to hear first-grade children at the end of the year say, "Oh, look at how babyish I was when I wrote that!"

In the primary grades there are many opportunities for writing various kinds of letters. After a trip or after seeing a school play, the teacher and children can write thank-you notes. If a child is out ill, classmates can write friendly letters to him or her. If parents are invited to visit the class to see some class project or play, the class can write invitations.

Children should be encouraged to write many different kinds of letters and to develop the proper attitudes, habits, and skills necessary for letter writing. They should understand that in order to receive letters, they must write them, and that it is discourteous not to answer a letter. They should be helped to develop the necessary skills in letter writing.

In the Primary Grades

1. Answer letters promptly.
2. Proofread all letters.
3. Since a letter is a means of communication, make sure your handwriting can be read easily.
4. Make sure your letter makes sense.
5. Know that there are many different kinds of letters.
6. Use the proper punctuation.
7. Try to make friendly letters interesting.

In the Intermediate Grades

1. Know all the primary-grade skills listed above.
2. Know the forms for different letters.
3. Know that there are five parts to a friendly letter: heading, salutation, body, closing, and signature.
4. Know that a business letter has the same form as a friendly letter, but the inside address is added and, sometimes in typed letters, the signature identification is added.

5. Know that headings are conventional.
6. Know that the salutation, closing, and signature in a friendly letter express the relationship between you and the reader.
7. Know that accurate dates and return addresses are important.

Example of a friendly letter:

172 Rogers Avenue
Princeton, New Jersey 08540
March 10, 1980

Dear Jennifer,

Your visit is going to be the most exciting event of the year. The whole family is going to come to a picnic in our back yard, and we'll have fried chicken and blueberry pie.

I can hardly wait for you to come. You'll be sleeping in my room and I can show you my photo album and you can play with my dog Brutus. Come soon.

Your cousin,
Elizabeth

Example of a thank you note:

December 2, 1980

Dear Artie,

I want to tell you how much I enjoyed the picture that you made for me! It is simply lovely. I brought it in to have it framed immediately, and it is now hanging in my study.

Please give my love to everyone. We are all looking forward to seeing you at the family reunion.

Love,
Aunt Diana

Example of an informal invitation:

Room 101
Eaton Elementary School
April 3, 1980

Dear Mr. and Mrs. Jones,

Our class is presenting a play in our room on April 21 from one-thirty to two-thirty. We would be pleased to have you come.

Sincerely yours,
Mrs. Jones's Fifth Grade

Example of a business letter:

1571 Conrad Avenue
Brockley, California
94501
July 9, 1980

Jones Electrical Company
932 Railing Avenue
Oakland, California 94604

Gentlemen:

The ABC Corporation in Brockley informs me that you stock the LT-0140 tube for the 1972 model television set manufactured by Grant. The model number is RBC-143V67.

Since the tube is easily replaced, ABC has suggested I order it from you by mail. My check for the cost of the tube plus mailing is enclosed. Please send it to the above address.

Yours truly,
Samuel Potts

Outlining

Outlining helps students organize long written compositions or papers. An outline should serve as a guide for the logical arrangement of material. Closely related to classification and categorizing, outlining should begin to be developed in the primary grades.

Young children tend to overgeneralize and, until they are able to make discriminations, they will not be able to classify. By the time children come to school, they are able to make many discriminations and are beginning to classify. (See Chapter 3.)

Developing readiness for outlining in the primary grades includes the following skills:

1. Five-year-olds learn to put things together which belong together—blocks of the same size in the same place; clothes for each doll in the right suitcase; parts of a puzzle in the right box; scissors, brushes, and paints in the spaces designated for these materials.

2. First graders may separate things that magnets can pick up from things they do not pick up by using two boxes—one marked "Yes" and the other marked "No." They can think of two kinds of stories—True and Make-Believe Stories. They can make booklets representing homes, dividing the pictures they have cut from magazines into several categories—living rooms, dining rooms, bedrooms, and so on. They can make two piles of magazines labeled "To Cut" and "To Read." [9]

3. Second-grade pupils continue to put things together which belong together—such as outdoor temperature readings and indoor temperature readings, valentines in individual mail boxes in the play post office, and flannel graph figures made to use in telling a story in the envelope with the title of the story. In addition, seven-year-olds begin to understand finer classifications under large headings; for example, in a study of the work of a florist, plants may be classified as "Plants which Grow Indoors" and "Plants which Grow Outdoors." Indoor plants may be further subdivided into "Plants which

[9]Although grade designations are given, teachers must take the individual differences of students into account. Some first-graders may be at a third-grade level; others may be at a first-grade or lower skill-development level.

Grow from Seeds," Plants which Grow from Cuttings," "Plants which Grow from Bulbs," and so on. After visiting the local bakery second graders, who are writing and drawing pictures of the story of their trip, can list the details in two columns—"Things We Saw in the Store" and "Things We Saw in the Kitchen."

4. Third-grade boys and girls have many opportunities to classify their ideas and arrange them in organized form. During a study of food in their community one group put up a bulletin board to answer the question: "What parts of plants do we eat?" The pictures and captions followed this tabulation formulated by the third graders:

Leaves	Seeds	Fruits	Roots
cabbage	peas	apples	carrots
lettuce	beans	oranges	radishes
spinach	corn	plums	

The file of "Games We Know" in one third grade was divided into two parts by the pupils—"Indoor Games" and "Outdoor Games." Each of these categories was further subdivided into "Games with Equipment" and "Games without Equipment." After a visit to the supermarket a third-grade class booklet was made by the children with stories and pictures of the trip. The organization of the booklet with its numbered pages was shown in the Table of Contents:

OUR VISIT TO THE FOOD MARKET

Developing skills in outlining in the middle and upper grades includes these skills:

Beginning with grade four, pupils often need to use and make outlines for reporting information found in reading a variety of references; listening to tape recordings, radio, and television; experimenting to find answers to questions; observing; and interviewing people who can help with the question at hand. *As the need for making an outline arises*, pupils may consult their English books to find out about the rules involved. Such suggestions as the following can be put in the pupils' own words and kept on a chart for reference:

Use Roman numerals for the main topics, putting a period after each Roman numeral.

Use capital letters for subtopics, with a period after each capital letter. Indent the subtopics.

Use ordinary (Arabic) numerals for details under subtopics and small letters under the details for less important points. Put a period after each number and letter.

Begin each topic with a capital letter, whether it is a main topic, a subtopic, or a detail. Do not put a period after a main topic, a subtopic, or a detail. Do not put a period after a topic unless it is a sentence.

Keep Roman numbers, capital letters, ordinary numbers, and small letters in straight vertical lines.

Topics are usually phrases, sometimes sentences. Do not mix phrases and sentences in the same outline.

Sets and Outlining

An exercise involving sets can be used with both primary- and intermediate-grade students to help them recognize that outlining and classification are closely related. Ask students to think of the set of all the books in the library. This is a very general set:

Books in
the library

Next ask students to state the kinds of books one would find in the library. By doing this we are becoming less general:

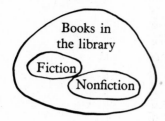

Now ask students to state what kinds of books one would find in the set of fiction books and what kinds of books one would find in the set of nonfiction books:

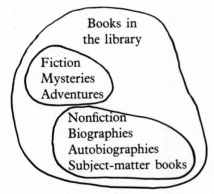

Ask the children to name a particular mystery or adventure book. At this point we are becoming very specific:

Now ask the students to put this information in outline form.

Here are samples of exercises, according to grade levels, which should help children de-

velop the skill of outlining through understanding classification.

PRIMARY GRADES

Family Names

Directions

On the line above each group write the appropriate family name or main topic. Although the different groups in each exercise belong to the same general class, the differences between the groups may be indicated by adding a descriptive word to the family name you choose.

Horse
Cow
Dog

Tiger
Wolf
Bear
Moose
Fox

FOURTH OR FIFTH GRADE

Organizing

Directions

At the head of the exercise is a list of words. Take each word and ask: "Does this word belong in Group I or Group II?" When you are sure of your answer, write the word under its main topic.

Exercise

Chicago, Arizona, Vermont, California, Los Angeles, Tulsa, Georgia, Baltimore

I. States

   A.
   B.
   C.
   D.

II. Cities

   A.
   B.
   C.
   D.

Outlines—Time Order

Directions

Study the following list. Select your main topics, and arrange them in time order. Then arrange your subtopics.

Exercise

Changes in Transportation

horseback, pioneer forms, modern forms, covered wagon, railway express, pony express, motor truck, airplane

I.

   A.
   B.
   C.

II.

   A.
   B.
   C.

FIFTH OR SIXTH GRADE

Levels of Abstraction

Here are some items in columns. Each column describes one item. Each word tells you more, or less, information about the item than all the others. Put a "1" in front of the word that tells the least, a "2" in front of the word that tells the next least, and so on until the highest number is placed beside the word telling the most. The word that tells the least is the most general word—such as "animal," whereas the word that tells the most is the most specific—such as "John Doe."

Example

   3   A—John Doe
   1   B—Animal
   2   C—Human

   _____ A—Animal
   _____ B—Lassie
   _____ C—Collie
   _____ D—Dog

   _____ A—Rock
   _____ B—Nonliving
   _____ C—Rock formations
   _____ D—Mt. Everest

   _____ A—Tree
   _____ B—Living organism
   _____ C—Spruce
   _____ D—Plant
   _____ E—Evergreen

   _____ A—Mammal
   _____ B—Living organism
   _____ C—Arthur Hale
   _____ D—Human
   _____ E—Animal

   _____ A—Machinery
   _____ B—Automobile
   _____ C—Cadillac
   _____ D—Vehicle

   _____ A—Wheat
   _____ B—Grain
   _____ C—Plant
   _____ D—Living organism

Notetaking

Students are not concerned with notetaking until they begin writing long reports or papers. Then notetaking, like outlining, is taught as a tool. Students in the intermediate grades should learn that notetaking:

1. is done when writing long reports.
2. is necessary when many different books are to be used.
3. is used to organize material.

Students learn to use index cards in notetaking because they are easy to handle and arrange. The cards should contain legible writing and the following information:

1. Name of author, title of book, publisher, date of publication.
2. The topic of the report and the subtopic to which the particular note applies should be written at the top of the card.
3. The recorded information may be a summary, figures, a definition, a quotation, or the like.

Intermediate-grade students are learning that notes consist of groups of words that help one remember important material. They learn that notes do not have to be written in sentence form, but book information *is* written in a special form. By the fourth grade the form is as follows: author's last name is written first, a comma separates the last name from the first name, and the title of the book is capitalized and underlined. A comma and page numbers follow the title. For example:

Wiese, Kurt, You Can Write Chinese, pages 45–50.

By sixth grade the bibliography also includes the date of publication. The teacher should initiate a discussion on the importance of knowing this factor.

For practice in notetaking, students read a particular paragraph and take notes on it. A discussion on the groups of words that were taken down as reminders of what was read ensues. The teacher collects the paragraphs and asks students if they can give an oral report on what they have just read, using their notes. The teacher also explains that it is relatively easy for them to give reports on the paragraph because:

1. It is still fresh in their minds.
2. It was not very long.
3. The discussion by many students on the same or similar paragraphs reinforced their recall.

Before students are asked to write a report using notes, the teacher should give them notetaking practice as outlined above with two, three, and more paragraphs on a similar topic from different sources. Students should take notes on these paragraphs and put them together in a short report.

Examples of Children's Writing Correlated to Other Subject Areas

By correlating writing with other subjects, children see that there are many purposes to writing. They will also realize that, unless they have some skill in written expression, they will have difficulty in other subjects as well.

The box includes some material that one fifth-grade class published in their monthly magazine related to science.

HYPOTHESES

Room 10 of School X has been studying hypotheses, which are possible solutions to a problem. This involves testing by experimentation and observation, and using the 5 senses. In connection with our study of "How Do Plants Grow?" we have divided into groups, each group testing a different hypothesis. They are as follows:

1. Plants need light in order to grow. (Liz, Mary Kate, Jerry, Beth, Mary)
2. Two seeds of different kinds can grow together. (Susan, Lyell)
3. One seed grows better than many. (David, Woody)
4. Plants can't grow when constantly wet. (Bo)
5. The placement of the seed in the soil affects the growth of the seed. (Bill, Tish)
6. Water is necessary for growth. (Chris, Karl)
7. Plants need fresh air to grow. (Mark)
8. Some seeds grow faster than others. (Patty, Bob, Ben, Webb)
9. Plants grow best in the shade. (Bill, Bruce, Richard)
10. Plants can grow without soil. (Muffy, Sammie)

This project was correlated with our study of making headlines and writing articles for a newspaper. Below is one of the results of this activity.

Plant Experiments Go On!

Sept. 25. Grade 5 made plant hypotheses today. For the last few days our class had been saving milk cartons for plant experiments. The hypotheses were:

Plants need light in order to grow.

2 seeds of different kinds can grow together.

One seed grows better than many.

Plants can't grow when constantly wet.

The placement of the seed affects the growth.

Water is necessary for growth.

Some seeds grow faster than others.

The different people in the class performed these experiments. They are still going on.

Most of the results are unknown to us. You either know or are going to find out whether or not these hypotheses are true.

Headlines on our Controlled Experiments

In connection with their study of controlled experiments, the class decided to write head-

lines and articles for a newspaper. Following is an example:

"GERM" EXPERIMENTS GOING ON

The fifth grade started an experiment with germ cultures on November 8. It was a controlled experiment using three different things—rinsed hands, washed hands, and dirty hands. The germs were placed in petri dishes containing food germs. We found out that the dirty hands had some staph germs on them. The rinsed hands didn't have as many germs as the dirty hands, and the washed hands had hardly any germs at all.

The headlines on controlled experiments were stimulated by the children's visit to a newspaper. They worked with various parts of a newspaper and differentiated between newspaper reporting and writing stories. The students' newspaper unit stimulated many exciting writing activities. For example, children acted as reporters on sports, food, fashion, television shows, movies, and so on. They discussed the differences between reporting events and writing reviews of shows. The following is one "reporter's" article on the visit to the News Post Building.

FIFTH GROUP TOURS NEWS POST BUILDING

The fifth grade started on their trip to the News Post Building at 9:30. With the class was their teacher, Mrs. R., the room mother, Mrs. H., and the assistant room mother, Mrs. D. We arrived at the News Post Building at 10:00. This was the first fifth grade ever to visit a newspaper office in Baltimore. They showed us the linotype and the teletype machines. We saw how a paper was put together, and how pictures were made. We went to the Editorial Department and met the editor. We saw how the papers were bundled and sent to the trucks. At the end of the tour everybody received a metal slab with his name on it. We arrived home at 11:45, almost lunchtime.

It is even possible to correlate writing exercises with mathematics. One student decided to put this article in one of the monthly magazines:

NUMBER BASES—WHAT FUN!

We have been working with other number bases in arithmetic than our number base of 10. We have discovered that working problems with the number bases 2 and 5 are fun. Below is the way we set up our problems:

Base Five (Quinary)	Base Ten (Decimal)
332	332
433	433
1320	765

Mary has written 2000 in bases 2 and 5:

Binary (Base Two)	Quinary (Base Five)
11111010000	31000

Can you write 1984 in both of these number systems?

In social studies some students became interested in the comparison of educational methods and techniques that existed in the past with those of the present. These students wrote an article for the monthly magazine:

SCHOOLS HAVE CHANGED!

The Pilgrims' life in school wasn't so easy. There were very strict teachers who were usually men. When children whispered in school, they got so much punishment it seemed like they had burned the school down. Most of the time, they had to wear the whispering stick. This was a piece of wood that they had to hold inside their mouth. There was a string at each end which was tied behind their neck. They also had to have whippings very often. Then it was a lot different from our schools. When we learn things we like to know why, but then they just memorized their lessons and other things, so that they could do the problem all right, but they didn't understand it. I'm sure everyone is glad they are going to school now, rather than a long time ago.

An eighth-grade class produced a newspaper related to their social studies classes. They were learning about the Renaissance, and the newspaper was to be a replica of events that might have taken place at that time. The front page of a paper produced by a highly gifted child is reproduced on page 246. There is humor, knowledge, organizational ability, and handword in its production.

Summary

This chapter has presented the ingredients teachers need to develop and implement a good writing program in their classes. First, the general aspects of writing applicable to both the creative and practical areas were presented. The interrelationship of writing to other language arts was discussed. Unless students have knowledge of spelling, punctuation, and word usage, and are able to write in some legible form, they will have difficulty with written expression. For best results in writing, teachers must provide a physical and emotional environment in which children do not feel threatened. Adequate time and opportunities for writing must be provided by the teacher. Although writing style is difficult to define, it is noticeable when present; some children exhibit style in the intermediate grades. The use of the magazine in the classroom as a stimulus for writing was discussed. Evaluation of written expression was reviewed, and teachers were cautioned against giving grades to primary-school pupils for their written work.

The skills necessary for becoming an effective writer were presented and sequentially developed at both primary- and intermediate-grade levels. Some of the skills included: punctuation, capitalization, writing sentences, and paragraphing. Standards for giving book reports, writing various types of letters, outlining, and notetaking for long reports were discussed. The correlation of writing with other subject-matter

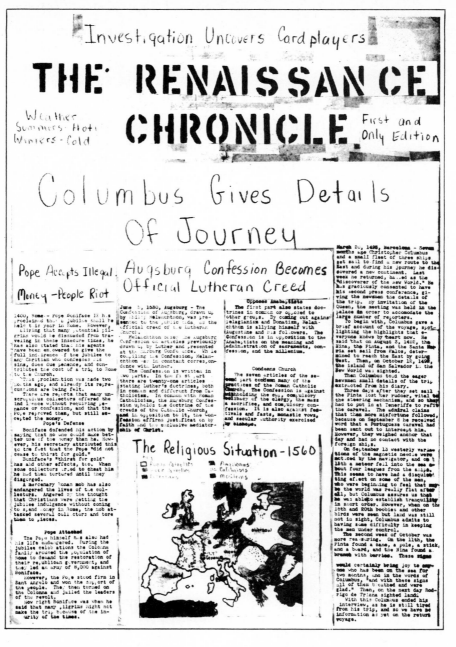

areas was analyzed, with examples from elementary-grade classrooms. A Diagnostic Checklist for "General and Practical Aspects of Writing" was also presented.

Now that you have read this chapter, you should have mastered the given teacher competencies presented at the beginning of the chapter.

Two examples of practical writing lesson plans are presented at the end of this chapter. Using these as a guide, see if you can construct another one.

Student's Name:
    Grade:
    Teacher:

Diagnostic Checklist for General and Practical Aspects of Writing

I. *Punctuation*	Yes	No

A. Primary Grades

The child
1. places a period at the end of a sentence.
2. places a period after abbreviations.
3. places a question mark at the end of question sentence.
4. places a comma to separate day from year (February 11, 1980).
5. places a comma to separate city from state (Albany, New York).
6. places periods after numbers in a listing (1. candy 2. cake, and so on).
7. places periods after Mr., Mrs., and Ms.
8. places a period after an initial.
9. places an apostrophe in some contractions, such as *can't, he's.*
10. places an apostrophe in possessive singular, such as *girl's, boy's.*

B. Intermediate Grades

The child is able to
1. master all items of previous years.
2. use apostrophes in more contractions, such as *let us*/let's, *will not*/won't.
3. use apostrophes in singular and plural possessives, such as *Jones's, Joneses', children's, babies', mice's.*
4. use hyphens between syllables in separating a word at the end of a line.
5. use an exclamation mark to express strong emphasis or emotion.
6. use a period or an exclamation mark for a command.
7. use a comma to separate items in a series.
8. use a colon after the salutation in a business letter.
9. use a comma to set off a quotation.

10. place quotation marks before and after a quotation.
11. use a comma to help make sentences clearer.
12. use a comma in figures containing more than four digits.
13. use commas with transitional words such as *however, indeed, that is, for example, in fact,* and so on.
14. use quotation marks for special words in a sentence.
15. use quotation marks for setting off the title of a poem, short story, magazine article, chapter, and so on.
16. use a colon to set off a list of items.
17. underline the title of a book.

II. *Capitalization*	Yes	No

A. Primary Grades

The child capitalizes
1. persons' names.
2. the first word of a sentence.
3. the greeting in a letter.
4. days of the week.
5. months of the year.
6. titles of persons such as Mr., Mrs., Miss, and Ms.
7. first word of the closing of a letter.
8. names of states.
9. names of cities.
10. names of streets.
11. the pronoun "I."
12. the first word of every line in a poem (except for the poetry of some modern poets).

B. Intermediate Grades

The child capitalizes
1. all items listed for the primary grades.
2. names of countries.
3. names of towns.
4. names of avenues.
5. names of roads.
6. any word used as a name such as *Father, Mother.*
7. titles of books.

8. titles of poems.
9. titles of stories.
10. titles of movies.
11. titles of magazines.
12. names of languages.
13. names of buildings.
14. names of companies.
15. the first word of a direct quotation.
16. names of institutions.
17. historical periods.
18. names of nationalities.
19. a direction that names a definite area.
20. in outlining, the first word of each main topic, subtopic, and detail.

III. *Sentences*	Yes	No

A. Primary Grades

The child is able to
1. write simple sentences in the active voice.
2. recognize that sentence fragments are not sentences.
3. recognize that a sentence expresses a complete thought.
4. recognize that a sentence may be as brief as one word such as "Go!" and that "you" is understood in such a sentence.
5. recognize statement sentences.
6. recognize question sentences.
7. recognize command sentences.

B. Intermediate Grades

The child is able to
1. master all items of previous years.
2. write exclamatory sentences.
3. expand sentences by adding descriptive words.
4. combine sentences.
5. recognize run-on sentences.
6. separate run-on sentences.
7. recognize misplaced modifiers.
8. correct sentences with misplaced modifiers.

IV. *Paragraphs*	Yes	No

A. Upper Primary Grades

The child is able to
1. recognize that a paragraph consists of a number of related sentences that develop the main idea.
2. recognize that the related sentences are arranged in some order to make sense.
3. state the topic of the paragraph.
4. keep to the topic.
5. know when to begin a new paragraph.

B. Intermediate Grades

The child is able to
1. master all items of previous years.
2. recognize the topic sentence in a paragraph.
3. write a topic sentence for a paragraph.
4. develop a paragraph using different kinds of details such as examples, comparison/ contrast, cause and effect, description, and definition.
5. write a group of paragraphs on a topic.
6. express ideas clearly.
7. express ideas logically.
8. present ideas creatively.

V. *Letter Writing*	Yes	No

A. Primary Grades

The child is able to
1. write announcements.
2. write friendly letters.
3. write thank you letters.
4. write get well letters.
5. write invitations.
6. write the five parts of a friendly letter.
7. address an envelope for a friendly letter including the zip code.

B. Intermediate Grades

The child is able to
1. master all items of previous years.

2. write business letters using appropriate language.
3. write the six parts of a business letter.
4. order something by mail.
5. write information in a concise manner.
6. write a letter of complaint.
7. write a letter of apology.
8. address a business envelope including the zip code.

VI. *Reporting*	Yes	No

A. Primary Grades

The child is able to
1. choose a topic to report on.
2. choose a title for the topic.
3. keep to the topic.
4. maintain some logical order in reporting.
5. dictate a review about a television show he or she has watched.
6. proofread the report.

B. Intermediate Grades

The child is able to
1. take notes to write a report.
2. maintain logical order in reporting.
3. find information related to the topic.
4. use the encyclopedia for information.
5. use the card catalogue to find information.
6. write a bibliography.
7. prepare an outline before writing the report.

VII. *Outlining*	Yes	No

A. Primary Grades

The child is able to
1. Make discriminations.
2. begin to classify objects:
   a. put things together that belong together
   b. group things under large headings

B. Intermediate Grades

The child is able to

1. use outlines for reporting information.	
2. use Roman numerals for the main topics.	
3. put a period after each Roman numeral.	
4. use capital letters for subtopics.	
5. indent subtopics.	
6. use ordinary Arabic numerals for details under subtopics.	
7. use small letters under the details for less important points.	
8. put a period after each number and letter.	
9. begin each topic with a capital letter.	
10. write an outline in phrase form.	
11. write an outline in sentence form.	

LESSON PLAN I

Primary-Grade Level*

Behavioral Objective

Students show that they are able to use punctuation signals, such as question marks and exclamation points, by placing them correctly in sentences.

Preliminary Preparation

Have available the following items:

1. Large cardboard figures of a question mark and an exclamation point.
2. Full-page pictures of facial expressions signifying surprise, a questioning or quizzical look, and no discernible expression.
3. Transparencies with sentences requiring question marks, periods, and exclamation points.
4. Overhead projector.

Introduction

"We've been working with writing sentences, and we've talked about how important it is to know when to end a sentence. We've learned that a period tells us a sentence is at an end. Who remembers some other things that we talked about? We said that in speaking we can show surprise by expressions on our faces and also by our voices. I have some pictures that I'd like you to look at. Can someone tell me what kind of expression this person has on his face? Yes, he looks as though

*This lesson plan is used with an advanced group of third graders. (Exclamation marks are usually not introduced until the fourth grade.)

he may be asking a question. Can someone make up a question that he may be asking? Good. Let's look at another picture. Yes, she seems surprised. Who can make up a sentence showing surprise? Good. Today we're going to learn about the signals that show surprise and questions in writing. We call these signals punctuation marks."

Development

"When we are writing question sentences and sentences that express surprise, we can't use our voices or facial expressions to help us get others to understand our meaning. This symbol [hold up large cardboard symbol] is called a question mark and this one [hold up large cardboard symbol] is called an exclamation point. We use the question mark symbol at the end of question sentences, and we use the exclamation point at the end of sentences that show surprise or some other strong feeling. I'm going to hold up a few more pictures and I'd like someone to tell me which symbol they would use. [Hold up a number of pictures and have children choose symbols.] Now I'm going to construct a question mark and exclamation point on the chalkboard. After I do so, I'd like you to make three of each of them on your papers. Now we'll see if you can put the correct symbol at the end of the sentences that I'll show you. For example, what symbol would you put at the end of this sentence? *How old are you?* Yes, a question mark. What about this sentence, *Oh, that is pretty!* Yes, an exclamation point. Number your papers from one to five and let's see who can put all the correct signals at the end of each of these sentences:

1. What is your name
2. I love it
3. This is fun
4. Who is she
5. What color is it

"Let's read each sentence and state what signal it should have. Now I'd like each of you to write one question sentence and one sentence that shows surprise or some other strong feeling."

Summary

Elicit from students when to use a question mark and when to use an exclamation point. Pull together the main points of the lesson.

LESSON PLAN II

Intermediate-Grade Level

Behavioral Objective

Students will be able to recognize that notes should fit into only one main topic area.

Preliminary Preparation

Overhead projector, transparency of a student's notes, main headings.

Introduction

"We've discussed the importance of having a good outline when we write a long report or composition. What are some of the reasons we gave? Yes, good. We also talked about the various kinds of outlines. Who remembers some? Today, I'd like you to look at this transparency. It contains notes from a student report called 'Why Accidents Occur.' You don't know this student because he doesn't go to our school. Look for one moment at the notes that this student took and also his main headings. Today we're going to discuss whether this student took good notes and give our reasons for our opinions. From the discussion we should be able to make some suggestions for good notetaking procedures."

Development

"I'd like everyone to categorize the notes into this student's main headings." (Teacher walks around the room while pupils are working and offers her assistance.) After a while she asks whether anyone is having difficulty classifying the notes. A number of children raise their hands and say that they are. The teacher asks them why. One pupil states that some of the notes fit into more than one main heading, and a number of students agree. Another pupil says that he can't put the notes under the proper heading because he isn't sure about their meaning. The teacher asks some students to read what they have put under main topic I. It turns out that students do not agree. The same is done for main topic II and main topic III. The teacher again asks why this has happened. Students reply that they all interpreted the notes differently, and they could fit under more than one heading.

Summary

The teacher asks students what they have learned that could help them to become better note takers from this activity concerning notetaking and main topics. Students reply that the main topics must be clearly stated and not overlap. The notes must also be precise and exact, so that there is no question as to where they belong.

The teacher then states, "Tomorrow we'll look at this student's notes and main topics again. We'll see if we are able to rewrite them so that they can fit properly under the main headings."

Following are the student's main topics and notes:

Why Home Accidents Occur

    I. Failure to see danger.
    II. Failure to use things correctly.
    III. Failure to make repairs.

Student's Notes

1. slippery floors
2. bathroom light switch
3. cellar stairs dark
4. ladder broken
5. medicines on shelf
6. light cord bare
7. pots on stove with handles out
8. throw rugs
9. using tools carelessly
10. toys on floor
11. box on stairs
12. putting penny in fuse box
13. thin curtains over stove

Suggestions for Thought Questions and Activities

1. A child in a fourth-grade class has good ideas, but also has difficulty in expressing them in a written composition. How would you go about helping this child?

2. A class enjoys writing activities, but most of the students do not revise or proofread their papers. What are some things that could be done to stimulate these children to revise and proofread their compositions?

3. What are some techniques that can be used to stimulate interest in outlining?

4. You have been chosen to present a talk to teachers in your school on the skills needed for written expression. How would you present this talk so as to gain and maintain audience interest? What skills would you emphasize in your talk?

5. State some creative ways to combine reading and writing.

SELECTED BIBLIOGRAPHY

Applebee, Arthur N. "ERIC/RCS: Writing and Reading." *Journal of Reading* 20 (March 1977): 534–537.

Furner, Beatrice A. "An Oral Base for Teaching Letter Writing." *Elementary English* 51 (April 1974): 589–594; 600.

Mellon, John C. *National Assessment and the Teaching of English*. Urbana, Ill.: National Council of Teachers of English, 1975.

O'Hare, Frank. *Sentence Combining: Improving Student Writing without Formal Grammar Instruction*. Champaign, Ill.: National Council of Teachers of English, 1973.

Rosenberg, Sheldon, ed. *Sentence Production: Development in Research and Theory*. New York: Halsted Press, 1977.

Rubin, Dorothy. *The Vital Arts: Reading and Writing*. New York: Macmillan, 1979.

Sullivan, Howard J., et al. "Effects of Systematic Practice on the Composition Skills of Frist Graders." *Elementary English* 51 (May 1974): 635–641.

eleven

Written Expression as a Creative Act

EXAMPLES OF TEACHER COMPETENCIES

1. The teacher will be able to state and apply conditions necessary for the development of creativity in children's written expression.
2. The teacher will be able to state and use motivating techniques for stimulating creative writing.
3. The teacher will be able to state and apply ways to stimulate children in the creation of poetry.
4. The teacher will be able to determine whether students value, appreciate, or have an interest in writing creatively by observing whether students voluntarily write stories or poems.

INTELLIGENCY

I think of the Hippopotamus
As quite an intelligent fellow;
(Not owing to the fact that he's
Very fat; and his teeth are yellow)
I think he's wise
Because of his eyes,
So solemn and big
When opened up wide.

And I also think
(Though I may be wrong)
That he does not boast
That he's more strong
Than any of the other animals
Of the forest
And though a passing tourist
May not envy him,
I do.

JANET M.
Fifth Grade

Introduction

Creative writers usually have "an itch to write." They allow their imagination to roam freely and give play to it. Their curiosity is never satisfied. They are always searching for the meaning of things and attempting to explain their findings in their own words. Creative writers are explorers; they are always seeking. They are miners, always digging deeper for keener understanding.

Creative writers are aware of the world in which they live. They are sensitive to their environment and are acute observers of it. They are concerned with what is happening around them and have compassion for others. Being perceptive and feeling persons, they are able to "dwell in the skin of others."

In order to create, they sometimes destroy old ideas. Sometimes they build on past conceptions to generate new ones. They are always open to new ideas and recognize the importance of evaluating their creation as objectively as possible.

They recognize that creativity takes time. It cannot be commanded or demanded! It is a personal thing.

This chapter will look at how students' experiences, coupled with the teacher's help, can awaken or stir the creative spark. After reading this chapter, you should be able to answer these questions:

1. Can children in the primary grades write creatively?
2. What are some stimulating techniques for creative writing?
3. What are some ingredients necessary for creative writing?
4. What techniques can be used to stimulate children to create poetry?
5. What are some poetic forms that can be used to stimulate children's poetry writing?
6. What is the teacher's role in helping to foster creativity in students?

Creative Written Expression in the Primary Grades

Children in the primary grades have a multitude of ideas. They love to listen to stories and enjoy creating their own. In kindergarten, children should be encouraged to tell stories about the many different things around them. When teachers listen to their kindergarten and first-grade children, they discover that many of the things they say about the world around them are in poetic form. Young children seem to play with words and to delight in saying and repeating words. Teachers should take advantage of the opportunities that present themselves and record these utterances. Children enjoy listening to and seeing their first creations in print. Their imaginations should be given free rein. Their lively imaginations are ready to blossom forth in writing, if they are properly encouraged and stimulated. There are a number of restraints that may act as deterrents—learning manuscript and mastering spelling, among others. If every time children write something on paper, the teacher corrects and criticizes it, the children will cease to put their ideas on paper.

These efforts at creative writing by two first graders were not corrected, even though they are not perfect. Once the stories were written, they were displayed on the bulletin board (p. 258).

By accepting the writing as it is presented, the teacher is encouraging these children to write again. They should not have to recopy the paper a number of times to achieve perfection. After the children have finished their self-expression, corrections can be made.

Children should be allowed to use any words they wish regardless of whether they can spell them correctly. They should also not be censored or made to choose only a topic the teacher has selected. Primary-grade teachers have a great responsibility, because what they do in school may influence students' attitudes toward writing all through their lives.

Matthaew D. W.
I ate an apple
I Have an ache
Do You? Have One.
The End.

Julie I see a
mouse? He is
scared to look
at me

Children's Imitative Writing

As was stated in Chapter 10, young children's writing tends to be imitative. Many times they copy cooperatively composed stories, or imitate what they read. Teachers should not be critical of this.

As long as the use of words and the ideas are the child's own, the writing is unique. Later on, one hopes, as children continue to write, they will develop styles of their own.

The Teacher's Role in Creative Writing

Teachers can help to foster creativity in students. The attitude and understanding of teachers, as well as their manner of teaching, will influence students' creative development. Teachers who demand one way of doing things will thwart pupils' desires to "look beyond" or to try new paths; teachers who stimulate students to be more divergent will be encouraging creativity within them.

When students are helped to realize that they have worthwhile things to write about, if they take the time to search within themselves, they are being helped to discover they can write.

Stimulating Creative Written Expression

The more creative the teacher, the greater students' chances will be for realizing their creative potential. Teachers cannot inject creativity into their students, but they can provide an atmosphere in which children feel free to explore, to make mistakes, and to take chances.

Motivation is an important facet of creativity, and is necessary for all learning. Teachers can create situations, either through using everyday events or through preplanned happenings, which can help motivate students to want to create. Although the best motivation is internal, outside stimulators can get the individual aroused and involved. Once students are motivated, a mood and desire to write must be created.

Creative writing stimulators can emanate from a variety of media—pictures, literature, tapes, discussion, records, films, dramatic activity, and so on. Motivational devices can be used to heighten awareness on the part of the child, and act as a springboard to stir the student's imagination.

The teacher must be careful not to expect results from all students. As individuals, children will be motivated by different stimuli, so a diversity of techniques and devices should be used to encourage responses from as many students as possible.

Motivating Techniques Here are some motivating techniques to help stimulate creative writing:

1. Hold up a papier-mâché "animal" which has the characteristics of many different animals. Tell the children that this "creature" is very confused. It doesn't know who it is or where it comes from. It needs help from the children. Perhaps they can find a name for it, and tell where it came from, what it does, and how it lives.

2. After reading some books the children can be asked questions that stimulate creative thinking in writing. In fifth or sixth grade the children might read *A Wrinkle in Time*, in which the main characters visit a gray planet devoid of sunlight, inhabited by gray people. The children could then be asked to write on the following problem: How would you as a human being adapt to this gray planet?

3. Hold up a number of pictures and ask students to write creative stories about them. In the primary grades a picture stimulus can be used as an experience story, with the teacher and pupils writing the story together.

4. Ask children to imagine they have an animal that can talk. Ask them to tell of their experiences with this animal.

5. Ask children to imagine they are living in a house of the far-distant future, and tell what this house is like: its furniture, its appliances, its kitchen utensils.

6. Children imagine that they live at the bottom of the sea. Ask them to tell of their adventures. For a fantastic account of such an adventure they can read *Twenty Thousand Leagues Under the Sea* by Jules Verne, and for a scientific account that may seem stranger than fiction they can read Rachel Carson's *The Sea Around Us*.

7. Children imagine that they own a spaceship which can take them to another planet. Ask them to tell of their experiences.

8. Children write an imaginative theme beginning with the sentence, "There is only one hour to wait. . . ."

9. "Who am I?" Students develop biographical mysteries.

10. Children imagine they are machines, and write a story from the machine's point of view.

Brainstorming, which was discussed in Chapter 4, lends itself to providing a warm-up for creative writing, as well as other creative activities. (See Chapter 4 for brainstorming techniques.)

Some Ingredients for Creative Writing

Experiencing, getting in touch with one's feelings, and having many opportunities to write are necessary ingredients for writing. Ideas are not created in a vacuum. Children need a rich and varied literary environment to which they can add their first-hand knowledge and experiences. Good literature not only gives students models of human thinking but also makes students more sensitive to the elements needed for good writing.

Students need time to write, to incubate and mull over ideas. They need a place where they can write undisturbed by others. Pupils need a classroom environment which is psychologically safe, a place in which they feel free to share ideas with others and to look within themselves.

Description: An Essential Writing Ingredient

Good writers are usually good observers of the world around them. They are perceptive and sensitive to their senses—of touch, smell, hearing, tasting, and seeing. Children need many experiences in these areas. They must recognize the importance of each sense and how each helps them communicate with themselves.

Here are some activities that help students become more sensitive, keener observers of their environment, and help them to develop descriptive ability:

1. The children are asked to close their eyes and put their hands into a number of different bags held near them. Each bag contains a different item—such as a piece of liver, cold spaghetti, or ice-cold grapes. The children are asked to describe each item. As they do so the terms they use are put on the board. (Ice-cold grapes elicit very good descriptions.)

2. Each group of students is given a box which contains one item. Students must try to figure out what the item is using their sense of hearing.

3. One student comes to the front of the room, while all others close their eyes. The student then describes someone in the class. The children, without opening their eyes, try to guess who the person is.

4. Children are asked to describe a building that they have to pass on the way to school. After they have described the building in writing, the teacher should take the whole class to visit the building to see how accurate the descriptions are.

5. Students can be asked to describe odors that come from the school cafeteria on a particular day.

6. Students are asked to describe the sounds of a busy traffic intersection.

7. Students may be asked to describe a favorite holiday, telling how it seemed to them when they were about five years old, and comparing how it seems now.

8. Students can be asked to describe a costume they would like to wear to a ball.

9. Students may describe a character from a favorite television show.

10. The teacher sets up this scenario and the children describe the person they saw:

Scenario

Beforehand, the teacher asks two outsiders each to bring an item into the classroom as he or she is talking to the students. The first person brings in a brown paper bag, the second brings a sheet of paper. The two persons put the items on the desk and leave. Then the teacher looks at the desk, notices the items, and says, "Oh! This isn't mine. It belongs to someone else." The teacher asks the children if they had seen who left the brown paper bag on the desk. The teacher asks them to write a description of the person who brought the item. After the children write their descriptions, some of them are read aloud for comparison. Later the visitor who brought the brown bag is invited into the classroom so that the children can see how accurate their descriptions are.

Exercises in description help children to be more perceptive of the world around them, and aid them in developing characters for their stories.

Creating Word Images: Figures of Speech

Children are exposed to figures of speech from listening to the language around them before they come to school. Many children, depending on their backgrounds, will use word images in their speech. People use figures of speech in conversation in order to communicate better.

As with the rest of our speech, the use of word images does not depend on knowledge of their labels. Since children use verbs, nouns, and other parts of speech without knowing their names, so they can use figures of speech. Many students may depend heavily on slang to convey their meaning.

When children begin to read, they encounter figures of speech that help the reader to see vivid word pictures. (See "Figures of Speech" in Chapter 9.)

Although students use figures of speech quite well in oral expression, they seem to have more difficulty with them in reading and writing. Perhaps children use such expressions in speech quite naturally and are not aware that they portray word images. Teachers must therefore try to get students to recognize that some of the phrases that brighten up speech can also be usefully incorporated in their writing. However, teachers must also recognize that since figures of speech are a form of inference, not all children will be able to work with figurative language. (See "Figures of Speech" in Chapter 9.)

Intermediate Grades: Developing Word Imagery   The teacher can record a number of expressions commonly used by students, and then ask why and when students use these expressions. The children should be encouraged to generate a number of word images about a specific event. The word images they include in their writing give readers a more lucid picture of the event. One event the teacher might describe for such an activity follows:

A boy and girl are dancing at a school dance. The boy is very clumsy and keeps stepping on the girl's feet.

Students, using word pictures, have to express how the boy and girl feel.

When students have generated a number of expressive phrases that start with "as" or "like," which compare two unlike things, the teacher states that these figures of speech are called *similes*. After analyzing some of the other phrases given by students which compare two unlike objects or concepts, but which do not start with "as" or "like," the teacher tells students that these phrases are *metaphors*.* If students have described inanimate objects with human characteristics, students should be told that these figures of speech are *personification*.

Students can then be encouraged to give further examples of similes, metaphors, and personification. They seem to have the least difficulty with generating and recognizing similes, because they are introduced with "like" or "as." Metaphors seem to be more difficult for students to recognize and make up, because there is no introductory word cue.

Although children in primary grades are both exposed to and using similes such as skinny as a toothpick, pretty as a picture, happy as a lark, quiet as a mouse, and so on, they do not have to learn the term "simile" for these phrases. However, by fourth grade "simile" can be introduced, and by fifth grade both "metaphor" and "personification" can be learned.

Hyperbole or "gross exaggeration" can be introduced in the intermediate grades. Again, students use this type of figure of speech in their everyday language, but they must be made aware of its potential in written form. For example, students might say:

---

*Often the term metaphor is used in a generic (general) sense to cover all forms of figures of speech. Therefore, simile, personification, and so on, might be referred to as metaphors.

I walked a million miles today.
I am dead tired.
He missed by a mile.

Students should be encouraged to discuss how these terms help readers to get a clearer understanding of what they are saying. When a writer says that someone "prattled on for an eternity," he or she is not only telling us that the person talked for a very long time, but the writer is also giving us his or her feelings about it. If the writer had enjoyed the company of the person talking, the writer would not have said that the person prattled on for an eternity.

Students should be helped to understand the use of hyperbole in advertising. The term "hype" is used very often in our culture, especially by the advertising industry in connection with television and movie advertisements. Exaggerated words such as "blockbuster," "death-defying," "shocker," "stupendous," "stupefying," "sensational," "amazing," and "unbelievable" are often used to describe the production they are promoting. Students should be able to generate many more terms.

Another technique that is frequently used by writers is that of *oxymoron*. (See Chapter 9.) *Oxymoron* is the combining of contraries (opposites) to portray a particular image or to produce a striking effect. These word contradictions attract our attention and present the author's feelings or ideas indirectly and expressively.

An oxymoron with which students may be familiar is "the poor little rich girl." Usually this word contradiction is accompanied with sarcasm, that is, the person saying it is actually ridiculing the girl while expressing a seemingly sympathetic phrase. In other words, the writer does not feel sorry for the girl. However, it is possible for the phrase "the poor little rich girl" to mean that the girl has a lot of material possessions, but she does not have other things such as love, understanding, parents, and so on.

Some other examples of familiar oxymorons used in sentences follow:

1. Parting is such *sweet sorrow*.
2. A *loud silence* followed the improper remark.
3. This is one of those occasions for *making haste slowly*.
4. She lives in *happy ignorance*.
5. He is suffering from *benign neglect*.
6. They are the *best* of *enemies*.
7. She was *conspicuous* by her *absence*.

The oxymoron "the dawn of night" would probably be one that would be used in connection with Dracula. For example, Dracula would be more interested in the "dawn of night." "Night is day" for Dracula. Students can probably come up with some interesting oxymorons in relation to the adventures of Dracula, one of the living dead.

Overworked Phrases

Teachers need to encourage students to try to avoid using overworked phrases—phrases that have been used over and over again. For many people, it is often easier to use a common phrase than to think of a fresh and original way to say something. For example, the phrases presented earlier, such as "pretty as a picture," "happy as a lark," "quiet as a mouse," and "skinny as a toothpick," would be considered overworked phrases.

Children need to be helped to recognize that strong, active, and descriptive words are better than general and static ones. For example, see how the sentence *They removed the obstacle* can be made into a more vivid and graphic sentence by changing the verb *removed* to one of the following verbs: *erased, demolished, obliterated, destroyed, liquidated, wiped out, deracinated, smashed, scattered,* or *displaced*.

Connotative Meanings[1]

Intermediate-grade level children should begin to realize that when we speak or write we

[1]Dorothy Rubin, *Reading and Learning Power* (New York: Macmillan, 1980).

often rely more on the *connotative* meanings of words than on their *denotative* meaning to express our real position on the topic discussed. The connotative meaning of a word includes the denotative meaning, the direct, specific meaning of the word. But the connotative meaning also includes all *emotional senses* associated with the word. The connotative use of a word therefore involves an understanding of more than a simple definition. When you respect a word's connotative meanings, you will use the word precisely and effectively.

"Credulous" and "trusting" are two words that have a similar denotative meaning: "ready to believe or to have faith in." However, if you refer to someone as a "trusting person," you are saying he or she has the admirable trait of believing the best of someone or something. If you refer to the same person as "credulous," you are saying that he or she lacks judgment, that he or she foolishly believes anything. Although both words have the same denotative meaning, in their very different connotative senses one is complimentary and the other belittling or insulting. Connotative meanings are obviously vital to the art of saying the right thing the right way. Writers rely on connotative meanings all the time, especially when they want to influence their readers. Whether a word influences positively ("trusting") or negatively ("credulous") makes a great difference to what is actually said.

Many words also have different overtones or associations for different persons. For example, the term "mother" can bring forth images of apple pie, warmth, love, and kindness for one, whereas for another it can mean beatings, hurt, shame, fear, and disillusionment.

Some words lend themselves more readily to emotional overtones or associations than others. For example, the term "home" can bring forth both good or bad associations based on the past experiences of the individual. However, the term "dwelling," which has the same specific definition as "home," does not bring forth the emotional overtones that "home" does.

Teachers can help their students recognize that a number of words have substitutes that more aptly express the meaning that an author wishes to communicate. Students can be challenged to come up with words that carry negative, positive, or neutral meanings. For example, a building that people live in could be a barn, a castle, or a dwelling.

Character Development

In developing characters children must be aided in avoiding stereotyping. A researcher who worked with intermediate-grade pupils was trying to help them improve their imaginative writing. The researcher used a short piece, "How to Tell the Good Guys from Bad Guys" by John Steinbeck (*The Reporter*, March 10, 1955). In the piece Steinbeck's son, Catbird, points out to his father that you can always tell the plot of a television Western at the beginning of the program, because the good guy is wearing a white hat and the bad guy wears a black one. The man in the gray hat is either good at the start and then turns bad, or is first bad and then turns good. A reading of this piece opens up an excellent opportunity for class criticism of some of the character portrayals on television.

To develop their critical abilities, children can be asked to watch a number of different television shows and describe which characters are one-dimensional, or not very realistic, and which characters are multi-dimensional, or more lifelike and realistic. Students can then state what the differences are. A combination of methods which help make a character come to life can be listed as:[2]

1. Describe the characters—how they look and so forth.
2. Show them in action—what they do.

[2]Adapted from Henry Larom, "Sixth Graders Write Good Short Stories," *Elementary English* 37 (January 1960): 20–23.

3. Tell what they say—this can lead into attempts at dialogue.

4. Show what other people think about them.

5. Tell what they think about—what goes on in their heads.

Rather than merely requiring pupils to write character sketches, have them present the characters in a happening, so that they are real people in action. Such an event includes all those things that could take place in a given situation or scene.

The Development of Suspense

In order to develop suspense, children must learn not to give all their information at once. They must learn to postpone, to give just enough to whet the appetites of their readers. In putting events together children must try to have something in each situation which will heighten the desire of the reader to want to go on with the story. Reporting suspenseful stories will help children learn this technique, as will choosing good suspense stories for analysis, to see how the author achieved suspense.

Writing about Events

In order to help children to write about situations, events, or scenes, they should be given many experiences. Children might present a short skit, which the rest of the class can then write about, telling exactly what took place and describing the characters and the action. The teacher can show a scene clip from a movie or a scene from a television show and the students can write a description of it.

In developing skills in writing there is no set order in which elements must be presented by the teacher. The important thing is that children be aided in mastering writing skills and that they be given *many opportunities to write*.

Creating Poetry

In Chapter 9 it was shown that children ranked poetry as the least liked of all literature. However, if children are properly exposed to poetry and allowed to create it, what delightful creations they can produce!

WHAT AM I?

I am a monster.
No, now I'm a dog!
Now I'm a bluebird,
And now I'm a log!

Now I'm a cat,
Now I'm a rat!

Now a mouse,
In a house!

I'm a lizard
No, I'm a blizzard

Now I've turned into a hat;
And now once again
Into a cat!

RICHARD

Kenneth Koch in his book, *Wishes, Lies, and Dreams,* demonstrates how he was able to get elementary-school children reading and writing poetry. His formula includes a fundamental belief that all children are able to create poems. They must be encouraged to put their thoughts down, and not fear recriminations because of misspellings, lack of neatness, or improper word usage; there must be a proper classroom environment, as well as knowledge of some techniques for poetry writing.

One technique used to stimulate poetry writing was to ask children to start their poems with "I wish." According to Koch: "The idea helped them to find that they could do it, by giving them a form that would give their poem unity and that was easy and natural for them to use: beginning each line with 'I wish.' " One of the main problems children have as writers is subject matter. Using a technique like "I wish"

Puppet shows by students develop writing capabilities.

helps and encourages children to be "imaginative and free." [3]

Some other successful methods employed were to:

1. Put a comparison or a sound in every line.
2. Write dream poems.
3. Write lie poems; to say something in each line that wasn't true.

Children were helped to write by ". . . removing obstacles, such as the need to rhyme, and by encouraging them in various ways to get tuned in to their own strong feelings, to their spontaneity, their sensitivity, and their carefree inventiveness." [4]

Another technique that helps children in poetry writing is exposure to many poems. "Jump or Jiggle" by Evelyn Beyer can be read as a "loosening up" exercise for the class. This can be followed immediately with Iris Tiedt's poem "What Can You Do?" After each poem is read children should be asked where they think the idea for the poem came from. A poem in a similar vein, "I Speak, I Say, I Talk" by Arnold L.

Shapiro, can also be read. At this point children should be asked if they would like to try writing a poem together. To stimulate the class, words in groups of two, similar to those given below, are listed, and the children contribute their ideas orally. Some children may want to write their own pairs, and should be encouraged to do so. [5]

Cows
Dogs

Ants
Worms

Cats
Fish

Boys
Girls

I
Birds

Since teachers do not know which poems will ignite the creative spark in their students, they should expose them to a variety. After listening to Amy Lowell's "Falling Leaves," and a number of other poems about fall, some children wrote these poems of their own:

FALLING LEAVES

I am going to rake some leaves,
Red, yellow and brown.
I am going to rake some leaves
All over the ground.
But they all keep falling down
Without making a sound.

LYELL

AUTUMN

The leaves are falling to the ground.
They don't even make the tinest sound.

They flutter, flutter when they fall;
Big and large, tiny and small.

MARY

[3]Kenneth Koch, *Wishes, Lies, and Dreams* (New York: Chelsea House, 1970), p. 7.
[4]Ibid., p. 25.

[5]A. Barbara Pilon, "Lighting the Candle to Children's Creative Language Powers," *Elementary English* 50 (April 1973): 568.

After listening to Elinor Wylie's "Velvet Shoes," Dorothy Aldis's "Snow," and Robert Frost's "Stopping by Woods on a Snowy Evening" a child wrote:

WINTER

Winter is here bringing a chill.
Watch the sleds whiz by
Every once in a while making a spill.
Let's go out and sled, just you and I;
The saucers twist, to and fro,
Here they come, there they go.
Horse drawn sleighs sometimes drive by;
The people in them wave and say, "Hi!"
Let's go out, just you and I!

BETH

Carl Sandburg's "Fog" stimulated this poem:

NIGHT'S SILENCE

All is still. The lilacs stand as if they had never moved before. The sunset lingers behind the stock still hill. The grass no longer sways in the breeze. Everything is still and silent. This night is a long and silent night. Who knows what will happen next?

LAURA

As has been stated, teachers must recognize that what stirs one child may not necessarily interest another. Not all students love all the poems presented in class, and teachers should be very careful about "gushing." It's one thing to be genuinely enthused about a poem; it's another to try to force-feed it to students. Children seem to be able to sense sincerity and honesty. Let the children know that you, too, do not "love" all poetry. Since you are sharing poems with the class, ask them to bring in some of their favorites, as well as some of their parents' favorites. This usually sparks an interest in poetry, a necessary first step in the creation of poems.

Poetry of the Senses

The poetry books used by the class should offer sights, sounds, and colors that stimulate children to want to produce their own creations.

Mary O'Neill's *Hailstones and Halibut Bones: Adventures in Color* has stimulated many students to create color poems. This prolific writer has also published *What Is that Sound!*, which encourages children to create "sound" poems; while her book, *Fingers Are Always Bringing Me News*, makes children more aware of utilizing the sense of touch in writing.[6] (See "Listening for Appreciation" in Chapter 5 for more on poetry of the senses. See also Chapter 8 for "Vocabulary of the Senses.")

Music and Poetry

The teacher should use a number of different stimuli because it is difficult to determine what will act as a catalyst to creation. Music can stir poetic creation in children because both have their own unique rhythms. Children respond very readily to the sounds as well as the rhythms of music, so music might stimulate children to "hear" poems.

As a result of listening to Tchaikovsky's "Quartet in D Major" some children wrote poems. A sample of a boy's poem reflects the sonorous sounds, whereas the girl's is preoccupied with the soft sounds.

POETRY AND MUSIC

Galloping, galloping, over the hills;
With two Toms, and six Bills.
Boy this is a lot of fun;
I hope we never get done.
Ride and ride all afternoon;
The horses' feet make such a tune.

BILL

POETRY AND MUSIC

Exciting music, soft and low and bouncy;
   a beautiful show.
The violin singing, Oh how lovely.
Never a mistake, skimming along.
Beautiful music, humming a song.

ABBE

[6]Ruth Kearney Carlson, "The Creative Thrust of Poetry Writing," *Elementary English* 49 (December 1972): 1183–1184.

Fun with Different Poetic Forms

Children can become excited over the many different kinds of literary forms used in writing poetry. Children may even be encouraged to make up their own. To act as guidelines to the great diversity of poetic forms, children should be exposed to the triangle, quadrangle, and diamante poetic forms created by Iris Tiedt.[7] Haiku, cinquain, concrete poetry, and newspaper poetry are other types of poetic forms children can experiment with in their creative endeavors.

Haiku   *Haiku* is one of the oldest forms of Japanese poetry. It consists of three lines composed of seventeen syllables—five in the first and third lines, and seven in the second. Since Japanese and English syllabication are not similar, haiku lends itself more readily to Japanese writing, and the 5-7-5 syllabication pattern is not always adhered to in English.

The most important factor in haiku is the feeling that is supposed to be portrayed in the poem. The themes are usually concerned with beauty and nature. The theme should be clearly stated and the location, time of day, or season is usually incorporated in the poem. Nothing is too insignificant to be noticed by the poet.

The 5-7-5 syllabication cannot be used until children are in the intermediate grades and have been exposed to syllables. Therefore, rather than stressing syllables, theme, feeling, and simplicity rendered in three lines can be stressed. Here are some examples *not* based on syllabication:

> The sun—
> brightly afire
> warms all.
>
> Flowers—
> opening their arms
> to love.

Samples of haiku based on the syllabication pattern include:

[7]Pilon, op. cit., p. 568.

THE MORNING MIST

> The morning mist crept
> over my lawn as I slept
> at the crack of dawn.

WINTER

> The sleds flew forward
> like birds flying in the sky.
> We played until dark.

The tanka verse is a five-line pattern of Oriental verse arranged in a 5-7-5-7-7 poetic pattern of thirty-one syllables. Although it has the same qualities as haiku, its form is not as delicate, because of the addition of the two seven-syllable lines.

Lanterne is another syllabic pattern of 1-2-3-4-1, which is arranged in the shape of a lantern. Ruth Carlson discusses both tanka and lanterne verse in her books, *Sparking Words: Two Hundred Practical and Creative Writing Ideas* and *Writing Aids through the Grades*. An interesting variation, given by Carlson, is that of the chained lanterne, which joins several verses in the form of a linked or chained lantern:

> One Small Egg
>
> One
> Small Egg
> Freckled gray.
> Warmed by mother
> Crack!
> ◇   ◇   ◇
> Crack, Crunch
> a small hole
> Crack, its larger
> Eyes
> ◇   ◇   ◇
> Crack!
> A mouth
> A small head
> A small gray wing
> Peep![8]

[8]Carlson, op. cit., p. 1179.

Cinquain   Cinquain is based on a five-line pattern. People writing in cinquain have varied this five-line pattern; for example, one variation consists of a first line with five words, while each subsequent line has one less word. The result is an upside-down pyramid five lines high, ending in one word.

Another five-line pattern consists of a first line with one word, the second line with two words, the third with three, the fourth with four, while the fifth line reverts to the one-word length of line one. Some persons also give specific purposes for each line, which is helpful in guiding neophyte writers:

First line: states the theme
Second line: describes the theme
Third line: the theme is in some action
Fourth line: gives a feeling of the theme
Fifth line: states another word for the theme.

Many elementary- and college-level students seem to prefer the second pattern of 1-2-3-4-1, with a specific purpose given for each line. An example is:

Fog,
white blanket
covering the universe
how still and quiet
Peace.

Iris Tiedt has invented four new poetry patterns that seem to be successful frames for ideas. The first of these, the diamante (dee ah mahn' tay), is a seven-line diamond-shaped poem structured as:[9]

Line 1: subject noun (one word)
Line 2: adjectives (two words)
Line 3: participles (three words)
Line 4: nouns (four words)
Line 3: participles (three words)
Line 2: adjectives (two words)
Line 1: noun, opposite of subject (one word).

[9]Iris M. Tiedt, "Exploring Poetry Patterns," *Elementary English* (December 1970): 1083–1084.

A second form by Tiedt is the septolet, which consists of seven lines (fourteen words) with this pattern:

Line 1: one word
Line 2: two words
Line 3: three words
Line 4: two words
Line 5: one word
Line 6: two words
Line 7: three words.

Tiedt's third form, the quinzaine, involves fifteen syllables in three lines (7-5-3), which make a statement followed by a question.

The fourth pattern, called the quintain, is a five-line progression of 2, 4, 6, 8, and 10 syllables respectively.

Concrete Poetry   Concrete poetry seems to be a favorite among children of all ages, who enjoy experimenting with many of the poetic styles utilized by modern poets. Concrete poets are concerned with the arrangement of words on a page and feel that their purpose is to be simultaneously perceived and read. Children can use any object that they desire as their stimulus, and develop a poem using the concrete form of the object as an outline. Stimuli can range from an outline of a cat to a child's hand. (See below.)

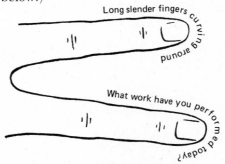

The concrete poem (page 269) was written by a child about a large blue-and-orange ball placed at the top of stairs.[10]

[10]Carlson, op. cit., p. 1182.

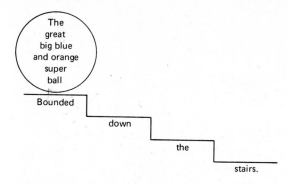

Newspaper Poetry Newspaper poetry, a poetic form that can be used to stimulate children's poetry writing, is similar in many ways to concrete poetry. Newspaper poets, like concrete poets, are concerned with the arrangement of words on a page, and feel that these should be simultaneously perceived and read, that is, the visual presentation is part of the poetic experience. However, newspaper poets rely on the appearance of the words and their arrangement for the desired effect, whereas concrete poets are more concerned with a specific object.

Children of all ages enjoy creating newspaper poetry, which involves choosing words from newspapers and magazines that express certain feelings or thoughts. These words can be of various sizes, shapes, and colors. The children arrange them in a pattern that best expresses the thought or feeling they would like to portray.

Constructing newspaper poetry is an enjoyable undertaking. It is a good idea for teachers to construct their own newspaper poems before they attempt this activity in class, because only then will their enthusiasm for this activity be genuine.

On the specified day for the construction of newspaper poems, teachers should make sure that each newspaper poet has an ample supply of newspapers and magazines, paste, a pair of scissors, and *sufficient time*.

To stimulate interest in poetry in which the medium is an important part of the message, the teachers can expose children to some poems by Edward Lear and Alastair Reid. Children will probably delight in Edward Lear's "Nonsense Botany" in which the visual is a very important aspect of the poem. In *Ounce Dice Trice*, Alastair Reid has such poems as "Counting" and "Odds and Ends," in which the visual appearance of the words and their arrangement on the page are part of the poetic experience.

Teachers can also relate back to their own efforts with newspaper poetry, which should be on display. They should emphasize again that the size, shape, color, and arrangement of the words are part of the poetic feeling, thought, or expression. Teachers could then present a number of themes that the children could use, but they must be sure to say that these are only ideas or springboards for the children, and that the children can make up their own.

Limericks

Most persons especially enjoy listening to limericks. Limericks consist of a five-line pattern. The first, second, and fifth lines of a limerick rhyme with one another, and the third and fourth lines rhyme with each other. The first, second, and fifth lines have three beats, whereas the third and fourth lines have two beats. Limericks are supposed to be funny, silly, and ridiculous.[11] (See "Listening for Appreciation" in Chapter 5.)

> There was a Young Lady of Norway,
> Who casually sat in a doorway;
> When the door squeezed her flat,
> She exclaimed, "What of that?"
> This courageous Young Lady of Norway.
>
> EDWARD LEAR

A Special Supplement of Children's Written Expression in the Primary and Intermediate Grades

By being exposed to the writing of many children, teachers will be in a better position to judge the level and ability of their own pupils. Since children very much enjoy reading other children's creations, and being read to, these may also act as stimuli for children to write on their own. Some schools keep bound volumes of children's works in the school library.

On many occasions, teachers discover they have students with great creative writing potential in their classes. Such students may have gone unrecognized because they are shy or taciturn. In this supplement the story, "The Flower," is reproduced as an example of creative writing from a young girl who, although very quiet in class, was articulate in print.

A representative sample of primary- and in-

[11]See Mary McDonnell Harris, "The Limerick Center," *Language Arts*, (September 1976): 663-665, *for information* on developing a limerick learning center.

termediate-school children's creative writings is also included. Since many of the hopes, wishes, and dreams of all children are similar, regardless of nationality, color of skin, or place of residence, the sample is made up of writings by children from all these backgrounds.

Children wrote stories about what they would like to be when they grew up. Then the stories were rewritten and corrected by the pupils, so that they could be displayed along with pictures they drew to illustrate the stories. Some of the compositions still had some spelling errors, and the teacher gave students correct spelling without criticism.

> I am a Policeman.
> I have a car.
> I catch robbers.
> I lock them up.
>
> RICHARD

> This is me when
> I am little.
> This is when I am
> big. When I am
> big I will be a
> nurse. I will work in
> the hospital.
> I will be taking care of sick people.
>
> ABBY

Sometimes young children reveal their private lives through their poems. This story was dictated to her teacher by a first grader:

MAD AND HAPPY

> Sometimes I talk to my brother,
> He doesn't listen.
> He doesn't listen.
> Sometimes I talk to my mother.
> She doesn't listen.
> Sometimes I talk to my father.
> He doesn't listen.
> My mommy and my brother can't hear me
> My daddy can't hear me.
> He doesn't listen.
> I am mad.
>
> LISA ANN

Children seem to enjoy listening to and writing tall tales. Here are a few tall tales written by intermediate-grade students:

A TALL TALE

Before the dinosaurs came from Venus, a giant came from Mars. He was 15 miles high and he wasn't very smart either. When he lay down he made the English Channel. He took his bath in the Indian Ocean, and he went swimming in the Atlantic Ocean. After his swim, when he put his hand on land, he made the Great Lakes. When he sat down to eat lunch he made the Grand Canyon. Then he made sand castles which are the Great Smokies. Then he went back to swim. He made all the valleys, plus he broke a dam which let the ice from the Antarctic into the States, where we have glaciers.

MARK

A TALL TALE

I once knew a man 20 yards tall. He pulled up trees, roots and all and made a flute of some sort. He played high notes and low notes that sounded like the wind. Some people say the wind is really silent and it is the giant playing on his flute.

PATTY

This tall tale was written by a fifth grader to explain why persons have different colors of skin.

One day all the gods were having a meeting to decide what this year's project was going to be.

One said, "How about a raindance party?" Everybody replied "no" because they had one last year. Another request was to have a bowling party, but all the bowling balls were being repaired.

Then God of Light had a good idea that everybody agreed to and that was to paint a giant picture of what the place looked like below the clouds of the sky.

Everybody had a job. God of Light was to light the sky and to make sure that everything went smoothly. God of Dark was to darken the sky and take over when God of Light was tired. When he was in the sky everybody was to stop work and rest, for this was the biggest project they (meaning the gods) ever had done. All the other gods were in charge of painting the picture and getting the other materials needed.

In choosing colors they chose red, yellow, brown and black. For the painting board they just got a fluffy cloud and flattened it out so it would be easier to paint on. It took one day to get set up and get all the materials needed. Everybody went to sleep to get all rested up for the big project they were to start the following day.

All gods were up early, for they were very anxious to start on the painting. Everybody got a paint brush and was assigned to a certain place, all except ZeZeus who was God of Dumbies and Clowns. He was forever getting in trouble or lousing things up. All the gods told him to stay away from the painting because this was the biggest and the best project they had ever done. Oh, how ZeZeus wanted to paint, but he couldn't even go within twenty feet of the painting or he would get yelled at.

ZeZeus thought when everybody is sleeping I'll go with my flashlight and look at the painting and maybe even paint a little bit. So when everybody went to sleep ZeZeus went with his flashlight to the painting. He looked at the painting and thought what a beautiful painting. There on the painting were hills full of grass, trees all leafy and green, water so blue, people so rosy cheeked, and flowers so delicate. He wanted to paint so bad that he picked a spot to paint, got a brush, and opened all the paint cans. Then he started to paint. He thought nothing can go wrong now and when the people wake-up they will thank me over and over again. Everybody will want me to paint now. Then ZeZeus heard a noise; when he turned around to see what the noise was he turned all the cans of paint upside down and down went the paint.

Everybody woke-up right away and began yelling at ZeZeus. When they looked down they saw that each paint can spilled paint in different parts of the world. Some people's skin was black, some red, some yellow and some brown. Where paint didn't fall the people stayed white and to this day people have different color skins.

THE
N
D

The following poem, written by an intermediate-grade child, seems to show her rather fatalistic acceptance of things.

I USED TO BE. . . .

I used to be a ball of string,
Until I was unraveled;
They tossed me over and all around,
And I became all baffled.

I used to be a ballerina,
Until I broke my toe;
But now I have to sit and watch,
It makes me sad you know.

I used to be a daffodil,
Blooming in the spring;
But now that summer is nearing,
I'll try another thing.

I used to be a doorbell,
Always being pushed;
But now the people moved away,
And I'm no longer bushed.

I used to be a little bear,
Nearing hibernation;
But now I better get in step,
And join my generation.

I used to be so many things,
So busy and so tired;
But now I think I should relax,
Because I've just retired.

This fourth grader seems to have enjoyed making his monster, which goes very well with his short poem:

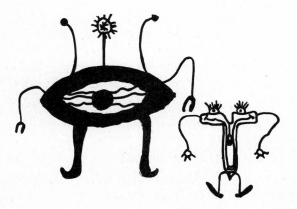

MONSTERS

Monsters, Monsters,
Giant Monsters,
Monsters, Monsters,
All over my pansters!

This excellent contribution by a twelve-and-a-half-year-old was written after she had read a number of Edgar Allan Poe's stories. It is clearly imitative of Poe's style, but the ideas, the words are the child's, who has gained confidence that she can write.

THE FLOWER

I looked forward to greeting my sweetheart the day I set out early in the morning to walk to her house. I had done this many a time before so this was not new to me. The houses, the cobblestone way, the tall leafy oaks—everything the same. I walked on with not a care in the world until I saw—the flower. It was, and still is, the most beautiful thing that I have ever seen. The color of it was a soft pure, creamy white that shone like silk. I am not a horticulturist so I cannot tell you its name. It looked somewhat like a rose but much fuller and fluffier. It had many, many petals which gave it a look like a ruffled gown. My words do not do it justice, for it was so beautiful that just one look at it would make its beholders want it like nothing before.

The flower was in a garden of many varied flowers—all of which were very beautiful, but the flower of which I have spoken surpassed all without a doubt. The garden was situated approximately one half mile off the main road, on a dirt path. I had passed the garden before, as I have used it to shorten my journey, but I had not noticed the flower previously. Now that I had seen it though, I decided it would make quite a lovely gift for my beloved. So I hastened to pick it. But it was not to be. Just as I touched the velvet stem, just as I was to pull it from its place, a dog, a monstrous, contemptible, hideous dog jumped up from the ground with such a snarl I had never heard before. I had seen him before but had taken little notice of him. He had seemed a placid enough fellow. But now, this beast that I looked at, surely this was no beast at all, but a demon in disguise. I can remember distinctly a glare in his eyes that froze me in my steps. I thought that now I truly knew what it was to see a dog's lips curl. And oh, that terrible growl I have mentioned before. This was the most remarkable thing about him. His whole body seemed to tremble with it. He started out with a low grumble that grew louder and louder till I thought my eardrums would burst. I thought to myself no lion could outroar this small persistent dog.

After I recovered my sense I wasted no time in escaping from his growls. I was quite lucky in that there was a fence. I shudder to think of my fate had there been no fence.

So, I proceeded to my sweetheart's without the flower. This sequence was to happen many times. Everytime I passed the flower and was about to pick it the dog would leap into the air and become a ferocious beast. And each time I passed it, it seemed the flower became more and more beautiful, making it more and more irresistible. You cannot imagine the agony I went through. How I stealthily crept up to the flower, how I held in my hands the graceful stem so many times but each time having to give in to the dog. At night his body haunted my dreams. During the day I heard his unearthly screams persistently. Always on my mind was the flower, the beautiful flower. I feared for my sanity.

I had no idea who was the master of the brute. Indeed, I often wondered if he possessed one. I had seen not one house along the path. I had always thought the land there unoccupied by humans. Nevertheless, whether occupied or not by humans I knew what I was to do to maintain my sanity. The dog would have to be gotten rid of. From my point of view it was quite a simple task. Not once had I seen any humans about, much less the dog's master. As I have said before the dog was always quiet until I started to pick the flower. The more I thought about it, the easier the deed seemed. I felt better than I had in weeks, but I was anxious to get the deed done with so I could possess the impossible—the flower.

It was a little after noon when I started out to the flower. My legs seemed to acquire a briskness of pace I had never known them to have. When I reached the flower, I stopped for a moment—

unsure. In all my time spent thinking of killing the dog I had never given much thought to detail. But then, a wild instinct drove me on. My feet clambered over the fence and before I realized it I was standing on the other side. My heart was pounding furiously as I took a step toward the sleeping dog. I was almost upon him when some instinct of his own must have awakened him for I had proceeded upon him with the utmost of caution. I saw the dog make ready for attack but before he could do so I sprang on to him. It was a thrilling battle but I never once doubted as to whom would come out the victor. I was merely a tool for my hate and revenge. They commanded me and I carried out their commands. When I had accomplished my task, I buried the dog in the garden and would have picked the flower then if not for the blood and dirt which covered me like a blanket. I found a stream not too far from the flower and I cleaned myself there. By the time this was accomplished it was quite dark, so I spent the night beside the stream.

Such a lovely night I have yet to see again. It was pitch black, without a star in the sky. I had a great feeling of satisfaction and relief. I was at last free of the hideous beast. My dreams were untormented, my thoughts still on the flower but this time with content for in the morning I would have it for mine.

I arose earlier than usual the next morning and upon doing so rushed to the flower at last. My feelings, I cannot describe, so content, so happy, so joyous was I that morning—until I reached the flower. I thought in frenzy at first that I was in the wrong garden. But no, I remember the bush and trees, everything there the same, untouched, except for the flower. Where could it be? I searched every branch of the bush but not a trace of the flower was to be found. Then, as I hung my head low in despair my eyes caught sight of something under the bush. It was a flower, but surely, surely, not the flower! Its stem was broken and coarse; its petals were crumpled and squashed and had the color of a grotesque brown that seemed to have soaked out all the life that had once lived in the flower. For yes, it was the flower. At the very tip of one of the brown petals was a very minute tinge of white. A white that could not be mistaken. Yet as I touched it, the pureness of the white disappeared and in its place the dullness and drabness of the brown became apparent.

SHARON ANNE

After a brainstorming session, a fifth-grade class wrote these statements about an ideal school:

I would like a school that would give me a complete education in five minutes. It would be the best education in the world. Then in half an hour, I would have the best college education in the world, which would enable me to live in the best house in all the world. That is the kind of school I would like.

RICHARD

1. Having a pencil write what you tell it to write.
2. Being able to read for an hour and having a little Merry-Go-Round by each desk filled with books.
3. Having a soda fountain by each desk.
4. Having a ferris wheel for the ramp.
5. Riding a horse to the board and the horse writes for you.
6. Having a robot to fan you when it's hot.

SUSAN

The Ideal School to me is very different. It is fun, educational (as much or more than other schools), and short. It would have teaching machines that cost absolutely nothing to run so no taxes would be needed. The machines could change your I.Q. from 50 to 175. The school building would have desks that could be used in many different ways. At the right upper side there would be a candy dispenser that would give you different kinds of candy free. At the upper left hand side would be a fountain which would make any kind of drink you want. The pencils on the desk would write your whole paper without making any mistakes, and it would go so fast you could do a year's work in a day. Buttons on your desk that have the names of subjects written on them would be able to give you any information you wanted.

CAROL

The children were told to allow their imaginations to wander while answering these statements:

1. If I could fly . . .
2. If you wore no shoes the sidewalks would have to be . . .

Here are two responses:

If you wore no shoes, the sidewalks would have to be —flubber! If I fell down on flubber . . . well, it's something you have to experience.

If I could fly, I would fly to the top of my room and fool my sister. I would fly in and out of buildings, but I would not fly too high. I might become myself again.

ABBE

If you wore no shoes, the sidewalks would have to be made out of pillows. Each pillow would be attached to the next in order to form a belt. The belt would revolve and would have turn-offs to all the houses.

If I could fly, I would fly back through history. I would meet famous people before they became famous.

BETH

In this poem and story children have projected themselves into the animal world. They have chosen an animal they thought they might like to be, and then have written a story from that animal's point of view:

A DOG

If I were a dog
I'd walk down to the stream
And catch a hog in a dream.

I'd chase a rabbit
As quiet as I could

I'd go back home
and go to sleep
And wait for another day.

BRUCE

I'M A BROOK TROUT

There is always something fishy going on in the sea, but I'm used to it. I have 126 brothers and 116 sisters. I'm 16 months old and I have had some adventures. One adventure was when I was swallowed by a shark. Mighty fish saved me. Another adventure was when I was caught by a fisherman, but managed to slip away that night. Of my 242 brothers and sisters, 57 of them are on the dinner table, and 29 of them have been eaten by other fish. The rest of them and I are lucky.

BILL

In this short story a child has allowed her imagination to run free:

HARRY'S HORROR HOUSE

Harry was a devil. His hobby was scaring people to death with his brand new horror house. Harry got this horror house from his Uncle Scats for his 40,000th birthday. Harry set it up in his backyard. Now he would wait for his first victim. So by and by an elderly lady devil came walking by and saw his sign that went like this:

> For only 1 thin
> dime you can have
> a horrible
> DEATH!   10¢

The elderly devil thought this was so cute. "Imagine," she said loud enough for Harry to hear, "a horrible death for only a dime. I must try that."

So she paid her dime, walked in the horror house. And the poor devil . . . it was the last time she was ever heard of again.

P.S. Neither was Harry when his Mother found out.

ABBE

It is sometimes interesting to ask students to think about certain concepts and what they bring to mind. In these activities, intermediate-grade students were asked about poetry:

Poetry is a beautiful thought put down on paper.

ALICE

Poetry is like fire. Fire can be almost anything. It can be dancers dancing and prancing and dancing again. It can also be made with rage and sometimes beautiful too.

ROBIN

The concept of happiness generated these responses:

WHAT HAPPINESS IS TO US

A forest of dogwood and thousands of daisies in the field.

The feeling you get when you think of a small bird chirping merrily on the branch of a willow tree by a pond. It is the feeling of proudness you get when you have done something well and receive praise for it.

A family that is bound together with love. A bouncing baby beagle.

Playing games with other children. Doing something to please someone. Eating an ice-cream cone with other children.

A new born kitten or puppy just opening his eyes for the first time to see the world. A lovely tulip opening up its petals to greet you.

Swimming in the waves in the ocean. Ice-skating in circles on a frozen pond when nobody is around.

When intermediate-grade level students were asked to state what beauty means to them, they wrote:

WHAT BEAUTY IS TO US

A peacock's tail.
Baby animals being born.
A snowflake that is falling to the ground.
The outside in the spring.
When something is very quiet and still.
A falling star.
A full moon surrounded by dancing stars.
The late days of fall.

Student's Name:
Grade:
Teacher:

Diagnostic Checklist for Written Expression as a Creative Act

I. *Description*	Yes	No

A. Primary Grades

The child is able to
1. describe a person in the class.
2. describe a character from a television show.
3. state descriptive words using each of the five senses.
4. state descriptive words that appeal to the senses.
5. use some word images.

B. Intermediate Grades

The child is able to
1. master all items of previous years.
2. describe a scene.
3. use simile.
4. use metaphor.
5. use personification.
6. use oxymoron.
7. use hyperbole.

II. *Character Development*	Yes	No

A. Primary Grades

The child is able to
1. describe the appearance of an imaginary character.
2. state how other people feel about the imaginary character.
3. tell what the imaginary character would say in certain situations.

B. Intermediate Grades

The child is able to
1. describe the feelings of an imaginary character.

2. show the character in action.
3. relate the character to other characters.
4. present dialogue between and among characters.
5. tell what the imaginary character thinks about.

III. *Poetry*	Yes	No

A. Primary Grades

The child is able to
1. write "wish" poems ("I wish . . .").
2. write "dream poems" ("I dream . . .").
3. write "lie" poems (say something in each line that isn't true).
4. put a comparison or a sound in every line.
5. write poems on any topic he or she wants.
6. write "sound" poems.
7. write concrete poems.
8. write newspaper poems.

B. Intermediate Grades

The child is able to
1. master all items of previous years.
2. write limericks.
3. write haiku poems.
4. write cinquain poems.
5. write tanka and other poetic forms.
6. write poems using figures of speech.

IV. *Stories*	Yes	No

A. Primary Grades

The child is able to
1. write about what he or she would like to be when he or she grows up.
2. write an imaginary story.
3. finish the statement "If I could fly . . .".
4. finish the statement "If I wore no shoes . . .".

B. Intermediate Grades

The child is able to

1. master all items of previous years.
2. write a tall tale.
3. choose a topic for an imaginary story.
4. choose a title for an imaginary story.
5. write a beginning paragraph for a story.
6. write a story in proper sequence.
7. write a concluding paragraph for a story.
8. use dialogue in a story.
9. write many and varied imaginative stories.
10. produce suspense in his or her stories by not giving all of the information at once.

LESSON PLAN I

Primary-Grade Level

Behavioral Objective

To be able to identify, describe, and project images of an unseen object in terms of its tactile sensory impressions.

Preliminary Preparation

"Feel" box. This would be prepared by the teacher before the lesson and would contain a variety of objects which produce sensory impressions. A cardboard box with a "window" cut in it, covered with a curtain, works very well.

Introduction

Pass around an object (pine cone) for everyone to touch. Elicit descriptions from different points of view from the students. Ask them: What did it feel like? How would you describe it? What do you think it is like to be a pine cone on a tree swinging in the breeze? What do you think it would feel like to have someone pull you off the tree?

Tell the children that they have been spending a lot of time writing. Talking about how writing can be improved, discuss what help is needed in describing things.

Introduce the "feel" box, and explain that there are a variety of objects inside the box and each should produce many sensations. Tell the students that they are going to work with description.

Development

At this point directions should be made clear. Each student will reach into the box while blindfolded and the teacher will be sure that they pick up only one object by guiding their hands to an object. Students can hold it, feel it, smell it, and explore all aspects of their objects. After they have held the object for a moment, they are asked to state some words to describe it. The words are put on the board. From these descriptions, children will be asked to name the object.

Some objects that could be used:

a peeled grape	sponge	crumpled tinfoil
cooked spaghetti	toothbrush	chalk
a cotton ball	velvet	flannel
piece of netting	sandpaper	fur
thimble	cornflakes	deflated balloon

After students have had a chance to study their objects, they each contribute a description to be presented to the rest of the class.

After a number of children have used the "feel" box, the children are told they will be divided into groups of four. Each group receives a box with an object inside it. The students describe the object, and from this description other pupils try to guess what the object is.

Each group is given a chance to describe their objects.

Summary

Pull the main points of the lesson together. Help students to recognize the importance of description and how it helps us to "see" an object better. The teacher tells students that tomorrow an object will be chosen and then the class will write about it together, as if the class were the object. Students are asked to think about how they would feel if they were chocolate sundaes or kites flying in the sky. If someone wants to, he or she can borrow the box, collect some new objects, and challenge the rest of the class to guess what they are.

LESSON PLAN II

Intermediate-Grade Level

Behavioral Objectives

To be able to sell a fictitious product by writing an original slogan and jingle.

To be able to act out (in front of the class) "their own TV commercial" to aid in selling the product.

Preliminary Preparation

Large posters containing some of the following selling slogans can be scattered on the walls throughout the room:

Try it, you'll like it!

Pucker power.
The taste you hate twice a day.
I can't believe I ate the whole thing!
Everybody doesn't like something, but nobody doesn't like . . .
I'd rather fight than switch.
They don't want tuna with good taste, Charlie! They want tuna that tastes good!
You've got the frizzies!

Mounted advertisements from magazines and newspapers.
A tape recording of a well-known TV and radio advertisement.
A box wrapped in plain brown paper with the word TRAZZLE written boldly across the front.

Introduction

We have spent some time on critical listening and reading activities, discussing propaganda and bias in relation to advertising. We have discussed the various techniques that advertisers use in promoting their products. Who remembers some?

Students state: the appeal to one's sense of prestige, economy, sex, the use of color, repetition, bold print, and so on.

We also gave examples of each of these. Who can give one? Yes, the use of a very dignified-looking gentleman surrounded by books and selling pain-killer.

Listen to this tape recording. A technique is being used that we have not yet discussed. (Tape is played which has a jingle with a catchy tune.) Today we will set up our own advertising companies, decide on a product, determine how to advertise that product using jingles or slogans, and then act the ad out.

Development

"Before we separate into our advertising company groups, I'd like everyone to look at this poster. What does it contain? Yes, lots of quite well-known selling slogans. Let's see how well we know the products that they are supposed to represent. Very good! You see how the slogan helps you to remember. Now we'll divide into five advertising companies. Each company will be responsible for preparing a slogan or jingle for this product." (Teacher introduces TRAZZLE to students.) "You must decide what TRAZZLE is, and prepare the slogan or jingle that you feel best suits it." (Students are divided into companies.)

Teacher walks around room offering assistance. After about a half hour, or whenever the teacher sees that students are ready, they are asked to present their commercials. The students do not state what TRAZZLE is. The other groups will try to guess the type product from the slogans or jingles.

Summary

Pull main points of lesson together.

Tell students to think about the kind of television program they would want to use to advertise their products. "Perhaps we will attempt to write such a show ourselves. We'll discuss this next time."

Summary

The teacher must understand that creativity cannot be commanded or taught, but it can be fostered in children by using a variety of motivating techniques. The essentials for putting creative stories together were presented with a major emphasis on description, since the development of children's perceptions of the world is an important factor in writing. In order to interest children in writing poetry, a number of techniques were discussed—such as exposing children to many different poems. Such poetic forms as cinquain, haiku, tanka, lanterne, concrete and newspaper poetry were presented so that children could experiment with different poetic forms.

A special supplement on primary- and intermediate-grade children's writings was given with samples of children's writing. No differentiation was made as to the quality or locale of the writing, but examples illustrated that children at all levels of capability can be stimulated to write. However, they must receive guidance and help from their teachers. A Diagnostic Checklist for "Written Expression as a Creative Act" was also presented.

Now that you have read this chapter, you should have mastered the given teacher competencies presented at the beginning of this chapter.

Two examples of writing lesson plans are presented at the end of this chapter. Using these as guides, see if you can construct another one.

Suggestions for Thought Questions and Activities

1. Discuss motivating techniques to stimulate interest in written expression.
2. Construct a creative lesson plan in the area of written expression.
3. How would you stimulate children to write poetry?
4. Discuss a number of topics that could be used to initiate a creative writing lesson.
5. You have been appointed to a committee to judge children's creative writing. What problems do you think you might encounter in this task?
6. You have been invited to give a talk to the annual meeting of teachers in your school system. The suggested topic is how you encourage the creative spark in your students. Write out your talk.
7. Choose ten poems to stimulate interest in concrete and newspaper poetry writing.

SELECTED BIBLIOGRAPHY

Applegate, Mauree. *When the Teacher Says, "Write a Story."* New York: Harper & Row, 1965.

Blake, Howard E., and Jaqueline Shachter. "Promoting Composition and Literature: A Schoolwide Thematic Program." *Elementary English* 51 (May 1974): 625–630.

Bradley, Buff. *Growing from Word Play into Poetry.* Palo Alto, Calif.: Education Today Co., 1976.

Brewton, John, and Sara Brewton. *Laughable Limericks.* New York: Crowell, 1965.

Carlson, Ruth. *Writing Aids through the Grades: 186 Developmental Writing Activities.* New York: Teachers College Press, 1970.

Cavanaugh, William. *Introduction to Poetry.* Dubuque, Iowa: W.C. Brown, 1973.

Day, Robert, ed. *Creative Writing in the Classroom: An Annotated Bibliography of Selected Resources (K–12).* Urbana, Ill.: National Council of Teachers of English, 1978.

Emmett, William. *Anthology of Concrete Poetry.* New York: Something Else Press, 1967.

Evertts, Eldonna. *Explorations in Children's Writing.* Urbana, Ill.: National Council of Teachers of English, 1970.

Harris, Mary M. "The Limerick Center." *Language Arts* 53 (September 1976): 663–665.

Hopkins, Lee Bennett. *Pass the Poetry, Please: Using Poetry in Pre-kindergarten-Six Classrooms.* New York: Citation Press, 1972.

Jackson, Walt, and Lew Musil. "Becoming a Concrete Poem." *Language Arts* 54 (March 1977): 290–293.

Koch, Kenneth. *Rose, Where Did You Get that Red?* New York: Random House, 1973.

———. *Wishes, Lies and Dreams: Teaching Children*

to Write Poetry. New York: Chelsea House Publishers, 1970.

Larrick, Nancy. *Somebody Turned on a Tap in These Kids: Poetry and Young People Today*. New York: Dell, 1971.

Lear, Edward. *Limericks*. Cleveland: World, 1965.

Livingston, Myra C. *When You Are Alone It Keeps You Capone: An Approach to Creative Writing with Children*. New York: Atheneum, 1973.

Mearns, Hughes. *Creative Power: The Education of Youth in Creative Arts*. New York: Dover, 1958.

Myers, R. E., and E. Paul Torrance. *Invitations to Speaking and Writing Creatively*. Boston: Ginn, 1965.

Rubin, Dorothy. "Developing Writing Skills," in *The Primary Grade Teacher's Language Arts Handbook*. New York: Holt, Rinehart and Winston, 1980.

————. "Developing Writing Skills," in *The Intermediate Grade Teacher's Language Arts Handbook*. New York: Holt, Rinehart and Winston, 1980.

Troop, Marian. *The Limerick Book*. New York: Grosset, 1964.

Whisnant, Charleen. *Word Magic: How to Encourage Children to Write and Speak Creatively*. Garden City, N.Y.: Doubleday, 1974.

Witucke, Virginia. *Poetry in the Elementary School* Dubuque, Iowa: W.C. Brown, 1970.

Wolsch, Robert. *Poetic Composition through the Grades: A Language Sensitivity Program*. New York: Teachers College Press, 1970.

twelve

Gaining Proficiency in Spelling

EXAMPLES OF TEACHER COMPETENCIES

1. The teacher will be able to state methods for teaching spelling.
2. The teacher will be able to state the relationship of spelling to other areas of the language arts.
3. The teacher will be able to state difficulties that students may encounter, which may impede correct spelling.
4. The teacher will be able to state spelling generalizations which should be taught.
5. The teacher will be able to plan and execute spelling lessons based on students' needs, interests, and ability levels.
6. The teacher will be able to incorporate spelling into other subject-matter areas.
7. The teacher will observe students' spelling in their writing and act positively by preparing and presenting spelling lessons based on the errors which appear most frequently.
8. The teacher will be able to define homophone and homograph.
9. The teacher will be able to determine whether students value, appreciate, or have an interest in spelling correctly by observing whether:

a. Students' former spelling errors are appearing less frequently in writing.
b. Students voluntarily attempt to look up the correct spelling in the dictionary.
c. Students ask the teacher about the spelling of words of which they are not sure.

Introduction

TEACHER: "Spell sago, mucilaginous, ephemeral, cyst, copal."
PUPIL: "Why?"
TEACHER: "Because I say so!"
PUPIL: "But, they are so hard and I never heard the words before."
TEACHER: "No matter. The harder the words you have at first, the easier spelling will become."

Choosing rare and very difficult spelling words, which were almost unpronounceable, was part of a lesson illustrated in an early edition of Noah Webster's *Blue Back Speller*, a child's basic primer. Such words as "sago," "copal," and "cyst" were selected for mastery by the elementary-school child. It was not until the latter part of the nineteenth century, when psychologists became involved in determining how children learn to read, that changes in the teaching of spelling also began.

The interaction of reading, language, and spelling was also demonstrated in Webster's *Blue Back Speller*. Here are some excerpts to serve as examples:

"Analysis of Sound in the English Language" had to be memorized exactly. It began with this definition:

> Language or speech is the utterance of articulate sounds or voices, rendered significant by usage, for the expression and communication of thoughts.

All other explanations were written similarly as if to obscure meaning. Children had to memorize passages, without understanding them, since teachers rarely offered explanations. (Perhaps they, too, had difficulty in interpreting the passages.) The *Speller's* format consisted of a page of the alphabet and a page of syllable combinations. The prose content of the *Speller* consisted of didactic sayings, admonishing children to be good and do their duty. A reading page consisted of several paragraphs, each concerned with an entirely different topic. For example:

A good child will not lie, swear, nor steal. He will be good at home, and ask to read his book; when he gets up he will wash his hands and face clean; he will comb his hair and make haste to school; he will not play by the way as bad boys do.

As for those boys and girls that mind not their books, and love not the church and school, but play with such as tell lies, curse, swear and steal, they will come to some bad end, and must be whipt till they mend their ways.

January begins the year, and the first day of that month is called New Year's day. Then people express to each other their good wishes, and little boys and girls expect gifts of little books, toys, and plums.

There are five stages of human life, infancy, childhood, youth, manhood, and old age. The infant is helpless; he is nourished with milk—when he has teeth he begins to eat bread, meat, and fruit, and is very fond of cakes and plums. The little boy chuses some plaything that will make a noise, a hammer, a stick or a whip. The little girl loves her doll and learns to dress it. She chuses a closet for her baby-house, where she sets her doll in a little chair, by the side of a table, furnished with tea-cups as big as a thimble.

As soon as the boys are large enough, they run away from home, grow fond of play, climb trees to rob birds' nests, tear their clothes, and when they come home their parents often chastise them. O how the rod makes their legs smart. These are naughty boys, who love play better than their books.[1]

A peculiar feature of the book concerned social relations.[2] The "young man, seeking for a partner for life," is advised to "Be not in haste to marry," and the young woman to:

> Be cautious in listening to the addresses of men. Is thy suitor addicted to low vices? is he profane? is he a gambler? a tippler? a spendthrift? a haunter of taverns? and, above all, is he a scoffer at religion? Banish such a man from thy presence,

[1]Clifton Johnson, *Old Time Schools and School Books* (New York: Dover, 1963), p. 177.
[2]Ibid., p. 178.

his heart is false, and his hand would lead thee to wretchedness and ruin.

For married people there are suggestions of this sort:

> Art thou a husband? Treat thy wife with tenderness; reprove her faults with gentleness.
> Art thou a wife? Respect thy husband; oppose him not unreasonably, but yield thy will to his, and thou shalt be blest with peace and concord; study to make him respectable; hide his faults.

Although Webster combined spelling and reading in one text (along with pre- and post-marital advice), it should be stressed that spelling is not synonymous with reading. (More will be said about this later.) Before Webster's book, which was based on Dilworth's spelling book, spelling in textbooks was not uniform. Even the most highly educated spelled the same word in different ways, as is documented in letters, records, and other manuscripts. Webster brought standardization and order to spelling, almost single-handedly counteracting the chaos that had previously existed.

A woodcut portrait of Webster, which made him look like a porcupine, was used in "Old Blueback," which caused a great deal of controversy concerning the book. But this controversy helped publicize and advertise it, and as a result Webster's *Speller* became very popular.

Before the *Speller* was published, spelling had only been taught incidentally, but Webster's book made it an important subject. Spelling matches were held and prizes were given, which absorbed a great amount of children's time and energy. Spelling matches also became a recreational event, and great competitive exhibitions were held.[3] Although the educational value of these events has been questioned, many vestiges of spelling matches remain to this day.

Spelling is not emphasized as much today as it was in the nineteenth and a great part of the twentieth century, but the skill is important for

[3]Ibid., pp. 167–184.

effective communication in writing. Numerous spelling errors detract from the ideas being presented, and the writer who makes many errors is usually looked on as lacking in education.

Since confusion exists as to the place of spelling in the school program—how it should be taught, and when it should be formally taught—these areas and others will be discussed in order to help teachers to establish an effective and viable spelling program for students.

After reading this chapter, you should be able to answer these questions:

1. How is spelling related to other language arts areas?
2. What is the spelling controversy? Explain.
3. How are words chosen for spelling lists?
4. What criteria should be used for choosing words for classroom study?
5. What are some of the spelling problems that a left-handed child could have?
6. What can the teacher do to stimulate pupils' spelling consciousness?
7. Why is there confusion about the terms homonyms, homophones, and homographs? Explain.
8. What spelling generalizations should be taught?
9. Can you explain the inductive method of teaching spelling?
10. What is the word study plan? Describe the steps involved in this method.
11. What are some possible difficulties in learning to spell? Explain.
12. What is the place of the dictionary in the spelling program?

General Aspects of Spelling

The Relationship of Spelling to Other Language Arts Areas

Spelling and reading are related through vocabulary. A child who has difficulty in recognizing a word will have difficulty in trying to reproduce its sequence of letters from memory. Reading and spelling can be seen to be closely related, since many of the abilities required for one are also required for the other. For example, learning to read and to spell requires the ability to discriminate visually among words. Generalizations concerning phonic analysis, structural analysis, and vocabulary development are the same as those in spelling. If vocabulary is poor and articulation not adequately developed, both reading and spelling usually suffer.

Good reading and spelling seem to go together. The more often a word is met in reading, the greater the likelihood that the word will be learned and used in writing. Although there are some good readers who are poor spellers, the opposite is rarely true. Children who have difficulty in learning the relationships between sounds and the symbols that represent them will usually have difficulty in spelling.

Although there are similarities between reading and spelling, the acts of reading and spelling are different. In reading, the child starts with visual symbols and then must think of corresponding sounds; whereas in spelling, one hears the word and has to think of the corresponding symbols. The act of spelling involves encoding (going from sounds to letters), while the act of reading involves decoding (going from letters to sounds). Spelling often requires the motor activity of writing letters to stand for the sounds heard.

Ability to spell enhances a pupil's creative writing, for the pupil does not have to concentrate on the mechanics of words but can be involved in the act of creating.

The Spelling Controversy

English

I take it you already know
Of tough and bough and cough and dough?
Others may stumble, but not you
On hiccough, thorough, slough and through?
Well done! And now you wish, perhaps
To learn of less familiar traps?

Beware of heard, a dreadful word

That looks like beard and sounds like bird.
And dead; it's said like bed, not bead;
For goodness sake, don't call it deed!
Watch out for meat and great and threat,
(they rhyme with suite and straight and debt).
A moth is not a moth in mother.
Nor both in bother, broth in brother.

And here is not a match for there.
And dear and fear for bear and pear,
And then there's dose and rose and lose—
Just look them up—and goose and chose,
And cork and work and card and ward,
And font and front and word and sword.
And do and go, then thwart and cart.
Come, come, I've hardly made a start.

A dreadful language? Why, man alive,
I'd learned to talk it when I was five,
And yet to write it, the more I tried,
I hadn't learned it at fifty-five.[4]

AUTHOR UNKNOWN

The "spelling controversy" is concerned with whether children should be taught spelling based on lists of words or whether generalizations should be used to teach spelling. Linguistic approaches to spelling emphasize the phoneme–grapheme relationships of words and analyzing groups of words by generalized rules. In the analysis, not only must the pupil know that each phoneme has a grapheme representation but the pupil must also learn how to listen for individual phonemes and notice their position and the sequence in which they occur.

Linguistic approaches to spelling instruction are not new. Many schools do not incorporate linguistic principles in the spelling curriculum because administrators believe there is no relationship between the way a word is said and how it is spelled. Because of the innumerable irregularities in spelling words, the subject was taught in the past by rote memorization, without any attempt at phonetic analysis. It was taught

[4]Harold G. Shane, *Linguistics in the Classroom* (Washington, D.C.: Association for Supervision and Curriculum Development, 1967), p. 50.

with spelling lists based on graduated levels of difficulty and containing words selected for their usefulness in writing. During the past two and a half decades an attempt has been made to emphasize the aural–oral aspect of spelling in relation to vocabulary. It was felt that, by being able to recognize words and *phonograms* or *graphemic bases* (a succession of graphemes that occurs with the same phonetic value in a number of words [at, ack]), children would be able to synthesize a large number of words on their own. As a result, there has been a greater emphasis on generalizations in spelling. Although there are not many scientific studies in this area, some researchers have attempted to establish sets of rules which would explain spelling.[5]

A study initiated in 1949 at Stanford University found that the phoneme–grapheme representation was regular in 80 percent of the 3,000 words analyzed. This was considered to be too narrow a sample, and it was suggested that if more words were added, the results would verify that the *orthography* (accepted spelling usage) was inconsistent to the point where the study would be considered unreliable. An extensive study to examine the degree of consistency of the phoneme–grapheme relationships of 17,000 words, closely representative of the American-English lexicon of an educated U.S. citizen, was undertaken. Since modern computer technology was used, it was possible to make large-scale analyses that would have been too tedious earlier. It was found that American-English orthography is more consistent with the spoken language than has been thought, especially when several components of the sound system underlying the orthography were examined. These are:

1. Position in syllables.
2. Syllabic stress.

3. Internal restraints. These refer to the specific letter that precedes or follows a letter (its environment).

The investigators did not claim their study made a firm case for the linguistic approach to spelling. It was stated that even though a phoneme is represented by a given grapheme in stressed (accented) or unstressed syllables 80 percent of the time, this fact may not help in the spelling of words. The restriction of the phoneme–grapheme correspondences to special positions keeps the results from applying to larger generalizations.

In the next phase of the study of phoneme–grapheme regularity in words, the earlier findings were used to predict the spelling of 17,000 different words. It was found that, by relying on phonological cues alone, researchers could spell over 8,483 words correctly from the list of 17,000. Therefore, even a limited knowledge of the phonological relationships can help provide some ability to spell words, while the additional knowledge relating to *morphology* (the study of the construction of words and parts of words) and *syntax* (the ways in which words are arranged relative to each other in utterances) would be even more helpful to correct spelling.[6,7,8]

Ernest Horn, an authority on spelling, and an opponent of the use of rules and generalizations, claims that there is no justification for assuming that students can deduce the spelling of words from generalizations. For Horn, there is no escape from the need for teaching directly a large number of common words which do not conform to any phonetic or orthographic rule.[9]

[5]Ruth H. Weir and Richard Vonezky, "Spelling to Sound Correspondences," in *The Psycholinguistic Nature of the Reading Process* (Detroit: Wayne State University Press, 1968).

[6]Richard E. Hodges and E. Hugh Rudorf, "Searching Linguistics for Cues in the Teaching of Spelling," *Elementary English* 42 (May 1965): 527–533.

[7]For the detailed report, *see* Paul R. Hanna et al., *Phoneme–grapheme Correspondences as Cues to Spelling Improvement* (Washington, D.C.: Office of Education, U.S. Department of Health, Education and Welfare, 1966), U.S. Project No. 1991.

[8]Paul R. Hanna et al., *Spelling: Structure and Strategies* (Boston: Houghton Mifflin, 1971).

[9]Ernest Horn, "Some Issues in Learning to Spell," *Education* 79 (December 1958): 229–233.

He claimed that:

> Like many worthwhile things, there does not seem to be any short cut to learning to spell. Although some phonetic generalizations hold true consistently, e.g., initial consonant sounds like "b," time is better spent in learning to spell needed words rather than learning generalizations. This is true for most spelling rules.[10]

In the late 1960s Horn compared the research on phoneme–grapheme regularity to his own extensive research in spelling. He claimed that the studies (his own and the generalization research) are in substantial agreement on the number of ways in which various phonemes are spelled, as well as on the relative regularity of the spellings of sounds. However, the investigations unfortunately differed in the meaning of the term "regular." In Horn's study *regular* means "the total number of ways in which the sounds are spelled irrespective of the word position or other phonological [refers to speech sounds] or morphological [deals with the construction of words and parts of words] factors."[11] In the linguistic study the term *regular* takes into account the phonological factors of stress and the environmental conditions in words and syllables, including such morphological factors as compounding and affixation and the use of approximately 300 specialized rules.[12]

Although Horn seems to have softened his stance toward the contribution of phonemics to spelling, he still feels that caution is necessary when making conclusions. For example, he says that:

> . . . in the evaluation of the claims for high regularity in phoneme–grapheme relations, two limitations should be kept in mind: first, the pronunciations chosen for analysis are those given in Webster's New International Dictionary, second edition. These pronunciations, according to the dictionary, are those found in deliberate and careful speech, elsewhere called formal speech. In many words, these pronunciations vary from those found in informal cultivated speech. Second, the degree of regularity obtained by sophisticated research workers using several hundred rules to guide them, and the use of a computer to perform the tedious analysis, seems far removed from what can be achieved by students with the abilities and tools they have or can be given.[13]

Other researchers claim that although a speller who uses the rules consistently can spell about 80 percent of all phonemes correctly, that speller would only be able to spell about half of the 17,000 most common English words correctly, because these words contain several phonemes.[14]

It is obviously futile to teach a rule in which there are more exceptions than words which conform to a pattern. Therefore, generalizations should only be taught if enough cases conform to the rule. Some studies on phoneme–grapheme relationships have been done with enumerated specific rule generalizations and the percentage of time that words followed the rule. Some investigators have claimed that a rule should not be taught unless it holds true at least 75 percent of the time.[15,16] However, this should depend on the words. There are some frequently used words which may conform to a rule pattern, whereas a number of less frequently used words may not conform to the same rule generalization. The percentage of these latter words that conform to a rule pattern may not be as high as 75 percent, even though the most often used words almost always conform to the

---

[10]Ibid., p. 232.

[11]Ernest Horn, *Teaching Spelling: What Research Says to the Teacher*, National Education Association, 1968, p. 22.

[12]Ibid.

[13]Ibid., p. 23.

[14]Dorothea P. Simon and Herbert A. Simon, "Alternative Uses of Phonemic Information in Spelling," *Review of Educational Research* 43 (Winter 1973): 115–137.

[15]Theodore Clymer, "The Utility of Phonic Generalizations in the Primary Grades," *The Reading Teacher* 16 (January 1963): 252–258.

[16]Lillie Smith Davis, "The Applicability of Phonic Generalizations to Selected Spelling Programs," *Elementary English* 49 (May 1972): 706–712.

same pattern. For example, the "silent *e*" rule, which is usually taught in the early primary grades, only has 63 percent applicability.[17] This 63 percent includes many frequently used words. Therefore, the rule should be taught as a phonic generalization.

The "spelling controversy" continues, and perhaps it would be best if a balanced approach prevailed. Those words which follow phoneme–grapheme patterns should be taught with rule generalizations, while those words which do not fit any pattern should be taught as separate entities.

What Words Should Be Taught?

The problem of compiling a spelling list is difficult. A first-grade child who comes to school with a speaking vocabulary of approximately 2,500–3,500 words may want to know how to spell some of these words. The problem becomes more complex because the child may have from 7,500 to 25,000 words in his or her listening capacity. It is not inconceivable that the child may want to use some of these words in writing.

A 1915 study based on a 1,000-word count of adult literary writing and correspondence found that there were 300 most common words which made up three-fourths of all the writing analyzed. It was also discovered that the first 1,000 most common words made up more than nine-tenths of the material.[18]

During the late nineteenth and early twentieth centuries there was a proliferation of similar studies published in the United States, stating those words which were of the greatest use in written communication. Some vocabulary lists, such as Rinsland's 1945 one, were derived from various types of students' spontaneous writing.[19] It seems that like adults, children employ a few words most often, but that the complete number of words they use is very large.

The question of what factors should be considered in compiling word lists for children has still not been definitively answered. One school of thought is that children should learn to spell those words which they will need for adult writing. Another is that spelling lists should be composed of words children frequently use.[20,21] From a psychological point of view, those words should be taught which the child needs, has an interest in, and can use. If the child learns words only for a weekly spelling test, and does not use the words again, the chances that the child will retain them are not good. New learning will probably interfere with past learning, and the earlier words may soon be forgotten.

Homonyms or Homophones or Homographs?

Confusion may exist among the terms *homonym*, *homophone*, and *homograph* because some authors are using the more scientific or linguistic definitions for the terms and others are using the more traditional definitions. *Homonyms* have traditionally been defined as words that sound alike, are spelled differently, and have different meanings; for example, "red, read." However, many linguists use the term *homophone* rather than homonym for this meaning. Linguists generally use the term *homonym* for words that are spelled the same, pronounced the same, but have different meanings; for example, "bat" (the mouselike winged mammal) and "bat" (the name for a club used to hit a ball). "Bat" (baseball bat) and "bat" (animal) would traditionally be considered a homograph (words which are spelled the same but have different meanings), but linguists usually define *homographs* as words which are spelled the same but

[17]Ibid., p. 709.

[18]Leonard P. Ayres, *A Measuring Scale for Ability in Spelling* (New York: Russell Sage Foundation, 1915).

[19]Henry D. Rinsland, *A Basic Vocabulary for Elementary School Children* (New York: Macmillan, 1945).

[20]Ernest Horn, "Research in Spelling," *Elementary English Review* 21 (January 1944): 6–13.

[21]James A. Fitzgerald, "What Words Should Children Study in Spelling?" *Education* 79 (December 1958): 224–228.

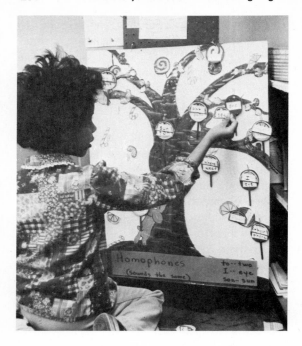

have *different pronunciations* and *different meanings;* for example, "lead" (dense metal) and "lead" (verb).[22]

The teacher should be aware that different textbooks in language arts may be defining the three terms somewhat differently, and should be familiar with the various systems and definitions in use. An attempt to find out which terms students have been exposed to, and continued use of them, will establish consistency, at least until pupils are old enough to understand the differences.

In this text the term homonym will be used interchangeably with homophone. The generic definition of homograph is also used; that is, homographs are words which are spelled the same but have different meanings and the words may or may not be pronounced the same.

Spelling and the Left-handed Child

Oftentimes left-handed students, who have learned to write in cursive with the hook-wrist

technique, produce many spelling errors. This occurs because the students tend to cover the first part of the word as they write. They often forget that they have already inserted a letter and repeat it while their hand blocks what they have written. Such students may be prone to delete letters as well if they think they have already inserted the letter.

Since these problems are usually unique to left-handed students using the hook-wrist technique, teachers should be especially vigilant with them. Although teachers should not attempt to change the writing techniques of such students, they should carefully observe their spelling errors. If the errors consist of deletions and insertions of similar letters, the teacher should ask the students to spell the words orally. If they can do so correctly, their spelling errors are probably caused by their method of writing. Such students should be cautioned to be on guard for this kind of error and to get into the habit of lifting their hands from the papers more often. Proofreading papers before they are submitted also helps. (See sections on the left-handed child in Chapter 13.)

Spelling and Children Who Speak Nonstandard English

Sociolinguists have suggested that phonological and grammatical factors may be interfering with culturally different students' ability to read. Although reading and spelling are related by their use of common word symbols, they are not similar (one requires decoding, the other encoding), as we have seen. However, they both require the ability to discriminate visually and are based on adequate auditory discrimination. It is therefore logical to assume that many phonological interferences that impede reading also hinder spelling. Studies have shown this to be true.

It therefore is imperative that teachers who work with children who speak nonstandard English be aware of phonological and grammatical factors which may interfere with standard Eng-

[22]Pose Lamb, *Linguistics in Proper Perspective* (Columbus, Ohio: Merrill, 1967), p. 138.

lish usage. Teachers must recognize that many of the spelling problems that these students have can be traced to their speaking a variation of English. The students who speak nonstandard English are spelling the words the way they "hear" and "say" them. And they should not be faulted for this. Vowel variations may produce a set of homonyms; for example, pin = pen and beer = bear. Simplification of final consonant clusters can produce another set of homonyms; for example, guest = guess, past = pass, and walked = walk. The weakening of final consonants creates yet another set of homonyms; for example, road = row and seat = sea.

Children who omit the *r* before vowels, as well as consonants, may produce another set of homonyms; for example, Carol = Cal, Paris = Pas, and guard = god. Those students who omit the *l* from a word may also be forming another set of homonyms; for example, toll = toe, help = hep, fault = fought, and tool = too. It can be seen that students who hear "toe" for "toll" will certainly have difficulty in spelling or reading "toll." [23]

A student who speaks nonstandard English may spell the plural of "desk" "desses" because desk = des, and a closed-syllable word that ends in *s* is made plural by doubling the final consonant and adding *es*.

Teachers need to be familiar with the sound and structure system of persons who speak nonstandard English to minimize confusions. The following dialogue between a second-grade student and his teacher aptly exemplifies this point. The child asks his teacher to spell the word "rat." The teacher replies, "r-a-t." The child says, "No, ma'am. I don't mean rat mouse. I mean right now!" [24]

Another problem that children who speak nonstandard English may have concerns the dictionary. Students who look up words under

[23]William Labov, *The Study of Nonstandard English* (Champaign, Ill.: National Council of Teachers of English, 1970), pp. 65–67.
[24]Diane N. Bryen et al., *Variant English* (Columbus, Ohio: Merrill, 1978), p. 207.

the wrong spellings because of their difficulty in recognizing standard spellings are going to be frustrated. In order to spell words in standard English, these students must be able to hear the phonological differences between standard and nonstandard English, make discriminations between them, and be able to pronounce the words in standard English. The importance of the aural–oral approach in learning standard English has been discussed in various sections of this text and will not be repeated here. Activities for auditory and visual discrimination have also been presented in other chapters. But it is important to remember that difficulties or interferences in one area of the language arts will most assuredly manifest themselves in another area as well.

Should Spelling Be Taught in the First Grade?

Some teachers will answer that question with a resounding "no." But most first graders who are reading and writing realize that certain symbols stand for oral sounds. Once they learn to decode the mysterious symbols, they also want to encode them in written form. They want to write stories, and in order to do this they need help in spelling. Teachers can help by spelling words either on the board or on the students' papers. It is difficult to anticipate all the words the first grader will want or need, especially if the teacher is encouraging creativity. But the sooner teachers help pupils to gain needed techniques—such as being critical analyzers of language, gaining skill in phonics, noticing regularities in phonograms or graphemic bases, noticing unusual spelling, and discovering rules—the sooner pupils will become independent spellers.

Developing a Spelling Consciousness

Students need a reason for spelling and a desire to spell correctly. If students do not see the purpose of spelling correctly, and do not develop a spelling consciousness, they usually will not spell correctly. An intermediate-level student whose spelling was so poor that it was difficult to read what he had written was a very creative writer. But it wasn't until the class produced a monthly magazine incorporating their writings and activities that the student made a concerted effort to learn to spell. He wanted other members of the class to be able to read his poems and stories. He had found a purpose for learning to spell.

A spelling consciousness is a desire to spell correctly, the ability to recognize that a word is misspelled, and an awareness that one is unsure about the spelling of the word. Students who make a conscious, concerted effort to look up or ask about any word that they are unsure of are developing a spelling consciousness. Students who have a well-developed spelling consciousness are usually knowledgeable in phonics, have good auditory and visual discrimination, and evidence a desire to spell correctly.

A Technique for Helping Upper-Intermediate-Level Students Gain Insights into Spelling

Presenting a list of words *not* known to be in students' listening capacities often helps them gain insights into spelling. The words are given rather hurriedly, no words are repeated, and they are not presented in context. After they have been spelled by the students, the teacher begins work on an entirely different topic without giving knowledge of results for the spelling words. After a few minutes the teacher stops and asks students if anything is bothering them about the spelling experience they have just had. Discussion is encouraged not only about what is wrong with the technique used for presenting the words but also with the words chosen for presentation. From this discussion students can discover a number of salient factors, which can be classified into three categories:

I. Spelling readiness.
II. What students need to know in order to be able to spell.
III. The proper presentation of spelling words.

I. Spelling readiness.
   1. Mental ability.
   2. Muscular ability.
   3. A need to express oneself in writing.
   4. Experience in the area of language.
II. What students need to know in order to be able to spell.
   1. Meaning of the word.
   2. Able to read and pronounce words.
   3. Able to hear and discriminate the sounds represented by letters.
   4. Able to copy letters correctly.
III. The proper presentation of spelling words.
   1. The spelling words should be clearly enunciated.
   2. Each word should be presented in a sentence so there is no confusion with possible homonyms or homophones.
   3. The word should be repeated after it has been presented in context.
   4. After all the words have been presented, knowledge of results should be given right away so that erroneous responses can be immediately corrected.

Practical and Applied Aspects of Spelling

Spelling in the School Day and Choice of Spelling Words

The allotment of time for formal spelling lessons should not be more than fifteen minutes a day, or about seventy-five minutes a week. With an increase of subject matter in the curriculum at the elementary-school level, the justification for more time is not warranted. However, during the school day there are many opportunities for incidental learning in spelling, and the teacher should take advantage of these. Spelling is related not only to many other language arts areas but to other areas of the curriculum as well. For example: A sixth-grade class in a social studies unit is working with famous people from other continents. The spelling words for the children include:

continent	Asia
globe	India
atlas	Africa
America	Japan
Europe	Israel

During the lesson the teacher asks a question concerning two women leaders whom they have read about and about whom the class has already talked. The teacher says, "I'll give you a hint. One of the women's first names is spelled almost like the country she used to head." Many children are able to correctly give Indira Gandhi as the woman, and India as her country.

Another opportunity for choosing spelling words would be at holiday time or in reference to the seasons. Children who want to write about the holiday or season must know how to spell applicable words.

A teacher can also use children's interests or hobbies as an impetus for choosing spelling words. They may be chosen according to specific generalizations or rules, or grouped around a particular phonogram family.

A perceptive teacher should be alert to all of the opportunities that present themselves during the school day for choosing words that students need. The important thing is that a variety of sources should be used, rather than just one specific spelling text or workbook.

Correlating Spelling with Written Expression

Spelling can be correlated with writing so that children can use the words and see a purpose for learning to spell them. For example:

a fifth-grade class wrote short Halloween stories. They tried to use as many of the spelling words that they could in order to make good stories. These stories were included in their monthly magazine.

Halloween and Spelling "This week our spelling words have to do with Halloween and we will write Halloween stories with them":

Halloween	skeleton	scare
ghosts	frightening	costumes
goblins	enchanted	pumpkins
witch	mysterious	trick
steeple	October	spooks

THE PUMPKINS

It was *October* 24, one week before *Halloween*. Some *pumpkins* were thinking about how they would have to become Jack-o-Lanterns. Eoww, it was awful! They were trying to think of a way to get out of it. Then one pumpkin had an idea. "We could all dress up like *spooks* and *scare* people," he announced. "It's a good idea and *trick*," said another pumpkin. "We could dress up like *ghosts*, *goblins*, *witches*, and *skeletons*," said a boy pumpkin. "No skeletons. We're too fat. Anybody could guess who we were," said an old wise pumpkin. "You can all meet on the church *steeple* to get the *costumes*," said two tailors.

The week passed slowly. Finally Halloween came. The pumpkins crept to the steeple. It looked *enchanted* and *mysterious*. The costumes were hung up on hangers. Everybody found a costume. They looked very *frightening*. The only trouble was that the ghosts couldn't fly.

BETH J.

HALLOWEEN

On *October* 31st, which you all know is *Halloween*, in our town it is a very *enchanted*, *frightening* and *mysterious* night. There are *pumpkins* on top of church *steeples*. There are *goblins*, *ghosts*, *witches*, and lots of other *spooks* playing *tricks* on everyone. These are not *costumes* of *skeletons* and things, these are the ones that haunt and *scare* you. But the next morning you'd never know it happened.

KARL D.

Spelling Stories on Veteran's Day   "During the week of November 11th we study Veteran's Day, developing a list of words which become our spelling words. We write stories using these words":

veterans	armistice	peace	fight
world	bravery	freedom	soldiers
danger	dangerous	fought	war
			family

VETERAN'S DAY

Right from the Revolutionary *War, freedom* has been *fought* for. In the Civil War it was for the freedom of the slaves. *Soldiers* were killed and their *families* wondered what happened to them. They knew it was *dangerous*. *Peace* has been thought to have been made many times, but it didn't last. The *world* is full of the thousands of *brave* soldiers who fought for their rights. The hope of Veteran's Day will last forever.

WEBB

Correcting Spelling Errors in Other Subject-Matter Areas

Teachers want to transfer learning from one subject-matter area to another. Using spelling words from mathematics, social studies, and science lessons will help considerably. When a child answers a question correctly, but the answer is marked wrong because of incorrect spelling, the student will probably become resentful and confused because the situation seems unfair. If the teacher wishes to test students' knowledge, misspellings should not count against the subject-knowledge grade. If such errors occur on a spelling test, then misspelled words would count as wrong.

The teacher should correct misspelled words on all written papers, but students will feel more positively toward spelling and will attempt to spell the word correctly in the future if they are not penalized for spelling errors. Seeing the errors and having them corrected immediately on all papers will give students a better chance to stamp out erroneous responses before they have become permanently set in their minds.

Spelling at the Primary-Grade Level

A number of determining factors operate in the grade placement of words: the usefulness of the word, the difficulty of the spelling word, the development of phonic principles, the development of combining forms, the learning of prefixes and suffixes, and the frequency of word use in the child's writing.

Although some words may be considered more difficult than others, often the uniqueness of the word lends itself to making it easier to learn to spell than is true of more common words. There are many difficult words a primary-grade child uses. But since children use some of these words frequently in their writing, it would be useful for them to know the correct spelling of such words.

An appropriate time for children to learn spelling words which are similar occurs when they are learning certain phonic rules in the primary grades. For example, while children are learning the phonogram *at,* and have already worked with most initial consonants and consonant substitution, they can also learn to spell a number of other words in the *at* family. These words can be put into simple sentences and illustrated with pictures: This is a *"cat."*

When children learn open and closed syllables, they can also learn a generalization: Words which end in closed syllables that have one consonant preceded by a vowel usually double the consonant before adding endings. For example:

run   running
chat   chatting

Teaching Spelling through Induction and Deduction

Inductive and deductive teaching strategies lend themselves very well to the teaching of spelling rules. An inductive strategy for teaching spelling generalizations includes the placement of a number of words on the board which portray a regular pattern. Students attempt to discover the generalizations. In order to assure students' discovery of the proper rule, the teacher should continue to put examples on the board which conform to the rule. (See the lesson plan for syllabication using nonsense words in Chapter 7 and the lesson plan at the end of this chapter for the development of inductive teaching lessons.)

In the deductive method of teaching a spelling rule the generalization is given first. Then a number of words are examined by students to determine which ones fit the rule.

These two teaching strategies are part of the discovery method. Both require students' discovery of the objective, instead of its explicit statement by the teacher. The discovery technique is conducive to greater learning retention and transfer of learning if it motivates students and encourages them to continue in their endeavors.

Teachers must recognize that not all children can learn through these techniques. The amount of guidance given by the teacher will determine how successful children will be in deriving rule generalizations.

A Model for Discovery Lessons[25]   A model proceeding from most difficult to least difficult

²⁵Gary R. McKenzie and Elaine D. Fowler, "A Recipe for Producing Student Discovery of Language Arts Generalizations," *Elementary English* 50 (April 1973): 596.

is presented for developing lessons which help students discover generalizations. In using the model the difficulty of the pattern to be discovered and the abilities of the students must be taken into account. Three other cautions stressed are:

1. Make sure the students can use the examples.
2. Be sure the examples fit the rule. Generalizations are rarely *always* true—only usually—and an example that doesn't fit will prevent recognition of the pattern.
3. When children are led through the steps with questions, try to make the questions specific enough so that they will know what to look for.

Teachers first select a principle and then give examples to illustrate the principle, as in the model on page 296.

Example of a Primary-Grade Exercise to Discover a Generalization Inductively   Children are given a listing of one-syllable words and endings:

run   running
bat   batting
can   canned

The teacher should instruct pupils to look closely at all the one-syllable words, and then look at all the one-syllable words with endings. The teacher should pose two questions: What do all the one-syllable words have in common? What happens to all the one-syllable words when an ending is added? The students should be able to state that all the one-syllable words end in consonants and the consonant is preceded by one vowel. When adding an ending to such words, the consonant is doubled.

After the generalization is learned, children can use deduction on new words to which it would apply.

Most Difficult		*Least Difficult*
1. Provide students with both positive and negative examples and ask them to describe attributes of the examples.	1. Provide students with positive examples and ask students to describe each one separately.	1. State the rule to students.
2. Ask students to group examples into sets according to patterns. When groups are formed, ask students to state the basis for classification.	2. State that these all illustrate a single rule to be discovered by comparison, or ask, "How are these alike?"	2. Provide an example pointing out attributes in the rule. Repeat with other positive and negative examples.
3. Ask students to compare, within the set illustrating the desired rule, to find the missing pattern.	3. Have students contrast with negative examples. State how all positives are the same, and different from negatives, in the form of a rule.	3. Have students classify new examples and explain choices.
4. State as a rule.		
5. Apply as a new test.		
6. Apply to new cases.		

Add the ending *ed* to the following words:

pin	bat	shop
beg	can	mop

Add the ending *ing* to the following words:

beg	shop	sun
can	get	bet
fan	run	cut
let		

Noun Plural Generalizations for the Primary and Intermediate Grades

AN ENGLISH TEST

We'll begin with box, the plural is boxes.
But the plural of ox should be oxen, not oxes.
One fowl is a goose, but two are called geese,
Yet the plural of mouse is never meese.
You may find a lone mouse, or a whole nest of
     mice,
But the plural of house is houses, not hice.
If the plural of man is always men,
Why shouldn't the plural of pan be called pen?
The cow in the plural may be called cows or kine,
But a bow, if repeated, is never called bine;
And the plural of vow is vows, not vine.

If I speak of a foot and you show me two feet,
And I give you a boot, would a pair be called beet?
If one is a tooth and a whole set are teeth,
Why shouldn't the plural of booth be called beeth?
If the singular's this, and the plural these,
Should the plural of kiss ever be written keese?
We speak of a brother, and also of brethren,
But though we say mother, we never say mothren.
Then the masculine pronouns are he, his, and him,
But imagine the feminine, she, shis, and shim!
So the English, I think you all will agree,
Is the funniest language you ever did see.

ANONYMOUS

Here is a list of generalizations for the teaching of noun plurals for grades one through six. These rule generalizations contain many commonly used words which conform to rule patterns. Rules 1 and 3 are usually taught in the primary grades, whereas all others are usually taught in intermediate grades. There is no hard-and-fast rule as to when the rules should be taught.

Noun Plurals That Usually Conform to Rule Patterns

1. An *s* is added to nouns such as: tree, airplane, truck, wagon, puzzle, boy, girl, horse, table.

2. An *es* is usually added to nouns which end in *s, ss, sh, ch,* or *x,* making an extra syllable:

bus, buses	bench, benches
glass, glasses	box, boxes
dress, dresses	brush, brushes

3. Nouns that end in *y* with a consonant before the *y*, change the *y* to *i* and add *es*:

baby	babies
story	stories
candy	candies

This rule generalization has many commonly used words which conform to the rule pattern.

4. Nouns that end in *o*, with a consonant before the *o*, usually add *es* to make the word plural:

cargo	cargoes
domino	dominoes
hero	heroes
tomato	tomatoes
potato	potatoes

Some nouns that end in *o* are made plural by adding *s:*

piano	pianos
solo	solos

5. Nouns that end in *f* or *fe* usually are made plural by changing the *f* or *fe* to *ves:*

knife	knives
shelf	shelves

Some nouns that end in *f* are made plural by adding *s:*

chief	chiefs
roof	roofs

Noun Plurals That Do Not Conform to Rule Patterns

1. Some nouns are made plural by changing the letters within the word or adding letters so that the spelling is changed:

foot	feet
man	men
mouse	mice

ox	oxen
tooth	teeth
goose	geese
child	children

2. Some nouns are the same in both the singular and the plural:

bison	bison
deer	deer
grouse	grouse
salmon	salmon
sheep	sheep

More Commonly Taught Spelling Generalizations: Intermediate-Grade Level

1. Words ending in silent *e* usually drop the *e* before the addition of suffixes beginning with a vowel, but usually retain the final *e* before the addition of suffixes beginning with a consonant. A suffix is a letter or a group of letters added to the end of a root word to change its meaning (*ing, ous, ary, able, ion, y,* and so on). Baking—suffix begins with a vowel so *e* is dropped. Blameless—suffix begins with a consonant so the *e* is retained. (*See* number 3 in the next section for the spelling of words ending in *ce* and *ge* when the suffix *able* is added.)

2. The letter *q* is always followed by *u* in common English words:

queen	quiet	quaint
queer	quick	quite

3. When the sound is long *e*, it is *i* before *e* except after *c*, and when sounded like *ā* as in weight or neighbor, it is *ei*.

		Exceptions
receive	reign	weird
receipt	eight	either
ceiling	believe	neither
conceited	siege	sheik
vein	yield	leisure
neighbor	field	codeine
weight	niece	protein
neigh	brief	

4. In order to retain the hard *c* sound when adding endings beginning with *i, e,* or *y*, add a *k* before the ending:

picknicking   trafficking
mimicker   frolicking
panicky

Some Spelling Rules for Prefixes and Suffixes

A *prefix* is a letter or a group of letters which is placed in front of a root word and which changes its meaning. A *suffix* is a letter or a group of letters which is placed at the end of a root word and which changes the meaning of the word. Here are some of the most common prefixes and suffixes found in intermediate-grade readers:

Prefixes

in	not
un	not
re	back
pre	before
con	with, together
ex	out of, beyond, away from
dis	not
de	off, away from

Suffixes

ness	quality of
less	without, free from
tion	result or product of an act
ful	containing, having qualities of
ish	like
ly	like, in a specified degree or manner
ment	outcome of an action
ous	full of
ure	state of, denoting action
able	capable of

1. The prefix *dis* and the prefix *mis* are spelled with one *s:*

disappear   misunderstand
distrust   mistrust

When the root word begins with *s* there will be two *s*'s, one for the prefix and one for the root word.

dissatisfied   misspell
dissimilar   misstep

2. If a root word begins with *l* or *r,* the negative prefix usually changes to *il* or *ir:*

illegal   illogical
irregular   illiterate

3. Words or syllables ending in *ce* or *ge* retain *e* before the suffix *able* in order to retain the soft *c* and soft *g* sound, and in all other words ending in a final *e* the *e* is usually dropped:

pleasurable   believable
enforceable   salable
manageable   likable
lovable

Steps in Learning to Spell

These guides are especially useful in helping children learn words that follow no pattern:

1. Look at the word.
2. Pronounce each word correctly.
3. Look carefully at each part of the word as it is pronounced.
4. Say the letters in sequence.
5. Cover the word and try to recall it by first saying it and then spelling it orally and in written form.
6. Check to see if the word is correct.

Spelling Study Plans   The two major study approaches to spelling are the study-test plan and the test-study plan. Investigations of the two plans have invariably found the test-study plan to be superior. Here is a typical test-study plan:

1. A preliminary test is given to determine the child's general spelling-achievement level.
2. A pretest is given at the beginning of each week's instruction, based on a week's list of words.
3. The child's misspelled words become his or her weekly list of words to study.
4. The child follows a series of steps, enumerated in the previous section, in learning to spell the words.
5. The words are presented in context and students usually must put each word into a sentence.
6. At the end of the week, the child is usually

given a test to determine spelling mastery of words studied.

The study-test plan is organized in a similar manner except that there is no pretest. Regardless of the child's ability to spell the words, all those in the lesson become the spelling words.

Spelling activities are presented each day during the week, which gives students practice in the spelling, reading, and writing of words. Usually a spelling quiz is given at the end of the week to determine whether spelling proficiency in the words has been accomplished.

Some studies have shown that students do better on weekly review tests when they receive a portion of the words each day and are tested daily on each portion than when they receive all the words at the beginning of the week and do not receive daily quizzes.[26] This procedure is based on sound learning principles because we know that distributed practice is better and tends to bring more sustained learning than massed practice.

Activities and Exercises for the Overlearning of Words   Drill and practice in the spelling of words, especially for those that do not follow a pattern, are used so that the child will overlearn correct spelling of the words being studied. Overlearning of the words helps children sustain their learning over an extended period of time, rather than just for a weekly spelling test. Therefore, drill, used for the purpose of helping children gain skills that need to be overlearned, is justified.

However, teachers must be cautioned against having children learn spelling words by writing them ten, twenty, or more times. This is a poor practice which develops negative attitudes toward spelling. Many times the students engaged in such an activity will write the word in rote fashion, without thinking. Some inventive stu-

[26]Herbert Rieth et al., "Influence of Distributed Practice and Daily Testing on Weekly Spelling Tests," *The Journal of Educational Research* 68 (October 1974): 73–77.

dent might employ the "mass-production" practice of copying one letter at a time in a straight row down the page in order to finish this onerous task as quickly as possible. This practice does not help the student to learn to spell.

There are many ways that are fun to achieve overlearning of needed skills. Examples are crossword puzzles, spelling Lotto, anagrams, filling in missing blanks, and others.

The Spelling Test

If the spelling test is used as part of the teaching–learning process, it is being used correctly. The test should be used for diagnostic, review, and reinforcement purposes. Teachers and students can determine through the test specific difficulties the student may be having.

In giving the spelling test the teacher should very carefully articulate each word, present the word in a sentence to avoid confusion with other homonyms, and then repeat the word again. Students should receive knowledge of results immediately after the test, so that they either get reinforcement or can avoid erroneous responses. A good technique, discussed in Chapter 19, is to have students write their spelling test words twice. One copy is submitted to the teacher; the other is retained for feedback.

Children should not exchange papers after a spelling test. This common practice actually impedes the learning of spelling words and may be detrimental to the individual child. Children need knowledge of their own results—not someone else's. A child who is not doing well does not want to share this with another child. Humiliation does not help children to gain positive attitudes toward spelling, school, or themselves.

Possible Difficulties in Learning to Spell

Difficulties in learning to spell include many factors which also impede development of word recognition skills. These include:

1. Perceptual problems due to either organic or experiential factors.

2. Problems in pronouncing, which might be due to faulty listening.

3. Inadequate knowledge in the area of phoneme–grapheme representations.

Auditory and visual discrimination are necessary readiness activities for spelling. Unless students are able to hear and see differences between and among letters, they will not be able to spell. Chapter 7 discusses some of the phonic skills that a child needs for word recognition. All of these skills are necessary for proficiency in spelling. Children must be aware of all the sounds in the word, and as much attention should be paid to the medial and ending sounds as to the initial ones.

Unless children are able to pronounce words properly, they will not be able to spell them correctly. Studies have shown that children with speech difficulties usually make many spelling errors; spelling errors reflect speech inaccuracies.[27,28] Substitutions, omissions, distortions, and additions in spelling are usually made by students who make similar speech errors. (See Chapter 6.)

It appears that primary-grade children's difficulties with beginning spelling are due to: mispronunciations, lack of phonic skills, inability to make proper phoneme–grapheme relationships, omission of letters, reversing or transposing of letters, insertion or deletion of letters, and confusion of words that sound alike but are spelled differently (homonyms or homophones).

Spelling Demons Studies of errors and lists of words most often misspelled have been made. Here is W. Franklin Jones's famous list of "100

Spelling Demons" which was compiled in 1913 and used for a very long time:

One Hundred Spelling Demons of the English Language[29]

which	can't	guess	they
their	sure	says	half
there	loose	having	break
separate	lose	just	buy
don't	Wednesday	doctor	again
meant	country	whether	very
business	February	believe	none
many	know	knew	week
friend	could	laid	often
some	seems	tear	whole
been	Tuesday	choose	won't
since	wear	tired	cough
used	answer	grammar	piece
always	two	minute	raise
where	too	any	ache
women	ready	much	read
done	forty	beginning	said
hear	hour	blue	hoarse
here	trouble	though	shoes
write	among	coming	tonight
writing	busy	early	wrote
heard	built	instead	enough
does	color	easy	truly
once	making	through	sugar
would	dear	every	straight

Another popular list was published in 1951. It is based on the misspellings of students in grades two through six:

Fifty Spelling Demons for Second, Third, Fourth, Fifth, and Sixth Grades[30]

am	going	pretty	time
and	goodby	received	to
because	guess	Saturday	today
coming	Halloween	some	tomorrow
cousin	have	sometimes	too

---

[27]James Carrell and Kathleen Pendergast, "An Experimental Study of the Possible Relation between Errors of Speech and Spelling," *Journal of Speech and Hearing Disorders* 19 (September 1954): 327–334.

[28]David R. Stone, "An Analysis of Spelling Errors," *Education* 84 (October 1963): 116–118.

[29]W. Franklin Jones, *Concrete Investigation of the Material of English Spelling* (Vermillion, S.D.: University of South Dakota, 1913), p. 24.

[30]James Fitzgerald, *A Basic Life Vocabulary* (Milwaukee, Wisc.: Bruce Publishing, 1951), pp. 144–150. Copyright 1951 by James A. Fitzgerald.

didn't	here	Sunday	two
don't	I'm	teacher	very
everybody	January	teacher's	we
February	know	thanksgiving	write
for	Mrs.	that's	writing
friend	name	their	you
from	now	there	your
getting	our		

Homonyms or homophones often cause spelling problems for students. Here is a list of homonyms which are often substituted for one another.

Homonym Demons

too—to—two	hole—whole
peace—piece	stake—steak
red—read	pane—pain
meet—meat	sight—site—cite
wood—would	coarse—course
bear—bare	plain—plane
dual—duel	do—due—dew
affect—effect	forth—fourth
led—lead	passed—past
pore—pour	fair—fare
principle—principal	hour—our
knot—not	threw—through
heard—herd	heel—heal
tale—tail	one—won
die—dye	write—right
route—root	toe—tow
so—sew	air—heir
ring—wring	gate—gait
know—no	way—weigh
soar—sore	rode—road

Table 12.1 presents typical errors, causes, and suggested corrective measures in spelling.[31]

Dictionary Skills

A dictionary is a very important reference book, not only for elementary-school students but for all students. It is helpful in supplying the following information to a student:

1. spelling
2. correct usage
3. derivations and inflected forms
4. accent and other diacritical markings
5. antonyms
6. synonyms
7. syllabication
8. definitions
9. parts of speech
10. idiomatic phrases

The function of dictionaries is not to regulate but only to describe. This is true for word meanings and pronunciation of words. The lexicographers who compiled the dictionary polled many persons and recorded the ways in which these participants pronounced words. The pronunciation was then recorded by way of diacritical marks under appropriate entries in the dictionary.[32]

Etymology deals with the history of a word. The dictionary is invaluable in supplying the etymology of a word. The semantic approach adds interest to the study of vocabulary because it refers to the way a word has been used in the past; it is the study of word meanings. The dictionary also aids students in choosing the correct meaning of homographs.

The Systematic Development of Dictionary Skills

Alphabetizing   Although most adults look on the task of alphabetizing as an easy and elementary one, there are persons who have problems with this skill. Some reading authorities have stated:

It is difficult for an adult who has led the child through such a sequential process to sense that learnings as mundane as alphabetizing may be

---

[31]David H. Patton, "How to Correct Spelling Errors: A Teacher's Diagnostic Spelling Chart," *Education Today,* Spelling Bulletin No. 54 (Columbus, Ohio: Merrill), pp. 364–366.

[32]Leroy Barney, "Dictionary Skills and Punctuation Habits as Aids to Children's Writing," in *Language Arts in the Elementary School: Readings* (Philadelphia: Lippincott, 1972), p. 448.

table 12.1 Typical Errors, Causes, and Suggested Corrective Measures in Spelling

Causes	Typical Errors	Corrective Procedures
Incorrect visual image	docter for doctor nitting for knitting familar for familiar	Make pupils conscious of the need to see each letter in the word. Break the words into syllables. Have pupils visualize the words. Look at the word for strong visual image.
Inaccurate pronunciation and inaccurate auditory memory	lighting for lightning pospone for postpone erl for oil chimley for chimney choclet for chocolate	Pronounce each word accurately on initial presentation. Pronounce words in concert with class. Listen for inaccurate pronunciation. Check individual pupils for doubtful enunciation. Repeat several times the part of the word which is difficult to enunciate.
Insertion and omission of silent letters	lite for light lineing for lining no for know ofen for often tabl for table gost for ghost stedy for steady lisen for listen	Silent letters cause many difficulties in spelling. Since these letters do not appear in an auditory image, special stress must be placed on the visual image. Observe each part of the word and have pupils practice writing the part likely to cause trouble. Provide practice exercises to fix habits of dealing with silent letters.
Confusion of consonant sounds	acke for ache parck for park gudge for judge visinity for vicinity sertain for certain	Practice for correct image of the word. Children need to know that some letters have more than one sound. S may sound like s or z. C may sound like s or k. G may sound like g or j.
Confusion of vowel sounds	holaday for holiday turm for term oder for odor salery for salary rejoyce for rejoice	Have pupils break word into syllables, and look at its parts. Practice for correct visual image of the word. Practice writing the word for the kinesthetic feel of the letters.
Confusion of double vowels	reel for real quear for queer	Double vowels often take the sound of the single letter or another vowel combination.
Inaccurate formation of derivatives	stoped for stopped haveing for having flys for flies sincerly for sincerely omited for omitted	Work for more vivid image of word endings. Emphasize auditory image of endings. Break words into syllables. Have children observe the word in its parts. Call attention to generalizations pertinent to regular ways of adding endings.

Causes	Typical Errors	Corrective Procedures
		Stress closer understanding of adding suffixes. Provide practice exercises on word endings.
Reversals or transposition of letters	gose for goes form for from bread for beard	Pronounce the word distinctly. Have pupils listen for sequence of each sound in the word. Practice for correct visual image.
Incorrect meaning—homonyms	dew for due our for hour hole for whole sum for some	Illustrate use of the word with commonest meaning. Use pairs of words in sentence to distinguish what each means. Provide practices on homonyms and stress word meanings at all times.
Phonetic spelling applied to non-phonetic words	bin for been gon for gone sum for some	While spelling embraces phonetics, pupils must be taught to look for numerous exceptions in our unphonetic language. They cannot rely on sound alone. They must realize that their visual memory must be their guide in many new words and word parts.
Confusion of words that are similar in sound	an for and were for where merry for marry effect for affect cents for sense	This error is often due to faulty auditory acuity. Care should be given to enunciation of these words. Pronounce the words in pairs and give the meaning of each.
Lack of acquaintance with phonetic elements	ivlize for result haw for how inbean for imagine	For pupils very deficient in phonetic sense or training, begin work with simple visual-auditory training (attaching beginning consonant sounds to appropriate letter symbol). Use kinesthetic approach also. Provide phonics readiness training.
Poor handwriting	stors for stars temt for tent	Provide practice on letter forms which cause special difficulty. Emphasize accurate information of each letter. Guide pupils in size, shape, slant, and spacing between letters and words.
Nervousness	Inaccuracies due to lack of control for deliberate thinking.	Check child's health. Be sure vision and hearing are not defective. Remove all possible tensions.
Carelessness	Errors due to poor concentration and careless habits of word study.	Stimulate pride in work well done. Praise all improvement.

exciting discoveries for the child and, at the same time, be fraught with hazard.[33]

This matter of alphabetical arrangement of words may seem very elementary, but a surprising number of able high school students do not have this basic information.[34]

Objectives (Primary Grades)

I. Alphabetizing
   A. Able to arrange letters in alphabetical order.
   B. Able to arrange words none of which begin with the same letter in alphabetical order.
   C. Able to list words several of which begin with the same letters.
      1. Able to alphabetize words according to both first and second letters.
      2. Able to alphabetize words according to third letter.

Objectives (Grades 3, 4, 5, 6)

II. Location of words in the dictionary
    A. Able to open the dictionary halfway and to note with which letter words begin in this location.

    B. Able to open dictionary by quarters and to note with which letter words begin in this location.

    C. Able to open the dictionary by thirds and to note with which letter words begin in this location.

    D. Able to open the dictionary at certain initial letters such as *g*, *n*, *s*.

    E. Able to use key words at the head of each page as a guide to finding words.

    F. Able to find brief lists of specific key words.

    G. Able to use key words to find words following key words.

    H. Able to use key words to find words preceding key words at end of page.

    I. Able to use key words to find words anywhere on page.

Objectives (Grades 3, 4, 5, 6)

III. Pronunciation and the dictionary
     A. Able to sound out unfamiliar words using diacritical markings.

Objectives (Grades 1–6)

IV. Multiple meanings—homographs and the dictionary
    A. Able to use the dictionary to select meanings to fit the context.

Objectives (Grades 3, 4, 5, and 6)

V. Using the dictionary to build up a vocabulary of synonyms and antonyms.
   A. Able to give the synonyms of stated words.
   B. Able to give the antonyms of stated words.

Objective (Grades 5 and 6)

VI. The etymology of a word and the dictionary
    A. Child is able to give the meanings of the parts of a word. (See activities in Chapter 8 under "Vocabulary Expansion.")

An Activity to Stimulate Interest in the Dictionary

See how well children can answer these ten questions using the dictionary. They should use it to find the meanings of words they do not know and then answer each question.

1. In what countries do centaurs live?
2. Where is Mount Everest?
3. Was Prometheus the goddess of fire?

---

[33]Guy L. Bond and Eva Bond Wagner, *Teaching the Child to Read* (New York: Macmillan, 1966), p. 69.

[34]Emmet Albert Betts, *Foundations of Reading Instruction* (New York: American Book Company, 1957), p. 671.

4. Is a songstress a man who writes songs?
5. Is Miss. an abbreviation for Missus?
6. Is haiku a Hawaiian mountain?
7. Did Andrew Jackson fight in the Civil War?
8. Is a statute a work of art?
9. Is a quadruped an extinct animal?
10. Is a centipede a unit of measurement in the metric system?

The questions can also act as stimuli for initiating other activities. For example, looking up "haiku," the children will discover that it is a type of poem, and they may decide to try to write some haiku poems. Some children may want to learn more about Prometheus and other mythological figures, and others may become interested in various mountain ranges.

A Look at Children's Spelling Series

There seem to be more similarities than differences among the various children's spelling series published in the late 1970s for the 1980s. In almost all of the major series, handwriting is incorporated with spelling; dictionary and proofreading skills are stressed; there is an emphasis on spelling patterns; high-frequency words are presented; attempts are made to provide for individual differences; other language arts areas are incorporated with spelling; and many review and gamelike activities are presented. Most of the series emphasize sound–symbol relationships and simple decoding skills at the first-grade level. The books are visually appealing, and there is some concern for stimulating creativity in children's writings. Some of the spelling books alert teachers to dialect differences. For example, in *The World of Spelling* the teacher is told that standard pronunciation varies from region to region and that there is no single "superior" standard American English pronunciation. However, spelling is uniform even when pronunciation is not. Books in the upper grades provide help for children who speak a so-called "*r*-less dialect." [35]

It appears that spelling texts are beginning to more closely resemble language arts texts. Spelling is related to the other language arts areas, so the integration of spelling with the other areas is laudable, and this integration should be carried over into the language arts program. The question of whether a separate spelling text is necessary comes to mind. A separate spelling text is probably warranted because the incorporation of a complete spelling program in the language arts text would make the children's language arts text too large.

[35]Thomas Owen et al., *The World of Spelling* (Lexington, Mass.: Heath, 1978).

Student's Name:
Grade:
Teacher:

Diagnostic Checklist for Spelling (General)

I. *Dictionary*	Yes	No

A. Primary Grades

The child is able to

	Yes	No
1. supply missing letters of the alphabet.		
2. arrange words none of which begin with the same letter in alphabetical order.		

3. list words several of which begin with the same letter.
4. list words according to first and second letters.
5. list words according to third letter.
6. find the meaning of a word.
7. find the correct spelling of a word.

B. Grades 3, 4, 5, 6

The child is able to
1. locate words halfway in the dictionary.
2. open the dictionary by quarters and state the letter with which words begin.
3. open the dictionary by thirds and state the letters with which words begin.
4. open the dictionary at certain initial letters.
5. use key words at the head of each page as a guide to finding words.
6. use the dictionary to select meanings to fit the context (homographs).
7. use the dictionary to build up a vocabulary of synonyms.
8. use the dictionary to build up a vocabulary of antonyms.
9. answer questions about the derivation of a word.
10. use the dictionary to learn to pronounce a word.
11. use the dictionary to correctly syllabicate a word.
12. use the dictionary to get the correct usage of a word.
13. use the dictionary to determine the part(s) of speech of the word.
14. use the dictionary to gain the meanings of idiomatic phrases.

II. *Spelling*	Yes	No

A. Primary Grades

1. The child recognizes that letters represent sounds.
2. The child has a need to spell because he or she wishes to write.

3. The child is able to spell a number of words that he or she continually has met.
4. The child can spell a number of words that have similar phonograms (a succession of graphemes that occurs with the same phonetic value in a number of words—often a rhyming unit of a "family" of words). For example, *ake, an, at, ight, ine.*
5. Noun plurals:
   a. The child adds an *s* to nouns such as tree, airplane, girl.
   b. The child adds an *es* to nouns which end in *s, ss, sh, ch,* or *x,* making an extra syllable. Example: bus—buses or busses; glass—glasses; bench—benches; box—boxes; brush—brushes.
   c. The child correctly spells nouns that end in *y* and have a consonant before the *y* by changing the *y* to *i* and adding *es.* Examples: baby—babies; candy—candies.
   d. The child correctly spells nouns that end in *y* with a vowel before the *y* by adding *s* to make the word plural. Examples: boy—boys; day—days.
6. The child can add some endings that begin with a vowel to a closed syllable (one-syllable words) by doubling the consonant before adding the ending. Examples: can—canned; run—running.

B. Intermediate Grades

1. The child has mastery of all items in previous grades.
2. Noun Plurals
   a. The child recognizes that proper nouns follow the regular rules for *s* and *es* plurals. Examples: Bobs; the Joneses.
   b. The child recognizes that nouns that end in *o* with a consonant before the *o* usually add *es* or *s* to make the word plural. Examples: domino—dominoes; piano—pianos; auto—autos.
   c. The child recognizes that nouns that end in *o* with a vowel before the *o* add *s* to make the word plural. Examples: radio—radios, cameo—cameos.

d. The child recognizes that nouns that end in *f* or *fe* usually are made plural by changing the *f* or *fe* to *ves*. Examples: knife—knives; wife—wives. Some nouns ending in *f* or *fe* form the plural by adding *s*. Examples: chief—chiefs; roof—roofs; safe—safes.

e. The child recognizes that nouns that end in *ff* usually add *s* to the word to form the plural. Examples: staff—staffs; sheriff—sheriffs.

f. The child recognizes that some nouns are the same in both the singular and plural. Examples: deer—deer; salmon—salmon; fish—fish; sheep—sheep.

g. The child recognizes that some nouns do not follow any rule patterns for plurals. Examples: foot—feet; child—children; goose—geese; tooth—teeth.

3. The child recognizes that a multisyllabic word that ends in a closed syllable usually doubles the consonant before an ending beginning with a vowel *if* the accent falls on the final syllable. Example: occur—occurring.

4. The child recognizes that most words ending in final silent *e,* except those ending in *ce* or *ge,* usually drop the *e* before adding *able.*

5. The child recognizes that words ending in final silent *e* usually retain the *e* before adding a suffix beginning with a consonant.

6. The child recognizes that words ending in final silent *e* usually drop the *e* before the addition of suffixes beginning with a vowel.

III. *Homonym Demons*	Yes	No
A. The primary-grade child spells such homonyms as to, too, two; so, sew; and red, read correctly.		
B. The intermediate-grade child spells such homonyms as peace, piece; pore, pour; principal, principle; route, root correctly.		

IV. *Spelling Consciousness (Primary and Intermediate Grades)*	Yes	No
A. The child generally spells words correctly in most of his or her written work.		
B. The child looks up a word that he or she is not sure of.		
C. The child asks the teacher about a word he or she is not sure of.		
D. The child asks for help in spelling if he or she needs it.		

Diagnostic Checklist for Spelling (Specific)

The child makes spelling errors on spelling tests and in written work in the following areas: (See Table 12.1 for typical errors, causes, and suggested corrective measures.)

	Specific Errors	
1. Consonants		
initial		
medial		
final		
blends (clusters)		
digraphs		
2. Vowels		
short		
long		
digraphs		
diphthongs		
followed by *r*		
3. Prefixes and suffixes		
4. Homonyms or homophones		
5. Omits letters		
6. Inserts letters		
7. Doubles letters		
8. Noun plurals		
9. Monosyllabic words		
10. Multisyllabic words		

LESSON PLAN I

Primary-Grade Level

Objective

Students will be able to define homophone and give five examples of homophones correctly spelled in a sentence.

Preparation

A number of humorous sentences composed of homophones are on the board:

I two no the weigh.
No, that is write to.
Hour friend is sew hungry two.
Meat him on the rode.
The tail was sew funny.
The heard of cattle is hear.

These sentences would also be on the board, but the underlined word is omitted.

Word		Sentence
meat	1.	I like to eat ____.
meet	2.	I have to ____ my friend.
one	1.	She has only ____ toy.
won	2.	She ____ the game.
hour	1.	This ____ seems so long.
our	2.	____ picture is the best.
right	1.	John is always ____ .
write	2.	I like to ____ letters.
to	1.	I am going ____ the zoo.
two	2.	I have ____ cookies.
too	3.	I want a cookie, ____ .
sew	1.	It is fun to ____ clothes.
so	2.	I felt ____ sorry for him.
weigh	1.	How much does that ____ ?
way	2.	Do you know the ____ to town?

Introduction

A number of sentences are on the board. "Can anyone read them aloud for us? Good! Although you can read them for us, is there something funny about these sentences? Remember, we've worked with words that are spelled alike but have different meanings. Who can tell me what such words are called and give me an example? Yes, homographs, and the example of 'saw' and 'saw' is very good. Today we're going to work with words that are often misspelled because they are mistaken for one another."

Development

"I am going to give you a number of words in sentences. After you spell the words on your papers, we'll discuss what some of these words have in common."
Give these words and sentences to the children:

Word	Sentence
meat	1. I like to eat meat.
meet	2. I have to meet my friend.
one	1. She has only one toy.
won	2. She won the game.
hour	1. This hour seems so long.
our	2. Our picture is the best.
right	1. John is always right.
write	2. I like to write letters.
to	1. I am going to the zoo.
two	2. I have two cookies.
too	3. I want a cookie, too.
sew	1. It is fun to sew clothes.
so	2. I felt so sorry for him.
weigh	1. How much does that weigh?
way	2. Do you know the way to town?

Have the children volunteer to pronounce and put in the correct spelling of the word that belongs in the blank. If any errors are made, help to correct them immediately. After all the words have been inserted in the blanks, ask the children what a number of the words have in common. They should come up with the statement that many of the words sound alike, but are spelled differently and have different meanings. Tell the pupils that such words are called homonyms or homophones. Ask them for more examples.

Summary

Pull the main points of the lesson together. Give the students a number of sentences with pairs of homophones and ask them to choose the correct word for the sentence. For example:

1. John is the _____ person _____ help us _____ the letter.
   right/write   to/two   write/right
2. He is the _____ who _____ the game.
   one/won   one/won
3. He has already played _____ games.
   too/two

4. Some girls do not like to _____ .
<u>sew/so</u>

5. _____ is good for you to eat.
<u>Meat/Meet</u>

The class might enjoy the following "whimsy." Some children might try to make up their own.

"Well," said Homonym, "it's true
I can't do what you can do,
And furthermore I don't want to . . .
For I had four cents for the fair,
But it didn't make sense to go in where
I'd wear a tie that was not in a knot,
So instead I watched blue smoke that blew
And then flew straightway up the flue.
Now tell me, Homograph, can you
See things from my point of view?
For I, sir, ay yes, I eye a dear deer,
And a hare with a hair that is half of a pair
While I pare a pear beside a new gnu
And shoo a bare bear away from my shoe—
And all this I do at ten to two, too!

AUTHOR UNKNOWN

They might also enjoy listening to Eve Merriam's poem *Nym and Graph* about homonyms and homographs, from the book *It Doesn't Always Have to Rhyme.*

LESSON PLAN II

Intermediate-Grade Level

Objective

Students will be able to derive the hard "c" spelling rule. Students will be able to apply the rule so that they can spell the following words correctly when given orally: mimicking, picnicking, frolicker, trafficker, panicky.

Preparation

A letter with many spelling errors written on large lined paper:

Dear Miz P,
    I just was askt to apair in a skool pla an i reely wanna. the techa said i ned hlp in spekin if i wan te be init. Plez hlp me.

Ami

Introduction

"I'd like to show you a letter that someone asked me to read. Perhaps you can help me decipher it. I just can't seem to make it out. What's the problem? Yes, there are so many spelling errors that it's difficult to read. What's the purpose of writing a letter that no one can read?

"In order to help us to become better spellers, we've been working with a number of different spelling rules. Who remembers some of the things we have said, not only about spelling rules but about all rules? Yes, very good! Before we can come up with a rule, there must be enough cases that fit the rule. Who remembers some of the spelling rules that we have derived? Yes, the 'ie' rule, the soft 'c' and soft 'g' rule before the suffix 'able.' Today, we are going to be involved with a spelling rule that also concerns some suffixes. Who can tell us what a suffix is?"

Development

"I am going to give you a list of words to spell. After we all spell them, I'll call on some volunteers to put the words on the board. After they are on the board, we will all try to see if we can come up with any rule for these words. Listen carefully while I give the words. First I will state each word; then I will put it in a sentence; and then I will restate the word. Here they are:

mimicker	notice
picnicking	ice
frolicking	practice
mimicking	police
panicky	noticing"
trafficking	

Ask for volunteers to put the words on the board. After each word is put down make sure the spelling is correct. If the "k" has incorrectly been omitted, insert it. Ask volunteers to pronounce each word. Ask the children to pay particular attention to the "c" sound at the end of words. For example, "mimicker" and "notice." The two sounds are different—in "mimicker" the "c" represents a hard sound, whereas in "notice" the "c" represents a soft sound.

Ask the children what would happen to the sound represented by "c" in the word mimicker if the "k" were left out. For example: mimicer—how would it be pronounced? It would be pronounced with a soft "c." Why? It is followed by an "e." Ask the children to say what they think the spelling rule is. The teacher should elicit the following rule: Words that end in "c" add a "k" before "i," "e," and "y" in order to retain the hard "c" sound.

Summary

Pull together the main points of the lesson and give the students a number of words to spell to which they can apply the hard "c" rule.

Summary

Spelling should not be taught as an end in itself, or for the outmoded belief that the brain is a muscle that needs exercising through memorizing. It should be used as a tool to help children to communicate better through writing.

It has been shown that in order to be an effective speller, certain methods of instruction, attitudes, and understanding must be taken into consideration. Here is a list of some of these:

1. Students have a need to, and want to, spell correctly.
2. Spelling instruction should be systematic, as well as provide for incidental learning.
3. Spelling should be correlated to all subject-matter areas. However, caution should be exercised so that a child who, for example, misspells the word "triangle" in a mathematics test is not penalized in his or her math grade. The word should be correctly spelled for the student, so that the student can correct the error.
4. The test-study technique is superior to the study-test technique. If children are able to spell all the words in a pretest correctly, there is no need for them to spend time studying those words.
5. Spelling words should always be presented in context.
6. Children should be helped to understand that tests are useful for diagnostic and review purposes.

In the first part of this chapter the general aspects of spelling were discussed. It was shown how spelling is related to the other language arts, and how difficulties in one area will affect others. Research and information on the "spelling controversy," involving generalizations and spelling word lists and which method of teaching is more useful, were presented. A dual approach was advocated as the solution yielding the greatest benefits for the most children. It was recommended that generalizations be introduced when enough cases warrant a rule being formed. Spelling and the left-handed child and spelling and the child who speaks nonstandard English were analyzed, with suggestions for the teacher.

In discussing spelling consciousness, it was emphasized that unless children have a need and a desire to spell correctly, they may not do so.

The more practical and applied aspects of spelling were presented next. Although the teacher should not spend more than fifteen minutes a day on spelling lessons, there are many opportunities for incidental spelling learning. An alert and perceptive teacher would correlate spelling lessons with many of the ongoing activities in the classroom. Methods of teaching spelling through induction and deduction for words lending themselves to generalizations, as well as word study plans, were presented. Spelling demons, homonym demons, and other spelling difficulties that students might encounter were also outlined.

The last part of the chapter presented a course of action for the systematic development of dictionary skills. Objectives for each dictionary skill were given. A Diagnostic Checklist for "Gaining Proficiency in Spelling" was also presented.

Now that you have read Chapter 12 you should have mastered the given teacher competencies presented at the beginning of this chapter.

As a further aid, two examples of spelling lesson plans are presented at the end of this chapter. Using these as a guide, see if you can construct another one.

Suggestions for Thought Questions and Activities

1. You are involved in a debate on whether to use spelling generalizations to teach spelling. Choose one side—either *for* or *against* the use of spelling generalizations to teach spelling. Support your argument in a research paper.
2. Think up some spelling activities or games that are fun.
3. Develop a creative lesson plan in spelling.
4. What do you feel are the best methods that can be used in presenting spelling words? Explain.

5. A mother writes a note to her son's teacher saying that she is most distressed that her son received a grade of 100 percent on his mathematics paper even though he made many spelling errors when he named the geometric figures. What do you think about this situation? How would you help parents to understand your position better?

6. How would you correlate the teaching of spelling with the other language arts areas?

SELECTED BIBLIOGRAPHY

Anderson, Paul. *Resource Materials for Teachers of Spelling*. Minneapolis, Minn.: Burgess, 1968.

Boyd, Gertrude. *Spelling in the Elementary School*. Columbus, Ohio: Merrill, 1971.

Emery, Donald W. *Variant Spellings in Modern American Dictionaries*. Urbana, Ill.: National Council of Teachers of English, 1973.

Fitzgerald, James A. *The Teaching of Spelling*. Milwaukee, Wisc.: Bruce Publishing, 1951.

Furness, Edna. *Spelling for the Millions*. Nashville, Tenn.: Thomas Nelson, 1977.

Geedy, Patricia S. "What Research Tells Us About Spelling." *Elementary English* 52 (February 1975): 233–236.

Hanna, Paul. *Spelling: Structure and Strategies*. Boston: Houghton Mifflin, 1971.

Hanna, Paul, et al. *Phoneme grapheme Correspondences as Cues to Spelling Improvement*. Washington, D.C.: U.S. Department of Health, Education and Welfare, 1966.

Horn, Thomas, ed. *Research on Handwriting and Spelling*. Urbana, Ill.: National Council of Teachers of English, 1966.

Personke, Carl. *Comprehensive Spelling Instruction: Theory, Research and Appreciation*. New York: Intext Educational Publishers, 1971.

Peters, Margaret. *Spelling: Caught or Taught?* New York: Humanities Press, 1967.

Rubin, Dorothy. "Developing Spelling Skills," in *The Primary Grade Teacher's Language Arts Handbook*. New York: Holt, Rinehart and Winston, 1980.

———. "Developing Spelling Skills," in *The Intermediate Grade Teacher's Language Arts Handbook*. New York: Holt, Rinehart and Winston, 1980.

"Spelling: Encoding English." (Special Topic) *Elementary English* 52 (February 1975): 221–257.

Tiedt, Iris M. *Spelling Strategies*. San Jose, Calif.: Contemporary Press, 1975.

White, Mary Sue. *Word Twins*. New York: Abingdon Press, 1961.

Zutell, Jerry. "Some Psycholinguistic Perspectives on Children's Spelling." *Language Arts* 55 (October 1978): 844–850.

thirteen

Gaining Skill in Handwriting

EXAMPLES OF TEACHER COMPETENCIES

1. The teacher will be able to state differences between manuscript and cursive writing.

2. The teacher will be able to teach the construction of letters, both capital and lowercase, in manuscript and cursive.

3. The teacher will be able to state the relationship of proximodistal and cephalocaudal development to handwriting.

4. The teacher will be able to state ways in which to help the left-handed child learn cursive writing.

5. The teacher will observe the students' handwriting and act positively by planning lessons based on the needs of students.

6. The teacher, together with students, will determine standards for handwriting.

7. The teacher will provide a classroom environment conducive to handwriting. It should include proper lighting, desks and chairs of the right size for students, adequate samples of handwriting on display within the visual range of all students, and an affective environment that is nonthreatening.

8. The teacher will be able to state ways in which handwriting is related to other language arts areas.

9. The teacher will be able to plan lessons integrating handwriting with other language arts areas.

10. The teacher will be able to state the most common errors in cursive writing.

11. The teacher will be able to determine whether students value, appreciate, or have an interest in handwriting by observing whether they write legibly.

PEANUTS ®  **By Charles M. Schulz**

© 1958 United Feature Syndicate, Inc.

Introduction

"Yesterday we had to write, 'I will be quiet,' a hundred times. I figured out a way to finish fast. First I wrote 'I' all the way down the page, then 'will,' then 'be,' and so on . . ."

"We spend so much time on handwriting. I hate it. Everything must be so exact."

"Even though I get everything right, I still get a poor grade. All because of my handwriting. It's not fair. I'm left-handed and whenever I write, my paper gets all smudged."

"I remember I had just struggled to learn to write one way when before I knew it, they were teaching me another way to write. You would think we had nothing better to do."

"When I grow up, I'll have a secretary do all my writing for me. I'll just speak into a dictaphone and let her type what I want."

"I don't see any purpose to it. It's dumb spending so much time on handwriting exercises when there are so many more interesting things to do and learn."

Are the criticisms of these students justified? What is the place of handwriting in today's schools? How much time should be spent teaching handwriting? Should handwriting be taught as an end in itself? What must the teacher know concerning child growth and development when teaching handwriting? What about cursive writing? Is cursive faster than manuscript? Should everyone have to learn to write legibly?

Before answering these questions, let us consider what it would be like if there were no books and all written material had disappeared. How would scientists do their work if there were no means for record-keeping or for putting down findings? For that matter, could anything be preserved through the ages if there were no writing? Obviously, humans without the ability to write would not have been able to advance to the high technological and cultural stage that presently exists.

Before the widespread availability of telephones and personal transportation over good roads, handwritten letters, both personal and business, were the principal means of communication. With the revolution in transportation and electronic communication, plus the widespread availability of low-cost typewriters, good handwriting has become almost a lost art. The lack of emphasis on handwriting exercises is warranted because of the deluge of knowledge that has taken place. The relative apportionment of time between gaining new knowledge and learning to learn must be weighed against time spent in learning to produce a "fine script." Legible writing is still a necessity for almost all persons in our literate society. Even those who use dictaphones almost all of the time must still get their ideas across on paper at one time or another. Handwriting needs to be taught, but not as an end in itself. It should be a communication tool.

In this chapter the background information necessary for understanding the development of handwriting skill in students will be presented. The sequence of steps for teaching both manuscript and cursive and, finally, the ways of diagnosing specific handwriting problems and determining how well the handwriting program has been received by students will be discussed.

After you finish reading this chapter you should be able to answer these questions:

1. How is handwriting related to other language arts areas?

2. What is the relationship of child growth and development to handwriting?

3. Why is manuscript writing used in the early-primary grades?

4. How can the teacher provide a physical and affective environment conducive to producing good handwriting?

5. How does a teacher know whether a child is ready for manuscript handwriting?

6. Should there be a transition to cursive writing? If so, when should this take place?

7. What does research have to say concerning the tools of handwriting?

8. What are the differences between manuscript and cursive writing?

9. How can the teacher help the left-handed child?

10. What are some of the problems that students encounter in cursive writing?

Historical, Psychological, and General Factors Pertaining to Handwriting

Handwriting in Antiquity

In the days of antiquity handwriting was a necessity not only for written expression but so that one could learn to read. Children had to copy the "school-boy's book" from the teacher's model. This was their text. For example, a "teacher's copy" contained a series of model passages for children to study. In the early stages of school the teacher would have to copy these passages for the children, but as soon as they could write, they would start copying the lessons themselves. At a later time children would take them down from the teacher's dictation. Since the teaching of reading letters was

so essential to the teaching of writing, it was to everyone's advantage that reading and writing be taught together.[1]

In learning to construct letters two methods were employed alternately. One went back to the beginning of the Greek school, and consisted of guiding the children's hands until they got used to the shape of the letter. The other consisted of stamping letters into the waxed surface of a writing tablet and then coaxing students to follow the outlines of the letters with "prickers."[2]

The Relationship of Handwriting to the Language Arts and Other Subject-Matter Areas

Handwriting mixes well with other language arts areas, and with all other subject-matter areas as well. Children who want to communicate their ideas in written form must learn to write and, it is to be hoped, to do so legibly.

Students engaged in listening, discussing, and reading are accumulating many experiences which they might like to share with others through writing. The more activities in which children are engaged, the more opportunities and possibilities will present themselves for writing. Children working with puppets may decide to write their own skits, and the students who read the parts must have legible scripts. Even if the parts of the play are typed, the writing must be legible enough so that the typist can copy it. Announcements of the performances, or invitations which are distributed to other classes, will also have to be written carefully and neatly.

If others cannot read what the student has written because it is illegible or difficult to read, ideas cannot be shared. Students should realize that handwriting is a tool which aids them in conveying their ideas in written form.

[1]H. I. Marrou, *A History of Education in Antiquity* (New York: New American Library of World Literature, 1956), pp. 215–216.

[2]Ibid., p. 365.

Sometimes students "fudge" their handwriting. If a child is unsure of how to spell "receive," both the *i* and *e* in cursive writing can be made to look the same by either omitting the loop in both letters or inserting a loop in both letters. It is then up to the teacher to decide what the letter is. The student may be either deliberately or subconsciously avoiding learning how to write legibly because he or she has problems in spelling. The teacher must relate this student's handwriting problem to spelling difficulties.

The Influence of Handwriting on Written Expression Storytelling is basic to the child's development in written expression. Many times, after children tell the teacher and class something orally about pictures they have brought in, the teacher will write their explanations as captions for the pictures. The children copy these in their own printing. The transition from oral composition to the complex process of written composition creates certain problems. Learning how to manipulate a pencil and to form letters in a specific way can be difficult and tension-producing. Learning to move a pencil fast enough to catch a thought is impossible. "Thoughts have to be slowed down to accommodate the pencil."[3] (Although children cannot duplicate their oral fluency in written composition, the accomplishment of writing may be its own compensation.)

The children's composing ability is also slowed during the transition from manuscript to cursive writing. Students must learn a new skill and integrate it into the writing process. Even if children are allowed to "print" after learning cursive writing, they may have lost this original skill through disuse.

If the transition from manuscript to cursive is made too early in a child's life, the child is more involved with learning "how to write" than in actually composing. This raises the question: Which is more important—the sort of handwriting the child uses or the creative process itself? (More will be said about this in a later section.)

Relationship of Child Growth and Development to Handwriting

Learning to write is not a mechanical, lower-level reflex response, but a thinking process, entailing activity of the cortical nerve areas. Smooth motor coordination of eye and hand, control of arm, hand, and finger muscles are acquired in the process of learning to write and are needed for legible results. Learning to write also requires maturity adequate for accurate perception of the symbol patterns. Writing from memory demands the retention of visual and kinesthetic images of forms not present to the senses, for future recall. . . . From earliest infancy, the eyes guide the hand, and the hand may be considered the instrument which carries out impulses received from the visual organs. The capacity for graphic representation, such as writing requires, depends on the motor function of the eye and is coordinated with the eye movements.[4]

Learning to write is a complex skill which requires specific motor muscle control and thinking ability. In order to write, a child must be at a certain maturational level, have had certain background experiences, and be motivated to want to write. The child's perceptual-motor skill development is essential. The term "perceptual-motor skills" refers to the coordination of perceptual processes (the awareness of objects or data through the senses) with motor responses. All observable responses are essentially perceptual-motor in nature, since the motor component is basic to the perceptual component. For example, walking, speaking, and writing are dependent on cognitive direction, on stimuli from the moving muscles themselves, and on stimuli from the external environment.[5]

[3]Mary J. Tingle, "Teaching Composition in the Elementary School," *Elementary English* 47 (January 1970): 73.

[4]Gertrude Hildreth, *Learning the Three R's* (Minneapolis, Minn.: Educational Test Bureau, Educational Publishers, 1947), pp. 583–584.

[5]Morris E. Eson, *Psychological Foundations of Education* (New York: Holt, Rinehart and Winston, 1972), pp. 395–396.

By the time children come to school they have acquired diverse skills, such as speech and walking, largely as a result of the maturational process, or internal growth. The school's role is to build on this foundation and help children correct any faulty habits that they may have developed.

In order to produce a particular letter, children must have a definite mental image of it and of the way in which the strokes are formed. This serves as a guide for motor development. The image, or perception, which gives meaning to sensations, guides initial practice for motor control and also inhibits the development of faulty habits.[6] If children have an incorrect perception of the letter to be reproduced, obviously they will form the letter incorrectly.

The techniques of learning perceptual-motor skills are similar to those used in learning other skills and concepts. For example, concept and motor development involve generalizations and discriminations. In order to write, children's motor responses must develop from a disorganized whole to differentiated part responses. They must then integrate these parts into an organized whole.

Studies have identified a "critical phase" for providing training in the development of motor skills; training before the neural mechanisms have attained a state of readiness (the critical phase) is useless.[7]

In order to have some understanding of the readiness levels for learning handwriting, the teacher should be aware of the sequence of physical development: cephalocaudal development, which is development from the head to the tail region (from the top downward), and proximodistal development, which is development from the central axis of the body out toward the extremities. Knowledge of proximodistal development is important in understanding left-handed children's problems when they are faced with learning to write from left to right. (This will be further discussed in the section on the left-handed child.) From proximodistal development we know that motor skills which depend on coordination of the larger muscles in the shoulder will appear before specific hand motor skills. From cephalocaudal development we know that children will be able to use their hands before they use their legs.

Teaching handwriting is a most complex task. The child learns to write letters from the top of the page down and to proceed from left to right. This follows developmental laws and for right-handed people is based on natural development. Human perceptual-motor activity is usually initiated from the one, dominant side of the body, even though humans are bilateral, or two-sided. By the time children enter school they usually show a fairly consistent preference for their right or left hand. There are also preferences in the use of eyes and feet; by the time children come to school they have usually also established these preferences. Such preferences concern laterality or sidedness. People are said to have a dominant side if their hand, eye, and foot preferences are similar. When people have a dominant hand on one side and a dominant eye on the other, they are said to have crossed dominance. Individuals who do not have a consistent preference for an eye, hand, or foot are said to have mixed dominance. It has been hypothesized that children who have crossed or mixed dominance may tend to have reversal difficulties in reading and writing, but studies done in this area have not been definitive. Children with crossed dominance can perhaps shift from a left-handed orientation to a right-handed one in writing, but this might cause difficulties for them. (See the next section.)

A teacher can easily test whether a child has crossed or mixed dominance in a child. To determine hand dominance, a teacher can observe which hand the child uses to throw a ball, write, or open a door. The teacher can tell which eye is dominant by observing which eye the child

---

[6]Beatrice A. Furner, "An Analysis of the Effectiveness of a Program of Instruction Emphasizing the Perceptual-Motor Nature of Learning in Handwriting," *Elementary English* 47 (January 1970): 61.

[7]Eson, op. cit., p. 398.

uses to look through a microscope, telescope, or an open cylinder formed by a roll of paper. Foot dominance can be easily determined by observing which foot the child uses to kick a ball or stamp on the floor with.

Teachers should be cautioned that crossed or mixed dominance in a child does not mean that the child will have a problem, although the possibility exists. The teacher should give special attention to those children who are having reversal problems by emphasizing left to right orientation for writing.

The Left-handed Child

A person's preference for one hand and skill in using that hand determines whether he or she has a dominant hand. Although young children may have mixed hand dominance, as they get older their preference and use of one hand usually increases. The theories concerning why a child becomes left-handed are many, but none are conclusive. Physiologists say the left side of the cerebrum controls the right side and vice-versa. Among those who hold the cerebral dominance theory of laterality, some believe that the child is born either right- or left-handed and any attempt to change the child from his or her dominant hand will cause emotional problems, such as stuttering and reading disorders. Others claim that handedness is a result of environmental factors, such as training and social conditioning. The heredity–environment debate over handedness has continued for generations without any resolution. Those who believe in the social-development theory of learned handedness believe that since there are many advantages in our culture to being right-handed, it should be trained and not left to chance,[8] especially if the child shows no definite preference. However, it would be very difficult and

unwise to attempt to change left-handedness in a child of age six, who has overlearned this motor pattern.

It has been suggested that handedness can be changed if the following favorable factors prevail:[9]

1. The child is under six years of age.
2. The child uses both hands interchangeably.
3. The child has no handicaps.
4. A trial period shows no permanent difficulty.
5. The child is agreeable to the change.
6. The child has a right-handed person to imitate.
7. The child is above average in intelligence.

Children should not be put on the defensive because they are left-handed. They should not be coerced into becoming right-handed, nor should they be continuously nagged about their left-handedness.

From the early twentieth century to the present time there has been a decided increase in left-handedness, due to the greater prevalence of permissiveness and naturalness in child-rearing practices.

To better understand the left-handed child's problem in writing we must refer to proximodistal development—development from the midpoint of the body to the extremities. Right-handed children move their right hands from left to right naturally. Left-handed children find moving their left hand from left to right against their natural inclination.

Try this simple experiment to illustrate the point: Bring both hands to the center of your body. Now, move both hands out away from your body. The right hand will follow a left to right path corresponding to the English pattern of writing; the left hand follows a right to left path. Ask some left-handed students to write a *t*. Observe carefully how they make the horizontal line. Most of them, unless they have been well conditioned, will draw the line from right to left.

Left-handed children have a greater susceptibility to reversal problems—for example, read-

[8]Gertrude Hildreth, "The Development and Training of Hand Dominance: I. Characteristics of Handedness; II. Developmental Tendencies in Handedness; III. Origins of Handedness and Lateral Dominance," *Journal of Genetic Psychology* 75 (1949): 197–275.

[9]Ibid., pp. 199–275.

ing the word "was" for "saw"; writing from right to left "℮ for 9" and ⌐ for 7." (See "Spelling and the Left-handed Child" in Chapter 12 and "Helping the Left-handed Child with Writing" in this chapter.)

Sex Differences in Handwriting

Teachers should recognize the maturational differences among all students and between males and females. When girls start school they may be, on the average, more mature than boys. Girls usually reach puberty about two years before boys. This factor has been used to explain differences in school performance between the sexes. It may well be that girls are readier than boys to learn certain skills—such as handwriting—which require specific motor coordination. Maturational differences between the sexes may account for the greater number of males who have difficulty with handwriting.

The perceptive teacher does not start all children writing at the same time. Many boys may need extra readiness activities. Pressuring children to attempt a skill for which they are not ready can frustrate them and cause them to develop negative feelings toward the activity. This may also help to explain why so many males dislike handwriting, and usually do not write as well as females.

Perceptual-Motor Learning and Handwriting

The way in which letters are formed, accompanied by verbal descriptions, should be emphasized in teaching handwriting. Students should practice the construction of letters based on their observations and the verbalizations, and then should analyze their own errors. Although handwriting skill is based on perceptual-motor learning, many school systems do not use perception in the teaching of handwriting.[10] For

example, a 1960 nationwide study of handwriting procedures preferred by teachers reported that copying, exercises and drills, tracing, rhythm exercises, and manual guidance were most favored by teachers, in that order. A commercial system was used as the basis of instruction in 82 percent of all school systems.[11] Although the trend is away from the tracing of letters, it is still being used by a number of commercial handwriting workbooks. As a result, many teachers use methods which emphasize only the motor aspect of handwriting. Children are involved in copying or tracing, without really noticing letter formation as a guide for motor practice.

Should Children Trace?

Although tracing is practiced in school, and it is found in most commercial handwriting systems, evidence for its effectiveness is hard to find. Reports showing positive effects are not experientially based.[12] The experimental studies that have been done have all either found no benefit or have reported negative transfer in improving copying or writing performance.[13]

Studies on copying versus tracing as a type of practice in handwriting instruction have shown that copying is superior to tracing at all grade levels.[14,15] It has been hypothesized that copying is superior to tracing because the task

---

[10]Furner, op cit., pp. 61–69.

[11]Virgil E. Herrick and Nora Okada, "The Present Scene: Practices in the Teaching of Handwriting in the United States—1960," in *New Horizons for Research in Handwriting*, Virgil E. Herrick, ed. (Madison: University of Wisconsin Press, 1963), pp. 17–32.

[12]M. Montessori, *The Discovery of the Child* (Madras, India: Kalak shetra, 1966).

[13]See Marcia Bernbaum et al., "Relationships Among Perceptual-Motor Tasks: Tracing and Copying," *Journal of Educational Psychology* 66 (October 1974): 731–732.

[14]Edward Hirsch and Fred C. Niedermeyer, "The Effect of Tracing Prompts and Discrimination Training on Kindergarten Handwriting Performance," *The Journal of Educational Research* 67 (October 1973): 81–86.

[15]Eunice N. Askov, "Handwriting: Copying versus Tracing as the Most Effective Type of Practice," *The Journal of Educational Research* 69 (November 1975): 96–98.

of copying is more difficult; therefore children must concentrate more, and this makes the letters more memorable. Another reason may be that children must visualize the letter form in order to copy it, whereas in tracing this is not necessary.

Tracing tends to foster bad habits more than anything else. For example, when children see the typical broken line activity found in many workbooks (⎺⎪-┼-) they tend to focus their attention on marking the line, despite the best efforts of the teacher to stress correct starting points for the strokes and the sequence of making the strokes. The broken line receives the children's overwhelming attention and they frequently will carelessly begin the movement of their pencils at any convenient point and will repeat strokes, going back and forth over them in order to "cover" the broken line completely.[16]

If tracing is used in school, and the likelihood is great that it will be because many commercial handwriting systems incorporate it in their programs, teachers should make sure that students are constructing the letters correctly. Some teachers may want to delete this activity entirely.

Importance of Feedback in Learning to Write

Feedback is an important component in learning to write, for it allows the child to detect errors and correct them. The more skilled the individual is, the more quickly and readily the errors are sensed and corrected. Knowledge of results and practice are the two most important ingredients for achieving skill in both cognitive and motor learning. In handwriting, movement is more complex than most people think. Frank Freeman, an authority on handwriting, has pointed out that when we write a single letter or word, the pressure of the fingers on the pencil or pen and the pressure of the pencil or penpoint

are continually changing. Feedback is very important in properly sensing when the pressure is incorrect, since changes in pressure are most complicated and delicate. For example, if the pressures are wrong in force or timing, the movement is incorrect; as a result the letter will be incorrectly formed. The child learns about pressure changes through the feeling of movement.[17] To become proficient at sensing and correcting movement automatically while writing, children must grow internally; they must mature. They also need practice, with knowledge of the results. To attempt to teach children handwriting at ages two or three, when they do not yet have the necessary hand muscle development, would usually be an exercise in futility.

The Physical Environment Conducive to Handwriting

The physical environment of the classroom is important in the teaching–learning situation, as we have already learned. In teaching handwriting the furniture must be convenient for the individual child. Lighting is also important. If there is a glare from the sun or from light falling at a certain angle, it will affect the writing position of the child. The teacher should try to arrange the furniture and adjust the blinds so that there is a minimum of glare.

Every child should be able to see a permanent alphabet and a sample of Arabic numbers. The room should have many pictures with words written in manuscript or cursive, corresponding to letters that are being learned in class.

Although it seems obvious that room temperature should be at a comfortable range, so that children are not so hot that their hands perspire when they write or so cold that they have difficulty holding their pencils, this can still be a problem in some schools.

[16]Leona M. Foerster, "Teacher—Don't Let Your First Graders Trace!" *Elementary English* 49 (March 1972): 431.

[17]Frank N. Freeman, *Teaching Handwriting: What Research Says to the Teacher*, No. 4 (Washington, D.C.: National Education Association, 1954).

and have a conference with the student. The teacher should point out that illegible handwriting makes it difficult to read his or her paper. The teacher can also tactfully point out that if his or her writing doesn't become more readable, it might be misinterpreted or other persons might not bother to read the paper.

In this way chances for developing a good attitude in the student toward both the teacher and the lesson will be increased.

Handwriting Exercises as Discipline—No!

Teachers who use handwriting exercises for disciplinary purposes are telling their students that handwriting is a punishment. This type of activity will set students against handwriting activities, deter them from developing a legible handwriting, and adversely influence the handwriting of those who have already mastered a fine script. Using handwriting in this way is poor practice. Some students may even begin to write illegibly as a kind of subconscious revenge on the teacher. Others who stoically bear the punishment learn "how to beat the system"—writing each word down the page as rapidly as possible rather than in sentence form. This can have ruinous results on their handwriting.

Creativity and Handwriting

Since handwriting involves imitating or copying specific forms produced by the teacher or seen in handwriting books, it is a process in conformity, which is the antithesis of creativity. Is it possible to be creative in the area of handwriting? The answer is: Yes, if the teacher works at it; if lessons are stimulating; if handwriting is coordinated with other areas; and if the teacher respects the individuality of students.

In order to stimulate interest in handwriting, a teacher can ask this provocative question: How can illegible handwriting be hazardous to you? Answers might look like this:

The Affective Domain and Handwriting

Students who feel threatened or are fearful will not be able to write as well as those who feel secure. Although handwriting requires concentration (some tension is prevalent in all concentrated activities), the tension should not be such that children can hardly hold their pencils.

The teacher should be warm, understanding, and friendly. Students whose letters are not exact copies of the model should not be embarrassed by having their papers singled out for direct criticism. If teachers observe that a number of errors are recurring, they can either plan a class or group lesson on such errors or work individually with students. Students should feel comfortable in the classroom; they should feel that the teacher will help them with their particular problems, and that they are not expected to produce perfect papers. They should know that everyone's handwriting is not the same.

Students acquire negative attitudes toward handwriting when they are penalized in other subject areas because of it. If a student's answer to a question is correct, but the teacher takes points off the grade for poor penmanship, the child will feel negative about handwriting lessons. The teacher should certainly take note of certain of the student's handwriting difficulties

1. In following directions—going the wrong way.
2. In visiting someone—going to the wrong house.
3. In filling a prescription—filling it out incorrectly.
4. In following doctor's orders—taking medicine at the wrong time or taking the wrong medicine.
5. In writing a note to a friend—misinterpretation of note because of handwriting.
6. In taking exams—teacher being unable to read it.
7. In taking spelling tests—marking words incorrectly when grading because teacher can not differentiate between the *i* and *e* or the *o* and *a,* and so on.

The handwriting lesson coordinated with other activities can also be creative. Students can become more perceptive to how letters are formed by using their bodies to imitate letters. They can start with simple formations such as the *t* and proceed to more difficult ones. Children who become adept at this game can correlate it with spelling. A number of students can join together to spell words which other students "read" aloud. Or words are suggested to groups of children, which they spell correctly with their bodies.

The children, together with the teacher, can also make up rhymes or jingles with which to practice letter formation in either manuscript or cursive.

Even though models for the proper formation of strokes and letters are given and the students are expected to "duplicate" them, the teacher must recognize individual differences in handwriting. If specimens of many adults' handwriting are made available, it can be seen that no two individuals' ways of writing are the same. These adults may have spent hours copying letters to get them as close as possible to the model, but other factors—such as personality, speed of writing, coordination, and motivation—have affected their handwriting output. This is true even for adults who, during their school days, learned to produce letters as exact replicas.

The teacher should emphasize individual improvement in handwriting rather than similar standards for all. Handwriting scales or standards may be used, but, by respecting the individuality of students and providing realistic goals, attitudes toward handwriting will be improved.

It can be seen that creativity can exist in the handwriting class, but the teacher must provide the proper affective environment, respect individual differences, and provide motivating techniques.

Teaching Manuscript Writing

Background of Manuscript Writing

Manuscript writing is a simplified form taken from the monks before the invention of printing. It has been called by many different names—print script, joined script, script manuscript, Italian cursive, and so on.[18] Today many use the terms "manuscript" and "printing" interchangeably.

Block printing refers to that style of writing where all letters are capitalized: BLOCK PRINTING LOOKS LIKE THIS. In the business world some persons are required to print—such as salespersons and clerks in stores in the larger cities. But "printing" to many means manuscript, or to some the use of a typewriter.

Some persons use the term "printing" to differentiate it from writing. This is quite misleading and erroneous. By implying that printing, or manuscript, is not actually handwriting, the impression is given that it must inevitably be replaced by "true" handwriting, or cursive.

Marjorie Wise, an English graduate student, introduced manuscript writing to this country while at Columbia University during the early 1920s. She brought it from England, where manuscript writing was in wide use. The claims for its use by educational authorities in Great

[18]Edith Underwood Conrad, *Trends in Manuscript Writing* (New York: Bureau of Publications, Teachers College, Columbia University, 1936), p. 3.

Britain and the experiments conducted by authorities at Teachers College, in public as well as private schools, have attributed these values to manuscript writing:

1. It is easy for children to learn because of the simple strokes.
2. Children can obtain satisfactory results early without drill on movement or form.
3. The letter forms are so simple that all of the children can see their difficulties and correct them.
4. The children learn one alphabet for both reading and writing.
5. This type of writing satisfies children's keen desire to write. (One important skill children want to accomplish on entering school is to learn to write.)
6. Unnecessary curves, loops, flourishes, and long joining strokes are omitted; therefore, the results are more legible than in cursive writing. This elimination of extra strokes also speeds up writing.
7. The pen may be lifted when going to the next stroke. This apparently lessens fatigue and the resulting strain on children's immature muscles.
8. Even children with poor muscular control can produce readable results.
9. The use of simple letter forms lessens the tendency toward children's "eyestrain" in reading and writing. There are fewer movements of the eyes required when reading manuscript writing. In fact, it is as easy to read as typewritten material.
10. Manuscript writing facilitates children's work in beginning reading.
11. Children who have written manuscript for a number of years can equal the speed of those using cursive writing, and in most cases exceed it.[19]

Readiness for Manuscript Writing

The fact that maturation is an important factor in readiness for writing has been stated a number of times. Although maturation is internal growth and cannot be speeded up, there are many readiness activities in which children should be engaged in order to be prepared for writing. For example, children should participate in working with scissors, in drawing, in making geometric shapes, in working with clay, in using tools, and in other activities that demand the use of eye–hand coordination. Since children's large muscles develop before their hand muscles, children should initially use large butcher paper or the chalkboard for drawing and writing. Learning to distinguish left from right is a vital readiness activity for writing. In teaching children to write, the teacher will continuously be stressing the left to right progression.

Before writing, children should be able to recognize and discriminate between and among letters of the alphabet, should have established a dominant hand, and should have a desire to write. Children should feel that learning to write is very important for them. They must be able to follow directions, have an adequate attention span, be able to make geometric figures (such as circles and squares), be able to make a straight line, and know left from right.

Most children will want to learn to write because they feel that writing and reading will somehow unlock the door to the adult world. Even as early as kindergarten children are attempting to write their names and to copy letters from the board or from posters around the room. Most first graders do not have to be coaxed into learning to write. This desire will soon be dissipated if the handwriting exercise becomes an end in itself, and if children are asked to draw endless pages of strokes, circles, or letters.

When children are first learning to write all of their efforts will go into attempting to make the letter with the correct strokes. Their reinforcement will be the knowledge that they have correctly completed this task. However, children should always be given a purpose for writing, and activities should be stimulating and interesting. More will be said about this later in the chapter.

Sitting Position

In order to assure that children will be sitting comfortably at their desks, the teacher must

[19]Ibid., p. 3.

make sure that desks and seats are at the correct height for the children. A child should be able to sit erectly with both feet flat on the floor, so that they can sustain his or her weight. The child's forearms should rest on the desk ready for writing. The nonwriting hand should hold the paper in its place and the chair should be close enough to the desk so that the child does not have to bend forward too much. The desk should be cleared of all unnecessary material.

Paper Position

In manuscript the position of the paper is the same for both right- and left-handed children. The paper is placed straight in front of the child so that the bottom edge is parallel to the edge of the desk, although many children, especially left-handed ones, find that it may be more comfortable writing with a slight slant.

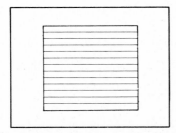

Position of paper for right- and left-handed children.

Pencil Position

The hand holding the pencil must be relaxed but not so much so that the forearm's muscles do not function properly. The pencil should be held loosely by the thumb and second finger. The side of the second finger touches the pencil, while the index or first finger acts as a guide.

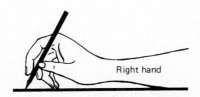

Right hand

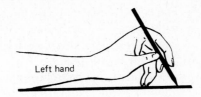

Left hand

The first finger should rest nearer the point of the pencil than the thumb. The thumb and first finger should not be drawn in or tightly pressed against the pencil. The left-handed child usually holds the pencil closer to the point.

Handwriting Tools

In the first grade primary pencils—thicker, rounder, larger, and with softer lead than ordinary pencils—are usually used. Educators generally recommend the use of a pencil with a large diameter because they feel that first graders lack control of fine muscular coordination. However, this recommendation is based more on subjective observation and evaluation than on scientific data. Very few scientific studies have been done in this area. Interestingly, the ones that have been done have found that the size of the handwriting tool has no effect on the child's writing performance.[20] Since the studies in this area are so few, it is difficult to make any definitive statements concerning pencil size. The best practice would be to have a supply of both primary and regular pencils available. Some children may find pencils with large diameters too awkward to work with and prefer a regular pencil, whereas some children may do better with a primary pencil. Whatever pencil is used, it should be well sharpened and long enough to hold comfortably.

Some studies have been done on whether ballpoint pens, felt pens, or pencils affect the quality and performance of children's writings. According to the studies, it seems that primary

[20]M. E. Wiles, "Effect of Different Size Tools on the Handwriting of Beginners," *Elementary School Journal* 43 (March 1943): 412–424.

graders perform better with ballpoint or felt pens than with pencils.[21] Furthermore, studies have shown that even first graders perform better with a ballpoint or felt pen.[22]

From the studies it seems that children in the third grade or lower should be allowed to use either ballpoint or felt pens for writing assignments, especially compositions. They should be allowed to continue the use of pencils for such subjects as arithmetic and spelling, where there is a substantial amount of erasing and where there seems to be no significant difference in the child's performance as a result of the writing instrument used.

Paper

Since beginning handwriting involves large free strokes, children are usually given large sheets of blank newsprint on which to write. The teacher usually makes several parallel folds in the paper creating "spaces" between which letters are formed. As children's hand muscles develop, it is felt that they will become more adept at writing within greater limitations; therefore as children gain coordination, lined paper is introduced, beginning with spaces about one inch in height. There is generally a dotted or light-colored line running in the middle of the inch to guide the child when making lowercase letters. This type of paper usually alternates light and heavy lines ½ inch apart, and is ruled horizontally on both sides. It is approximately 8½ × 10½ inches. In second grade the paper is approximately 8 × 10½ inches, with alternate light and heavy lines ⅜ inch apart, ruled horizontally on both sides. In grade three students generally use the 8 × 10½-inch paper with alternate light and heavy lines ¼ inch apart, ruled horizontally.

Researches on providing special paper for beginning handwriting have been very few. Two researches, one in 1943[23] and one in 1971,[24] found that the width of the ruled paper had no significant effect on a child's writing performance. A more recent study in 1976 involving kindergarten children also found that the traditional practice of providing special paper for beginning handwriting was not a justified practice. The researchers stated that the width of the writing space (one inch or one-half inch) had no differential effect on the quality of beginning handwriting, and the use of paper with closed ends (vertical lines at the right and left margins to enclose the writing space) did not improve the placement of letters in the writing space.[25]

The D'Nealian Handwriting system incorporates the findings from this recent study into its program. In the D'Nealian program beginning writers start writing on one-half-inch ruled paper with a dotted mid-line, usually referred to as a third-grade writing paper. This paper is used from kindergarten through third grade. At fourth grade in the D'Nealian system the children change to standard notebook paper with about one-third-inch rules, which is a typical size for adult writing.[26] (See section on "Using Handwriting Workbooks" for more on the D'Nealian Handwriting method.)

The Chalkboard

Since children seem to enjoy writing on the chalkboard they should be given the opportunity to do so. While writing at the board children stand at approximately an arm's length from the board, writing at their own eye level. A half-piece of chalk is held between the thumb and

---

[21]Joseph Krzesni, "Effect of Different Writing Tools and Paper on Performance of the Third Grader," *Elementary English* 48 (November 1971): 821–824.

[22]S. Tawney, "An Analysis of the Ballpoint Pen versus the Pencil as a Beginning Handwriting Instrument," *Elementary English* 44 (January 1967): 59–61.

[23]Wiles, op. cit.

[24]Krzesni, op. cit.

[25]Glennelle Halpin and Gerald Halpin, "Special Paper for Beginning Handwriting: An Unjustified Practice?" *The Journal of Educational Research* 69 (March 1976): 267–269.

[26]Donald N. Thurber, *D'Nealian Handwriting* (Glenview, Ill.: Scott, Foresman, 1978), p. 8.

first two fingers, and writing proceeds from left to right.

When the teacher uses the chalkboard he or she should make sure that the words to be copied by the children are level with their eyes. The teacher's writing should be clear and legible. In order to achieve firm bold letters, the teacher also should use a half-piece of chalk and exert sufficient pressure on it. The teacher should make sure that the spacing of letters allows each to be clearly distinguished from any other. He or she should be able to write fast enough so as not to slow down any discussion in progress. It is also important that the teacher write in such a way that he or she does not obstruct the pupils' view of the board. Both right- and left-handed teachers walk from left to right as they are writing on the chalkboard. However, left-handed teachers will have to be especially careful about making their horizontal lines proceeding from left to right, overcoming the natural inclination to go from right to left. The teacher's writing should be of high quality because the children will use it as a model.

Beginning Instruction in Manuscript Writing

Children need to learn to make the basic strokes and shapes necessary for handwriting. They have already had practice in working with large paper and with making geometric shapes. Now, they will learn to make special shapes using one-inch spaced paper with the half-inch dotted line. The basic shapes needed for lowercase and capital letters consist of:

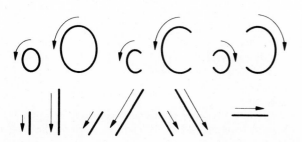

Children are introduced to the proper construction of the shapes one at a time. Large and lowercase circles can be taught together, as well as large and small vertical lines. The teacher should observe whether students are able to space the shapes properly and keep them within the lines of the paper. Some children may not be able to do this. There will be many other children who are ready to begin handwriting when they enter first grade. This range represents the normal ability span teachers can expect to find in their classes. Teachers must recognize this phenomenon and be prepared to work with a wide range of differences among their students.

In teaching how to write, the teacher will help children make the shapes by giving these instructions:

Straight lines—Start at the top and go down. "We always start at the top and go down."

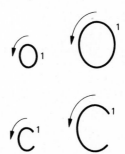

Circles—Start at the two o'clock position. "Does everyone see the 2 on the clock? Good, we all start at that point and go around this way."

Circles and parts of circles.

The teacher continues in this manner until the children are able to make all the necessary shapes. Children are told: "Each stroke is made separately. Lift your pencil after each stroke."

To give children further practice in making these shapes, and for stimulating interest, the teacher can make some pictures out of circles, lines, and so on. The teacher can then ask children to try to draw other things using the shapes they have learned.

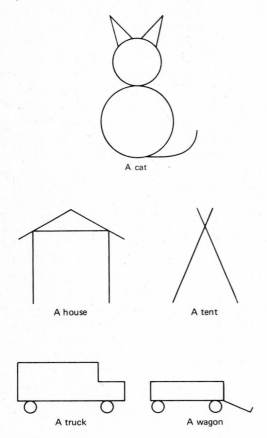

A cat

A house   A tent

A truck   A wagon

Teaching Handwriting in the Primary Grades

Handwriting will be more meaningful if the letters are taught in relation to what is being learned in class. Children should not be taught to write letters in rote fashion, according to the alphabet, but in relation to the phonics lesson in progress. For example, before teaching the letter *b*, children should have had auditory and visual discrimination exercises for this letter,

and they should be able to state words that begin with the letter.

To keep the attention of children, the teacher should pass out paper for writing after children have been shown how to construct the letter. First the children should be given time to put their first names on the paper. All of the children should have sample nameplates on their desks from which to copy their names. The teacher should then ask children to watch while he or she forms the letter on the board. The teacher might ask some children to volunteer to make the letter with him or her at the board.

The teacher should give explicit instructions on how to draw the letter as he or she constructs it. Children are told to follow exactly what the teacher is doing when he or she writes the letter. After each stroke the teacher stops and looks to see whether any child is having undue difficulty. The lesson proceeds in this manner until the letter is completed.

It is desirable for children who are beginning to write to have a work sample at their desks. This saves pupils from constantly having to shift attention from the board to the desk when copying letters.

Here are some instructional recommendations to help teachers who are working with a perceptual-motor program in handwriting:

1. Develop the appropriate mental set for perceptual learning by involving the children in establishing the problem for each lesson.

2. Guide children to observe the formation of the letter or procedure under study. The child must build a mental image of the letter or feature of writing skill involved (such as spacing or size), as well as how it is formed. This cannot be inferred from a still model presented in a copybook, worksheet, or chart.

3. Provide many guided exposures to the stimulus in order to build perception. For example, guide children to watch the formation of a letter several times, focusing on a different aspect of the formational process each time.

4. Use methods of instruction which require a mental response from each child concerning the for-

mational process, not just motor responses. This facilitates the building of a perception. It can be done through asking children to verbalize the formational process in their own words, having children think about the movement of a letter, or visualize or write a letter as it is described by another child.

5. Use multisensory stimulation. Since people seem to perceive best through varying modes, but all people appear to respond best to multiple modes, it is important to use visual, auditory, and kinesthetic exposure, rather than just visual as is provided by a still model of a letter.

6. Stress self-correction by giving the children a means of comparing their procedure and the desired one. This comparison will serve to build accurate perceptions and can then be used as a basis for practice.

7. In practice, keep the emphasis on comparison and improvement, rather than on writing numerous samples. While a program must provide instruction toward developing speed in handwriting, stamina in writing for longer periods, and fluency, these aspects should be developed separately from direct emphasis on perceptual and motor development of a particular formational procedure.

8. Consistency of letter formation and materials is essential in all writing presented to children and in all performance situations. All teachers from kindergarten through sixth grade should use the style of writing adopted by the school system. A great deal of interference in the building of perceptions occurs when inconsistent models are presented. Further, whenever children see the written form or write, materials should be consistent in line width and style with those used in instruction. Teachers should carefully examine worksheets and workbooks to determine that positive reinforcement is insured. When children are asked to write on unlined paper, narrow lines, or in too small a space, negative influences in both perceptual and motor aspects will result.

Whenever possible, the written form should be presented to children on lines to build perceptions of size relationships, spacing, and alignment. Writing on lined chalkboards and using the manuscript or cursive form on lined worksheets and charts facilitate this.

9. Care should be taken to keep expectations in terms of quantity of writing consistent with that which children can be expected to achieve. Further examination of the results of this study in terms of speed of writing will be enlightening to many teachers. If the average first grader can write only 16 to 17 letters per minute, this amounts to only 160 to 170 letters in ten minutes, or about thirty words. Certainly in terms of motor development, many first graders could not be expected to write steadily for a longer period than this. Similar comparisons can be made for second and third graders.

10. In functional use teachers should consider the positive or detrimental effects to perceptual and motor development of extensive use of unsupervised writing or copywork, prior to the development of skills of writing. Surely many other areas of the curriculum are more crucial than handwriting, and teachers ought not refrain from use of handwriting as a tool when it is important to the child's development in another area. However, many times when copywork is used as a form of independent activity, it is of questionable value to the child and may be detrimental to handwriting. Other activities involving recreational reading, listening, and the like may be more creative and of greater value to the child.

By careful examination of procedures utilized in teaching handwriting and in its use in the classroom, and through application of the procedures suggested above, teachers can improve instruction in handwriting in both the perceptual and motor aspects of learning.[27]

The Handwriting Lesson Related to Other Activities   As has already been stated, children must see a purpose in what they are doing. Rather than having children write lines or pages of a specific letter, stroke, or combination being learned, the teacher should incorporate this with other activities, such as written expression. In first grade children can write letters to their parents telling them what they have learned. The teacher tells children that although they should try to form all the letters as well as they can, they are expected to pay special attention to the letter they have just learned. (See sample notes and letters in Chapter 10.)

The teacher can easily combine the handwriting lesson with a listening activity. Children

[27]Furner, op. cit., pp. 68–69.

can be asked to listen carefully and see how well they can follow directions and how well they can construct the letter *b*. When the teacher has everyone's attention he or she should say: "On the first line make two capital letter *b*s and three small letter *b*s." After the children have finished each line, the teacher can call on individual children who have the correct answers to construct the letters on the chalkboard.

The purpose of good handwriting is legibility. Therefore the teacher should stress that legibility be carried over to other subject-matter areas—such as spelling, social studies, writing compositions, and so on.

Using Handwriting Workbooks

Many teachers use handwriting workbooks which give explicit instructions on the presentation and formation of each letter. Consistency is important, so the school should use the same series for all its handwriting classes, since the construction of some of the letters differs among different publishers. It can be confusing to learn to construct a letter in one way and in the next grade have to learn to construct it another way. For example, the capital letter *I* is constructed with and without two horizontal lines by different publishers of handwriting workbooks:[28,29]

Noble and Noble (left) *and Lyons and Carnahan* (right).

Similarly, some publishers use whole circles in constructing letters, while others use half-circles or arcs:

a B b D d g P p q

[28]J. Kendrick Noble, *Better Handwriting for You,* Book II (New York: Noble and Noble, 1972).

[29]B. F. Skinner, *Handwriting with Write and See,* teacher's ed. (Chicago: Lyons and Carnahan, 1968), p. 17.

Zaner-Bloser workbooks teach the construction of *a* as:[30]

The letter is lowercase *a*. Make a backward circle touching the mid-line and baseline. Begin at midline, pull down straight to the baseline, touching the right side of the circle.

In the construction of B b, D d, P p, and g the whole circle is also used.

Noble and Noble workbooks teach the construction of *a* as:

Starting at the two o'clock position and written to the left, then a straight line coming down.[31]

Some commercial systems have first-grade children construct capital letters so that they occupy the full space from the top to the baseline. Later on, letters are reduced in size, and capitals occupy slightly less than a full space.

A complete sample of the Zaner-Bloser alphabet in manuscript form and samples of a few letters from other handwriting systems appear on page 333. Notice how these letters differ in construction from the Zaner-Bloser letters.

The D'Nealian Handwriting method published by Scott, Foresman deviates from the traditional handwriting systems by making its manuscript letters as similar as possible to their cursive counterparts; this way the transition to cursive is very easily made. With the exceptions of *f, r, s, v,* and *z,* manuscript letters become

[30]Walter B. Barbe et al., *Creative Growth with Handwriting,* teacher's ed. (Columbus, Ohio: Zaner-Bloser, 1975), p. T26.

[31]Noble, op. cit.

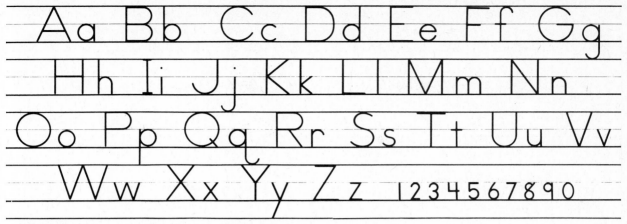

figure 13.1 *The Zaner-Bloser Creative Growth Alphabet*[32]

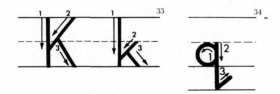

cursive letters with the addition of simple joining strokes.

The D'Nealian method capitalizes on children's desire to imitate adults and their older brothers and sisters. In the D'Nealian method children do not first learn circles, straight lines, and slant lines, and then learn to join these parts into letters. They start writing immediately. Most of the letter forms are made with a continuous stroke rather than with separate strokes. The beginning writer lifts his or her hand from the paper only after each letter rather than after each stroke. In the D'Nealian method, manuscript letters are slanted, beginning writers use one-half-inch ruled paper with a dotted mid-line (paper generally used in the third grade in most

other systems), and spacing is taught from the very beginning.

A sample of the D'Nealian Manuscript Alphabet and D'Nealian Numbers is on page 334.[35]

Teaching Cursive Handwriting

Transition to Cursive

Reasons given against the teaching of manuscript writing in Great Britain in the early 1920s were later cited in support of making the transition to cursive writing in the primary grades in the United States. Such arguments by British educators included:

1. Loss of fluency and speed through the use of the somewhat disconnected letters of manuscript writing.
2. Children would not be able to read the cursive writings of others.
3. Manuscript writing would result in a uniform stereotyped handwriting and destroy individuality. Were this the case, grave dangers would ensue in banking and business, making forgery an everyday occurrence.[36]

[32]Barbe, op. cit.

[33]Mary E. Bell et al., *I Learn to Write* (New York: McCormick-Mathers, 1978).

[34]Fred M. King, *Palmer Method Handwriting* (Schaumburg, Ill.: A. N. Palmer Co., 1976).

[35]Thurber, op. cit.

[36]Marjorie Wise, *On the Technique of Manuscript Writing* (New York: Scribner's, 1924), p. x.

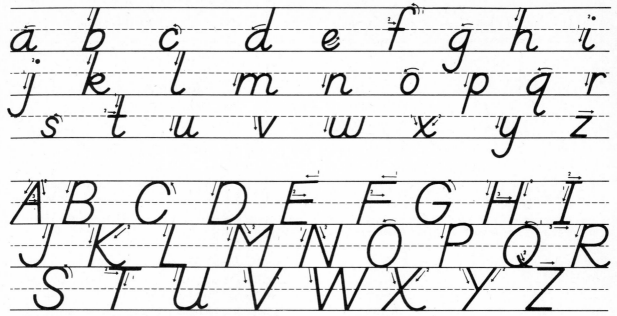

figure 13.2   *The D'Nealian Manuscript Alphabet*

figure 13.3   *D'Nealian Numbers*

Most studies have found no differences in speed between manuscript and cursive writing. People who learned manuscript can write as rapidly as those who write in cursive.[37] As a matter of fact, it has been stated that people who acquire great speed are usually rhythmical writers, and that manuscript writing is more suitable for rhythm than cursive.[38]

The belief that manuscript writing must be slower may be because an individual's style has become "contaminated" at some time or other with instruction in the cursive style. And children who write in manuscript have not had as much practice as those who are taught the traditional cursive style.[39]

It seems that much of the pressure to change to cursive writing comes from parents and the children themselves. Children observe that their parents and older siblings write in cursive and they want to write that way too. They feel it is too "babyish" to write in manuscript. Parents feel that it is childish to write in manuscript and pressure schools to teach cursive writing. When parents notice children writing in cursive, they feel that somehow the children are "progressing" in learning.

[37]Gertrude Hildreth, "Manuscript Writing after Sixty Years," *Elementary English* 37 (January 1960): 3–13.
[38]Wise, op. cit., p. xii.
[39]Gertrude Hildreth, "Simplified Handwriting for Today," *The Journal of Educational Research* 56 (February 1963): 330–333.

The myths concerning manuscript writing still hold sway, and so cursive writing is taught in most schools sometime during the primary grades. There are a few school systems that allow children to make the transition at the end of first grade or at the beginning of second, claiming that they have the necessary hand development for cursive, but this is poor practice. The children have spent all of the first grade learning to write in manuscript. Most have acquired this skill and they can now use it as a tool for written expression. If they are made to change at the end of first or at the beginning of second grade, they have had very little time for reinforcement of the skill that they spent all their first school year learning. Looking at it from the viewpoint of the child, the changeover can seem frustrating and useless. Nevertheless, many children do pressure for learning cursive writing even before they have mastered manuscript.

In view of this discussion, it is probably better to begin the transition to cursive at the end of second or the beginning of third grade. If the school system starts cursive in first grade or the beginning of second, teachers should do the best they can, recognizing that not all children will have the necessary coordination.

Many school systems use commercial handwriting programs, which usually determine at what time the transition to cursive will be made. Even though these programs advocate teaching cursive at specific grades, school systems do not have to follow such suggestions. Workbooks should never be used as ends in themselves or allowed to dictate the kind of program schools should have. Commercial programs should be utilized as aids which are integrated into the whole program.

Examples of letters in the transition to cursive follow for a number of publishers:

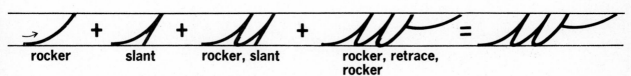

rocker　　**slant**　　**rocker, slant**　　**rocker, retrace, rocker**

figure 13.4　　*Peterson Handwriting (Macmillan)—Latter Part of Grade Two*[40]

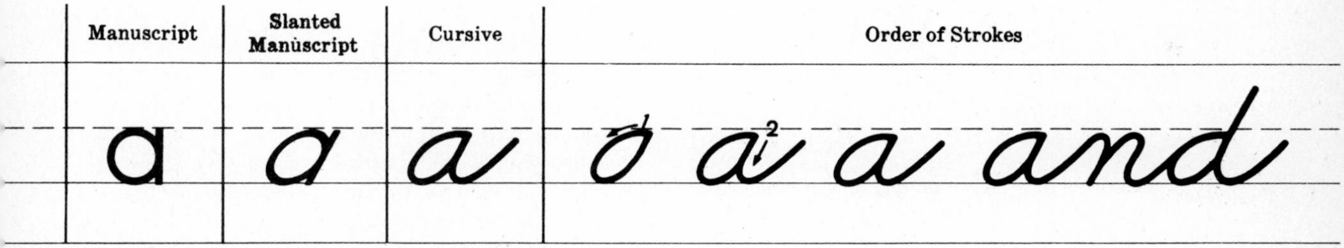

Manuscript	Slanted Manuscript	Cursive	Order of Strokes
a	a	a	a a a and

figure 13.5　　*Noble and Noble—Beginning of Grade Three*[41]

---

[40]Patricia M. Hawks, *Adventures in Handwriting,* Book Two (New York: Macmillan, 1975), p. 45.

[41]Noble, op. cit., Book 3, p. 12.

| Step 1 | Step 2 | Step 3 | Step 4 |

figure 13.6 *McCormick (Mathers)—Middle of Grade Two*[42]

figure 13.7 *Zaner-Bloser—Beginning of Grade Three*[43]

figure 13.8 *D'Nealian Handwriting (Scott, Foresman)—Middle of Grade Two*[44]

figure 13.9 *Palmer Method Handwriting—Middle of Grade Two*[45]

A study in 1960 found that vast differences existed among the publishers of handwriting series:

There is not agreement among commercial systems of handwriting on the formation of a single uppercase cursive letter. Greatest uniformity is found for letters *A, J* and *M* (three forms each) and *O* (two forms). Greatest variation in form is found for *B* (seven), *F* (ten), *I* (seven), *P* (eight), *R* (ten), and *T* (eight). For lowercase cursive letters general agreement is found for *a, i, l, m, n, s* and *t.* Showing greatest variation are *c* (six), *g* (five), *r* (six) and *y* (five). Among cursive numerals there is agreement on formation of *1* and *0.* There is greatest variation on numeral forms for *2* (eleven) and *3* (eight).

The differences among cursive forms for the same letter are more subtle for the most part than those found in manuscript form but may be classified generally as (1) inclusion or elimination of loop strokes, (2) use or elimination of end strokes,

[42]Bell, op. cit., Book 2–2, p. 2.
[43]Barbe, op. cit., Gr. 3–T, p. 4.
[44]Thurber, op. cit., Gr. 2, p. 47.
[45]King, op. cit., Transition Gr. 2, p. 40.

(3) use or elimination of beginning strokes other than loops, (4) direction and curvature of end strokes, (5) straight versus curved portions, (6) overlapping versus non-overlapping loop strokes, (7) major differences in basic letter structure and (8) length of loop below the baseline.

This evidence reveals the need for any teacher of handwriting to know the nature of the differences in letter formation in manuscript and cursive symbols. This knowledge will enable him to identify the help a child needs to move from one form of manuscript to a particular form of cursive letter formation. This evidence suggests also the importance of an elementary school staff agreeing on a particular form of upper- and lowercase letter formation for both manuscript and cursive styles.[46]

The similarity in the formation of a number of letters in different handwriting systems seems to be increasing rather than decreasing, with the exception of the Scott, Foresman D'Nealian method; however, some differences still exist among the various handwriting programs. Commercial systems still seem to introduce cursive at different times; they still differ on the formation of some letters; they still differ in their method of teaching the construction of the letters; and they may or may not have children make letters touching the top line.

If teachers are uncertain about the construction of a letter, they should refer to the teacher's edition of the workbook series in use in their school. Because of the differences in the formation of a number of letters among various publishers, it is less confusing to children learning to write if the teacher's and the workbook examples of letters are identical. Children should be helped to understand that there are different ways to form letters, and that each person's handwriting is unique, but while learning to write, only similar forms should be used.

[46]Virgil E. Herrick, *Comparison of Practices in Handwriting Advocated by Nineteen Commercial Systems of Handwriting Instruction* (Madison, Wisc.: Committee on Research in Basic Skills, University of Wisconsin, 1960), pp. 47–50.

Differences between Manuscript and Cursive Writing[47]

In making the transition to cursive, children should first be made aware of the differences between the two styles. The teacher may write a word on the chalkboard in both cursive and manuscript and try to get the children to see the differences for themselves. After some response, the teacher can write a few more words very carefully in both cursive and manuscript, and note if the children can discern further differences. The teacher can also demonstrate written words on large newsprint paper. With manuscript writing the paper should be put on the board with masking tape in a squared-off position; for cursive the paper should be put in a slanted position.

Cat big jump

Children should state these differences:

Manuscript	Cursive
1. Letters are straight.	1. Letters are slanted—parallel to one another.
2. Paper is straight.	2. Paper is slanted—to the left for right-handed persons and to the right for left-handed persons.
3. Pencil is lifted from the paper after each stroke.	3. Pencil is not lifted from the paper until the whole word is finished.
4. The letters are all separate.	4. The letters are all connected.
5. The letter *t* is crossed, and the *i* and *j* are dotted after the completion of the letter.	5. The *t* is not crossed, and the *i* and *j* are not dotted until after the completion of the word.
6. Certain letters are more circular.	6. Certain letters are more oval—egg-shaped.

[47]The differences are for the traditional manuscript and cursive systems. Many of the differences would not apply to the Scott, Foresman D'Nealian method or any other method similar to the D'Nealian method.

Readiness for Cursive

To construct letters in cursive a child must have achieved enough coordination to write in manuscript. He must also have a strong desire to write in cursive, which is often evidenced by the slant a child starts to insert in his or her manuscript writing. Children will also verbalize a desire to "really learn to write."

During the transition stage the teacher should be presenting material in cursive to help children to read cursive writing. They should achieve facility in reading cursive before they attempt to write it. The teacher should also help students acquire the vocabulary and strokes for cursive writing. Again, not all children will be ready for cursive at the same time, so the teacher will have to form groups which will learn cursive at different times.

Paper for Cursive Writing

Grade three uses paper which is 8½ × 10½ inches with alternate light and heavy lines ¼ inch apart, ruled the long way.

Grade four usually uses 8 × 10½-inch practice paper. It has ⅜-inch ruling on one side, ruled the short way, and ⅜-inch alternate light lines. The ink paper is 8½ × 10½ inches with ⅜-inch ruling on both sides, ruled the short way.

In grades five and six, a similar type of paper is used. Practice paper is usually 8½ × 11 with ⅜-inch ruling and no margins. The ink paper is 8½ × 10½ inches with ⅜-inch ruling on both sides, ruled the short way.

Position of Paper

In cursive writing right-handed students should slant their papers to the left, and the lower left corner should make an approximately 30- to 40-degree angle with the edge of the desk. The teacher must be especially careful that left-handed children have their papers slanted in the

proper position so that they do not develop a hook-wrist position. The paper should be slanted to the right and the lower right-hand corner should make an approximately 30- to 40-degree angle with the desk edge.

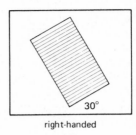 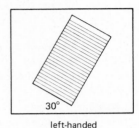

right-handed   left-handed

Paper positions for right-handed (*left*) and left-handed (*right*) children.

Pencil Position

The pencil position for cursive is similar to that for manuscript.

Presentation of Cursive Writing in the Classroom

Since we know that children should be able to read cursive before they write it, they should have seen many examples of cursive handwriting and the teacher should be presenting lessons mostly in cursive. Differences between the two forms of writing should also have been discovered by the children.

As in manuscript writing, cursive letters are not presented in alphabetical order. There are differences of opinion as to how to introduce cursive, as can be seen by the handwriting programs of various publishing companies. One way is to proceed from the letters that require the easiest and least number of strokes to the letters that require the more complex and greater number of strokes. Another method would be to present those letters which are the most often used by children. Whatever method is used to introduce children to cursive writing, the letters should be put into words at each lesson, so that children can see how they are connected in the word.

The teacher should always stress the importance of legibility and help children see the purpose of the lesson. Although they must first concentrate on learning the proper strokes before cursive writing becomes a communication tool, handwriting should not be made an end in itself. Pages and pages of undercurves, overcurves, upper and lower loops act as a deterrent to developing a "good script." If the children are using the newly learned skills in some activities, such as the following, it will encourage them to try to write their best:

1. Writing a thank you note to someone.
2. Writing to a sick classmate.
3. Writing a letter to a friend.
4. Writing a letter to parents.
5. Making a poster for display.
6. Requesting material or information from a firm or organization.
7. Writing papers for display on the bulletin board.
8. Writing invitations to parents.
9. Writing invitations to other classes in school.
10. Writing letters to children in other countries, states, communities.
11. Writing birthday cards.
12. Writing cards for holidays.
13. Writing reports and creative stories.

It should be stressed that cursive writing should be introduced by a method which will ". . . become routine as rapidly and efficiently as possible in order that it may be used functionally by a person to express and record his thoughts and feelings for others to read."[48]

Constructing Cursive Letters

Cursive letters are made up of straight and curved lines. The straight lines become slanted when the paper is tilted either to the right or left, depending on whether the writer is left- or right-handed. The curved lines are used in the beginning and endings of letters and in connecting letters:

The three basic beginning strokes may be taught through three basic letter forms:

i,
n,
a.

The *i* is basic for all of the sharp-top and loop, or undercurve letters:

i, u, w,
r, s, t,
e, l, b,   *h, k,*
            f, j, and p

The *n* is basic for all the round-top or overcurve letters. In this group are:

n, m, v, y, z, and x

The *a* in some handwriting systems is basic for oval forms or downcurve letters.

a, c, o, d, g, and q [49]

Most of the letters of the alphabet end with an undercurve, except: *y, z, g,* and *j,* which end with an overcurve.

[48]Virgil E. Herrick, "Manuscript and Cursive Writing," *Childhood Education* 37 (February 1961): 264–271.

[49]Emma Harrison Myers, *The Ways & Hows of Teaching Handwriting* (Columbus, Ohio: Zaner-Bloser, 1963), pp. 60–62.

The o, b, v, and w do not end in an undercurve but with an undercurve swing from the top of the letter, which is called a "tick-stroke" or a "check-stroke." Ending strokes are made approximately the height of small letters and swing out as though another letter were to be added. Their length is about the same as the space from letter to letter in words.

Combining Letters[50]   A letter ending in an undercurve stroke and joined to a letter beginning with an understroke is the simplest kind of joined letter combination:

i t it l b lb

e s es r e re

m e

me

Another combination of letters is that of overcurve endings and overcurve beginnings:

g n gn

g y gy

Combinations of overcurve endings and undercurve beginnings result in an over-under curve, or compound connecting stroke:

y e ye g l gl

j u ju

The compound under-over stroke occurs when undercurve endings and overcurve beginnings come together as in:

[50]Ibid., pp. 73–75.

i m im l y ly

e x ex a z az

The compounds made up of the check-stroke ending joined to an undercurve beginning stroke result in combinations such as:

w r wr v e ve

b l bl o s os

When the check-stroke ending is joined to a downcurve beginning the connecting stroke results in combinations such as:

b a ba

w o wo

o a oa

v o vo

When the teacher presents a new letter or combination, it should also be presented in a word so that children can see the relationship of the letters to the whole word.

Slant in Cursive Writing   Slant is the direction of the downstroke. In order to attain the proper slant, the paper and writing tool must be held correctly. While writing, the paper should be moved to keep it directly in the line of vision. An even stroke is obtained by pausing briefly at the end of the downstroke before adding the next stroke. The downward stroke of all letters should be parallel. Children can test their slants by drawing lines along the downstroke:

label

Irregular beginning and ending strokes may cause problems in word spacing between words. Such spaces should be equal to the size of one letter:

Baby cries

Correct

Baby cries

Too close

Baby cries

Too wide

The baby cries

Irregular

Alignment in Cursive   Alignment is necessary for legibility. All letters must rest on the baseline, and all should have proper relative height. A pupil may test for alignment by drawing a straight line across the top of his or her letters:

Poor

Spacing   Uniform spacing is necessary for ease in reading. Spaces are left between letters and words. A problem in slant will result in a problem in spacing. Too much slant causes crowded letters; lack of slant causes wide spacing between letters. Another cause of letters being too close together is that the paper is not moved often enough in writing across the page:

make   make

Correct   Too wide

make   make

Too narrow   Irregular

Size   Size refers to the uniform, correct height and width of letters:

cloud   cloud

Correct   Too small

cloud   cloud

Quality of Line   The quality of the line depends on correct writing tools and good paper. A heavy line quality signifies that the writing tool is held too firmly. A light line quality means the writing tool is held too lightly. A tremulous line quality would mean that the writing movement is too slow.

Examples of Letter Constructions   Since the undercurve is the easiest form to make, children usually begin learning letters with this stroke. In presenting the letter teachers should first demonstrate at the chalkboard how to construct a long undercurve stroke used in lowercase letters. Making sure they have the attention of the whole class, teachers demonstrate the stroke and describe what they are doing. They then ask the children to make the stroke and incorporate it into lowercase letters. As the first letters are constructed, it is helpful for teachers to count off each step of the process, while verbalizing what is being done. Some examples follow.[51]

[51]Rochester Public Schools, *A Course of Study in Handwriting* (Rochester, Minn., 1964), pp. 77–92.

Undercurve Letters

Count 1, 2, 3. Start on baseline and curve upward to the dotted line. Stop and retrace downward halfway, and curve out on the baseline. Dot.

i

Count 1, 2, 3, 4. Start on the baseline and curve upward to the dotted line. Stop and retrace downward halfway and curve out on the baseline. Repeat steps two, three, and one. Stop and swing out to right.

u

Count 1, 2, 3. Start on the baseline and curve upward to the dotted line. Stop and come down in a straight slant past the baseline and form a loop. Dot.

j

Overcurve letters

Count 1, 2, 3. Start on the baseline and make an overcurved line back to the baseline. Repeat step one. Swing up from the baseline in a curved line.

n

Count 1, 2, 3. Start on the baseline and make a slanted overcurved line back to the baseline. Make an upward curved line. Swing out to the right.

v

Count 1, 2, 3. Start on the baseline and make a slanted overcurved line back to the baseline. Make an upward curved line. Cross the hump with a slanted straight line.

x

Oval Letters or Downcurve Letters

Count 1, 2. Make an oval, stop, and make a slanted straight line down to the baseline and curve up.

a

Count 1, 2. Make an oval, and go straight up. Stop and retrace slanted straight line down to the baseline and curve up.

d

Count 1, 2. Make an oval. Stop and make a loop below the line.

g

Upper Loop Letters

Count 1, 2. Start on the baseline and make an undercurve line. Form a loop and swing up at the baseline.

e

Lower Loop Letters

Count 1, 2, 3, 4. Start on the baseline and curve upward. Stop; make a slanted straight line down below the baseline. Form a loop and make an oval on the baseline. Swing out on the baseline.

There are several definite letter groups for the teaching of capital letters.

Oval Group

Count 1, 2. Start with an oval, which rests on the baseline. Make a loop and connect with the first part of the letter. End with a swing stroke.

Count 1, 2, 3. Begin letter with a slight curve and good slant to the baseline. Make a small loop, standing upright, touching the baseline. Rest oval part on the baseline. Continue with an upstroke, making an open loop. End with a swinging stroke.

Boat Endings

Begin with a midpoint upswing. Make a straight line to the baseline. Retrace on a straight line.

Swing out with an oval. Make an open oval half the height of the letter. Make an oval resting on the baseline. Finish with a boat swing.

Begin with an up-push to the left from below the baseline. Make a nice curved upstroke to the left. Return back straight to the baseline. Curve left. Boat ending.

Start the letter on the baseline with an upcurve, and make the loop at the top open. Make a deep curve which is about one-half the height of the loop. Make a curved downward stroke, resting it on the baseline. Make a boat swing, and finish.

Cane Group

Start with a cane stroke, loop one-third space high. Bring first stroke to the baseline. Start second part of the letter with a slight curved downward stroke to the baseline. Retrace and make a loop tying it to the center of the cane stroke. End with an upswing.

Start with a cane stroke like the *H*. Start second part of the letter with a double curve. Make a loop and tie in the center of the cane stroke. Make a double curve and rest it on the baseline. Finish with an upstroke.

Upper Loop Group   Begin the letter with an underswing about one-half the height of the letter. Keep loop open. Make a downward double curve resting on the baseline. Finish with a graceful curve below the baseline.

Start with an indirect upward sweep from below the baseline. Keep loop well rounded. Make upper loop larger than the lower loop. Make an open loop below the baseline and cross it on the baseline. Finish with an overcurve.

A complete set of cursive letters from three different handwriting systems follows:

Helping the Left-handed Child with Writing

Left-handed children need special help not only in the formation of letters and digits but in the positioning of the paper, the placement of their hands, the position of their wrists, the placement of their arms, and the grip of their writing instruments. Although manuscript writing is not much different for left-handed children, the teacher should pay special attention to them to make sure they are following the left-right progression and are holding the writing paper in place with their right hands.

When left-handed children are learning cursive the teacher must be especially careful that left-handed writers avoid the hook-wrist technique by having the paper slanted to the right, opposite to the direction for right-handers. If

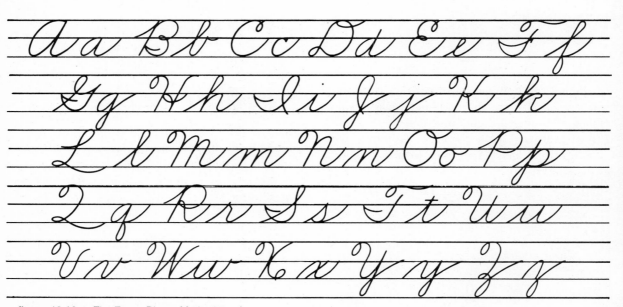

figure 13.10   *The Zaner-Bloser Method* [52]

[52]Barbe, op. cit.

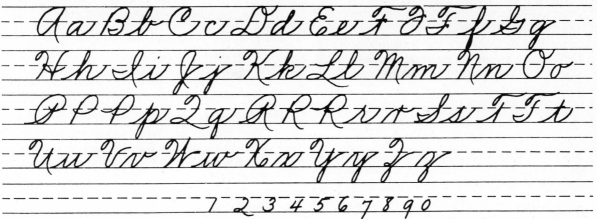

figure 13.11   *The Palmer Method* [53]

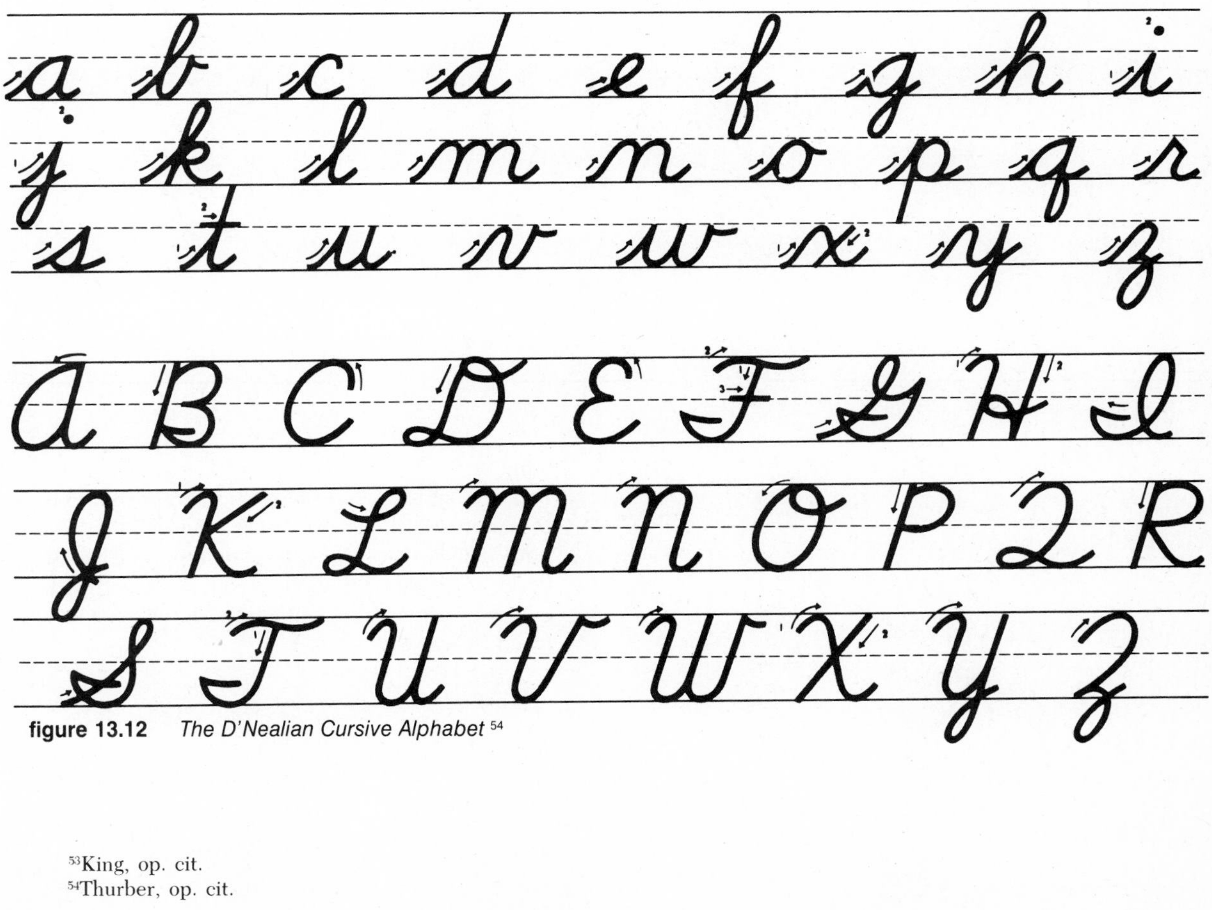

figure 13.12   *The D'Nealian Cursive Alphabet* [54]

[53]King, op. cit.
[54]Thurber, op. cit.

pupils arrive in an upper grade habituated to the hook-wrist technique, all the teacher can do is make sure that they use a ballpoint pen so that they will not smear their writing. No attempt to change the students' technique should be made at this late stage in their development, as more harm than good may be the result.

Enstrom has done a good deal of research on the writing of the left-handed child, using a camera and sketch pad. From his observations, he found that fifteen approaches used by left-handed writers could be detected: the position of the paper, arm, pen, and so on. The criteria used to evaluate various techniques employed by the writers were:

1. The quality of the handwriting product.
2. The rate of writing.
3. Ability to produce neat, smear-free papers.
4. Healthy body posture.

Here are Enstrom's findings and conclusions:

The efficiency testing revealed that in Group I three of the six techniques used are efficient in quality, rate, ability to produce smear-free papers, and considerations of healthful body posture. These techniques are used by 69 percent of the writers in this group. They bear the classification identifications I-E, I-D2, and I-F, and are pictured below, from left to right, in order of desirability:

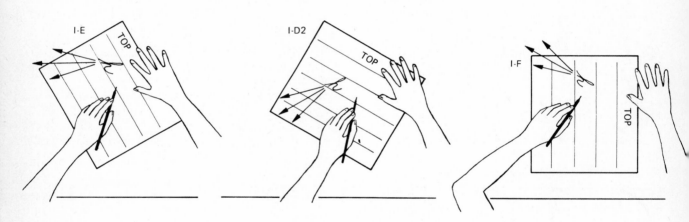

Only one adjustment in Group II can be recommended, and then only where it seems inadvisable to make radical changes because of habit formation, daily writing pressures, or a pupil's lack of desire to change. Only 20 percent of hooked writers use this more efficient approach, which is pictured below:

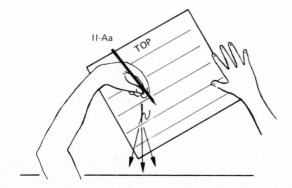

While quality and rate are high, the probability of ink-smearing is inherent in this technique. Other variations of the hooked-wrist method either test low or involve possible health hazards, with no advantage in quality or rate—and so cannot be recommended.

The following conclusions can be drawn from the study as a whole:

1. There are more left-handed writers in the classroom than are usually reported in the literature. This was true in the study area and will probably be found to be universally so as more studies are made. The problem of left-handed handwriting is sufficient in scope to warrant the inclusion of the subject in teacher preparation courses.
2. The study clearly revealed the most efficient ways of writing with the left hand. Three of the six Group I techniques are superior, all things considered, and are identified, in order of efficiency, as I-E, I-D2, and I-F (see page 346).
3. It can further be concluded that very few, if any, "hookers" can be changed beyond grade four. The best "cure" for the problem is prevention in the first place—a responsibility of primary teachers. Helping the hooker find the most desirable way of writing with a hooked technique is the best answer in advanced grades. The study indicated the best solution for these pupils to be the II-Aa position (see page 346). Instructions for these pupils would be:

   a. Place the paper exactly as a right-handed pupil would place it.
   b. Keep the writing wrist on edge.
   c. Use maximum flexing of the wrist during the writing process.
   d. Ignore all hand-position instructions intended for all other pupils.
   e. Use a ballpoint pen.

Lest there be misunderstanding, the disadvantages of this position at best should be reviewed: (1) the hand does not move very freely in carrying the work across the page, particularly if the hand perspires; (2) the probability of smearing is inherent in this approach; again, especially if the hand tends to perspire.

4. The study revealed that successful writing with the left hand is strictly a teaching problem, not a pupil problem. Where teachers understand how to help these beginning writers, pupils write successfully, with great speed and ease.[55]

[55]E. A. Enstrom, "Research in Left-handedness as Related to Handwriting," *Public School Digest* 12 (1959–60 School Year).

Handwriting Problems and Difficulties

Kinds of Handwriting Problems

Studies have shown that there are a number of letters that cause special problems for children. In manuscript, reversals often occur in the letters *S*, *N*, *D*, and *B* and in the digits *3*, *7*, and *9*. To avoid them the teacher should not teach the letters *b* and *d* at the same time. Only after the children have overlearned how to construct the letter *b* should the children be taught to make *d*. Since left-handed children are more prone to make reversal errors, the teacher should give special help to such students, continuously stressing the left to right sequence.

Letters which occur most frequently in writing and that are most often incorrectly formed, leading to illegible handwriting, are: *a*, *b*, *d*, *e*, *h*, *i*, *n*, *r*, and *t*.[56]

In the 1960s a study of manuscript handwriting difficulties of first graders was made. The investigation resulted in a ranking, by difficulty, of all lowercase and capital letters. Starting from most to least difficult, these letters are:

q	u	K	F
g	M	W	P
p	S	A	E
y	b	N	X
j	e	C	I
m	r	f	v
k	Z	j	i
U	n	w	D
a	s	h	H
G	Q	T	O
R	B	x	L
d	T	c	o
Y	z	V	][57]

According to this list, q, g, p, y, j, m, k, U, a, and G are manuscript-writing demons which need special attention.

[56]Freeman, op. cit., p. 28.
[57]Edward R. Lewis and Hilda P. Lewis, "Which Manuscript Letters Are Hard for First Graders?" *Elementary English* 41 (December 1964): 855–858.

Studies have shown that, among capital letters, the cursive *I* has been found to be the greatest problem. Of the small letters, the cursive *r* ranks as the greatest troublemaker, as it is often confused with cursive *i* or *s*. It has been found that *r*, *a*, *e*, and *t* account for almost 50 percent of the illegibility errors in handwriting.[58]

In cursive writing, combinations of letters usually cause more difficulty than single letters. The combinations that contribute to illegibility are:

be	by	om	wa
bi	oa	on	we
bl	oc	va	wi
bo	ol	ve	wo
br	of	vi	wr
bu	ou	vy	

From inspection it can be noted that all these combinations include either the check-stroke to undercurve, the check-stroke to downcurve, or the check-stroke to overcurve as in: *oa*, *on*, *bo*, *vy*, *wa*, and *wr*.

Other problems found to cause illegibility in children's and adults' writing are:

1. failure to close letters, such as *a* and *o*.
2. the closing of looped strokes.
3. a tendency to make unnecessarily large or long loops.
4. the making of slanting or straight-up strokes, rather than curving ones.
5. careless crossing of the *t*.

The teacher should be aware that some handwriting problems may be caused by spelling problems. (See "The Relationship of Handwriting to the Language Arts and Other Subject-Matter Areas.")

Evaluation of Handwriting

Although teachers and students may use evaluation scales to measure students' hand-

writing, both should recognize that such scales are only guides. That is, students' handwriting should not be expected to conform exactly to the scales. The teacher must allow for individual differences in handwriting, as in all other areas. Individual handwriting improvement, rather than absolute standards, is the criterion that should be used for judging or evaluating progress.

Scientific measuring scales can be useful in helping both teachers and students know what kind of handwriting to expect from students at various grade levels. There are a number of commercial scales used as standards of measurement. In order to determine the level the teacher slides each child's sample along the scale until one is found that comes close.

The Zaner-Bloser publishing company provides a scale for each grade from one through high school. Samples of five degrees of quality are given for each grade: high, good, medium, fair, and poor. To use the scale, these steps are suggested:[59]

1. Pupils practice writing the sentence to familiarize themselves with the words and phrasing.
2. Pupils write the sentence on another paper.
3. The papers are classified roughly into three groups—good, medium, and poor.
4. Each paper is compared with the scale by placing the child's sample below each step until a matching value is found. This value (or score) is assigned to the child's sample.
5. Each child may evaluate his or her own sample by sliding it up and down the scale until the student finds a matching quality.

Measuring scales can be useful if they are not employed as ends in themselves but rather as guides for individual improvement. (Samples of the Zaner-Bloser scale are on pages 349–50.)

Students Set Handwriting Standards A viable technique for stimulating self-improvement in handwriting is one in which the teacher

[58]Myers, op. cit., p. 139.

[59]Clinton S. Hackney and Emma H. Myers, *Ready! Set! Go!*, teacher's ed. (Columbus, Ohio: Zaner-Bloser, 1969), p. 48.

figure 13.13 *Samples of Zaner-Bloser Manuscript and Cursive Handwriting Evaluation Scales*[60]

Specimen 1—High for Grade 3   Similar manuscript writing may be given a mark of A, and writing better than this may be evaluated accordingly.

We are learning many new things about space. How far in space would we need to travel to reach the first planet?

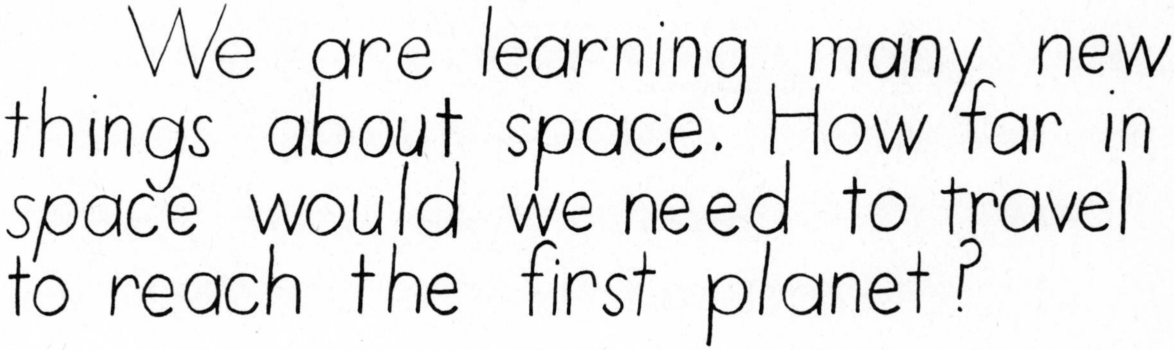

Specimen 2—Good for Grade 3   Similar manuscript writing may be given a mark of B.

We are learning many new things about space. How far in space would we need to travel to reach the first planet?

Specimen 5—Poor for Grade 3   Similar manuscript writing may be given a mark of E, and writing poorer than this may be evaluated accordingly.

We are learning many new things about space. How far in space would we need to travel to reach the first planet?

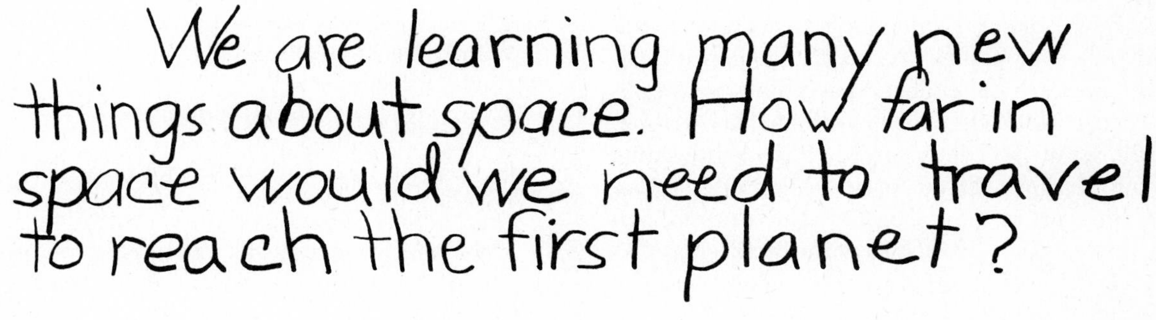

[60]Zaner-Bloser Staff, *Creative Growth with Handwriting: Third-Grade Evaluation Scales* (Columbus, Ohio: Zaner-Bloser Company, 1974).

Specimen 1—High for Grade 3   Similar cursive handwriting may be marked A, and writing better than this may be evaluated accordingly.

My name stands for me. I want to write it well.

Specimen 2—Good for Grade 3   Similar cursive handwriting may be marked B.

My name stands for me. I want to write it well.

Specimen 5—Poor for Grade 3   Similar cursive handwriting may be marked E, and writing poorer than this may be evaluated accordingly.

My name stands for me. I want to write it well.

encourages students to develop their own handwriting standards. Standards that are cooperatively developed can be on display in the classroom. All of the children have their own scales against which they evaluate their handwriting. The students determine which handwriting sample they will use each week to determine if they are making progress. The areas for improvement are discussed with the teacher.

The checklist the class develops may be either general or specific. For example, a general checklist could be stated in this question form:

1. Is my spacing of letters adequate?
2. Is my spacing of words adequate?
3. Are all my letters slanted in almost the same way and direction?
4. Are my letters uniform in size?
5. Did I close all my letters?
6. Do all my looped letters have the proper loop?
7. Are all my letters resting on the baseline?

More specific diagnostic charts and pupil-designed standards can also be used by students to evaluate their handwriting progress. The diagnostic chart can have samples of all strokes necessary for good cursive writing and examples of each. Students can diagnose their handwriting by checking the chart to see whether they are constructing letters correctly by making these strokes properly:

	Example	Letters
1. Undercurve	*(e)*	*e i t u*
2. Downcurve	*(r)*	*a c d g o*
3. Overcurve	*(r)*	*m n v x*
4. Undercurve and retrace	*i*	*s w*
5. Upper loop	*l*	*e l b h k*
6. Lower loop	*f*	*f j p*

Examples of common errors:

1. Failure to close letters	*a d o*
2. No loops where needed	*l b f*
3. Letters too close together	*are*
4. Not enough space between words	*one boy*
5. Letters are too small or too large	*boy*

Students should recognize that as they learn new skills in handwriting they are expected to add these to their checklists. Students who have specific difficulties may want to add such problem areas to their checklists, even though they have not been chosen as checklist items for the group as a whole.

Teacher Evaluation Checklist Teachers can use this evaluation chart to determine whether they are teaching handwriting to pupils well:

1. Does each child write legibly and easily?
2. Have I developed good position habits of the body, arms, hand, pencil, and paper in my pupils?
3. Do the children have an appreciation for the value of handwriting as a tool of written expression?
4. Do they take pride in being able to express their thoughts and ideas in good written form?
5. Are the mechanics of handwriting sufficiently proficient among the class so as not to hamper the expression of thoughts and ideas?
6. Do I present my lessons in such a way that the children discover their own errors and willingly proceed to correct them?
7. Are the aims of my handwriting lessons simple, understandable to children, and possible to attain within the scope of one or two lesson periods?
8. Do I encourage proofreading and self-evaluation on the part of the pupils?
9. Has the handwriting of my pupils improved?
10. Has the number of poor writers been reduced?
11. Is my own handwriting always a good model?[61]

The teacher may also ask children to save samples of their work so that they, their parents, and the teacher can see the students' handwriting progress.

Summary

The historical, psychological, and general factors concerning handwriting were presented. In order to develop a good handwriting program for all students, it was stated that the teacher must know about the developmental growth patterns of children and, in particular, about proximodistal development. This knowledge of growth from the midpoint to the extremities

[61]Myers, op. cit., pp. 142–143.

Student's Name:
Grade:
Teacher:

Diagnostic Checklist for Gaining Skill in Handwriting

I. *Handwriting readiness (K–1)*	Yes	No

A. Concepts and terminology

   1. Location and direction

      The child recognizes the following terms:
      a. above/below
      b. around
      c. first, second, last
      d. left/right
      e. start/stop
      f. top/middle/bottom

   2. Relationships

      The child is able to
      a. recognize similarities in objects.
      b. recognize differences in objects.
      c. classify like objects.
      d. recognize objects that are bigger or smaller.
      e. put things in order.

   3. Communication

      The child
      a. communicates orally.
      b. expresses a desire to write.
      c. attempts to write.
      d. is beginning to read.

B. Visual Perception

   The child is able to
   1. differentiate between and among letters.
   2. recognize similarities in words and letters.

C. Auditory Perception

   The child is able to
   1. listen with sustained attention.
   2. follow oral directions.

D. Motor coordination

The child has
1. eye-hand coordination.
2. large motor control.
3. specific motor control.
4. a dominant hand.
5. proper handwriting position.

II. *Learning handwriting*   Problem Letter(s)

A. Manuscript

The child has problems with forming
1. lowercase letters.
2. capital letters.

B. Cursive

The child has problems with forming
1. lowercase letters.
2. capital letters.

C. Specific Problems

The child has problems with
1. spacing of letters.
2. spacing of words.
3. spacing within words.
4. spacing between sentences.
5. slant of letters.
6. size of letters.
7. alignment.
8. loops (failure to put in).
9. loop (unnecessary insertion of)
10. letters (not closed).
11. letter endings.
12. letter joinings.

D. Other problems

The child has problems with
1. neatness.
2. holding of pencil.
3. position of paper.
4. sitting position.

LESSON PLAN I

Grade—Early Primary-Grade Level

Objectives

Students will be able to recognize the letter "G g" when orally given as the initial consonant of a word.
Students will be able to state words beginning with the letter "G g."
Students will be able to read some words beginning with the letter "G g."
Students will be able to construct the letter "G g."

Preparation

A bulletin board is to be filled with pictures beginning with the letter "G g."
A picture of a clown's face with the letter "G" as his ear held by the teacher.
The following words with blanks in front __ o, __ irl, __ reen, __ ood, __ ame are put on the board.

Introduction

"We have been constructing alphabet letters and we have talked about how much fun it is to be able to write letters and have our families read what we say. What alphabet letters have we been working with? Who remembers? Yes, an 'F.' Good. Yes, I remember the fish. Can anyone guess what I have for you today? I'll give you a riddle. He makes children laugh. He is at a circus. He does tricks. Who is he?

"Yes, a clown. Now, yesterday we met the alphabet letter that we are going to work with today. Let's see who remembers what it looks like and what we called it. Everyone look at the clown. The letter we are going to work with is some place on the picture of the clown. When you find it, raise your hand. I'll walk up and down the room so that everyone can see the picture. Has everyone seen it? Good! What is it? Yes, the letter 'G.' Where was it on the clown? Yes, it was the clown's ear. We are going to see how many words we can list that start with 'G g,' and we are also going to learn to write the letter 'G g.' "

Development

Ask all the children in the class who have a first name that begins with "G" to stand. Ask them to state their names. Ask all children who have a last name that begins with "G" to raise their right hands. Ask children to state their last names. Children who have a "g" in any place in their names are now asked to raise their left hands. Have these children tell where the "g" is in their name by showing their name cards. Next tell the children that you will give them a number of riddles and all the answers have to begin with "G g":

Who can think of a color that starts with "g"?
Who can think of a word which is the opposite of boy?

What word is the opposite of stop?
What do children like to play?
What is the word that is the opposite of bad?

The teacher should then ask children to look around the room and see how many words they can state that start with "G g." After the children have given a number of such words, the teacher tells them that they are going to learn to construct the letter "G g."

"Now let's see how to make the big letter 'G.' Everyone watch. Start at the top, at about two o'clock, go around to the left and stop at about four o'clock. Now make a straight line from the center out. Who would like to try it at the board? Good!"

Give out paper.

"Now let's all make it together—'G.' Let's all make a small 'g.' "

Give instructions for the construction of the lowercase "g."

"Who would like to come to the board? Let's all do one together. Good! Who would like to put the lowercase 'g' in the blanks?

___ ame   ___ irl   ___ ood   ___ reen

"Listen carefully. See how well you can follow directions. On your papers see how well you can make two capital or big letter 'G's, two small 'g's, and one capital 'G' in a row. Do it. What good direction followers you are, and what good writers you are.* Now let's write a letter telling our parents how well we can write and what we have done."

*The number of activities would depend on the group of children and their attention span. If children get restless, it is best to stop and pull the lesson together before the letter writing takes place.

Dear Mommy and Daddy,
    I can write the letter "G g."
                                    Love,
                                    Susan

Summary

"What have we done today? We worked with the letter 'g.' We said words that begin with the letter 'g.' Can you figure out what letter we're going to work with tomorrow? I'm going to bring in something that we drink. It comes from a cow. I bet you all know what it is."

LESSON PLAN II

Grade—Early Intermediate-Grade Level

Objectives

Students will be able to construct these letter combinations with the proper connecting strokes, slant lines, undercurve, downcurve, and spacing: "bl," "st," "cl."

Preparation

1. Have on display the proper formation of combinations "bl," "cl," and "st," in the following words: blame, blue, class, clue, clear, steer, stain, stair, star.
2. Put this letter on a transparency:

241 Clearview Street
Clearwater, Florida
May 10, 1978

Dear Mr. Clancey,

    I am answering your advertisement about a job for the summer. I would like an interview. My address is: 731 Thompson Street Clearwater, Florida

Sincerely yours,
John Brown

3. Have overhead projector available.

Introduction

"We've been writing letters. Who remembers some of the things we said about writing letters? Good, many of you remember the main points we made about the form of the letter. Who remembers another very important statement we made? Good! The letter we write should be easy to read and the word we used was 'legible.' "

Display the transparency of the letter on the overhead projector. Tell the students that they will be concentrating on the construction of some combinations with which they seem to be having difficulty.

Development

Ask students about the letter on display, and discuss whether the person writing the letter would get the job he wanted. Discuss the students' problems about letter writing, and elicit their comments on specific problems. Choose a few of these problems and practice correcting these.

"A problem we seem to have concerns making the 'bl,' 'cl,' and 'st' combinations. Can you think of a number of words which begin with these combinations so that we can practice them? It would also be fun to make some humorous sentences with the words."

Children may offer such words as:

black	blame	blew	clear	clue	stair	stove	steer
blue	bloom	clothes	claim	clean	stem	store	

These sentences may be offered:
The blue bloom blew in the breeze.
The clean clothes clung to the clothesline.
The steer walked up the stairs to the stove.

Students are asked to observe the teacher while the "bl," "cl," and "st" combinations are constructed in the words blue, bloom, blew, clean, clothes, steer, stair, and stove. Students are then told to construct the sentences, paying special attention to the combinations being practiced. After the children have finished writing the sentences, they are asked to make up their own "funny sentences" using words that begin with the "bl," "cl," and "st" combinations. The teacher tells students that they can share their sentences with the rest of the class by putting some of them on the chalkboard in their best handwriting.

Summary

The main points of the lesson are pulled together. The teacher gets the children to explain what they have done and tells students that tomorrow they will practice some other combinations which seem to be giving a number of children difficulty.

helps teachers to understand the readiness of students for handwriting, and also gives teachers an insight into some reversal difficulties that the left-handed child may encounter. Providing a good physical and affective environment, one in which children will be comfortable and free from fear, is essential. The teacher must also understand about individual differences in handwriting, and respect individuality. Creativity in handwriting lessons can be achieved by inventive teachers who use stimulating techniques and integrate handwriting with many other ongoing activities.

The manuscript program in handwriting was then given, and the factors necessary for teaching manuscript effectively were presented. The various factors necessary for teaching cursive effectively were discussed in the hope of helping teachers who are unfamiliar with or unaccustomed to teaching handwriting and to give them confidence in their ability to do so.

Specific handwriting problems which are found to cause the most difficulties for students were introduced. These included reversal problems with the letters *S, N, D,* and *B* and with the digits 3, 7, and 9. Methods for overcoming the problems were discussed. In cursive writing certain combinations—such as *be, bi, bl, bo*—often cause difficulties. To help in evaluating handwriting, checklists and diagnostic charts were given, so that students can determine whether they are improving. A Diagnostic Checklist for "Gaining Skill in Handwriting" was also presented at the end of the chapter.

The handwriting program presented in this chapter advocates handwriting improvement based on individual differences, not on conformity to absolute standards.

Now that you have read this chapter, you should have mastered the given teacher competencies presented at the beginning of the chapter.

As a further aid, two examples of handwriting lesson plans are presented at the end of this chapter. Using these as a guide, see if you can construct another one.

Suggestions for Thought Questions and Activities

1. A left-handed child is writing in cursive with the hook-wrist movement. What would you do to help this child?
2. Think up some handwriting activities that will be fun for the class and list them.
3. Develop a creative lesson plan in either cursive or manuscript writing.
4. Should only manuscript writing or only cursive writing be taught? Why? Should there be a transition from manuscript to cursive? If so, how should it be made?
5. You have been appointed to a special curriculum committee on handwriting which is charged with the responsibility for choosing the handwriting system to be used in your school. What information would you have to gather in order to be able to make an effective contribution? Would you use a commercial system or would you develop your own? Explain.

SELECTED BIBLIOGRAPHY

Anderson, Dan. "Teaching Handwriting." *What Research Says to the Teacher: No. 4.* Washington, D.C.: National Education Association, 1968.

Burns, Paul. *Improving Handwriting Instruction in Elementary Schools,* 2d ed. Minneapolis, Minn.: Burgess, 1968.

Chappell, Warren. *A Short History of the Printed Word.* New York: Knopf, 1970.

Fairbank, Alfred. *The Story of Handwriting* (New York: Watson-Guptill, 1970.

Foerster, Leona B. "Let's Be Realistic about Handwriting Evaluation." *Elementary English* 51 (May 1974): 741–742.

Herrick, Virgil. *New Horizons for Research in Handwriting.* Madison, Wisc.: University of Wisconsin Press, 1963.

Horn, Thomas, ed. *Research on Handwriting and Spelling.* Urbana, Ill.: National Council of Teachers of English, 1966.

Howell, Helen. "Write On, You Sinistrals!" *Language Arts* 55 (October 1978): 852–856.

Myers, Emma. *The Whys and Hows of Teaching Handwriting.* Columbus, Ohio: Zaner-Bloser, 1963.

Scribe: A Handbook of Classroom Ideas to Motivate the Teaching of Handwriting. Stevensville, Mich.: Educational Services, 1976.

fourteen

Word Usage —"Traditional Grammar" and "New Grammar"

EXAMPLES OF TEACHER COMPETENCIES

1. The teacher will be able to define grammar according to its linguistic definition.

2. The teacher will be able to state differences between word usage and grammar.

3. The teacher will be able to state differences between traditional grammar and the new grammar.

4. The teacher will be able to diagnose students' needs in word usage, and prepare lessons to help them to correct terms in speech and writing they had previously used incorrectly.

5. The teacher will be able to prepare lessons for students based on sentence expansion.

6. The teacher will be able to state the parts of speech in traditional grammar and give examples of each.

7. The teacher will be able to define the following terms used in English series so that they are acceptable to such linguists as Bloomfield and Hockett: phoneme, morpheme, syntax, grammar, allophone, suprasegmental phonemes, affixes.

8. The teacher will be able to define and explain "word classes" in structural grammar.

9. The teacher will be able to define and give examples of function or structure words.

10. The teacher will observe students' speaking and writing behavior and act positively by preparing lessons based on their needs.

11. After listening to tapes of students' speech, the teacher and students will cooperatively plan lessons to correct some faulty word usage. They will generate some other terms to use in place of colloquial ones, such as "ain't."

12. Teachers working with children who speak nonstandard English will be

able to recognize that their syntactic, morphological, and phonological patterns differ from standard English patterns.

13. The teacher will be able to determine whether students value, appreciate, or have an interest in speaking and writing with good usage by observing whether students incorporate what they have learned about word usage in their everyday activities.

Introduction

We often hear it said that the teaching of grammar is too formal and impractical. Originally grammar was not created to help with teaching nor was it supposed to help children acquire the mechanics of their native tongues. Grammar, then as now, was at the level of linguistics. It was an advanced science which was purely speculative and theoretical.[1]

Although the Western tradition of grammar emanated from the ancient Greeks, the analysis of language dates back as far as 1000 B.C. in India.[2] The science of grammar in Greek antiquity was originally confined to the analysis of poetry. Around the first century B.C., the teaching of grammar expanded to become the methodical study of the elements in language. This subject matter was similar to what we call "grammar."

Although the Greeks were not as successful in analyzing the structure of language as they were in developing Euclid's geometry, Dionysius Thrax did produce an exceptional grammar book, which was in use until the twelfth century. Its use actually extends right up to our own day, since it has influenced all subsequent grammar books. The grammar of Dionysius was an abstract formal analysis of the Greek language, broken down into its simplest elements, and then meticulously defined and classified.[3]

It wasn't until the third century A.D. that

some supposedly "practical exercises" in morphology appear on school papyri—there was a writing board with the verb on the back carefully conjugated into all forms (voice, tense, person, and number) of the optative and participle. Although this activity has been determined to be at the level of the primary school, because of the type of exercise used, it was probably part of secondary-school education.[4] Even though the teaching of grammar during the Roman period was intended for the secondary school, somehow it extended downward into the primary school, almost exactly paralleling the situation that exists today.

Despite the knowledge that grammar does not help with speaking or writing (which will be discussed shortly), there is still emphasis on this topic in some schools. Perhaps this is so because of the prestige that has long been attached to the term "grammar." In Roman schools the "grammaticus" had more prestige than a mere schoolmaster, even though, measured absolutely, it was not much. Another reason may stem from certain misconceptions. Those persons who believed in faculty psychology (the brain is a muscle that needs to be exercised) felt that grammar was good for mental discipline. If one believed in this theory, then one also believed that exercising the brain would bring about a transfer of learning.

Because grammar was used by the Greeks for the analysis of poetry, it was thought that teaching grammar would help children to interpret literature—which seems logical. It was also believed that knowledge of grammar would help

---

[1]H. I. Marrou, *A History of Education in Antiquity* (New York: New American Library of Literature, 1964).

[2]Burt Liebert, *Linguistics and the New English Teacher* (New York: Macmillan, 1971).

[3]Marrou, op. cit., pp. 235–237.

[4]Ibid., p. 238.

PEANUTS ®   **By Charles M. Schulz**

© 1958 United Feature Syndicate, Inc

in reading comprehension, in writing, in punctuation, in word usage, and in teaching sentence structure. Although a number of studies in the early twentieth century destroyed this theory,[5,6] grammar continued to be taught in schools.

In the early 1960s it was stated that "teachers have been shown in one experiment after another that the systematic study of traditional grammar has a negligible or, because it usually displaces some instruction and practice in composition, even a harmful effect upon the improvement of writing." [7] Yet traditional grammar is still taught in many classrooms.

Some more recent studies have shown that while traditional grammar still has no positive effect on students' compositions, the teaching of transformational grammar does seem to have some positive results for writing. Teachers are cautioned against inferring from this that the study of grammar will "improve" sentence structure. It was the emphasis on sentence combining practices, associated with grammar study, that produced beneficial results, not grammar study alone.[8] (See "Reading and Written Expression" in Chapter 10.)

[5]Franklin S. Hoyt, "Studies in English Grammar," *Teachers College Record* 7 (November 1906): 1–34.

[6]L. W. Rapeer, "The Problem of Formal Grammar in Elementary Education," *Journal of Educational Psychology* 4 (March 1913): 125–137.

[7]Robert L. Ebel, ed., *Encyclopedia of Educational Research* (New York: Macmillan, 1969), pp. 451–452.

[8]J. C. Mellon, *Transformational Sentence Combining: A Method for Enhancing the Development of Syntactic Fluency in English Composition*, National Council of Teachers of English Research Report No. 10 (Champaign, Ill.: National Council of Teachers of English, 1969).

An often-quoted example, which further lends empirical credence to research proving that traditional grammar does not help children in speaking or writing, is the case of the child who left this message for his teacher after writing for some time on the chalkboard: "Dear Teacher: I have wrote 'I have gone' one hundred times, like you said, and I have went home."

To this day confusion exists about the teaching of grammar—whether it should be taught, when it should be taught, and how it should be taught, and what should be taught. The relationship between grammar and word usage is also not very clear. There is disagreement between linguists and nonlinguists concerning traditional and "linguistic" grammar. Each side is intent on proving the wisdom of its position. Additional complications exist because of the various divisions within the field of linguistics itself—for example, psycholinguistics, descriptive or structural linguistics, and transformationalism.

After reading this chapter you should be able to answer these questions:

1. What is meant by the term grammar?
2. What are the differences between grammar and word usage?
3. Should elementary-school children learn the terminology of the new grammar? Explain.
4. Must students know the terminology of traditional or new grammar in order to be able to speak or write better? Explain.
5. Does the teaching of grammar help children in writing? Explain, and give reasons for your answer.
6. What are the major differences between traditional and the new grammar?

7. Should grammar or word usage be taught in school? Explain.

8. What aspects of structural grammar can be used in the elementary-school classroom? Explain.

9. What aspects of transformational grammar can teachers use in their classrooms?

10. What is the place of grammar in the primary grades?

11. What should teachers know about the grammar of students who speak nonstandard English? Explain.

Theoretical Aspects of Grammar

Definition and Role of Grammar

Grammar, according to Robert Pooley, a well-known grammarian, is defined as:

. . . the study of the way a language is used; English grammar is the study of how English is used. In other words, grammar is the observation of the forms and arrangements of English words as they are employed singly and in combination to convey meaning in discourse.[9]

When a student says, "He ain't no friend of mine" (an example of poor usage), it is as grammatical as "He isn't any friend of mine" (good usage). There is no such thing as good, bad, or poor grammar. Grammar, which is merely descriptive, does not establish any standards and it is not prescriptive.

Nelson Francis, another authority on grammar, seems to have derived his definition from Pooley's. Francis defines grammar as a form of behavior, a field of study or a science, and as a branch of etiquette:

The first thing we mean by "grammar" is "the set of formal patterns in which the words of a language are arranged in order to convey larger meanings." It is not necessary that we be able to discuss these patterns self-consciously in order to

be able to use them. In fact, all speakers of any language above the age of five or six know how to use its complex forms of organization with considerable skill; in this sense of the word—call it "Grammar 1"—they are thoroughly familiar with its grammar.

The second meaning of "grammar"—call it "Grammar 2"—is the branch of linguistic science which is concerned with the description, analysis, and formalization of formal language patterns . . . grammar in the first sense was in operation before anyone formulated the first rule that began the history of grammar as a study.

The third sense in which people use the word "grammar" is "linguistic etiquette." This we may call "Grammar 3." The word in this sense is often coupled with a derogatory adjective: we say that the expression "He ain't there" is bad grammar. What we mean is that such an expression is bad linguistic manners in certain circles.[10]

One of the main differences between Pooley's and Francis's definitions of grammar is in the area of "bad grammar." Where Pooley carefully avoids any reference to "bad grammar," Francis, in his linguistic etiquette definition, uses such phrases as "bad grammar" and "bad linguistic manners." Since grammar is not prescriptive, one should avoid using the phrase "bad grammar." Pooley employs the term "usage" to cover the range of choice and discrimination in grammar. In this text "usage" is the term employed when discussing how one *should* speak.

The grammar of most language is discussed in terms of syntax and morphology. *Syntax* is the patterning of words; it is "the way in which words . . . are arranged relative to each other in utterances,"[11] to convey meaning. "The function of syntax is to study the order of words in meaningful discourse and to attempt to explain the relationship between word order and mean-

[9]Robert C. Pooley, *Teaching English Grammar* (New York: Appleton-Century-Crofts, 1957), p. 104.

[10]W. Nelson Francis, "Revolution in Grammar" in *Readings in Applied English Linguistics*, 2d ed., Harold Byron Allen, ed. (New York: Appleton-Century-Crofts, 1964), p. 70.
[11]Charles F. Hockett, *A Course in Modern Linguistics* (New York: Macmillan, 1969), p. 77.

ing . . . the subject-verb-object pattern of the common English statement is one example." [12] "The cat scratched John" conveys a different meaning from "John scratched the cat," because the order of the words has been changed.

Morphology deals with "the construction of words and parts of words"[13]—for example: ox, oxen; he, they; drive, drove, driven; and girl, girls.

Defining Traditional Grammar

Traditional grammar has most often been used in schools. It is based on Latin and Greek, leading to the description and analysis of English in terms of these languages. Traditional grammar is prescriptive, in that one must adhere to specific rules:

> One such rule forbids the use of the prevalent "It is me." Another commands the speaker or writer never to use who instead of whom. Still another clarifies a point of usage thus: "But means but except when it means except." And never use a conjunction to start a sentence, nor a preposition to end a sentence with. During World War II, Winston Churchill's radio addresses were checked against possible security leaks by an official reader; when this official undertook to rearrange a sentence to conform to this mistaken rule, Churchill asserted himself as follows: "This is the kind of arrant nonsense up with which I will not put." [14]

Instruction in traditional grammar is the classification of the parts of written sentences into nouns, verbs, adjectives, adverbs, prepositions, conjunctions, pronouns, and interjections—which are called parts of speech. It is also concerned with what makes up a sentence, and with the individual's ability to differentiate between phrases and various kinds of clauses.

[12]Pooley, op. cit., pp. 104–105.
[13]Leonard Bloomfield, *Language* (New York: Holt, Rinehart and Winston, 1966), p. 207.
[14]Carl A. Lefevre, *Linguistics, English and the Language Arts* (Boston: Allyn and Bacon, 1970), pp. 21–22.

Here are definitions of the terms most frequently used in traditional grammar:

1. Nouns: the names of persons, places, or things.
   a. Proper nouns: names of particular persons, places, and so on, and usually capitalized.
   b. Common nouns: all other nouns not capitalized.
2. Verb: a word that shows action or state of being.
   a. Transitive verb: requires an object.
   b. Intransitive verb: does not require an object; for example, the verb "to be."
3. Adjective: modifies a noun or pronoun.
4. Adverb: modifies a verb or adjective.
5. Pronoun: used in place of a noun.

Diagraming and Parsing in Traditional Grammar Parsing and diagraming sentences were means of dissecting them into various parts supposedly to help students see the relationships among the parts. The sentence: "The happy girl ran swiftly" would be diagramed as:

```
    girl          |        ran
 _____ | _____
 \  the | happy   |   swiftly  /
```

The sentence: "An old man swiftly ate the apples," which has an object, would be diagramed as:

```
   man       |     ate      |   apples
 _____ | _____ | _____
 \  An | old |  swiftly   |   the  /
```

Parsing included further explanation of each word in exact terminology. The verb "ran" in the first example would be explained as: irregular, active voice, indicative mood, past tense, and so on.

Diagraming and parsing are not endorsed as activities in the elementary-school classroom. Nor are they recommended for other students unless they are especially interested in studying and learning about language. Whether or not these exercises are given in the classroom, teachers should be familiar with them, since some language arts programs do include them.

Defining Linguistics

Linguistics is the science of language and, according to linguists, language is speech—the spoken form is more nearly the language than the written form. Linguists are concerned with the empirical study of children's oral language and in developing explanations for their acquisition of language. Their interest in writing is secondary and extends only insofar as writing represents speech. Linguists seek to describe, not prescribe; they tell us how we speak, not how we should speak. They are interested in analyzing sentences uttered by the speakers of the language. The sentence "Go to the store" is a well-formed one; whereas "Store the go to" is not. Linguists are concerned with the rules that speakers follow. Most speakers of a language usually cannot state the rules of their language. Linguists find and describe the implied "rules."

Linguistics is not concerned with helping children to acquire language nor in helping them to write. It has little to do with the *teaching* of language arts skills, nor can grammar instruction help children acquire speech or writing. By about age three-and-a-half a child has acquired the adult structure of language. He or she did not need "overt" or "conscious" knowledge of the rules to achieve this phenomenal feat.

Defining Usage

Confusion has existed as to the differences between grammer and usage, and the role that usage plays in language. Although individuals who say: "I ain't going no place" and "He don't know nothing" are not considered to have "poor" or "bad" grammar, they are exhibiting poor word usage.

As stated previously, grammar merely "describes" the way an individual speaks; it does not impose standards. Usage, however, "makes choices, expresses preferences, takes sides, creates standards. . . ." Usage is to grammar as etiquette is to behavior. Behavior simply is what people do; etiquette sets a stamp of approval or disapproval on actions or sets up standards to guide actions. Usage involves propriety, idioms, and word choice.

Pooley says:

"... there is a close relationship between grammar and usage where the propriety of use of certain word forms is governed by the history of its grammatical forms. For example, the past tense of the verb *stick* is *stuck* because of the history of the development of this verb. The irregular form can be explained by reference to historical grammar. . . . When a fifth-grade child says or writes sticked as the past tense of stick, he is following the same process which produced such current past tense forms as "helped" or "wept" from verbs which once had a change of vowels in the past tense. To correct the child at the moment of his use of "sticked" calls for a consideration of propriety—that is, usage—rather than of grammatical history.[15]

(See the second half of this chapter for examples, activities, and further clarification of usage.)

The New Grammar

In order to determine whether differences between old and new grammars are significant, and whether these differences warrant that the new grammar be taught, particularly in elementary schools, a clearer understanding of both grammars must be given. One reason that confusion exists between old and new grammars is because old words, such as "grammar," are being used but new meanings are being stipulated for them. A number of new "grammars" have sprung up in the past few decades, and it is likely that more will be produced. Some of these new grammars are more complete than the old, and are more difficult to use. Noam Chomsky, one of the leaders of the transfor-

[15]Pooley, op. cit , pp, 106–107.

mational movement, says: ". . . the teaching of new grammar prematurely and abstractly to children incapable of really understanding it would be disastrous, even though the grammar itself might be acceptable to a linguist."[16]

Much of the ferment leading to the present changes in grammar was due to the work of such people as Jespersen and Bloomfield in the early 1900s. Jespersen tried to explain irregularities in the English language. He questioned the "idealness" of Latin or Greek and forced a re-evaluation of the source of our standards of usage.[17] Bloomfield also began to describe the language as it was spoken, as it exists, rather than as it should be.[18] Such questioning and attempts at finding answers to perplexing questions relating to traditional grammar paved the way for the new grammars.

The new linguists were not interested in prescribing or in making judgments on what is or is not correct. They were only interested in describing usage. New terms were developed and descriptive grammar was born.

Understanding the Language of the Linguists

Although it is questionable whether children must know the terms that the linguists employ, teachers should have some familiarity with them. This is especially important since a number of English textbooks at the elementary-school level are incorporating some of the new terminology. The task of familiarizing teachers with the new linguistics is not an easy one because of the various systems in existence and the different means of classifying and codifying phonemes. Before elaborating on these points,

some basic definitions of terms are necessary for better understanding:

Phonology: A branch of linguistics that deals with the analysis of sound systems of language.

Phoneme: Smallest unit of sound in a specific language system. A phoneme is a class of sounds. (See Chapter 7.)

Allophones: Variants of the same phoneme; they are phonetically similar to other members of the phoneme class to which they belong. The [p] at the beginning of pin and the [p] at the end of tip are allophones of the phoneme /p/. Brackets are typically used to indicate allophones; slanted lines are used to indicate phonemes. (See Chapter 7.)

Suprasegmental phonemes: Pitch, stress, and juncture or pause are significant sound units, or phonemes, because they influence meaning. The term suprasegmental refers to "the vocal effects of pitch, stress, and juncture, which accompany the linear sequence of vowels and consonants in utterances."[19]

Stress: "An accentual system in which the differences are largely in relative loudness or prominence is called a stress system, and the contrasting degrees of prominence are called stresses or stress-levels."[20] Stress can relate to differences in the prominence of various parts of a word or sentence. Some linguists identify three levels of stress, whereas others indicate four. Some linguists also use different symbols to record stress levels.

The accent or stress phoneme with which elementary-school children usually become familiar in their work with the dictionary is the primary stress /'/. They learn that stress is important in helping to convey meaning. For example, the stress or accent in the following words will help determine the meaning of the word:

[16]Noam Chomsky and Morris Halle, "Some Controversial Questions in Phonological Theory," *Journal of Linguistics* 1 (1965): 104.

[17]Otto Jespersen, *The Philosophy of Grammar* (New York: Henry Holt, 1924).

[18]Leonard Bloomfield, *Introduction to the Study of Language* (New York: Henry Holt, 1914).

[19]Harold G. Shane, *Linguistics and the Classroom Teacher* (Washington, D.C.: Association for Supervision and Curriculum Development, 1967), p. 110.

[20]Hockett, op. cit., p. 47.

re cord' (verb) to set down in writing; to make a record
rec' ord (noun) a recording; preservation of something in writing
re fuse' (verb) to reject
ref' use (noun) something worthless[21]

Some dictionaries indicate stress in different ways; teachers should discuss and point out these differences to students, in order to avoid confusion.

Pitch: The different frequency levels in utterances. The regulation of the amount of tension on the vocal cords determines the pitch level. The more tense an individual is, the higher the pitch. Although most linguists agree that there are four identifiable degrees of pitch, there is no agreement on the symbols used to record the various pitch levels.

Pitch in combination with stress is necessary in order to convey or receive a message properly. In the following dialogue, the second and third lines use the identical word; but the two sentences do not sound the same, nor do they have similar meanings.

> TERRY: What are you doing?
> LAURA: Playing.
> TERRY: Playing?
> LAURA: Yes.

Juncture: The way in which phonemes in a language are joined together in an utterance; the way in which an utterance begins and ends. It is a vocal device for indicating grouping in a linear progression of vowels and consonants, so that divisions into words and constructions—including sentences—can be perceived.[22] Juncture, or pause, is usually divided into four types. Again there is no unanimity among linguists in the use of symbols representing various types of junctures or pauses.

Juncture helps people to distinguish between such words as: nitrate and night rate. These words sound different because of different transitions between successive vowels and consonant phonemes. The transition between the /t/ and the /r/ of nitrates is muddy. The /t/ of night is clearly finished; then the speaker starts afresh with the /r/ of rates.[23]

Dialect: A variation of a language sufficiently different to be considered a separate entity, but not different enough to be classed as a separate language. These differences occur in vocabulary and pronunciation and, to a limited extent, in grammatical construction.[24]

Graphemes: The written representation of phonemes.

Graphemic Base: A succession of graphemes that occurs with the same phonetic value in a number of words (*at, ack, ight, et,* and so on).

Morpheme: The smallest individually meaningful elements in the utterances of a language.[25]

Allomorph: A morpheme which is represented by alternate phonemes. For example, the genitive (possessive) English morpheme is represented phonemically by the symbol /z/. But because the pronunciation of this morpheme is conditioned by the preceding consonant, the same morpheme is written differently in different environments. For example, in boy's it is written /z/; in cat's it is /s/; and in fish's it is /iz/.[26]

Affixes: Prefixes which are added before the roots (bases), and suffixes which are added to the end of roots (bases), are called affixes.

Morphophonemic system: The ways in which morphemes of a given language are variously represented by phonemic shapes can be regarded as a kind of code.[27]

[21]*Webster's New Twentieth Century Dictionary, Unabridged,* 2d ed. (Cleveland, Ohio: World Publishing, 1970), pp. 1508, 1519–1520.
[22]Shane, op. cit., p. 107.

[23]Hockett, op. cit., pp. 54–55.
[24]Pose Lamb, *Linguistics in Proper Perspective* (Columbus, Ohio: Merrill, 1967), p. 138.
[25]Hockett, op. cit., p. 123.
[26]Liebert, op. cit., p. 104.
[27]Hockett, op. cit., p. 135.

The English Phonemic System

The new grammar of English utterances is more complete and complex than the old. The old grammar surprisingly covered only a portion of our English utterances. But linguists have not agreed on the number of phonemes in American-English, nor on the way to represent some of the phonemes, and so a great deal of confusion exists.

People speak differently in differnt regions of the United States. As a result, linguists may record systems of language which are unique to their specific areas. Leonard Bloomfield's system is based on the standard English that prevails in Chicago, and some of the phonemes he records differ from those of other linguists. Some linguists treat suprasegmental features—such as pitch, stress, and juncture—as phonemes; others do not.

Difficulties are further compounded by inconsistencies in the representational symbols used for various phonemes. The same phoneme is written /ʃ/ in I.P.A. (International Phonetic Alphabet), /š/ by Charles Hockett, /ʃh/ in i.t.a. (initial teaching alphabet), /ʃh/ by Paul Roberts, and /sh/ in some dictionaries.[28]

Some linguists rationalize these differences by saying that consensus is often hard to come by. This may well be, but laypersons should not be expected to make comparisons among experts who differ in something as fundamental as an alphabet. Unlike the case in most other highly technical fields, the lay public in its daily work is intimately concerned with these representational symbols. The average person is in continuous contact with the primary reference work which uses these symbols—the dictionary. If students are taught one system in school, and then find another system in the dictionary or in other sources, their confusion will certainly be justified. It would appear that linguists have a responsibility to their students, as well as to the public, to agree on a common or standard set

[28]Liebert, op.cit., p. 94.

of representational symbols from which they may take exception in publications of more limited distribution, such as scholarly journals. This is, however, an exceedingly difficult task due to the various dialects that exist in American-English.

English Morphemes

The phonemes of a language have no meaning unless they are combined in certain sequences to form morphemes. Descriptive linguists define morphemes as the smallest element that has meaning. (Some transformationalists, such as Noam Chomsky, disagree with this definition.) Morphemes include word bases, grammatical inflections, and derivational prefixes and suffixes. Morphemes are categorized into free forms and bound forms—"cat" is a free form because it can pattern independently; that is, it can occur in many environments without having any attachments. When /s/, a bound form, is added to "cat" to form "cats," a new morpheme is formed which conveys the meaning of more than one cat. Bound morphemes cannot stand independently. They are usually the grammatical inflections and derivational affixes of nouns, verbs, adjectives, and adverbs. This same /s/ bound form can be used to form other meanings— "cat's," meaning possession, and "cats' " showing plural possessive. The single phoneme /s/ in these examples is three different morphemes.

Inflectional affixes are the suffixes which give words the characteristics of tense, number, and gender. The past tense of the verb play is played; the past tense of want is wanted. He, she, it are examples of gender. Number refers to whether something is singular or plural—boat, boats.

Derivational affixes determine in what class a word will be, whether it will be a noun, verb, adjective, or adverb. For example: (base) prince + (affix) ly becomes (adjective) princely.

In order to discern the full meaning of morphemes, they must be seen in context. Although we may know the lexical definitions of the word "saw," unless we hear the word in context we will not be able to determine its meaning. As was already discussed, pitch, stress, and juncture are called phonemes by some linguists because they affect the sound unit and help to give a word its precise meaning. There are ways of expressing words which convey a meaning different from the lexical meaning. When someone says, "Are you kidding!" he is definitely not asking a question.

Word Classes

Some of the terms used in traditional grammar are also used in new grammar, but they are presented differently and some new meanings have been stipulated. Nouns, verbs, adjectives, and adverbs are the major parts of speech according to structural linguists, and are categorized as word classes. James Sledd, a structural linguist, defines a noun as:

> . . . any word belonging to an inflectional series which is built like "man," "man's," "men," "men's," or "boy," "boy's," "boys," "boys'," on either or both of the contrasts between singular and plural numbers and between common and possessive or genitive cases, and on no other contrasts.[29]

Other structural linguists stipulate numbers to designate nouns, verbs, and so on. Fries assigns 1, 2, 3, and 4 to these terms. Class 1 words fit into the blanks in this pattern: The _____ carried _____ . Class 2 words fit into these blanks: The horse _____ the man; or into this blank: The horse _____ brown. Class 3 words fit into these: The horse carried the _____ man. Class 3 words pattern with Class 1 words. Class 4 words are more movable. They fit this blank: The horse _____ carried the man. But

they may also be moved to other positions; that is, the pattern could be: The horse easily carried the man; or the horse carried the man easily. Class 4 words pattern with Class 2 words.[30] (Although Fries' complex system, using numbers and other designations to analyze sentences, is not widely followed, many of his concepts are used in other forms.)

Function or Structure Words

Function (structure) words, according to structural linguists, include all those words in a sentence that are not classified as major parts of speech. They are used to show the structural or functional relationships of the major parts of speech. They also do not change in form, as form or word classes do. Here is a list of function words which are important for indicating structural meaning; they are used to show the structural relationship of the major parts of speech in a sentence:

Noun markers (noun determiners): Include definite and indefinite articles, possessives, demonstratives, and cardinal numbers. They usually begin a noun group (a noun and its modifiers), serving as a cue that the following word is a noun or functions as a noun. *Examples:* Articles (a, an, the) are always noun markers: *The* boy ran. Possessives (my, our, your, his, her, their): *My* dress is red. Demonstrative (this, that, these, those): *This* dress is pretty. Cardinal numbers or quantitative terms (one, two, three, and so on; some, many, each, and so on): *One* girl is here.

Verb markers (auxiliaries): Signal that a verb will soon follow. *Examples:* (am, is, has, have, did, will, and so on): He *will* arrive shortly.

Negatives: Indicate that a structural unit is

---

[29]James Sledd, *A Short Introduction to English Grammar* (Chicago: Scott, Foresman, 1959), p. 70.

[30]Charles C. Fries, *The Structure of English: An Introduction to the Standard of English Sentences* (New York: Harcourt, Brace, 1952).

not positive. *Examples:* (not, never, no, and so on): She is *not* here.

Question markers: Usually placed at beginning of sentences to indicate that the sentence is a question. *Examples:* (who, where, what, why, how, whom, and so on): *Who* are you?

Prepositions (phrase markers): Precede noun or noun units combining with them to make phrases that usually act as modifiers. *Examples:* (about, amid, above, across, against, before, into, behind, and so on): They ran *into* the woods.

Qualifiers (intensifiers): Precede and modify adjectives and adverbs. *Examples:* (very, rather, quite, considerably, and so on): He is a *very* old man.

Subordinators (clause markers): Usually begin dependent clauses. *Examples:* subordinating conjunctions (although, before, until, if, when, and so on); relative pronouns (who, whom, whomever, whichever, and so on): I will not leave *until* you go.

Coordinators (conjunctions): Used to join words having the same or parallel function as in compound subjects. They are also used to produce compound predicates, objects, and compound sentences. *Examples:* (and, but, nor, and so on): The boys *and* girls were happy. We will go with you, *but* we will not enjoy it.

Sentences and Sentence Patterns In order to determine the meaning of sentences, according to structural linguists, it is necessary to know the syntax (which is the position of words in the sentences) and the morphology (which is the form of words with affixes and inflectional endings). Sentence pattern or word order would determine whether the word class is a noun, verb, adverb, or adjective. In the sentence "*Vons* eat," although *Vons* is a nonsense word we know that it is a noun, because it occupies a particular place in a specific sentence frame. Here are five sentence patterns that seem to occur the most frequently in the English language:

1. Pattern: *Noun Verb (intransitive)*
   Birds fly.

2. Pattern: *Noun Verb (transitive) Noun (direct object)*
   Boys eat cake.

3. Pattern:

Noun	*Verb (transitive)*	*Noun (indirect object)*	*Noun (direct object)*
John	gave	Jane	the candy.

4. Pattern: *Noun Verb (linking) Noun*
   John is a boy.

5. Pattern: *Noun Verb (linking) Adjective*
   Jane is pretty.

These common sentence patterns are all declarative, and are given in the active voice.

Special Notes

1. An intransitive verb cannot take an object, and a sentence containing an intransitive verb does not require an object to complete its meaning.

2. A transitive verb can take an object; that is, it can carry over an action from a subject to an object.

3. Verbs such as *be, become, smell, sound, taste, feel, look, seem,* and *appear* are called linking verbs because they often link a subject with a word that in effect renames or describes the subject.

Transformational Grammar

Transformational grammarians build on the work of the structuralists, but they go further into the area of generating sentences. Transformational grammar is concerned more with syntax. It has strict rules for combining morphemes (the smallest word unit) into simple phrases and for combining phrases into sentences. Noam Chomsky, whose name has become almost synonomous with transformational or generative grammar, in 1957 divided his grammar into three parts:

1. "Phrase structure," which is the most elemental unit of our language.
2. "Transformational structure," which includes "obligatory transformations" and "optional transformations."
3. Morphophonemics.[31]

For example, agreement between subject and verb is obligatory, whereas the insertion of adjectives or negatives is optional.

When the obligatory transformations are applied to the phrases in Part 1, and if the appropriate word-form rules of Part 3 are applied, the result would be a grammatical English sentence. If only obligatory transformations are supplied, the sentence will be a kernel sentence. All other English sentences are generated from kernel sentences by optional transformations. For example, the sentence: "The girl eats" is a kernel sentence. It has the attributes of being a simple, active, declarative sentence with no adjectives, adverbs, negatives, and so on. If we were to change the sentence to the following variations, they would all be transforms of the kernel:

1. The pretty girl is hungrily eating the red apple.
2. Is the happy girl eating that big apple?

[31]Noam Chomsky, *Syntactic Structures* (The Hague, Netherlands: Mouton, 1957).

3. The sad girl is not eating the big red apple.
4. The big apple is not being eaten by the pretty girl.

Example of Sentence Transformations

Kernel sentences consist of noun phrases and verb phrases. They are declarative, active, and affirmative. Transforming consists of sets of rules. Here are some symbols that will be used in diagraming and analysis:

S: stands for sentence
NP: stands for noun phrase
VP: stands for verb phrase
⟶: stands for "is made from" or "consists of"
S→NP + VP

In order to generate a sentence we must choose words from the class of nouns and verbs; for example, "Jane" and "eats." "Girl eating" is the kernel sentence generated, and it would look like this when diagramed:

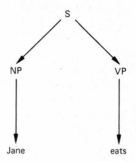

Rigorous rules are presented for combining morphemes into simple phrases. For example: a noun phrase is NP → Determiner (Det.) + Noun. This rule indicates that a noun phrase may be composed of a determiner (article, demonstrative, or possessive) and a noun (common noun, proper noun, collective noun, concrete or abstract, or a pronoun). A verb phrase is VP → Auxiliary (Aux.) + Verb Expression. Strict rules determine what variety of combinations a verb phrase may contain.

Here is an example of a tree diagram of the sentence: "The students will eat the food," using transformational rules:

S → NP + VP

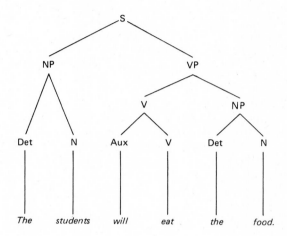

Sentence → S
S → NP + VP
NP → Det. + N
VP → V + NP
V → Aux. + V
NP → Det. + N
Det. → the
Aux → will
N → students
N → food
V → eat

Other sentences of this type can be generated by merely inserting words in each category as required by the rules.

In summary, according to Chomsky the phrase structure rules operate on the vocabulary to produce underlying strings. The transformational rules are the ones which produce the sentence (surface structure). These rules convert one string into another. The underlying phrase marker contains the deep structure from which meaning is derived. The sentences that are produced are the surface structure. In general, apart from the simplest examples, the sur-

face structures of sentences are very different from their deep structures. Chomsky says:

> The grammar of English will generate, for each sentence, a deep structure, and will contain rules showing how this deep structure is related to surface structure. The rules expressing the relation of deep and surface structures are called "grammatical transformations." Hence, the term "transformation-generative grammar." In addition to rules defining deep structures, surface structures and the relation between them, the grammar of English contains further rules that relate these "syntactic objects" (namely, paired deep and surface structures) to phonetic representations of meanings on the other. A person who has acquired knowledge of English has internalized these rules and makes use of them when he understands or produces (sentences) . . .[32]

Chomsky also states that the study of grammar is the study of linguistic competence. When one talks of "competence" in grammar, the reference is to the individual's knowledge of grammar, which is considered to be innate (unconscious knowledge). Performance, or the actual observed use of language, involves such factors as memory restriction and extralinguistic beliefs concerning the speaker and the situation.

A Summary of the Comparison of Traditional Grammar with New Grammar

Table 14.1 presents a summary of the differences between traditional and linguistic approaches in grammar.[33]

A linguistic approach is more helpful to teachers and students than traditional grammar because it is based on the English language and it only describes rather than prescribes. However, the emphasis on linguistics in classrooms has not extinguished the confusion that exists concerning teaching grammar in school. Al-

[32]Noam Chomsky, *Language and Mind* (New York: Harcourt Brace Jovanovich, 1972), p. 106.
[33]Liebert, op. cit., p. 37.

table 14.1

Traditional	Linguistic
Based on reason, authority, philosophy.	Based on careful observation of language data.
Concerned with written language, especially great works of literature.	Concerned with all phases of language: spoken, written, recorded in any form. Often emphasis on spoken language.
Until recently, considered the language of the vernacular to be inferior. Especially disparaged English because it had few inflections.	Considers the language of all communities of equal value.
Attempts to "fix" language into one, unchanging form.	Views language as a constantly changing phenomenon.
Has as its purpose the eradication of errors in usage (prescriptive approach).	Investigates language as it actually is used (descriptive approach).
Syntax based on Latin-Greek inflectional system.	Syntax based on English word-order system.
Uses form, function, and meaning indiscriminately in defining terminology.	Separates form, function, and meaning into different systems; tends to favor form and function over meaning.

though linguistic texts may use different terminology and present their material in different ways, the teacher's emphasis tends toward the prescriptive. Furthermore, the new grammar is highly structured and requires learning parts of speech, so that what started out as merely describing language, with no emphasis on what should or should not be taught (linguistics), has entered the classrooms as a series of prescriptions for teaching via the new grammar.

For example, in a number of linguistic texts, this description would be given for a noun:

A noun is a word like apple, beauty, or desk. That is, it is a word that patterns as apple, beauty, or desk. It is a word that occurs in positions like those in which apple, beauty, and desk occur, such as:

I saw the *apple*. The *apple* tastes good.
I saw the *beauty*. The *desk* is too low.

Traditional grammar would define a noun as:

"A noun is a word that names a person, animal, place, thing, or group. Examples of nouns are italicized below.

The *girl* rode the *pony* in the *corral*."

Since researchers have shown that the teaching of grammar does not help in the various language arts areas, how can one, just by changing the terminology and enumerating examples of nouns rather than classes of nouns, justify the teaching of grammar? Linguists have stated that their field is purely descriptive, but it is difficult to reconcile this claim with the many linguistic texts intended for teaching parts of speech. Little evidence exists to support the value of grammar based on linguistics.

Should grammar be taught in the elementary school and, if so, which grammar? Will the new grammars help children in speaking, reading, and writing better than the old grammar?

Some linguists beg these questions. Paul Roberts states:

It is not to be expected that the study of grammar, no matter how good a grammar it is or how carefully it is taught, will effect any enormous improvement in writing. Probably the improvement will be small and hard to demonstrate, and for the large number of students who lack the motivation or the capacity to learn to write, it will be nonexistent. But even these students can learn the grammar, and it is valuable for them to do so. For grammar is the heart of the humanities, and like other humane studies, its ultimate justification is that it informs the mind and teaches its own uses.[34]

[34]Paul Roberts, "Linguistics and the Teaching of Composition," *The English Journal* 52 (May 1963): 335.

Nonstandard English and Its Grammar

As we have said, linguists cannot completely standardize the phonemic system of the English language because of speech differences in different regions. They describe language based on specific local dialects, and no one of these descriptions is any more correct, or better, than any other. In describing the language of children who speak nonstandard English, it was found that there are a number of phonological, as well as structural, differences between standard and nonstandard English.

Teachers must accept their students as they are, and not judge their speech patterns adversely. They should recognize that these children's speech patterns are different, and that the patterns perform functions similar to those of standard English with similar but different rules. Teachers must also devise methods to help these children to acquire standard English. (See Chapters 5 and 6 for activities and a discussion on teaching English as a second language.)

Word Usage, Traditional Grammar, New Grammar: Practical Aspects for the Elementary School

The Teacher and Word Usage

Young children are self-centered and, according to Piaget, it is not until children must become social that their language becomes more logical and less egocentric. Children coming to school have just emerged from this stage. Language is used in order to communicate, and the more closely the language of children resembles the speech norms of those around them, the more effective will they be in communicating. Similarly, the more opportunity children have to communicate, the more skillful will they become in the use of language.

Since usage is concerned with the way people speak, children can be made to understand that there would be no communication if people involved in listening and speaking did not use common word sounds and meanings.

The emphasis in school should be on using standard English. The range of standard English is broad and includes formal, informal, and colloquial usage. Which type is used depends on the particular situation or circumstance. Formal speech occurs in writing scholarly articles or planned lectures; informal usage is the spoken language of the elementary school. It was Charles Fries, a well-known linguist, who recommended that teachers concentrate on using standard informal usage rather than literary language in teaching children.[35]

When children come to school they speak in a particular way. Children's speech is intimately tied up with their "selves" and their feelings about themselves. Some children come from homes using good speech patterns; others use illiterate speech. Some children speak more immaturely than others. For example, young children tend to overgeneralize and usually regularize irregular verbs. The past tense of "to go" becomes "goed" rather than "went." By the time children come to school, they have often learned the correct past tense of "to go" and it has become a normal part of their speech. If not, the teacher should correct the children, but in such a way that it does not damage their self-concept or deter them from speaking. By accepting what the children have said, by reinforcing their oral statements, and by responding with the correct form of the word, the teacher can help the children. If a child says, "I goed to the movies yesterday," the teacher's response might be, "Oh, you *went* to the movies yesterday. Good! Tell me about what you saw." The correct form is emphasized, yet the child's statement is accepted and further conversation is stimulated.

Grammar study is not needed to develop

[35]Charles Carpenter Fries, *American English Grammar* (New York: Appleton-Century-Crofts, 1940), pp. 289–290.

good usage. The teacher does not have to require pupils, orally or in written expression, to learn the principal parts of the verb "to go" in order to speak correctly. Pooley claims that drilling on correct usage of irregular verbs actually results in children's "cheerfully continuing to maltreat these verbs in speech and writing."[36] Since children speak in a specific way, they must be weaned from faulty habits and helped to form others through correction and practice.

Before behavior can be modified so that a habit is changed, students must identify the problem and learn to think about what they are saying. This can be difficult, because when we speak we are concerned with *what* we are attempting to say, rather than the form in which we say it.[37] If the teacher calls attention to the word that needs to be changed, without embarrassing the student, and provides the proper form of usage, the odds in favor of success will increase.

The teacher must be careful to make students feel free to express themselves and not immediately set restrictions for them. Since language is oral, living, and changing, individual differences exist, and there is no arbitrary "good" or "bad." The question is whether the usage is appropriate and based on the situation. If children are constantly reprimanded each time they speak, they soon will speak less.

The teacher should avoid correcting children each time they do not speak in complete sentences. Teachers have been influenced by the definition of a sentence as expressing a complete thought. So when children do not express themselves in a sentence, it is assumed that they are not expressing a complete thought. But ideas can be expressed by one or two words or phrases.

Teachers must also be aware that they are models for students, who will often imitate not only a teacher's speech patterns but his or her mannerisms and voice tones as well.

Instruction in Word Usage

Although studies have shown that knowledge of grammar does not help in writing or speaking, a great deal of time is spent on syntax and parts of speech in the classroom. Students are given sentences to dissect—stating which is the noun, verb, adjective, and so on—and grammar is taught as an end in itself. This is not useful. Time is best spent in school on speaking and writing English. The parts of speech may be introduced incidentally when children are working with sentences or sentence patterns.

The main emphasis in the elementary-school grammar program should be on word usage and building and manipulating sentences. (The latter will be treated in more detail later in this chapter.) Since studies have shown that word usage helps in writing, the important questions are: What word usage should be taught and who sets the standards for what should be taught?

> Good English is that form of speech which is appropriate to the purpose of the speaker, true to the language as it is, and comfortable to speaker and listener. It is the product of custom, neither cramped by rule nor freed from all restraint; it is never fixed, but changes with the organic life of the language.[38]

This definition of standards is broad, but Pooley's 1960 "particulars," ranging from an elementary level to a more complex one not ordered on any grade level hierarchy, are excellent and still valid. He claims that some usage problems are rather easily overcome, whereas others persist into adult life:[39]

---

[36]Pooley, op. cit., p. 107.

[37]A. F. Watts, *The Language and Mental Development of Children* (London: George G. Harrop, 1944), p. 65.

[38]Robert C. Pooley, *Grammar and Usage in Textbooks on English*, Bureau of Educational Research Bulletin No. 14 (Madison, Wisc.: University of Wisconsin, 1933), p. 155.

[39]Robert C. Pooley, "Dare Schools Set a Standard in English Usage?" *The English Journal* 49 (March 1960): 179–180.

1. The elimination of all baby talk and "cute" expressions.

2. The correct uses in speech and writing of *I, me, he, him, she, her, they, them*. (Exception, *it's me*.)

3. The correct uses of *is, are, was, were* with respect to number and tense.

4. Correct past tenses of common irregular verbs, such as *saw, gave, took, brought, bought, stuck*.

5. Correct use of past participles of the same verbs and similar verbs after auxiliaries.

6. Elimination of the double negative: We don't have *no* apples, and so on.

7. Elimination of analogical forms: *ain't, hisn, hern, ourn, theirselves*, and so on.

8. Correct use of possessive pronouns: *my, mine, his, hers, theirs, ours*.

9. Mastery of the distinction between *its*, possessive pronoun, and *it's, it is*.

10. Placement of *have* or its phonetic reduction to *v* between *I* and a past participle.

11. Elimination of *them* as a demonstrative pronoun.

12. Elimination of *this here* and *that there*.

13. Mastery of use of *a* and *an* as articles.

14. Correct use of personal pronouns in compound constructions: as subject (Mary and I), as object (Mary and me), as object of preposition (to Mary and me).

15. The use of *we* before an appositional noun when subject; *us* when object.

16. Correct number agreement with the phrases *there is, there are, there was, there were*.

17. Elimination of *he don't, she don't, it don't*.

18. Elimination of *learn* for *teach*, *leave* for *let*.

19. Elimination of pleonastic [redundant] subjects: *my brother he; my mother she; that fellow he*.

20. Proper agreement in number with antecedent pronouns *one* and *anyone, everyone, each, no one*. With *everybody* and *none* some tolerance of number seems acceptable now.

21. The use of *who* and *whom* as reference to persons. (But note, *Who did he give it to?* is tolerated in all but very formal situations. In the latter, *To whom did he give it* is preferable.)

22. Accurate use of *said* in reporting the words of a speaker in the past.

23. Correction of *lay down* to *lie down*.

24. The distinction between *good* as adjective and *well* as adverb: He spoke *well*.

25. Elimination of *can't hardly*, *all the farther* (for *as far as*), and *Where is he (she, it) at?*

Pooley claimed that "this list of twenty-five kinds of corrections to make constitutes a very specific standard of current English usage for today and the next few years." He conceded that "some elements in it may require modification within ten years; some possibly earlier." Conspicuous by their absence are these items which were on usage lists years ago and which survive in the less enlightened textbooks:

1. Any distinction between *shall* and *will*.
2. Any reference to the split infinitive.
3. Elimination of *like* as a conjunction.
4. Objection of the phrase "different than."
5. Objection of "He is one of those boys who *is*."
6. Objection of "The reason . . . is because . . ."
7. Objection to *myself* as a polite substitute for *me* as in "I understand you will meet Mrs. Jones and myself at the station."
8. Insistence on the possessive case standing before a gerund.

According to Pooley: "These items and many others like them will still remain cautionary matters left to the teacher's discretion. In evaluating the writing of superior students, teachers could call these distinctions to their attention and point out the value of observing them. But this is a very different matter from setting a basic usage standard to be maintained. It is fair to say the items listed in the basic table lie outside the tolerable limits of acceptable, current, informal usage; those omitted from the base table are tolerated at least, and in some instances are in very general use."

Teachers should analyze the speech patterns of children in their classes and determine which speech terms are the most frequently misused. These would then be eliminated by a carefully worked out plan. For example, if children are continually using certain terms incorrectly, a tape recording of their speech could be made. Before it is played back, the teacher can call attention to the term that is being used incorrectly. Since children are habituated to speaking the way they do, they must first identify a bad habit before they can change it. They must also want to change it, and they must get help in doing so.

One motivating technique can be a number of short oral skits, in which the teacher incorporates a number of items with which children need help. The skits can be tape recorded so that the students are reinforced by hearing themselves using correctly stated terms or expressions.

A technique used in the fifth and sixth grades requires a tape recording of a person going for a job interview. The interviewee exhibits incorrect speech usage and colloquialisms. After discussing why this person would have difficulty in getting the job, students can be asked to give some helpful suggestions to him or her for the next interview.

The teacher can also ask children to listen to each other's speech and help plan some word usage lessons based on what they hear.

In order to help children become more sensitive to their language, intermediate-grade students could discuss the importance of speaking well and the role of the linguist. Students can then be told that they are going to be classroom linguists, who describe how someone speaks. The students tape children's speech during many classroom activities, as well as during lunch, free play, and physical education. (All children who are being taped should know about it and give permission for the taping.)

When the tapes are played back, students should be asked whether children use the same kind of English in all activities. They should be encouraged to describe differences that exist in speech in the various activities recorded.

The Utilization of Traditional Grammar in the Classroom

The only justification for traditional grammar's use is when it contributes to students'

understanding of language and helps them to communicate better in oral and written forms. Studies have shown that diagraming, which was much used by upper-grade teachers, does not significantly improve a student's language ability. Similarly, the ability to parse or state the various parts of speech of a sentence does not aid a student's writing ability. Can we justify its place in the classroom?

If traditional grammar is properly used in the classroom, it can help children to use language better and to be more sensitive to language. This links knowledge of grammatical terms with the way they are used. The emphasis in all exercises should be on word usage and the way words are used in sentences—not on parsing. The sample exercise given below is based on this dual approach.

Weakness noted in pupils' oral and written language	Suggestions for functional practice
What do we need to know about *nouns* in order to speak and write effectively?	
Approximately Grades 3 and 4 Using sentences that are weak and lacking in variety because of careless choice of nouns.	Write a sentence on the chalkboard such as: "The tiny boat sank." Cover the noun to show how important it is. Find nouns in other sentences. List the nouns in an interesting picture. Copy sentences from pupils' work omitting the nouns, such as "_____ grow in south Jersey." Have pupils suggest nouns to fill in the blank (trees, cranberries, vegetables, and so on). Show how the nouns change the meaning of the sentence. Suggest nouns that fit a sentence better than other nouns, such

as: "A terrified man ran away." "Man" might be changed to "thief," "tramp," and so on. Apply this procedure to pupils' own written work.

Pulips may also choose the best noun when several are given: "With a (yell, shriek, cry) of (fear, dismay, terror), the mountain climber fell into the (hole, pit, opening)."

Verbs and Nouns as Homographs   Some exercises help children to be better readers of homographs (words which are spelled alike but have different meanings). (See Chapter 8 and the discussion on homonyms, homophones, or homographs in Chapter 12.) Children are given a number of sentences containing homographs used as either nouns or verbs. The emphasis should be on how the word is used in the sentence, since that will determine the meaning of the sentence.

This is a sharp *saw.*
Help me *saw* this tree in half.

You have a long *climb* ahead of you.
Let's *climb* that mountain.

The wounded man left a *trail* of blood.
The police will *trail* him until he is caught.

Adjectives as Modifiers in Writing   Written description is very important. Children should be involved in various activities to develop this skill. A useful method of teaching adjectives would be to show them as qualifiers or modifiers, which help a person to describe some object, place, or thing better. By giving examples, children will see how adjectives are used in writing. Children can be asked to describe a picture of a man. Just stating that the picture

is of a man does not give the class very much information. If it is further stated that he is a tall, fat man the class is better able to distinguish him from the class of all men.

Structural Grammar in the Classroom

Activities in structural grammar are concerned with sentence patterns. Earlier in this chapter, five basic sentence patterns were given. The simplest one consists of a noun and verb, such as:

Subject	Predicate
Noun or Pronoun	Verb (Intransitive)
Birds	fly.

If a determiner is added, it would read:

Determiner	Verb
Noun or Pronoun	
The birds	fly.

Children in the third, fourth, or fifth grade can be asked to participate in these activities using the pattern given above:

1. Write two sentences similar to the pattern. For example:

Men work.
Dogs bark.

2. Choose another word which would fit in the place of "fly" in the sentence "Birds fly," which would make sense.
3. Choose another word which would fit in the place of "birds" in the sentence "Birds fly," which makes sense.
4. Add some words to describe the birds.
5. Add some words to describe "fly." For example: Do the birds fly swiftly or slowly?

The most frequently used pattern is:

Noun	Verb	Noun
	Transitive	
Boys	eat	cake.

Students can be asked to:

1. Choose another word to replace "boys" in the pattern.
2. Choose another word to replace "cake."
3. Write two sentences similar to the pattern.
4. Add some words to describe "boys."
5. Add some words to describe "cake."

In the sentence pattern:

Noun	Verb	Noun
	Linking	
Mary	is	a girl.

students can be asked to:

1. Write two sentences similar to the pattern given above.
2. Choose another word to replace "Mary" in the pattern.
3. Choose another word to replace "girl."

Transformational Grammar's Place in the Classroom

Transformationalists—those linguists who emphasize sentences, the positioning of words in sentences, and the expansion of sentences—seem to offer a fruitful approach to helping students in writing. *Good* teachers, when dealing with supposedly traditional grammar, have always emphasized that the way words are used in a sentence determines the meaning of the sentence. Teachers in the elementary grades need not use all of the linguists' terminology or rules, but they can help children see how to construct a great many sentences from one sentence in the pattern: $S \rightarrow NP + VP$. Students can state sentences to fit this pattern and then transforms (variations) of these sentences can be given. For example: "She is happy" is changed to "Is she happy?" Students need not learn the complicated rules of transformation to make this change.

As children's language expands, due to an increase in short-term memory, the teacher can help them carry this expansion over into their writings. For example, when young children first start writing sentences, they tend to be short and simple:

I can run.
I can play.
I can jump.

As children gain in language competence, they tend to increase sentence length by adding the conjunction "and."

I can run and I can play and I can jump.

Gradually, the teacher helps children to delete the conjunction, "and," and the verb, "can," from the sentence and insert commas. Now the sentence reads:

I can run, play, and jump.

The instructor can also teach students to write more descriptively by helping them expand their sentences. "The cat runs" does not tell us very much about which cat is running, where it is running, or how it is running. The addition of certain kinds of words to the sentence will help children with both oral and written communication.

Some activities for both primary- and intermediate-grade students follow.

Primary Level

1. Given the following words, see how many sentences you can make:

a	funny	happy
the	clown	is
		man

2. Make one sentence out of the following three sentences:

The dog barks.
The cat meows.
The horse neighs.

Intermediate Level

1. Given the following words, see how many sentences you can make using all the words:

on	who	a
hungry	tired	dog
bag	and	was
car	in	red
brown	slept	the
white	the	and

2. Make one sentence out of the following three sentences:

The sailor is tall and thin.
He walks with a limp.
He became involved in a fight with some men.

As was already stated, knowledge of the terms "adjectives" and "adverbs" or "noun phrases" or "verb phrases" will not make any difference in developing writing skill. Being involved in the act of writing and knowledge of word usage will make a difference. When students are describing something, the teacher can say that "red" is an adjective and, since it tells us something about a noun, it modifies or qualifies the noun. Such comments add to learning and, as in all other areas of the language arts, balance and moderation are key words. Word usage must be taught, but only as a tool to help children to communicate better, not as an end in itself.

The Place of Morphology in the Classroom

An exciting prospect for students and teachers lies in the area of morphology, which can help students to understand the structure of words, as well as expand their vocabularies. The emphasis should be on extending meaning vocabulary by combining affixes and combining forms or roots, rather than in the analysis of morphological units.

The table on page 380 consists of some prefixes and combining forms and some vocabulary words derived from them. See how many words you can define. (See Chapter 8 for segment on vocabulary expansion.)

The Treatment of Grammar in Elementary English Series Textbooks

From a survey of the treatment of grammar in some of the major language arts series now in use in schools, it appears that grammar holds a prominent position in most of those series. It also appears that many of the series are combining the new grammar terminology with the old or traditional terminology. Almost all of the texts of the late 1970s separate grammar from word usage. The emphasis is on sentence patterns, sentence types, and sentence analysis rather than diagraming. Sentences are analyzed in terms of subject-predicate structure, and parts of speech are emphasized. The trend toward the generating of sentences and sentence expansion and combining, which was noticeable in the early 1970s, is continuing, which is good in the author's opinion. The trend away from diagraming is also good; however, the strong emphasis in many texts on sentence structure analysis and the naming of parts of speech is not. The emphasis should be on sentence writing. There is nothing wrong with students learning the parts of speech and being able to name them, but continuous drill in this area is not warranted. For example, when children are expanding sentences and using descriptive phrases, the labels for the descriptive words or phrases can be given. However, the naming of the parts of speech should not become an end in itself, nor should the analysis of sentences. Recognition

Prefixes	Combining Forms	Vocabulary Words
a-without	anthropo-man	anthropology, apodal
ante-before	astro-star	astronomy, astrology
arch-main, chief	audio-hearing	audiology, auditory, audition, audible
bi-two	auto-self	automatic, autocracy, binary, biped
cata-down	bene-good	benefit, catalog
circum-around	bio-life	biology, biography, autobiography
hyper-excessive	chrono-time	chronological, hypertension
hypo-under	cosmo-world	microcosm, cosmology
in-not	gamy-marriage	monogamy, bigamy, polygamy
inter-between, among	geo-earth	interdepartmental, geology
mis-wrong, bad	gram-written or drawn	telegram, mistake
mono-one, alone	graph-written or drawn, instrument	telegraph, monarchy
post-after	logo-speak	theology, logical, catalogue
re-backward, again	macro-large	macrocosm, return
trans-across	micro-small	microscope, transatlantic
	mis-hate	misanthrope, misogamist
	poly-many	polyglot
	retro-backward	retrorocket
	pod-foot, feet	pseudopod
	scope-instrument for seeing	microscope
	phobia-fear	monophobia
	theo-god	theocracy
	pseudo-false	pseudoscience

practice helps make students aware of the different types of sentences that they encounter in their everyday reading; it also gives students experience in working with the various sentence types. The key, however, is in giving students the real writing experience needed to generate the various types of sentences.

Teachers and Textbooks

Teachers should not be intimidated by textbooks. They should not be afraid to deviate from the book and try out some of their own ideas. If teachers want to help students to be more creative, they will have to behave more creatively themselves. If there is something in the text that violates certain principles or that is not "appropriate" for some students, teachers need not slavishly adhere to the text. On the other hand, if the text presents some ideas that teachers feel are needed and seem promising for their students, teachers should use these as springboards to generate their own ideas. The textbook is only a guide to some of the possibilities that are available to teachers and students. The teacher as the manager, the innovator, and the organizer, based on the needs and interests of the students, is the determiner of what to include rather than the textbook writers.

It appears that an eclectic and pragmatic approach with an emphasis on word usage is the one that is most valuable in the teaching of grammar. Teachers can use vocabulary from traditional grammar, as well as some of the new terminology, and the sentence patterns provided by descriptive grammar can also be used as an aid in gaining insight into language. However, the emphasis should be on speaking and writing, rather than on diagraming or drill on parts of speech. The expansion and generating of sentences from generative transformational grammar, without its accompanying prescriptiveness, is useful in the writing program.

Student's Name:
Grade:
Teacher:

Diagnostic Checklist in Word Usage for Standard English[40]

	Yes	No
1. Elimination of baby talk.		
2. Correct usage in speech and writing of pronouns such as *I, me, he, him, she, her, they, them.* (Exception: *it's me.*)		
3. Agreement of subject and verb.		
4. Agreement of pronoun and antecedent: "The men and women went to work. They were late."		
5. Correct past tenses of common irregular verbs, such as *saw, gave, took, brought, bought, stuck.*		
6. Correct use of past participles after auxiliaries: *has gone, had gone, was gone.*		
7. Elimination of the double negative: "We don't have *no* apples," and so on.		
8. Elimination of analogical forms such as *ain't, hisn, hern, ourn, theirselves,* and so on.		
9. Correct use of possessive pronouns such as *my, mine, his, hers, theirs, ours.*		
10. Mastery of the distinction between *its*, possessive pronoun, and *it's, "it is."*		
11. Placement of *have* (or its phonetic reduction to *v*) between *I* and a past participle.		
12. Elimination of *them* as a demonstrative pronoun.		
13. Elimination of *this here* and *that there*.		
14. Mastery of use of *a* and *an* as articles.		
15. Correct use of personal pronouns in compound constructions: as subject (Mary and I), as object (Mary and me), as object of preposition (to Mary and me).		
16. The use of *we* before an appositional noun when subject; *us* when object.		
17. Correct number agreement with the phrases *there is, there are, there was, there were.*		
18. Elimination of *he don't, she don't, it don't*.		
19. Elimination of *learn* for *teach*, *leave* for *let*.		

[40]Adapted from ibid.

20. Elimination of pleonastic (redundant) subjects: *my brother he, my mother she, that fellow he.*
21. Proper agreement in number with antecedent pronouns *one* and *anyone, everyone, each, no one.* With *everybody* and *none* some tolerance of number seems acceptable now.
22. The use of *who* and *whom* as reference to persons. (But note,"Who did he give it to?" is tolerated in all but very formal situations. In the latter, "To whom did he give it?" is preferable.)
23. Accurate use of *said* in reporting the words of a speaker in the past.
24. Correction of *lay down* to *lie down.*
25. The distinction between *good* as adjective and *well* as adverb: He spoke *well.*
26. Elimination of *can't hardly, all the farther* (for *as far as*), and "Where is he (she, it) at?"

Summary

Some knowledge of the structure of our language is desirable. It can obstruct learning and the love of good language if presented at the wrong time with the wrong approach to the wrong subjects.

> There is no evidence that memorization of rules would help the native speaker to improve his acquired capacity to invent and interpret new sentences without recourse to book-learned rules. Such a prescriptive requirement might even undermine the student's creative use of introspection in language study and deprive him of his natural birthright.[41]

Grammar, which is composed of both morphology and syntax, is concerned with the study of the way language is used. Since it is merely descriptive, there is no good, bad, right, or wrong grammar. Word usage is differentiated from grammar in that standards are involved and choices are made in the areas of speaking and writing. Traditional grammar, which is based on Greek and Latin, has been taught in school as a prescriptive system; it is composed of rules from which one cannot deviate. New grammar, which is based on linguists' description of American-English, is replacing traditional grammar in many school systems. However, confusion exists because of the complexity of the new grammar and because of the lack of agreement among linguists on both terminology and methods of classifying the phonemic system.

At the beginning of this chapter a discussion on the source of the new grammars—such as structural and transformational grammar—was given. Students who speak nonstandard English use a grammar that deviates in structure from standard English, but that is not wrong or bad.

Word usage activities, as well as methods of

[41]Lefevre, op. cit., p. 323.

LESSON PLAN I

Primary-Grade Level

1. Students will be able to recognize when the word "saw" should be used in a sentence.
2. Students will be able to state four sentences using the word "saw."
3. Students will be able to write four sentences correctly using the word "saw."

Preparation

A picture of a grocery store scene is not visible. A newsprint paper with four prepared questions is not visible. A table with a sign saying "Mystery Table" and a large black cloth covering it is in front of the room.

Introduction

"Yesterday we talked about some of the things we saw on our way to school. Today we will be writing sentences about some of the things we looked at using the word 'saw.' Before we begin, I'd like everyone to look at our mystery table and try to imagine what is under the table cover."

Development

"There are a number of different things under the cover of the table. I'm going to call on a number of you to come to the table, look under the cover, and then tell us what you saw."

Each child comes to the table and tells what he or she saw. Ask the children why they used the word "saw" rather than "see" when they told about what was under the table cover. Ask them whether it sounds right to say, "A little while ago I see a little doll under the cover," or "A little while ago I saw a little doll under the cover."

Help them to come up with the generalization that the word "saw" is used when something has already taken place, whereas "see" is used when something is presently taking place.

Hang and display the grocery store picture. Ask children to look at the picture closely and see if they can answer these questions:

What did the lady buy?
What kind of machine do we use to find how much our groceries cost?
Where do we go to pay for our groceries?

Cover the picture. Ask the following questions:

What did you see that is good for breakfast?
What did you see that is good to drink?
What vegetables did you see?
What did you see that is not for sale?

Ask children how they would begin each sentence, and why they would begin each sentence with "I saw."

Summary

Pull main points of lesson together. To determine if they are using the word "saw" correctly, ask children if they can tell about some things they saw on the way to school.

LESSON PLAN II

Intermediate-Grade Level

Behavioral Objectives

Students will be able to recognize incomplete sentences.
Students will be able to construct sentences which convey complete thoughts.
Students will be able to define "communication."

Preparation

On display is an enlarged comic strip of two cartoon characters saying the following words to one another:

Are They Communicating?

Conversation I	Conversation II
Character A: "You"	Character A: "Oh!"
Character B: "Are?"	Character B: "You, too?"
Character A: "I"	Character A: "Yes!"
Character B: "They"	Character B: "Oh!"

Introduction

"We've been working with improving our sentences so that we can say what we mean better. Who remembers some of the problems we talked about that could take place if someone receives the wrong message? Yes, in an emergency, phoning for help, and so on. Good! We said that if we don't give correct information or complete information we would not get the right kind of help.

"I would like everyone to look at the bulletin board and our two cartoon characters. In which conversation are they involved in having a communication problem. Why? Have any of you ever had any problem in communication? Today, we are going to work with the area of communication and the importance of being able to state and write complete thoughts."

Development

"Before we can decide if our two characters are communicating, we have to know what 'communicate' means."

During the discussion the teacher should elicit responses from students concerning the meaning of the term "communication." It should be defined as "an exchange of ideas; both the speaker and listener are able to understand and respond to one another."

"Now that we all can define communication, in which conversation in the cartoon are the characters not communicating, and why not?"

A discussion should develop concerning the conversations. Students should recognize that the characters in Conversation I are not communicating because they do not have enough information to be able to respond logically. In Conversation II, even though it is as brief as Conversation I, the characters are communicating because they are conveying a complete thought. Ask students to change Conversation I so that the characters would be able to understand one another using the words they already are saying. A number of different kinds of conversations should be elicited. For example:

Character A: "You are going, aren't you?"
Character B: "Are you?"
Character A: "I probably will, but Chip and Nutty aren't."
Character B: "They told me that they would be able to go."

After a number of possible conversations have been thought up, put the following phrases and sentences on the board and have the children decide which are complete sentences. Then convert the phrases into complete sentences:

1. The parents named.
2. The baby was.
3. Run!
4. John and Mary.
5. Look!
6. He called.
7. The two girls were.
8. The man ran.
9. He jumped.
10. Running through the woods.

Summary

Pull the main points of the lesson together. Have students give examples of complete and incomplete sentences.

presenting traditional and new grammars in the classroom, were discussed. Activities showing how transformational generative grammar can contribute to children's maturity as writers, if used in a nonprescriptive way, were also suggested. Meaning-vocabulary expansion, an area of morphology, was named as an area to be explored by teachers and students.

The treatment of grammar in some elementary-grade English textbooks was investigated. Although a number of authors of such texts disavow the importance of knowledge of grammar in helping students to speak and write better, there is nevertheless an emphasis on parts of speech in some texts. It appears that many books are using an eclectic approach, drawing from traditional, structural, and transformational grammar. A Diagnostic Checklist on "Word Usage for Standard English" was also presented.

Now that you have read this chapter you should have mastered the given teacher competencies presented at the beginning of this chapter.

As a further aid, two examples of lesson plans are presented at the end of this chapter. Using these as a guide, see if you can construct another one.

Suggestions for Thought Questions and Activities

1. You are a teacher in a middle school, grades 4 to 6, who has just been placed on the curriculum committee to help develop the grammar program in your school. What information must you have to be able to make an effective contribution? What kind of program would you advocate? Why?

2. You have just been appointed to a committee whose responsibility is to present the new language program, based on transformational grammar, to parents. How would you go about doing this in an informative and creative way?

3. Develop a creative lesson plan in the area of word usage concerned with the double negative.

4. How would you help a child who speaks in nonstandard English to acquire standard English sentence structure? Explain.

5. Using knowledge of transformational generative grammar, develop a sentence expansion lesson plan avoiding the use of prescriptiveness.

6. You are to be on a panel which will discuss the merits of the teaching of grammar in your elementary school. What position would you take? Why?

SELECTED BIBLIOGRAPHY

Bach, Emmon. *An Introduction to Transformational Grammar*. New York: Holt, Rinehart and Winston, 1964.

Bloomfield, Leonard. *Language*. New York: Holt, Rinehart and Winston, 1966.

Chomsky, Noam. *Current Issues in Linguistic Theory*. The Hague: Mouton, 1964.

Corcoran, Gertrude. *Language Arts in the Elementary School: A Modern Linguistic Approach*. New York: Ronald Press, 1970.

Fromkin, Victoria A., and R. Rodman. *An Introduction to Language*, 2d ed. New York: Holt, Rinehart and Winston, 1978.

Gleason, H. A., Jr. *Linguistics and English Grammar*. New York: Holt, Rinehart and Winston, 1965.

Golden, Ruth I. *Improving Patterns of Language Usage*. Detroit, Mich.: Wayne State University Press, 1960.

Hall, Robert A. *Linguistics and Your Language*. Garden City, N.Y.: Doubleday, 1960.

Hockett, Charles F. *A Course in Modern Linguistics*. New York: Macmillan, 1958.

Hughes, John P. *Linguistics and Language Teaching*. New York: Random House, 1968.

———. *The Science of Language*. New York: Random House, 1962.

Hunt, Kellogg W. *Grammatical Structures Written at Three Grade Levels*. Urbana, Ill.: National Council of Teachers of English, 1965.

Kennedy, Arthur G. *English Usage*. New York: Appleton-Century-Crofts, 1942.

Lamb, Pose. *Linguistics in Proper Perspective*, 2d ed. Columbus, Ohio: Merrill, 1977.

Lefevre, Carl A. *Linguistics, English, and the Language Arts*. Boston: Allyn and Bacon, 1970.

Liebert, Burt. *Linguistics and the New English Teacher*. New York: Macmillan, 1971.

Pooley, Robert C. *Teaching English Grammar*. New York: Appleton-Century-Crofts, 1957.

——. *The Teaching of English Usage*, 2d ed. Urbana, Ill.: National Council of Teachers of English, 1974.

Postman, Neil, and Charles Weingartner. *Linguistics: A Revolution in Teaching*. New York: Dell, 1966.

Roberts, Geoffrey R. *English in Primary Schools*. London: Routledge & Kegan Paul, 1972.

Rosenberg, Sheldon, ed. *Sentence Production: Development in Research and Theory*. New York: Halsted Press, 1977.

Rubin, Dorothy. "Developing Word Usage Skills," in *The Primary Grade Teacher's Language Arts Handbook* (New York: Holt, Rinehart and Winston, 1980).

——. "Developing Word Usage Skills," in *The Intermediate Grade Teacher's Language Arts Handbook* (New York: Holt, Rinehart and Winston, 1980).

Shane, Harold G. *Linguistics and the Classroom Teacher*. Washington, D. C.: Association for Supervision and Curriculum Development, 1967.

Thomas, Owen. *Transformational Grammar and the Teacher of English*. New York: Holt, Rinehart and Winston, 1965.

Preparing
For
Instruction

fifteen

The Teacher as Manager of the Language Arts Program

EXAMPLES OF TEACHER COMPETENCIES

1. The teacher will be able to state factors that profoundly influence children's learning in school.
2. The teacher will be able to explain the role of planning in the language arts program.
3. The teacher will be able to discuss the importance of student-teacher planning in the language arts program.
4. The teacher will be able to explain how lesson plans are used as tools for teachers.
5. The teacher will be able to state the parts of the lesson plan.
6. The teacher will be able to construct lesson plans in all language arts areas.
7. The teacher will be able to explain how the classroom physical environment influences learning.
8. The teacher will be able to explain how proxemics influences verbal communication.
9. The teacher will be able to describe "self-fulfilling prophecy."
10. The teacher will be able to explain why he or she is the key to a good language arts program.
11. The teacher will be able to state some of the criteria that are used to evaluate teaching performance.
12. The teacher will be able to explain the role of teacher-competency-based objectives in evaluating teaching performance.
13. The teacher will be able to state factors that affect teacher performance.
14. The teacher will be able to explain how self-evaluation helps teachers gain insight into their teaching performance.
15. The teacher will be able to state criteria for effective evaluation.

It is the supreme art of the teacher to awaken joy in creative expression and knowledge.

ALBERT EINSTEIN

Introduction

There are a number of factors which profoundly influence children's learning in school. These factors range from teachers' insight into their own personalities to the physical surroundings which include the school plant, the classroom, the walls of the rooms, the corridors, the play area, and so on. All of these variables will determine how teachers organize for learning and how they manage the learning environment. Although teachers are not managers in the business sense, they are responsible for a group of pupils and are interested in the "largest return" for an investment of time, energy, and money. Many persons would frown on looking at human behavior as an "output" and would claim that such an attitude is dehumanizing. But is it?

Are not teachers interested in making a positive, beneficial difference to the learning of their students? "A teacher is a person engaged in interactive behavior with one or more students for the purpose of effecting a change in those students."[1] In order to accomplish this goal teachers must have rules or methods and also ways to evaluate whether the desired learnings have been achieved. And they must not make unfounded assumptions about the abilities of their students.

It is not possible to give an exhaustive, indepth discussion of all the components with which teachers must deal in this chapter. However, unless teachers understand their roles, the firm foundation on which a strong language arts

program can be mounted cannot be established. In the *Second Handbook of Research on Teaching* the statement is made that the:[2]

> . . . teacher's primary task is to design and engage pupils in learning activities sufficiently engrossing that pupils find those activities substantially more attractive than proscribed alternatives (which often have attractions of their own). Under these circumstances, maintaining "the students' absorption in the task at hand" and getting their attention are tasks of great immediacy and importance both for instructional and managerial reasons.

How teachers gain students' attention and keep them engaged in these tasks is a most important concern of educators. The successful accomplishment of this concern depends on the teaching technique and incentives that are used, the teacher's personality and motivating techniques, providing challenging seat work, the ability to make smooth transitions from one topic to another, and a knowledge of individual differences.

Teacher Planning for Learning

Teacher planning is an essential part of the language arts program, as well as any other program. Planning helps guide teachers in making choices about what to include in the language arts program, how to organize the program, and how to develop it. Effective planning also helps teachers to clarify their thinking about objectives, students' needs, interests, and readiness levels, as well as what kinds of motivating techniques to use. Good planning guarantees the wisest use of time, assuring that balance and sequence will prevail in teaching–learning activities.

[1]John D. McNeil and W. James Popham, "The Assessment of Teacher Competence," in *Second Handbook of Research on Teaching*, Robert M. W. Travers, ed. (Chicago: Rand McNally, 1973), p. 219.

[2]Robert Dreeben, "The School as a Workplace," in *Second Handbook of Research on Teaching*, Robert M. W. Travers, ed. (Chicago: Rand McNally, 1973), p. 466.

Student-Teacher Planning

Student-teacher planning is rapidly becoming accepted by teachers and is effective if properly used. The role of the teacher in planning with students must consist of a judicious balance between accepting students' contributions and managing and controlling the teaching–learning situation. For pupil-teacher planning to be productive, teachers must recognize that students' involvement in some decisions will help these students to become more self-reliant and more interested in the planned activity.

Teachers must also realize that student-teacher planning will only work if students are helped to plan. Such planning should begin in the pri-

mary grades, where the teacher and children discuss and plan the topics and activities that they will engage in during morning and afternoon sessions. The teacher can assure wise decision-making by helping students to understand why they should not plan certain activities consecutively. They should also state scheduling constraints, such as group plans, seat work, special art periods, special music periods, and so on.

In the language arts areas students should be given opportunities to express the kinds of activities in which they would like to engage. For example, if students are interested in puppetry, creative dramatics, or writing skits, time for these activites should be planned.

SCENARIO: TEACHER-PUPIL PLANNING

Lower-intermediate grade:—ten boys, nine girls, one female teacher. A suburban school with children from a middle socioeconomic background. The classroom contains desks clustered together in groups of four. Learning centers are visible in easily accessible areas.

Time: beginning of the school day
Date: middle of the week (middle of the school year)

Action

Children arrive in classroom. They are smiling and chatting with one another. Mrs. Hill greets each of her students and seems to have something special to say to each. After the children have settled down, Mrs. Hill asks if anyone has anything special that they would like to share with the class. Four children raise their hands. Mrs. Hill asks each to share his or her special item. After the children share their special items, Karen comes to the front of the room and reads her favorite poem. Mrs. Hill thanks her, and then she reminds Seth that tomorrow he will be reading his special poem to the class. "Remember," Mrs. Hill says, "you do not have to know the poem by heart. The poem you choose to

read to the class should be one that you enjoy and that you think your classmates will enjoy hearing. I'm very pleased with the poems everyone has chosen to share with us. Some of them have also been really funny."

A child comes to the chalkboard on which a large sheet of paper is attached with masking tape. Mrs. Hill says, "Cynthia is ready to write our plans for the day. Let's help her. Don't forget to carry over any of our unfinished plans from yesterday."

A child raises his hand. Mrs. Hill calls on him. The child says, "Yesterday, we said that we would finish making our hand puppets and that we would begin working on our scripts for the puppet shows." "Good," says Mrs. Hill, "let's put that down." Many of the children in the class show agreement by saying "yes," by vigorously shaking their heads, or by making some affirming comment to a neighbor. Another child raises her hand. Mrs. Hill calls on her. "We challenged Mr. Smith's class in dodgeball yesterday." "That's right, we did, didn't we? Well, I've talked to Mr. Smith and we've decided if it's all right with you that we would begin the tournament this afternoon."

A child raises her hand. "We have to continue working on our science experiments." Another child raises his hand and says that Mrs. Hill had asked that someone remind her and the class to set aside some time to work on their word puzzle booklets. Another child raises her hand and says that they were supposed to leave time to work in their groups on role playing their special stories on life in colonial times. Mrs. Hill says, "I'd like to add something, too. Let's put down continuing to work with the metric system in our learning center, writing a story about a child's life in the colonial period, reading groups, math groups, and working on individual projects in our learning centers."

This is what the plans looked like:

Finish making hand puppets
Work on scripts for puppet shows
Dodgeball tournament with Mr. Smith's class after lunch
Continue work on science experiments
Work on word puzzle booklets
Role play stories on life in colonial times
Work with the metric system
Write a story on a child's life in the colonial period
Reading groups
Math groups
Work on individual projects in learning centers.

Mrs. Hill thanks Cynthia for writing everything so clearly on the large newsprint paper. She then asks if anyone has any questions. Seth raises his hand. Mrs. Hill calls on him. Seth says, "Mrs. Hill, you said that as long as we finished our special assignments we could work in any of our interest areas that we wanted. Well, John, Mary, and I will need extra time to work on our science experiment, and we need to do it today. Is that all right?" "Why don't I meet with the three of you in a moment to discuss this and see what we can work out."

Children without any cue from Mrs. Hill begin work at their seats, in learning centers, and in groups. Mrs. Hill walks around the room, nods approval to some, says "good" to others, and stops to ask a question or two. She then goes to meet with John, Mary, and Seth.

Teaching and the Lesson Plan

Lesson plans are tools or aids for teachers. They serve as guides and are necessary for good teaching. Although experienced teachers use more succinct lesson plans than a novice would, the plans are always useful. It is not necessary for experienced teachers to put down every question that they will ask or write in every detail, because they are better able to anticipate children's questions and utilize students' cues to provide meaningful and interesting lessons.

The beginning teacher, on the other hand, is more insecure and so tends to prepare more detailed lesson plans. This is good until experience takes over. Although the detail of the planning will vary according to the individual instructor, the parts included in the lesson plan are similar.

The success of any lesson depends on the preplanning and preparation for the lesson, as well as its execution. If students' past experiences, interests, and previous learnings are not considered in the plan, there is less likelihood for a successful lesson. Similarly, the teacher must estimate the proper amount of time necessary for the lesson, know the availability of materials and books needed for the lesson, and have prepared any special charts, displays, work papers, and so forth that are to be used in the lesson.

Many times a lesson may act as a springboard for a number of other lessons. Subsequent lessons may extend, reinforce, review, or provide application.

Classroom Physical Environment

The discussion so far in this chapter has focused on the teacher and planning. However, the physical environment in which teachers and pupils are housed can and does affect the teaching–learning situation, as well as the teachers' and students' behavior.

Environmental psychology, which is still in its infancy, is a field of extreme importance. It focuses on behavior in relation to physical settings. "Physical settings—simple or complex—evoke complex human responses in the form of feelings, attitudes, values, expectancies, and desires and it is in this sense as well as in their known physical properties that their relationships to human experience and behavior must be understood."[3]

It is important for teachers to recognize that

[3]Harold M. Proshansky, et. al., "The Influence of the Physical Environment on Behavior: Some Basic Assumptions," in *Environmental Psychology*, Harold M. Proshansky, et al., eds. (New York: Holt, Rinehart and Winston, 1970), p. 28.

PARTS OF THE DAILY LESSON PLAN

The lesson plan presented here has five parts.

1. The Objectives for the Lesson

Objectives should be stated in behavioral terms (that which can be directly observed and is able to be measured). This part is primarily for the instructor. The more precise teachers are in stating objectives, the better they will be able to plan and execute a successful lesson.

2. The Introduction

The introduction includes the following three areas:

a. Relating the lesson to the students' past experiences.
b. Using motivating techniques to gain the attention and interest of students.
c. Informing pupils about the purpose for the lesson.

Students' knowledge of the objectives of the lesson is important because it helps them to know what they are expected to accomplish.

3. The Development

This is the "heart" of the lesson. Each step in the sequence is enumerated. (The more experienced the teacher is, the less detail is given.) The questions, examples, materials, and activities used to help the students to attain the objectives are stated.

4. Summary and Evaluation

a. The summary ties the loose ends together and makes sure that learning is complete.
b. The behavioral objective should be restated and the evaluation should consist of evidence that the desired outcomes have been achieved.
c. The progress and interest of the children may be noted and standards of work evaluated.
d. Next steps and assignments may be defined.

5. The Preliminary Preparations

This involves any special arrangments that are necessary for the execution of the lesson plan, such as the arrangement of furniture in the classroom and special equipment or materials.

the constraints of the classroom physical setting will influence behavior as well as the ongoing activities. Windowless rooms and fixed desks will evoke one kind of student behavior; classrooms with windows and mobile desks and walls will evoke a different kind. For example, if a teacher arranges students' desks in five straight rows, five desks to a row, and emphasizes that the desks must remain in these exact positions, students' physical, emotional, and social behavior will be restricted. A certain atmosphere exists in the class, and the teacher is looked on as authoritarian and dominant. In such an environment communication can only take place with students adjacent to, behind, or in front of the individual. Since desks may not be moved, communication is not very satisfactory, and there are a number of other difficulties:

It almost encourages shy children to be inarticulate and to rely on the teacher to be their interpreter. The girl who answers a question or offers a comment from the front of the room may be quite inaudible to those sitting behind her, and she will certainly be unable to see their reaction to what she says. The boy who speaks from a seat near the back will probably be heard by the rest of the class, since he will have to use more volume in order to be heard by the teacher; but he will be little better informed than the girl at the front about the reactions of his fellow pupils, since he will be looking, for the most part, at the backs of their heads. Some children enter cheerfully into the competition to secure the teacher's attention and approval. Others find the whole situation threatening and become intellectually crippled by it. Others, of course, prefer to form their own systems of communication in their own part of the classroom.[4]

Such a classroom obviously does not lend itself to a good language arts environment where students feel free to communciate, probably because of the teacher's lack of knowledge in the area of proxemics.

Proxemics concerns the relationship of humans and space. It is a form of nonverbal communication which can have an effect on pupil-

[4]Elizabeth Richardson, "The Physical Setting and Its Influence on Learning," in *Environmental Psychology*, Harold M. Proshansky, et al., eds. (New York: Holt, Rinehart and Winston, 1970), p. 387.

teacher, as well as pupil-pupil, communication. Whether students sit at the front, center, side, or back of the classroom and the placement of the teacher in the room will determine to a degree the kind of verbal communication that can take place.[5] (See the bibliography for materials on proxemics.)

Other factors that teachers must take into account in the physical environment of the classroom concern heating, lighting, and acoustics. A room that is too hot or too cold, or one in which there are many competing stimuli, or one filled with glare will detrimentally affect the learning behavior of children.

Teachers must recognize that the physical setting of the classroom is an important and dynamic part of the learning environment because of the direct force it exerts on students' physical and mental well-being. The physical, emotional, and social environment all interact and help to establish the teaching–learning climate. Throughout this textbook, where appropriate, the various environments of the classroom have been analyzed in relation to the specific area under discussion. The emphasis has been on maintaining a comfortable, nonthreatening environment where mutual respect and trust can reign and where there is a balance of competition and cooperation.

A good language arts program cannot prevail where children feel intimidated, are isolated, and are reluctant to express themselves.

Teacher Assumptions

Teachers should recognize the dynamic interplay of variables described so far throughout this chapter. The more teachers know about their students, the better they are able to plan well for them. However, teachers must be cautioned against the self-fulfilling prophecy—where

teachers' assumptions about children come true, at least in part, because of the attitude of the teachers, which in turn becomes part of the children's reactions in the classroom. For example, if a child comes from a home environment not conducive to learning, the teacher may assume this child cannot learn beyond a certain level and thus may treat the child accordingly. If this happens, then the teacher's assumptions could become part of the child's own self-concept, further reinforcing the teacher's original expectations.

The Teacher as the Key to a Good Language Arts Program

Although a school may have the best equipment, the most advanced school plant, a superior curriculum, and children who want to learn, it must have "good teachers" so that the desired kind of learning can take place. With today's emphasis on accountability, the spotlight is even more sharply focused on "The Teacher." When conversation turns to "teacher evaluation," *everyone* seems to be an expert. But despite the surge in educational research, no definitive agreement exists as to how to evaluate teachers. If we were to go back through the ages we would find such familiar comments as:

> The teachers today just go on repeating in rigamarole fashion, annoy the students with constant questions and repeat the same things over and over again. They do not try to find out what the students' natural inclinations are, so that the students are forced to pretend to like their studies; nor do they try to bring out the best in their talents. As a result, the students hide their favorite readings and hate their teachers, are exasperated at the difficulty of their studies, and do not know what good it does them. Although they go through the regular course of instruction, they are quick to leave when they are through. This is the failure of education today.
>
> CONFUCIUS (*c.* 551–479 B.C.)

---

[5]*See* Peter Delefes and Barry Jackson, "Teacher-Pupil Interaction as a Function of Location in the Classroom," *Psychology in the Schools,* 9 (April 1972): 119–125.

When he [Abelard's teacher] lit the fire, he filled the house with smoke not with light.

PETER ABELARD (A.D. 1079–1142)

It seems as though time has stood still when we discuss teachers. If we were to ask a number of persons to state the qualities of a "good" teacher, we might produce a statement that reads like this:

> Good teachers need the eyes of an artist to know the varying personalities in their midst. They need a philosopher's insight to be able to deal with each individual. They are blessed with a "democratic spirit" and treat each person as someone worthy of dignity and respect, who is capable of self-direction. They have the patience of Job. They help those who need help to help themselves. They are astute diagnosticians. Their analytical ability is well developed. Their ebullience and enthusiasm know no bounds. Their experiences are manifold, their knowledge of the highest; and their judgment is superb.
> *Our Problem*—There are only mortals on earth. Teachers, too, are human beings.
> *Solution*—We must work within our limitations—be optimistic and idealistic, but realize that man is fallible.

However difficult it is to generate universally agreed upon statements and evaluative criteria, teachers must realize that they are always under scrutiny, formalized or not. For example, the first day that teachers enter their classrooms, the way they walk, their facial expressions, the way they speak, what they say, how they say it, their voices, their mannerisms, what they are wearing, their ages, their modus operandi, even their genders—all these and more affect their students, regardless of grade level. Will teachers measure up?

There are no precise measurements for determining what makes a good language arts teacher, nor are there commonly accepted instruments for determining good-teacher traits in general. One might ask, "Shouldn't a language arts teacher be superior in the area of communication skills?" But all teachers should be able to express themselves well, for we usually gain our first impression of individuals from their ability to communicate. How many of us have been impressed with a beautiful or handsome face only to have the image shattered when the person began to speak?

Good teachers are insightful about themselves and sensitive to the individual differences in their students. This is especially true of language arts teachers. They also recognize that there are certain skills and knowledge that they need in order to be called teachers.

Problems with Teacher Evaluation

Is teaching an art or is it a skill which can be scientifically analyzed? Research on the evaluation of the teacher and teaching has not been very productive, for many investigators claim that it is difficult to determine "good teaching."

> . . . practice has been seriously weakened by the false belief that there are scientific conclusions which correspond to good teaching. Teacher educators err when they promote teaching skills that are approximately consistent with scientific conclusions as if these skills were certain, confirmed answers about how a teacher should proceed to effect desirable consequences in learners.[6]

However complex and difficult the task may be, teachers are being evaluated by their students, supervisors, administrators, and indirectly by parents. When students report that they dislike school it is largely because of the teacher. Hardly anyone would refute the importance of the teacher's role in the classroom, and so, despite the obstacles, it becomes necessary to evaluate teachers and what they do in the classroom.

There is no unanimity on what factors affect teaching performance and student learning, or

[6]John D. McNeil and W. James Popham, "The Assessment of Teacher Competence." In Robert M. W. Travers, ed., *Second Handbook of Research on Teaching* (Chicago: Rand, McNally, 1973), p. 241.

on the objective criteria for evaluating teacher performance. Who is to do the evaluating? What kinds of instruments should be used? How consistent will the administration of the evaluative instrument be? How will the data be used? All these questions add to the problem.

Effective teaching is usually determined by a teacher's ability to produce desirable changes in students' learning behavior. If evaluation were only based on such changes, the task of teacher evaluation would be somewhat simplified. Students could be given pretests at the beginning of the term and posttests at the end of the term. The students' achievement, based on desired outcomes, could then be determined. But there are recognizable difficulties with this method. One is the assumption that students' achievements or nonachievements are directly due to their teachers. This is not so. As we have seen, there are many variables which affect student learning, such as home environment, ability level, motivation, peers, television, illness, and so on. What on the surface may appear to be simple is really not. In one class, children may produce better results on standardized tests than in another, but they may have grown to dislike the subject matter so intensely that they will avoid it in the future. These learned attitudes are not desirable, and will remain with the students longer than the subject matter they have learned. How should such teachers be evaluated?

It is beyond the scope of this book to try to answer or resolve the teacher-evaluation controversy. We will concern ourselves with possible descriptions and means for evaluating

---

TEACHER EVALUATION

Teacher: Socrates

A. *Personal qualifications*	Rating:	
1. Personal appearance	5	Dresses in an old sheet draped about his body.
2. Self-confidence	5	Not sure of himself—always asking questions.
3. Use of English	4	Speaks with a heavy Greek accent.
4. Adaptability	5	Prone to suicide by poison when under duress.
B. *Class Management*		
1. Organization	5	Does not keep a seating chart.
2. Room appearance	4	Does not have eye-catching bulletin boards.
3. Utilization of supplies	5	Does not use supplies.
C. *Teacher-pupil relationship*		
1. Tact and consideration	5	Places student in embarrassing situation by asking questions.
2. Attitude of class	2	Class is friendly.

D. *Techniques of teaching*		
1. Daily preparation	5	Does not keep daily lesson plans.
2. Attention to course of study	3	Quite flexible—allows students to wander to different topics.
3. Knowledge of subject matter	5	Does not know material—has to question pupils to gain knowledge.
E. *Professional attitude*		
1. Professional ethics	5	Does not belong to professional association or PTA.
2. In-service training	5	Complete failure here—has not even bothered to attend college.
3. Parent relations	5	Needs to improve in this area— parents trying to get rid of him.

Recommendation: Does not have a place in education—should not be rehired.

Source: John Gauss (El Cajon, Calif.), *Phi Delta Kappan* 43: outside back cover, January 1962. By permission.

those characteristics, traits, and competencies which language arts teachers should possess in order to present a good language arts program.

Teacher-Competency–Based Objectives[7]

One of the biggest problems in evaluating teachers is the lack of objective criteria. Evaluation cannot go far unless these are determined. Educators are attempting to generate explicit competency-based objectives, and, although this movement is gaining momentum, it is also gaining critics. No one set of teacher behaviors has yet been agreed on and it is unlikely that this will happen. Objectives will vary according to individual value orientation. And this is as it should be. However, competency-based programs seem to be a step in the right direction.

The definition used for "competency" in these programs is the "ability to do." Competency-based instruction embraces two essential characteristics. The first concerns *learning objectives;* these are defined in behavioral terms, so as to make their assessment easy, and are known by both learner and instructor. The second concerns *accountability,* so that the learner can demonstrate achievement of the competency at the required level and in an agreed upon manner. Competency-based programs are usually also personalized; that is they are self-paced and the student has some choice in the selection of objectives and learning activities. In competency-based education one is judged in terms of whether one has achieved a set of objectives and not on one's ranking relative to a specific group.[8]

Although teachers may possess specific competencies, this is no guarantee that students will

[7]It should be emphasized that the teacher competencies presented in this book are not an inclusive set. They are merely examples which should act as a guide for teachers. Each student is unique and will many times require personalized teaching-learning strategies.

[8]W. Robert Houston and Robert B. Howsam, "Change and Challenge," in W. Robert Houston and Robert B. Howsam, eds., *Competency-based Education* (Chicago: Science Research Associates, 1972), pp. 3–4.

learn from them. Yet it is less likely that students will learn from teachers who do not possess certain competencies.

In Chapter 18 information on the construction of behavioral objectives will be given. Also, at the beginning of each chapter in this book you have met examples of teacher competencies in various areas. These should all be helpful in judging the competence of a teacher.

Factors Affecting Teacher Performance

Although researchers claim there is not enough evidence to determine what good teaching is, students seem to have no difficulty in identifying traits that they feel a "good teacher" should possess. In numerous action researches with students the traits that come up most often are:

1. Remembers what it was like to be a student.
2. Respects all students.
3. Is interested in students.
4. Listens to students.
5. Allows students to express their feelings.
6. Encourages students.
7. Projects a nonthreatening environment.
8. Uses motivating techniques.
9. Includes pupils in planning.
10. Plans well.
11. Is willing to learn.
12. Makes learning fun.
13. Is knowledgeable in all areas.
14. Is knowledgeable in subject taught.
15. Is interested in subject taught.
16. Is enthusiastic.
17. Is creative and encourages creativity.
18. Uses many different techniques of teaching.
19. Uses a variety of materials and media in teaching.
20. Speaks well.
21. Has a nice appearance.
22. Has a good sense of humor.

The factors named—which include teacher characteristics, teaching methods and materials, and knowledge of subject matter and learning theory—are all areas in which teachers should have competence in order to be effective instructors.

A teacher who is enthusiastic, warm, and friendly; who knows the interests, needs, and readiness levels of individual students in the class; who uses the experiences and interests of the students to plan cooperatively for them; who employs a variety of teaching procedures such as discussion, review, questioning, and discovery; who uses a wide variety of materials and resources; and who knows adequate techniques for student evaluation is *a good teacher*.

Self-Evaluation

Good teachers evaluate themselves continuously in terms of how well their students do and how well they perform in relation to established criteria.

A self-evaluation method using videotape can be effective in giving teachers insight into their teaching performance. Teachers can list certain criteria as a guide for evaluation of performance; videotape themselves in action at different times of the day during different activities over one week; and then view the tapes to rate their abilities with these measures in mind. To insure objective rating, other teachers whom the teacher respects and trusts could be invited to comment on the teacher's performance. Student evaluations should also be encouraged.

Here are a number of questions that teachers can ask themselves in order to determine the effectiveness of their classroom performance:

1. Did I capitalize on students' interests?
2. Did I help to stimulate the students?
3. Was I usually enthusiastic about the lesson?
4. Was I clear in the presentation of objectives for the lesson?
5. Were my questions clear and easily understood?
6. Were my questions thought-provoking?
7. Did I use positive reinforcement?

8. Did I provide for individual differences?

9. Did I allow for adequate student-teacher interaction?

10. Did I allow adequate time for group discussions?

11. Was I always prepared?

12. Did I use various materials?

13. Did I speak clearly and distinctly, varying the pitch, tone, and volume of my voice?

14. Was I always able to make myself heard?

15. Did I make good use of the language arts periods?

16. Did I adequately prepare for the students in the various language arts lessons?

17. Did I use the games and gamelike activities as an integral part of the language arts lesson, rather than as ends in themselves?

18. Did I use games and gamelike activities and simulation activities to help children to overlearn certain skills?

19. Did I help students to understand the purposes of teacher-made and standardized tests?

20. Did I use teacher-made tests for diagnostic purposes?

21. Did I use teacher-made tests for review purposes?

The only way that many of these questions can be adequately answered is by observation of students' behavior. By videotaping lessons, teachers can better observe classroom behavior, including their own. This method will help teachers to evaluate progress in teaching areas in which they are weak by comparing videotapings over a period of time.

Evaluating the Teacher in Action

What criteria are used in judging teacher performance? The accompanying boxed material shows two hypothetical teachers in action. Which teacher is more effective?*

*Although these are two hypothetical classroom scenes, similar events can readily be observed in many schools.

SCENARIO ONE

Upper-elementary grade—11 girls, 4 boys, 1 male teacher. An inner-city school with children from a low socioeconomic background. The classroom contains five straight rows of desks, five to a row. In the upper right front of the classroom a TV set is prominently in view. The front chalkboards contain these instructions:

Bd. #1—Do pp. 81–84 in your English books.
Bd. #2—Two sentences about Halloween are on the board.
Bd. #3—Class spelling words. Spelling book p. 40. Write each word five times neatly.

The children are told to:

1. Finish the story.
2. Make interesting sentences.
3. Proofread.

Action

Children arrive in classroom after recess. They are still energized from their outdoor activities and some generalize this feeling to the classroom environment. They are highly agitated about some event that has occurred in the playground. The teacher sits on the sidelines and says nothing. The children exchange accusations with one another. After about five minutes the teacher walks to the front of the room and points to board #1, board #2, and to board #3. He says: "Do this work!" The teacher then walks to the back of the room with one boy. He and the boy sit down at a desk at the far end of the room and play chess for one hour and ten minutes.

Let's see what took place during this hour: One quite physically mature girl—we'll call her Jane—is still apparently rather agitated about events which had transpired during recess. She points a finger of accusation at a very heavy-set girl—whom we'll call Laurie—who is seated at a nearby desk. "It's all your fault," Jane says. "No, it isn't," says Laurie. At this point another girl, sitting next to Jane, also turns and points to Laurie and says vehemently, "Oh yes it is. I was standing in front of you and I heard you." Now two more girls and Jane stop what they are doing (they were supposed to be working on word usage problems in their language books) and also attack Laurie verbally. The accused Laurie, who has apparently learned how to survive such bombardments, completely ignores them. She does not raise her head from her book. She appears to be working on spelling words. Jane, who has never attempted to do any work, stands up, goes to the TV set, and turns it on. She sits down in the chair in front of the TV set and glues her attention to it. At this point everyone in the classroom also looks at the TV set—everyone, that is, except the chess players, the teacher, and one boy.

After about one hour and ten minutes (at 2:20) the teacher, Mr. D. Ense, terminates the chess game and goes to the front of the room, pointing in rapid succession at boards #1, #2, and #3. Then he says, "You know this has to be all finished before you can go home. [The class will be dismissed at 2:45.] Those who haven't been doing their work had better get to it."

Comment

Since a learning experience constitutes an interaction between a learner and the environment, we could say that the students were having learning experiences of a kind. However, what kind of learning was taking place is another matter. For effective learning, the teacher must try to structure and organize the classroom situation in such a way as to stimulate experiences and maximize total learning. The preplanning, the organization of learning experiences, and other preliminaries necessary for effective learning are not readily visible when an operating classroom is being observed. They must be inferred from the ongoing activities seen in the classroom. However, whatever the organizational pattern, if proper attention has been paid to the "learning prerequisites" and if they have been well planned, the results would be readily discernible in the learning behavior of the children.

It is difficult to infer that desired learning was taking place from the behavior of these students. The only child who was totally engrossed in his task was the boy playing chess with the teacher. Although chess is a challenging game, for a teacher to spend one hour and ten minutes with only one child, while the rest are left to fend for themselves, seems a misapportionment of time and a poverty of judgment. Mr. D. Ense could have taught more of the children to play chess, and could then have overseen several games with the objective of helping students to develop strategies necessary for playing and winning the game.

We should also wonder about Jane, the girl who did not appear to be doing anything. Jane is only at a first-grade reading level. The work she was asked to do was not within her readiness. How could she read a fifth-grade English book, which was the one assigned by the teacher? And why should she learn to spell words that she can't even read?

Using the students' criteria given earlier in this chapter, how would you rate Mr. D. Ense's teaching performance?

SCENARIO TWO

Upper-elementary grade—14 girls, 12 boys, 1 male teacher
Same inner-city school.

The classroom contains desks clustered together in groups of four. In the front of the room there are six desks in a semicircle facing a chalkboard. A large map is visible. A bulletin board has an exhibit called "Creative Stories from Other Continents" on display, including a list of the continents and various countries being studied. Next to the list are spelling words related to the countries and continents being considered.

Another board contains class plans for the day. The teacher is working with a group of six at the chalkboard. Children who are at their desks seem to be engrossed and busy.

Action

The teacher, Mr. K. Now, says, "We've been working with different continents and countries and we have combined this with our language arts lesson and working with the newspaper. Yesterday we allowed our imaginations to roam and we wrote some very creative stories. We've talked about some of the countries and their leaders who have been in the news lately. Who remembers some of the countries and leaders we have been talking about?"

A child raises his hand and suggests Japan and Hirohito.

Mr. K. Now says, "Yes. Why were we talking about Hirohito?"

A student raises his hand and tells about the president's visit with the Japanese emperor and where and why this visit took place.

Mr. K. Now responds with "Good!" He then asks that someone go to the board to point out Japan on the map.

Many children enthusiastically raise their hands. Someone is chosen who quickly and aptly points out the country.

"Good," Mr. K. Now says. He then asks, "Who are two women leaders who have been in the news that we have also talked about? I'll give you a hint. One of the women's first names, is spelled almost exactly like the country she used to head."

Many children raise their hands again. The teacher calls on a boy who proudly says, "Indira Gandhi." He also offers to point out India on the map. The teacher thanks him and nods, and the student quickly points out India.

A discussion ensues about why India has been in the news so much. The teacher then asks the name of the other famous woman leader who has been in the news. A girl is called on and answers correctly. She says, "Mrs. Thatcher, the Prime Minister of England."

The teacher says, "Good. You really seem to know your world affairs and your countries. Let's see how good you are in categorizing countries according to their continents. I have an outline map for each one of you, and I'd like you to see if you can put the continents in the right areas and then insert the countries that I have listed on the board. Does anyone have any questions? Let's do one together to make sure everyone understands."

He points to an area on one of the outline maps, and asks, "Can everyone see where I am pointing?

Okay, what is this continent?"

Almost everyone calls out, "North America!"

"Correct," says Mr. K. Now. "Looking at the list on the board, which country would you place in this continent and approximately where would you put it?"

Again, many of the children call out the correct answer.

"Good. Let's see how many of you can finish this on your own."

The children start working and Mr. K. Now goes around the room checking other papers and stopping to help those who need it. After some time has elapsed, the teacher goes over the correct answers with the group to give them feedback on the results. He helps students summarize what they have done and asks them to check the news for exciting things that are happening in other areas of the world so that they can add those to their list.

"Tomorrow," Mr. K. Now says, "we're going to be combining outlining with our study of continents and countries. Then we're going to use the outline as a guide to learn more about the country we choose to study. I would like you to think about which country you want to get to know better. At your seats, review some of the things we talked about concerning outlines. This sheet should help you."

During the lesson with this group, other children moved about the room freely. Two children came to the front of the room to ask the teacher questions. After getting an answer the children returned to their seats. Rather than calling another group to the front of the room, the teacher asked the class what game they would like to play when he had finished with the group at the bulletin board. When the game was over, the teacher continued reading a Sherlock Holmes story to the children, but first he challenged the children to try to solve the mystery in the story.

The next scheduled activity concerned description. This was a "whole class" activity. Each student had a number of mystery items in a box or bag. A student would have to describe a hidden item using only one sense. The words used to describe the items were written on the board. These words would then be used in the pupils' writing. Lastly, Mr. K. Now and his students discussed their plans for the next day.

Comment

From observation of the students, desirable learning seems to be taking place in this classroom. The teacher is sensitive to individual differences in students. Pupil-teacher planning was in evidence. He used a variety of teaching materials and meth-ods, and he employed stimulating techniques and encouraged creativity. He correlated the language arts to other subject-matter areas. Preplanning and organizing for learning were evident from these on-going activities. Mr. K. Now appears to be an effective teacher.

Criteria for Effective Evaluation

The principles concerning effective evaluation, which are discussed in Chapters 18 and 19, should certainly be used for teacher evaluation. Good evaluation is based on an adequate and valid collection of data. It is important that judgments not be made on one or two casual observations.

In order to adequately evaluate the two teachers in our scenarios, or any other teachers, they must be observed a number of times in a variety of teaching situations. Teachers, as well as students, can have their "off days."

The criteria used for evaluation should be known to both teachers and their evaluators. Criteria that are cooperatively selected, defined, and agreed on are usually the most effective for such evaluation purposes, and mutual goals prevent teachers from feeling threatened.

Teachers play many and varied roles both inside and outside the classroom. How teachers perform in the classroom will depend on how they visualize their roles. Teachers who see themselves solely as conveyers of knowledge and who are subject-matter oriented will behave one way. Teachers who see themselves as student-oriented will behave another way. One may not necessarily be a more effective teacher than the other.

The method of instruction should not be evaluated; rather, the effectiveness with which the teacher utilizes the method should be weighed. And the personality of the teacher should not be evaluated but the manner in which the teacher promotes an atmosphere conducive to learning. It is beyond the scope of this book to discuss methods of teaching, teaching problems, and supervisors' ways of evaluating teachers. Many excellent books already exist in these areas. (See the bibliography for a listing of such books.)

Summary

Teachers are managers of the teaching–learning environment because they are responsible for a group of students and because their purpose is to make a positive and beneficial difference to their students' learning. Good planning, the use of lesson plans as aids, the inclusion of students in planning, and a good physical environment greatly influence the teaching–learning program. Teachers themselves are key factors in the teaching–learning environment. Knowledge of self-fulfilling prophecy, evaluation, self-evaluation, and competency-based objectives helps teachers gain greater insights into themselves.

SELECTED BIBLIOGRAPHY

Ashton-Warner, Sylvia. *Teacher*. New York: Simon and Schuster, 1963.

Barker, Roger. *Ecological Psychology*. Stanford, Calif.: Stanford University Press, 1968.

Bernard, Harold W. *Mental Health in the Classroom*. New York: McGraw-Hill, 1970.

Craik, K. M. "Environmental Psychology," in *New Directions in Psychology*, T. M. Newcomb, ed. New York: Holt, Rinehart and Winston, 1970.

Dennison, George. *The Lives of Children*. New York: Random House, 1969.

Do Teachers Make a Difference? Department of Health, Education and Welfare Report No. OE-58042. Washington, D.C.: U.S. Government Printing Office, 1970.

Dreeben, R. *The Nature of Teaching*. Glenview, Ill.: Scott, Foresman, 1970.

Elliot, Velma L. "Peer Evaluation for Teachers? Why Not?" *Elementary English* 51 (May 1974): 727–730.

Flanders, Ned A. *Analyzing Teaching Behavior*. Reading, Mass.: Addison-Wesley, 1970.

Holt, John. *How Children Fail*. New York: Pitman, 1964.

Houston, W. Robert, and Robert B. Howsam, eds. *Competency-based Teacher Education*. Chicago: Science Research Associates, 1972.

James, Shirley M. "CBTE and Trends and Practices in the Reading Program." *The Reading Teacher* 29 (December 1975): 267–271.

Kounin, Jacob S. *Discipline and Group Management*. New York: Holt, Rinehart and Winston, 1970.

Kozol, Jonathan. *Death at an Early Age*. Boston: Houghton Mifflin, 1967.

McNeil, John D. *Toward Accountable Teachers: Their Appraisal and Improvement*. New York: Holt, Rinehart and Winston, 1971.

McNeil, John D., and W. James Popham. "The Assessment of Teacher Competence," in Robert M. W. Travers, ed. *Second Handbook of Research on Teaching*. Chicago: Rand McNally, 1973, pp. 218–241.

O'Donnell, Holly S. "Accountability for What?" *Elementary English* 51 (May 1974): 721–726.

Rogers, Carl R. *Freedom to Learn*. Columbus, Ohio: Merrill, 1969.

Rosner, Benjamin. *The Power of Competency-based Teacher Education*. Boston: Allyn and Bacon, 1972.

Rubin, Louis J., ed. *Facts and Feelings in the Classroom: Views on the Role of the Emotions in Successful Learning*. New York: Viking, 1974.

Silberman, Charles E. *Crisis in the Classroom*. New York: Random House, 1970.

Stuart, Jesse. *To Teach, To Love*. New York: Penguin, 1973.

Travers. Robert M. W., ed. *Second Handbook of Research on Teaching*. Chicago: Rand McNally, 1973.

Waskin, Yvonne. *Teacher-Pupil Planning for Better Classroom Learning*. New York: Pitman, 1967.

Watson, D. M. "Directions in Proxemic Research." *The Journal of Communication* 22 (December 1972): 443–459.

sixteen

Organizing for Instruction

EXAMPLES OF TEACHER COMPETENCIES

1. The teacher will be able to explain how organizing for instruction affects the teaching–learning program.

2. The teacher will be able to discuss the factors that are taken into account in organizing for instruction.

3. The teacher will be able to describe the types of groups into which children are organized.

4. The teacher will be able to explain the procedure used in organizing for instruction in the classroom.

5. The teacher will be able to explain why student involvement in grouping for instruction is important.

6. The teacher will be able to determine when student involvement in grouping should take place.

7. The teacher will be able to explain how the stigma usually attached to grouping can be discarded.

8. The teacher will be able to describe his or her role in the management of groups.

9. The teacher will be able to describe different types of individualized programs.

10. The teacher will be able to describe characteristics of informal and formal individualized programs.

11. The teacher will be able to explain for whom individualized programs work.

12. The teacher will be able to describe how to individualize instruction in a language arts area.

13. The teacher will be able to describe what a learning center is and explain how it is used in the classroom.

14. The teacher will be able to state and describe the steps involved in preparing a learning center.

15. The teacher will be able to explain the reasons for using multimedia in learning centers.

16. The teacher will be able to explain the purposes for preparing bulletin boards in the classrooms.

The child is the starting-point, the center, and the end. His development, his growth, is the ideal. It alone furnishes the standard.

JOHN DEWEY

Introduction

Ms. Hart arrived especially early the first day of school to make sure everything in her classroom was in order. When she arrived, she was relieved to see that everything was as she had left it the day before, and that the custodian had not changed her desk arrangements.

Ms. Hart had worked for a long time to prepare her classroom for her students. She looked at the Communication bulletin board and smiled. "It does look pretty good," she said to herself. She was especially pleased with her Jigsaw bulletin board because it made the room look so bright and cheerful. (She had known there was a reason for saving all that gift-wrapping paper.) "The cutouts of various sizes and designs with the words PUZZLED? ASK QUESTIONS! should certainly attract attention," she thought to herself.

Ms. Hart had arranged the desks and chairs in clusters of four in a semicircle. She wanted to allow for easy access to all the learning centers, which were placed around the periphery of the room. (See the diagram on page 409). At the far left, she had placed her grandmother's hooked rug and rocking chair. Surrounding the rug at right angles were the bookcases filled with books at various readability levels. Ms. Hart had read practically all of the books for her college course in children's literature. The colorful book jackets that she had collected through the years were on display on top of the bookcases. Ms. Hart beamed when she looked at the warm, homey setting. "Children should enjoy reading there, and it will be perfect for storytelling or for reading stories to the class," she thought.

Ms. Hart's anthill, goldfish aquarium, and plants had been placed near the science center. Because of Ms. Hart's special interest in words and vocabulary expansion, she had prepared a special learning sequence in this area. She would help the children see how the learning of a few word parts could help them in learning many of the terms used in the metric system. Ms. Hart felt especially proud of her media corner, which housed the media equipment, and in which the listening and music learning centers were located. Ms. Hart had prepared some of the tapes for the listening center, and she had brought in some of her favorite tapes for the music appreciation learning sequences. She hoped that her puppet stage would stimulate children to make their own puppets, write scripts, and present puppet shows. The math center, writing center, art tables, and round reading table for group work were all as she had placed them. Even the line she had strung for the hanging of the groups' weekly behavioral objectives was still there. (See section on student involvement under "Grouping within Classes.")

Ms. Hart sighed and thought, "What a lot of work!" And she was right. It had taken a great amount of time, effort, planning, decision-making, and work to organize this classroom for optimum teaching and learning.

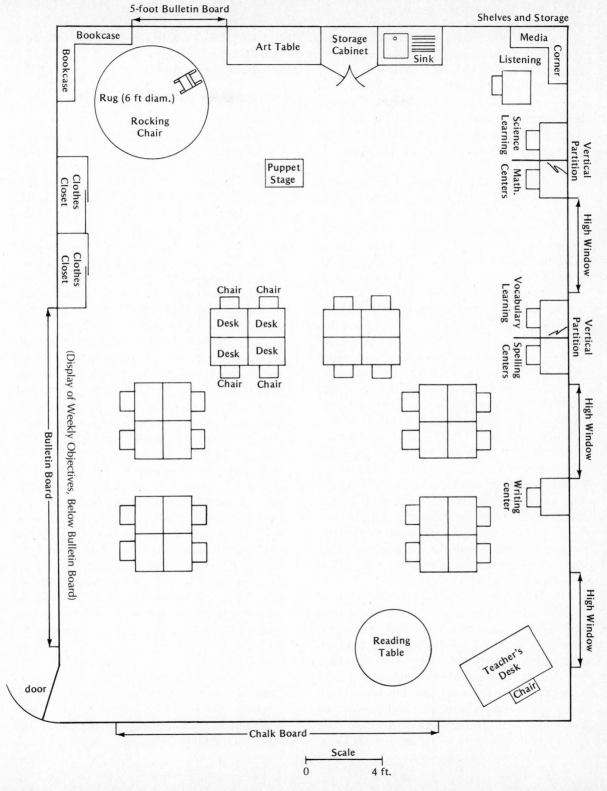

5-foot Bulletin Board

Bookcase

Bookcase

Rug (6 ft diam.)

Rocking Chair

Clothes Closet

Clothes Closet

Art Table

Storage Cabinet

Sink

Shelves and Storage

Media

Listening

Corner

Science Learning Centers

Math. Learning Centers

Vertical Partition

High Window

Puppet Stage

Chair Chair

Desk Desk

Desk Desk

Chair Chair

Vocabulary Learning Centers

Spelling Centers

Vertical Partition

High Window

(Display of Weekly Objectives, Below Bulletin Board)

Bulletin Board

Writing center

High Window

Reading Table

Teacher's Desk

Chair

door

Chalk Board

Scale

0   4 ft.

Ms. Hart is a new teacher. She is excited about her fourth-grade teaching assignment, and she wants to be a perfect teacher—well, almost perfect. After looking over everything in the classroom, Ms. Hart feels that she is starting in the right direction. She has tried to make the room into an attractive and inviting learning environment that reflects her philosophy of education.

Ms. Hart realizes, however, that this is only the first step. She still has not decided on how to organize for instruction within her self-contained classroom. She respects the fact that each student is a unique individual; the importance of individual differences was stressed in many of her college courses. She agrees with the principle of adapting instruction to the needs, interests, and ability levels of each of her students, and she wants to organize an educational program within her classroom based on individual differences. Ms. Hart's problem is in deciding on the kind of program. There are so many individualized programs. The one thing that Ms. Hart is certain about is that she wants a program that provides for both group and individual instruction.

Ms. Hart is making a good start. She has established a physical environment that is conducive to both individual and group activities. The kind of organizational pattern Ms. Hart chooses will depend on the students she has. Some organizational patterns work better with some groups of students than with others. Also, some patterns work better in one curriculum area than in another.

Ms. Hart will have to wait a little while to see what works best with her group of students. She will probably try a few plans. First, she must learn about each of her students. Through observation, informal tests, and standardized tests she can gain information to help her determine what will work best for her unique group of students. There is no one correct way to organize for instruction. There are a number of ways, and some work better for certain groups

of students and teachers than others. Ms. Hart will find this out.

How to Organize for Instruction

To find one plan of class organization that can be executed effectively by all teachers with all children is as difficult as finding a word to rhyme with orange.

EMMETT A. BETTS

Teachers' decisions concerning how they will organize their classes for instruction are vital because they will affect the entire teaching–learning program. Teachers certainly should take the individual differences of all the students into account, and should try to provide for their individual needs. However, it simply is not practical and is probably not possible to provide a completely individualized program for each student in each specific language arts area. Children need experience in working with small groups, large groups, and with the whole class. Working with various groups helps children gain learnings that they cannot obtain from working individually.

Teachers in organizing for language arts instruction must provide for group instruction as well as individualized instruction. Activities such as choral speaking, creative dramatics, puppetry, plays, discussion groups, and so on all require working with others. In a classroom organized for both individual and group instruction, students learn to work both cooperatively and independently. Being courteous and respecting the rights of each individual are the basic tenets of any viable program organized for instruction.

Grouping within Classes

Although a combination of individual and group instruction is advocated, we need to look at each separately to get a better understanding of individualized and group instruction.

Types of Groups

Children are organized into groups to make instruction more manageable. A teacher during any school day usually works with the whole class as a unit, with small groups, with large groups, and with individual students. Some groups are *ad hoc* ones, formed for a specific short-range purpose and dissolved when the purpose has been accomplished, and some groups are ongoing ones.

Student Selection in Groups

Usually the basis for selection in language arts groups such as reading, punctuation, capitalization, word usage, and spelling is the achievement levels of students. During the first few weeks of the term, teachers collect data concerning the achievement levels of each of the students in their classes through observation, informal tests, and formal tests. After evaluating the collected data, tentative groups are organized. The number of groups in a skill area depends on the amount of variability within the class. For some areas, there may be three or four groups; for some, there may only be two groups; for some, the teacher may decide to work with the whole class as a unit; and for some areas, the teacher may have a number of children working individually. The grouping pattern is a flexible one and the goups themselves are recognized as flexible units; children can easily flow from one group to another.

In a number of language arts areas, as well as other subject-matter areas, groups are formed based on interest rather than achievement levels. Working in groups in some language arts activities such as choral speaking, creative dramatics, role playing, plays, and discussion groups

allows students of various ability levels to work together. When students have an opportunity to work with others, they usually are able to establish a better basis for mutual understanding and respect.

Student Involvement in Grouping

Student involvement is vital for any program to work effectively. To encourage student involvement, the teacher explains to the students the manner in which the groups are being organized and the purposes for the groups. The students are told that they may ask to move to any group at any time if they feel that they are ready for something another group is learning. Students may also sit in with any other group to either relearn a skill, review a skill, or to learn something that they might have missed when it was taught to their group because they were absent.

At the beginning of the week, the behavioral objectives for each skill area are planned with each group. The behavioral objectives are clearly printed on large newsprint paper. The sheets for all the groups for each area are then clipped together and hung on a small line that has been strung for this purpose. Students are encouraged to go through the objectives at any time to see if there is something that they would like to learn, relearn, or review. Students then speak to the instructor and make arrangements to come to the group when the specific skill they wish to acquire is being taught. Some students who feel that they are ready for higher-level skills will ask to sit in with another group on a trial basis, or a teacher can invite certain students to sit in with other groups. The main factor is that students have the opportunity to move freely from one group to another. Also, by encouraging students to make decisions about their own learning, teachers are helping students to become more self-reliant and independent learners.

Grade Level for Student Involvement in Grouping

There is no set level to which one can point and say, "*That* is the correct level at which to include student input in grouping decisions." Some intermediate-grade level children who have never had the opportunity to contribute to planning or decision-making will not be ready to work in a program with a strong emphasis on student participation, whereas some primary-grade level students who have been involved in some planning and decision-making will be ready. The teacher will need to involve the inexperienced children gradually in planning and decision-making. If teachers encourage some student involvement from the day that children begin school, by the intermediate grades many students should be more independent and involved learners.

Teachers' Responsibility in Student Involvement in Grouping Decisions

Involving students in decision-making and planning does not mean that teachers give up their role as planner and decision-maker. Teachers are still the individuals responsible for the major decisions in the classroom. If children wish to plan for activities that are neither feasible nor desirable, teachers must help the students to recognize that they cannot do this. Teachers must help the students to be responsible and discriminating planners and decision-makers. This is difficult because responsible decision-making and planning require value judgments. A number of primary-grade level students, as well as intermediate-grade level students, may not be able to make such value decisions. Teachers will obviously have to use their judgment to determine the ability of their students to make certain decisions.

The Stigma Attached to Grouping

The stigma generally attached to grouping is usually discarded when students know that they can move freely from one group to another. By explaining the purposes for the groups and by having the students involved in the planning, students probably will not feel humiliated because they are not at another level. Students do not want to work at their frustration levels; therefore, they usually will not resent working at a lower level, which is at their instructional level. They will also probably not ask to move to a group working at a higher level if they feel that they cannot do the work at that level.

Names usually are chosen for the various ongoing groups rather than numerals, such as one, two, three, and so on. The students usually choose the names for their groups, and this helps give a sense of identity to the group. When students understand the purposes of grouping and have information about what the various groups are doing, names such as "Bluebirds," "Robins," and "Jays" are not used as cover-ups for fast, medium, and slow. The names never can act as cover-ups—everyone always knows who the fast, medium, or slow "birds" really are.

Teacher Management of Groups

A teacher makes the following remarks to the rest of the class: "Don't bother me now. I'm working with this group. It's their turn now. You've had yours."

Is the teacher who made these remarks a good classroom manager? The answer is probably "No." A good classroom manager is able to deal with more than one situation at a time. A teacher working with a group should be aware of what is going on not only in the group with whom he or she is presently working, but also with the other children in the class. A teacher cannot "dismiss" the rest of the class because he or she is working with a particular group. Even though the children have been provided with challenging work based on their individual needs, the teacher must be alert to what is going on. A teacher who ignores the rest of the class while working with one group will probably have a number of discipline problems. The following scenario presents an example of a good classroom manager. Notice especially how Ms. Mills is able to manage a number of ongoing activities at the same time. Notice how she is always aware of what is going on in her class, and notice how she prevents problems from arising.

SCENARIO

One teacher and six children are seated at a round table engaged in reading. The rest of the class is involved in a variety of activities: a number of children are working individually at their seats or at learning centers; one child is seated in the rocking chair reading; two children are working together; and a group of children are working together in the rear of the room.

The teacher says to her group at the round table, "We've talked about what inference means, and we've given examples of it. Who can tell us what we mean by inference?" A few children raise their hands. Ms. Mills calls on one, and he gives an explanation of inference. "Good," says Ms. Mills. "Now, I'd like you to read the paragraph about Mr. Brown and then tell us what inferences you can make about Mr. Brown. Be prepared to support your inferences with evidence from the paragraph."

Ms. Mills looks at each of the children as they are reading. She then glances around the room. She says, "Judy, may I see you for a moment?" Judy comes to Ms. Mills. The teacher asks Judy in a very quiet tone if she can help her. She says, "Judy, you look confused. What's wrong?" Judy says that she is having trouble figuring out a question. Ms. Mills tells Judy to work on something else for about ten minutes, and that then she will help her. As Judy goes back to her seat, Ms. Mills again quickly glances around the room. As her eyes catch some of the children's, she smiles at them. Ms. Mills then looks at the children in her group. She sees that they are ready. Ms. Mills asks them what inferences they can make about Mr. Brown. All the children raise their hands. Ms. Mills calls on one of the children. He makes an inference about Mr. Brown. Ms. Mills asks the rest of the group if they agree with the inference. Two students say that they do not agree. Ms. Mills asks all the students to skim the paragraph to find clues that would support their position. Ms. Mills again looks around the room. A child approaches Ms. Mills and asks her a question. Ms. Mills answers the question and then goes back to the group. After a while Ms. Mills and the group discuss whether they have accomplished what they were supposed to. They then discuss, for a moment, what they will be doing next time. They all go back to their seats. Before Ms. Mills calls another group, she checks off in her plan book the objectives that have been accomplished by the group. She also makes some remarks in her record book about the individual children in the group. Ms. Mills puts down her book and walks around the room to check on what the students are doing. She smiles to a number of the students, says "good" to some others, helps Judy with her problem, and listens in on the group that has been working together on a special project. Ms. Mills asks the group how they are doing and how much more time they will need before they will be ready to report their progress to her and the class. Ms. Mills then goes back to the reading table and calls the next group.

Individualized Instruction

The many different types of individualized programs range from informal ones, developed by teachers or teachers and students together, to formal ones, which are commercially produced. It is beyond the scope of this book to give a description of the organizational patterns or the individualized programs that exist; books have been written on these. (See bibliography.)

However, a brief description of some of the characteristics of both informal and formal individualized programs would be helpful.

Informal Programs

Informal programs can vary from teacher to teacher. However, most of the programs usually use behavioral objectives, which are taken from curriculum guides, study guides, and instructors' manuals. To accomplish the objectives the teachers usually cull activities and materials from a number of sources; the teacher and student confer periodically; and the teacher keeps a check on the student's progress by keeping adequate records.

Formal Programs

A variety of different commercial programs exists, and they have a number of things in common. Most of the programs use behavioral objectives for each curriculum area. Usually each curriculum area is divided into small discrete learning steps based on graduated levels of difficulty. A variety of activities and materials generally combined in a multimedia approach is used, and usually built into the commercial programs is a system of record-keeping, progress tests, and checklists.

Some Common Characteristics of Formal and Informal Individualized Programs

In almost all individualized programs, students work at their own pace. Learning outcomes in individualized programs are based on the needs, interests, and ability levels of the students. Activities are interesting and challenging, and they usually employ a multimedia approach. The activities are based on desired outcomes, students work independently, and there is some system of record-keeping.

For Whom Does Individualized Instruction Work?

Students who have short attention spans, who have difficulty following directions, and who have reading problems will obviously have difficulty working independently. Teachers will have to help these students set limited, short-range objectives that can be reached in a short period of time. For those students with reading problems, the teacher will have to rely very heavily on audio tapes to convey directions. Students who are slow learners (see Chapter 17) will also need special help; special programs will have to be devised for them. Students who have no discernible achievement problems but who have never worked in an individualized program before will also have difficulty unless they are properly oriented to the program. (Note: Do not confuse the need to work independently in an individualized program with the need to provide for the individual differences of each student in the class. For example, a child who is a slow learner will usually have difficulty working independently, but the teacher still needs to provide an individual program for this child based on his or her special needs.)

Some Common Sense about Individual Programs

Preparing individual outcomes and a specially tailored program for each student in each specific subject area can be a monumental task. Therefore, what is generally done is to use outcomes and programs already prepared, either informally (teacher-made) or formally (commercially made), and then match these to the needs of individual students. For such an individualized program to work effectively, teachers must have a variety of individualized programs available for their students, and teachers must know the individual needs of each student. (See section on learning centers.)

In the following scenario, an example of how one fifth-grade teacher individualizes instruction in one language arts area is presented:

SCENARIO

In going over Susan's papers Ms. Mills finds that the pupil consistently makes many spelling errors. Ms. Mills decides to have a conference with Susan about this. Ms. Mills begins the conference by praising Susan's ideas and by telling Susan that she enjoys reading her stories. "However," Ms. Mills says, "you have so many spelling errors that it detracts from the story." Susan says she is aware that she has a spelling problem, but that she has always had a spelling problem. "I guess I just can't spell," says Susan. Ms. Mills tells Susan that since she is a good reader and writer she really should not have a spelling problem. She also tells Susan that since she likes to write, it would be helpful to be a better speller. Susan says that she definitely does want to spell better. "Good!" says Ms. Mills. "The first step to improving in something is knowing that you have a problem." "Let's both look at some of your papers and see if we can come up with a program that will help you. We'll meet tomorrow to discuss this further."

The next day Ms. Mills and Susan have another conference. Ms. Mills asks Susan if she noticed anything special about the words she misspelled. Susan says that she is not sure, but she seems to have problems with word endings. She never knows when to drop a final *e*, change a *y* to an *i*, or double a consonant. Ms. Mills says, "Good, I noticed the same things. Did you know that there are a number of spelling rules that you can learn that will help you? As a matter of fact, in the spelling learning center we have just the program for you. Let's go to the center so that we can look at it together."

Ms. Mills and Susan proceed to the learning center. At the center, Ms. Mills shows Susan a modularized instructional spelling program. The teacher chooses the module that deals entirely with spelling endings. Ms. Mills and Susan go over each step of the module together. The spelling module is composed of the following steps: (1) directions for using the module; (2) pretest; (3) behavioral objectives; (4) learning activities; (5) student self-assessment; (6) postassessment; and (7) recycling.

After going over each step of the module with Susan, Ms. Mills makes sure that Susan is able to operate the audio equipment that is used in the module. Ms. Mills then tells Susan that she can work at her own pace, and that if she needs any help, she should not hesitate to come to her. Susan thanks Ms. Mills and says that she is looking forward to starting as soon as possible. "It looks like fun," she says, "because there are so many different kinds of activities, and I especially enjoy doing word riddles and puzzles."

It is probable that Susan is on her way to becoming a better speller. However, Ms. Mills's job is not over. She must continue to check on Susan's progress and then, together with Susan, determine whether the student is ready to go on to another area or whether she needs further remediation.

Record-Keeping

Since Susan is only one of many students in Ms. Mills's class, and since many of the students are working in different areas at different levels, Ms. Mills cannot rely on her memory to recall exactly what each student is doing and at what level each student is working. Ms. Mills, therefore, has established a record-keeping system. She has a folder for each student in the class. In the folder she keeps a record of each student's progress in each area. For example, Ms. Mills, after meeting with Susan, went back to her file drawer to pull Susan's folder. She wanted to record that Susan is attempting to accomplish certain behavioral objectives in the area of spelling. She also wanted to record the specific program Susan is working in and the date that Susan started the program.

A teacher and student working together.

Susan's folder contains a number of items: a checklist of activities; a record of standardized achievement test scores, intelligence test scores, diagnostic test information, and criterion-ref-

erenced test information. In the folder there is also a sheet listing the particular behavioral objectives that Susan has attempted to accomplish up to that time. Next to each behavioral objective is the program chosen to achieve it, as well as the starting and completion dates.

Learning Centers in the Classroom

The concept of learning centers is not new. Good teachers have always recognized the importance of providing "interest centers" for their students based on their needs and ability levels. However, in the past most of the science, art, library, listening, and fun centers were just "interest attractions"; they usually were marginal to the ongoing teaching–learning program rather than an integral part of it.

As used today, learning centers are an important and integral part of the instructional program. They are more formalized and recognized as vital to a good individualized program. A set area is usually set aside in the classroom for instruction in a specific curriculum area. Aims for learning centers may be developed beforehand by teachers or cooperatively by teachers and students. Some of the requirements for a good learning center are as follows:

Outline of Steps in Individualizing a Spelling Program for Susan Based on Her Needs

1. Susan has a spelling problem.
2. Susan's spelling problem is observed by Ms. Mills.
3. A conference is set up between Susan and Ms. Mills.
4. At the conference Susan recognizes that she has a spelling problem.
5. Both Susan and Ms. Mills decide to diagnose Susan's spelling problem.
6. In diagnosing Susan's spelling problem, Ms. Mills and Susan analyze the types of spelling errors Susan consistently makes to determine if a pattern exists.
7. Another conference is set up between Susan and Ms. Mills.
8. Susan and Ms. Mills, following an analysis of Susan's papers, determine Susan's spelling problem.
9. Ms. Mills decides on a program to help Susan overcome her spelling difficulties.
10. Ms. Mills intorduces Susan to the program.
11. Susan begins work in the program.
12. Ms. Mills periodically checks on Susan's progress.
13. Ms. Mills keeps records on Susan's progress.

1. Is in an easily accessible area.
2. Is attractive.
3. Provides for students on different maturational levels.
4. Has clearly stated behavioral objectives so that students know what they are supposed to accomplish (outcomes).
5. Provides for group and team activities as well as individual activities.
6. Allows for student input.
7. Asks probing questions.
8. Has some humorous materials.
9. Provides activities that call for divergent thinking.
10. Uses a multimedia approach.

11. Has carefully worked out learning sequences to accomplish objectives.

12. Has provisions for evaluation and record-keeping.

Designing a Learning Center

In the following plan for developing a learning center, notice the similarity to the development of a lesson plan.

1. Motivating technique: necessary to attract attention. This could be realia (real objects), pictures, humorous sayings, and so on.

Example: Familiar commercials with pictures are listed on learning center bulletin board·(propaganda learning center).

2. Behavioral objectives: necessary so that students know what they are supposed to accomplish (outcomes).

Examples: (propaganda learning center)

   a. Define "propaganda."
   b. Define "bias."
   c. Explain what is meant by a propaganda technique.
   d. List five propaganda techniques.
   e. Describe each of the five propaganda techniques you chose and give an example of each.
   f. Listen to a tape of ten commercials and identify the propaganda technique used in each.
   g. Listen to a tape of a political speech and state what propaganda techniques the politician uses.
   h. Team up with another student and using a propaganda technique, role play a commercial to be presented to the class.
   i. Using one or more propaganda techniques, write a commercial about an imaginary product.
   j. Tape-record the commercial created by you on the imaginary product.

3. Directions to accomplish objectives: necessary so that students know what to do to accomplish objectives. Step-by-step instructions are given for the students to accomplish the objectives. Students are told to:

   a. read behavioral objectives so that you know what you are supposed to accomplish

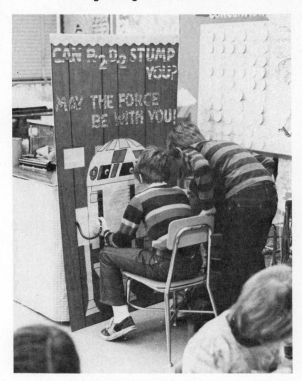

Children working in a language arts learning center

   b. go to file drawer one, which contains the learning activities to accomplish objective one.
   c. complete each learning activity and record your progress on each before you go on to the next objective. (This depends on the learning center. In some learning centers, the students must accomplish the objectives in sequence; in others this is not necessary. For the propaganda learning center, some of the learning objectives must be accomplished in order. Obviously, before students can write a commercial using propaganda and bias, they must be able to define "propaganda" and "bias," they must be able to explain propaganda techniques, they must be able to recognize them, and they must be able to give examples of them.)

Summary of Steps in Preparing a Learning Center

1. Select a topic.
2. State objectives.

A media corner in a learning center

3. Identify experiences.
4. Collect materials.
5. Prepare activities.
6. Make schedules (which children use center and when).
7. Prepare record forms (each student using center must have one).

Multimedia in Learning Centers

Ms. Mills recognizes that successful individualized programs usually have learning centers that use a diversity of instructional materials to accommodate the individual differences of students. As a result, Ms. Mills has included in each of her learning centers learning sequences that use such instructional materials as textbooks, library books, programmed materials, sets of pictures, realia (real things), commercial and teacher-prepared audio tapes, filmstrips, films, TV, radio, tape recorders, maps, globes, manipulative materials, and games.

The media corner itself is not a learning center, but a conveniently located storage and extra viewing place. Each learning center has its own viewing area. The media corner has two "homemade" carrels, which are helpful for viewing films and filmstrips if the learning center is occupied.

Ms. Mills realizes that she is extremely fortunate to be in a school system that not only recognizes the importance of the use of a variety of media to help students to achieve learning objectives, but which provides the funds necessary to acquire the materials. (She also has a friend who helped her make the carrels for the media center.)

Bulletin Boards

In the introduction to this chapter, Ms. Hart had worked hard to prepare some bulletin boards to arouse the interests of her students, to use as a motivating technique for the unit on communication, and to make the classroom a

A language arts bulletin board

more pleasant and attractive learning environment. Throughout the term, the bulletin boards in Ms. Hart's room change to reflect the ongoing projects and activities in the classroom. Also, under Ms. Hart's guidance, students participate in the planning and putting together of the bulletin boards. (See the bibliograhpy for a listing of some books with good bulletin board ideas.)

Summary

How a teacher organizes for instruction will greatly affect the teaching–learning program. In organizing language arts instruction, the teacher ought to provide for both group and individualized instruction. Teachers organize students into groups to make instruction more manageable. However, there are times when the needs of a child will be better served by an individualized program than by group instruction. Many individualized programs exist. Teachers should be familiar with a number of these so that they can match specific programs to the needs of individual children. Learning centers are an important part of the instructional program and vital to a good individualized program.

SELECTED BIBLIOGRAPHY

Breyfogle, Ethel, et al. *Creating a Learning Environment: A Learning Center Handbook*. (Pacific Palisades, Calif.: Goodyear Publishing, 1976).

Brown, James W., et al. *AV Instruction: Technology, Media and Methods*, 5th ed. New York: McGraw-Hill, 1977.

Carroll, Anne W. *Personalizing Education in the Classroom*. (Denver, Colo.: Love Publishing, 1975.

Charles, C.M. *Individualizing Instruction*. St. Louis, Mo.: C. V. Mosby, 1976.

Coplan, Kate, and Constance Rosenthal. *Guide to Better Bulletin Boards*. Dobbs Ferry, N.Y.: Oceana Publishing, 1970.

Davidson, Tom, et al. *The Learning Center Book: An Integrated Approach*. Pacific Palisades, Calif.: Goodyear Publishing, 1976.

Flanigan, Michael C., and Robert S. Boone. *Using Media in the Language Arts: A Source Book*. Itasca, Ill.: F. E. Peacock 1977.

Forte, Imogene, and Joy Mackenzie. *Nooks, Crannies, and Corners: Learning Centers for Creative Classrooms*, rev. ed. Nashville, Tenn.: Incentive Publications, 1978.

Gerlach, Vernon S., and Donald P. Ely. *Teaching and Media: A Systematic Approach*. Englewood Cliffs, N.J.: Prentice-Hall, 1971.

Helton, George B., et al. "Grouping for Instruction 1965, 1975, 1985." *The Reading Teacher* 31 (October 1977): 28–33.

Marland, John, et al. *Classroom Learning Centers*. Belmont, Calif.: Fearon-Pitman Publishers, 1973.

Petreshene, Susan S. *Complete Guide to Learning Centers*. Palo Alto, Calif.: Pendragon House, 1978.

Shiman, David A., et al. eds. *Teachers on Individualization: The Way We Do It*. New York: McGraw-Hill, 1974.

Smith, James A. *Classroom Organization for the Language Arts*. Itasca, Ill.: F. E. Peacock, 1977.

Talbert, E. Gene, and Larry E. Fraser, eds. *Individualized Instruction: A Book of Readings*. Columbus, Ohio: Merrill, 1972.

Voight, Ralph Claude. *Invitation to Learning I: The Learning Center Handbook*. Washington, D.C.: Acropolis Books, 1974.

Wayant, Louis. *Learning Center II: Practical Ideas for You*. Paoli, Penn.: Instructo McGraw-Hill, 1977.

Weisberger, Robert A. *Developmental Efforts in Individualized Learning*. Itasca, Ill.: F. E. Peacock, 1971.

seventeen

Individual Differences: Teaching Special Children

EXAMPLES OF TEACHER COMPETENCIES

1. The teacher will be able to explain who "exceptional" children are.
2. The teacher will be able to define the term "learning disability."
3. The teacher will be able to list the levels of mental retardation and state the descriptive terminology that is presently being used to classify retarded persons.
4. The teacher will be able to discuss the significance of the phrase "adaptive behavior" in defining mental retardation.
5. The teacher will be able to discuss the identification bias of children labeled "educable mentally retarded."
6. The teacher will be able to discuss what the label "average" child means.
7. The teacher will be able to state the characteristics of the "gifted" child.
8. The teacher will be able to discuss the significance of knowing about the mental age span in the regular classroom.
9. The teacher will be able to describe the characteristics of the "borderline" or "slow-learning" child.
10. The teacher will be able to describe the kinds of language arts experiences that should be planned for the borderline or slow-learning child.
11. The teacher will be able to describe instructional provisions for the gifted child in the language arts area.
12. The teacher will be able to explain what is meant by "mainstreaming," able to describe how it is implemented, and able to give an example of how children in a regular classroom can be prepared for a mainstreamed child.

All the children of all the people have a right to an education.

PUBLIC LAW 94–142

Introduction

Public Law 94–142 advocates a free appropriate education for all children in the least restrictive environment. This has brought to the fore the importance of the uniqueness of each child. In the regular classroom there is usually a wide range of ability levels, which generally includes the borderline (slow-learning) and the gifted child.[1] As a result of Public Law 94–142, exceptional children may be mainstreamed into the regular classroom. In order to be able to work with such children, all teachers, not just special education teachers, must become more knowledgeable of exceptional children. The more teachers know about the children with whom they work, the better able they will be to provide for their individual differences and needs.

In this chapter, language arts methods are provided that are most applicable for those children whom teachers currently have in their regular classrooms, such as the borderline child and the gifted child; however, they may also be adapted for children who may be mainstreamed. Public Law 94–142 requires that exceptional children have individualized programs specially prepared for them. These individualized programs are too varied to be presented in a text with as broad a scope as this one. Teachers who have mainstreamed children in their classrooms are, therefore, encouraged to go to special education texts for more in-depth coverage. (See the bibliography for a listing of books that deal specifically with the subject.)

[1]Although gifted children are classified as exceptional children, they are generally found in the regular classroom. Borderline (slow-learning) children are not classified as exceptional children in the revised AAMD definition.

Mental Age Span in the Regular Classroom

The teacher in a regular classroom usually has students with a mental age span of five years. It can be more. Mental age (MA) refers to a child's present level of development; it helps to indicate the child's present readiness. As children progress through the grades the span between the borderline (slow-learning), average, and gifted child gets wider.

Children enter school based on chronological age rather than mental age; however, instruction needs to be geared to their mental ages rather than their chronological ages. For example, a child of six with an IQ ($\frac{MA}{CA} \times 100$ = IQ) of 75[2] has a mental age of 4.5, and a child of six with an IQ of 130 has a mental age of 7.8. (See Table 17.1 on page 422.) Obviously, these children need extremely different programs even though both are chronologically the same age.

Even teachers who believe in individual differences and who attempt to develop an individualized instructional program for each child in their class will not be able to build a meaningful program for their students unless they are knowledgeable of the cognitive styles that children at different intellectual levels possess.

The "Average" Child

The first question that comes to mind whenever anyone labels someone an average child is: Is there really an "average" child? Actually, there probably is not. Every child is an individual and as such is unique and special. However, for research purposes we tend to look upon the average child as that individual who scores in the IQ range from 90 to 110. Studies are based on averages. Averages are necessary as criteria

[2]Teachers may have children with IQs as low as 68 in their regular classrooms because borderline children's IQs range from approximately 68 to 85.

table 17.1   Comparison of Mental Ages

Grade	CA	75 IQ MA	85 IQ MA	100 IQ MA	115 IQ MA	130 IQ MA
K	5.6	4.2	4.8	5.6	6.4	7.3
1	6.0	4.5	5.1	6.0	6.9	7.8
	6.6	5.0	5.6	6.6	7.6	8.6
2	7.0	5.3	5.11	7.0	8.1	9.1
	7.6	5.7	6.5	7.6	8.8	9.9
3	8.0	6.0	6.8	8.0	9.2	10.4
	8.6	6.5	7.3	8.6	9.9	11.2
4	9.0	6.8	7.7	9.0	10.4	11.7
	9.6	7.2	8.2	9.6	11.0	12.5
5	10.0	7.5	8.5	10.0	11.5	13.0
	10.6	8.0	9.0	10.6	12.2	13.8
6	11.0	8.3	9.4	11.0	12.6	14.3
	11.6	8.7	9.9	11.6	13.3	15.1
7	12.0	9.0	10.2	12.0	13.8	15.6
	12.6	9.5	10.7	12.6	14.5	16.4
8	13.0	9.8	11.0	13.0	15.0	16.9
	13.6	10.2	11.6	13.6	15.6	17.7

Example: An eight-year-old child with an IQ of 115 has a mental age of *9.2*.

$$IQ = \frac{MA}{CA} \times 100$$

$$115 = \frac{x}{8} \times 100$$

$$x = 1.15 \times 8$$

$$x = 9.2$$

or points of reference. Only after we have determined the criteria for "average" can we talk about "above or below average."

The Borderline Child or the "Slow Learner"

The borderline child is usually described as a dull average child who is borderline in his or her intellectual functioning. As already stated in an earlier section in this chapter, these children's IQ scores range from approximately 68 to 85. As a result, they generally have difficulty doing schoolwork. Borderline children are not,

however, equally slow in all their activities or abnormal in all their characteristics. It is difficult at times to differentiate borderline children and children with specific learning disabilities from underachievers produced by disadvantaged environments.[3]

Providing Instruction for the Borderline Child

Teachers in regular classrooms have many times been frustrated because they have had children who do not seem to be able to learn

[3]Samuel A. Kirk, Sister Joanne Marie Kliebhan, and Janet W. Lerner, *Teaching Reading to Slow and Disabled Learners* (Boston: Houghton Mifflin, 1978), p.3.

material that is considered "average" for the specific grade level. Not only is the teacher frustrated, but so is the child. A child who according to an individual IQ test scores in the 68 to 85 range would have difficulty working at grade level. Because of social promotion (children are promoted according to chronological age rather than achievement) children are moved along each year into a higher grade. As slow learners go through the grades, their problems generally become more pronounced and compounded unless they are given special attention.

The term slow learner is probably a misnomer, because the term implies that a child needs more time to get a concept, but eventually will acquire it. Actually, there are some concepts that slow learners cannot acquire no matter how long they work on them because slow learners usually cannot work in the abstract. Obviously, the teacher should not use inductive or deductive teaching techniques in working with slow learners. Slow learners generally can learn material if it is presented at a concrete level. Slow learners usually must be given many opportunities to go over the same concept; slow learners must continue practice in an area beyond the point where they think that they know it, in order to *overlearn* it. The practice should be varied and interesting to stimulate the students. Many games and gamelike activities could be used for this purpose. Slow learners have a short attention span, so learning tasks should be broken down into small discrete steps. Slow learners generally need close supervision, and they may have difficulty working independently. Distractions must be kept at a minimum, and each task should be very exactly defined and explained. It is necessary to define short-range goals, which slow learners can accomplish, to give them a sense of achievement. Slow learners are usually set in their ways, and once they learn something in one way, they will be very rigid about changing.

The teacher should recognize that individual differences exist within groups as well as between groups. Obviously, there will be individual differences among slow learners.

Language Arts for the Borderline Child

In Chapter 3 you learned that children who are advanced in language development have a better chance for success in school than those who are not. Slow development of language is a noticeable characteristic of slow-learning children. The teacher recognizes that these children need many opportunities to express themselves orally and that they learn best at a concrete level. The teacher should, therefore, plan his or her program for slow-learning children to include many *first-hand experiences* where the children can deal with real things. The teacher can take the children on trips to visit farm animals, zoo animals, the firehouse, the police station, factories, railroad stations, farms, and so on. In planning for the trip, the teacher should use the same good practices that are used for all children. The teacher should discuss the trip with the children beforehand and give them the opportunity to help plan for the trip. After the trip the teacher should encourage the children to discuss what they saw. The teacher and children could then cooperatively write an experience story about the visit. (See Chapter 7.)

In helping slow-learning children acquire new words, the teacher should recognize that these children will learn and retain words that they will use in their everyday conversation more readily than abstract words. It therefore helps for the teacher to associate the new words with their pictorial representations, real objects, or actions. Slow learners must repeatedly hear and see these words in association with objects, pictures, or actions in order to learn them. As mentioned in the previous section, the children must *overlearn* the word. (Overlearning takes place when you continue practice even after reaching the point where you feel you know something quite well.) Slow-learning children not only have problems in working with abstract words, they also have difficulty dealing with words in isolation. Cohen's study has shown that the slower students are in academic progress, the more difficult it is for them to deal with words in isolation, unrelated to a totally meaningful experience. Her study has also found that the reading aloud of stories that are at the interest, ability, and attention span level of the children is an excellent means of helping the children to develop vocabulary and sentence sense.[4] After listening to a story, the children should be encouraged to engage in some oral expression activities. All children need many opportunities to express themselves, and slow learners are no exception. A child who feels accepted and is in a nonthreatening environment will feel more free to contribute than one who feels threatened or embarrassed.

In providing language arts instruction the teacher should provide opportunities for the slow-learning child to work with other children. Oral expression (speech stimulation) activities such as choral speaking, finger play, and creative dramatics are good for these purposes. The child should be given opportunities to share with the other children; all children seek approval of peers as well as of adults.

Gifted Children

Gifted children fall into the category of exceptional children because this group of children deviates greatly from "average" children.

When one talks about the gifted, immediately visions of small children wearing horn-rimmed glasses and carrying encyclopedias come to mind. This is a myth. There are many definitions of the gifted. In recent years the definition of the "gifted" has been broadened to include not only the verbally gifted with an IQ above 130 or 135 on a Stanford-Binet intelligence test but also those individuals whose performance in any line of socially useful endeavor is consistently superior.

Marland's national definition in a congressional report alerts educators to the multifaceted aspects of giftedness:

Gifted and talented children are those identified by professionally qualified persons who by virtue of outstanding abilities are capable of high performance. These are children who require differentiated educational programs and services beyond those normally provided by the regular school program in order to realize their contribution to self and society.

Children capable of high performance include those with demonstrated achievement and/or potential ability in any of the following areas:

1. General intellectual ability.
2. Specific academic aptitude.
3. Creative or productive thinking.
4. Leadership ability.
5. Visual and performing arts.
6. Psychomotor ability.[5]

Characteristics of Gifted Children

Gifted children, on the average, are socially, emotionally, physically, and intellectually superior to "average" children in the population. Gifted children have, on the average, superior general intelligence, a desire to know, originality, common sense, will power and perseverance, a desire to excel, self-confidence, prudence and forethought, and a good sense of humor, among a host of other admirable traits.

Instructional Provisions for Gifted Children

Gifted children need special attention because of their precocious learning abilities.

[4]Dorothy H. Cohen, "The Effect of Literature on Vocabulary and Reading Achievement," *Elementary English* 45 (February 1968): 209–213, 217.

[5]S. P. Marland, *Education of the Gifted and the Talented* (Washington, D. C.: U.S. Office of Education, 1972), p. 10.

However, when gifted children are not given special attention, they still usually manage to work on grade level. As a result, gifted children are often ignored. Regrettably, gifted children are actually the most neglected of all exceptional children. Attention is given to those who have "more need." Margaret Mead, the renowned anthropologist, has written about this attitude toward the gifted:

> Whenever the rise to success cannot be equated with preliminary effort, abstinence and suffering, it tends to be attributed to "luck," which relieves the spectator from according the specially successful person any merit. . . . In American education, we have tended to reduce the gift to a higher I.Q.—thus making it a matter of merely a little more on the continuity scale, to insist on putting more money and effort in bringing the handicapped child "up to par" as an expression of fair play and "giving everyone a break" and to disallow special gifts. By this refusal to recognize special gifts, we have wasted and dissipated, driven into apathy or schizophrenia, uncounted numbers of gifted children. If they learn easily, they are penalized for having nothing to do; if they excel in some outstanding way, they are penalized as being conspicuously better than the peer group, and teachers warn the gifted child, "Yes, you can do that, it's much more interesting than what the others are doing. But, remember, the rest of the class will dislike you for it."[6]

Gifted children, like all other children, need guidance and instruction based on their interests, needs, and ability levels. Although gifted children are intellectually capable of working at high levels of abstraction, unless they receive appropriate instruction to gain needed skills, they may not be able to realize their potential. Gifted children should not be subjected to unnecessary drill and repetition. Gifted children gain abstract concepts quickly. They usually enjoy challenge and have long attention spans.

Teachers who have gifted children in their self-contained classrooms can provide for those children to work at their own pace in many areas through individualized programs.

Language Arts for the Gifted Child

Gifted children's language development is usually very advanced. They generally have a large stock of vocabulary and delight in learning new words. According to Terman, a noted psychologist, who did monumental research on the gifted, nearly half of the gifted children he studied learned to read before starting school; at least 20 percent before the age of five years, 6 percent before four, and 1.6 percent before three years. Most of these children learned to read with little or no formal instruction.[7] Other studies seem to corroborate these findings. However, these findings should not be taken to mean that gifted children can fend for themselves, and that teachers should spend more time with others. It does mean that the teacher must provide alternate programs for gifted children. To not recognize that these children are reading when they first enter school and to make them go through a program geared to "average" children can be devastating.

Gifted children usually have wide-ranging interests that they pursue in extensive depth; they read voraciously, and they are impatient with detail. They are usually able to work in a number of activities simultaneously; therefore, the teacher must provide a rich and varied program for the gifted so that they have the opportunity to work in many areas. Speech stimulation activities such as choral speaking and creative dramatics give gifted children an opportunity to work with children on all ability levels. This is important for both gifted children and for children of various other ability levels;

---

[6]Margaret Mead, "The Gifted Child in the American Culture of Today," *The Journal of Teacher Education* 5 (September 1954): 211–212.

[7]Lewis Terman and Melita Oden, *The Gifted Child Grows Up*, Genetic Studies of Genius, Vol. 4 (Stanford, Calif.: Stanford University Press, 1947).

children who work together in activities that tap the special abilities of all the children will usually learn to understand each other better.

Mainstreaming

The impetus of mainstreaming was triggered by Public Law 94–142. Public Law 94–142 is a federal law that is designed to give handicapped children a "free appropriate public education." It requires state and local governments to provide identification programs, a special education, and related services such as transportation, testing, diagnosis, and treatment for children with speech handicaps, hearing impairments, visual handicaps, physical disabilities, emotional disturbances, learning disabilities, and mental retardation handicaps. Public Law 94–142 also requires that whenever possible, handicapped students must be placed in regular classrooms. *Mainstreaming* is the placement of handicapped children in the least restrictive educational environment that will meet their needs.

Handicapped children who are moved to a regular classroom are supposed to be very carefully screened. Only those who seem able to benefit from being in a least restrictive environment are supposed to be put into one. The amount of time that a handicapped child spends in a regular classroom and the area in which the child participates in the regular classroom depend on the individual child. Some children who are moderately mentally retarded (trainables) may spend time each week in a regular classroom during a special activity such as a story hour.

For mainstreaming to be successful, classroom teachers must be properly prepared for their new role, and teachers must enlist the aid and cooperation of every student in their class. Classroom teachers must prepare their students for the mainstreamed child by giving them some background and knowledge about the child. The amount and type of information given will, of course, vary with the grade level. Regular classroom teachers should also have the students involved in some of the planning and implementation of the program for the mainstreamed child.

For example, if teachers are expecting physically handicapped children to be admitted to their class, they can help to prepare their students by reading some books to them that portray a physically handicapped child in a sensitive and perceptive manner. Teachers might read some excerpts from Helen Keller's *The Story of My Life* or Marie Killilea's book *Karen*. After reading the excerpts teachers can engage the students in a discussion of the handicapped child's struggles, fears, hopes, concerns, goals, and dreams. Teachers can then attempt to help the children in their classes recognize that they have feelings, hopes, and fears similar to many handicapped children's. Teachers should also help their students to understand that a child with a physical handicap does not necessarily have a mental handicap. As a matter of fact, many handicapped persons are very intelligent and able to make many contributions to society. The teacher can then discuss with the children how they think they can make the new child who is coming to their class feel at home. The teacher might also use special films and television programs to initiate interest in the handicapped and to help gain better insights about them. (See section on "Television: Making It Part of the Communicative Process" in Chapter 5 and see the bibliographies in Chapter 9 and at the end of this chapter for books on the handicapped.)

Besides preparing the children in the regular classroom for the mainstreamed child, an individualized program must be developed for each mainstreamed child in cooperation with the child's parents, the special education teacher, or consultants. The progam should be one that provides a favorable learning experience for both the handicapped child and the regular classroom students. That is, the integration of a handicapped child should not take away from the program of the regular classroom children.

To assure that this is not done, it has been advocated that there be modifications in class size, scheduling, and curriculum design to accommodate the shifting demands that mainstreaming creates; that appropriate instructional materials, supportive services, and pupil personnel services are provided for the teacher and the handicapped student; that there be systematic evaluation and reporting of program developments; and that there be adequate additional funding and resources.[8]

Who Are the Exceptional Children?

The phrase "exceptional children" is applied to those children who deviate so much from "average" or normal children that they require special attention. Exceptional children deviate from the "average" child in "(1) mental characteristics, (2) sensory abilities, (3) neuromuscular or physical characteristics, (4) social or emotional behavior, (5) communication abilities, or (6) multiple handicaps. . . . "[9] More specifically, with slight variation from state to state and author to author, exceptional children have been classified as (1) gifted, (2) educable mentally retarded, (3) trainable mentally retarded, (4) custodial mentally retarded, (5) emotionally disturbed, (6) socially maladjusted, (7) speech-impaired, (8) deaf, (9) hard of hearing, (10) blind, (11) partially seeing, (12) crippled, (13) chronic health cases, (14) multiple handicapped, and (15) learning disabled.

Levels of Mental Retardation

Although there are many definitions of mental retardation, the one that is most generally used is the revised AAMD definition. In defining an individual who is mentally retarded, the

American Association on Mental Deficiencies (AAMD) states in its revised 1973 definition that:

> Mental retardation refers to significantly subaverage general intellectual functioning existing concurrently with deficits in *adaptive behavior*, and manifested during the developmental period.[10] (italics are author's)

"Adaptive behavior" is a crucial phrase in the AAMD definition, and it is one that is often ignored. Many mildly retarded individuals function quite well outside the school environment and their mild retardation is not noticeable. They are able to adapt socially, emotionally, and physically, that is, they have sufficient communication skills, sensory-motor skills, and socialization skills to function in society as independent and self-reliant individuals if they are helped to acquire vocational skills.

The AAMD definition classifies individuals according to the severity of their mental retardation. The scale for determining the levels of mental retardation is based on individual intelligence test scores. (The cutoff for the different levels varies according to the IQ test used.) However, there are also available levels of adaptive behavior that correspond to the intellectual categories of mild, moderate, severe, and profound retardation. (See Table 17.2.)

In the revised AAMD definition, mental retardation refers to an IQ of 67 or below. Children with an IQ above 67 are not considered retarded. There is a category in the earlier AAMD definition called *borderline* retardation which has been deleted from the 1973 revision. The IQ range for the borderline level is approximately 68 to 85. This group of children has many times been referred to as *slow learners*. This group of children is between the "average" child and the mentally retarded child. Special emphasis has been given to this group of children because most classroom teachers have chil-

---

[8]Resolution passed by the 1975 Representative Assembly of the NEA.

[9]M. Stephen Lilly, *Children with Exceptional Needs: A Survey of Special Education* (New York: Holt, Rinehart and Winston, 1979), p. 17.

[10]H. Grossman, ed. *Manual on Terminology and Classifications in Mental Retardation*, rev. ed. (Washington, D.C.: American Association on Mental Deficiency, 1973), p. 11.

table 17.2   IQ Ranges for the Levels of Mental Retardation

| | Intelligence Tests | |
	Stanford-Binet	Wechsler
Mild retardation	67 to 52	69 to 55
Moderate retardation	51 to 36	54 to 40
Severe retardation	35 to 20	39 to 25
Profound retardation	19 and below	24 and below

dren in this IQ range in their regular classrooms, but many teachers may not know how to provide for them.

As was stated earlier, there are a number of different definitions of mental retardation. These different definitions usually have different IQ cutoffs for mental retardation, and whether a child is classified as mentally retarded or not is many times dependent on the definition of mental retardation that is being used. Since different school systems or states may use different definitions of mental retardation, a child may be considered mentally retarded in one school system or state but not in another. School systems also usually use the term *educable* to refer to mildly retarded children, *trainable* to refer to moderately retarded children, and *custodial* to refer to severely and profoundly retarded children.

Identification Biases of Children Labeled "Educable Mentally Retarded"

It appears that the incidence of educable mental retardation is not equally distributed across all segments of the population. There is a tendency to label more boys as educable mentally retarded than girls. This may be because boys are usually more likely to be mischievous than girls and as a result are more likely to be candidates for referral than girls. There also seems to be a highly disproportionate number of children from lower socioeconomic status

homes who are labeled educable mentally retarded. Studies show too that minority children are overrepresented in this group.[11]

The teacher is usually the person who first identifies the child as having a problem. Many times, as already stated, the child is referred for special testing because of nonadaptive social behavior. After the referral the child is given a number of standardized tests, of which the IQ test is the most influential in determining whether a child is retarded or not. Since studies have shown that children from minority groups and from lower socioeconomic classes usually do not do as well on IQ tests as children from the rest of the population, it is not surprising to find children from these groups disproportionally represented in the group of children labeled "educable mentally retarded."

It cannot be emphasized enough how careful teachers must be in using such terms as "mentally retarded," "emotionally disturbed," and "learning disabled" to label a child. Once labeled, the child is hardly ever able to shed that label, even though the child has been incorrectly labeled. Often children so labeled continue to function at a particular level because they, themselves, have incorporated the image that others have of them into their own self-concept. (See the section on "Teacher Assumptions" in Chapter 15.)

Learning Disabilities

The definition of learning disabilities is one that needs special attention because there is so much confusion concerning this term. Researchers have found that the characteristics of children labeled "learning disabled" vary so much that it is impossible to list common characteristics. The way the term is used seems to vary not only from state to state but from school district to school district within a state.[12]

[11]Lilly, op. cit., pp. 61–62.
[12]Lilly, op. cit., p. 21.

Although there is a great amount of confusion and controversy concerning the term "learning disability" and although studies have shown that there is in existence a multitude of definitions and synonyms for this term, there is one definition that is most widely accepted and acted on. The definition that is usually given for learning disabilities is that proposed by the National Advisory Committee on Handicapped Children:

> Children with special learning disabilities exhibit a disorder in one or more of the basic psychological processes involved in understanding or in using spoken or written language. These may be manifested in disorders of listening, thinking, talking, reading, writing, spelling, or arithmetic. They include conditions which have been referred to as perceptual handicaps, brain injury, minimal brain dysfunction, dyslexia, developmental aphasia, etc. They do not include learning problems which are due primarily to visual, hearing, or motor handicaps, to mental retardation, emotional disturbance, or to environmental disadvantage.[13]

Summary

Teachers usually have children with a wide range of ability levels in their classrooms, which generally include borderline (slow-learning) and gifted children. Now, because of mainstreaming, many teachers can expect to have physically handicapped children, children with emotional problems, children with learning disabilities, and children who are mildly and moderately mentally retarded in their classes at some time. Teachers must, therefore, be prepared for their new role, and an individualized program must be developed for mainstreamed children in cooperation with the children's parents and the special education teacher or the consultant. In this chapter, language arts methods are provided that are most applicable for dealing with borderline and gifted children; however, they

[13]*National Advisory Committee on Handicapped Children: First Annual Report* (Washington, D.C.: U.S. Office of Education, 1968), p. 34.

may also be adapted for some of the children who may be mainstreamed.

Exceptional children are those children who deviate so much from the average that they require special attention. The category of exceptional children includes the gifted as well as the physically handicapped, the emotionally disturbed, and the learning disabled. Adaptive behavior is an important factor in defining individuals who are mentally retarded. Teachers must be especially cautious in using such terms as "mentally retarded," "emotionally disturbed," and "learning disabled" to label a child. Labels are difficult to shed.

SELECTED BIBLIOGRAPHY

Aiello, Barbara, ed. *Making It Work: Practical Ideas for Integrating Exceptional Children into Regular Classrooms*. Reston, Va.: The Council for Exceptional Children, 1975.

Baskin, Barbara Holland, and Karen H. Harris, eds. *The Special Child in the Library*. Chicago: American Library Association, 1976.

Charles, C. M. *Individualizing Instruction*. St. Louis, Mo.: C. V. Mosby, 1976.

Dexter, Beverly L. *Special Education and the Classroom Teacher: Concepts, Perspectives, and Strategies*. Springfield, Ill.: C C Thomas, 1977.

Dunn, Lloyd M., ed. *Exceptional Children in the Schools: Special Education in Transition*. New York: Holt, Rinehart and Winston, 1973.

"The Gifted and the Talented." (Special Feature) *Today's Education* 65 (January/February 1976): 26–44.

Kirk, Samuel A., et al. *Teaching Reading to Slow and Disabled Learners*. Boston: Houghton Mifflin, 1978.

Knight, Lester N. *Language Arts for the Exceptional: The Gifted and the Linguistically Different*. Itasca, Ill.: F. E. Peacock, 1974.

Labuda, Michael, ed. *Creative Reading for Gifted Learners: A Design for Excellence*. Newark, Del.: International Reading Association, 1974.

Laycock, Frank. *Gifted Children*. Chicago: Scott, Foresman, 1978.

Lilly, M. Stephen. *Children With Exceptional Needs:*

A Survey of Special Education. New York: Holt, Rinehart and Winston, 1979.

"Mainstreaming." (Special Feature) *Today's Education* 65 (March/April 1976): 18–32.

Macmillan, Donald L. *Mental Retardation in School and Society.* Boston: Little, Brown, 1977.

Parks, A. Lee, and Thomas N. Fairchild. *Mainstreaming the Mentally Retarded Child.* Austin, Tex.: Learning Concepts, 1976.

Paul, James L., Ann P. Turnbull, and William M. Cruickshank. *Mainstreaming: A Practical Guide.* Syracuse, N.Y.: Syracuse University Press, 1977.

Roucek, Joseph S., ed. *Slow Learner.* New York: Philosophical Library, 1970.

Scofield, Sandra J. "The Language Delayed Child in the Mainstreamed Primary Classroom." *Language Arts* 55 (September 1978): 719–723; 732.

Terman, Lewis M., and Melita H. Oden. *The Gifted Child Grows Up*, Genetic Studies of Genius, Vol. 4. Stanford, Calif.: Stanford University Press, 1947.

Turnbull, Ann P., and Jane B. Schulz. *Mainstreaming Handicapped Students: A Guide for Classroom Teachers.* Boston: Allyn and Bacon, 1979.

Witty, Paul, ed. *Gifted Child.* Westport, Conn: Greenwood Press, 1972.

eighteen

The Evaluative Process and the Language Arts Curriculum

EXAMPLES OF TEACHER COMPETENCIES

1. The teacher will be able to describe and explain the concept of evaluation.
2. The teacher will be able to explain the relationship of evaluation to the educative process.
3. The teacher will be able to state evaluative criteria for language arts.
4. The teacher will be able to state what is included in the language arts curriculum.
5. The teacher will be able to define "principle" and generate some language arts principles.
6. The teacher will be able to define "objective" and "goal."
7. The teacher will be able to explain what a behavioral objective is and generate some behavioral objectives.
8. The teacher will be able to state some objectives in the cognitive and affective domains.
9. The teacher will be able to discuss the importance of decision-making, planning, and materials to a language arts program.
10. The teacher will be able to state a variety of language arts activities that he or she would like to involve his or her students in.

The Concept of Evaluation

The word evaluation seems to bring shudders to most people. Although some individuals may look on evaluation as necessary, it is often considered an intrusion on privacy and is avoided for as long as possible. The following remarks were overheard in one school. Do they sound familiar to you?

PERSON A: "Shh, everyone be alert! Keep the kids quiet! We're being evaluated!"

PERSON B: "Oh no! Don't tell me we're being evaluated again. We just finished testing our students."

431

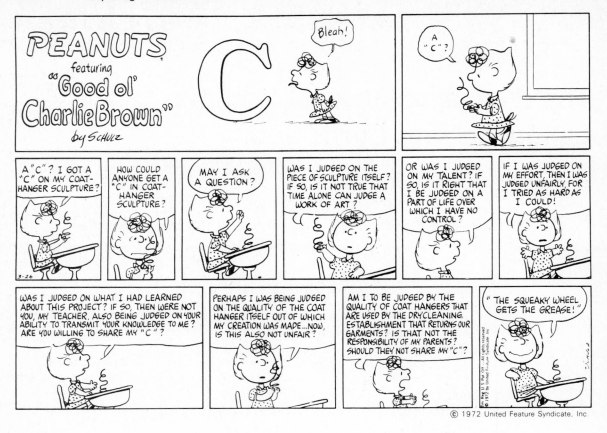

To some, evaluation and testing are synonymous. But they are not.

"'Evaluation' designates a process of appraisal which involves the acceptance of specifc values and the use of a variety of instruments of observation, including measurement, as the bases for value judgments."[1] Good evaluation occurs at the beginning, during, and at the end of the educative process; is based on an adequate collection of data; and is done in terms of desired objectives and standards. Evaluation involves making value judgments, and is therefore larger in scope than measurement, which is limited to quantitative descriptions. Since evaluation is a process carried on by humans, good evaluators avoid emotional bias in their judgments by using measurement techniques and other assessment instruments.

The Relationship of Evaluation to the Educative Process

Evaluation is a necessary, ongoing process that should be present throughout the general educational and language arts programs.

Figure 18.1 shows how the evaluative process influences and is influenced by the educational program. It also illustrates the interrelationships between and among the various parts of the educative system.

Although this text is concerned only with the

[1]Ralph W. Tyler, "The Functions of Measurement in Improving Instruction," in *Educational Measurement*, E. F. Lindquist, ed. (Washington, D.C.: American Council on Education, 1951), p. 48.

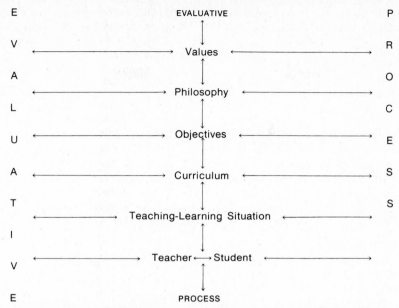

figure 18.1   *Evaluation is a continuous and integral part of the educative process.*

language arts curriculum in the elementary school, it is important for readers to recognize that evaluation of the educational process as a whole will influence the kind of language arts program that will be developed, how it will be taught, and how students and teachers will be assessed. For example, if the Board of Education in a particular school system believes in stringent censorship, it may outlaw certain books. This would affect the objectives of the children's literature program, which would in turn affect all the kinds of materials used in the classroom. This would influence the teaching–learning situation. The ramifications are many.

Evaluative Criteria for the Language Arts

A good evaluative system should meet these criteria:

1. Determine *what* is to be evaluated in the language arts program.

2. Recognize evaluation as a *means*, not as an end.

3. Take into account the *principles* of the language arts program.

4. Encompass all *objectives* valued in the language arts program.

5. Facilitate *teaching and learning* of language arts.

6. Enhance self-evaluation in the language arts.

7. Provide appropriate assessments so that the best possible communication concerning progress in the language arts is made.

8. Recognize the · limitations of assessment techniques.

The Language Arts Curriculum

The language arts curriculum includes everything in the school environment which is planned prior to instruction to promote the teaching–learning process. Therefore, the physical environment in the classroom, the materials, the equipment, and the activities would all be part of the language arts curriculum.

When the teacher and students use materials and are actively engaged in experiencing planned activities, instruction has begun. They are then involved in the teaching–learning process.

Principles of the Language Arts Program

At the inception of a language arts program principles and objectives must be agreed on by teachers, students, and the school administration so that adequate assessment and fair judgments can be made concerning the effectiveness of a specific program. Principles are rules, while objectives are ends or terminal behaviors. Established rules must be used as guides for the entire language arts program. For example, if the principle chosen is: "A teacher should consider the individual differences among students in the planning, organization, and execution of the language arts program," then these are some factors which should be observed:

1. Were the materials chosen based on the needs, readiness levels, and interests of students?
2. Were children grouped for instruction based on their readiness levels?
3. Were lessons based on the students' readiness levels?
4. Were students free to make choices based on individual interests?

The material discussed in Part One and Part Three of this book provides some of the principles of a good language arts program. For example, the chapter on creativity could be the basis for these principles:

1. A nonthreatening environment should prevail in the classroom so that children feel free to express their ideas and to make intelligent and creative guesses.
2. A physical, social, and intellectual atmosphere should be provided which is conducive to creativity.

If these principles have been included as guides for the language arts program, then here are some classroom scenes which might be observed:

1. Students freely sharing ideas and involved in a variety of language arts activities.
2. Students using many different ways to solve problems.
3. Students free to move around the classroom from one activity to another at will.
4. Classroom furniture and materials arranged so that students can move about without disturbing others.

Some further principles that might be selected from the chapters in Parts One and Three would include statements about pupil-teacher planning and the interrelatedness of the language arts.

How many principles can you generate?

Defining Objectives and Goals

Although the terms objectives and goals have the similar lexical (dictionary) meaning of ends, and refer to outcomes, some educators have used these terms differently. Goals are generally employed in developing long-range plans, whereas objectives are more often used with short-range plans—daily lesson plans, for instance. Goals are used many times with the phrase "to develop," which is somewhat at variance with the dictionary definition since "to develop" implies an ongoing process rather than an end.

Understanding Behavioral Objectives*

The Uses of Behavioral Objectives

Since the publication of Robert Mager's[2] now classic book on behavioral objectives, there has been a great amount of discussion concerning the use of such objectives. The three main in-

---

*Such terms as instructional objectives, performance objectives, or learning objectives can be used in place of behavioral objectives if they are stated in behavioral terms.

[2]Robert F. Mager, *Preparing Instructional Objectives* (Palo Alto, Calif.: Fearon Publishers, 1962).

structional functions put forth for using behavioral objectives are:

1. Direction for teaching and curriculum development.
2. Guidance in evaluation.
3. Facilitation of learning.[3]

Although the research done on behavioral objectives is not conclusive, it does suggest certain effects that facilitate learning. For example, behavioral objectives help provide direction for the learning of students, and they help students to differentiate between relevant and incidental content by their knowing what is expected of them. Other functions of behavioral objectives are:

1. They provide organization of the subject matter.
2. They serve as a management function, enabling students to better manage their time and learning experiences in accordance with the goals of the course.
3. They provide feedback to learners; that is, learners can compare their performances with the criteria contained in the objectives.
4. They serve as task reinforcers; that is, students who know they are mastering a certain set of goals will be more effective than those whose only reinforcement is a grade at the end of the term.

Some persons who object to the use of behavioral objectives in evaluation claim that only trivial educational outcomes will be emphasized, because these are the easiest to make operational, while the really important outcomes will be ignored. W. James Popham, Director of the Instructional Objectives Exchange at the University of California, refutes this claim, stating that just the opposite is true:[4]

[3]Phillipe C. Duchastel and Paul F. Merrill, "The Effects of Behavioral Objectives on Learning: A Review of Empirical Studies," *Review of Educational Research* 43 (Winter 1973): 53–69.
[4]W. James Popham, "Probing the Validity of Arguments against Behavioral Objectives," in Robert J. Kibler, et al., *Objectives for Instruction and Evaluation* (Boston: Allyn and Bacon, 1974), pp. 10–11.

. . . if you were to ask a social science teacher what his objectives were for his government class and he responded as follows, "I want to make my students better citizens so that they can function effectively in our nation's dynamic democracy," you would probably find little reason to fault him. His objective sounds so profound and eminently worthwhile that few could criticize it. Yet beneath such facades of profundity, many teachers really are aiming at extremely trivial kinds of pupil behavior changes. How often, for example, do we find "good citizenship" measured by a trifling true-false test. Now if we'd asked for the teacher's objectives in operational terms and had discovered that, indeed, all the teacher was attempting to do was promote the learner's achievement on a true-false test, we might have rejected the aim as being unimportant. But this is possible *only* with the precision of explicitly stated goals.

In other words, there is the danger that because of their ready translation to operational statements, teachers will tend to identify too many trivial behaviors as goals. But the very fact that we can make these behaviors explicit permits the teacher and his colleagues to scrutinize them carefully and thus eliminate them as unworthy of our educational efforts. Instead of encouraging unimportant outcomes in education, the use of explicit instructional objectives makes it possible to identify and reject those objectives which are unimportant [while retaining those that are worthwhile*].

Defining Behavioral Objectives

Behavioral objectives describe what students will be able to do after they have achieved their goals. With the use of behavioral objectives, teachers can very readily evaluate students' performances. Behavioral objectives help teachers to clarify their thinking in the preparation of lesson plans because they have to identify precisely what learning behaviors should be exhibited at the end of a lesson. For example, if instructors were to state as an objective: "to develop the understanding that. . . ," how would they know whether students had gained such

*Author's addition.

understanding? They wouldn't, because the phrase "to develop" implies an ongoing process, while the term "understanding" is a construct— something which cannot be directly observed or directly measured. The teacher must aviod using terms which defy direct observation. All stated learning outcomes must be of observable rather than covert (hidden) behavior. A good behavioral objective should include terminal behavior; that is, the objective should state what behavior the student would exhibit in order to demonstrate his or her accomplishment of the desired end. It should state the criterion or test by which the end can be evaluated. The teacher competencies stated at the beginning of each chapter may also be regarded as behavioral objectives; however, as stated earlier, they usually do not include the standard to measure the success of the performance nor the conditions under which the behavior is to be performed.

Objectives in the Cognitive Domain

B. S. Bloom's *Taxonomy of Educational Objectives*,[5] which is concerned with the cognitive domain, is helpful in determining those objectives concerned with thinking that students should achieve in any discipline. This taxonomy is based on an ordered set of objectives ranging from the more simplistic thinking skills to the more complex ones. Bloom's objectives are cumulative in that each objective includes the one preceding it. As a result, evaluation, the highest level in the taxonomy, includes all the preceding objectives in the hierarchy.

Here are the six major categories in Bloom's taxonomy of objectives in the cognitive domain:

1. *knowledge:* deals with definitions and statements of facts in various subject-matter fields
2. *comprehension:* enables people to explain or summarize a statement
3. *application:* enables people to use knowledge and understanding to solve a problem

4. *analysis:* enables people to separate a whole into its elemental parts
5. *synthesis:* enables people to put the elements together into a whole
6. *evaluation:* enables people to make judgments using all preceding cognitive skills.

In order to facilitate the writing of behavioral objectives, samples of some verbs, which describe various cognitive behaviors, follow:

Verbs to Use in Writing Behavioral Objectives in the Cognitive Domain

recognize, identify, find
illustrate, examine
prove, construct, differentiate, relate
estimate, compare, distinguish between
analyze, generalize from data
deduce, formulate hypotheses, integrate
synthesize, evaluate

Taxonomy of Objectives in the Affective Domain

The affective environment is concerned with the feelings and emotional learnings of students. Affective learnings are longer lasting than much of the subject matter of the course and usually exert a dynamic and directive influence on the individual's future involvement with the subject matter. Because knowledge in the affective domain is so important, teachers must have a better understanding of these emotional understandings and also some means of evaluating whether students' affective learnings are favorable or not in specific areas. Before teachers can determine what changes should take place, they must have knowledge of what is happening in their classrooms and also what kinds of objectives are involved in the affective domain.

A taxonomy of educational objectives in the affective domain is presented in a helpful handbook for the teacher.[6] These objectives in the

[5]B. S. Bloom, ed., *Taxonomy of Educational Objectives—The Classification of Educational Goals, Handbook I: Cognitive Domain* (New York: McKay, 1956).

[6]David R. Krathwohl, Benjamin S. Bloom, Bertram B. Masia, *Taxonomy of Educational Objectives—The Classification of Educational Goals, Handbook II: Affective Domain* (New York: McKay, 1964).

affective domain are ordinally arranged or ranked according to the degree of "internalization" involved; that is, the first category, *receiving*, is one which has a lesser degree of internalization than that of *responding*, and responding has a lesser degree of internalization than *valuing*, and so forth. In other words, each successive level in the affective domain is in a continuum employing a greater amount of internalization as the categories move on. The fifth category, *characterization by a value*, or value complex, has the greatest degree of internalization; at this level it would involve behavior that is an important or essential part of individuals and their lifestyles.

Following are samples of verbs which can be used to describe various behaviors in the affective domain:

Verbs to Use in Writing Behavioral Objectives in the Affective Domain

volunteer, take part, choose, offer, give
help, share, practice, respond, accept

Constructing and Generating Behavioral Objectives

Cognitive Domain

In formulating behavioral objectives the exact outcomes must be stated in observable terms for ease of evaluation. Following are examples of behavioral and nonbehavioral objectives at different levels of the cognitive domain, which illustrate how much easier it is to evaluate in terms of behavioral objectives:

1. Behavioral objective: Knowledge Level
   Student will be able to state three words that rhyme with man in one minute with 100 percent accuracy.
   Nonbehavioral objective:
   To develop the understanding of rhyming words.

2. Behavioral objective: Knowledge and Application Level
   Students should be able to state the *"ie"* spelling rule and list ten words to which it applies within an exam period and with 90 percent accuracy.
   Nonbehavioral objective:
   To develop the understanding of the *"ie"* rule in spelling.

3. Behavioral objective: Synthesis Level
   During a handwriting lesson students will be able to construct the letter *n* in cursive with the proper slant, round-top, or overcurve without lifting their pencils from their papers while writing the following words: name, none, nap.
   Nonbehavioral objective:
   To develop the understanding of writing the letter *n*.

Affective Domain

1. Behavioral objective: Responding Level
   Students will volunteer to take part in the production of a class play.
   Nonbehavioral objective:
   Students enjoy play production.

2. Behavioral objective: Organization Level
   Students will formulate standards for cursive writing, which they will use in evaluating their cursive writing papers.
   Nonbehavioral objective:
   Students appreciate good handwriting.

Decision-Making, Planning, and Materials for a Language Arts Program

Planning for the language arts program includes decision-making. When the teacher decides to arrange the desks in the classroom in a semicircle rather than in straight rows, a decision has been made based on the teacher's values. The teacher who recognizes the importance of students' visual contact for more effective aural (listening) and oral (speaking) communication will develop a program different from the one for children who are always sitting behind one another.

Similarly, teachers who choose a variety of materials from many sources are making decisions that will affect the kind of language arts program they will present. Their programs will be different from those of teachers who use only one source for materials. If teachers decide they want to use a multimedia approach to teaching, further decisions concerning the kinds of materials employed in their lessons must also be made. For example, will the lesson be more effective if only printed materials—such as books, bulletins, or pamphlets—are used, or should cartoons and charts be brought into the classroom? Cartoons give some comic relief if they are at the comprehension level of the students, and charts graphically illustrate some of the points made in the written material. Such questions as to whether the print is too small, or whether the words used in printed materials are at the children's reading level, must also be considered if evaluation of children's accomplishments with the material is to be valid.

Should visual aids such as pictures (photographs of individuals, places, animals, objects), picture slides, television, filmstrips, videotapes, or motion pictures be used? This decision would depend on the amount of time allotted to the lesson, the availability of the visual aids, which facilities are provided, and whether there were other more effective ways to obtain the desired objectives.

Should audio aids—such as tape recorders, record players, the radio, or plays—be brought into class? Again the answer would depend on the objectives and what is being stressed in a particular lesson. For example, if the lesson focuses on some aspect of speech improvement,

a video- or audiotape recorder would be an invaluable tool, if it is properly used.

Teachers must decide on the kinds of concrete materials they will need for the language arts program. Often such decisions must be made months before the materials are to be used because of the long lead time necessary for delivery. In this case planning must take place before the beginning of the school year. This would be particularly true if the teacher wants students to learn to express themselves, for instance, as in puppet making. If the teacher wants to coordinate a writing lesson with an art period, various kinds of construction paper and other art supplies must be made available to give children the choice of a range of materials.

It can be seen that planning and decision-making are an ongoing process that complement one another. The better the planning and the more timely the decision-making, the more effective the language arts program will be.

Planning Language Arts Activities

Teachers who decide at the beginning of the year that they want to involve their students in a variety of language arts activities will plan accordingly. Although it is not possible to plan the details of specific lessons beforehand—because the needs, interests, and readiness levels of the students are not yet known—decisions should be made concerning the possible kinds of activities that will be considered for the program.

Teachers might use the "Suggested Activities List" as an assessment aid to help determine whether they are providing a sufficient variety of activities for their pupils.

What other activities can you think of for the language arts program?

Suggested Activities List

Suggested Activities	Check each activity as your pupils have completed experience with it.				
1. Writing and sending friendly letters					
to sick classmates					
to other classes					
for Junior Red Cross booklets					
to invite guests					
to thank someone					
Signing and addressing cards for birthdays, holidays, Valentine Day					
Addressing envelopes properly					
Using charts or books to check the letter form					
2. Telephoning					
Making and answering a call					
Referring to books for good telephone manners					
Use of directory (making class directory)					
3. Introducing people					
Various situations involving introductions					
Using books to check rules					
4. Taking part in discussions					
Setting up rules with the group					
Stating the problem clearly					
Constantly referring to books					
Sifting out the part which answers the question					
5. Having an interview					
Listing questions to ask					
Keeping notes					
Summarizing					
Reporting					
6. Experimenting with creative expression					
Writing endings for stories					
Telling story heard in music					
Writing stories of pictures (what happened before the picture, what is happening in the picture, what will happen after the picture)					

Suggested Activities List (Continued)

Suggested Activities	Check each activity as your pupils have completed experience with it.				
Giving impressions of rain, wind, snow, smoke					
Finishing lines when a part is given					
Choral reading					
Writing words for tunes					
Writing original poems					
7. Writing business forms					
Writing business letters for materials, arrangements, and so on					
Referring to form in books					
Addressing and mailing packages					
Filling in blanks for mail orders, money orders, checks, and so on					
8. Taking part in dramatizations					
Reading parts from books					
Spontaneous conversation (characters change each time)					
Writing and giving original plays					
Using puppets					
Writing and recording a radio script					
Creative dramatics					
9. Making announcements					
10. Giving directions					
11. Carrying verbal messages					
12. Making summaries (varied types)					
13. Making outlines					
14. Taking notes					
15. Activities growing out of books					
Who's Who in Books (riddles)					
Drawing pictures of favorite parts to recommend a book					
Making an anthology of favorite poems					
Sharing poems, jokes, riddles					
Keeping an individual record of books read					
Reading orally to lower grades					

Suggested Activities List (Continued)

Suggested Activities	Check each activity as your pupils have completed experience with it.				
Making an annotated bibliography					
Making and using a table of contents for a book					
16. Working in committees					
Serving as chairperson					
Contributing to committee's report					
17. Using a code to find and correct errors					
18. Keeping samples of best handwriting and evaluating them					
19. Keeping a spelling dictionary of difficult words (individual)					
20. Planning bulletin boards					
Selecting materials					
Writing captions for pictures					
21. Producing a newspaper					
Writing "morning news"					
Selecting and rejecting materials					
Writing headlines					
Proofreading					
22. Conducting a meeting					
Serving as chairperson					
Writing minutes					
Electing officers					
23. Making class or individual books					
Making a cover and title page					
Making a table of contents					
Writing a preface and dedication					
Planning and writing content					
Drawing illustrations with captions					
Making an index					
Making a bibliography					

Summary

Evaluation is a continuous, ongoing process consisting of value judgments based on adequate measurement and other assessment techniques. It involves more than grading and testing. In order to plan for an effective language arts program, decisions must be made as to what principles and objectives will act as guides for the program. Choices must also be made for the various kinds of materials and activities that will be used. The teacher who chooses a variety of materials and activities has different values from those of the teacher who is content with no variety. Such value decisions will determine the kind of language arts program that will evolve.

SELECTED BIBLIOGRAPHY

Adams, Georgia S. *Measurement and Evaluation in Education*. New York: Holt, Rinehart and Winston, 1964.

Berger, Allen, and Blanche Hope Smith, eds. *Classroom Practices in Teaching English, 1973–1974, Language Activities*. Urbana, Ill.: National Council of Teachers of English, 1973.

Bloom, Benjamin, and David R. Krathwohl. *Taxonomy of Educational Objectives, Handbook I: Cognitive Domain*. New York: McKay, 1956.

Eson, Morris E. *Psychological Foundations of Education*. New York: Holt, Rinehart and Winston, 1972.

Hoover, Kenneth H., and Paul M. Hollingsworth. *Learning and Teaching in the Elementary School*, 2d ed. Boston: Allyn and Bacon, 1975.

Kibler, Robert J., et al. *Objectives for Instruction and Evaluation*. Boston: Allyn and Bacon, 1974.

Krathwohl, David R., Benjamin Bloom, and B. B. Masea. *Taxonomy of Educational Objectives, Handbook II: Affective Domain*. New York: McKay, 1964.

Kryspin, William J., and John F. Feldhusen. *Writing Behavioral Objectives: A Guide for Planning Instruction*. Minneapolis: Burgess, 1974.

Mager, Robert F. *Preparing Instructional Objectives*, 2d ed. Belmont, Calif.: Fearon-Pitman Publishers, 1975.

Nachbar, Cornèlia. "Accountability Is Not a Dirty Word," *Elementary English* 51 (May 1974): 717–720; 730.

O'Donnell, Bernard, ed. *Aids to Curriculum Planning of English Language Arts K-12*. Urbana, Ill.: National Council of Teachers of English, 1973.

Plowman, Paul D. *Behavioral Objectives*. Chicago: Science Research Associates, 1970.

Popham, W. J., and E. L. Baker. *Establishing Instructional Goals*. Englewood Cliffs, N.J.: Prentice-Hall, 1970.

Smith, Fred M., and Sam Adams. *Educational Measurement for the Classroom*, 2d ed. New York: Harper & Row, 1972.

Wilhelms, Fred T., ed. *Evaluation as Feedback and Guide*. Washington, D.C., Association for Supervision and Curriculum Development, 1967.

nineteen

Evaluation of Student Performance and Progress

1. The teacher will be able to state students' language arts goals and objectives.

2. The teacher will be able to discuss the importance of student assessment as part of the evaluative process.

3. The teacher will be able to state criteria for a good test.

4. The teacher will be able to describe standardized tests and explain what their greatest value is.

5. The teacher will be able to describe different kinds of teacher-made tests.

6. The teacher will be able to explain what a criterion-referenced test is and compare criterion-referenced tests to norm-referenced tests.

7. The teacher will be able to explain the importance of knowledge of results.

8. The teacher will be able to explain what "assessment as diagnostic" means.

9. The teacher will be able to state and describe the steps in a diagnostic pattern.

10. The teacher will be able to explain how to involve the student in diagnosing a problem.

11. The teacher will be able to explain how students' errors should be described.

12. The teacher will be able to explain the importance of observation in evaluating behavior.

13. The teacher will be able to discuss the problems involved in grading.

14. The teacher will be able to explain why the parent-teacher conference is a most effective means of reporting pupil progress.

Introduction

Children coming home from school are often asked: "What did you do in school today?" The reply frequently is: "Nothing."

One would hope that desirable learning is taking place, and that this is noticeable in children's behavior, without the children being aware of it. How can we measure this? What are the language arts goals and objectives for assessing students' learning behaviors? How can learning behavior be determined? What is the place for student self-evaluation? What problems are there in grading students' work? How should pupil progress be reported? This chapter will attempt to answer these questions.

Students' Language Arts Goals and Objectives

Both educators and lay persons recognize the importance of goals such as:

1. Encouraging creative thinking.
2, Developing essential listening skills.
3. Developing the ability to listen critically and selectively.
4. Becoming aware of good speech.
5. Developing an appreciation for a rich, expressive vocabulary.
6. Developing the ability to write creatively.
7. Developing a spelling consciousness.
8. Developing an appreciation for good literature.

However, such general goal statements do not aid in assessing students' language arts behavior. To do this it is necessary to describe *what* student behaviors should be present in order to indicate achievement of the goals. Objectives that are stated behaviorally—which exactly describe the operations that learners must perform to acquire the objectives—solve a large part of the assessment problem. Once the desired result is defined, the measurement is actually contained in the statement of the objective. For example, the objective is described as: Students will be able to state the "hard *c*" rule generalization in spelling and apply the rule to the following words: panic, picnic, traffic. Then the test is: The child is asked to write the "hard *c*" rule and spell panicky, picnicker, and trafficking. (See Chapter 18 for help in constructing and generating behavioral objectives.)

Assessment for Evaluation

Examinations are formidable, even to the best prepared, for the greatest fool may ask more than the wisest man can answer.

C. C. COLTON

The positive values of measurement outweigh the negative connotations associated with assessment. Measurement is useful for diagnostic, review, and predictive purposes. It can be used as a motivating technique for students, as well as a basis for grades and promotion. Through student assessment, teachers are also able to reevaluate their own teaching methods.

In order for measurement to be an effective part of the evaluative process, teachers must master varied measurement techniques and be able to administer and interpret them. Such measurements include standardized tests and teacher-made tests. Direct observation of student behavior is also necessary in order to collect data for valid evaluations.

Criteria for a Good Test

Whatever tests teachers choose for assessment, the tests should all meet these criteria:

1. *Objectivity:* The same score must result regardless of who marks the test. Since essay questions do not lend themselves to a high degree of objectivity, the users of such tests should give specific directions for scoring, and should make the essay question as explicit as possible.

2. *Validity:* The appraisal instrument should measure what it claims to measure. There are differ-

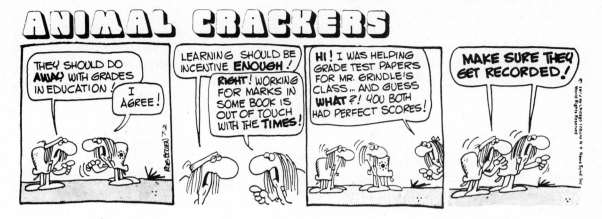

ent kinds of validity, but language arts teachers will be concerned primarily with the content of a test. In order to determine content validity the test should be compared with course content.

3. *Reliability:* The test is reliable if it consistently produces similar results when repeated measurements are taken of the same students under the same conditions.

4. *Suitability:* In selecting or preparing a test, the teacher must determine not only whether it will yield the type of data desired but also whether the test is suitable for the age and type of students and for the locality in which the students reside.

Standardized Tests[1]

Standardized tests are commercial tests which have been constructed by experts in the field and are available from publishers. In developing these tests a large representative sample of students have been used for research and reliability, more than is possible with a teacher-made test. The greatest value of standardized tests is their consistency or sameness.

Standardized tests contain exact instructions

[1]Oscar K. Buros's *Mental Measurements Yearbook* is an important source on standard tests. A teacher can use this reference to obtain information about specific tests or to locate tests in specific areas.

on how to administer them. These instructions must be followed by all testers so that they can compare scores for different students or groups of individuals. The comparison is easily made, since each standardized test has available a set of norms based on the national sample. Norms are average scores for a given group of students, which help teachers to learn where their own students stand in relation to others in the class, school system, city, state, or nation. Although a child may be doing average work in a particular class, the child may be above average when compared to other norms. Similarly, it is possible for a child to be doing above average in a third-grade class, but to be below average for all third graders in the nation.

Teachers must be cautious in their analysis of test results. They should not be intimidated by standardized tests and they must recognize the limitations of these tests. Teachers must determine whether a test is appropriate for their students. If the class has not covered the work in the standardized test, it obviously would not be valid. Differences in student populations must also be taken into account in interpreting test results.

Other important factors concern the students themselves in the test situation. Students who are overly anxious or upset by a test, who are tired or hungry, or who lack motivation will not perform as well as others not burdened in these ways. Such factors will adversely affect test performance. Read Dick Gregory's disturbing words:[2]

> The teacher thought I was stupid. Couldn't spell, couldn't read, couldn't do arithmetic. Just stupid. Teachers were never interested in finding out that you couldn't concentrate because you were so hungry, because you hadn't had any breakfast. All you could think about was noontime, would it ever come? Maybe you could sneak into the cloakroom and steal a bite of some kid's lunch out of a coat pocket. A bite of something. Paste. You can't really make a meal of paste, or put it on bread for a sandwich, but sometimes I'd scoop a few spoonfuls out of the big paste jar in the back of the room. Pregnant people get strange tastes. I was pregnant with poverty.

Teacher-made Tests

Teachers can get quick feedback on student learning behaviors by constructing appropriate informal tests. Since these tests to a large extent help to determine students' grades, they must be carefully constructed so that valid results are achieved. For example, if contractions are being taught in class, the test should cover contractions only.

Kinds of Teacher-made Tests Tests are usually classified into essay and objective types. The teacher must decide which kind is the most applicable for the area being tested. Although language arts lends itself more to essay tests, both these and objective tests can be used. Objective tests allow for more comprehensive coverage of an area, while essay tests cover subject matter to a greater depth. Objective tests are also more easily graded because there is usually only one correct answer for a given question. Since essay tests are subjective, they are more

difficult to grade. Studies have shown that the same essay, graded by different teachers, will receive as many different evaluations as the number of teachers rating the essay.[3] Similarly, an essay graded by a teacher in the morning may receive a different rating if it is graded by the same person in the evening or the next day.

These suggestions may help teachers to determine when to use essay tests:

1. The group to be tested is small, and the test will not be reused.
2. The instructor wishes to do everything possible to encourage and reward the development of student skill in written expression.
3. The instructor is more interested in exploring the students' attitudes than in measuring achievements.
4. The instructor is more confident of his or her proficiency as a critical reader than as an imaginative writer of good objective test items.
5. The time available for test preparation is shorter than the time available for test grading.[4]

In devising essay-test questions the teacher should avoid ambiguity, making the questions as specific as possible, with explicit directions. For example:

Poor: Explain the poem _____.

Better: Compare the poem _____
to the poem _____
in terms of the author's ability to portray the idea of "fatalism."

An essay is defined as "a test item which requires a response composed by the examinee, usually in the form of one or more sentences, of a nature that no single response or pattern of responses can be listed as correct, and the accuracy and quality of which can be judged subjectively only by one skilled or informed in

---

[2]Dick Gregory, *Nigger: An Autobiography* (New York: Dutton, 1964), p.44.

[3]B. Claude Mathis, John W. Cotton, Lee Sechrest, *Psychological Foundations of Education* (New York: Academic Press, 1970), pp. 614–620.

[4]R. L. Ebel, *Measuring Educational Achievement* (Englewood Cliffs, N.J.: Prentice-Hall, 1965), pp. 109–110.

the subject."[5] A good example of this type of essay question in an English class is one asking the student to write on "How I Feel about Poetry" or "How I Feel about Poe's Stories." It is impossible to assess correctness of content, and the grader must make a subjective judgment of quality.

Such topics have value when the teacher wants to evaluate students' ability to write logically and to organize the subject matter, as well as when students' ability to use proper word usage and punctuation is to be investigated. If this is the purpose of the essay, students should be told so before the test.

Essay questions are also useful for measuring divergent thinking, since there are no correct answers in a test of this kind. However, the difficulty comes in determining what criteria to use in measuring creativity.

Objective tests include true-false, multiple-choice, fill-in, and matching questions. For example, a fill-in test where students have to put in the correct word could be devised to show understanding of the homonyms "to," "too," and "two." Put the correct word in the following sentences:

I _____ (to, two, too) want to go.

He went _____ (to, two, too) town.

The children have _____(to, two, too) balls.

Criterion-Referenced Tests

Criterion-referenced tests are based on an extensive inventory of learning objectives in a specific curriculum area. The objectives are presented in behavioral terms. (See Chapter 18.)

Criterion-referenced tests are designed to diagnose specific behaviors of individual students. They are used to gain more information about the students' various skill levels, and the information is used to either reinforce, supple-

[5]As cited by Stalnaker, in Mathis, et al., op. cit., p. 613.

ment, or remediate the skill-development area being tested. The test results help the instructor plan specific learning sequences to help the students master the objective they missed.

Criterion-referenced tests are not norm-based; that is, they do not provide a means for comparing students to a standardization sample or a norm group. Criterion-referenced tests are concerned primarily with mastery of behavioral objectives, which are based on classroom curriculum. On criterion-referenced tests an individual competes only with him- or herself. There is very little difference in appearance between a norm-referenced test and a criterion-referenced test; however, differences do exist, as has already been noted, in the purposes for the tests. An example of a question from a criterion-referenced test and the specific pupil behavioral objective to which the test question correlates follow:

General area: reading comprehension (interpretation)
Specific area: drawing inferences
Behavioral objective: The student will draw inferences about the personality of the main character based on the content of reading material.

The child is asked to read a short story carefully. After the child has finished reading the story, the child is asked to answer questions based on the story. An example of a question based on the given behavioral objective follows:

What can you infer about the personality of Dennis?

The child is then asked to choose the best answer from the given statements. (Note that in criterion-referenced testing *every* test item is related to a corresponding behavioral objective.)

Criterion-referenced tests can be commercially produced or teacher-made. Many individualized programs use criterion-referenced tests. (See Chapter 16.)

Knowledge of Results

Since feedback is essential in correcting faulty responses, teachers should always go over tests as soon as possible—immediately after the test is the best time. One technique that helps students eliminate errors is to have them write their answers twice. Students fold their papers vertically in half. They then write their answers on one side of the paper and at the end of the test they copy the answers on the other side of the paper, which is then ripped down the creased edge. One sheet is given to the teacher; the other is retained. When the test is reviewed immediately afterward, the student gets immediate knowledge of results.

Assessment as Diagnostic

Appropriate instruction stems from and is interwoven with accurate and pertinent diagnostic information. Diagnosis is ongoing and is necessary for prevention as well as for remediation. In diagnosis the teacher is interested in emphasizing or defining the nature of the student's language arts difficulty and the conditions causing it. To do this the teacher must first *identify* at what level the student is in each language arts area. This is done by using both standardized and informal tests. The teacher must then *appraise* the student's present level of performance in relation to his or her potential. (See the section on intelligence tests in Chapter 2 and the section on "Who Is a Disabled Reader?" in Chapter 8.) After appraisal, the teacher does extensive diagnosis to discover the specific conditions and abilities that underlie the student's performance in a particular area. Then the teacher helps the student to set attainable goals in the particular area.

A Diagnostic Pattern

Step I: Identification The teacher must first *identify* the student's present status in a partic-

ular problem area. The teacher does this by describing in detail the individual student's performance in the specific problem area. For example, if a student is having difficulty in reading, the teacher would describe in detail what phonic skills the student possesses, what word attack method the student consistently uses, how large the student's sight vocabulary is, how well the student reads orally, what difficulties the student encounters when he or she reads orally and what errors he or she makes, how accurate the student is in comprehending silent reading material or how accurate the student is in comprehending material when it is read to him or her. Informal tests as well as standardized achievement tests are used to help determine a student's present performance in an area.

Step II: Appraisal After determining the student's performance level in a particular area, the teacher must *appraise* the student's performance in relation to his or her potential. For example, in the area of reading, the teacher first determines the student's reading performance (see Step I), and then the teacher determines the student's reading expectancy. The teacher then tries to determine if there is a discrepancy between the student's reading performance as determined by achievement tests and the student's reading expectancy. (See the section on "Who Is a Disabled Reader?" in Chapter 8.)

Step III: Diagnosis At this step the teacher is interested in discovering the specific conditions and abilities that underlie the student's performance in a particular area. The teacher observes the student while the student is in the activity causing him or her difficulty to try to find the conditions influencing his or her performance. For example, while reading, does the student display any anxieties? Does he or she have any habits such as subvocalizing (moving lips while reading), pointing to each word, and so on? Next, the teacher tries to determine whether the abilities involved in the specific skill area are causing the difficulty. For example, lack of phonic skills may be due to deficiencies in auditory or visual discrimination (perceptual problems) or lack of memory (retention problems). Through further diagnostic testing and observation, the teacher tries to determine whether the problem is due to organic or experiential factors. Obviously, if the teacher suspects an organic problem, he or she should refer the student to a skilled professional or medical doctor for further testing. The teacher also tries to determine whether the student's problem is due to the student's attitude or motivation.

Student Involvement

The only purpose for diagnosis is to determine what is causing a student's problem so that a program can be developed to help a student overcome the difficulty. Student involvement is crucial. Unless the student recognizes that he or she has a problem, unless the student understands what that problem is, and unless the student is interested in overcoming the problem, nothing much will probably be accomplished.

The teacher can help the student to become involved in the following ways:

1. The teacher should help the student recognize his or her strengths as well as weaknesses.
2. The teacher should not overwhelm the student with a listing of all his or her difficulties at once.
3. The teacher should try to elicit from the student what the student thinks his or her language arts problems are, why the student feels that he or she has these problems, and what the student feels are the causes of his or her language arts problems.
4. The teacher and the student together set attainable goals for a specific problem area.
5. Together, the next learning step is determined.

Describing Student Errors

So that evaluation is diagnostic, the nature of student errors must be pointed out as clearly as possible. The student should understand exactly what the teacher is saying.

The "Poor handwriting!" on a student's paper will not help a child correct the problem. The teacher should help the student understand that an illegible paper cannot be read and that communication is therefore not taking place. Examples of legible handwriting against which children can judge themselves should be available. Teachers should also point out specific problems in constructing letters so that the children can improve in this area. For example, the teacher could say: "In writing the *e* for cursive you are not forming your loop, so that it is difficult to tell the *e* from the *i*'s." (See the diagnostic checklists at the end of each language arts subject-matter chapter.)

Observation of Students' Learning Behaviors

The best method for determining whether students have learned something is to observe whether they are actually using what they have learned. For example, it is one thing to be able to pass a paper-and-pencil test on proper punctuation in letter writing, but it is something else to apply these principles when actually writing letters, whether in or out of school. Another example would be the difference between stating the importance of being courteous and giving examples of courteous behavior on a paper-and-pencil test, and behaving in a courteous manner at all times.

Direct observation is helpful to the teacher who wants to become aware of the attitudes, interests, and appreciations of students. For example, teachers can observe whether students are volunteering to participate in discussion and to work in group projects, and whether they voluntarily take books from the library and read them. Teachers can also learn about students' interests by observing what they do in their free time.

So that observations are of value, teachers must be as objective as possible and avoid making generalizations about students' behavior too early in the process of getting to know them. For example, by observing that Jane on one or two occasions is reading mystery stories, the teacher states that Jane likes mysteries. This may be so, but it may also be that she is just "trying them out." Jane may actually like only a few of them and she may read only one or two a year.

Student Self-Evaluation and Group Evaluation

The same procedure applies to self-evaluation as took place in teacher evaluation of the student. First it is necessary to formulate objectives in order for students to feel a need for evaluating some aspect of their achievements. They then determine what kinds of assessment methods they will use, and collect data. Conclusions are formed after the data have been analyzed.

The only difference between group evaluation and self-evaluation is that the group makes all the decisions.

In language arts classes teachers and students usually combine their efforts to develop standards for different activities. Examples of standards by which students can evaluate themselves are presented in the various subject-matter chapters.

Difficulties in Grading

FATHER: "Well, son, how are your marks?"
SON: "They're under water."
FATHER: "What do you mean under water?"
SON: "Below 'C' level."

We usually do not joke about our own grades, for they often affect our subsequent learning behavior. Grades may act as positive reinforcement for those students with good grades, but they negatively reinforce those with poor marks. Yet when pupils are overly concerned about grades, the grades may become more important than learning the material.

Grading is a complex topic. Some educators feel that traditional grades should be discarded, and "replaced with something more informative, more diagnostic, and more harmonious with students' own motivations."[6]

The subjectivity inherent in grading brings up the problem of unreliability.

A child returned home from school with his report card for his mother's inspection. "But, dear," she said, "what's the trouble? Why do you have such poor grades this month?" "There's no trouble, Mom," was the quick reply. "You know yourself things are always marked down after the holidays."

Different criteria may be used by different teachers as a basis for grading. For example, one teacher may use a composite of the students' test scores, while another may use the effort exerted by the student in class work. In the second case, a student who receives "A's" on all language arts papers, but according to the teacher is not exerting an effort, may not get an "A" on his or her report card. Some teachers lower the grade if neatness counts in their evaluation. Student absences, lateness, deportment, and show of interest can all be factors in determining a grade.

There are teachers who award grades based on pupils' achievement in relation to ability. A child with high ability would be expected to do more than a student with low ability. As a result, low-ability children doing less good work might get higher grades than high-ability students doing higher-quality work which was nevertheless not up to teacher expectation.

For grades to have any significance and uniformity, school systems must determine the criteria for grading. Students and parents should be informed as to what the criteria are. The grade will be a more accurate evaluation of stu-

[6]Fred T. Wilhelms, "Evaluation as Feedback," and Clifford F. S. Bebell, "The Evaluation We Have," in *Evaluation as Feedback and Guide*, Fred T. Wilhelms, ed. (Washington, D.C.: Association for Supervision and Curriculum Development, 1967), pp. 6 and 45.

dent performance if a number of valid measurement techniques are used and other information is given.

Other Criteria Affecting Grades

"The teacher said I must learn to write more legibly," the child told his mother, "but if I do, she'll find out I can't spell."

Should teachers lower grades when a paper is messy or if there are spelling errors if the answers are correct? Should teachers lower grades because of poor handwriting if the ideas are creatively expressed? These questions are important to both students and teachers. Although it is important to recognize the interrelatedness of such factors, and although transference of learning to other areas is desirable, teachers must grade according to the degree that objectives have been achieved. If a teacher cannot decide whether an *i* is an *e* on a spelling test, then the teacher is justified in marking the word incorrect and asking the child to write more legibly. However, in an outlining test, or in the writing of a creative composition, the teacher should not "grade down" a paper with spelling errors or one that is not neat. The incorrect spelling should be corrected by the teacher, although the error will not count in the grade. Neatness is more difficult to handle. However, as children gain respect for their own work and take more pride in it, it is to be hoped that they will attempt to be neater.

Reporting Pupil Progress to Parents

"How is my child doing?" is the question parents most often want the teacher to answer. The method used to report pupil progress will reflect the kind of program prevalent in the school. The report to parents, which consists of specific compartmentalized sections of the curriculum in which a letter or percentage grade is given, probably reflects a curriculum taught in a compartmentalized way. If the report is vague and nebulous, the curriculum probably is also. If the report is direct, informative, and individualized, an unusual curriculum probably lies behind it. Such a report would consist of a combination of grades and written reports, as well as parent-teacher conferences.

The parent-teacher conference is the most effective way of reporting pupil progress. So that these conferences give the greatest value, teachers should have a progressive sampling of the student's work available. Teachers must be friendly, interested, and allow for an exchange of ideas with parents. It is also important for teachers to recognize that, although they have twenty-five or thirty students in the class, this particular child is the most important one to the parents because he or she is theirs.

Teachers should help parents to understand the grading system and should discuss the children's ranking in relation to the class, national norms, and their own abilities. Most importantly, since this conference is primarily an exchange of ideas, teachers should encourage parents to give some insights into the children that would be helpful in teaching them. Remember, it is doubtful that anyone knows these children better than their parents. If the children need any special help, teachers should point this out to parents and explain precisely what they can do.

Parent-teacher conferences need not take place only during the reporting period. Whenever a need for a conference arises is the right time to call for one. However, teachers should remember that successful parent-teacher conferences require careful planning and effort.

Summary

Student evaluation is a necessary component of effective teaching and learning. Teachers must be knowledgeable about a variety of measurement techniques and be able to use these to collect data for more accurate student evaluation. Diagnosis is an important part of any instructional program, and teachers should be aware of the steps in determining a diagnostic pattern. Grading is a complex task that requires establishing some uniform criteria for dependability and consistency, and parent-teacher conferences are the best form of pupil-progress reporting. The greater the participation of teachers and students in the evaluative process, the more successful and the more productive the language arts program will become.

SELECTED BIBLIOGRAPHY

Ahman, J. Stanley. *Evaluating Pupil Growth*, 2d ed. Boston: Allyn and Bacon, 1963.

Anderson, Robert H., and Cynthia Ritsher. "Pupil Progress," in R. L. Ebel, ed., *Encyclopedia of Educational Research*. New York: Macmillan, 1969, pp. 1050–1060.

Berger, Allen, and Blanche Hope Smith, eds. *Classroom Practices in Teaching English, 1972–73, Measure for Measure*. Urbana, Ill.: National Council of Teachers of English, 1972.

Blue, Reginald. "Accountability to Children." *Elementary English* 52 (January 1975): 51–52; 72.

Glasser, William. *Schools without Failure*. New York: Harper & Row, 1969.

Gorow, Frank F. *Better Classroom Testing*. San Francisco: Chandler Publishing, 1966.

Hillerich, Robert L. "A Diagnostic Approach to Early Identification of Language Skills." *The Reading Teacher* 31 (January 1978): 357–364.

Hopkins, Charles D., and Richard L. Antes. *Classroom Measurement and Evaluation*. Itasca, Ill.: F. E. Peacock, 1978.

Langdon, Grace, and Irving W. Stout. *Helping Parents Understand Their Child's School*. Englewood Cliffs, N.J.: Prentice-Hall, 1957.

Murray, Thomas R. *Judging Student Progress*, rev. ed. New York: McKay, 1962.

Theobald, John. *Classroom Testing: Principles and Practices*, 2d ed. New York: Longmans, Green, 1974.

Wilhelms, Fred T., ed. *Evaluation as Feedback and Guide*. Washington, D.C.: Association for Supervision and Curriculum Development, 1967.

Summary of Part Three

Good teachers must have a multifaceted set of skills and a broad range of learning, including insight into themselves as teachers. So that effective teaching can prevail, teachers must be able to provide an optimum physical environment in the classroom and realize that this environment affects the emotional, social, and intellectual milieu. Proper classroom management, combined with good lesson-planning techniques, and knowledge of how to organize for instruction help to produce an effective teaching–learning situation.

Teachers must be concerned with the individual differences of their students in planning their instructional programs. They must realize that they have children with a wide range of ability levels in their classrooms and be prepared to provide instruction for each child according to his or her need. Individualized programs as well as group instruction should be utilized. Teachers must also be prepared to work with exceptional children (children who deviate so much from the "average" that they require special attention) because many exceptional children are being placed in regular classrooms.

The evaluative process should be an integral part of the language arts program. It is continuous, beginning at the inception of the language arts program and going on throughout the school year. Effective evaluation is a complex task based on accurate measurement as well as other assessment techniques. It involves more than measurement. Planning and decision-making are also required.

Evaluation is done in terms of desired outcomes. The more explicitly such objectives are stated, the more effective the evaluation will be. Behavioral objectives, which are stated in terms of overt student behavior, describe what students will be doing to show achievement of the goals. These are the easiest and most effective ways to evaluate students.

Assessment of students' learning behaviors

requires an adequate and accurate collection of data and knowledge of diagnosis. Teachers must know about standardized tests and should be adept at constructing teacher-made tests. One difficulty in grading arises from the different criteria used as a basis for grading. When properly planned, the parent-teacher conference is most effective in reporting pupil progress.

Teacher evaluation is the most difficult and controversial of all the evaluation areas. The criteria for effective teaching have not yet been determined, and research in this area has not been definitive. Competency-based objectives seem to be a good approach to establishing such criteria, although there are a number of critics of this evaluative method. It is doubtful whether one set of criteria is desirable or can even be established.

It is important not to make judgments or evaluations based on only one or two casual observations. Effective evaluation demands an adequate and valid collection of data taken over a long period of time.

Suggestions for Thought Questions and Activities for Part Three

1. Design a mini-language arts lesson using videotape. Rate yourself as a teacher according to criteria set up in Chapter 15.

2. In evaluating a child's work, what methods would you use to diagnose any problems the child may have? What kinds of procedures would you suggest for alleviating any such problem or problems?

3. As a teacher, how would you evaluate your success in presenting a language arts program to students?

4. You have been selected to serve on a school committee whose responsibility it is to evaluate the language arts program in the school. How will you proceed? *Hint:* What factors must you take into account? What assessment techniques will you use?

5. Choose two of the teachers you had in school. One should be someone you feel was your best

teacher, the other should be one you feel was the worst. State the characteristics of each. Compare your list of characteristics with others generated by the class.

6. Read the following short selection. Then determine whether any language arts principles are being violated. If a principle is being violated, explain how the principle is being violated by the teacher and state the language arts principle(s).

Ms. X asks all the second graders in her class to open to page 26 in the language books. She says, "Since so many persons had trouble with the inductive phonics lesson the other day, everyone will review it again. No questions. Let's begin. I have everything planned for you and I want to make sure we finish it all. Sit up straight. Don't turn around. Pay attention. I know we've been working one hour straight, but we have to finish."

Epilogue

At the beginning, the center, and the end of the educative process is the child, whose proper development is the ideal.

Teachers are the guides, stimulators, energizers, and helpers. They hold keys to unlock the storehouse of knowledge.

Language is the "spiritual food." It is the means by which individuals share thoughts and feelings.

This book has attempted to provide teachers with the language arts skills and knowledge they will need to help students to lead richer, fuller lives. The emphasis has been on the child as an active, curious, imaginative, and creative experiencer of life. Through the language arts, the child's world is expanded. The child grows and reaches new intellectual and emotional heights.

To take a child by the hand and help lead the child into the good life, while safeguarding and fostering his or her uniqueness, is an awesome task. Teachers need all the help they can get. One would hope that this book has been one aid.

Glossary

Accommodation. Child develops new categories rather than integrating them into existing ones—Piaget's cognitive development.

Affective environment. Concerned with the feelings and emotional learnings that students acquire.

Affixes. Prefixes *(which see*)* that are added before the root word and suffixes *(which see)* that are added to the end of a root word.

Alliteration. This is the repetition of usually the initial consonant sound or sounds in two or more neighboring words or syllables.

Allomorph. A morpheme *(which see)* that is represented by alternate phonemes *(which see)*.

Allophone. Variants of the same phoneme *(which see)*.

Ambidextrous. Able to use both hands equally well.

Analogies. Analogies are relationships between words or ideas.

Antonyms. Words opposite in meaning.

Articulation. Production of speech sounds.

Assimilation. A continuous process which helps the individual to integrate new incoming stimuli to existing concepts—Piaget's cognitive development.

Association. Pairing the real object with the sound of the word.

Auding. Highest level of listening which involves listening with comprehension.

*Which see refers to the immediately preceding word that is defined elsewere in the glossary.

Auditory acuity. Refers to the physical response of the ear to sound vibrations.

Auditory discrimination. Ability to distinguish between sounds.

Auditory fatigue. A factor which inhibits hearing; temporary hearing loss due to a continuous or repeated exposure to sounds of certain frequencies.

Aural. Refers to listening.

Basal reader approach. An approach involving a basal reader series. This approach is a highly structured one. It uses a controlled vocabulary, and skills are sequentially developed.

Base. Same as root *(which see)*.

Behavioral objective. Statement which describes what students will be able to do after they have achieved their goal.

Bibliotherapy. The use of books to help individuals to cope better with their emotional and adjustment problems.

Bilingual. Using or capable of using two languages.

Binaural situations. Being in the presence of two or more conversations.

Brainstorming. Generating many different ideas without inhibition.

Choral speaking. The saying aloud, in unison, of a poem or prose selection by a group.

Cinquain. A poetic form based on a five-line pattern.

Closed syllable. A syllable having a single vowel and ending in a consonant. The vowel is usually short; for example, căn.

Clusters.   Clusters represent a blend of sounds.

Cognitive development.   Refers to development of thinking.

Cognitive domain.   Hierarchy of objectives ranging from simplistic thinking skills to the more complex ones.

Combining forms.   Usually defined as roots borrowed from another language that join together or that join with a prefix, a suffix, or both a prefix and a suffix to form a word; for example, *aqua/naut*.

Communication.   Exchange of ideas.

Competency-based instruction.   Embraces two essential characteristics: learning objectives, defined in behavioral terms; and accountability.

Concepts.   A group of stimuli with common characteristics.

Concrete poetry.   Concerned with the arrangement of words on a page using the actual or approximate forms of an object as an outline.

Connotative meaning.   This meaning includes all emotional senses associated with the word.

Consonant blends.   A combination of sounds blended together so that the identity of each sound is retained.

Consonant clusters.   Same as consonant blends (*which see*).

Construct.   Something which cannot be directly observed or directly measured—such as intelligence, attitudes, and motivation.

Creative dramatics.   An informal dramatization by the child using his or her imagination.

Creative process.   Refers to Wallas' stages of preparation, incubation, illumination, and verification.

Creativity.   Knowledge plus imagination plus evaluation—defined according to Parnes; no universally agreed upon definition.

Criterion-referenced tests.   These are based on an extensive inventory of learning objectives in a specific curriculum area. They are not norm-based.

Critical listening.   A high-level listening skill whereby the individual is able to detect bias, propaganda, and so on in oral presentations.

Crossed dominance.   The dominant hand on one side and the dominant eye on the other.

Culturally deprived.   Child comes from a poverty-level home, in which parents are illiterate and perhaps indifferent to the child; this child may or may not be culturally different (*which see*).

Culturally different.   Refers to those children whose parents have usually been born in another country and who speak a language other than English; it may also refer to a child who is born in the United States, but English is not the dominant language spoken in the child's home.

Curriculum.   Includes everything in the school environment planned prior to instruction.

Deductive teaching.   Students are given a generalization and must determine which examples fit the rule; going from general to specific.

Denotative meaning.   This is the direct, specific meaning of the word.

Derivatives.   Combinations of root words with either prefixes (*which see*) or suffixes (*which see*) or both; for example, prefix (re) plus root word (play) = replay. (*See also* Stems.)

Desist technique.   Any technique used to control misbehavior.

Dialect.   A variation of language sufficiently different to be considered separate, but not different enough to be classified as a separate language.

Digit span.   Refers to amount of words or numbers an individual can retain in his or her short-term memory.

Digraph.   Usually consisting of either two consonants or two vowels which represent one speech sound; for example, ch, ai.

Diphthongs.   Blends of vowel sounds beginning with the first and gliding to the second. The vowel blends represented by two adjacent vowels; for example oi. For syllabication purposes diphthongs are considered one vowel sound.

Divergent thinking.   The many different ways to solve problems or to "look at things."

Elaboration in speech acquisition.   When the parent or adult figure expands a baby's word or words into a complete sentence.

Environmental psychology.   Focuses on behavior in relation to physical settings.

Equilibrium.   According to Piaget, a balance between assimilation (*which see*) and accommodation (*which see*) in cognitive development (*which see*).

Evaluation.   A process of appraisal involving specific values and the use of a variety of instruments in order to form a value judgment.

Exceptional children.   Those children who deviate so much from the "average" that they require special attention.

Experience story.   A basic teaching technique in reading founded on experiences of students.

Function or structure words.   All those words in a sentence not classified as major parts of speech.

Goals.   A synonym for objectives (*which see*), but usually used for long-term plans.

Grammar.   The study of the way language is used; composed of syntax (*which see*) and morphology (*which see*).

Grapheme—phoneme relationship.   Letter-sound relationship.

Graphemes.   The written representation of phonemes.

Graphemic base.   This is a succession of graphemes that occurs with the same phonetic value in a number of words (ight, ake, at, et, and so on). Same as phonogram (*which see*).

Haiku.   A Japanese poetic form consisting of three lines composed of seventeen syllables—5 in the first and third lines and 7 in the second.

Halo effect.   A response bias which contaminates an individual's perception in the area of rating or evaluation.

Haptics.   Nonverbal communication through touch.

Hearing.   Lowest level in the hierarchy of listening; the physical perception of sound.

Homographs.   Words which are spelled the same but have different meanings (see Chapter 15).

Homonyms.   Words which sound alike, are spelled differently, and have different meanings (*see* Chapter 15).

Homophones.   Same as homonyms (*which see*).

Hyperbole.   Gross exaggeration as a figure of speech.

Illumination.   Part of the creative process in which the individual achieves an "insight" into the problem.

Imitation in speech acquisition.   Child attempts to voice the sounds voiced initially by the parent figure.

Incubation.   Part of the creative process in which the individual "mulls over the problem."

Inductive teaching.   Students discover generalizations by being given numerous examples which portray patterns; going from specific to general.

Inference.   Understanding that is not derived from a direct statement but from an indirect suggestion in what is stated.

Intake of language.   Listening and reading.

Intelligence.   Ability to reason abstractly.

IQ.   Intelligence Quotient; mental age divided by chronological age multiplied by 100.

I.P.A.   International Phonetic Alphabet.

Juncture.   Refers to the way in which phonemes (*which see*) in a language are joined together in an utterance; the way in which an utterance begins and ends; pause.

Kinesics.   Study of the gestures which may or may not accompany speech. (message-related body movement)

Language.   A learned, shared, and patterned, arbitrary system of vocal sound symbols with which people in a given culture can communicate with one another.

Language arts.   The major components are: listening, speaking, reading, and writing.

Language-experience approach.   A nonstructured emerging reading program based on students' experiences, and which incorporates all aspects of the language arts into reading.

Lanterne.   A poetic pattern of 1, 2, 3, 4, and 1 words in a line, arranged in the shape of a lantern.

Learning center.   This is an integral part of the instructional program and vital to a good individualized program. An area is usually set aside in the classroom for instruction in a specific curriculum area. (See Chapter 16.)

Limerick.   A five-line pattern in which the first, second, and fifth lines rhyme with one another, and the third and fourth lines rhyme with each other.

Linguist.   An individual engaged in the systematic study of language.

Linguistics.   The science of language.

Listening.   Middle of hierarchy of listening in which the individual becomes aware of sound sequences, and is able to identify and recognize the sound sequences as words; many times the term "listening" is used in place of auding (*which see*).

Main idea.   This is the central thought of a paragraph. All of the sentences in a paragraph develop the main idea.

Mainstreaming.   This is the placement of handicapped children in the least restrictive environment that will meet these children's needs.

Masking. A factor which inhibits hearing; sounds interfere with the spoken message.

Measurement. Part of the evaluative process; involves quantitative descriptions.

Memory span. The number of discrete elements grasped in a given moment of attention and organized into a unity for purposes of immediate reproduction or immediate use; synonym for digit span (*which see*).

Metaphor. The comparison of two unlike objects without using "like" or "as."

Morpheme. The smallest individually meaningful element in the utterances of a language.

Morphology. Involves the construction of words and word parts.

Morphophonemic system. The ways in which the morphemes (*which see*) of a given language are variously represented by phonemic (*see* phoneme) shapes; can be regarded as a kind of code.

Motivation. Internal impetus behind behavior and the direction behavior takes; drive.

Newspaper poetry. The arrangement of words on a page that helps express the poet's message.

Objective. An end; an outcome; usually used for short-range plans.

Onomatopoeia. The use of words whose sound suggests the sense of the word.

Open syllable. A syllable having a single vowel and ending in a vowel. The vowel is usually long; for example, gō.

Oral. Refers to speaking.

Outgo of language. Speaking and writing.

Overworked phrases. Those phrases that have been used over and over again to describe something.

Oxymoron. Word contradictions which are used to portray a particular image.

Pantomime. Creative dramatics without speech; only facial and body actions are used to convey thoughts or actions.

Personification. The giving of human characteristics and capabilities to nonhuman things such as inanimate objects, abstract qualities, or animals.

Phoneme. Smallest unit of sound in a specific language system; a class of sounds.

Phonics. Relationships between letter symbols of a written language and the sounds they represent.

Phonogram. Same as graphemic base (*which see*).

Phonology. Branch of linguistics (*which see*) dealing with the analysis of sound systems of language.

Physical environment. Refers to any observable factors in the physical environment which could affect the behavior of an individual.

Pitch. Refers to the different frequency levels in utterances.

Prefix. An affix (*which see*); a letter or a sequence of letters added to the beginning of a root word which changes its meaning; for example, *re* plus *play* = *replay*.

Preparation. Part of the creative process relating to the background of experiences.

Principle. Refers to rules or guides.

Projective technique. A method in which the individual tends to put himself or herself into the test situation.

Proxemics. Study of the effects of space or distance on human interaction; a form of nonverbal communication.

Proximodistal development. Muscular development from the midpoint of the body to the extremities.

Reading. The getting of meaning from and bringing of meaning to the written page.

Reinforcement. Any stimulus which usually causes the individual to repeat a response, such as praise.

Reliability. The extent to which a test instrument consistently produces similar results.

Role playing. A form of creative dramatics in which dialogue for a specific role is spontaneously developed.

Root. Smallest unit of a word that can exist and retain its basic meaning; a base; for example, play.

Simile. The comparison of two unlike objects using "like" or "as."

Skimming Reading rapidly to find or locate information.

Sociogram. A map or chart showing the interrelationships of children in a classroom and identifying those who are "stars" or "isolates."

Speech correction. Applies to children who are referred to a clinician for speech help and who are generally not so helped in the regular classroom.

Speech improvement. Applies to the ongoing classroom speech program.

Speech stimulation activities. Refers to oral expression activities which help to develop better speech, voice, and body movements.

Standardized tests. Commercial tests using a large representative sample of students upon which a set of norms is based.

Stem. Any word construction to which an affix (*which see*) can be added. All roots are stems, but all stems are not roots. A stem may consist of a root plus an affix; for example, in *replays, play* is the root, *replay* is the stem to which the suffix *s* is added.

Stress. Part of the accentual system in which differences in a syllable or words are largely in relative loudness or prominence.

Suffix. An affix (*which see*); a letter or a sequence of letters added to the end of a root word, which changes the grammatical form of the word and its meaning; for example, *prince* plus *ly = princely*.

Suprasegmental phonemes. These include pitch, stress, and juncture, which are significant sound units because they influence meaning.

Syllable. A vowel or a group of letters containing one vowel sound; for example, blo.

Synonyms. Words similar in meaning.

Syntax. The patterning of words or the way in which words are arranged relative to each other in utterances.

Tanka verse. A five-line pattern arranged in a 5, 7, 5, 7, 7 poetic pattern of thirty-one syllables.

Teaching. Involves intent, rules, and goals (according to Kingsley Price); no universally agreed upon definition.

T.E.S.L. (Teaching English as a Second Language). Concentrates on helping children who speak a language other than English or nonstandard English to learn English as a language.

Telegraphic speech. A child is able to receive and convey a message, even though it is beyond the child's digit span (*which see*).

Topic sentence. It states what the paragraph will be about by naming the topic.

Traditional grammar. Based on Latin and Greek, leading to the description and analysis of English in terms of these languages; prescriptive.

Usage. Involves the way people speak; preferences and choices in language are made according to formal or informal usage.

Validity. A test instrument that measures what it claims to measure.

Verification. Part of the creative process in which the individual tests the "insight" gained in the illumination (*which see*) period.

Word classes. The major parts of speech according to linguists; for example, nouns, verbs, adjectives, and adverbs.

Appendix A:
Checklist for Choosing Language
Arts Textbook Series

According to the Educational Products Information Exchange Institute, a nonprofit consumer-supported organization, ninety-five percent of classroom instruction can be attributed to classroom materials.[1] Even if the percentage is exaggerated, hardly anyone would deny that textbooks play a prominent role in the instructional program. Because of their importance, teachers need to be critical textbook consumers. Although in the past decade children's textbooks seem to be becoming more similar than different, textbook series are generally unique in what they tend to stress, the terminology they use, and usually in the presentation of their material.

The general checklist on pages 460 and 461 should help in choosing language arts textbook series.

[1]Donald H. Graves. "Language Arts Textbooks: A Writing Process Evaluation" *Language Arts:* (October 1977): p. 817.

General Checklist for Choosing Language Arts Series

	Excellent	Good	Fair	Poor

1. *Physical Characteristics*

   a. Print
     (1) Clear
     (2) Readable
     (3) Proper size
     (4) Proper spacing between lines
   b. Paper
     (1) Good weight
     (2) Durable
     (3) Non-glossy
   c. Binding
     (1) Reinforced
     (2) Book held firmly in its cover

2. *Content (general characteristics)*

   a. Valid information, i.e., information is related to topic being studied
   b. Covered in proper depth for particular grade level
   c. Based on objectives that have been chosen for specific language arts areas
   d. Emphasis on interrelatedness of listening, speaking, reading, and writing
   e. Emphasis on listening
   f. Emphasis on speech-stimulation activities such as creative dramatics, discussions, puppetry, choral speaking, and so on
   g. Emphasis on creative writing
   h. Emphasis on practical writing skills such as punctuation, capitalization, word usage, and some spelling

3. *Readability*

   a. Vocabulary is suitable to particular grade level
   b. Sentence length is suitable to particular grade level

4. *Features*

   a. Variety of activities
   b. Creative presentation of material
   c. Objectives presented at beginning of each
      lesson
   d. Index is complete
   e. Glossary—special terms used in text are
      defined
   f. Bibliographies—include up-to-date mate-
      rials
   g. Summaries at end of each chapter

5. *Visual Content or Illustration*

   a. Charts and graphs are included
   b. Pictures and cartoons included

6. *Treatment of Minorities*

   a. Every group of people is treated with dig-
      nity and respect
   b. No group is stereotyped
   c. Each group is accurately portrayed

7. *Treatment of Gender*

   a. Males and females are treated as equals
   b. Stereotypes are avoided

8. *Provisions for Individual Differences*

   a. Special aids for slow learners
   b. Challenging material for the gifted

9. *Teacher's Manual*

   a. Includes helpful suggestions
   b. Provides extra activities
   c. Provides activities for special children
   d. Provides creative ideas

Appendix B:
Readability Formulas

The Fry Readability Formula is simple and fast to compute. It can be used at the primary grades as well as other grade levels.

Average number of syllables per 100 words

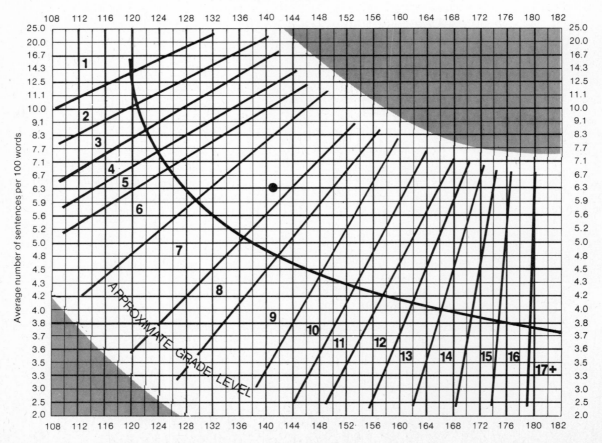

EXAMPLE:		SYLLABLES	SENTENCES
1st Hundred Words		124	6.6
2nd Hundred Words		141	5.5
3rd Hundred Words		158	6.8
	AVERAGE	141	6.3

READABILITY 7th GRADE (see dot plotted on graph)

HOW TO USE THE FLESCH READABILITY FORMULA[1]

To estimate the readability ("reading ease" and "human interest") of a piece of writing, go through the following steps:

Step 1. Pick Your Samples

Unless you want to test a whole piece of writing, take samples. Take enough samples to make a fair test (say, three to five of an article and 25 to 30 of a book). Don't try to pick "good" or "typical" samples. Go by a strictly numerical scheme. For instance, take every third paragraph or every other page. (Ordinarily, the introductory paragraphs of a piece of writing are not typical of its style.) Each sample should start at the beginning of a paragraph.

Step 2. Count the Number of Words

Count the words in your piece of writing. If you are using samples, take each sample and count each word in it up to 100. Count contractions and hyphenated words as one word. Count numbers and letters as words, too, if separated by spaces. For example, count each of the following as one word: *1948, $19,892, e.g., C.O.D., wouldn't, week-end.*

Step 3. Figure the Average Sentence Length

Figure the average sentence length in words for your piece of writing. If you are using samples, do this for all your samples *combined.* In a 100-word sample, find the sentence that ends nearest to the 100-word mark—that might be at the 94th word or the 109th word. Count the sentences up to that point and divide the number of words in those sentences in all your samples by the number of sentences in all your samples. In counting sentences, follow the units of thought rather than the

[1]Rudolf Flesch, *The Art of Readable Writing* (New York: Harper and Brothers, 1949), pp. 213–216. Copyright by Rudolf Flesch.

punctuation: usually sentences are marked off by periods; but sometimes they are marked off by colons or semicolons—like these. (There are three sentences here between two periods.) But don't break up sentences that are merely joined by conjunctions like *and* or *but.*

Step 4. Count the Syllables

Count the syllables in your 100-word samples and divide the total number of syllables by the number of samples. If you are testing a whole piece of writing, divide the total number of syllables by the total number of words and multiply by 100. This will give you the number of syllables per 100 words. Count syllables the way you pronounce the word; e.g., *asked* has one syllable, *determined* three, and *pronunciation* five. Count the number of syllables in symbols and figures according to the way they are normally read aloud, e.g., two for $ ("dollars") and four for *1916* ("nineteen sixteen"). However, if a passage contains several or lengthy figures, your estimate will be more accurate if you don't include these figures in your syllable count; in a 100-word sample, be sure to add instead a corresponding number of words after the 100-word mark. If in doubt about syllabication rules, use any good dictionary. (To save time, count all syllables except the first in all words of more than one syllable; then add the total to the number of words tested. It is also helpful to "read silently aloud" while counting.)

Step 5. Count the "Personal Words"

Count the "personal words" in your 100-word samples and divide the total number of "personal words" by the number of samples. If you are testing a whole piece of writing, divide the total number of "personal words" by the total number of words and multiply by 100. This will give you the number of "personal words" per 100 words.

"Personal words" are:

(a) All first- second-, and third-person pronouns except the neuter pronouns *it, its, itself,* and *they, them, their, theirs, themselves* if referring to things rather than people.

(b) All words that have masculine or feminine natural gender, e.g., *John Jones, Mary, father, sister, iceman, actress.* Do not count common-gender words like *teacher, doctor, employee, assistant, spouse.* Count singular and plural forms.

(c) The group words *people* (with the plural verb) and *folks.*

Step 6. Count the "Personal Sentences"

Count the "personal sentences" in your 100-word samples and divide the number of "personal sentences" in all your samples by the number of sentences in all your samples. If you are testing a whole piece of writing, divide the total number of "personal sentences" by the total number of sentences. In both cases multiply by 100. This will give you the number of "personal sentences" per 100 sentences.

"Personal sentences" are:

(a) Spoken sentences, marked by quotation marks or otherwise, often including speech tags like "he said," set off by colons or commas (e.g., *"I doubt it."—We told him: "You can take it or leave it."—"That's all very well,"* he replied, *showing clearly that he didn't believe a word of what we said.*)

(b) Questions, commands, requests, and other sentences directly addressed to the reader (e.g., *Does this sound impossible?—Imagine what this means.—Do this three times.—You shouldn't overrate these results.—This is a point you must remember.—It means a lot to people like you and me.*) But don't count sentences that are only indirectly or vaguely addressed to the reader (e.g., *This is typical of our national character.—You never can tell.*)

(c) Exclamations (e.g., *It's unbelievable!*)

(d) Grammatically incomplete sentences whose full meaning has to be inferred from the context (e.g., *Doesn't know a word of English.— Handsome, though.— Well, he wasn't.—The minute you walked out.*)

If a sentence fits two or more of these definitions, count it only once.

Step 7. Find Your "Reading Ease" Score

Using the average sentence length in words (*Step 3*) and the number of syllables per 100 words (*Step 4*), find your "reading ease" score on the How EASY? chart printed on page 467.

You can also use this formula:

Multiply the average sentence length by 1.015 . . . .
Multiply the number of syllables per 100 words by .846 . . . .

Add

Subtract this sum from 206.835

Your "reading ease" score is . . . .

The "reading ease" score will put your piece of writing on a scale between 0 (practically unreadable) and 100 (easy for any literate person).

Step 8. Find Your "Human Interest" Score

Using the number of "personal words" per 100 words *(Step 5)* and the number of "personal sentences" per 100 sentences (*Step 6*), find your "human interest" score on the How INTERESTING? chart printed on page 467.

Or use this formula:

Multiply the number of "personal words" per 100 words by 3.635 . . . .
Multiply the number of "personal sentences" per 100 sentences by .314 . . . .

The total is your "human interest" score . . . .

The "human interest" score will put your piece of writing on a scale between 0 (no human interest) and 100 (full of human interest).

In applying the twin formulas, remember that the "reading ease" formula measures *length* (the longer the words and sentences, the harder to read) and the "human interest" formula measures *percentages* (the more "personal" words and sentences, the more human interest).

For further interpretation of your scores, use the following table.[2]

[2]Ibid., pp. 149–151.

Meaning of Reading Ease Score

Reading Ease Score and Description of Style	Average Sentence Length	Average Number of Syllables per 100 Words	Writing Typical of Style	Estimated School Grades Completed	Estimated Percent of U.S. Adults
0–30 Very difficult	29 or more	192 or more	Scientific (professional papers)	College	4½
30–50 Difficult	25	167	Academic (textbooks)	High school or some college	33
50–60 Fairly difficult	21	155	Quality magazines *(New Yorker, Business Week)*	Some high school	54
60–70 Standard	17	147	Digests *(Reader's Digest, Time)*	7th or 8th grade	83
70–80 Fairly easy	14	139	Slick fiction *(Ladies' Home Journal)*	6th grade	88
80–90 Easy	11	131	Pulp fiction (Westerns, confession magazines)	5th grade	91
90–100 Very easy	8 or less	123 or less	Comics	4th grade	93

How Easy?

Words per Sentence	Reading Ease Score	Syllables per 100 Words
		120
		125
		130
	100	135
Very easy	95	
	90	140
Easy	85	145
	80	
Fairly easy	75	150
	70	155
5	Standard — 65	
	60	160
10	Fairly difficult — 55	165
	50	
15	45	170
	Difficult — 40	175
20	35	
	30	180
25	25	185
	20	
30	Very difficult — 15	190
	10	195
35	5	
	0	200

How to Use This Chart: Take a pencil or ruler and connect your "Words per Sentence" figure (left) with your "Syllables per 100 Words" figure (right). The intersection of the pencil or ruler with the center lines shows your "Reading Ease" score.

ⓒ 1949 by Rudolf Flesch

How Interesting?

Percent of "Personal Words"	Human Interest Score	Percent of "Personal Sentences"
23		
22		
21		
20		
19		
18		
17		
16		
15		
14	100	
13	90	
12		
11	Dramatic — 80	
10	70	
9	60	100
8		90
7	Very Interesting — 50	80
6	40	70
5		60
4	Interesting — 30	50
3	20	40
2	Mildly Interesting	30
	10	20
1		10
	Dull	
0	0	0

How to Use This Chart: Take a pencil or ruler and connect your "Personal Words" figure (left) with your "Personal Sentences" figure (right). The intersection of the pencil or ruler with the center line shows your "Human Interest" score.

ⓒ 1949 by Rudolf Flesch

Appendix C:
The Sociogram

A sociogram is a map or chart of interrelationships among the individuals within a group and shows the role of each person within the group. The sociogram must meet specific criteria if it is to fulfill its function. The basis of the choice of student associates must be real and not hypothetical. The test must be a means to an end, never an end in itself. The results should be carried out in arrangements for living as these are desired by all members. The application is immediate; the action is not to be taken for some vague period in the future.

STEPS IN ADMINISTERING

1. *Choosing the question.* The first task in making a sociogram is to devise a question which will draw from the members of the group expressions of their true feelings regarding other members. The question should deal with a situation which has meaning to every group member. It should be clear and concise.

The most meaningful sociogram is obtained if students feel that they will gain something they need by accurately recording their opinions.

2. *Asking the question.* The question should be presented to the group in an informal and natural manner; that is, in such a way that it does not take on undue importance. In addition, when the question is put to the members of the group, they must be satisfied on two counts. First, they will want assurance that their replies will be kept confidential. Second, they will want and deserve some good reasons for answering the question.

Teachers should always feel free to answer any questions that may occur to the group, both before and during the writing of answers to the sociogram question, and should treat the occasion in a businesslike manner. The most important things to remember about administering the test are:

a. To include the motivating elements in the introductory remarks.
b. To word the question so that children understand how the results are to be used.

c. To allow enough time for questions to be answered.

d. To emphasize *any* boy or girl, so as to approve in advance any directions the choice may take.

e. To present the test situation with interest and some enthusiasm.

f. To say how soon the arrangements based on the test can be made.

g. To keep the whole procedure as casual as possible.

In administering this project, the teacher should provide each student with a 3" x 5" card. In the upper left corner of this card, the student should write his or her name. Below it, he or she should write the names of students with whom he or she prefers to associate, listing them in order of preference.

```
Sharon J.
    Seth    J.
    Carol   S.
    John    S.
```

3. *Collating the names.* In collating the names and choices appearing on the students' cards, the teacher uses the Sociometric Tabulation Form—example below.

4. *Plotting the sociogram.* The choices of the students are portrayed graphically on the sociogram. Circles symbolize girls and squares boys. Each symbol contains the name of a given student. Different colors for the lines designating each of the three levels of choices can be used.

The plotted sociogram is a beginning, not an end. It raises questions rather than answers them. Perhaps its greatest value is that it directs the attention of the teacher

Sample Sociogram

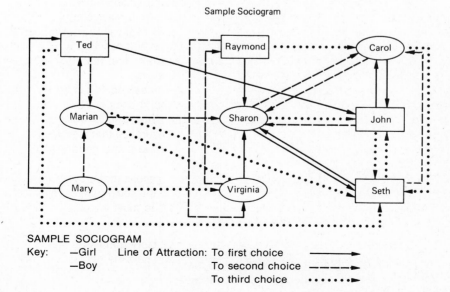

SAMPLE SOCIOGRAM

Key: —Girl   Line of Attraction: To first choice ⟶

       —Boy   To second choice – – –►

                                    To third choice •••••►

to certain aspects of group structure which will lead to further valuable observation of individual and group behavior.

5. *Interpreting the sociogram.* To a person looking at a sociogram for the first time the whole thing may seem to be a meaningless jumble of circles, lines, and triangles. The first problem, then, is to trace the pattern and gradually see its significance. A good way to begin reading a sociogram is to concentrate on one person and follow all lines that lead from and to him (*note* sample sociogram).

6. *Preparing the sociogram.* The first step is to arrange the last names of the students in alphabetical order, although this is optional. The second step is to list these names in the column at the left and in the row across the top. The "chooser" is shown in the left column; the "chosen" in the top row. The third step is to enter the choices by number—1, 2, 3, and so on—in the chart at the intersection of the row at the right of the choosing student's name and of the column under the chosen student's name (*see* the tabulation form below).

BRIEF INTERPRETATIONS

At first glance a sociogram, such as that shown in the sample, is confusing. Even without close inspection, however, it can be seen that Sharon and Henry received a large number of choices. It can also be seen that the choices are fairly well distributed among students.

Tabulation Form Showing Choices of Students

Chooser \ Chosen	Sharon J.	Seth J.	Carol S.	John S.	Marian E.	Virginia F.	Ted M.	Raymond H.	Mary L.
Sharon J.		1	2	3					
Seth J.	1		2	3					
Carol R.	2	3		1					
John S.	2	3	1						
Marian E.	2	3					1		
Virginia F.	1				3			2	
Ted M.		3		1	2				
Raymond H.	1		3			2			
Mary L.					2	3	1		

In the sample sociogram it can also be seen that Mary is an isolate. None of her three choices was reciprocated, and she was not chosen by anyone else. The choices of Sharon, Seth, Carol, and John indicate that they make up an in-group.

Chosen as								
First Choice	3	1	1	0	0	0	2	0	0
Second Choice	3		2	2	2	1	0	1	0
Third Choice	0	4	1	2	1	1	0	0	0
Total	6	5	4	4	3	2	2	1	0

Index